THE OFFICIAL® PRICE GUIDE TO OLD BOOKS & *Autographs*

**FROM THE EDITORS
OF THE HOUSE OF COLLECTIBLES**

D0057822

**SEVENTH EDITION
THE HOUSE OF COLLECTIBLES
NEW YORK, NEW YORK 10022**

©1988 Random House, Inc.

℧ This is a registered trademark of Random House, Inc.

All rights reserved under International and Pan-American Copyright Conventions.

Published by: The House of Collectibles
201 East 50th Street
New York, New York 10022

Distributed by Ballantine Books, a division of Random House, Inc., New York and simultaneously in Canada by Random House of Canada Limited, Toronto.

Manufactured in the United States of America

Library of Congress Catalog Card Number: 84-643007

ISBN: 0-87637-313-9

10 9 8 7 6 5

TABLE OF CONTENTS

MARKET REVIEW

Buyer activity has greatly increased in the rare book market since the recession-inspired doldrums of the early eighties, but the shortage of really fine material available for purchase is preventing a thorough resurgence of the hobby. This past year's auction season in both New York and London slid by with the appearance of only two or three libraries that could be called noteworthy. The fine libraries that reach sale today are essentially of a different nature than those sold in the 1950's and 1960's: much smaller (really tiny by the old standards of book collecting), more specialized, and generally of a higher grade of condition. One factor in this trend was, of course, the wholesale volume buying of rarities by institutional libraries from about 1960 into the early 1970's. During that period huge quantities of important first editions, early illustrated works and other significant books were permanently taken off the commercial market. "Permanently" may not be a 100% accurate term, as some of these institutions have subsequently sold their duplicates, but most of these books will not be coming on the market again. Today, institutional libraries are doing practically no buying of rare books, as the special endowments and funds set aside for that purpose have long since been depleted.

Private collections which embody the traditional ideals of book collecting are still seen today, though very occasionally. Even when these collections are small, as they invariably are, one still cannot fail to be impressed by the effort and cost involved in building them under current conditions. Such a collection was that of Paul Francis Webster, sold by Sotheby's in New York on April 24, 1985. Webster, a song writer, had died the previous year at the age of 77. This was actually his second book collection, as he had earlier formed one which was sold by Parke-Bernet (not then affiliated with Sotheby's) in the 1940's. This second collection required only 181 lots to catalogue, and one of those was a bookcase! Compared to the Abbey or Phillipps libraries sold during the fifties and sixties in marathon sales with multi-volume catalogues, it was a minuscule library indeed, but a brilliant one. Webster owned all four Shakespeare folios, no mean feat in this era despite the fact that coffee baron Henry Folger had over 70 copies of the First Folio alone in the 1920's. Webster also had complete sets of all Presidential autographs and signers of the Declaration of Independence, including the rarity of rarities, Button Gwinnet. Additionally, the library included a first edition of Dickens' Pickwick in the original monthly parts and a choice selection of illuminated manuscripts: not the sort of illuminated manuscripts that would have turned heads 50 years ago, but excellent ones in light of modern availability.

Less traditional but no less appealing was the library of Lindley Eberstadt, which passed through the same galleries on May 1, 1985. The name Eberstadt, as veteran collectors are well aware, is firmly linked to rare Americana via the firm of Edward Eberstadt, rare book dealers (now defunct, but active for something like half a century). The Lindley Eberstadt collection was not, however, part of the Eberstadt stock but a private library. It was—once again—a small collection. Sotheby's elected to include general properties to round out the sale. There were numerous highspots. Zenas Leonard's *Narrative*, a rare "overland travel" published in 1839 at Clearfield, Pennsylvania, fetched $8,800 against a house estimate of $5,000 to $6,000. An early tidbit of Hawaiian interest, Damon's *A Trip From the Sandwich Islands*, published at Honolulu in 1849, reached $605. Far outdistancing its estimate was a copy of Metcalf's *Indian Warfare*, 1821, which got to $1,760 compared to a published presale figure of $600 to $800.

It is not at all unusual today for some of the better auction sales to be derived from what the trade calls "mixed properties," that is, books consigned by a number of different owners. As fine collections become less abundant, the alternative for auction houses is to meld several modest ones together. Such was the case in New York on February 2, 1985 in a sale of rare books featuring atlases, travel books, natural history, science and works in various other fields. This was not a "name" sale but there was enough of real merit included to bring heavy buyer competition. Peter Martyr's *Travel in the West and East Indies, 1577*, sold for $8,800. It had a good provenance, having once belonged to the celebrated Pennsylvania book lover Boise Penrose. But this sale was far more notable for its array of color plate natural history books, one of the largest selections of the type to be dispersed in recent memory. In bulk, as well as in value, the star lot was a virtually complete set of the John Gould color plate "imperial folios" dealing with birds and mammals. This comprised 43 volumes, all of them of immense size and bound more or less uniformly in two shades of green morocco with lavish gilt tooling. The auction house felt, and understandably so, that it would be a pity to break such a set unless circumstances absolutely warranted. Of course this presented the need for a buyer with almost unlimited funds plus unlimited storage space, as the 43 volumes weighed close to one ton. It was decided to take a dual course: the set was catalogued as a single lot, with an estimate of $425,000 to $450,000, followed by the stipulation that it would be immediately broken if its reserve failed to be met. The reserve figure was not, of course, announced, but based upon the prevailing practices it can be safely estimated around $250,000 or a quarter million dollars. Inasmuch as single copies of Audubon's *Birds* have sold for more than that, it should have been an attractive bargain at $250,000 for the right party. Nevertheless, it could not be brought up to the estimate, and the house promptly placed its Plan Two into operation. The individual works were sold title by title, but even this did not prove totally successful. A few sold far over the estimate, some under the estimate, and several were withdrawn after failing to reach their reserves. One of the better sales was $82,500 for the eight volumes of *Birds of Australia*, which the house had estimated at $60,000 to $75,000 and probably reserved at no more than $35,000. Also satisfactory was $28,600 for *The Birds of Great Britain*, a perennial favorite. This had carried an estimate of $25,000 to $30,000, which proved virtually on the nose (meaning a reserve of perhaps $15,000 or slightly less). Among the failures were *The Birds of New Guinea*, estimated at $25,000 to $30,000, and *The Mammals of Australia*, which carried a $30,000 to $35,000 estimate and a reserve of probably $17,500. In any event, it is unlikely that a comparable offering of Gould's massive and colorful publications will be seen in the auction gal-

A FULL

ACCOUNT

OF THE

PROCEEDINGS

In Relation to

Capt. KIDD.

In two LETTERS.

Written by a Person of Quality to a Kinsman of the Earl of *Bellomont* in *Ireland*.

LONDON,

Printed and Sold by the Booksellers of *London* and *Westminster*. MDCCI.

This brief tract (fifty-one pages) gives a biographical sketch of pirate Captain Kidd and an account of his trial. Captain Kidd was commissioned to search out pirates in the Atlantic, but instead became a pirate himself. No hard evidence of pirating was obtained against him, so he was finally charged with killing one of his sailors and was executed. The "person of quality" responsible for this work has never been identified.

leries for some time. How many such sets could still be intact or even partially intact?

Autograph material in the upper price ranges enjoyed a particularly sound year, better in fact than any within the past four or five. There was a definite note of traditionalism in the market with some of the heaviest action centering upon American historical material. At the Philip D. Sang sale, held on March 27, 1985, fine Americana archival items were offered in quantity and some of the lots went surprisingly high. The sale's biggest shocker was a price of $104,500 for a photo of Lincoln and his son Tad, signed by Lincoln. It had been estimated at $10,000 to $15,000 and thus exceeded its estimate by close to 1,000%.

THE CARE AND REPAIR OF BOOKS

For all the fragility of paper, books are basically durable objects if they are not subjected to harsh treatment. If this were not so, illuminated manuscripts and incunabula from the Middle Ages would not survive today in such quantities. Even utterly ignored and untouched for 500 years, such as was a Gutenberg Bible found in a church belltower in Germany, a book will fare pretty well. The binding, if made of leather, will dry out and crack, but internally there should be no serious damage.

The chief enemies of books are:

(1) Fire. Fire has totally or partially destroyed many important libraries, often as the result of war (for example: the burning by Caesar's troops of the Alexandrian library and by British troops of Washington's Library of Congress in the War of 1812), and sometimes by accident (such as the Duke of Cavendish's collection, in which Caxtons perished). Light or moderate fire damage to a book can be repaired. The binding can be replaced, and the page-ends, if scorched, trimmed down. When scorching is serious, it may be better to have the book taken apart and the leaves mounted, if the book's rarity warrants this kind of expense. Any experienced bookbinder can restore a fire-damaged volume. This is why fire-damaged books are so rarely seen on the antiquarian market or in collections.

To guard against fire striking one's library, a collector should be careful to take certain precautions. If you have a library room filled with books, be certain the rugs are fire-retardant. Do not keep draperies or curtains on the windows. Have a minimum of furniture in the room, and nothing upholstered or "overstuffed." If you can bear the ugliness of metal bookshelves, use them, as they will hold up better in a fire. If an open fireplace is in the book room, make certain that no books or papers are kept too near it, and do not allow the fire to burn while the room is unoccupied. Keep the book room as neat as possible and there will be less danger of fire; have no books stacked on the floor or on tables. Glass-enclosed bookcases are safer against fire than open shelves. Have a small fire extinguisher handy in the book room and in the adjacent room or hallway. When the book room is unoccupied, and especially overnight, keep the door shut.

And remember—if a fire does break out, save yourself before you save your books!

(2) Water. Water damage comes via floods, fires, and plumbing problems. Whether or not a soaked book can be salvaged depends upon its paper quality. Books printed on good rag paper can usually be resuscitated, but must be taken apart and the leaves dried out individually (a job for an expert). Books printed on coated paper, such as modern art books, are a total loss when wet. So are newspapers. Vellum stands soaking pretty well. There is not much advice to be given in the way of guarding against water damage, except (a) do not choose rooms with overhead plumbing pipes for library rooms and (b) cover books carefully when taking them out of doors in bad weather.

(3) Excessively dry or humid air. Dry air results in damage to leather bindings. Humid air can breed mold and mildew, and curls paper. The ideal humidity for books is around 50%, give or take ten points either way. If you live in a humid climate and do not use a dehumidifier, open shelf bookcases are better than those with glazed doors. Enclosed cases lock in the moist air and prevent the books from "breathing."

(4) Rough handling. Books that are roughly or improperly handled do not survive very long without some kind of injury. Care in handling applies to all books, not only those which appear delicate. A big brawny folio can be damaged just as easily as a Revolutionary War pamphlet, in fact perhaps more easily, as ten or fifteen pounds worth of pages makes a strain on the binding. Any book opened too wide is sure to crack its hinges. Never force an open book to lie flat on a table for purposes of copying from it. Early bindings with metal clasps require special attention. To open such a binding, **do not tug at the clasps**, as this will break them. Gently squeeze the outer edge of the book and the clasps will pop open by themselves. To close, squeeze again and fit them into place. But remember that many old books, especially those with vellum covers, have swelled over the years, and the clasps will not fit into the catches unless a great deal of pressure is applied. In these cases it is wise to leave the clasps undone, as you only risk breaking the binding with undue squeezing.

(5) Improper storage. Books can be damaged—gradually and imperceptibly but damaged nevertheless—by being shelved in the wrong way. The common mistakes are: stacking books flat on their sides, one atop another; wedging them in too tightly on a shelf; allowing books to flop about on unfilled shelves; and shelving on the fore-edge. This latter practice, shelving on the fore-edge, is the cause of most spinal ailments in books of folio and larger sizes. When a big book has loose sections or covers, chances are very good that, somewhere in its life history, it was shelved for a long period of time on its fore-edge. It is of course tempting, when one has a book too tall for the shelf, to place it sideways, but that temptation must be avoided. The weight of the pages will pull away from the binding and, even if you do not end up with a broken book, the result is sure to be a saggy one. Stand oversized books on the **top** of your bookcase, supported by serviceable bookends or other supports. If this is not possible, and they must be placed in the case, lay them flat on their sides, but **without other volumes atop them**.

(6) Sunlight. Books stored for long periods of time in cases or on shelves that receive direct sunlight will show some "mellowing" of the spines, es-

pecially those bound in cloth. In planning a library room, try to situate cases where they will receive a minimum of direct sunlight.

(7) Insects. Various insects can do damage to books. They will not normally eat the paper, but the dye on cloth and buckram covered books. Bookbinders' dye contains some ingredient that insects find appetizing. The best safeguard is to hire a professional exterminator and have him treat the entire house, including the library room, at regular intervals. Never spray insecticides into a bookcase, or directly on books; this can cause more harm than the bugs.

The choice of a bookcase or other shelving unit ought to be a matter of concern for any serious collector. The comfort and preservation of your books will depend to some degree on it. Do not choose a bookcase for its physical appearance. Many times, a mediocre-looking case has all the right qualities for keeping a collection of rare books.

ANTIQUE BOOKCASES. It is understandable that some persons whose interests run to early printed books, fine bindings and the like, prefer to house their books in an antique bookcase so that the case will harmonize in appearance with the books. It is not necessarily a bad plan, so long as the case is well made and decently preserved. Too often when purchasing an antique bookcase the buyer is so awed by its outward details—by little carved gargoyles or brass trimming—that its interior is overlooked. **Check the inside first.** Are the shelves adjustable? It is troublesome, to say the least, to keep books (except miniature ones) in a case with unadjustable shelves. Are all the shelf supports present? Are the grooves into which they fit rotted, cracked or otherwise damaged? Are all the shelves present? (A case with an interior height of six feet ought to have at least five shelves.) Are the shelves sagging, cracked, or splintery? Are they sturdy enough to support the weight of heavy books? (Often an antique "bookcase" is really a china cabinet, with very flimsy shelving. A case with an interior width of five feet ought to have hardwood shelves no less than one inch thick.) And what of the case itself? Is the backboard firmly attached? Do "air spaces" appear anywhere—an indication that the wood is no longer solidly joined?

Whether or not a case should be enclosed—that is, equipped with glass-panel doors—is a matter of debate. There is good and bad to be said of glass-door cases. They help in keeping dust away from the books; at the same time they prevent air circulation.

Check the measurements of the case, especially its **interior depth**. An interior or shelf depth of less than twelve inches is not likely to prove satisfactory, unless you collect novels or other books of rather small size. A 14-inch depth is best. Of course, if your collection includes atlas folio volumes, no case but a specially constructed one will give enough depth.

WALL SHELVING. Wall shelving is sold today in many handsome designs, and often is more attractive than cases. There is no harm in using wall shelving, so long as the wall is sturdy and the hardware securely installed.

BOOKENDS. When a shelf of books is not filled to capacity, bookends or a good substitute must be used to prevent the volumes from tumbling around. Most bookends sold in gift shops are not serviceable; they may be neat looking but fail to do the job. The best are the metal L-shaped type, in which the lower portion slides beneath the first several books. These are strong enough to support heavy cumbersome volumes, and are inexpensive (purchaseable for less than $1 a pair).

Do not attempt to store books on (or in) anything but shelves. Books kept in boxes do badly, while those piled in closets or garages are liable to suffer serious injuries.

SLIPCASES AND BOOK-BOXES. Some collectors prefer to have slipcases or folding boxes made for their rarer volumes. If you like to encase your books in this way, by all means do so; but it is really unnecessary except for fragile items or part-issued books, not to mention that it is extremely expensive. A morocco-backed box costs from $50 to $100 to construct, and slipcases backed in leather run only slightly less. To have a fine old binding enclosed in a box, its spine not visible on the shelf, is considered a crime by most bibliophiles.

BOOK REPAIR. No attempts should be made by an amateur to repair the bindings or pages of costly rare books. This work is best left to a bookbinder. However, the collector ought to learn enough about book maintenance and repair to do restoration work on volumes of low or moderate price, which are not financially worthwhile to consign to a professional.

PROFESSIONAL REPAIR AND RESTORATION. Bookbinders can do wonders with damaged old books. A 300-year-old book cannot be made to appear new (who really wants it to?), but most kinds of defects are repairable. First it must be determined **when** a book should be placed for repair, and what sort of repair should be ordered. Usually the binder will make suggestions, offering various alternatives from which you may choose. If the binding is broken or badly worn, there will be a choice of trying to salvage or replace it. A new binding can be created, in which remaining portions of the old leather are inlaid into a leather of similar grain and color. The old spine—or what's left of it—can be reset into a new spine. This is expensive, more expensive than simply having the book rebound, and probably not worthwhile unless the book has some special appeal by way of retaining the original binding (say a Caxton or Wynkyn deWorde printing, or an American book of the 17th-century), or the binding carries unusual decoration or marks of ownership. Otherwise, to preserve a plain 16th or 17th century binding just because it was the book's original covering, when a fresh new binding would be sturdier and preserve the volume better, seems unnecessary.

When pages or gatherings are loose, the book may need resewing. If the paper is too fragile to permit resewing, the leaves can be attached to guards. When guards are used, it is generally not possible to recase the volume—that is, return it to the original binding—because the page ends will protrude from the fore-edge. A new binding is necessary.

A book in really poor condition, with the binding broken and many pages torn or mutilated, can have its leaves mounted and the mounts bound into a new binding. Once mounted, they are not likely to suffer any further damage. While a book with mounted leaves may have a slightly peculiar look, it is sound bibliophilic principle to have this done. Put off too long, the book may reach a point where even mounting cannot save it.

Do not order a new binding if the old one is in substantially sound condition. A loose cover can be rehinged, missing leather can be replaced.

AMATEUR REPAIRS YOU CAN DO. Check your books occasionally for possible damage, separating those which must be given to a binder from volumes you can safely deal with yourself. Do not hesitate to perform minor operations, but **practice first** on waste paper or worthless books.

LOOSE BINDINGS. Loose cloth bindings can usually be repaired by opening the book about midway, laying it face downward, and brushing glue along the inner side of the spine. Do not use cement-type glues; polyvinyl acetate, such as Elmer's Glue-All, does the job best. Use it sparingly (this applies to all book repairs done with glue). When completed, place rubber bands around the book and allow it to dry for several hours.

CRACKED INNER HINGES. Inner hinges can be strengthened by folding a narrow strip of paper and pasting it along the hinge. The paper should be about as heavy as index card paper for best results. Make sure it is neither too short or too long.

TORN SPINES. Spines are best treated by simply brushing a small quantity of glue on the torn sections, pressing them firmly into place, and allowing them to dry under the pressure of a rubber band.

TORN LEAVES. Leaves are mended by lightly daubing the torn edges with glue, placing the leaf between sheets of waxed kitchen paper, and drying (with the book shut) under a moderately heavy weight. (An object weighing two or three pounds will supply about the right pressure.) Tissue paper can be used instead of waxed paper if you wish; it will adhere to the tear and, when the excess is torn away, help to hide the repair.

NOTATIONS OR UNDERLININGS. Markings done in pencil are easily erased. When these are in ink, nothing removes them satisfactorily, and it is probably wise not to make the effort. The paper could be damaged by using strong cleansers or scraping. Besides, the notations might be of interest and could even, possibly, provide evidence on the book's previous ownership.

CARE OF LEATHER BOOKBINDINGS. Leather bindings are more attractive and valuable than cloth but also require more upkeep. Leather, being an animal substance, has natural oils when new. As it grows old the oil dries out and the leather brittles. It can crack, peel, or powder. Red "dust" on your bookshelves is a sure indication of dry bindings. At that point emergency treatment is necessary. It won't cure damage that's already occurred but halt further deterioration. With regular, periodic care, any leather binding bought in good condition should remain so. But don't buy a shabby binding in the belief that it can be easily refurbished as this is impossible.

Leather bindings must be dressed. This may not be a pleasant chore but it's something the book collector has no choice about. Actually, dressing leather can be rewarding. Just be sure to get a good preparation and use it intelligently: too much will leave the binding sticky and greasy. Any leather dressing, except those containing dyes, is suitable for bookbindings. However you will get better results with one made expressly for bindings such as British Museum Leather Dressing, rather than shoes or saddles. This, the "old stand-by" of the book trade, was once hard to get in America. Collectors sent to London for it and paid any price. Today it can generally be had in the states. A small amount is applied with a cotton swab, rubbing in a circular motion thoroughly over the entire leather portion of the binding. The book is then set aside for a half hour or so (longer in humid weather), giving the dressing time to soak in, and the book is buffed up with a clean dry cloth before replacing on the shelf. Dressing is applied lightly to gilded areas of a binding, as the gilding could be removed. Remember that the aim in dressing leather is to give it a drink, much like watering a plant, not to raise a polish. Most old leathers will not polish and should not be expected to.

About once every six months is the proper schedule for dressing leather bindings.

COLLECTOR'S TERMINOLOGY

ADDENDA (or ADDENDUM). Material added to the rear of a book.

ADVANCE COPY. Some publishers make a practice of issuing advance copies ahead of the normal edition, either to gain final approval of the author or send to reviewers, or both. Sometimes they will be identical to the regular edition but more often not, at least to the extent that they will be identified as advance copies. If the only difference is in the style or color of binding, it is just about impossible to know if such copies represent an advance issue or simply a BINDING VARIANT, which could have occurred in the ordinary trade run. There is generally some collecting enthusiasm for advance copies, as they represent an early state of the text. There is always a chance, outside though it may be, that an advance copy might carry notations by the author.

AGENT (AUCTION). The purpose of an auction agent is not merely to place bids in sales the bidder cannot attend, as this could just as easily be done by mail. Rather, he is expected to inspect lots in which the client is interested, to be certain there are no defects omitted in the catalogue, and to use his supposed expertise in bidding. Most agents are booksellers, sometimes retired. In Europe, the vast majority of auction bidders are dealers. The usual commission for purchases is 10%, nothing if the agent is unsuccessful.

ALDINE PRESS. See MANUTIUS, ALDO.

ALL EDGES GILT. One of the few bibliographical terms that explains itself. This means that all three edges of the leaves (top, bottom and foredge) have been dipped in gold gilt. It is abbreviated as a.e.g.

ALL PUBLISHED. When a book or partial set is said to be "all published," it indicates there were no further additions—so far as the bookseller can determine—even though they appear CALLED FOR. There is no guarantee, however, that publishing projects which have lain dormant many years might not suddenly be reactivated, leaving the purchaser with nothing more than half a horse.

ALTERNATIVE TITLE. Up to about 1850, and in some cases later, many publishers would provide books with two titles: the first or basic, by which it was generally known, and a second. The purpose of the alternative title was to give the public some hint (often more than a hint) of what the book was about, assuming this would promote sales. It was employed with both fiction and non-fiction. The result would be something like "Thaddeus Whimple; or, The Strange Tale of an Adventure at Sea." In rare instances, books came to be known better by the alternative than the main title. It is sometimes called a secondary title.

ANA. This is another term for ephemera. Johnsoniana is material relating, in some way or other (sometimes very remotely), to Samuel Johnson. Included under the heading are letters by, about, or to; pamphlets about; books with references to; newspaper accounts of; even personal articles owned by. The collecting of ana (or -ana, if you prefer) is widespread among those whose interests rest with a particular author or historical personality. Although someone may have written only one or two books, or none, collections of tens of thousands of items can be built around him. Institutional libraries are notorious collectors of ana.

ANONYMOUS. The reasons for authors wishing to publish with anonymity have been various through the ages. During periods of religious persecution, anything that smacked of criticism of the group holding power was best published (and printed, and sold, and read) anonymously. Political repression also produced floods of anonymous writing, much of it in the form of pamphlets. In the 17th and 18th centuries persons of position, such as titled Englishmen, often did not wish to launch literary efforts under their own name, fearing failure or, more likely, that the material would be considered unbecoming to their character. In this fashion did many a sober lord—or even clergyman—churn out the spiciest pornography, or at least what passed for it.

The identification of anonymous authors is sometimes easy, often difficult, most often impossible. Contemporary sources may shed light, such as the conversations of Boswell with Johnson (who usually knew who wrote everything). When offering an anonymous book whose author has been identified, the bookseller will place the name in brackets. A bracketed name does not necessarily mean an anonymous book, however. The standard work on the subject is by Halkett and Laing, a book that receives more wear than most on the reference shelves.

ANTHOLOGY. An anthology is a collection, in book form, of a number of short writings, not always by the same author. The earliest anthologies were of poetry but in recent years short stories, criticisms, essays, science fiction, and other topics have appeared profusely in anthology form. The material may be new, but more likely previously published.

ANTIQUARIAN BOOKSELLING. The 17th century saw the rise of antiquarian bookselling in England, France and elsewhere. Few catalogues were issued at first. Most early shops were in clusters, such as those in St. Paul's Churchyard, London. They were almost all in large cities, as towns and villages did not draw many collectors. By today's standards they were extremely small. Ten thousand volumes was a gigantic stock for a bookshop of Samuel Pepys' day, only a portion of which would be second-hand. They were primarily stalls, much of the material displayed on the sidewalk and very little within. The PENNY BOXES that became such a favorite of the bargain hunters in later years were probably not present, but prints, engravings, maps and such were sold by at least some.

The stall-type shop continued in popularity in the 1700's, but larger stocks were carried and there was more effort to cater to the special needs of collectors. London and Paris were the antiquarian book centers of the 18th century; others of note were Leipzig, Munich, Frankfurt, Vienna, Leyden, Amsterdam and Antwerp. The emergence of the scholar-dealer, the man who was a collector at heart and studied his merchandise with interest, did not occur until the early part of the 19th century. By this time antiquarian bookselling was big business and a number of the leading dealers made very comfortable livings. The BOHN brothers of London are generally credited with giving birth to modern rare-book dealing. With sizable libraries of fine books coming on the market regularly, stock building was not difficult. By 1900, there were at least half a dozen English dealers who boasted inventories in excess of half a million volumes. Several German booksellers at this time had stocks much larger.

As no single dealer can stock every book ever printed on his shelves, there is much dependence in the trade upon other members and a close association between all. Often the largest will depend upon the smallest to supply a title requested by a customer (see QUOTES).

ANTIQUE. When applied to paper, antique usually means a quality or appearance resembling the finer grades of olden times, when the proportion of rag pulp was much higher than today. However, most "antique" paper does not rely upon a rag content but a special sort of grass called Esparto that is quite hardy. When used of the binding, the term can be taken to mean a style of decoration that has a look of antiquity but in fact is modern or at least not contemporary with the book. If the book was printed in the 15th or 16th centuries, it is common for such bindings to feature RAISED BANDS on the spine and sometimes even CLASPS and CORNERPIECES. Stamped pigskin and vellum bindings are also frequently made when an early printed book or manuscript needs rebinding. There is seldom any attempt to fool purchasers into believing the binding is old, as the mere cost of application is usually more than the original binding would have been worth.

APPRAISALS. A number of antiquarian booksellers will appraise libraries or individual books. So much depends upon condition and a thorough examination of each item that it is well to contract with an appraiser who has sufficient time to devote. In choosing an appraiser, one should also try to select someone who has dealt in the sort of material the library contains. It is a folly to call in an authority on Americana to valuate a collection of Portuguese literature. Some appraisers will perform without ever seeing the books. They merely ask that a list be sent, from which they figure values. This, of course, is most unsatisfactory, unless the person compiling the list is an expert bibliographer equipped to describe volumes in anatomical detail; and if that were the case he could probably also appraise them.

The relationship of appraised prices to potential realizations on the auction market is questionable. When one is contemplating placing books for auction, the gallery can usually make better estimates than an independent appraiser. Collectors often think in the reverse: that the independent man, having no connection with the auctioneer, will give a more truthful statement. But the auctioneer, it should be remembered, has experience determining what sort of books do well in his sales and his guesses are apt to be nearer the mark. In any event, one should not expect actual prices to be carbon copies of appraisals, as too many indeterminable factors are involved (such as a snow storm on sale day).

Appraisals are more difficult to obtain—accurate ones, at any rate—when one has an ultra-specialized collection. There are few appraisers who have thorough knowledge of miniature books or early advertising memorabilia, to name just two of many topics. Appraisal fees are quite stiff but worth it if a good job has been done.

AQUATINT. This is a method of etching which stresses soft tone and shade, similar in effect to mezzotint. Aquatints bear a resemblance to wash drawings. It was first used in primitive form, with unsatisfactory results, in the 17th century. Perfection of the process is generally credited to the French artist LePrince, who used it from 1768. At first it was almost ignored in much of Europe, though British artists seized upon it. Many British books of the late 18th and 19th centuries were illustrated in aquatint, sometimes printed in color and on other occasions colored by hand. When printing in colored aquatint, it was necessary to use a separate plate for each color. A few famous artists, such as Goya and Picasso, have done a good deal of experimentation with aquatint.

ART PAPER. The shiny, coated stock upon which most art books (or at least their illustrations) are printed is art paper. Attractive enough when new, it does not grow old gracefully and is ruined by the least contact with water. Also, dirt and stains cannot be removed from it without eating into the surface.

AS NEW. A used book which does not look used is considered to be as new. It is seldom applied to books more than about 20 years old and is basically a British expression. American booksellers prefer "mint," which means the same.

ASSOCIATION COPY. An association copy is a book that has been associated, in one way or other, with a famous person. This could be a result of coming from his library, or containing some HOLOGRAPH writing of his; or it might be that the author inscribed the book to him, which is the most common case. However it is unfair, under present definitions, to term any book inscribed by the author an association copy (see PRESENTATION COPY). Some feel that any person the author gave a book to must have been well known to him and hence of association interest, but this is not so; inscriptions are obtained at autograph parties by persons the author does not know and will never again see. The intimacy of the inscription is meaningless in an attempt to discover familiarity. Association can only be claimed in instances where the inscription is addressed to a person who can be proven an acquaintance of the author. However, it is not at all necessary that the second party should possess any great fame to make the item desirable. Rather, his or her relation to the author and effect on the author's career is of more importance. For instance, a book of Oscar Wilde's inscribed to Robert Ross would be considered an ideal and valuable association item because of the influence they exercised in each other's lives, even though the fame of Ross on his own is rather inconsequential.

Association copies are generally thought of in terms of modern literature, but there are examples from the early days of printing and even among medieval manuscripts, though of course not frequent. As one can imagine, association copies are often the subject of forgeries, but the experts in the trade do a good job of weeding them out.

AUCTIONS. Auction sales have long been resorted to for the dispersal of books and consequently for their purchase. It is probable that auctions of manuscript scrolls and the like occurred in ancient Rome, as almost everything passed through the auction market (including people!) in the ancient world. Auction sales devoted exclusively to books were introduced in England in the 1670's and were almost immediately successful. Far more volumes, both in quantity and quality, went over the block in olden times than presently, as the majority of the world's rare books were in private hands, a far different situation than now exists.

The choice of whether to place a library in the hands of an auctioneer and take one's chances in an UNRESERVED SALE, or negotiate a sale with a bookseller (who must re-sell at a profit), is not an easy one. At an auction, the vendor receives the full price realized for his merchandise, less the commission charged by the house, which may vary from 10% to 15% or more. Thus if a book is sold at an auction for $100, the vendor may receive from $80 to $90, whereas a book for which a dealer will charge $100 will not gain the seller a similar amount. The average mark-up in the antiquarian book business is 100%, but it may vary considerably. Still, this is not a fair indication, because many auction battles occur between dealers who must re-sell and therefore the realizations are apt to be a cut beneath retail prices.

The conditions of sale at most auctions prevent returns except where obvious errors have been committed in descriptions. Most auction houses devote careful attention to their descriptions, however, and employ experienced cataloguers. Sometimes nothing will be taken back in any case, even if one opens the binding and finds all the leaves missing, so it is well to read the conditions (printed on the inside front wrapper of the catalogue, or nearby) with care. Lots comprising several books are never accepted back, no matter what goes wrong.

AUSTRIA, NATIONAL LIBRARY OF. Located in Vienna, the Austrian National Library is the former Imperial Library, for many years one of the glories of the old Imperial Burg of the city. Since the 18th century, when the present structure was erected (rebuilt in the 20th), it has been ranked one of the foremost libraries of Europe. The Hapsburg family did much to bring it to prominence and some of their portraits are to be seen in the library today. During the 18th and 19th centuries, when Vienna was the principal city of the German world, it received gifts from all corners, including many private collections and papers of celebrities. One of the major acquisitions was the Oriental library of Baron Von Hammer-Purgstall, who died in 1857. Among earlier collections, the Austrian National Library possesses a portion of the manuscripts owned by MATTHIAS CORVINUS; the 15,000-volume library of the Fugger banking family; and the library of Tycho Brahe, pioneer Danish astronomer. The beginnings of the Austrian National Library date to 1493, when it began as the Hofbibliothek. When the Jesuits were expelled from Austria in the 18th century, a number of their finer manuscripts were absorbed. When threatened by the French at the revolution, many of its rarities were whisked away into storage. The list of major holdings is long: a 6th century manuscript on purple parchment, written in gold and silver; fragments of the Book of Genesis from a 4th century Bible; a 5th century textbook of medicinal herbs with illustrations; a map of the roads of the Roman Empire, dating from 160-180 A.D.; a miniature octagonal Koran dated 1545, worn as an amulet; Mexican Indian writings on leather; a manuscript of Livy's Roman History brought by St. Suitbert from Scotland in the 7th century, etc.

AUTHORIZED EDITION. The term "authorized edition" is usually used with reference to biographies that have the approval of the subject. It implies the existence of other, unauthorized versions, which is not always the case. The term is used to draw public interest, and to guard against the chances of an unauthorized version popping up later. One drawback of authorized editions is the popular feeling that if the subject saw fit to authorize the book, it cannot contain any startling revelations.

BACKBONE. One of the many terms used for the spine of a book. Shelfback and back are two others.

BACKED. This usually means the spine has been recovered, either as a repair or decoration, in a different fashion than the binding. Most backing is amateurishly done by owners to save or replace the spine, as a binder will almost surely think of something more attractive. But in some cases it is used to indicate a half binding, such as "cloth boards backed in vellum," which is misleading; one does not know if the vellum was applied with the binding or glued on with cement by a do-it-yourselfer.

BASKERVILLE, JOHN. Baskerville was the most exceptional English printer of the 18th century, and really the only one of genius in his age. His name has become so renowned that many persons are apt to believe all his books are very scarce, which is not the case, but eager competition makes him costlier than the average English book of their day. The oddity of Baskerville was that he lived in a time of little inspiration, so that his accomplishments are all the more striking. It may be said that Aldus was influenced by Jenson, Gryphus by Aldus, the Elzevirs by Plantin, but Baskerville was removed by at least a century and studied examples of their work, and held a high opinion of the Elzevirs. Long before starting up as a printer, he designed type on which he spent the equal of a fortune in modern money. His first book was printed in Birmingham in 1756. Almost all his productions were masterpieces, but devoid of all but the slightest ornament. Baskerville's volumes are built along the most simple, clean, fluid, classic lines; his type a delicate roman. The paper he used was also above the average, as he intended his books to appeal to connoisseurs. However, they were not issued in elegant or special bindings.

Of particular note was his four-volume edition, in quarto, of Addison's writings. A few of his books were imprinted with the identity of the Elzevir press, not as forgeries but merely out of recognition of his respect for them.

BASTARD TITLE. Another name for half title, that is, the leaf before the title page which carries the title, in small letters, but no other information is a "bastard title." It is a holdover from the INCUNABULA period, when title pages were nothing more than this, and survives as a useless appendage, but tradition dies hard in the world of book design. To maintain decorum, some bibliographers refer to it as "bas title." As the bastard title came first in chronological sequence, it is not aptly named.

BAY PSALM BOOK. The Bay Psalm Book was the first full-length American-printed book, issued at Cambridge, Massachusetts, from the press of STEPHEN DAYE in 1640. The name derives from the Massachusetts Bay Colony; the actual title is "The Whole Book of Psalms." Only 11 copies are known to exist. The most recent sale was in 1947, when a specimen fetched the then record price of $151,000 at New York's Parke-Bernet Galleries. It was bought by Dr. Rosenbach and sold eventually to Yale University. All but one of the 11 are in public or institutional libraries. A copy was unexpectedly discovered in 1934, when an Irishman found it among family possessions and sold it to an American dealer, who retained it for his personal collection. However, this collection has since been institutionalized. Had it remained outside the U.S. it would have been unique as all other specimens were on American soil.

It is not known how many copies were printed. The figure is placed between 100 and 300, which is little more than a guess. The average size of editions of commercially published works in England in 1640 was considerably more, but it is felt Daye would not have risked a large edition as there were few book buyers in the colonies. In any event, the majority seem to have quickly perished, probably owing to heavy use and the lack of sturdy bindings. By the mid-1700's it was collected as a rarity, though it brought only a fraction of the price of most celebrated European books. During the late 1800's and even into the 1900's many New England attics were combed for copies, as the public heard of the prices being fetched.

BERTHELET, THOMAS. An English printer of the second quarter of the 16th-century, Thomas Berthelet was quite prolific, turning out more than 200 books, and a typographer of some skill. His books are all in BLACK LETTER or gothic, but better designed and arranged than is the case with many of his contemporaries. His illustrated books, which are unfortunately few, are especially fine. Most of the woodcuts are done after the German fashion, with heavy shading and attention to small detail, rather than the crude and angular manner of those who engraved for PYNSON and WYNKYN DeWORDE. While Holbein, the German master painter, was staying at the court of Henry VIII, he did some illustrating for Berthelet, notably the title page of "Institution of a Christian Man," 1537. Berthelet's press was notable for its many productions of the works of English authors and poets, including Chaucer, Gower, etc. His mark consisted of a well-executed engraving of "Lucrecia Romana" putting a knife in her chest.

BEST EDITION. "Best edition" is a term often seen in catalogues but of doubtful meaning. It is seldom clear whether it is the best printed, best bound, has the best illustrations, the best text, or is best in some other (or collective) way. Generally the authority for this lofty distinction is the personal opinion of the bookseller, who may or may not be qualified to pass judgment. But the best edition, whether truly best or not, is never the first.

BEST SELLER. The origin of the modern best seller lists, which appear in magazines and newspapers (and seldom agree) can be traced to 1895, when the American Bookman began publishing a list limited to six titles. The term is frequently misused. There is no single "best seller list," though one often hears it referred to as some omnipotent power that sends down messages. If a book appears as #76 on a list compiled from sales in a Sacramento shop, the author can boast of being on the best seller list. Publishers, too, often release their own lists of best sellers from their current selections, and if someone is tenth on the Zoonsday Press list, he likewise has a best seller. But to genuinely have a best selling book means to sell many copies, whether the item ever appears on a list or not. Publishers naturally encourage the compiling of lists, as they bring publicity, but authors are paid strictly on the basis of copies sold, no other consideration.

BEVELED EDGES. In the days when thick WOODEN BOARDS were a common feature of bookbindings, their edges were often beveled, or cut to a slanting angle. Their presence is only noted by the most meticulous cataloguers as they have no bearing on the value of the book.

BIBLIOGRAPHY. In everyday understanding, a bibliography is a list of books: cookbooks, books on the Vietnam War, books on toy trains. To most librarians, a bibliography is a list of works by a single author (called an author bibliography), in which the compiler attempts to record every specimen of the subject's writing that has ever appeared in print. But in a more sweeping, general sense, bibliography is the study of books: their history, origin, anatomy, appearance and value.

Bibliography in its more refined forms is a new science, not yet walking upright, but its beginnings are rather ancient. What study may have been done of the evolution of physical properties of books by scholars of the primitive societies we have no way of knowing. As books were collected in early Egypt it is likely there was some curiosity about their background, but any writings or studies that might have been carried out no longer exist. The Greeks must have come into possession of a sizable number of Egyptian papyri and undoubtedly made an attempt to catalogue them; certainly the Imperial Romans catalogued their libraries. Had Rome lived on beyond 476 A.D. the science of bibliography might have progressed better, but the Dark Ages put all such things at a virtual standstill. Readers of the Middle Ages had no more interest in the history of books than in speculating if the earth were really flat, or the seas contained dragons.

The Renaissance and the invention of printing in the 15th century marked a new era. There were many fresh libraries built and scholars engaged in research never before carried out. Encyclopedias printed toward the close of the 15th century attempted to give information on the origin of printing. Much of it was erroneous, but at least it was a beginning. In the 16th century, bibliographies in the modern fashion of subject catalogues appeared. As the total of printed books was still comparatively small, some early bibliographers set out to catalogue every one that had been issued since Gutenberg's 42-line Bible. Of course it was an impossible task; not by weight or numbers, but because facilities were inadequate. It is only in recent years that we are fully realizing the amount of work produced by incunabula printers. At one time it was thought there were less than 20,000 titles issued in the 15th century; then the estimate was increased to 30,000; now we know the real figure is well over 60,000, perhaps near 100,000. Though far more specimens of early printing existed in the 16th century than today, they were widely scattered and it was far beyond the abilities of any editor to harness more than a fraction.

The first full-scale effort at cataloguing all European books was Gesner's "Bibliotheque Universalis," which appeared in four volumes at Zurich in 1545–55. Incomplete as it was, it served as the foundation for many later works and is still useful. At the time of the Gutenberg Bicentennial in the 17th century, there were attempts to make special catalogues of incunabula. An ambitious Scotsman, Dr. Robert Watt, published his "Bibliotheca Britannica" in four volumes in 1824, which surveys the whole of British literature and touches upon continental. By this time bibliography had its rough edges polished down. The greatest English bibliographers of the early 19th century were its booksellers and auctioneers, men like HENRY BOHN and THOMAS THORPE, who made a more systematic study of rare books than had ever been done. It was largely as a result of their efforts that interest was stirred among private researchers. By the mid 19th century, investigation on manuscripts and early printed books had begun in earnest and many articles and papers appeared.

The first conclusive attempt to catalogue incunabula was the series of volumes compiled by Ludwig Hain from 1826 to 1838. Though incomplete, it remains a basic reference work and Hain numbers appear in many catalogues of antiquarian booksellers. The year 1837 saw the publication at Oxford of the "General Bibliographical Dictionary" in four volumes, a translation of a work which had appeared earlier in Germany. One of the major efforts to classify English literature was Lowndes' "Bibliographers' Manual," which ran through several editions in the 19th century. In 1881, the British Museum began publication of a 108-volume set of catalogues of its printed books, the largest bibliographical work up to that time.

Today the practice of bibliography is greatly advanced over a hundred or even fifty years ago. Modern scholars attack their subject with surgical precision, using ultra-violet lamps and a variety of technical gadgets to discover forgeries or hidden repairs. As a result, many of the old beliefs and traditions (see BINDING MYTH) have been exploded and others are in danger of toppling.

BIBLIOTHEQUE NATIONALE. The National Library of France is considered the finest library of the western world. Its beginnings date to the Middle Ages, at least to the reign of Charles V who kept the Bibliotheque du Roi (as the collection was then called) at the Louvre. Under Francois I (1515–1547) the Bibliotheque du Roi was united with the libraries of the

Orleans family and moved to the royal palace at Fontainebleau. Charles IX then transplanted the library to Paris, placing it in the College of Clermont. In 1622 it was brought to the rue de la Harpe. With this move came the appearance of the first printed catalogue, recording a modest holding of 6,000 items. But it was quickly to grow. The French kings were far more dedicated to book collecting (and collecting in general) than the English or German and gave their personal attention to the royal library. Aware of this, booksellers from all over the continent besieged its librarians with offerings, as well as personal visits. In 1714 the total was up to 70,000 volumes, then nearly 500,000 a century later. In 1908 it possessed 3,000,000 printed books. Today the total of all items, printed and in manuscript, is well beyond ten million.

The great period of growth was the 18th century, which saw it graduate from just another continental library to the first rank. Numerous private libraries of value were dispersed with the Bibliotheque du Roi purchasing heavily from many. Sometimes it bought whole collections intact, if it considered the contents sufficiently worthwhile. Others came as gifts. Two of the finest private collections acquired were those of Marie deMedici and her librarian DeTHOU. Others of note were the Colbert, DuFresne, and Mentel, which were not very celebrated internationally but nevertheless valuable. The Bibliotheque Nationale also contains the library of Cardinal Mazarin (1602–1661), one of the most brilliant of its time. It included a copy of the Gutenberg Bible bearing a RUBRICATOR'S note dated 1456, providing the book was off the press by then. The Gutenberg Bible is still sometimes called the Mazarin, because of this specimen.

The Bibliotheque du Roi also benefitted from some of the harsher political bombshells of the 18th century. When the Jesuits were sent out of France, many of the better items from their libraries were taken over. But this was nothing compared to the acquisitions which came on the heels of the revolution. As royalist families and supporters fled Paris, leaving their possessions behind, their libraries were freely looted for rarities. But such are the ill winds that build book collections, and sometimes destroy them.

The main building has been rebuilt and renovated a number of times, in an effort to provide greater space. The major reconstruction was carried out in the 1850's. But its collections have grown at far too rapid a pace to be adequately housed. Today many books are sent to Versailles to be stored, but the library remains overcrowded and years behind in indexing its acquisitions. The Bibliotheque Nationale is a copyright library, entitled by law to two copies of all books printed in France.

BINDER'S TICKET. The old fashion was for bookbinders to place a small ticket bearing their name and (usually) address on the front endpaper or pastdown of books they had bound and of which they were proud. As these tickets could be rather easily removed, they were abandoned in favor of stamping, usually in ink but sometimes in gilt. Binders' tickets and stamps are very tiny. Almost all hand or craft binders leave their mark. Edition binders seldom do, unless their name might appear somewhere in the credits along with the printer, paper maker, etc.

BINDING COPY. A book in dire need of a new binding is referred to as a "binding copy." The term is only applied to books whose bindings are in miserable condition, as it constitutes an admission of defeat. Sometimes binding copies are found to have no binding at all, not even the barest trace of leather on the spine. This is basically a British term. American booksellers often use the less glamorous "needs binding."

BINDING MYTH. The history of bookbinding was, until less than a century ago, one of the cloudiest in all the decorative arts. The progress of printing can be easily traced and the personalities involved identified from their productions; but very few early binders signed their work and concrete information proves elusive. Because of this, many traditions and myths grew up around certain binding styles, for which there was no good cause. As bindings from the library of 16th century French collector JEAN GROLIER were always admired, there were many speculations on their origin. Some thought Grolier bound them himself, which, though absurd, was widely believed for a time. Others firmly thought they were bound in Paris in such a shop, or at Venice by such a craftsman. After it came to be agreed that most Grolier bindings were of Italian origin, all sorts of names were advanced. Many fictional names were included, too, or at least they appear fictional today, for if any records concerning them once existed they have disappeared. There are binding myths surrounding every famous collector and most binders up to the 18th century, though many have been so soundly disproved they should have been long ago wiped from memory. However, some cataloguers and writers do their research from outdated reference works and are unaware of the latest findings, so these errors and groundless theories are allowed to live on.

Of the myths concerning binding styles, embroidered bindings are a good example of how romanticism can lead one astray. At one time someone must have seen an embroidered binding in the library of a convent, then went about telling how the nuns passed their hours by turning out examples of such work. Book collectors, who have always shown large doses of gullibility in these matters, ate it up and went on believing that embroidered bindings were the products of nunneries just as illuminated manuscripts of the Middle Ages had come down from monasteries. It was a pretty deceit but a deceit nonetheless, for no proof has ever been found linking any embroidered binding to any convent (see NUNS OF LITTLE GIDDING).

Myths regarding binders are no less entertaining and have turned a good deal of names into celebrities who would be very surprised to find themselves so regarded. Samuel Mearne is an example. Even if he were a prolific craftsman, there are far more bindings attributed to him than any one man could have produced. But in truth Mearne, for all the space given him in histories of binding, may not have been nearly so influential as some have contended. He lived in the 17th century, a time when many of the myths were a-brewing, and certainly must have operated as a bookbinder at one time or other; but there is no information to personally link him to any single binding, and the belief that he initiated the COTTAGE style cannot be supported.

Yet myths are tough to dissolve. Collectors have a love and respect for the old tradtions, which have given the hobby a good measure of color, and discovering a myth unmasked is like learning there is no Santa Claus.

BINDINGS. Bookbinding seems to have been introduced in Rome, either in the 3rd or 4th century A.D., but it was not an invention heralded by the blast of trumpets. In fact it is doubtful that anyone took notice of the event, as it was not recorded anywhere in Roman literature and the Romans liked to write down everything. It was merely a by-product of the development of the CODEX book. As soon as books were made into folded leaves instead of scrolls they needed a suitable covering. The very earliest bindings were probably plain uncovered wooden boards with a hide spine, what we today would call a half binding. In a short time this evolved into the full leather binding, which looked much like specimens of a thousand years later, and well they should have: they were constructed in precisely the same fashion, differing only in ornament. Early ornamentation consisted of painting and encrusting with jewels and walrus bone carvings, which later gave way to blindstamping and finally goldstamping.

The materials that have, over the centuries, been employed for binding books are numerous. While the most common (and satisfactory) are vellum, pigskin, calf, morocco, and the various derivations of cloth or muslin, bindings have been fashioned of antelope, shark, snake and even—yes— human skin! The use of human skin did not come about because of a shortage of other leathers. Rather, it was occasionally a practice in the Middle Ages to strip the skin of slain enemy soldiers and make different uses of it; bookbinding was only one. There are cathedrals in Europe where one may still see doors covered in human hide, though tour guides sometimes hesitate to mention the fact.

The average binding of the monastic era was made of boards covered in leather and supplied with CLASPS and so forth. In Italy the limp vellum binding, in which no boards were used and ties took the place of clasps, was more popular and eventually spread to Spain, Portugal, and, to an extent into France. Morocco was introduced from North Africa in the 15th century and used primarily for the bindings, with sumptuous gilding. Collectors like the Frenchman Jean Grolier made the 16th century the great age of decorative bindings, granting huge commissions to artist-binders to design and execute special styles for them. The finest bindings of the 16th century were made in Italy and France, but in the 17th century very excellent work was done in England, particularly in the way of "cottage" and embroidered bindings. Velvet or "plush" was occasionally used for binding from a very early period and enjoyed a sort of renaissance in the 16th and 17th centuries, particularly in France and Spain. It could not be gilded or blindstamped. To compensate for this, a number of metal objects were attached, including bosses, centerpieces, and anything the binder could dream up.

The collecting of book bindings, whether by country, style or period, is one of the major divisions of the hobby and has inspired many volumes of reference literature, much of which is now out of print and itself rare.

BINDING TIGHT. The binding, while scuffed or otherwise defaced, is nevertheless structurally sound and in no immediate danger of falling off. It is another in the long list of bibliophilic terms that try to cheer up the prospective customer.

BINDING VARIANT. In the case of TRADE BINDINGS after the introduction of publisher's cloth (c. 1823), where one would expect bindings to conform, not all copies of a particular edition may be bound uniformly. The difference may be only in color, or it could involve the style of lettering or even the quality of material. The most common reason for binding variants was the practice of publishers to bind only a portion of the edition, say a few hundred copies out of a total run of a thousand or more, to try them on the market before making a larger investment. If they failed to sell, the unbound remainder might be destroyed, sold as waste paper, or given over to another publisher at a fraction of the original cost. But if the book showed promise, the remaining stock might be bound in a more attractive covering. Books exported from Britain for sale in other countries often received secondary bindings, but these are not properly classed as variants. Collectors normally choose to believe that a variant constitutes an earlier state, but there is no guarantee unless the text or other factors give evidence.

BLACK LETTER. Also known as "gothic," this was the heavy, broad type in which early books were printed, including most incunabula. When moveable type was first introduced (c. 1450) in Germany, there was probably an attempt to fool the public into believing such books were actually manuscripts. To accomplish this the types were designed to resemble handwriting, and it happened that German script of the 15th century was based upon wide, inky, nearly unreadable characters. Black letter books remained in popularity long after the secret was out, but later printers tried their luck at modifying it and making it more pleasing to the eye. In Italy, where the humanistic hand of the Renaissance was written, gothic could not take hold. Instead a semi-gothic was used, which quickly gave way to roman or modern type. Black letter was widely used in England, where it was not effectively replaced by roman until the close of the 16th century. Its final stronghold was its birthplace, Germany, where it lingered into the 19th century, but by then was not recognizable as the type of Gutenberg and his associates.

BLAKE, WILLIAM. Blake was an English author, poet, philosopher and artist (1757–1827), considered by many far ahead of his time in concepts and techniques. At the age of 16 he executed an engraving of "Joseph of Arimathea," basing it upon work of Michelangelo, whose muscular free-moving figures were to provide an inspiration throughout his career. He was apprenticed to a minor engraver named James Basire, under whose eye he carried out drawings of prominent London buildings. Blake was caught up in the Gothic Revival of the later 18th century and into Romanticism. At this period in his life he spent long hours in the medieval monuments of London, studying the architecture, but mainly submerging himself in the mood of the Dark Ages, which became a powerful force in his life. Rejecting conventional artistic methods, he feuded with artists of his day, including Joshua Reynolds. But in later life he inspired many followers.

In the late 1780's, be began publishing unique illustrated editions of his mythical poems which he called "illuminated printing." They consisted of text and illustrations done in his hand, then engraved for printing. The first was "Songs of Innocence" in 1789. He also illustrated books for others, notably Young's "Night Thoughts," and Robert Blair's "The Grave," a poem. Though his work was praised by some critics it fell short of the public taste, as few people knew or cared what he was about. Resolved not to conform his approach to accepted standards, he continued in his own fashion, developing a style unprecedented in the history of art. In 1809, his one-man exhibit, for which he worked hard at a catalogue, fell flat. Discouraged, or perhaps casting about for new subjects or outlets, he did little for the next nine years. In 1818, surviving on a meager income, he was taken under the wing of painter John Linnell, who provided for his remaining years. It was under Linnell that he created much of his finest work, as the burden of financial worry was gone. His engravings for "The Book of Job" are of the Linnell period.

Though technical faults can often be found in Blake's illustrations, they remain the most creative and forceful in English art, fully alive and expressive of motion and thought, rather than mere pictorial designs. Many interpretations of his art, with its ghostly and tearful figures, have been attempted, but Blake seems too complex to reduce to simple terms. The present century has witnessed a revival of interest in his art and writing.

BLINDSTAMPED. Blindstamping has long been used in association with leather articles and has not been confined only to bindings. It did not make its appearance as a decoration for bindings until the 12th century, so far as we learn from surviving specimens. The procedure was to stretch vellum, pigskin or calf over heavy wooden binding boards and fasten it in place with nails. The leather would then be moistened with water and stamped with red-hot tools, just taken from the fire. These tools were made in two distinct styles. In one, the design—which might be an acorn or leaf—would be cut away and formed only an outline impression. In the other, the design was raised on the tool and the surrounding area cut away. Depending on which was used, the binding would either have designs that were recessed or slightly raised from the surface.

At first a good deal of imagination went into the design of these bindings. The binders had only a limited number of small tools or stamps at their disposal, so the artistry lay in the method by which they were arranged. With nothing more than a few leaf and arabesque stamps, a binder could produce excellent work, positioning them in panels, circles, triangles, and so forth. But, as with other good ideas, the need for economy and speed soon cheapened the craft. Large stamps were manufactured, which could decorate an entire cover of a small book in one impression, thereby making the process an assemblyline routine. In the case of folio volumes, where a single stamp would not suffice, a solution was readily found. The stamps were made in rolls, like a rolling pin, so that a continuous design would be repeated by simply rolling the stamp along the binding. It was only occasionally that a stamp of special design would be created for use on a particular volume or class of volumes. Some fairly good portrait stamps were used in Germany in the 16th century. Generally speaking, English blindstamped bindings were the most successful.

Sometimes the binder, if he felt he had turned out a presentable job, would sign his initials. Other times the collector who ordered the binding wanted his own initials, or name, or in rare instances, emblem included. As the tools used in blindstamping were often passed through the trade from one to another, as workmen died or sold out, it is possible to make a game of tracing them. Sometimes one finds the tools going from one country to another and zig-zagging across the continent. The finest blindstamped bindings of the INCUNABULA period were executed in Germany, particularly at Nuremberg. The house of KOBERGER released many of its productions in blindstamped calf coverings, which all exhibit a similarity. Blindstamped bindings continued to be made in Germany until the 18th century, by which time they were much debased and had little character.

Blindstamped bindings were sometimes, but not often, painted in gold or colors after stamping. The result was rarely satisfactory.

BLOCKBOOKS (or XYLOGRAPHIC BOOKS). Books printed from wooden blocks upon which all text (and illustrations, if any) were engraved by hand. Such books were printed in central Europe in the 15th century, in very small quantities. The process was grueling and the finished product often appeared very amateurish. At one time it was firmly believed blockbooks comprised the stepping-stone from manuscript to typography, a natural assumption, but doubt has now been cast. While existing blockbooks are crude and primitive, indicating a very early origin, historians argue that this results only from the limitation of the technique, which did not permit polished work. It is the opinion of some that blockbooks did not appear until after the Gutenberg Bible, c. 1450. This raises the obvious query: why fool with this method if typography already existed? The answer, as advanced by this body of critical thought, is that speculators wanted to cash in on the profits to be gained from printing but lacked the skill or materials to print as Gutenberg had done, so they resorted to this painstaking approach.

Regardless of when they were introduced, the majority of specimens definitely were produced after the printing press was known, in the 1460's and 1470's. By 1480, they had almost completely died out, but a few continued to be published as late as the first decade of the 16th century. The fact that they survived into the sixth decade of typography is surprising; no clear explanations can be offered. One thing is sure, however: they were all intended for the poorer classes and must have been far cheaper in price than large, sumptuous printed books. Usually they consisted of a few dozen pages with illustrations and a brief text, on such topics as the art of dying (Ars Moriendi), the Bible of the poor (Biblia Pauperum), etc. All specimens are of the greatest rarity. It is believed a good number have totally perished, leaving no trace, and that those recorded are but a fraction of what was produced.

BLURBS. The little sales talks given in antiquarian booksellers' (and auctioneers') catalogues are called blurbs, probably due to their brevity. The actual meat of the description—title, author, place of publication, date, etc.—is not part of the blurb. These are just formal details that must be gotten out of the way. The blurb only begins afterward and is generally marked by an indented line. While the anatomical description of a book is regulated by the rules of bibliography, the bookseller can let loose his spirit on the blurb: it is his moment of glory.

The purpose of the blurb is naturally to help sell the book. Even the most desirable books do not seem overly appealing by a cold statement of their physical points, so the bookseller tries to paint a rosier picture. The approach generally taken is to better acquaint customers with the particular edition, in the belief they may fail to order out of ignorance. To do this the bookseller or his cataloguer will attempt to find favorable references to it in bibliographies. Sometimes this is easy and sometimes not. Even if the edition is only mentioned in a bibliography, with no comment pro or con, the bookseller is safe in saying "cited by Smith." Or the bookseller can say something of his own. In the case of standard sets or other works of popular interest that have been continually reissued, he may resort to calling it "the best edition," which is open to interpretation. If this seems too strong, he may call it "a very good edition," "a significant edition," "a well-printed edition," or possibly "a neat edition," neat being an all-purpose word that frequently comes to the rescue. As all of these designations are more or less matters of personal opinion, the opinion of the buyer is apt to differ from that of the seller.

There is a trend these days toward longer and sometimes even witty blurbs. As an example, we are faced with these excuses for damage: "stains on some leaves, possibly the result of being read at evening by a monk holding an oil lamp"; "several leaves torn with loss of text, title mounted, binding broken, but all in all an excellent copy for a scholar of meager circumstances"; and, "playfully nibbled by the little creatures of the library."

BOARDS. The term "bound in boards," sometimes merely "boards," refers to a binding in which the sides are of plain board, perhaps covered in paper, with a cloth or buckram spine. Incunables and other early books were sometimes bound in uncovered wooden boards with a leather spine; the spine would occasionally be BLINDSTAMPED. Paper and strawboards were used later.

BODLEY, SIR THOMAS. An English book collector of the late Elizabethan and early Stuart eras (died 1613), Bodley donated his library to Oxford University, where it came to be known as the Bodleian, and gave money for its maintenance. The Bodleian is now one of the major rare-book libraries of England.

BOHN, HENRY GEORGE. Next to QUARITCH, Henry Bohn was the leading figure in the history of English antiquarian bookselling. There were three Bohn brothers—Henry, James, and John—who operated their separate bookshops. Henry, by far the most successful, was born in 1796. Until he entered the secondhand book business, the general system of compiling catalogues was archaic. Volumes would be classed by size, one line given each title, and nothing said regarding condition; often the style of binding was even ignored. Bohn introduced a detailed, conversational approach which won him acclaim. Instead of merely publishing lists to be distributed to readers at large, Bohn spoke their language. His stock was enormous, larger than any English (perhaps any European) bookseller up to that time, surpassed even in the modern age by only two or three firms. Also, it comprised a far greater proportion of rarities than was usual. Bohn personally attended many auctions and bought the finest items, sometimes as agent but often for stock. Most noted English collectors of the mid 19th century bought from him and depended on his advice in the building of their libraries. The first of his huge retail catalogues appeared in 1841. It was five inches thick and sold for a guinea, so was dubbed the Guinea Pig. This was followed by another monster in 1847, improved in format.

In 1842 Bohn hired Bernard Quaritch, newly arrived from his native Prussia, who stayed with him until 1847. In 1846 he established the now famous Bohn Library, which issued over 600 volumes of popular literature in inexpensive editions. The business concluded with his death in 1884 when he was 88 years old. In private life he spent much of his fortune on works of art and lived amid plush surroundings.

BOOKCASES. The history of bookcases dates very far into antiquity, though the earliest ones consisted of wall shelving rather than free-standing furniture. The method of storing scrolls in the ancient world was to place them in clay jars, with the title of the book or books written on the lid; these would then be arranged on shelving according to subject or author. If a work consisted of many volumes, the jars would be made larger. It was only when books were written out on folded sheets and bound in the present manner that the use of jars was abandoned and something resembling modern storage methods came into adoption. For more than a thousand years, however—up to about 1600—volumes were placed on the shelves with their spines inward and the foredges facing out, and instead of standing upright they were normally stacked. Consequently, early bookshelves made no provisions for tall volumes.

Free-standing bookcases were not a common article of the medieval household. Private parties who had books, and there were few who did, generally kept them in carved chests along with their plates, or linen, or in upright cupboards. The person who owned enough books to warrant the manufacture of a special receptacle was a rarity, and in these instances it was considered more chic to have a carpenter come and install shelves on the walls. Usually these would be open but sometimes provided with a swinging grate or ornamental grille. The modern bookcase as we know it was really a product of the Italian Renaissance. By this time books were beginning to be shelved upright and attention was given to the design and manufacture of cases, which were called presses. Some cases of the 16th century were made from wood encrusted with seashells, sparkling minerals, mother-of-pearl and so forth. Much fine carving was also done on them, particularly on English and German examples. The majority of these early cases were extremely large. Occasionally, the shelves were painted or gilded; the exterior might be gilded as well. Some early specimens that survive today show many layers of old paint, indicating that they were probably redone as often as the fabric of the home.

Glazed-door bookcases were not introduced until the 17th century and were popular mainly in England. They were also large and commonly provided with a wider lower section to receive oversized volumes. The doors would swing out rather than slide, and were often designed in the fashion of many small, square panes of window glass. The cases were usually richly carved and surviving specimens command high sums at auctions, but rarely appear on the market. It should be remembered that cases of this era were not the product of an established industry but were, in the main, created to the individual specifications of buyers. Most modern cases are unsuitable for collectors as the dimensions are small, the shelves do not adjust, and the materials are flimsy (including shelf brackets made of plastic).

BOOKENDS. The manufacture of bookends for the support of volumes on an unfilled shelf is of relatively modern origin. In early times a variety of substitutes were used when necessary, but as leatherbound books do not collapse as easily as cloth bound books there was less need for them. In ancient times, when books were written on papyrus and parchment scrolls, they were kept in clay jars. Even after the introduction of the CODEX or modern format, many owners kept their books stashed away in chests (see BOOKCASES). The sort of books common to medieval and early Renaissance libraries, bound in thick oak boards with clasps and catches, could easily stand without aid. It was only when soft bindings, such as LIMP vellum, started to be used for trade editions in the late 15th and early 16th centuries that books became weak-kneed. But nevertheless bookends were seldom called for, as limp bindings were in the minority and could easily be supported by the stouter volumes on the shelf; or so collectors and librarians of the time apparently thought. Today any partially stocked shelf is provided with a bookend of one sort or other, regardless of the circumstances, as it has become tradition.

In the past hundred years, as the craze for bookends took hold, they have been offered in every imaginable size, shape, design, material, quality, and price. There have been bookends featuring silver cherubs, miniature stagecoach wheels, ox heads, globes of the world, Spanish cannons, candlesticks, and a lengthy catalogue of other frolics. There have been a good many hewn from agate and petrified wood, too, which seem to continually turn up at seaside giftshops. In selecting bookends for a worthwhile library, rather than as showpieces in themselves, the collector should avoid being influenced by ornament. A bookend is useless, and may do harm, if it cannot perform its duty, and a large share of those sold in dime stores and variety outlets fall in this class. Even the most beautiful bookend in the world will not look well after a shelf of books has toppled over it.

A bookend must have strength to counteract heavy weight, far heavier than one might imagine. Even just two feet of National Geographic can exert a strong push, enough to send a frilly bookend flying. There are two types of bookends on the market, not counting the new experimental models which are not worthy of mention. The first operates purely by force of weight, the second by using the weight of the books instead of its own. This latter kind is called the "L" because of its shape. It is constructed of a plain length of flat metal bent in the middle at a 90−degree angle, to form an upright. One half is placed beneath the first few books on the shelf, thereby being anchored by their weight while having practically no weight of its own. While not decorative, this is the best (and by far cheapest) bookend that can be bought, and is used by almost all libraries. If there are fine bindings which might be scratched by the metal, the bookends can be covered in morrocco or a sheet of cardboard placed before the first volume next to the bookend.

Those which depend on their own weight tend to be less satisfactory, as a large book is apt to be more than a match for the heaviest of them. Those sold in giftshops usually weigh less than five pounds and thus are only useful if one has miniature books, or books that will stand by themselves anyway. A fairly good if unsightly bookend can be fashioned by gluing two bricks together, along the wide side, but it could hardly be sent to do battle with an Audubon elephant folio.

BOOK OF HOURS. During the Middle Ages many wealthy laymen, such as princes and merchants, commissioned prayer books to be transcribed for their private use. Usually they were made in the monastic scriptoriums, just as other manuscripts, and sometimes elegantly illuminated. A feature of Books of Hours (called Horae) is their consistent small size, as they were designed to be carried about to church services. They generally included Psalms, Litanies, and various Offices of the church. They were prized for their calendars, which frequently featured pictures of month by month activities (planting in spring, harvesting in fall, etc.), providing historians with valuable insights into medieval society and habits. The first half of the 15th century was the golden age of Books of Hours, as they were produced in vast quantities by the commercial manuscript industry, which often employed artists of great skill. France and Flanders turned out the finest specimens. There continued to be a trade in manuscript Horae at Paris long after printing had been introduced. Books of Hours were issued by many of the early printers, especially the French, and were occasionally given touches of color by an illuminator. This continued to the mid 16th century.

BOOK OF KELLS. An Irish manuscript of the 8th century A.D., the Book of Kells is considered by many the finest early illuminated manuscript surviving today. The work of missionaries who set up monasteries in Ireland not long after the fall of Rome, it contains illuminations of a very high quality, in the most brilliant and carefully applied colors, giving the impression it required many years to complete. It is in folio size and written upon heavy vellum. In spite of its great age—its condition is remarkably good and fresh. The Book of Kells is of interest to art historians as well as bibliographers, as it shows the attainment of Irish artists of the early Middle Ages, a time when little creative work was done elsewhere. It is housed in the library of Trinity College, Dublin. See HIBERNO-SAXON MANUSCRIPTS.

BOOK OF THE DEAD. It was a practice in ancient Egypt to bury a papyrus manuscript containing a special formula of spells and prayers with the dead, as well as food and earthly possessions. The text most often chosen thus came to be known as the "book of the dead." During the 18th and 19th Dynasties examples of great beauty were produced and are, strictly speaking, the earliest ILLUMINATED MANUSCRIPTS, though of course in scroll form rather than CODEX. Scholars have concluded that three basic variations of the text exist, though each separate manuscript is likely to differ widely from another. Such burials were naturally reserved for persons of position.

BOOKPLATES. Bookplates serve a dual purpose, to guard against theft (the reason libraries use them) and preserve the PROVENANCE or history of ownership. Many collectors think of neither, however, and use bookplates simply as a means of personalizing their volumes, or to follow tradition. Their use dates from the 15th century and over the years many designs of artistic merit have been created, sometimes by noted engravers. Most early bookplates were commissioned by collectors from local printers. It has only been in rather recent times that pre-printed plates have been available, on which the collector may write or stamp his name. Early plates were also not gummed on the back. The user had to apply his own paste, and in olden days this meant boiling dry glue or making a flour paste. Lumps were naturally frequent.

The sizes and styles of bookplates have varied a good deal, changing with the climate of artistic design and the personal whim of the collector, as they represent a branch of art in which the buyer normally dictated the format. In the Baroque era they tended to excessive ornament, with angels blasting away at trumpets and trailing banners through the air, and masses of grapes and other fruits piled about. In the Enlightenment most plates were subdued and used popular as well as classical subjects. The 19th century is looked upon as the golden period of bookplates, as the number of collectors using them rapidly increased and there was still individuality in design.

The collecting of bookplates, a subhobby that boasts a good many followers around the world, is not looked upon kindly by most bibliophiles. This has nothing to do with bookplates but the fashion in which they are obtained. Instead of merely collecting loose plates, some are stripped from old volumes, in the theory that the books are not seriously damaged by such vandalism. The truth is that they are, especially when an endleaf or pastedown has been cut. The removal of bookplates also destroys evidence of prior ownership, an important phase of bibliography.

Not all bookplates are of paper. Some have been printed on leather, such as morocco, as were the Robert Hoe plates. It is often said that one can determine more about a collector from his bookplate than his library, and in the days when collectors dreamed up their own designs this was perhaps so. Some collectors have sought to portray their occupation on their bookplate, others a daydream, still others their own likeness. Plates in which a photograph of the collector is surrounded by an engraved motto are common. Bookplates are frequently dated, but lacking other data it is usually impossible to know if the date is that of the collector's birth, the designing of the bookplate, or another milestone.

The question of whether or not to use bookplates is one the collector must decide for himself. If properly applied, they do no harm. They should never be affixed over an already existing plate, or in such a manner that they obliterate ownership inscriptions or other important-looking writing. The ideal place is the inside front cover, but if there is no space (or if the paste down consists of a fine manuscript that should be left alone) the alternative is the front free endleaf, either the RECTO or VERSO. One should never use plates if there is the least chance he will wish to be anonymous when the library is sold.

A bookplate does not provide conclusive proof of past ownership in cases of items having ASSOCIATION value, as there is a chance the plate could have been removed from a lesser book.

BOOK SCOUT. A book scout is one who searches for books that appear on a WANTLIST, selling them for a profit when located. Usually he works independently, carries no stock, and offers his services to dealers, collectors, and librarians alike. Scouts are mostly found in large cities that abound in secondhand bookshops. In the 19th and 20th centuries, in fact until about World War II, the number of book scouts in London was extraordinarily high. Some operated without any wantlists or established customers; they merely roamed about the smaller, less frequented shops for underpriced items. They would then offer them to the more prominent dealers who did a catalogue trade, and in this way might realize several pounds for a book in which they had invested no more than ten or twelve shillings. Finds this good were not uncommon, if one had the ambition to spend long hours in search and knew a worthwhile book when he saw it. Some scouts regularly brought bulging cartons of purchases from suburban London dealers to those in the city. Today the sport is a shadow of its former self for many reasons: almost all antiquarian booksellers issue catalogues, which are circulated through the trade; private parties with good books to seek the larger markets; and reference works furnishing pricing information are more common.

BOOK SIZES (or FORMATS). In the language of bibliography, the sizes of books are most often stated according to their format rather than by measurement. The common formats are folio, quarto, octavo, and duo-decimo. The format is determined at the very outset of a book's life, according to the manner in which the printer intends to fold his sheets. Regardless of the planned format of the book, the sheets are fed through the press in full size and then folded up later into quires. These are then collected and bound, whereupon the closed edges of the folded sheets are cut open—voila—a book is born!

If the original sheet is folded once it creates two leaves and becomes a folio, the largest of book sizes. If folded twice we have four leaves, or a quarto (called 4to). Fold again and there are eight leaves; an octavo, or 8vo. Keep going and you have progressively smaller sizes, and larger numbers: 12mo, 16mo, 24mo, 32mo, and 64mo. There is such a format as 128mo, though only seen on the very tiniest of miniature volumes.

If this appears complicated, it's just the beginning. If all sheets of printing paper were of equal size, the precise sizes of books could be determined by the format, save for the trimming done in binding, but they vary widely. The common sizes range from Atlas, about 34 by 26 inches, all the way down to Pott, a mere 16 by 12½ inches, with many between. Consequently, a printer can make a book in folio format from any of them, and end up with books of very different dimensions. If he starts off to print a folio on Atlas paper, the finished product will be in the area of 26 by 17 inches; if Pott, only 12½ by 8 inches, yet both are called folios. An octavo printed on Atlas will be about 13 inches high; on Pott 6¼ inches. Thankfully, however, the largest sizes of paper are not often used in commercial printing, so the problem is not so tricky as it could be. The tallest octavo one is likely to encounter is about 9 inches high and the tallest folio under normal circumstances no more than 18 inches. This of course still leaves one to wonder what might be expected of a book simply described as 8vo, 4to, etc. Some booksellers will say "tall 8vo" or "short 8vo" if the volume seems to differ much from the norm, but this like many other points in bibliography, is a matter of personal interpretation and experience. What is small to one bookseller (or auctioneer, or collector) is average to another and what is average to one is tall to the next.

As a general rule, folios and octavos can be anticipated to be rather sleek, at least 1½ times as tall as they are wide. Quartos, on the other hand, tend to be squarish and dumpy. The Gutenberg Bible is a folio; the productions of the Aldine Press generally small 8vo's; the Elzevir books either 12mo or 24mo. Most modern novels are 8vo's; coffee-table art books are folios, or overgrown quartos.

Yet another difficulty comes into play, too: some cataloguers do not bother to check the book and simply guess the format by its size, thereby making mistakes. To learn the format of a boundbook (as opposed to a paperback), one has but to count the leaves from one SIGNATURE letter to the next; if there are eight, the book is in 8vo, and so forth. Lacking signature marks, the sewing usually tells the tale.

BOOKWORMS. The bookworm is a hungry little maggot that feeds upon the leaves and bindings of books and has preyed upon libraries since the very earliest times. Apparently it found papyrus as appetizing as vellum and paper, as the Roman author Lucian calls attention to its evil deeds, and there are references to the worm in numerous other ancient works. It was the scourge of monastic libraries in the Middle Ages. There was no area of Europe free of the bookworm and it did not, as supposed by many, seek only filthy habitations. The nature and construction of medieval libraries greatly encouraged infestation, however, as they were damp, dimly lighted, poorly heated, and not well ventilated. The scarcity of early books that are not marred by wormholes testify to their widespread activity. Modern chemicals have virtually exterminated them. They have never been a problem in America. See WORMING.

BOSSES. Bosses were nails with large, sometimes decorative, heads, driven into the binding boards of early books. Their purpose was to guard the leather from rubbing. Bosses became uncommon after the early 16th century, except on large manuscript hymnals and the like. They were often used in conjunction with CENTERPIECES.

BOWDLERIZED. "Bowdlerized" is another term for censored or expurgated. It was named for Thomas Bowdler, who edited a cleaned-up version of Shakespeare in 1818, in which hundreds of subtle references and double entendres were destroyed. The butchery was then performed on other works. A Bowdlerized book, in which the censoring is willingly carried out by the compiler, must be distinguished from one censored as the result of public or legal pressure.

BRADFORD, WILLIAM. Bradford was a London Quaker who holds a very curious distinction: he was the first to set up printing presses in both Philadelphia (1685) and New York (1693). Though typographic excellence was next to impossible under prevailing conditions, he was an inventive workman and did much to help the progress of American printing. Born in 1663, he lived to the age of 89, spending the latter part of his life in New York. He was buried in New York's old Trinity Churchyard.

BREAKING COPY. "Breaking copy" is a term often used with reference to damaged books with engraved plates, which would be more profitable to break up and sell the plates individually than attempt finding a buyer for the volume as a whole. It is sometimes a difficult matter to decide, especially if the book contains a great many engravings. For instance, if a book with

50 engravings could be sold as a unit for $100 or the plates separately at $3, the bookseller may choose the former rather than wait the long time required to find individual buyers. Early printed books with leaves missing are also sometimes broken up, even if unillustrated, merely to sell as specimens of primitive typography. Here the figures are more likely to be in the dealer's favor, especially if the volume is thick. Four hundred incunable leaves might be sold at $2 each, making $800, against a value of perhaps less than $300 as a whole, if seriously incomplete. The problem is that this sort of arithmetic results in some near-perfect books being sacrificed.

BRITISH MUSEUM. The most valuable and significant, if not the largest, library in the English-speaking world, the British Museum is located in London on Great Russell Street. Its beginnings are not nearly as ancient as most European state libraries, but acquisitions of major private collections enabled it to quickly assume importance. In 1753 the British Government purchased the library of Sir Hans Sloane, noted physician and antiquary, with the intention of turning it into a national library. It contained 50,000 printed books and 2,000 manuscripts and was thought the finest private collection of its day. It was not for another six years, however, that it became available to the public. In 1759, it was combined with the libraries of Sir Robert Bruce Cotton, Robert Harley, and George II, already in government possession, and the title of British Museum was bestowed. Its headquarters at this time was Montague House. The present structure was not completed until 1847, and various additions (including the celebrated reading room) were made afterward.

At first the object of the British Museum was to collect materials in all fields of natural science and decorative art. While still retaining its character as an art and natural history museum, its oil paintings have been assigned to a separate institution, the National Gallery.

The creation of the British Museum provided a suitable repository for items of national interest. Boswell deposited a number of letters he received from Johnson in the British Museum, where they are still to be seen. Although growth was exceptional in the 18th century, the first half of the 19th century was the primary period of development. In 1817 the B.M. acquired the library of Charles Burney, containing 13,000 printed books, many of them incunabula, and 500 Greek and Latin manuscripts. A feature of this collection was its large showing of British newspapers, which Burney carefully saved as published and had them bound in convenient volumes, saving many from sure extinction. Then came the enormous library of George III in 1823, the 16,000 volume science collection of Sir Joseph Banks, and in 1830 the Arundel manuscripts from the Royal Society. But perhaps the major acquisition of the era was the library of Thomas Grenville in 1846, comprising some 20,000 carefully purchased books, including many first-rank rarities.

The B.M. suffered some damage during World War II but most of its treasures had been removed to coal cellars and were safe. Within a few years the losses had been largely replaced. Today it contains more than double the total of printed books and manuscripts it held in 1925. It boasts strong collections in all fields: fine printing, royal bindings, dime novels, early Slavic printing, miniature books, Oriental literature, etc. In 1970 the name was officially changed to "The British Library," but nearly everyone still says "British Museum."

BRITWELL. The collection gathered by William Henry Miller (1789–1848) and S. R. Christie-Miller at Britwell Court, commonly called the Britwell library, was one of the most celebrated English libraries of the 19th century. It was eventually sold at auction by Sotheby's in a long series of sales in the 1920's. Though containing many foreign books, its basic strength and appeal lay in its English literature, the majority in first editions. It included numerous Shakespeare source books. Dealers and agents from all parts of the world attended the sales, where record-breaking prices were commonplace. The largest single buyer was DR. ROSENBACH, many of whose purchases went into the libraries of FOLGER and HUNTINGTON.

BROADSIDE. A single printed sheet, in which one side is blank, to be tacked or pasted on walls, etc. is a broadside. The most common broadsides are proclamations, announcements, posters, and advertising matter of all kinds. Broadsides were very common in the Middle Ages, when they were written by hand, and usually called attention to some new law or royal (or papal) pronouncement. When typography was introduced, broadsides were printed before full-length books; or at least it appears so based on currently available evidence. The Gutenberg shop at Mainz specialized in this sort of thing. In England, as in most continental countries, publicly displayed broadsides were used to announce government proceedings long after the information could be obtained in newspapers. Broadsides of this nature, as they generally constitute the first printed reference to items of historical interest, often fetch high sums from collectors. Their survival was naturally not so secure as books, not being protected by a binding, and those displayed out of doors naturally fared badly in poor weather. It was a common practice among beggars in early times to strip broadsides from walls and sell them for pulping, a laborious job that could have netted only the smallest profit. Single sheets distributed for advertising purposes (usually to strollers on street corners) are more properly called handbills.

BROCHURE. "Brochure" is an advertising term for a pamphlet, which does not sound alluring enough to suit the tastes of admen ("send for our beautifully illustrated pamphlet on Caribbean vacations" does not seem to carry the same force). It is very rarely seen in catalogues or bibliographies, as bookmen have a preference for no-nonsense words; "a brochure on the Popist Plot" appears equally out of place.

BROTHERS OF THE COMMON LIFE. The monastery Brothers of the Common Life was the first to print books in Brussels, beginning in 1476. They produced almost exclusively religious works, including a very thick little Carmelite Breviary in 1480, and writings of the church fathers. They used gothic type. It was not unusual for a monastery to operate its own printing office, as this was done throughout Europe, especially in Italy. But the usual procedure was to recruit an established printer to come and oversee things, which does not seem to have been the case here. Nevertheless the quality of work was not inferior to the general Flemish standard of that early date.

BROWN, JOHN CARTER. Brown was an early American book collector (1797–1874), primarily interested in material relating to the history and development of America. A man of great personal wealth, he bought heavily throughout his lifetime and did much to stimulate interest in rare books and manuscripts. After his death his library was carried on for some years by his widow and sons, then presented in 1900 to Brown University in Providence, Rhode Island, which had been named for his father.

BUCKRAM. Buckram is a modern binding material, very much like cloth but tougher and somewhat more attractive. When libraries have their books rebound, it is nearly always in buckram. It is inexpensive and can be dyed all the colors of the rainbow, as well as gilt stamped. The "natural" shade, which is rather like a cross between straw and wheat, is preferred by many. Buckram bindings are often described in catalogues as cloth and vice-versa, a fact of life that collectors must endure.

BURNEY, CHARLES. Burney was a british book collector. In 1817 his library was acquired by the British Museum.

BYDDELL, JOHN. English printer of the post-incunabula era, Byddell's first office was located at the sign of Our Lady of Pity in London. He apparently discovered this device in Corio's *History of Milan*, 1505, and used it as his printer's mark as well. Following the death of WYNKYN DeWORDE in 1534 Byddell rented his shop at the famous Sign of the Sun in Fleet Street, which seems to suggest Byddell was doing a heavy trade. However there is little evidence of this, as only a small number of his publications have been recorded. He died around 1544, having been in business only about a dozen years. He signed his name Johan, following the custom of Latinization.

BYZANTINE MANUSCRIPTS. The second earliest school of manuscript production in CODEX form, the Byzantine manuscripts were successor to the late Roman or antique school. Considered to have begun around the 5th century A.D. in Italy, it spread quickly around the Mediterranean and into central Europe. The codex book (as opposed to the scroll) was still in its infancy and papyrus continued to be used for some manuscripts, though far less frequently than in the classical period. The Byzantine scribes, who were mainly churchmen and followers of monasteries, had one great advantage over those of later periods: manuscripts of classical authors and biblical writings were still to be had in the original texts. In spite of wars and plundering, a scribe could probably place his hands without difficulty upon an authentic text of Virgil, Pindar, Horace, or the Evangelists. If not, the copy that was available did not differ greatly, and represented far nearer the genuine than anything we possess today.

Yet the difficulties were enormous and there is no wonder that the Byzantine school progressed slowly. The fall of Rome in 476 left the western world virtually without a culture, and all that the most learned men could do was collect the fragments. Libraries were few and readers still fewer. Of all persons who lived in the 5th and 6th centuries, only a minute proportion could read or write intelligently, if at all. The only real arts which existed were craft trades. The climate was not suited to the manufacture of books, but books were made.

It is difficult to gauge the extent of the early Byzantine manuscript industry, as the scarcity of existing specimens can be partly attributed to the long passage of time. From what does exist, it is evident there was more than merely an effort to preserve texts; they were richly decorated as well, though in a different fashion than ROMANESQUE or GOTHIC manuscripts. The books were mainly in quarto and small folio size, containing full-page paintings at intervals in the text, almost exclusively of persons rather than scenes, battles, etc. The manner is flat and stylized, borrowed from the portrait style of classical Rome, in which everyone sports huge eyes, a tiny nose and Egyptian skin coloration.

Greek artists played a major role in the early history of Byzantine manuscripts, as Greece was a center of book production. Little change was to be seen in the general style for the first two or more centuries. The text was written in widely spaced lines, very straight and rigid, the ink quality far better than one might expect. Illustrated Bibles were made from a very early period; there is a portion of a 5th century specimen in Berlin. In the 8th century, the manuscript industry became far more extensive, both in size and scope, as Christian monasteries were dotted over almost the whole of Europe and virtually all turned out books. At a slightly later date there was a concerted effort to imitate classical Roman manuscripts, with moderate success, but by then the world of learning was far removed from the spirit of ancient Rome. Illuminations steadily improved and included a more liberal use of color, inspired by Byzantine church decoration. The 10th century in the south and south-east of Europe is usually looked upon as the outstanding age of Byzantine manuscripts. Much fine work was also done in Byzantium itself (modern Turkey), Syria, and elsewhere in the middle east. The British Isles, effectively removed from Byzantium, developed styles of their own.

CALF. Calf is the most common variety of leather for the binding of books, yet capable of being attractively decorated. The earliest leather used on CODEX bindings was undoubtedly calf. It has been used continually, in almost every area of Europe, down to the present day. From the 16th to the early 19th centuries, calf, in various styles and grades, was the usual covering for TRADE BINDINGS in Britain and then America. It has now, of course, given way to cloth and buckram, but continues to be used on limited editions and in rebinding old books.

During the Middle Ages and especially in the north and west of Europe, calf bindings were applied over wood and affixed with the usual hardware. Blindstamping was popularly employed on calf in the later Middle Ages, just as on vellum and pigskin. By the 15th century, a number of localized binding styles all utilizing calf had grown up in Germany and elsewhere, and some of the binders gained a measure of temporary fame. Nuremberg was the European center for exquisite stamped calf bindings. The introduction of gilt stamping in the late 15th century gave calf new life. The Italians, who had looked upon blindstamping with disdain, embraced gilding and carried it to lofty heights. Elaborate bindings in calf were made for princes, popes, wealthy merchants and traders, patrons of the arts. Yet calf in its humbler forms served well as trade bindings, either undecorated or stamped with simple conventional designs.

Calf is not so durable as either pigskin or vellum, though it has the advantage over vellum of not being affected so noticeably by changes in humidity. It does have a tendency to dry out, as do most leathers, and must be regularly oiled to retain its original freshness. Much of the splitting of spines and joints on calf bindings results from dryness. Calf comes in a variety of finishes and grains. The natural color ranges from a light milky brown, called coffee by some, to a strong deep mahogany.

CALLED FOR. Features or POINTS mentioned in bibliographies are said to be "called for." For instance, if a handbook written by Smith says that a blank leaf follows the title in a certain edition of a certain book, then the blank leaf is "called for." Authorities sometimes disagree on what an edition should or should not contain, however. And there is the further possibility that even if a copy totally agrees with Smith, Smith may have missed something. A bibliography is only as potent as the material used to compile it and poor Smith may have had to base his conclusions on a single—perhaps imperfect—copy. When booksellers and auctioneers use the term, they often fail to cite the source, stating simply "without the half title called for," as most specialist collectors are familiar with the reference works.

CALLIGRAPHY. Calligraphy is the art of handwriting. Its history is ancient, dating back to the clay tiles of Egypt and Sumeria. Surviving specimens of papyrus writings from the classical world are extremely rare but serve to demonstrate the styles of calligraphy in practice. It is evident that at Greece and Rome there were many professional writers, not only scribes who gained their living transcribing books but public letter-writers as well, serving the needs of illiterates. Though one often hears of "the Roman hand," this is a misnomer as there was no single style of writing. The calligraphy in books (scroll manuscripts) was usually far more sophisticated and stylized than in letters; the same is true of offical documents. The basic Roman book hand was UNCIAL. A page of Roman uncial looks foreign to our eyes today but represents, in its characters of equal size and clear definition, a forceful and flowing style. One characteristic of uncial is that the letters did not connect, and there were no spaces or breaks between words, but the alphabet was not written very differently than today.

Fine calligraphy continued to be practiced until the fall of Rome in the 5th century A.D., though it had undergone various changes. Uncials of later Rome were generally written more closely together, but still without connection. As local Italian writing styles grew up in the 6th century, the uncial hand was subjected to drastic adaptations. The average handwriting of the era was unrecognizable compared to court uncial but showed leanings to modern script. Illuminated manuscripts of the early Christian Era were almost entirely in stiff, carefully drawn uncials, but the average person wrote hastily.

The changes which occurred in court or monastic uncial were subtle. Starting about the 8th century the characters grew more and more squat, which was considered handsome. As this progressed it turned into the Carolingian hand, which is generally dated from the reign of Charlemagne. It featured characters more easily and naturally formed, as in ordinary writing, and used minuscule or small rather than majuscule or capital letters. However the style, just as uncial, was interpreted according to local tastes and use, and by no means developed equally or regularly throughout the continent.

The Italian Renaissance ushered in what may be termed modern hand-writing. The scripts of the humanists were considered ideals to be aimed at in court hands and even type designers were strongly influenced by them. The first roman types were said to be based upon the handwriting of Francesco Petrarch. This writing was far more practiced and skilled than it appeared to the casual observer at the time, requiring long study to perfect.

The materials used in writing over the years have played some role in developing scripts. In Greece and Rome steel pens were used, dipped in ink, but had points which bore little resemblance to modern pens. They were sharp and often struck holes through the papyrus, an accident which no longer occurred when vellum was introduced. Goose quills were probably not used until after the 6th century A.D.

In the 20th century there have been brave efforts to pump life into the dying art of calligraphy, occasionally with fruitful results. Fountain pens are now marketed with special "italic" nibs that give one the chance to write in neoclassical fashion, if one has some talent.

CANCEL. Cancel is a form of ERRATA. There are two ways in which errors are treated, aside from ignoring them: the use of an errata slip, in which the error is left with its bare face hanging out, and cancels. The cancel not only corrects the error but removes it. This might be done by pasting a scrap of paper containing the right word over the wrong, by tearing out the offending leaf and preparing a new one, or in any other manner. The choice of using an errata slip or a cancel is never easy, but as the errata slip is generally cheaper it tends to be more frequently employed. Cancel refers only to the replacement; that which is cancelled is known as the cancelland.

When a cancel has been used, collectors are naturally curious to know if the mistake was spotted before any copies had been released. If not, there will be two states of the book, one with the cancel and the other with the cancelland. Obviously, those with the cancelland are the earlier state, and would in most cases be preferred. But it may be that only a small number of copies were cancelled, which could make them more desirable. But in instances where a pasted-in cancel greatly reduces the value, there is always the chance someone will try removing it and hope the spot will go undetected.

Sometimes there is a cancelland without a cancel. This results when something is struck out (usually with thick black lines) but nothing added to take its place. It occurs commonly in catalogues to indicate sold merchandise, but in this case is not strictly a cancelland as there is no intention to retract what was printed. Cancellands without cancels which appear in early printed books are usually the result of censorship.

CAPTION. The most common meaning of caption is in the sense of "legend," or description accompanying an illustration. It may appear alongside the plate, beneath it, on a separate page, or wherever the publisher thinks proper.

CAROLINGIAN MANUSCRIPTS. Carolingian Manuscripts were an important school of textual and illuminated manuscripts which grew up in the 8th century A.D. as a development of Carolingian art. The revival of learning in the 9th century is thought to have played a major part in the growth of the school. It was confined mainly to France and Germany and was a forerunner of GOTHIC, though its influence gradually spread far. In terms of decoration, it borrowed from various other schools and resulted in a conglomerate of styles which, nevertheless, had originality. There was strong flavor of classical taste in many Carolingian manuscripts, though how much was accidental and how much actual copying is hard to say. It is presumed the Carolingian scribes and illuminators may have worked with early Christian manuscripts which for the most part no longer exist; they could also have derived inspiration from ancient fresco painting. Large, intricately drawn initials were a feature of Carolingian manuscripts, just as in HIBERNO-SAXON, but the work is not, on the whole, as meticulously done. The principal centers of the Carolingian manuscript industry were the Court School of Charlemagne, the Palace School, and other schools at Tours, Metz, and Reims. A good deal of Carolingian work is termed Franco-Saxon. Basically the Carolingian movement is better remembered for its contribution to the advance of CALLIGRAPHY than its artistic achievements, yet of course such manuscripts are now precious and of immense historical interest. The school was dead for all practical purposes by 1050, though stragglers who had been grounded in its ideals continued to work for some decades afterward.

CASES (PROTECTIVE). Book cases—that is, cases made by binders for individual books—come in several styles. The most prevalent is the slipcase, a box with one of its long ends open, into which the book fits snugly. When displayed on the shelf, the spine faces out as usual and one is hardly aware that the book is encased. A variation is the double case, in which the first slipcase is fitted into another, so that no part of the book remains visible; the spine of the case is then labeled for identification. Then there are double-half cases, which consist of two pieces that are slipped over opposite ends of the volume and meet in the middle, and others. The original purpose of cases was to protect fragile books, or keep ornamental bindings from being molested by other volumes, but today they have become a matter of routine in many libraries for any items of special value. Box-like cases are objected to by some, on the grounds that hiding a book (or at least its spine) removes much of the joy of ownership.

Most cases are made of cloth or buckram over boards. Leather is sometimes used but is costly and there is no logical justification for it. When publishers issue a volume or set described as "boxed," an ordinary slipcase, usually in paper-covered boards, can be expected. Publishers are not renowned for lavishing great sums of money on cases. Secondhand-books that were issued in cases have usually lost them along the way; if present they are likely to be pretty well worn.

CASLON, WILLIAM. Caslon was an English type designer (1692–1766). He was originally an engraver and did decorative work on gun barrels. In 1716, he opened an office in London as a typecutter and founder. The specimen sheet he issued in 1734, exhibiting the variety of characters and symbols he offered, is now considered a classic in the field. In 1742, he was joined in business by his son, William II, and traded under the name of William Caslon & Son. The firm was carried on by successive family members until the male line died out in 1873.

Caslon's types were reminiscent of the roman fonts that were used in incunabula days, with modifications to suit not only the time (more than 200 years had passed since Jenson and Torresanus unleashed their mighty productions on a sleepy world), but the English language as well. They were clean, light, straightforward characters with a grand and noble air, not embellished with any unnecessary ruffles or flourishes; above all they were easy on the eye and a considerable advance over the state of English type as Caslon found it. As Caslon slightly preceded BASKERVILLE, he is thought to have a strong influence upon him, and was responsible for a brief Renaissance in fine British printing.

The types pioneered by Caslon are still used today, especially for limited editions and other special productions. It is unfortunate that they are called "Old English," because true Old English is gothic or black-letter, which bears no relation to Caslon.

CASTALDI, PAMFILO. An Italian incunabula printer, Castaldi was a rival claimant to Gutenberg as the inventor of typography. Though supported by strong local legend (a monument was even dedicated to Castaldi in his native Feltre in 1868), bibliographers have never seriously considered him as a possible inventor of moveable-type printing. He has been proven the first printer to work at Milan, however. Nicholas Jenson and Ulrich Han are two other Italian-based printers who from time to time have been credited with introducing the process.

CATALOGUES. Antiquarian booksellers' catalogues have a most ancient history. They were in all probability circulated by the Egyptians and almost certainly by the Romans, who had a large and flourishing trade in old books. Printed catalogues appeared as early as the 17th century. Even well into the 19th, however, they were little more than handlists, providing no more information about each item than title, author, date, and sometimes style of binding. The first English bookseller to issue catalogues with detailed descriptions was Henry Bohn of London. His massive 1841 catalogue, called the Guinea Pig because it sold for a guinea, set the pace for the remainder of the century. It was five inches thick, bound in three-quarter morocco, and contained entries for 23,208 items.

The early habit was to collect many thousands of new acquisitions before compiling a catalogue and thereby keep each catalogue current far longer than is presently done. Some booksellers would publish a catalogue but once a year, others even less frequently. In this way a charge, sometimes rather substantial, could be made and a profit realized from the sale of catalogues. The most authoritative and useful catalogues prior to 1900 were those of Bernard Quaritch of London, issued in monthly parts but periodically collected and bound. They are still widely used for reference, though the prices are far outdated.

In this century the use of photography has created catalogues that put their ancestors to shame in the way of visual beauty.

Catalogues are a necessary arm of the hobby, though collectors take widely different views of them. Some collect files according to subject or dealer and have them bound or boxed for reference; others actually seek out early catalogues as their specialty. The majority do not have either the space or patience to save all catalogues received and merely clip out descriptions of items they buy.

CATCHWORD. Anyone who has handled old books (at least those prior to about 1820) has noticed that a loose word appears at the right-hand foot of each page of text, which corresponds to the first word of the next page. This was said to be done not to guide the printer, nor the binder, but to assist the reader. It is very likely, however, that the practice originated as an aid in collecting the GATHERINGS for binding, and was merely held over as a tradition long after it ceased to be very relevant. They are known as catchwords. They may perhaps have helped those who read publicly from books, such as ministers giving sermons.

CATHOLICON. The monumental work of Johannes Balbus de Janua, Catholicon figures prominently in the early history of printing, as an edition was published at Mainz, Germany, in 1460, less than a decade after the Gutenberg Bible. In the opinion of most (but far from all) authorities, it was printed by Gutenberg after he was wiped out by Fust's successful lawsuit (see GUTENBERG and FUST). The theory is that, having his press legally turned over to Fust and Fust's son-in-law Schoeffer, Gutenberg tried to start anew with a much smaller shop nearby the old. The 1460 Catholicon gives the place of printing—Mainz—and the date, but does not name the printer. This, however, would have been characteristic of Gutenberg, as he signed none of his earlier work. It is almost sure the Catholicon was not printed by Fust and Schoeffer, the only other printers known to be active in Mainz at the time, as by 1460 they were signing their books and used different types. If printed by Gutenberg, it must have been his final book.

CAVENDISH, WILLIAM. The Duke of Devonshire (1790–1858) was an English collector and owner of the famous Chatsworth Library. His holdings were particularly strong in English literature and early English printings, including Caxtons. Many of his books were destroyed in a fire, which his insurance company believed had suspicious origins. There is feeling to this day that Cavendish purposely set it to collect a claim.

CAXTON, WILLIAM. William Caxton was the first English printer. The year of his birth is disputed, as are a number of other circumstances of his life. The date 1412, which in the past was commonly accepted, is now generally altered to 1420 or 1422. He was born at Kent and, after serving an apprenticeship, became a mercer or dealer in yarn goods. In this trade he passed most of his early life, showing no mechanical skills or flair for literature. Around 1441, Caxton went to Burgundy and spent most of his adult life on the continent. In 1462, he became governor of the Merchant Adventurers at Bruges in Flanders. After spending several years at Utrecht he returned to Bruges in 1468. In 1471, he entered the service of the Duchess of Burgundy. It was under her influence that he performed his first effort with books, translating for her the *Recuyell of the Historyes of Troye*.

In 1471, he visited Cologne, staying until December of 1472, and apparently was there introduced to the art of printing (the first Cologne press was established in 1472). Back at Bruges in late 1472 or early the next year, he set about to give the city a printing press. He became associated with a Flemish calligrapher named Colard Mansion, who may already have been a printer. Some say Mansion taught Caxton printing, but this is now discredited. In any event a partnership was formed and the two issued the first English language book—the same *"Recuyell"*—in 1475. After printing perhaps two more books with Mansion, Caxton came home to England in 1476, alone, and founded a printing office in the parish of Westminster. The following year he published the first dated book printed in England, *"Dictes or Sayengis of the Philosophres."*

The career of Caxton continued to his death in 1491, aged about 70. It is not known how many books he printed but about 100 have been recorded. A number are probably extinct while others wait in the recesses of old libraries or storerooms to be discovered. Compared to the best French and Italian printing of the time, Caxton's books come off a sorry second. His fame has led many to assume that his talent as a craftsman and type designer must have been extraordinary, but this was not the case. He did, however, exert much influence upon his contemporaries and followers. He began with types modeled on German gothic and stuck with them to the end, though he modified them a number of times. This set the trend for English printers and it was not until a century after his death that they were replaced by the more graceful roman.

There is no question but that Caxton expended far more care on the preparation of texts than the physical beauty of his books. He executed a number of translations of foreign works, including the classics, and wrote lengthy prefaces and introductions that sometimes show droll wit. Caxton paints a portrait of himself as a lazy scholar, translating books for want of something better to do, then gets on a soapbox and denounces the changes in the English language since his boyhood. The service he performed by bringing printed literature to his countrymen, particularly to those who could not afford costly manuscript copies, was beyond measure. He did not confine himself to any special class of titles but published chronicles, books on games, religion, manners, poems, and so on. He was the first to print the works of Chaucer. A number of Caxton's books were illustrated, in crude but quaint woodcuts, by an artist or artists whose identity is no longer known.

The "craze for Caxtons" among collectors began in the early part of the 19th century and has gathered steam ever since. The finest collections are at the British Museum and John Rylands Library. In the U.S., the Morgan and Huntington libraries are notable for their Caxtons.

CENTERPIECES. Metal ornaments, fastened with nails to the centers of binding boards in the manuscript era and the first century of printing were called centerpieces. They were an outgrowth of BOSSES, metal nailheads intended to protect the leather. Originally five identical bosses were used on each board, but gradually the center one became larger and more decorative. The majority have fallen off and been lost.

CHAINED BINDINGS. Books produced in the Middle Ages were quite valuable, with hand painted miniatures and other decorations, so there was always a threat of theft. To guard them, monastic librarians introduced chaining, which flourished mainly in the 14th and 15th centuries. A length of iron chain, usually from 1½ to 2 feet long, was nailed to the wooden binding board. The other end was attached to a desk or bookcase shelf, depending on where the volume was kept. The bookcase shelf would be equipped with a metal rod, over which the free ends of the chains passed. The rod was then locked in place. To remove a volume it was necessary to unlock and slide out the rod.

The system was soon found unsatisfactory, as it prevented the free movement of books and hampered those carrying out studies. As soon as typography made books reasonably cheap there was no longer much danger they would be stolen. Also, the use of chains required bindings made of wooden boards, which went out of fashion in southern Europe in the 15th century. Chained bindings continued to be manufactured in England into the 16th century. Specimens are rare on the market. There would be a good deal more, had those who removed them from libraries taken care to preserve the chain, but in many cases it was discarded as useless (which it surely must have seemed then). A few chained libraries are still to be seen in Europe but they, too, are becoming scarce.

CHEAP COPY. Next to "poor copy" (which is almost never used), the worst a bookseller can term a volume is a "cheap copy." To merit such a rating there must be something, or a long list of things, seriously and usually irreparably wrong. It is not often used with reference to major rarities, as it seems awkward to call an item cheap and then ask several thousand dollars for it.

CHINESE PAPER. Chinese paper is a fine grade of specially prepared paper, quite thin, soft, and with a brownish hue. It is traditionally made from pulping bamboo bark, which has finer keeping qualities than most vegetable pulp. It is not used on a large scale in the printing industry because of the cost and is never seen in ordinary trade editions. It is an ideal surface for the printing of wood and steel engravings, and for many sorts of graphic art. Another name, very misleading, is rice paper.

CHISWICK PRESS. Chiswick Press was a London printing office founded in 1789 by Charles Whittingham. After being taken over by this nephew, also named Charles, it attained a large following for its well-designed and cheaply printed editions of famous books. Also notable were the woodcut volumes it printed. After 1830, the Chiswick Press was printer for WILLIAM PICKERING, one of the leading English publishers of the time. In 1896, New York's Grolier Club issued a detailed history of the Whittingham family, written by Arthur Warren. The popularity of the Chiswick Press spread into related fields; there have been a number of antiquarian bookshops, both here and abroad, using the name Chiswick.

CLASPS. The practice of furnishing bookbindings with metal clasps arose early in the Middle Ages, but just how early is questionable. Though surviving examples tend to be looked upon as ornamental, or at least quaint, this was not the original purpose. There were really two reasons for clasps. Medieval manuscripts were a task to produce and intended to last for centuries. As they were often taken outdoors when the monks were on the road, clasps kept the edges tightly shut, so that rain and snow would have a more difficult time penetrating. Also, the vellum leaves upon which they were written had a habit of curling or cockling; with clasps this was reduced. In reality they were of little service, however, as most users did not bother to re-catch them when finished with the volume. Books long left unclasped will often have swelled so much that closing the clasps is impossible, and should not be attempted, as the strain will only cause further and more serious injury.

The medieval manner of shelving books, with foredges pointing outward and the spines in, made life most unhappy for clasped volumes. The clasps proved a much too tempting vehicle for pulling them from their place, and in time many were damaged to such a degree they fell off and were discarded. A volume of the 15th or 16th century in which the original clasps are still in working order is somewhat unusual.

Their construction and operation was simplicity itself. Two leather thongs would be affixed to the lower cover, near the edge. At the tips would be little metal claws, which fitted into metal catches on the upper cover. The fit was usually so tight it was necessary to exert some pressure on the binding to open or close them. Some sprung open by themselves upon application of pressure.

Clasps were generally confined to bindings in which wooden boards were used for the covers. In the vast majority of cases two clasps were provided, but there were improvisations if the book happened to be of odd size. Small pocket editions might be given only a single clasp, along the center of the foredge while ponderous folios would receive four, the additional pair at the upper and lower edges.

They continued in use in Germany, Austria and eastern Europe long after becoming obsolete in other areas. Clasps were still common on German trade bindings as late as the second quarter of the 18th century, more than 200 years after they had ceased to be used in Italy, Spain, and France.

CLOTH BINDING. Prior to the 19th century all trade bindings were in materials other than cloth. The earliest trade bindings for printed books were heavy wooden boards and blindstamped leather, which was succeeded by a variety of methods and materials. As leather became costly, publishers tried to avoid it as much as possible. Many 17th century bindings, both in Britain and on the continent, were of boards with a calf or vellum spine. This remained the usual style in the 18th century, though some publishers used very cheap grades of leather—such as roan and skivver—in an attempt to retain "full" bindings. But in the early 19th century, the situation was becoming more intolerable, as labor and materials grew more expensive, and something new was called for. In 1823, according to most sources, a London publisher named WILLIAM PICKERING issued the first book bound in cloth, equipped with a paper label on the spine, and continued to use such bindings throughout his career. They were quickly adopted by others in Britain and the U.S., but were somewhat slower to catch hold on the continent; even today they are not popular in France.

Cloth has often been termed the ideal binding substance, for its cheapness, durability, variety of color, and ease of application. Much of this is undeniably true, and for works of reference or everyday books which are intended for heavy use there is nothing more suitable. One would certainly not wish to have a road atlas bound in gilded morocco (though in previous times they indeed were). But most collectors, even if not the reading public, lament the disappearance of leather, even though the cost of leather bindings would prohibit ownership of books to all but a slim class.

In the first several decades of cloth trade bindings, publishers let their fancies run wild. Cloth was something new and, just as when leather was new, every effort was made to ornament it as much as possible. It was both gilded and blindstamped, using patterns taken from notable bindings of earlier ages. But unlike the models, gilding of cloth was done with large panel stamps impressed by a machine, rather than small tools worked by hand. The purpose was to make customers forget leather, and this was more or less accomplished, as full bindings in leather decorated in similar style would have cost three times the price of cloth. Only connoisseurs who kept fine libraries retained any affection for leather; once it was gone the general public forgot it.

Beginning around 1860, pictorial cloth bindings started to appear. They were a great change from the rather somber and dignified examples ushered in by Pickering as they were alive with color and scenes from the book. Their aim was to catch the attention of bookshop browsers, a purpose now served by dust jackets. A book about exploration in India might have a portrait of a few natives riding elephants on the front binding board, and perhaps a giraffe (even though there are none in India) on the spine. Often the covers formed a sort of mural extending from back to front if held open. Thick papers were used so that a wide spine was provided for illustration. The cloth on these bindings was treated so that it was hard and shining, without any surface texture. In their time, they were looked on as frivolous by serious collectors, but today many of the better specimens (and there were some nifty ones) are admired. By 1890, they had just about ceased production.

Cloth bindings lose their strength of color when exposed to sunlight over long periods. Booksellers call this mellowing.

COBDEN-SANDERSON. His real name was Thomas James Sanderson and he was considered one of the most versatile geniuses ever to devote their talents to books, though quite an eccentric character. He was involved, at one time or other, in every phase of book production: publishing, printing, type design, paper making, ink making, binding. However, his interest in books did not begin until he passed 40 years of age.

He was born at Northumberland, England, in 1840. After spending three years at Cambridge University he dropped out in protest over the competitive system, choosing to study and learn in private. For a number of years thereafter he had no fixed profession or goal, though his intelligence would have qualified him for a number of careers. For a while he contemplated being a minister, then a surgeon, both of which he discarded. Around the age of 30 he became an attorney, but this did not satisfy his quest to do something creative and he followed it for only a short time. He took up manual labor, which was likewise unappealing. Upon being married to a Miss Cobden at the age of 42, he determined to start off fresh in life and changed his name to Cobden-Sanderson.

It was only a chance incident that led him to book making. Being entertained in the home of WILLIAM MORRIS, he expressed his love of craft trades and Mrs. Morris urged him to take up bookbinding. This he had never considered, nor is there evidence he had ever seen or admired fine bindings up to that moment, but the idea struck home. Within the week he apprenticed himself to a London binder, undoubtedly one of the oldest apprentices in the trade, and in less than a year was the proprietor of his own bindery, at 30 Maiden Lane. Friends thought this merely another of his passing fancies, that the next week or month would find him fumbling with something new. But such was not the case. He loved the work and was creating tooled bindings that rivaled the finest of their era. Soon a long roster of collectors and dealers became his regular clients and the business prospered.

After becoming so intimately associated with books, his affection for them was not satisfied merely by working as a binder. He decided to try his skill at designing and manufacturing books, trying to create the most beautiful and artistically perfect volumes ever produced. As his shop was called the Doves Bindery, he named his press Doves Press. It was formed in 1900, when he was 60 but still filled with enthusiasm and schemes for projects. His partner in the venture was Emery Walker, a talented printer who had introduced Cobden-Sanderson to the technical aspects of the craft. The Doves Press productions were in the form of limited and rather costly editions of well-known works, received with praise by critics and collectors. Feeling he had not long to live, and not wishing his Doves type to be used by others, he began in 1916 to throw handsful of it into the Thames, stealing out by night to perform the mission. He died in 1922 at the age of 82.

CODEX. The term "codex" applied to leaves bound in book form, in the present manner, as opposed to scrolls or tablets. The first codexes are thought to have originated in the 3rd or 4th century A.D. in Rome; the earliest existing specimens are of the 4th. The invention is generally credited to Roman legal clerics, who grew weary of cumbersome scrolls and cut them down to convenient size. At first they were probably bound in raw wooden boards with a leather spine, sewn together with heavy cord. The word is often pluralized as codices.

CODEX SINAITICUS. A 4th century A.D. Greek manuscript of the Bible, Codex Sinaiticus was discovered by the Russian scholar TISCHENDORF at Mount Sinai (hence the name) in 1859. He persuaded the monastery in which it was found to present it as a gift to the Czar of Russia. It remained in the library of St. Petersburg for a number of years, but after the revolution of 1917 the new government decided to dispose of many national treasures and eventually offered the Codex Sinaiticus on the market. At first it was quoted to an American bookseller for a price of more than one million dollars, which was rejected (the depression was in its darkest depths). Not bothering to follow up, the Russians allowed the British Museum to buy it in 1932 for £100,000, the equal of nearly $500,000. Its arrival in Britain and subsequent exhibition were attended with much ceremony and pomp; a public fund was established to meet the cost. It was later said that the American market would have gobbled it down, had it known the price was reduced to less than half a million.

COLLATION. To collate a book means to check that all leaves are present and in their proper order. Collation takes no notice of imperfect leaves; it is merely a roll call for completeness. In the case of most early books (at least those published before the advent of cloth for trade bindings), it is necessary to have a perfect copy for comparison, or a collation of a perfect copy taken from a reference work. In the old days of collating books, a simplified system was used that would fail to satisfy the creative imaginations of today's bibliographers. A collation of 1850 would read something like, "one blank, half title, 4 preliminary leaves, 326 pages, 16 pages of index and addenda, one blank." And that was that! No mumbo-jumbo, hieroglyphic symbols or mirror writing. Any person of normal intelligence could understand a collation, but not so now. Collations now describe books in scientific detail, and it's all done by means of signs and codes. Many collectors, including advanced specialists, never learn to read collation, just as some baseball players are never able to keep a scoreboard or piano players read music. Truthfully it is not necessary and if one is going to get ulcers over the matter it is not worth the effort.

The key to understanding collations is to remember that the leaves are always identified by their positions in the SIGNATURE, the gathering of leaves which formed the original sheet of paper fed into the press (see BOOK SIZES). In an octavo, the signatures will consist of eight leaves, in a quarto four, in a folio two. The signatures are referred to by their letters, which appear in the lower margin at the beginning of each new signature. Thus, the first leaf of a book is normally A1. The RECTO of the leaf is A1a, the VERSO A1b. The next leaf is A2, and so on, until the A signature is completed; then begins B1, B2, etc. There are variations to this method of collation but it is pretty widely used.

COLLECTED EDITION. There are two meanings of "collected edition." In its usual sense, collected edition (as in "first collected edition") refers to the first appearance in collected form of serial writings. Generally speaking, collectors are not overly thrilled with them, but try instead to locate the originals.

The term is sometimes, though confusingly, applied to editions popular with collectors—hence "collected editions"—but modern bibliographers seem willing to let this application go the way of the woolly mastodon. It was never really certain how much collected editions were collected anyway.

COLOPHON. The colophon was the forerunner of the title page, but it appeared at the rear of books instead of the front. It became the tradition of medieval scribes, when completing work on manuscripts, to record their name and place of residence, and sometimes the day on which the book was finished. This was done more or less out of vanity, to gain recognition for a job well done, but in the case of printed books such information became almost a necessity. Without it a printer or publisher could not identify an edition as his, which might result in legal difficulties if it were PIRATED or stolen by another printer.

The colophon in INCUNABULA usually came on the last printed leaf, though not always. Some books ended with a special typographic flourish, such as a display of typefaces in the printer's arsenal. In these instances, one must sometimes grope through several leaves to reach the colophon.

The average colophon was a model of simplicity: just a one-sentence acknowledgment in which the essential facts were contained. At times, however, it became lengthy, as in the case of Fust and Schoeffer, who rambled on about the wonders of the printed letters.

Colophons continued in use until the early 16th century, when they were replaced by title pages. Many printers still added a colophon, out of respect for tradition, at the ends of their books.

CONDITION. There is probably no point over which collectors and dealers (not to mention librarians, auctioneers, and others who buy or sell books) disagree more than condition. As no hard and fast rules exist, the terms used to designate condition are subject to personal viewpoint. There have been all sorts of attempts to improve the situation, the majority by persons of the highest intentions, but all have more or less failed. Some bibliophiles contend it is impossible to draw a fair picture of a book from a catalogue description. In many cases this is true. But buyer and seller could live far more happily if common, accepted meanings were attached to the hobby's terminology.

A book may safely be said to be in superb or mint condition when it does not deviate in the least from the state in which it was issued: not a corner should be creased, not a doodle appear on an endpaper. The word mint is generally reserved for modern books, however, as it seems the same as "uncirculated." In the case of a volume 200 or 300 years old, one would assume it has been handled or even—perish the thought—read, somewhere along the line. Therefore superb or some equally enthusiastic term is used for older books that have aged gracefully. But it is rare that a bookseller will have time to examine a common volume so thoroughly to be sure it merits such a rating, so it is usually seen only in connection with items of special interest (which have been collated backwards, forwards, and sidewise).

Minor injuries or blemishes are, except in the case of super rarities, passed over without comment in most catalogues because secondhand books are expected to display some indications of prior ownership. The collector should understand that most cataloguers only describe damage of a rather serious nature. Lesser faults are indicated when a book is listed as "a good copy," "used copy," or "fine reading copy." In the common law of bibliophilism, he is within his rights. The dealer need not list defects *if* their gravity is indicated in his summing-up. In other words, if the description says nothing but that a book is "a rather poor copy," the fact that it omits to mention missing leaves or a broken binding is no cause for complaint. Merely by warning the purchaser that the copy is poor, the bookseller has discharged his obligation. The collector who expects a volume so described to be in anything approaching decent condition has much to learn.

Generally speaking, the collector should avoid damaged books. Their purchase, even at a considerable discount, is apt to be later regretted, when one discovers they are nearly impossible to dispose of. This is especially true in the case of illustrated books lacking one plate out of a hundred or more. The collector is likely to believe that the reduction in price more than compensates for the loss of a single plate out of so many. In terms of the book's usefulness it does, but the copy is incomplete and the thought of that plate is apt to hang upon the collector's memory like an albatross. The only worthy excuse for buying damaged books is if the collector is of modest pocket and could not attain anything better. Even so, the collector had best kiss goodbye the money he spends, as poor copies are a poor investment.

CONJUGATE LEAVES. Conjugate leaves are leaves in a QUIRE (or gathering, or section; whatever term you choose) which are connected to each other. To understand how conjugates come about, it is necessary to realize that books are not printed upon those leaves but large sheets that are folded down. Each quire is a nesting of leaves, which can be seen by studying the edges of the pages at the head and foot of the spine. The word conjugate is a favorite of those who like to work out COLLATIONS. When a leaf is missing, its conjugate will likely be loose and in danger of being detached from the sewing (if it has not already disappeared). See SINGLETON.

CONSTANCE MISSAL. Although examples of very primitive Dutch printing exist which cannot be safely dated, the Constance Missal is the only whole book which stands a chance of being older than the GUTENBERG BIBLE. It is only a chance, because even the most advanced bibliographical methods cannot place a fixed date upon it and undoubtedly never will, while experts are divided on one side of the fence and the other. There are three copies in existence, one of which was purchased in 1954 by New York's Pierpont Morgan Library for more than $100,000, and numerous page fragments that were found in a binding. It is a small book, printed in a simple, attractive gothic resembling the types used by Fust and Schoeffer. The ends of the lines are not quite regular, which may point to an early date, but not nearly so irregular as in the Dutch fragments. It gives no hint as to its origin, place of printing, printer, or any other information. It was only brought to attention by the German bibliographer Otto Hupp in the 1890's having been ignored before that time. Hupp's contention was that it was printed by Gutenberg at Mainz, as a sort of practice or warm-up before attempting the 42-line Bible. He gathered mountains of evidence in an effort to prove this, but it was received as inconclusive. Although some of the types were extremely similar, it was hard to say they were identical. If Hupp's theory is believed, the Constance Missal would date from a period no earlier than about 1446 and no later surely than 1452. But weightier opinion seems to rest on the other side.

A popular theory is that the Constance Missal—which takes its name from Lake Constance in central Europe—was the work of an early Swiss printer, who may have worked for Gutenberg and then went off on his own. If this were the case, it is probably later by a year or two than the 42-line Bible, which would place it in the mid 1450's. But there is even a chance it could have been printed in Holland, possibly by the same man or men responsible for the mysterious Dutch fragments, and in this connection the name of LAURENS COSTER always surfaces, though few seriously relate him to the Constance Missal.

Hupp, who lived to be 90 and collected incunabula most of those years, found his copy in 1880 in a secondhand bookshop in Munich. For fifteen years he, too, ignored it, thinking it merely a curious example of early typography. Then he decided to trade it for something he wanted more, as his lack of wealth required him to swap on occasion. To gain a good bargain from the bookseller, he determined to learn as much as possible about the book, and this convinced him it was the work of Gutenberg. However, he still went ahead with the trade, as the book was now worth much more than he had supposed. The Morgan Library copy was discovered at the monastery at Romont, Switzerland, in 1915. At the 1940 Gutenberg Celebration in Munich, the Constance Missal was exhibited as the earliest printed book. Hupp died, enjoying the controversy to the end, in 1949.

CONTEMPORARY. This word is sometimes applied very loosely. In spite of the flood of reference works and sober discussions on such topics, there is no established criterion for its use. The dictionary definition of contemporary is "existing or occurring at the same time." If bibliographers adhered to this, the word would vanish from their vocabulary. Rather, they use it to mean "in the same age," and the limits of the age covered could be very broad. The period of history must be taken into account, for one thing. If one is dealing with a 7th century manuscript, a binding applied fifty years later (if it were possible to determine this) would qualify as contemporary, whereas a 1950 binding on a 1900 book would not. In fact, it is safe to say that a 10th century binding on a 7th century manuscript will be described as contemporary, as few but advanced specialists could safely distinguish a binding of the 10th century from one of the 7th, 8th, or 9th century. In the strict sense it is not contemporary, but most buyers will accept it as such without argument, even if their knowledge of the subject is more polished than the bookseller's.

As one advances in time the problem is compounded. Most incunables that clearly appear to have been bound in the 15th century are said to be in contemporary bindings, even if the book was printed in 1465 and not bound until 1495. It takes a sharp eye to know the difference between a 1495 and a 1525 binding, however, so errors creep in. Many a 16th century binding has been taken for earlier because it adorns an incunable. Beginning with the sixteenth century, contemporary is generally regarded to mean 25-year periods. Most bindings can be assigned by quarter centuries (first quarter of the 17th, third quarter of the 18th, etc.). This is done by signs of wear, which are inconclusive, also by decoration, quality of leather, method of application, and other factors. Luckily they underwent continual change, otherwise it would be a task to say what is or is not contemporary.

Such phrases as "near contemporary" and "closely contemporary" mean the binding falls outside the quarter-century limit (or whatever limit the bookseller is working with). When a binding is described as "not contemporary," it is too old to be termed modern. But "not contemporary" for a 16th century book could mean a binding applied in 1600 or 1875. MARGINAL NOTES are another can of worms.

COPLAND, ROBERT. An early English printer, stationer and bookseller, Copland carried on business at the sign of the Rose Garland in Fleet Street, London, from about 1515 to 1548. He was an assistant to WYNKYN DeWORDE, who had taken over CAXTON'S trade, and received a legacy in his will. One of the least talented of the English printers of his era, he published very little under his own name, though it is possible he may have printed for others, or subsisted largely by selling the publications of others.

COPLAND, WILLIAM. English printer of the mid 16th century, William Copland was a son, brother, or other younger relation of ROBERT COPLAND. He was employed in Robert's office until the latter's death in 1548, at which time he began on his own. A slovenly craftsman, it is obvious he gave little thought to the aesthetic qualities of typography. He printed a large number of cheap books, some of which carried crude but pleasing woodcuts, all rare and valuable today. Among his better-known publications was the *Story of the most noble and worthy Kynge Arthur*, 1557, and *The right pleasant and goodly Historie of the foure sonnes of Aimon*, 1554. He died in 1568, having been printing under his own banner two decades. His mark was a wreath enclosing his monogram, with his name (spelled Wyllyam Coplande) on a ribbon beneath.

COPPER PLATE ENGRAVING. Copper plate engraving was a process for producing prints and book illustrations. Of early origin, it was modified and improved in the early 18th century with the introduction of more refined techniques. Plates were prepared by the battery-hammer method, then smoothed by rubbing with pumice and oilstone. Though costly and time consuming, this approach gave the best possible surface for engraving. Later the industry employed steam powered rollers to prepare the plates, which did not give so even or responsive a surface. The majority of English illustrated books of the 18th century used copper plates. Hard steel replaced copper in the 1820's, parallel with the adoption of publishers' cloth for edition bindings. Copper plate engraving was never quite so popular on the continent as in Britain.

COPYRIGHT. The equivalent of a patent on a work of literature, a copyright prohibits another from using it, either in whole or part, without consent. Books published in the U.S. secure their copyright upon deposit at the Library of Congress and the issuing of a Library of Congress serial number. It extends 28 years and may be renewed another 28 after which time the work comes into public domain. Magazines are also copyrighted by their publisher, and thus all writing (and photographs, cartoons, etc.) appearing within their pages share in the copyright.

Prior to copyright laws, it was every writer, printer, publisher, and bookseller for himself. Private wars were waged and often reached court, where a restraining order might be obtained. But usually it was impossible to locate or identify the offending party, as such works were in the nature of "underground" publications (see PIRATED EDITION). The history of copyright laws is long and involved. The first attempt to outlaw piracy was the English Copyright Act of 1709—some 230-odd years after Caxton printed the first English book. However, it did not apply in Ireland, so Ireland instantly became a center for pirated works, and this continued until 1801. A revised Copyright Act appeared in 1842, placing limits of expiration of seven years after an author's death or 42 years after the first publication of the book. Consequently, the early 20th century witnessed an avalanche of editions (mainly cheap) of popular books that had appeared in the earlier part of Victoria's reign. The present U.S. copyright law was enacted in 1909.

COPYRIGHT LIBRARY. A copyright library—such as the Library of Congress in the U.S. and the British Museum—is one to which a publisher must submit his books to obtain a copyright. By law, copyright libraries are entitled to free copies (usually two) of every volume published in their nation, and the publisher must pay delivery charges. In the case of ordinary trade editions, there is seldom complaint, but where costly limited editions are involved the publisher sometimes balks at giving copies away. Periodic checks of holdings at copyright libraries always reveal missing titles, a result of publishers refusing to comply. Those who comply against their will occasionally submit damaged copies that could not be sold. This has caused outcry from bibliographers, who maintain that copyright libraries are losing prestige and building sloppy collections by taking handouts instead of purchasing their books.

CORDS. In hand (or custom) binding, the GATHERINGS of leaves are sewn on cords, which serve to hold them in place and secure them to the binding. The cords are laid crossways along the spine, their number (and thickness) depending on the size and weight of the book. A miniature volume will require only two or three, a folio four or five, depending on the binder's judgment. When the spine is covered with leather the cords result in RAISED BANDS, which divide the spine into compartments and provide a suitable basis for gilding. The ends of the cords are run through holes in the binding boards, pulled apart for flattening, and pasted down; they are then covered by the PASTE DOWN.

CORNERPIECES. Bindings were provided with cornerpieces as long ago as the manuscript age, prior to the invention of printing c. 1450. Originally they were plain sections of bent iron, hammered to the wooden binding boards with nails. They fitted over the four corners of the covers and were intended not as an ornament but to protect the edges from damage. After a time, however, the decorative potential of cornerpieces was seized upon. By the time printing came along, they had grown quite large and decorative, as had the various other items of hardware common to gothic bindings, extending as much as three inches along the outer covers and worked into artistic designs. Sometimes they would be triangle shaped, the edges cut into scallops, or punched out in the center; or there might be large spiked BOSSES in the center. As many early printers hired their own binders, each tended to develop certain styles of cornerpieces and can occasionally be identified by them; the cornerpieces used by KOBERGER of Nuremberg, for example, were very characteristic. By the early 16th century they had died out, used only when a special binding was called for, as they involved work and cost and were just not worth the effort. Bindings with cornerpieces were especially favored in Germany and Holland. There was a short-lived attempt to revive them in Holland at the close of the 17th century.

CORVINUS, MATTHIAS. Medieval king of Hungary, Corvinus lived from 1440 to 1490. Corvinus has been called the most enthusiastic book collector of his time, surpassing even the Italian popes and princes. The fact that he was somewhat removed from the centers of the book trade did not hamper his activities, as he employed agents to scout throughout the continent for fine items. In his royal palace at Buda was a special writing room or scriptorium, fashioned after the manner of Christian monasteries. There he employed some 20 scribes and artists to copy out texts and create manuscripts more beautiful than existed anywhere else. The splendor in which he lived is beyond modern belief. At his death his library was estimated by some to contain 50,000 volumes, though present guesses place the figure nearer 10,000. Nevertheless, all were of exceptional quality, and the value of the collection in terms of today's market would be in the multimillions of dollars. Unfortunately it was broken up, some of the more attractive manuscripts taken as war spoils by the Turks.

COSTER (or KOSTER), LAURENS JANSZOON. Coster was a 15th century Dutchman who has occasionally been suggested as an alternative to Gutenberg as the inventor of printing. To this day there is strong feeling in the Low Countries that Gutenberg was a rank impostor and that his fame belongs to Coster. A few serious bibliographers share this view, but the cause is losing ground due to insufficient evidence. A number of primitive fragments of Dutch-language printing do exist and appear to pre-date Gutenberg, but nothing conclusive can be learned of them.

It seems well established now that Coster was more than a myth, although BERNARD QUARITCH called him fictitious. He was apparently born around 1370 and was a church sexton (or coster—hence the family name) in Haarlem. Legend states that he was strolling in the woods sometime around 1430 when he carved a few letters from tree bark, then made ink impressions with them on paper. If this is true, he had invented nothing up to this point. Handstamps had long been in use in Europe and Coster was no more the first to stamp out letters than Newton was the first to be plunked on the head by an apple. But Coster saw possibilities in this simple device that had escaped others. After years of top-secret experimentation, the legend goes on, he perfected a system of using carved letters to duplicate handwriting, so that books could be made simply and cheaply. The press he used was the ordinary screwpress that had been employed in other industries for a long while. But, unlike Gutenberg, Coster's types were not made of metal. Gutenberg, after all, was a goldsmith by profession and had knowledge of casting metals, but Coster was only a simple church sexton. Exactly how Coster's letters were made is not known. The early scraps of Dutch incunabula appear to have been printed with wooden characters, but this has been challenged by some authorities on the grounds that individually carved types would show greater variation.

From this point the Coster Legend becomes less credible, which tends to cast doubt on the whole story. It is said that when the business was flourishing, as it eventually did, Coster could not meet the demand for school texts and religious works, so he began to take on helpers and apprentices. One was an evil German named Johann (meaning probably FUST, not Gutenberg) who ran away one Christmas Eve while the household was asleep, stealing a set of typefaces. He made good his escape back into Germany and set himself up as a printer in Mainz, announcing to the world that he was the true inventor of the art. Coster is thought to have died sometime between 1440 and 1445.

Until the close of the 15th century, there were people in Haarlem who had known Coster and some even who had worked for him who upheld the legend. They passed the story to their children and they passed it to theirs. In fact the house where Coster lived, which also served as his office, was venerated as a sort of shrine in Haarlem for many years, but no longer exists; it is thought to have burned. Yet the spot where it stood is still considered hallowed ground. Search as they might, bibliographers have not been successful in locating any documents that link Coster with printing. Unless this is done, the legend can only be regarded as a folk tale.

COTTAGE BINDING. Cottage binding was a style of decorative binding popular in Britain in the second half of the 17th century and, with modifications, well into the 18th. It was the first native English style that rivaled continental work for elegance. Usually executed in full morocco or calf, it comprised overall gilding of both covers. Many small tools were used, built into a design previously sketched on paper. The center portion (extending almost the length of the cover) might consist of a geometrical pattern formed with tiny floral and leaf tools, intermixed with gilded stars and rosettes of various sizes. The whole would be surrounded by a gilded panel, at the corners and sides of which would be more floral gilding. The term derives from the fact that the gilding along the inner sides of the panel resembles the gables of a cottage. Samuel Mearne, binder to Charles II, was long thought to have invented cottage, but current opinion doubts it. The presence of a cottage binding is evidence the book has come from the library of an affluent (if not necessarily prominent) early collector, as the average run of English binding of the time was a good deal plainer.

COTTON, SIR ROBERT BRUCE. Cotton was an English antiquary, and a collector of rare books, manuscripts, and medals (1571–1631). Born at Denton in Huntingdonshire, he was schooled at Cambridge and afterward settled in Westminster. Here he pursued his study of the old and curious, accumulating reference works on classical and ancient art, architecture, statuary, medals, etc. Among his principal collections was early manuscripts, which he purchased in much the same fashion, and with similar appetite, as SIR THOMAS PHILLIPPS, a countryman who followed him by two centuries. Cotton House, as his home was called, came to be filled with the gleanings from secondhand dealers and booksellers, and was a favorite of scholars. Cotton was knighted by King James I in 1603, raised to a baronet in 1611, and became a confidant of the king. A member of Parliament, he gradually fell out of favor as the result of unpopular writings. In a book he wrote on Henry III, he denounced monarchy; in a 1628 pamphlet he blasted away at the government, then headed by Charles I. A close friend of the Earl of Somerset, he was suspected of plotting the death of Sir Thomas Overbury and imprisoned for eight months. In 1629 his library was officially declared unfit for public inspection. When he passed away two years later, his son, Sir Thomas, fought to have the library turned over to him and succeeded. Sir John Cotton, grandson of Sir Robert Bruce, presented the Cottonian Library to the nation, and it was removed to Ashburnham House in 1730. In 1731 a fire occurred at Ashburnham House, destroying many of the finest items, but a large proportion escaped undamaged. In 1753 it became part of the British Museum.

CUNEIFORM. An ancient form of writing, cuneiform is generally believed to be the first practiced, prior even to Oriental alphabets. Cuneiform developed in the lower Tigris and Euphrates, that pioneer hotbed of human activity, probably the invention of the Sumerians. It quickly spread throughout the ancient world and was adopted in Babylonia, Mesopotamia, Assyria, and to some extent in Persia, though not until a later date. The Egyptians and Hebrews were the only two major races to use other alphabets. The first use of cuneiform is placed at about 4000 B.C., though this remains a rough estimate; Sumerian civilization flourished even before this date. The earliest method was to etch the characters into slabs of brick, less frequently into stone. This was satisfactory so long as the only necessary writing was the identification of monuments or tombs, but as society became more advanced it was impractical. One alternative was to impress the characters into terra-cotta or baked clay, which was extensively manufactured throughout the ancient east. Another, which did not develop until later, was the use of wax slates.

Cuneiform was used for every writing task, including legal proceedings and documents. When archaeological sites are explored in modern Iraq, or other regions whose ancestors wrote in cuneiform, many small and large clay tablets bearing these bizarre inscriptions are discovered. Until rather recent times the deciphering of cuneiform posed a sticky problem but today, thanks to the efforts of such scholars as Sir Henry Rawlinson, it can be interpreted without difficulty. Many tablets prove to be land grants, transfers of property, and various sorts of licenses, which conform surprisingly closely to more modern laws. The normal shape is not rectangular, as might be expected, but like a dinner roll, and quite thick. A single document might weigh as much as several pounds, so if early legal scribes complained of being buried under tons of work they were not far from correct.

Cuneiform was one of the longest surviving of the world's alphabets. It continued in use until about the 3rd century B.C. and for a long time was more widely written and understood than any other. It was based upon a series of four wedge-shaped symbols rather than letters and in this respect was more closely allied to Chinese than modern European languages. There were many huge libraries of cuneiform writings, notably that of Assurbani-pal at Nineveh, but only a fraction of specimens have been preserved.

CURIOSA. A heading which began to appear in catalogues from an early date and still continues, curiosa was at first mainly applied to books that might be considered pornographic, and in the Victorian age this included nearly every third volume. Today, however, most booksellers frankly list erotic items under "Erotica," or whatever classification they choose to use, as calling a spade a spade is more apt to promote sales among today's buyers. Now the term curiosa is more often applied to books which really are curious in nature, or at least appear so to the cataloguer. Early tracts on the making of porridge from chimney sweepings, or reports on the finding of mysterious footprints, are the sort of thing that qualify. To be fair, it should only be applied to little-known publications, not famous or common works on peculiar subjects. There are quite a number of collectors of curiosa, not specializing in any particular topic but accumulating the weirdest titles they can locate.

DAMP STAINS. "Damp stains" is a term used by many booksellers instead of Water Stains, because it sounds less offensive. The rippling seen in the leaves of many old books is not the result of dampness and this is not what is meant by damp stains. Books damaged by damp are ragged and musty rather than crisp, and often soiled in the bargain. Sometimes the trouble is only in the outer margin of a few leaves, in which event it is apt to be overlooked by the buyer or seller, or run through the entire volume. If one could know the physical history of each volume, there might be more sympathy for damp stained books. Some have suffered water damage as a result of fires; others have been in floods; still others were minding their own business on library shelves when a waterpipe in the ceiling overhead chose to go phut. Books which have been wet and then not properly dried are apt to develop a variety of other maladies, such as FOXING and warped bindings. Cloth bindings suffer more than leather from contact with water and are usually permanently disfigured. Calf and morocco return to their original state when dry; vellum carries its scars, but nobly.

The following procedure has been suggested for drying books that have gotten wet, but it must be done quickly: Mop up surface water by patting with a crushed napkin. Place a large sheet of waxed kitchen paper between each leaf that has become wet (if it chances to be an encyclopedia or other large volume this may require several dozen rolls). Get a wooden box, about twice the size of the book, and place a one-inch layer of pipe tobacco in it. Lay the book in this and sprinkle a few more leaves over it. Shut the box tightly and place in a dry location (preferably with a humidity under 60%) for several weeks. The staining will still be noticeable, but should be less serious than if proper aid were not given. After the stains have dried, there is almost nothing that can be done. French collectors have the whole book washed (less the binding, that is) but this never seems to do much good.

In climates where the humidity is continually above 70%, and frequently above 80%, damp staining can result merely by the volume standing in a case, though it will not be as severe as actual contact with water. It is more likely that constant high humidity will take its heaviest toll upon the binding, especially if it should be of vellum.

In many old books, particularly those printed in Germany, France and Switzerland from about 1590 to 1650, the natural paper discoloration is often mistaken for staining. There are many books of this period in which almost every leaf has turned a dark, mellow brown, while the margins stay white. This was caused by an effort to economize on printing papers. It is almost never seen in INCUNABULA.

DATES. The majority of medieval manuscripts were undated, nor did they contain any other information regarding their manufacture. Occasionally a scribe who was especially proud of his work would slip his name in, sometimes with a date, as was done more frequently by monastic laborers in other fields—the chalice signed at the base, for example, which most of us have seen in museums. Some think this was done so the volumes could not be accused of being outdated; an important consideration, as the monasteries often traded books back and forth and all wanted to get something decent in the bargain.

The Gutenberg Bible likewise was not signed or dated. Some say this was because Gutenberg and Fust wanted to sell it as a manuscript; others think they wished to avoid possible persecution or legal troubles; while many feel it was simply an omission that had no particular significance. The first dated printed book was the Psalter of Fust and Schoeffer, which appeared in 1457. The majority of incunables were dated but a large number were not. Until the 16th century, dates were normally carried in the COLOPHON, which appeared at the end of the book, as there was no title page in the modern sense. The early practice was to print dates in roman numerals. Some incunables appear with arabic dates but they are few and far between (Scotus of Venice was one who used them).

Many early books, from about 1510 to 1570, are dated in front and rear, as they carry both a title page and colophon. Sometimes the dates do not jibe, but are seldom more than a year apart. This results from the body of the book being printed before the title page; or it could be just the reverse. Dates are, of course, of primary importance in establishing the order of editions of a work, but often the book sleuth must delve deeper than surface evidence.

DAY, JOHN. English printer John Day was considered the most skilled in Britain in the 16th century. The facts of his career are only sketchily known, but fortunately a good number of his books are preserved. He is thought to have started in business around the Holborn Conduit in London in the 1540's and then moved to Aldersgate in 1549. At this early period he was in partnership with a journeyman printer named William Seres. Around 1550, the two went their separate ways, but it seems Day did some printing for Seres afterward, in the common practice of early printers to share the work of large editions. For a period of more than two decades, Day was the most successful printer-publisher in London, holding a position similar to that of Pynson a half-century before. He was the first to use Saxon letters, and modified the Greek and italic types that had been previously in use. For a time, it was necessary for Day to operate a number of printing offices simultaneously, to satisfy the enormous workload, which was very rare for an English printing establishment of the time. He died in 1584, very well advanced in age, having brought a long list of books into the world. One of his most famous publications was "*Psalmes in Metre with Music*," 1571, in small quarto, which now fetches a handsome sum. His mark consisted of a plaque with Renaissance border, wherein one youth awakens another with the call "arise, for it is Day," a clever play on his name.

DAYE, STEPHEN. Daye was the first man to print in America. He had been a locksmith in Britain and apparently did no printing prior to settling in the colonies. His press was located in Cambridge, Massachusetts, on the doorstep of Harvard College. Its first full length production was the BAY PSALM BOOK of 1640, crudely printed, which took its name from the Massachusetts Bay Colony. It is thought the actual presswork, or a good measure of it, was performed by Stephen's son, Matthew, then 20 years old. Daye died in 1668, aged about 74. See GLOVER, JOSE.

DeLUXE EDITION. A term that seems like it should mean a lot, "Deluxe Edition" often doesn't. Its use is only justified in cases where a book has been issued in two distinct states: ordinary copies for the general trade, and those which by superior design, type, paper, binding or other factors can be called DeLuxe. However, it is generally applied merely to good looking or finely bound books. It is probably best relegated to the world of advertising.

DeTHOU, J. A. A French book collector (1553–1617), DeThou was the librarian of Marie deMedici. DeThou was especially interested in specimens of fine printing and book production, which he never failed to outfit in personalized bindings. He began collecting when a child and built a large and attractive library while still in adolescence. His career as a bibliophile spanned more than 50 years. At first he was influenced by the bindings made for GROLIER, France's foremost collector of the first half of the 16th century. Those he chose for himself were more austere, comprising his arms stamped in gilt but lacking the overall strapwork and tooling of Grolier's bindings. Instead of gold, he chose to have his stamping done in silver, which is handsome and original but easily tarnishes. His bindings appear in four distinct divisions. Prior to 1587 he was a bachelor and his crest alone was used. After that year his wife's emblem is stamped beside, and the initials J. A. M. below. When she died, he ceased to use emblems, but employed a mourning wreath and his initial intertwined with hers. Upon marrying again in 1603, he readopted the old style, with his shield and that of his new wife.

The history of the library is of interest. When DeThou died in 1617, it was maintained intact. In 1677, having by then acquired much additional fame, it was sold en bloc to the Marquis de Menars, who at one swoop gained for himself immeasurable notoriety as a connoisseur. In 1718 he passed away and the collection was brought by Cardinal deRohan, who kept it intact. When he died his heirs tried for a time to keep it, knowing the Cardinal's wish and the importance of the collection as a unit, but financial difficulties made this impossible. In 1789 it was finally sold, to enrich the shelves of collectors throughout the world.

For a long while it was thought that the Eves brothers, particularly Clovis Eves, were responsible for the majority of DeThou's bindings, but this is now generally discredited, as are so many other fond old stories about bookbindings. Unlike Grolier, many of DeThou's bindings are in vellum, sometimes with gilt back. Although no decoration but arms was employed on the covers, the spine panels were sometimes very creatively gilded. Almost all have RAISED BANDS and a sort of classical, timeless appearance. They have lost something in esteem over recent years as a result of critical research into the characters and circumstances surrounding them.

DeWORDE, WYNKYN. One of the English incunabula printers, DeWorde was the best known aside from Caxton. He worked for some time in Caxton's office, perhaps playing a major role in his later publications, and took over the business upon Caxton's death in 1491. His career then stretched across 43 years, until his passing in 1534, in which time he issued more than 800 books. In addition to reprinting some of Caxton's books he published many new works, particularly those of native authors. Among his most well-known were the *Nova Legenda Angile* of 1516; Dame Juliana Berners' *Fyshing with an Angle* (1496); Voragine's *Golden Legend* (1527). He did much less literary work than Caxton, probably due to his greater output of titles. In terms of style his books are much like his master's, and in fact his earlier volumes were executed in Caxton's very type. Even at the close, when influences from Renaissance Italy and Spain were strong, he continued to follow Caxton's traditions. He used a variety of marks, which incorporated Caxton's monogram. All Wynkyn DeWorde imprints are very rare. At one time they were considered "Caxtons for the poor man," but no longer, because some bring fully as much as Caxton's.

DIDOT. The Didot family of French scholar-printers was credited with reviving classical learning on the continent. Their activities were very extensive and the fame of their books such that every gentleman of rank stocked his library with them, bringing them enormous wealth. The house had its beginnings with Francois Didot (1689–1759), whose name is closely associated with the literary world of Paris in his lifetime. Of his 11 children, two became printer-publishers: Francois Ambroise and Pierre Francois. Francois Ambroise was the real genius and it was under his direction that the name of Didot rose to eminence. Not content to merely publish, he strove to improve printing methods and made useful discoveries. He worked out an advance—or at least it was so considered at the time—upon Fournier's point system of grading the sizes of type. He designed his own type, known universally by the name of Didot, which was cut by Waflard. Unsatisfied with the sort of paper used for printing fine editions, he ordered the Johannot mill at Annonay to produce special stock for him, and thus was **papier velin de France** born. The Didot house soon became a tourist attraction and was visited constantly by travelers; Benjamin Franklin paid his respects in 1780. Franklin's grandson, B. F. Bache, was apprenticed to Francois Ambroise.

The other brother, Pierre Francois, operated his own publishing house. His business was considerably smaller but he was a printer of much skill and issued very beautiful volumes. Some of the most luxurious books of the period were his work, and command great sums today. He was appointed Printer to the Dauphin (subsequently Louis XVIII), an enviable position, in 1759. Later in his career he was more concerned with the manufacture of fine paper than in printing and established a paper mill at Essonne, which gave the Didots supremacy in printing, publishing, type design, and the supply of papers as well.

Francois Ambroise, who passed on in 1804, had two sons who also distinguished themselves as printers and carried the firm to new heights. One of them, Pierre, lived to the age of 92 and was the patriarch of French publishing for the last several decades of his life. He managed the Didot interests while his brother, Firmin, carried on the tradition of his father, designing type, inventing, innovating, and adding to the achievements of the house. His greatest invention was the process of stereotyping. In 1830, Firmin was offered the position of director at the Royal Printing Office, but declined, claiming the office had permitted its works to become too commercialized. However, his bust was placed in the Royal Printing Office after his death in 1836. But still this did not spell the end of the House of Didot, as Firmin's two sons stepped in to direct it. Ambroise Firmin, who lived to 1876, was one of the most popular publishers of his time, and a noted book collector. He issued numerous works on the history of printing. His personal library was sold for more than half a million dollars. During the height of its success, the Didot Press employed more than a thousand persons, the largest publishing operation up to that period. It also ran a retail shop where its books were sold.

DISBOUND. Ninety-nine out of a hundred new collectors mistake disbound to mean unbound, and it is difficult to blame them. A disbound item generally **is** unbound, but that is only an accessory after the fact. In its proper sense, to disbind something is to **remove it from a book**. Most disbound items on the market are individual tracts or sermons taken from religious works, ballads from songbooks, and such. So long as the material extracted is complete in itself, it stands to have bibliographical value, but not so much as the book as a whole. The major cause of disbinding is that some booksellers believe a few plays (or whatever) taken from an otherwise damaged volume will have greater sales appeal. When a book has been seriously damaged, such as the result of a fire, the salvaged portions are sometimes sold as disbound parts. Shakespeare's plays, rescued from crippled copies of the first four folios, are commonly seen as disbounds. Books from early Bibles and sections of geography books dealing with a certain country also frequently end up as disbounds.

DISCARD STAMP. When a book has been owned by a library, it usually must receive a discard or cancel stamp in order to be sold. This is a matter of procedure, to guard against stolen and hence unstamped books from its collection being sold. Cancels vary from small and unoffensive to large and very offensive. Normally the more prestigeous libraries (which think like book collectors) try to deface their outgoing volumes as little as possible. The discard stamps of some, such as Cambridge, are almost attractive. Usually, but not always, the cancel is struck directly over the ownership stamp. Most cancel stamps are worded in such a fashion that the book can still retain its dignity, such as "No Longer the Property of..." or simply "Cancelled." But far too many loudly proclaim that the book has been "Discarded," which—even if it should be a Gutenberg Bible—cannot but hurt its sales potential, especially if it has been discarded by a little library no one has heard of.

DIVINITY CALF. A smooth, hard-surfaced calf, divinity calf is not very much different than law calf in texture, used in former times for the binding of religious works. There are many objections to it, ranging from its color (a pale, rusty violet) to keeping qualities. It is an extremely cheap grade, used only in commercial works, and is never the recipient of elaborate tooling. The most common decoration for divinity calf is plain blocked covers, the corners intersecting in crosses like Easter buns. The division of calf into various grades dates back to the days when it was used to bind almost all classes of books, good and ill, and was marketed in a wide variety of colors and textures.

DIVISION TITLE. When a book consists of a number of distinct parts— not different volumes, but divisions within the same volume—it is usual to set them apart with divisional titles. In the early days of printing this was done almost automatically but seems to be dying out today, except in textbooks. The divisional title may give much information or little. The majority of early ones repeated most of the title page information and even stated the name of the printer, place of printing, and date. But in certain respects they would differ: if the GENERAL TITLE had been printed in red and black, the divisional titles would likely be only in black; if there was a fine decorative border on the general title, it would be lacking on the divisional titles. Disagreement in dates from one divisional title to another is not unusual, as books took a long time to print and one section might be on the shelf long before the whole work was completed. One must be careful to distinguish between divisional titles and two or more separate books bound together.

DOG EARED. Originally used of the corners of pages that had become ragged through creasing, "dog eared" is now applied to any pages that have the appearance of heavy use. One of the causes of dog earing is the habit of some readers to keep their place by turning down a corner or otherwise mutilating pages. This was a rather widespread practice at one time, but apparently modern readers are becoming less barbaric. The term is confined mainly to American catalogues; the British prefer "frayed." Such dogs as the beagle and basset hound, whose ears turn downward, are said to be responsible for the phrase: an open and shut case of bibliographers going to the dogs.

DOS-A-DOS BINDING. Dos-A-Dos binding is a very unusual sort of late medieval binding, practiced occasionally as late as the 17th century, wherein two books of equal size are joined like a loveseat: that is, the two lower covers are attached, so the foredges face in opposite directions. It originated in the monasteries, purely as a convenience measure. Monks frequently wished to carry two books about with them, but this necessitated a double chain at the waist. With a dos-a-dos binding, two books became one. Genuine examples are extremely rare.

DOUBLURE. In fine bindings, the PASTE DOWNS are sometimes made not of paper but some more elegant material, such as silk or thin leather. In these cases they are apt to be called doublures. Leather doublures are often gilded, sometimes in a very elaborate manner. In some bindings the exterior, though of good leather, is relatively plain, while the doublures are lavishly festooned. The proper term for this style is JANSENIST. Doublures did not come into their own until the 1600's. Cheaper bindings which still attempt a decorative appearance sometimes use doublures of brightly patterned paper. In the late 18th century and throughout much of the 19th century doublures were supplied in trade editions by means of heavy marbled paper. Those having rare books rebound shy away from ordering doublures, as they add a stiff sum to the already high cost of hand binding and the preference for them is on the decline.

DURER, ALBRECHT. Though principally a painter, German artist Durer (1471–1528) did a good deal of book illustration and also designed illustrations for others. Born at Nuremberg, he was apprenticed at the age of 15 to MICHAEL WOLGEMUT, who won fame as a woodcutter in the employ of the printer KOBERGER and was also an accomplished painter. Durer experimented in many techniques from an early age and never left off experimenting. Though he became a journeyman painter at the hands of Wolgemut, much of his early work was in silverpoint and woodcut. His first employment as a book illustrator was at Basel in 1493, where he executed the now famous woodcuts for Sebastian Brant's *Ship of Fools*. He was not very satisfied with woodcut as an art, however, and whenever possible made steel engravings and etchings, including the Apocalypse, Great Passion, Life of the Virgin, and others. His style gradually shifted from Flemish mannerist to Italian Renaissance, but the change was well absorbed by his strongly personal character. Most of his fame came after 1500. In the last two decades of his life, he was in heavy demand as a book illustrator; the total number of volumes to which he lent his handiwork was astronomical, but he also continued to work in oil, watercolor, silverpoint, drypoint, and other mediums. Though his woodcuts are powerful, they seem restrained by the limitations of the process, while his etchings show his full ability. There is a habit to ascribe any fine German woodcut book to Durer, or at least suggest he might have had a hand in it.

DUST JACKET (or WRAPPER). Though one may think of commercial dust jackets as having a modern origin, they were used in a primitive form as long ago as the 16th century. At that time, however, they were not printed. They seem to have evolved in Germany or Austria, first used as a protection for trade bindings in stamped vellum, which is easily rubbed. They were made of heavy paper, perhaps occasionally vellum, and completely wrapped around the binding. The title would then be written on the front cover, as book shops of the 1500's displayed their volumes in racks with the front cover faced out, rather than on shelves with the spine displayed as now. Sometimes the wrapper would be slightly torn open by the bookseller, so the binding could be seen. Very few specimens of early dust-wrapped books survive, but this must be partially due to their fragility and the habit of buyers to discard them after purchase. We are probably safe in guessing that Spanish, Portugese, and Italian books were seldom, if ever, wrapped. The earliest printed jacket dates from 1832.

EDGES. The edges of a book's pages are an important part of its makeup, especially in fine or rare editions. When delivered to the binder, the leaves of a new book are in uncut GATHERINGS, so he must separate them. The edges are also trimmed down somewhat, to make them perfectly even. Many early books were bound without their edges touched and thus show the ORIGINAL STATE of the paper, with the irregularities it retained from manufacture. Collectors value such specimens as virgins. Some modern books, especially novels, are given untrimmed or deckled edges out of tradition. Gilding of edges did not become a fad in Europe until the 1500's. Luxuriously bound volumes would be gilded on all three sides, others on the top and front, and the more humble just the top. Today many publishers (and almost all bookclubs) still color page tops, but rarely in gold; more likely yellow or green dye. MARBELIZING was another technique used to decorate edges, and of course there were FOREDGE PAINTINGS for the upper crust who could afford it. During the 16th and 17th centuries, less frequently afterward, gilded edges were GOFFERED or chased with tools to form indented patterns. Gilt edges as a whole were mainly popular in Italy, France, and Spain; less so in England and very much less so in

German speaking lands. Rare books with ample edges or margins are valued a good deal more than those which have been closely cut. See UNOPENED.

EDITIO PRINCEPS. The first printed edition of a work that had circulated in manuscript prior to the invention of typography was a editio princeps. Normally applied only to the Greek and Latin classics, which were seized upon by the incunabula printers not only because of their popularity but the fact that they required no payment or contract with the author. Also, the classics could be translated or edited at the publisher's whim, and many were butchered to fit printing schedules or other needs. Still, the editio princeps of the classics are highly regarded by collectors as well as literary historians, as they were prepared from early manuscripts and stood a chance of being truer to the originals than later efforts. By the close of the 15th century virtually every scrap of classical writing, important or not, had appeared in print; the majority had gone through a number of editions. The editio princeps of Aristotle, Ovid, Plato, Cicero and others whose books had existed well over a thousand years in manuscript somehow fit the term better than medieval authors. Caxton's first edition of Chaucer is seldom, for example, called an editio princeps.

ELLIOT, THOMAS. An English bookbinder of the first half of the 18th century, Elliot is believed to have worked for the Harleys and executed many choice bindings that were for long years ascribed to others. While research on his life and career is still in the embryo stage and many questions remain unanswered, it appears he was a far more important figure than previously given credit for.

ELSE FINE. A term frequently used by booksellers after a lengthy recitation of faults, else fine means the book still has some portions of its anatomy free from damage. Not of much comfort when found in a context such as "spine missing, covers loose, endleaves lacking, plates foxed, else fine." Of British origin, it has been successfully adopted by the American trade.

ELZEVIR. Next to the Aldus or Aldine press, the Elzevir printing house is the most illustrious of the early scholar-publishers who made the classics available to the common masses. The total number of books issued by the Elzevirs amounts to 1,608 according to the standard work on the subject, Willem's "Les Elzevir." Of these, 1,213 bear the Elzevir name or mark, the others being anonymous. Although the fame of the Elzevirs is founded upon their pocket editions, issued in large quantities for circulation across the continent, they did print books in standard formats as well, including a number of folios.

The firm began with Louis Elzevir, born at Louvain in 1540. He seems to have had no intention early in life to be a printer. In 1580, aged 40, he set up as a bookseller and binder in Leyden, Holland, at that time a bustling university town with strong demand for books. In 1583 he printed his first book and had issued more than a hundred titles by his death in 1617. However, the name of Elzevir was undistinguished until one of Louis' five sons, Bonaventure Elzevir, began on his own as a printer in 1608. Upon his father's death, he incorporated the two businesses and then took a nephew into partnership. It was Bonaventure who popularized the pocket classics and whose productions collectors find most desirable. There were also branches of the Elzevir press at Amsterdam and Utrecht, both important commercial centers. The final Elzevir title appeared in 1712 at Leyden, a span of activity of 129 years.

In terms of rarity, Elzevir volumes are among the most common of their era. However, there are a number highly valued and some, particularly from Bonaventure's early years, genuinely rare. During the middle part of the 19th century, a vogue for Elzevirs grew up in London, Paris, and elsewhere. As they were not difficult to find on the shilling stalls, collectors would make the rounds of shops regularly and then gather to compare their spoils. Tall copies, those not cut by the binder's knife, were most prized. The frenzy reached such a degree that collectors went about with rulers in their pockets when visiting bookshops and auctions. If someone located a copy of a particular edition a fraction of a centimeter larger than one owned by his friend, it was an occasion for celebration. Elzevirs were then classed according to the "right" and "wrong" editions, the right usually being one that carried the Leyden imprint under Bonaventure's reign. Today Elzevirs are collected somewhat more soberly, though size continues to be a consideration to those of the old school.

From a typographic standpoint, the Elzevir works are not remarkable, in fact surpassed by many presses of the time. They aimed toward a public uninterested in beauty of type or design; speed and cheapness were their basic goals. The size of type in their pocket editions is much too small to be comfortably read, and is closely crowded together to save paper. In the smaller details of ornamentation, such as page headings, initial letters, and so forth, they are equally undistinguished.

EMBROIDERED BINDINGS. Embroidered book coverings, made of fancy silks, velvets and similar cloths, were an English innovation, especially popular during the reign of Elizabeth I. They are thought to have come about to satisfy the demand among British collectors for ornamentation. During the early 16th century, when Italian and French books were sumptuously gold gilded, their British counterparts paraded in plain vellum or calf, occasionally stamped in blind. While these bindings seem attractive to us today, it is obvious that contemporary collectors were not at all enthusiastic over them. Yet there was no attempt to imitate the gilt bindings of southern Europe.

It is difficult to say how many embroidered bindings were actually created by professional binders. Probably very few. The majority may have been the handiwork of seamstresses; it is rather certain a portion were made by female household servants to pass idle hours. At one time they were ascribed to convents. It was said that Elizabeth executed embroidered bindings as a hobby, but this should be taken with a grain of salt. Embroidered bindings, even the bad ones, are rare today and do well on the market. They were also produced in France, but for a briefer period.

ENGRAVING. The art of engraving began in the ancient world, with stamps and seals. But the process was not used to print illustrations in the west until the late 14th or early 15th century. At this time woodcut prints began to appear around the area of the Rhine, as well as playing cards in which the designs were stamped from wood engraved blocks. A number of towns have been suggested as the birthplace of this innovation: Mainz, Nuremberg, Constance, Basel, Strasbourg. Nor is anything known of the identity of these early artists. The subjects were mainly saints and other devotional portrayals, suitable for those who could not afford paintings. In contemporary use, they were unframed, stuck directly to the wall by means of melted wax.

Wood engraving was next employed in xylographic printing, which is thought to have preceded typography. Engravings on steel were developed in the 15th century, as an improvement over wood, as they permitted more minute detail and delicate shading. It was introduced first in Germany and Italy. In the early 16th century steel engraving reached its height under ALBRECHT DURER. Later that century, the art was often used to make black-and-white copies of oil paintings.

When engravings are published as individual works of art, not to be included in books, the edition is limited to a certain number of copies, after which the plate is defaced. Collectors of engravings seek early impressions, those among the first taken from the plate, as fine lines sometimes wear down as the work progresses. To determine an early impression, it is usually necessary to have several for comparison. Engravings that have appeared in books seldom make the pulse of collectors beat fast, as many hundreds (sometimes thousands) of impressions have been made from the same plate. In cases where the engravings were printed as an integral part of the book, it is possible to have all the plates in an early state; but where there are folding illustrations and such, which are apt to have been run off separately, one can find early and late or intermediate stages in the same volume. In the case of books illustrated by Durer, Holbein, or other artists of renown, the plates have sometimes been removed by a previous owner.

ERASURES. When a bookseller receives a volume with pencil underlining and ugly notations, he may decide to clean it up before offering it for sale. This is generally done with a wad of art gum, the sort that comes in small bars resembling soap; or, if nothing better is available, the reverse end of a pencil. If one uses a hard, scratchy eraser, such as those intended for ink, the paper is almost sure to suffer. Collectors tend to have mixed feelings about notations. Only a few attempt to perform erasures; either the book is rejected or, if bought, lived with as is. Even if successfully erased, pencil markings will always leave impressions in the paper, like the lines of an engraving, because of the pressure of the point. Notations in early books (say prior to 1850) are more likely to be in ink, in which case there is no hope of ridding oneself of them. Many erasures seen in books were made by the very persons responsible for decorating them, often hastily done before putting them up for sale.

It sometimes happens that a person will inscribe his name in ink on the front flyleaf or (in olden days) the title page, then wish to conceal his identity when selling the book. This is solved by gouging with a steel scraper; cutting out the piece of paper with a scissor, or blotting ink over it, all of which result in sad disfigurement. Cutting is the gravest sin; there is no reason why it ever should be resorted to. Yet prior to 1800 this was the common method of removing ownership evidence, even in books of high value. One must always be sure it was a signature removed, not evidence showing the book to be a less valuable edition.

ERRATA. Translated from the Latin, errata means mistakes. Regardless of the amount of proof reading, errors are common to most books. Some are the fault of the printer, others of the author, and still others of the publisher. The printer may drop letters, print a line inverted, omit captions for illustrations. Errors by the author are more likely to be in the nature of misinformation, which are more embarrassing and difficult to detect. The transposition of Gilbert Stuart into Stuart Gilbert and other tricks of this sort could be blamed on either. The printer must be forgiven if he follows incorrect copy, as the duty of seeing things right rests with the author and publisher.

There are several ways in which all parties concerned wash their hands of errata, provided the bloopers are noticed before the work is placed in circulation. In the first four centuries of printing, many books carried an errata leaf at the conclusion, listing pages where errors had occurred and appropriate corrections. The errata leaf is still used in cases where the trouble is spotted early, and extensive corrections are called for. Sometimes it will happen that by getting one fact or name wrong, several dozen pages carry mistakes, as the error is repeated and compounded. More frequently seen is the errata slip, a small strip of paper which may be pasted in the book (either at front, rear, or the scene of the crime), or laid in loosely. Sometimes errata pages are also merely laid in. In these cases the collector will not look with favor upon copies from which they have vanished. However, there is always a question—seldom answerable—of whether all copies were issued with the errata. When the errata leaf is part of a SIGNATURE or quire, it can be assumed all copies possessed it. Otherwise, it is entirely possible batches may have gone out to a distributor before the errata leaf was even printed. In instances where the errata leaf has been GUARDED, it's a pretty safe bet that copies lacking it were released that way. If merely laid in, it's anybody's guess. Booksellers (and many collectors) prefer to look on the bright side. If the errata leaf is present, it is gloated over, as making the book bibliographically perfect. If not, it is looked upon as an "early copy," the lack of the errata leaf being used to bolster the contention.

ESTIENNE. The most famous family of French scholar-printers, the Estienne books were superior in design to almost any others of their era and traditionally held up as specimens of the most artistic typography. The founder of the dynasty, Henri Estienne, started printing in Paris around 1501 or 1502. French books were then modeled closely after manuscripts, which were still being made in quantity. The introduction of typography had not caused a total shift of attention to the printed book, so it was necessary for French printers to maintain a high standard. Henri's books were in a soft, graceful roman letter, and well received, but gave little hint of the subsequent glories of the House of Estienne.

The term scholar-printer has been applied to many names over the years, often without foundation, but the Estiennes were indeed scholars. Had they not chosen to become involved in the mechanical side of publishing, there is the feeling they could have been noteworthy poets or classical historians; yet their taste in decorative art was equal to their scholarship. The most celebrated member of the family, and the one whose volumes are most eagerly sought, was Robert Estienne, son of Henri. Some call him the greatest printer in history. From an aesthetic point of view, his books were faultless: the types are all in harmony, the pages perfectly laid out and balanced, without a stroke or flourish wasted. His were true Renaissance books, in full humanistic spirit.

Robert employed both CLAUDE GARAMOND and GEOFFROI TORY, the leading type designers and book artists in Europe. Garamond is thought to have fashioned much of his type, while Tory supplied the emblem of the olive tree, which for years served as the mark of the Estienne press and was copied by the Elzevirs (who also modeled their types after Garamond's). Robert did not print in nearly the quantity of Aldus, Gryphus, or others who dealt with the classics, nor were his merchandising aims similar. While the others attempted to bring fine literature to the level of the common people by reducing the cost of books, he glorified the ancient authors by dressing them opulently. His books were not cheap, nor printed in huge editions. Collectors of the early 16th century gloried in them, even if they did not read them.

Being a Protestant, Robert found he was unable to carry on work at Paris and fled to Geneva in 1550. His brother Charles operated the Paris office from 1551 and published many significant items, including an encyclopedia and works on medicine and science, which were his pet subjects. The Geneva branch flourished and when Robert died in 1559 was taken over by his son Henri. Under Henri's leadership typography was relegated to a secondary role, but his books were easily as good as those of ordinary printers. He was imprisoned for a controversial book he published in 1566 and forced out of business. Without the political and religious difficulties they faced, it is felt their accomplishments could have been even greater. The influence of the Estiennes on book design continued strong in each succeeding age, down to our own. During the Victorian age there was effort to revive their ideals. The name was Latinized as Stephanus, as one is apt to find it in catalogues and reference books.

EX-LIBRARY. At one time the term "ex-library" was used only of books from circulating libraries, applied today to all volumes bearing evidence of library ownership. Unless very rare, ex-library copies are considered less desirable, as they are likely to have received heavy wear. See DISCARD STAMP.

EXTENDED. When a leaf is described as extended, it means that it was short and has been filled out to full size by adding a new margin or margins, cut from paper of (hopefully) a similar color and texture. But why was it short? Usually there can be only two reasons, neither comforting: it was damaged (by heavy worming, burning, rat gnawing) or, worse, inserted from a smaller copy. In the latter case, the book is a SOPHISTICATED COPY— and if that sounds good, hasten to refer to the definition. If one leaf has been inserted from another copy, there is an excellent chance others have been, too. Extending might be done along any of the four margins but usually the inner.

EXTRA ILLUSTRATED. Extra illustrations are those inserted, usually by a private owner, in addition to ones already possessed. The practice was popular in Britain and to some extent on the continent in the 18th and 19th centuries. The model would be an ordinary edition of any book that lent itself to the hobby, such as a handbook of birds native to the British Isles. The owner would go about scrounging suitable plates wherever he might be able to find them, mounting them on fresh leaves fastened in the book with paste. When done with care, the result was sometimes pleasing, though most extra-illustrators did not know when to stop and created huge bulging books that threatened to burst their bindings. Only rarely was extra illustrating carried out by a discriminating collector who confined additions to illustrations of quality, such as watercolors, drawings, or engravings by noted artists. There are few collectors today who specialize in extra illustrated works.

FACSIMILE LEAVES. Before photostatic copies came into use, the term "leaves supplied in facsimile" usually meant pen facsimiles, in which the writer attempted to imitate the shape and size of the printed characters. Today this art has been lost, as there is no necessity for it, but prior to about 1890 it was possible to obtain a pen facsimile so close to the real thing that even an expert could be fooled. Penmen were so skilled in the craft that they could even duplicate engravings, or add portions of leaves to those damaged, with hardly any trace of where the type ended and the writing began. However, examples are also found which are not so well done, while others are nothing more than attempts to transcribe the missing texts without making the writing look at all like printing.

There was another way in which facsimile leaves were prepared in early times, too. The desired leaf would be traced from another copy, etched on stone and then used to make a printing impression. Of the two, pen facsimiles were normally more successful. A facsimile truly intended to deceive requires paper of the same age and texture as the book, not easily obtained in many cases. Most photo-copy facsimilies, unlike old soldiers, rapidly fade away and must be replaced.

FANFARE BINDING. Fanfare binding was a popular style of decorative binding which originated in France around 1560 and was imitated elsewhere, though the finest specimens are of French manufacture. It consists of heavily gilt ornament, usually with many small arabesque tools repeated around a large centerpiece, in conjunction with gilt borders and other lavishness. Generally such bindings were applied in full calf or morocco. The style was said to have evolved as a protest against the overly somber bindings executed for Henri III. It gained greater impetus in the Baroque age, as wealthy collectors vied with each other to own the best specimens. Around 1620, it began to decline and was obsolete by 1650, replaced by variations and adaptations.

FAQUES (or FAWKES), WILLIAM. An obscure English printer, Faques was notable for the fact that he was active in the incunabula period. He came from France. His real name was Guillaume Faques. From 1503 to 1508 he served as Royal Printer to Henry VII. His mark consisted of two interlocking triangles, one printed in white on black ground, a favorite English typographic trick of the day. His books are extremely valuable.

FAVORITE EDITION. A popular phrase in catalogues, "favorite edition" suggests the edition was at one time (but probably no longer) highly regarded. The sentiments may be copied from a bibliography in which the work was praised, or even from contemporary reviews (preserved in the jacket notes). But in 99% of cases, there is no reference given to whose favorite it might have been. A favorite (like a "collected" edition) is not the first, nor the rarest edition.

FAWKES (or FAKES), RICHARD. An English post-incunabula printer thought to have started in business in 1509, Richard Fawkes probably took over the trade of WILLIAM FAQUES, though their exact connection is doubtful. Some maintain Richard did no printing until 1519, that the date 1509 (taken from his "Salus Corporis") is a misprint, intentional or otherwise. If a misprint, he was perhaps William Faques' son; if he started in 1509 he may have been a brother. His books bear such a resemblance to those of PYNSON it is hard to believe this is a coincidence, more reasonable that he worked for Pynson at one time or other. He was uncommonly talented, though his books are so scarce and few in number that they are seldom available for study. The name, however one spells it, is an early form of Fox, which was too simple for the Tudor imagination.

FINE PRINTING. Any book attractively printed might be called an example of fine printing, but collectors will not allow the matter to rest so easily. Modern books issued by commercial publishers for sale to the general trade do not qualify. The type in which this book is printed may be said to be lovely. Lovely, after all, is a question of opinion. But it is merely standard type available to any printer. Books printed by individuals or presses which design their own type may rate as fine printing, if the type is well designed (often far from so). PRIVATE PRESS books are regarded as premier examples of fine printing. Generally speaking, any book in which the type and layout are of main consideration qualifies. It is not necessary that such books be limited editions, or kept from general public sale. All the productions of the early typographers were sold on the general market, yet some represent very excellent presswork. Had these men merely bought their types from foundries rather than having a hand in their design, their books might not be so respected. Collectors of fine printing are numerous, but it is hard to find two who agree on anything but the weather.

FIRST EDITION. Generally used to indicate the first appearance of a book in print, as opposed to a second or revised edition, first editions are valued by collectors, in the belief they constitute the truest version of the author's text. It is much easier to distinguish first editions of early works than those of the 19th and 20th centuries, as old-time publishers boasted with glee if a book was popular enough to merit more than a single edition and proclaimed it on the title page. Even when this was not the case, there is often enough secondary evidence to decide the matter. In dealing with books published since about 1820, it is sometimes necessary to have a library of reference works at hand. Even then, there are cases over which even the most qualified authorities disagree. Few subjects spur as many bibliophilic jousts as the question of which of two editions came first. After research on some of these puzzles the collector is nearly ready for the padded cell.

When one is in a bookstore, far away from his handbooks and checklists, he will have difficulty picking first editions. It is universally believed by collectors that booksellers are a careless lot who habitually offer valuable "firsts" at basement prices, but experience disproves such a notion. From time to time one may discover a bargain, especially if the author is rather obscure and more popular abroad than at home, but it will not happen often. Remember that the bookseller has a vast advantage. At his fingertips (in that mysterious little rear room to which he disappears at selected moments) are all the catalogues issued since the most remote times, and he is not about to make his customers presents of scarce material. In a shop, without access to the tools of the trade, one is at the mercy of his memory and knowledge, either of which may fail; but the bookseller depends upon neither when a sticky point is in question. So one must understand that he is working with a heavy handicap and that most of the low-priced books he encounters are not likely to be worthwhile first editions.

The field "modern first editions" has become one of the most active in the hobby, numbering countless collectors and a good many specialist dealers, such as London's Bertram Rota and New York's House of Books. Second and subsequent editions are very seldom admired, unless they carry major revisions or perhaps a new preface by the author. See FIRST IMPRESSION.

FIRST IMPRESSION. "Impression" and "edition" are taken to mean the same in everyday language, but actually are quite different. An edition may (but not necessarily) comprise several impressions; in the case of books for which heavy demand is anticipated, far more than several. An impression is a run of copies, large or small, ordered by the publisher from the printer. The printer then keeps the type set up, in the event more copies are needed. Thus, they are all technically "first editions," but not first impressions. Among bibliographers, first edition is synonymous with first impression, as collectors of first editions do not settle for any but the first impression.

FIRST PUBLISHED EDITION. The first commercially issued edition of a work that has previously appeared in a private printing not sold on the market is called the first published edition.

FLAP BINDING. Flap binding is an unusual style of binding, with a number of variations, produced in the late Middle Ages and early Renaissance. They are seldom collected as examples of fine binding, as no decoration was applied, but as only a small number exist they are rarities and deserve attention. Up to a point they are nothing more than ordinary LIMP vellum bindings, as were applied to tens of thousands of trade editions at the time. The difference is that a long wide flap of vellum extends out from the lower cover and folds around the FOREDGE. On its tip is a metal catch which hooks into a clasp on the upper cover. The purpose was to keep the edges of the leaves from damage. This may account for their more frequent use on religious tracts, as the clergy were notorious for hauling books about the countryside in foul weather. Some believe they gave the inspiration for later YAPP EDGES.

FLOATED COPY. A book in fragile condition, whose leaves have been floated onto glassine sheets for preservation, is a "floated copy." This naturally involves taking the volume apart and rebinding or RE-CASING it. Sometimes only the title page or selected leaves will be so treated. Lengthy books in which all leaves have been floated are unusual. Floating does not erase the original damage, nor improve the value of the book, it merely renders it easier and safer to handle and perhaps gives it a longer life.

FLY SPOTS. The little traces which flies leave upon the pages and bindings of books, to act as a remembrance of their visit, are fly spots. As it would require an entomologist to make distinctions, the term is loosely applied to all insect markings, so the fly is really blamed for much more than his due. Squeamish cataloguers prefer to use "spotting," which is confusing, as it could refer to FOXING or spots made by oil, grime, jam, or footprints. In bibliography, it pays to be frank.

FLYLEAF. Flyleaf is a term everyone has heard and thinks he knows the meaning of but often does not. When issued, most modern books have two flyleaves: the first and last blanks, somewhat thicker than those forming the body of the book. Sometimes they are decorated in the fashion of wallpaper, but normally plain. In early volumes, prior to about 1820, they were furnished by the binder and are not considered an integral part of the book. Often it is nearly impossible to determine if flyleaves are "called for" in a particular book. The front flyleaf is usually the repository for inscriptions. In common bibliophilic jargon, flyleaf is the same as endpaper, though ultrapurists may object.

FOLDING PLATES. No mystery here. Folding plates are precisely what they claim to be: pages of illustrations which fold out to a size larger than the book. They are uncommon prior to 1550 but became very popular in the first half of the 17th century and are seen in volumes of all sorts issued since then. Normally a folding plate folds once, in an outward direction, so that its full size is twice that of the book, but this is by no means a hard rule. Some folding plates (and cataloguers are perfectly within their rights terming them so) fold no more than an inch beyond the margin. Others comprise many folds, extending ten or twelve times the size of the book. Not all plates fold outward, either; some fold down, others up, and still others in all three directions. The larger the folding plates, the more likely they have been misfolded and damaged by careless owners.

FOLGER, HENRY. An American book collector (1857–1930), Folger built the finest library on Shakespeare gathered in the U.S. A partner of John D. Rockefeller in the Standard Oil Co., he began to collect in earnest in the 1890's, when the dispersal of many fine British collections placed desirable Shakespeare items on the market. His initial interest was in the FOUR FOLIOS, sets of which were rather easily obtainable to collectors of means, and he continued to purchase sets and single specimens until his death. No matter how many copies he may have owned at any given time, he seldom allowed the sale of any example to pass without placing a bid, which caused some collectors and critics (including Bernard Berenson) to accuse him of hogging. But the Folios, while the basis of the Folger holdings, were only a small portion of it. Included was much rarer material, such as early quarto editions of Shakespeare's plays, now virtually unobtainable. Anything having the least connection with the bard appealed to Folger. He also acquired many books relating to Elizabethan England. His quest for Shakespeare source books—works which might have provided inspiration for his plays or characters—was unmatched in the history of collecting. From a purely critical point, one may say he spent huge sums on nothing but hope and supposition in these cases, as sources are difficult to pin down, but such is testimony to his zeal. During the last two decades of his life, he was forced to compete with HENRY HUNTINGTON for many of the finer pieces. He built a gothic-style library with timbered ceilings in Washington, D.C., to house his books, opened to the public in 1932 as the Folger Shakespeare Library. It has since greatly expanded the scope of the original collection, adding many Elizabethan and later British books and reference material.

FOLIATION. The numbering of leaves in a book, rather than pages is foliation. Medieval manuscripts, if numbered at all, were foliated. The number would generally be written at the outer corner of the top of the right-hand leaf. This continued into the incunabula age. Many early printers foliated their books, usually in roman numerals. It was not until the mid 16th century that pagination almost universally replaced the earlier practice. Manuscript foliation is often inaccurate.

FOLIGNO DANTE. The EDITIO PRINCEPS or first printed edition of Dante appeared at the little town of Foligno in Italy in 1472, the work of a press operated by Johann Numeister. A beautiful production typographically, it was in small folio, containing 250 leaves, and probably had a comparatively small edition, 200 copies or less. The type was a very bold, large roman, resembling that used at Rome by ULRICH HAN, who might have been an associate of Numeister at one time.

Numeister was a German, as were almost all the first Italian-based printers, from the city of Mainz. As with most printers who came from Mainz, there is speculation he was an assistant or pupil of Gutenberg, or possibly of Fust and Schoeffer. In any event he wandered to Rome, where he was employed by either Han or SWEYNHEYM & PANNARTZ. From there he was invited to come to Foligno in 1470, where he printed a number of humanistic books. He went on to Perugia, becoming the first printer in that city, then returned to Mainz. Finally he came on the request of Cardinal d'Amboise to Lyons, where his second best-known work, the "Missale secundum usum Lugduni" was printed in 1487. The Foligno Dante is one of the most valuable of all printed books; it sold in the $1,000 range even before 1900, when common incunables could be had for $5.

FOLIO. Folio is the largest book format, in which the printer folds his sheets once to make two leaves, or four pages. During the early years of printing, from its inception to about 1470, folios were almost the only books produced, as typefaces were large and it was necessary for books to be gargantuan. The average folio, if such a thing exists, is from 12 to 14 inches in height by about 8½ to 9½ inches deep. Sizes vary much more than this, however, depending upon the original sheet used by the printer. Elephant folio is generally thought to be the maximum size, but this is untrue: there is one still larger. A folio printed from Atlas sheets will end up measuring (before being trimmed in binding) about 26 inches tall by 17 inches deep, while an Elephant is only a mere 23 inches by 14 inches on the average. Naturally these dimensions are subject to vary. The other sizes are roughly as follows:

Imperial folio, 22 by 15
Royal, 19 by 12
Demy, 17 by 11
Crown, 15 by 10

Post, 15 by 9½
Foolscap, 13 × 8½
Pott, 12 by 8

As can be judged from this, the differences are not merely in dimensions but shape as well. The Elephant folio, for example, is svelt and lean, whereas the Imperial is far more rotund, losing an inch in height but gaining it in breadth. The variance between Crown and Post, both about equal height, is not so noticeable. In the days of illuminated manuscripts, it was not unusual for choir books to attain a height of 30 inches and weigh more than 50 pounds. Spanish binders sometimes equipped them with metal wheels, nailed directly into the binding boards. Printed books of such size are most uncommon.

Although the terms to indicate folio formats were in common use until fairly recent times, booksellers have more or less abandoned them, feeling many customers were only confused by them. Had the system been replaced by measurement in inches, a good turn might have been done, but this has not generally been the case. Rather, descriptions will now read "large folio," "quite large folio," "tall folio," or "small folio," which is not saying very much.

FONT (or FOUNT). A font is a set of printing types, comprising upper and lowercase characters, numerals, punctuations, symbols, etc., all designed to harmonize with each other. Thus any separately created face of type is called a font; but one basic design (such as ITALIC) might, over the years, give birth to countless descendants, each in itself a font.

FOREDGE. The foredge is the outer edge of a book, opposite from the spine. The four sides are designated the spine, foredge, top (or head), and bottom (or foot).

FOREDGE PAINTING. Foredge painting is a method of painting the edges of a book's leaves with a scene or other picture, as the leaves are slightly fanned out. The book must be held in a special press while this is done. The foredge is then gilded to hide all traces of the painting, which appears only when the book is opened. Though originating as early as the 16th century, foredge painting did not reach its height until the 18th century. It was especially in vogue in Britain, where such books were presented as gifts to ladies of fashion. Some examples were rather pretty, but the majority could only be classed as mediocre as far as the quality of painting goes; undoubtedly it was the novelty that was appealing. The books chosen for such decoration were usually collections of poems or something equally delicate and proper. There are a number of collectors of foredge paintings, but the sport is hampered by the fact that originals are difficult to distinguish from recent imitations. Merely because a book is old does not guarantee that the painting is old. Even the experts are left speechless by some examples.

FOREL. Forel is the cheapest grade of vellum, used in many trade bindings of the 16th and 17th centuries. It is usually a darker, richer yellow than good vellum (which is nearly white) and has an oily, sometimes tacky surface. The term is only seen in catalogues of dealers who know or care enough about vellum to make the distinction, which is not a great many.

FORGERY. As with all arts, forgery plays some role in the world of books and manuscripts. Documents and autographs are naturally more often forged than printed material, as counterfeits of manuscripts are more easily produced and tougher to detect, if well done. Though spending much time studying the handwriting of a subject, the forger may expose himself by using the wrong paper or ink. To forge a letter, a blank leaf is extracted from a book printed while the subject lived. Old ink, however, is not so easily imitated. If the forger wishes to affix an early date to his work, he must write with a goose quill rather than a modern pen. Assuming he has attended to all these points, and is an expert at the game, there is still relatively little chance his handiwork will pass the experts. It is a critical age in matters of genuineness vs. forgery and today's dealers and auctioneers (not to mention librarians and even a good many private collectors) are well equipped with advanced detection apparatus.

Rather than try to forge the handwriting of a celebrated person, some feel they have a better chance by creating manuscripts that will be valued more for their age or historical content. A number of medieval text manuscripts have been forged, few convincingly. A favorite target of forgers at one time was manuscripts in the Erse and Celtic languages. Forgeries of complete illuminated manuscripts are very unusual, as the work is demanding and the odds on fooling anyone very slim. The really dangerous forgeries are those which have added something bogus to something genuine, such as illuminated borders in early manuscripts. Provided the manuscript is accepted as genuine, each decoration is likely to be appraised uncritically. The same can be said of painted initials in incunabula.

The most common forgery in modern books is the faked author's inscription, which haunts numerous first editions. This is an attractive vehicle for forgers, as it requires less composition than a letter and the fact that it appears in a book will impress some prospective buyers. Until recently these forgeries got through the market far more easily than others, but such is no longer the case. The only really successful forgeries of printed material were those of Thomas J. Wise. Where printed forgeries are concerned, it is necessary to invent an edition that did not exist rather than try duplicating a known rarity, which would be next to impossible. There were scattered forgeries of 15th century BLOCKBOOKS in Germany in the 1800's, made on old-looking paper and printed as crudely as possible, but they failed to deceive any authorities.

FOULIS BROTHERS. A pair of Scottish printers, Robert Foulis (1707–1776) and Andrew Foulis (1712–1775), were among the outstanding scholar-printers of their time. From their large and prosperous Glasgow office came exacting editions of the Greek and Latin classics, equal in design and accuracy to any that had ever appeared in the British Isles. They also published a large number of theological tracts and books on philosophy, which sold well throughout Britain. They strove to imitate the approach of 16th century master typographers, such as the ESTIENNES, PLANTIN, and ALDO MANUTIUS. Two university professors were employed to read their proofs to catch any possible errors. It was said that nothing received approval until it was read half a dozen times. The types used by the Foulis brothers were designed by Alexander Wilson, who used CASLON'S as his model. The Foulis Press made many contributions to the advance of printing, including a simplified Greek font and modernized title page, both copied by others. It issued more than 700 titles according to present count.

FOUR FOLIOS. "Four Folios" is the term by which the first four editions of the collected works of Shakespeare are known. All in FOLIO format, they were issued in London in 1623, 1632, 1664, and 1685. The frontispiece portrait they carry is often considered the only true likeness of Shakespeare. All are valuable, but the first and third far more than the second and fourth. The Third Folio is the rarest, long believed due to stockpiles of copies being burned in the Great Fire of 1666. This has now been shown to be untrue. Actually none of the four are very rare compared to some other books of their era, as they were issued in large quantities and well preserved by collectors, but their long-standing popularity has forced prices up to dizzying heights. See FOLGER, HENRY.

FOXING. The brownish spots that sometimes appear on the leaves of old books are called foxing. The origin of the term is a matter of conjecture. Some think it derives from Reynard the Fox, others from the archaic English Pepys' Diary. The damage results from an infestation of microscopic lice, which know no geographic boundaries and thrive well in a variety of climates. Dampness, however, is more likely to encourage foxing. If the spotting is light most collectors take it in stride, but sometimes it reaches unspeakable proportions; the cultures spread over entire leaves and grow dark in color, and can even be felt with the finger. At this stage the book is a terminal case and had best be consigned to the waste bin, unless it happens to be of unusual significance. Although foxing hits very old as well as quite new books, it prevails most in those of the Victorian age, from about 1840 to 1890, suggesting that the paper of that time may have contained a substance the lice found specially inviting. The research worker who attempts to pinpoint the cause can be further guided by the fact that foxing is most severe on **heavy** papers: flyleaves and illustration plates, rather than those of text. What it means is hard to say.

Several techniques are used to remove or lessen foxspots. One should really only attempt to lighten them, as total removal often results in putting a hole through the paper. Foxspots can be sanded gently with a fine grade of glasspaper, taking care to concentrate only on the spot and not the surrounding paper. They can also be touched (not rubbed) with a cloth dipped in hydrogen peroxide, then patted with a dry cloth or ball of cotton. This may have to be repeated many times before fruitful results are gained, if at all. Never buy a foxed book with the thought that it can be easily fixed up.

FRAKTUR. Fraktur is a style of gothic or black-letter type. In the incunabula period—the 15th century—the majority of printers experimented with one variety of gothic or another, originally based upon the heavy German legal script of the earlier part of the century. With the passing of years, as type design was taken out of the hands of printers and became a separate trade, gothic was modified, improved, and doctored in many ways. Different areas of Europe developed regional gothic, which came to be called by distinguishing names. Fraktur was most prevalent at Augsburg and Nuremburg in the POST-INCUNABULA period, when gothic had been almost totally dropped by French and Italian printers. It was modified still more in later years and became prominent in the U.S. through the Pennsylvania Dutch in the 18th century. Versions of fraktur, much diluted from its day of glory, continued to be used for German trade publishing until the 20th century.

FRONTISPIECE. An illustration, usually full-page, appearing opposite the title page is a frontispiece. After the second quarter of the 19th century, it was common for a sheet of tissue to be bound between the two, but the practice died out around 1900 except for fine or limited editions. More often than not the frontispiece in an old book is a portrait of the author. Abbreviated to "frontis."

FULL. In the sense of "full calf" or "full leather" this means the binding is fully covered in the material indicated, as opposed to a HALF or THREE-QUARTER binding in which the sides are composed of boards. However, while cataloguers may shout the claim with bloated pride, it is not always occasion for dancing upon rooftops, as there are other (more important) factors to be taken into account: the variety of the leather and its condition. Full roan, for example, is not nearly so desirable as a fine gilded half-morocco binding, even though one gets less leather, as morocco is far more costly, handsome, and durable. And if a binding is falling apart, or badly scuffed, the purchaser will hardly take solace in the fact that it is "full."

FUST, JOHANN. Johann Fust was the Mainz, Germany, moneylender who advanced a total of 1,600 gulden to GUTENBERG for his experiments with typography. In the Middle Ages there were no commercial banks to finance business ventures, so it was necessary to contract with private lenders. Fust gave the sum in two installments, to be repaid at 6%, but added a clause that he share in the profits of the enterprise. In 1455, he sued Gutenberg to drive him out of business and take control himself. From then until his death in 1466, he worked out of Gutenberg's Mainz office in partnership with Peter Schoeffer.

It has been suggested that Fust had a scheme to sell copies of the 42-line or Gutenberg Bible as manuscripts rather than printed books, and thus gain more respectability for them. Some historians in fact believe this was actually done, and that the existence of printing was not revealed to the world until the Fust and Schoeffer Psalter of 1457, which carried a COLOPHON plainly stating the truth. Fust was not a printer and it is doubtful he ever handled a piece of type or equipment during his whole association with the art. Many legends and curious stories were told of Fust in olden days. It was once believed in Holland that he stole the secret of printing from COSTER after being apprenticed in his shop, taking it to Mainz and claiming it for his own.

GARAMOND, CLAUDE. A French type designer (1480–1561), Garamond was one of the first to operate an independent type foundry, as almost all incunabula types were designed and/or cut by the printers themselves. His clients were spread across the continent, from Italy to The Netherlands, his types used in hundreds of books. Garamond was employed for a time by the ESTIENNES as designer and supervisor of style and layout. But most of his efforts were in his own offices, where he sketched, planned, experimented, cast, cut, and brought into the world the most beautiful fonts of type that had ever been seen. The roman series he designed in the 1530's for Robert Estienne was used, with slight alterations, as the basis of fine French typography for 250 years.

GATHERING. A group of printed leaves gathered together for binding, the term "gathering" has come to mean the same as SIGNATURE, a grouping of leaves made from a large folded sheet and then cut apart in binding. Each book will possess a certain number of gatherings, depending on the original format, and their study is of course important to the COLLATION, to discover if anything is missing. See BOOK SIZES.

GENERAL TITLE. When books are broken up into divisions, each having a sort of title page of its own (though perhaps not containing all the information expected of a title page), the opening title page which introduces the work is called the general title. The others go by the name of divisional titles.

GILL, ERIC. English sculptor, type designer, printer, and book illustrator, Gill was born in 1882, and studied at London's Central School of Arts and Crafts. In 1903 he began to work as a letter cutter and from then his interest in typography and fine book design grew. In 1924 he started illustrating books for the Golden Cockerel Press, of which his most noteworthy was probably the 1928 "Canterbury Tales." Though influenced by the classical in art, he strove to give the traditional new insights and developed a fresh, clear, straightforward style. His engravings are widely used in teaching graphic art. Some have placed him in a class with William Blake. He designed two major faces of type, Perpetua and the Gill Sans-serif. He died in 1940. Today there is increased interest in Gill's works.

GILT EXTRA. Bindings whose spines are richly GOLD TOOLED are "gilt extra." The term originated from the old practice of instructing binders to apply "extra" gilt when a really luxurious binding was desired. This presupposes that standard bindings were gilt in a simple fashion and can easily be distinguished from "gilt extra," but this is not always so. Nor can we tell, when a binding is very heavily gilt, whether this was done on instructions of the owner or by exuberance of the binder, or both. The distinction is very arbitrary; one dealer will use it in cases where another will not.

GIRDLE BOOK. A very quaint and unusual form of medieval bookbinding, in a "girdle book" the binding was equipped with a long thong of leather that hung on the belt of a monk. The churchmen of the Dark Ages were always taking their books about with them, so they could read the offices at the appointed hours. Rather than have the burden of carrying them, and thus risk losing them at the bargain, monastic binderies devised the girdle style of binding, so that the Book of Hours became a part of their uniform as much as their sandals and beads. The binding was of soft leather, usually calf, and in other respects no different than standard bindings of the time.

But it came to a great lip or protrusion at the lower edge, from which the leather extended outward, and would dangle from several inches to a foot from the waist. Girdle bindings were naturally applied only to small books that would be convenient to carry and thus are never found upon folios or other hulking works. They died out with the coming of printing in the 15th century. Specimens are hardly ever seen on the market, though some very attractive examples are to be found in European libraries.

GLOVER, JOSE. A minister from Sutton, England, Jose Glover came to America in 1634 and the following year was living in Boston. Concerned with the shortage of books in the New World which hindered learning and religious practice, he returned to England in search of printing equipment and a workman to operate it. The press was easily obtained, but apparently he could not interest an established printer to make the journey; and it is little wonder, for the English trade was so closely regulated that each had more work than he could handle. So he took STEPHEN DAYE, a locksmith, and his two sons, both of whom might have been apprentice printers, and set sail for Massachusetts in 1638. Before the ship arrived Glover developed smallpox and died. His widow carried on the project and helped to install the Dayes as first American colonial printers. See BAY PSALM BOOK.

GOFFERED. Goffered is a method of decorating the edges of leaves by tooling in blind, then applying a coating of gilt. The designs usually run along all three sides and consist of arabesques, circles, stars, or patterns borrowed from architecture. Of Persian origin, it became popular in southern and southwestern Europe as early as the first quarter of the 16th century and was applied to most fine French bindings. It was also widely used in Italy, to a lesser degree elsewhere; hardly ever north of Germany. Most popular French binding styles of the 17th century also incorporated goffering. By around 1700, it was dying out as new designs and fashions came into vogue. Also called chasing.

GOLD TOOLING (or GILDING). Gold tooling for the decoration of bookbindings was introduced to Europe from Persia, where it had long been practiced, in the final quarter of the 15th century. At first the designs were simple, consisting of blocking in panels, or peppering the sides with diamonds or other devices endlessly (and often sloppily) repeated. Beginning around 1510 really fine work was produced, usually at the order of wealthy collectors. This gave birth to a new form of artistic expression and many craftsmen employed in other fields turned to bookbinding, where the rewards were ample—at least for those favored with business from a GROLIER or DeTHOU. The style of tooling favored by Grolier, the most celebrated private collector of the 16th century, was naturally adopted or imitated by others. It consisted mainly of interlaced strapwork, the same pattern repeated on the upper and lower covers. For a long time libraries, particularly private, were judged by the gilding of their bindings and as a result far more was spent in rebinding rare books than their initial cost.

Next in importance to the Grolier style was probably the FANFARE of France, a product of the late Renaissance and Baroque eras. Such bindings consist of much exotic tooling, with fans, lozenges and so forth composed of many stamps and usually radiating outward from a central design. The impression of a fanfare binding is often like a flower with petals spread wide. However, while pots of gold were lavished upon them, they are really not equal as items of craftsmanship to the earlier styles, in which the pattern had to be designed with engineering precision. If one examines fanfare bindings critically he will often observe cases of haste making waste, where the wrong tool has been used, or placed upside down, or off the mark, whereas such instances in Grolier bindings are most uncommon. Collectors of the 17th century apparently did not care, so long as the binding was gaudy. Much the same can be said of English COTTAGE bindings, which were, however, somewhat more creative.

The earliest gilt tooled bindings were in dark calf, either its natural shade or black. Morocco was then very soon introduced and used throughout the 16th and 17th centuries for a good deal of the richest work, as it can be stained and polished somewhat better than calf. The method of applying tooling was to sketch out the design on the leather, lay gold leaf over each portion and press a heated tool into it. In execution it is not so easy as it sounds, however. It is exacting work and one miss can result in disaster.

The art of gold tooling began to fall into decay in the second quarter of the 19th century, when cloth replaced leather as a common covering for books. Persons disturbed by this turn of events attempted a revival, which was to some extent successful. Modern binders such as Zaehnsdorf, Cobden-Sanderson, Sangorski & Sutcliffe, etc., are known for their work with decorative tooling. The cost of applying such bindings today is sometimes greater than specimens from the so-called "golden age."

GOTHIC MANUSCRIPTS. Insofar as the Middle Ages were regarded by historians as "the gothic era," it is natural to presume that all or most medieval manuscripts would come under the heading of gothic. But this is not so. The gothic school of manuscript illumination only began in the early 13th century, as the Middle Ages were reaching their close and the first signs of the humanist revival were faintly seen in Italy. Previous to this time, other schools of writing and illuminating had been dominant in different parts of Europe: the HIBERNO-SAXON in the north and west, later the CAROLINGIAN, the WINCHESTER, and finally ROMANESQUE, which became gothic.

The gothic school represents the final phase of European manuscript illumination prior to the invention of printing c. 1450. It was also the most successful, both from an artistic and commercial point of view, and by far the most prolific, as it produced more books than all previous schools combined. The gothic school adopted what were considered the finest features of both Romanesque and the earlier Carolingian, both of which flourished throughout most of Europe. This meant heavy painted initial letters with grounds of burnished gold and/or silver, decorated page borders, very large script (later toned down), and pictures at various points in the text. At the beginning gothic work was confined, as had the earlier schools, to monasteries, but from c. 1350 onward a good deal was done by the commercial book trade, which was particularly active in France and the Netherlands. These manuscripts were made partially on the order of wealthy princes and other collectors, who were equally if not more zealous in their love of books than the monastic librarians. Some of the artists who worked on gothic manuscripts went on to paint altarpieces and portraits, though not always easily identified. The Van Eycks may have started in the manuscript trade. The majority of gothic manuscript illuminators did not sign their work and are thus unknown to us. Many went under pseudonyms, such as "the Master of the so-and-so Hours," and were known by previous work they had executed, just as did early panel painters. Yet many who are unknown, either by real or trade name, can be distinguished by a comparison of their style from one set of illuminations to another. For example, if a series of manuscripts produced at one center (let us say Brabant) are closely examined, it will be seen that certain subtleties of style are repeated from one to the other.

Many exquisite examples of gothic manuscripts are to be seen today in libraries and museums. In the opinion of some, the most outstanding is the Hours of Jeanne d'Evreaux, a late 13th century French manuscript in the Metropolitan Museum in New York. Another of exceptional merit is the Belleville Breviary in the Bibliotheque Nationale in Paris. By the end of the 14th century, the text in many manuscripts had taken a back seat to decoration, as they were produced and sold as objets d'art. Had printing not been invented, this trend could well have reached bizarre proportions. As it was, short works were frequently embellished with so much artwork that they resulted in thick volumes. The text would appear in a small rectangle in the center of the page, surrounded by a frame of painted sunbursts, pheasant quills, violets, cherubs, and anything else that came to the artist's imagination.

After printing appeared, the manuscript industry valiantly struggled on, first laughing off the newcomer and then being swallowed by it. The quality of work carried out from 1450 to 1470, contemporary with printing, was not inferior to what had gone before, but after 1470 manuscripts grew infrequent. A few of their makers, such as PETER SCHOEFFER, became printers or type designers.

GRAFTON, RICHARD. Grafton was an English printer of the mid 16th century who had a long and sometimes harrowing career, the most intriguing of the era from a biographical point of view. Grafton spent more than three decades in the trade, starting in 1537 in partnership with EDWARD WHITCHURCHE. From the beginning the two distinguished themselves above their contemporaries. In 1539–40 they printed the Cromwell or Great Bible and in 1538–39 the New Testament of Coverdale, which was partly printed by Regnault at Paris. The partnership was dissolved in 1541 and each went his separate way. Grafton, who served in the role of King's Printer, was in difficulty over the Act of the Six Articles, which brought about general turmoil and numerous beheadings in England. Although hounded a good deal of his life, once in grave danger of execution, he continued to maintain his publishing house. He died—of natural causes—in 1572, having printed a large number of books. His mark consisted of a barrel lying upon its side, from which a tree springs, but his name appeared in the form of monogramed initials.

GREEN (or GREENE), SAMUEL. The second printer in colonial America, Samuel Green was the successor to Matthew DAYE, the son of Stephen. Green was not a printer by trade but was called upon to keep the Cambridge press in operation when Matthew Daye died in 1649 at the age of 29; his work was good, though uninspired. He remained in business more than 40 years, until 1692.

GRIFFO, FRANCESCO. Griffo was a 15th and early 16th century type designer responsible for a number of original and artistic fonts. A native of the medieval city of Bologna, he was hired as type designer by ALDO MANUTIUS of Venice, who must have instructed him to come up with something novel and yet dignified, which could be compatible with good typography. His answer was a face based on the papal chancery script, used by the Italian humanists, a slanting letter that resembled roman but had greater style and character; thus was italic type born. Aldus tried it for the first time in 1501 and it became the talk of European printing circles. Within a short time dozens of printers had come up with their answer to the italic of Aldus and a merry publishing war was on. Griffo also fashioned creditable roman types, also used by Aldus. His work exerted wide influence, not only for its excellence but the fact that it appeared in the best sellers of their day, the publications bearing the Aldine dolphin and anchor, and was seen by far more people than any other 16th century type. The ESTIENNE family was one of Griffo's major contemporaries who used type styled after his.

GROLIER, JEAN. A French bibliophile (1479–1565), Grolier was noted for the luxurious bindings he commissioned for his library. He was in the service of Francois I and apparently affected by that monarch's love of Italian art. Almost all his books seem to have been bound in Italy. At one time it was believed Grolier was a professional binder and that many of the productions which carried his name were executed for others. Then historians, discounting that possibility, began to think he toyed with binding as a hobby and decorated his own books, but this is likewise untrue. These theories arose from the fact that most of his bindings were very similar in design, many identical, consisting of geometrical strapwork tooling on both covers. Some bear the motto "Io. Grolierii et Amicorum," meaning "Grolier and his friends." The names of these friends can only be guessed and their connection with his book-buying activities, if any, is not known.

Surviving to 86 years of age, and living at a time when beautiful books were like raisins in a cake, Grolier amassed a collection of about 3,000 volumes—huge for a 16th century private individual, spending out of his own pocket. It was dispersed in 1675, a large number of the volumes subsequently being lost or destroyed. In the past 300 years several fine collections of Grolier bindings have been put together, notably those of the British Museum and Bibliotheque Nationale. Some on the market are fakes. The Victorian age saw a profusion of bogus Groliers manufactured and foisted upon a rather gullible public, which ate them up. The great danger is that genuine Groliers, even though more than four centuries old, usually look new. The signs of age one would expect are seldom found: scratches or abrasions in the leather, fragments of tooling worn away, dryness, etc. This results from the fact that, being always in high regard, they have been meticulously cared for over the centuries, regularly dressed and delicately handled. It has been argued that Groliers commanded far higher prices than other bindings of equal or perhaps superior merit, simply for the fame of his name.

GRUB STREET. Grub Street was a street in London, inhabited in the 18th century by hack writers and struggling poets because it offered low rent. Thus it was common to call any piece of undistinguished writing "Grub Street Work." It was the spawning ground of many authors who went on to bigger and better things. The street was renamed in the 19th century for poet John Milton.

GUARDED. When a page comes free from a book there are several things that can be done, aside from bursting into tears. Obviously it must be reattached, but there are a number of ways of doing this. One is known as guarding. It consists of first attaching a blank stub at the proper place in the book, then gluing the inner edge of the page to this (which usually results in the outer edge protruding beyond the foredge). When one notices a page that appears "too large," guarding should be suspected. Of course, guarded leaves can be remargined, but this is not always done.

GUIDE LETTERS. In the illuminated manuscripts of the Middle Ages, initial letters were supplied in very elaborate fashion. Sometimes they would be nearly half the size of the page, painted in various shades of watercolor and burnished gold or silver. In addition, the illuminators (the artists who decorated manuscripts) would add long marginal extensions in many cases, curling around the lower part of the page and embellished with flowers, animals, or whatever seemed appropriate. When printed books were introduced, it was thought wise to make them resemble manuscripts as close as possible, to win public approval. To accomplish this, many features of the manuscript were retained, though usually modified. One was the illuminated initial. Instead of printing large initials, the space was left blank so it could be filled in by hand. However, as many of the artists employed in this work were totally illiterate and might paint the wrong letter, it was common for printers to place a tiny lower-case letter in the space as a guide. It frequently happened that the initials were never added, so the guide letters are still to be seen. The use of guide letters had become obsolete almost everywhere in the close of the incunabula period. In fact many printers had used them seldom or not at all. They were mainly prevalent in central and south-central Europe. They give quite an odd appearance, as if the page had forgotten to put its clothes on. In the 18th century collectors gave such volumes to artists to have the missing initials supplied, and for this reason one must look critically at incunables with beautifully decorated initials—especially if they seem rather more inspired by romanticism than contemporary ideas. On the other hand, there is nothing to be ashamed about if a volume is acquired with initial spaces bare; it is merely a fact of bibliophilic life.

GUTENBERG BIBLE. The name previously used to designate the Latin Bible issued from Gutenberg's Mainz office was the Mazarian, as a copy was found in the library of the celebrated French Cardinal. Then, this not being very descriptive, bibliographers christened it the 42-line Bible, based on the number of lines per page. It was a huge book, in large folio size and running to 641 leaves. It was generally bound in two volumes; as a result the volumes have sometimes become separated over the years, one perishing and the other surviving. On all accounts, it was a masterpiece of typography, as brilliant from a technical view as anything subsequently done, including all the work of William Morris and other limited editioners. How it could have been an experimental effort is puzzling. Some conclude that the perfection of the 42-line Bible is proof Gutenberg could not have been the inventor of printing, but that the art must have been practiced for a long time before.

It is not known how many copies were issued, but a portion of the edition was on vellum and the remainder on paper. The ratio of paper to vellum, if surviving examples are any indication, must have been about four to one. It is thought that as many as 300 copies, all told, might have been printed, of which less than fifty now exist. Though respected for its beauty and antiquity, it remained a fairly common article on the secondhand book market through the 17th century and even into the 18th century. In the mid 1700's a London bookseller named Richardson offered a specimen in his catalogue for £1. When one considers that the number of preserved examples is larger than for most incunables, some of which are known in but a single copy, it is easy to understand why it could have sold so cheaply. In the 18th century, one must recall, the majority of old and rare books were floating freely through the trade or in private collections, not in institutional libraries as today. So it was not a difficult matter for a collector of 200 years ago to obtain a Gutenberg Bible. It was only necessary to look and wait until one came up for sale, which was not likely to take very long. In the 19th century, the number of collectors greatly increased and Gutenberg Bibles set record prices almost whenever they were offered. Yet the supply was still good. Many changed hands during the century, some copies more than once.

There are many famous copies, the outstanding being that at Eton College, England, in its original blindstamped binding. Another was in the ROBERT HOE collection and was bought at his sale in 1911 by HENRY HUNTINGTON, now gracing the Huntington Library in California. In 1930 the Library of Congress purchased the copy belonging to Dr. Otto Vollbehr, now considered one of the finest in the U.S. There are other noted copies in the Berlin Library, British Museum, Pierpont Morgan Library, and The Gutenberg Museum of Germany. The Yale University copy was once owned by the monks of Melk Abbey, Austria. The specimen at the Bibliotheque Nationale in Paris is perhaps the most important historically, as it contains a RUBRICATOR's note dated 1456, proving the edition was printed by this time. How much earlier it might have appeared is a matter of speculation. See GUTENBERG, JOHANN.

GUTENBERG, JOHANN. The man generally credited with the development of typography was born at Mainz in Germany around the year 1397 (some say 1399, others 1400). He came from a family of social standing and was apprenticed to a goldsmith in his youth, a trade he apparently followed for a decade or more. From Mainz he supposedly went to Eltville and then to Strasbourg, where he manufactured eyeglasses and perhaps other things as well. Around 1435 he began taking on partners for a fixed fee, with some scientific invention as the goal. Whether or not it related to printing we have no way of knowing, but guesses are that it did. It is even possible that the invention of printing was made in Strasbourg, but nothing was published there. About 1446 Gutenberg returned to Mainz, filled with ambition but woefully short of funds. His years of experimentation and toil had left him without an income and his only prospects of reaping a fortune lay with its successful completion, for which he was not financially equipped. The problem was solved when a Mainz financier named JOHANN FUST agreed to advance 800 gulden, provided he was taken in the business. When this was used up and no books were yet ready to be sold, Fust came across with an additional 800 gulden. Finally, sometime around 1454–1456, about twenty years after the thought had first glimmered, the first full-length book printed from interchangeable type appeared: the 42-line Latin Bible, now called the GUTENBERG BIBLE.

However, this did not prove the end of Gutenberg's troubles. Fust, seeing that printing had the possibilities of gaining enormous wealth, pressed Gutenberg for repayment, with the object of forcing him out of the trade. Being already a partner in the firm, such as it was, Fust was well aware that Gutenberg could not settle the loans until copies of the Bible had been widely circulated. The action was judged in favor of Fust, who was awarded all of Gutenberg's printing equipment and title to the office.

Gutenberg, then nearly 60 years old, was broken. Half his adult life had been spent on the creation of the printing press, the most significant invention in the history of mankind, and it was snatched from him just when success was at hand. What he did directly following the suit is a matter of debate. Some believe he lived in anonymity for a time, then cast another set of letters and tried to compete with Fust. They point to the CATHOLICON of 1460 as a product of Gutenberg, but the evidence is not strong. Subsisting the last few years of his life on a pension of corn and wine, he died February 24, 1468, nearly blind and forgotten by the public.

It is really impossible to know what Gutenberg did or did not print. Prior to the 42-line Bible there were a number of small publications issued from his Mainz shop, such as calendars, indulgences and the like, which he may have executed single-handedly. When work was being done on the Bible, however, there was a workman named PETER SCHOEFFER present, who may have played a major role in its production. The name of Gutenberg does not appear on any piece of printing. Everything he issued, at least that we have evidence of, was anonymous. As with many artists and poets, the greater share of Gutenberg's fame came along after death.

GUTTA-PERCHA BINDING. A method of binding books without the use of stitching, Gutta-Percha binding consists of trimming the inner edges of the leaves, to eliminate the GATHERING fold, then gluing them together and to the inside of the spine. At first it was considered the ideal solution to the cost and labor of bookbindings and was used on all types of volumes, including those it should never have been: large, weighty art books, whose pages quickly pulled away from the spine. After a few years of experimentation in the late Victorian era it became obvious that gutta-percha was a poor substitute for genuine binding, though its cheapness made publishers hesitate to give it up. Today its use is almost strictly confined to paperbacks, and only on the lowest grade (in which the butler did it). As the glue dries out the spine is no longer flexible and opening the book causes it to crack. Once cracked it lies uneasy and the leaves gradually pull free, especially if the book is frequently used.

HALF-BOUND. One of the first phrases beginning collectors stumble over, half-bound simply means the book has a leather spine, which extends an inch or so along the covers, but the binding boards are either plain or covered in paper or cloth.

HALF-TITLE. The half-title comes before the title leaf and is usually the first printed leaf in the book. It contains merely the title of the work, in rather small type, and is usually blank on the reverse side. Sometimes, however, the reverse may list the author's previous books. See TITLE PAGE.

HAN (or HAHN), ULRICH. A German who settled in Rome and became one of the leading Roman incunabula printers, Han arrived in Rome in 1467 and provided the pioneer team of SWEYNHEYM & PANNARTZ stiff competition. Han's books were, on the whole, less pretentious, but sometimes advertised with a flourish. In one, his "Decretals" of 1474, he advised the public that other editions of the work (of which there were many) were "not worth a straw" by comparison. He worked at one time in collaboration with a printer named Simon Lucensis. There is a chance Han was actually the first printer in Rome, as Sweyheym & Pannartz also began in 1467, but this can neither be proved or disproved.

HARLEY, ROBERT, 1st Earl of Oxford. English collector (1661–1724) Robert Harley built one of the finest libraries of his time. Meticulous in his collecting activities, he employed a secretary who kept a detailed record of all purchases. He commissioned many of his volumes to be bound in a special style, which was afterward known as Harleian. His two sons carried on building the library, eventually acquired by the British Museum. It contains numerous rare and little-known early English books and manuscripts and is invaluable for research purposes.

HEADBAND. A decorative ornament at the head of the spine, where it meets the leaves, consisting of colored (or sometimes plain) thread worked over straw or other substance and sewn to the leaves is a headband. It has no utilitarian purpose. Sometimes tailbands are also used.

HEADLINE. A headline is the uppermost line of type on a page, set apart from the text, which identifies the book or chapter. It is usual for the headline on the lefthand page to give the title of the book, that on the right the chapter or division, but this is not always followed—nor are headlines always used. When a book has been trimmed down in binding, headlines are most vulnerable to be cut into, and thus the expression "headline shaved."

HEBER, RICHARD. An English collector (1773–1833), Heber was reputed to own the largest library of his time, running to better than 200,000 volumes. A long series of sales was required to disperse them. He had eight homes, four in Britain and four on the continent, several of which served as nothing more than storerooms for his books. Active at all the major auctions of the day, he bought heavily and was feared by other bidders. Generally he used no agent but came to bid in person, a favorite habit of early collectors, and his attendance was welcome in every gallery. It was his practice to purchase three copies of books: his display copy, in a fine binding, which would stand untouched on the shelf with its spine radiating; a reading copy, so he did not have to handle the display copy; and a lending copy. It was said that he kept most of his common books in disarray and disuse, piled with dust and cobwebs. His rare treasures were mostly stored in London, in his principal estates. When finally catalogued it was shown that the Heber library contained very little of real quality in comparison to its bulk. Many of Heber's better volumes were purchased by SIR THOMAS PHILLIPPS.

HEBREW, EARLY PRINTING IN. Two German printers resident in Italy share the distinction of issuing the first publication in Hebrew characters, in 1475. Meshullam of Pieve di Sacco printed a code book of rabbinical law, and Ben-Garton of Reggio Calabria a commentary on the Pentateuch. Hebrew printing then quickly spread through Italy, especially the smaller towns away from the major centers of Renaissance learning. In the 15th century Italy had a large Jewish population, comparable to that of the eastern European nations, and undoubtedly a good portion were book buyers. But many Italian Hebrew publications must also have been exported for sale, especially into Germany and Switzerland, possibly Hungary as well. Bologna, Ferrara, and Mantua issued many Hebrew books, but toward the close of the incunabula period Naples became the European center for Hebrew literature. Joshua Soncino, son of the scholar Israel Soncino, established a press in Naples which was taken over in 1492 by his son, Gerson. Gerson Soncino is often regarded as the foremost early Hebrew printer. He did not choose to remain long at Naples but moved about the continent from city to city and country to country. At first he tried remote Italian villages far from competition, then settled in France. Eventually he pushed east into Constantinople and ended his career in Salonika. The business, itinerant though it was, was carried on by his descendants, who landed—of all places—in Cairo in the 1560's. All in all the family was responsible for about 130 books in Hebrew. Gerson used types designed by FRANCESCO GRIFFO.

One of the most prolific printers of Hebrew works was a Christian named Daniel Bomberg, who came from Germany and settled in Venice, where he secured an exclusive privilege for the publication of Hebrew books. He held this right for 34 years, from 1515 to 1549, after which time other notable printers of Hebrew appeared in Venice. Unlike other cities, Venice's Hebrew publishing industry of the 16th century was almost totally controlled by Christians. Authorities consider some of the types which originated in Venice around mid-century as the finest Hebrew fonts ever cut. Some were the creation of an equally Christian Frenchman named LeBe, who had worked for Robert Estienne. Staying for a time in Italy, where he had considerable success with his Hebrew types, he returned to France and cut sets for other scholar-publishers, including Plantin.

The state of Hebrew typography declined somewhat in the 17th century, as did typography in general. Once out of the hands of Jews, it lost much of the drive of the incunabula age, and the anti-semitism which prevailed throughout western Europe did not encourage the appearance of Hebrew books. The ELZEVIRS did some spirited Hebrew printing, but only incidental to their usual trade, as they were neither Jewish nor scholars of Hebrew. By the 18th century Hebrew typography had reached a morose condition, not to be rejuvenated until the late 19th.

Most early books in Hebrew are very rare, as they were not likely to be printed in large editions. Collectors sometimes ponder why this should be so, as early Greek books are not especially scarce, and there were fewer Greeks in 16th century Europe than Jews. The answer is obvious; Christians who sought higher education learned Greek as a second language (along with Latin), but did not learn Hebrew. Thus the number of those who could read Greek was far in excess of those who could read Hebrew.

HENRI III. The King of France from 1574 to 1589, Henri III was a pivotal figure in the history of decorative bookbindings. He was a book collector, but not the scholarly humanist Francois I had been. In 1583 he issued a decree, perhaps the most unusual inside bibliography or out, that private citizens could not employ more than four diamonds on their bindings, while noblemen were permitted five and Henri himself given no restrictions. It was said this was done to curb inflation in the binding industry, caused by many wealthy individuals competing to have the most luxurious examples. The real reason may have been that Henri wanted to be sure his bindings were more decorative than others. Some of his bindings are most somber, however, in plain black calf, stamped with a death's head and crossed bones. This was not an emulation of the pirate flag, but one of Henri's many expressions of a fixation with death and morbidity. The period of his reign is jokingly called the puritan age of French bookbinding, from which it swiftly rebounded.

HIBERNO-SAXON MANUSCRIPTS. The Hiberno-Saxon is one of the earliest schools of manuscript illumination, the most significant artistically in the first centuries of the Middle Ages. The Hiberno-Saxon school can be traced as far back as the 6th century A.D., when manuscripts first began in production at the Irish monasteries. During the next several centuries large numbers were turned out in Ireland and other parts of the British Isles, though the Irish are generally conceded superior in design and beauty. Hibero-Saxon manuscripts follow a basic style, which depends upon lavish and detailed interlaced patterns, executed with absolute precision, and the use of many contrasting colors. While the grounds are worked up in one color, they are overlaid with touches of other shades, almost in a mosaic fashion. The whole effect is very pleasing and reflects a high order of artistic understanding. Initial letters were often painted very large, sometimes nearly the full size of the page, then decorated. But there was little in the way of miniatures, the painted scenes we associate with illuminated manuscripts. The Lindisfarne Gospels, written in the 7th century and now in the British Museum, has miniatures of the Evangelists. The best known and finest Hiberno-Saxon manuscript is the BOOK OF KELLS, 8th century, in Trinity College Library, Dublin. The oldest is the manuscript of Cathach of St. Columba, 6th century, in the Royal Irish Academy. The school continued to the 9th century, though later examples are somewhat lacking in brilliance. The style is seen occasionally in continental manuscripts of the period, but in these cases the work may have been done at monasteries run by Hiberno-Saxon monks.

HIND, ARTHUR MAYGER. Authority on the history of prints, engravings, and illustrated books, Hind was the author of many works on the subject. Keeper of Prints and Drawings at the British Museum, 1933–1945. His theories and discoveries shed much light on the development of woodblock printing and engraving, especially in its pioneer stages.

HOCHFEDER, CASPAR. The first printer in Poland, Hochfeder started at Cracow in 1475.

HOE, ROBERT. Hoe was an American collector of the late 19th and early 20th century and the son of Richard March Hoe, who manufactured the first U.S. flatbed and cylinder presses and invented the revolutionary Hoe Rotary Press. Robert assumed control of the printing press empire upon his father's passing in 1886. He was probably the most scholarly and attentive of early American collectors, as his long association with the technical side of printing had taught him much about the physical makeup of books. It is natural enough that his library centered around fine printing, including not only examples of the early presses, but notable workmanship throughout the centuries, including the private presses of his own time. Nor did he exclude manuscripts, and in fact owned an enviable collection of illuminated manuscripts, as well as fine bindings and other rarities. He was one of the founders of the Grolier Club and the Metropolitan Museum of Art. Even as early as the 1860's, his library was included in a listing of the finest book collections in New York. He always maintained that books, regardless of rarity, should be used and enjoyed. One of his pet peeves was the state of rare book collections in European libraries. He often told of occasions when he asked for a specific volume, only to be told it could not be found, or that it was covered with a layer of dust and soot.

Hoe's library was not large by European standards: only about 20,000 volumes as compared to the 200,000-plus of Heber and several million items (books and manuscripts) of Phillipps. However, it was gathered with a degree of care uncommon at the time. When rare books were pouring on the market, as they did for most of the 19th century, even the great collectors had a tendency to plunge and buy in quantity, in the theory that bad purchases would be mitigated by good. Hoe chose his books like a connoisseur. While many of the publicized European private libraries turned out to comprise a good share of junk, it could be said that at least 80% of Hoe's consisted of items of high quality, that have since greatly increased in value and desirability.

Hoe died on a trip to London in 1909. Unlike Morgan, always his rival, he expressed a wish that his books be sold by public auction, to afford collectors the sort of opportunity which allowed him to build his library. The sales were held in New York at the Anderson Galleries in 1911 and 1912, creating the biggest sensation in the world of book collecting up to that time. Well-known dealers and collectors from all parts of the world attended, making it the first truly international sale, while newspapers gave it considerable play. The largest single purchaser among private collectors was HENRY HUNTINGTON, through his agent George D. Smith. He acquired Hoe's vellum-printed Gutenberg Bible for $50,000, the highest price of the sale and a record for a printed book which stood for a number of years. The Hoe catalogues were issued in four parts of two volumes each, well prepared and lavishly illustrated. Copies with the lists of prices now bring stiff sums in themselves.

HOLOGRAPH. Holograph is defined as written by, in the hand of. An author's holograph manuscript is written out in his hand, ditto a holograph letter. The term occurs far more frequently in autograph than book catalogues. It is sometimes used in the latter to refer to inscriptions or notations in books but is really out of place; anything written in a book stands to be in holograph as books are not easily fed through a typewriter.

HORN BOOK. A horn book is neither a horn nor a book. It is an alphabet or other primer for very young students, pasted on a flat wood surface with a handle for convenience in using at class. The early method was to cover the sheet with transparent horn, giving rise to the name. It was thought preferable to give lessons in such form, rather than loose cards or sheets, for the sake of durability. They date from the late Middle Ages to mid 18th century. Genuine horn books are rare. Some specimens on the market are later concoctions that never saw the inside of a schoolroom.

HUNTINGTON, HENRY EDWARDS. Called by many the greatest American book collector, Huntington was born in 1850, the nephew of Collis P. Huntington, who controlled a west coast railroad empire. Henry collected very little until 1900. The library in his plush California home was furnished with standard sets in expensive tooled bindings, but nothing that would excite a collector. Afterward he began buying heavily, both rare books and fine art. Most of his books were acquired through the New York dealer George D. Smith then, after Smith's death, DR. ROSENBACH. At first he was interested mainly in INCUNABULA but eventually formed sprawling collections of Americana, English Poetry and Drama, early manuscripts, voyages and travels, and much else. Following the HOE sales in 1911–1912, Huntington spent more heavily on rare books than anyone up to that time, buying whole collections as well as choice single items. His appetite for incunabula often extended to large mixed approval lots, which dealers readily submitted and he seldom returned. When he died in 1927 his library, housed in a spacious building at San Marino, California, contained the largest and most valuable collection of early imprints in the U.S., as well as untold treasures in other fields. It has been kept intact as a research center and museum. A portion of his art collection, including Gainsborough's "Blue Boy," is also on view.

HUTH, HENRY. Huth was an English collector (1815–1878). Despite the competition of such other titans as Lord Spencer and Sir Thomas Phillipps, Huth succeeded in acquiring a large share of the most desirable rarities that came on the market. Upon his death his son Alfred continued the collection. Some of its more valuable pieces were presented as gifts to the British Museum, but the bulk of the library was sold by Sotheby's in the early 20th century. The total realization was more than £300,000.

ILLUMINATED MANUSCRIPTS. Illuminated means, to the average reader, something to do with electric lighting. The sense in which it is used in connection with medieval and other manuscripts is not so much different.

The "illuminations" were pictures, drawn in gold, silver, and watercolor, that shed light upon the text. At least this was the origin of the term. In reality many of the illuminations bore little relation to the subject of the book, but were used merely for ornamentation.

The first illuminated manuscripts were produced in ancient Egypt, in the form of decorated scrolls. However, the phrase is almost never applied to these specimens, as scrolls are considered a different race of animal. When CODEX books were first introduced in the 3rd and 4th centuries A.D. at Rome, they seem not to have been immediately adorned with pictures, but this came about shortly after. Manuscript illumination is known to have been practiced as early as the 5th century, as there are two surviving specimens in European libraries. In the 7th and 8th centuries, manuscripts of great artistry were produced by the monks of Ireland, including the precious BOOK OF KELLS. The craft was followed largely by monastic scribes until the end of the 14th century, when it became dominated by the commercial manuscript industry.

Before printing, which was not used in Europe until c. 1450, every book had to be written out by hand, letter by letter, page by page. The larger monasteries each had their scriptoria or writing room, where a group of trained scribes gathered with parchment sheets and pots of oily ink. The text to be transcribed would be read out by a lector, while a rule of absolute silence prevailed among the workers. It took a long time to complete a manuscript under such conditions and the text was just the beginning. The book was then handed over to a rubricator, who painted in the initial letters, headlines, and paragraph marks. After this it went to the illuminator (though sometimes the rubricator and illuminator were one), a qualified artist who added small pictures and/or decorations in the margins. He might also paint in large initial letters when the situation called for it. A good share of these men, though they may have possessed little or no formal art training, had much talent.

The great age of illumination, at least in more modern times, occurred in the 15th century, most strongly felt in France and Flanders. Many of the more elaborate specimens were executed by lay artists to the order of princes, kings, bishops and so forth. The invention of printing caught the manuscript trade at the height of its glory. Although collectors of means continued to prefer the manuscript, their days were numbered, as they could not hope to compete with the press. By 1470 the German manuscript industry had virtually ceased; those of Italy and Spain gave way soon after. France was the final stronghold of illuminated manuscripts, turning out specimens of quality even after the incunabula age, but by this time the printed book was unquestionably king and manuscripts were made only to suit special needs. In the 20th century, there has been a more or less unsuccessful attempt to revive the art among those interested in calligraphy as a hobby.

IMITATION LEATHER. Various grades and styles of imitation leather have been used in bookbinding in recent years, mainly in trade editions. Though imitation leather may appear genuine to the non-collector, it falls far short of convincing the experienced eye, and in fact borders on repulsive to anyone accustomed to the real thing. Imitation leather does not have nearly the keeping qualities of genuine, nor can it be dressed and polished. The surface, instead of being warm and rich, with a supple grainy texture, is flat and shiny, almost like a piece of waxed linoleum. Fabrikoid and leatheroid are two commonly used imitations.

IMPERFECT. Imperfect should only mean "slightly less than perfect," but in the world of books things do not go quite so easily. An imperfect book is lacking leaves; of this one can be certain. How many are lacking, and the state of those remaining, can only be guessed at. It is prudent to expect very little when such a word appears, as booksellers will not use it if something softer would serve the purpose.

IMPRESSION. Impression has at least two common meanings. Impression is used in the same sense as edition, particularly by limited-edition publishers, whose notices will read "of this impression, x number of copies have been printed." To trade publishers it means a batch of copies ordered from the printer, which may or may not constitute the entire edition (see FIRST EDITION). In advertisements one sees such phrases as "third impression before publication," indicating that advance orders prior to the official date of publication are strong enough to warrant stocking large quantities. Collectors naturally seek out the earliest of the early.

Impression also means the impression of type (or illustration plate) upon paper, and is seen in such contexts as "early impression," which means a print taken in the early stage of production, before the plate had a chance to wear down. This definition is, however, a matter of viewpoint; what looks early to the seller may not to the buyer. Very heavily inked plates are commonly termed "early," which is a mistake, as an old beaten plate can be inked just as heavily as a new. Rather, earliness should be judged according to the condition of the fine lines of the engraving, which may require another copy for comparison.

INCUNABLE, INCUNABULA. A word of Italian origin, meaning "in the cradle." It is applied to the earliest days of printing and hence to early printed books. The line is drawn at the year 1500; books printed later do not qualify. Being purists, bibliographers do, however, include the year 1500 in the incunabula class, as the 15th century is not considered to have ended until January 1, 1501. As the first printed books did not appear until 1450 or slightly later, a relatively brief span of only 50 years is covered; yet more than 60,000 books were issued in that time and the art of typography spread very far from its point of origin (see GUTENBERG, JOHANN).

Collecting of incunabula began in earnest in the 17th century, as the 200th anniversary of the invention was celebrated in Europe. But at this time, and for along while afterward, there was no serious effort to investigate the history of typography, circumstances surrounding the printing of incunabula, or the lives of the printers. Books of the 15th century were simply looked upon as interesting curiosities that added a certain class to one's library. This is unfortunate because collectors of three centuries ago had marvelous opportunities at their fingertips to unlock the secrets that puzzle historians today.

Scholarly interest in incunabula did not begin until the first quarter of the 19th century, long after they had begun drawing stiff competition at auction sales. Yet they remained rather common through much of the 19th century and could, but for the acknowledged rarities, be collected by anyone of reasonable means. Collections of incunabula numbering in the hundreds of specimens regularly came upon the market in London, Paris and even New York in the mid to late 1800's. One could purchase incomplete examples on London book stalls for as little as £1 as late as 1910. The dispersal of the HOE and HUTH libraries in the earlier years of this century did much to increase interest in early printing, which has grown steadily since. Today even the most common, poorly printed, and textually unimportant incunables are eagerly sought. The word is pronounced in the English-speaking world as "in-kwe-na-bull."

INDIAN BIBLE. Indian Bible is the name commonly given to an edition of the Bible in the Indian language, compiled by the Rev. John Eliot and published at Cambridge, Massachusetts, in 1663. It was also the first Bible of any kind to appear in the American colonies. The aim was to gain Indian converts.

INK. The most primitive writing ink, manufactured by the Egyptians and Hebrews, was a mixture of lampblack and vegetable glue. It may have originally been developed in China or India, where similar ingredients continue to be used. This formula was slightly modified with succeeding ages but remained basically unchanged until the early Italian Renaissance. The Romans may have possessed a somewhat better technique of ink making, but it is not apparent in surviving documents. The inks of the early Middle Ages were poor and tended to fade, suggesting that a shortage (or costliness) of materials may have prompted dilution. The quality then improved in certain areas of Europe. In HIBERNO-SAXON manuscripts, it was particularly sharp, though tending toward brown rather than the deeper black of earlier times. The monasteries undoubtedly made better ink than was available from tradesmen, as can be seen by matching monastic books with lay writing. Much of the ink of the Middle Ages had a tarry, greasy appearance. Toward the close of the gothic era ink became cheaper and more plentiful, but not always very satisfactory, resembling a sort of dim mud. Its lasting properties were no better than the modern commercial product, perhaps worse in some cases. This may have been due, in large measure, to experimentation with formulas. By the 15th century, most European inks were fairly standardized. The rise of graphic arts in the Renaissance led to the marketing of many grades and colors of ink, some very fine. The ink used by early printers was essentially the same as used by monastic scribes.

INSCRIBED COPY. When used in a bookseller's or auctioneer's catalogue "inscribed copy" generally means the copy carries an inscription, signed or unsigned, by the author. If nothing further is said, one can safely presume it is a very brief, insignificant message such as "with regards" or "for Miss so-and-so." Still, an inscribed copy always rates a little higher on the scale than a plain, even if the author is virtually forgotten. In the case of Hemingway or Shaw or anyone of similar magnitude, just a word is enough to add considerable value. Inscriptions are subject to forgery, just as letters and documents, but if a bookseller of reputation has given the item his blessing, one can be pretty certain it is genuine.

Occasionally the term is applied, incorrectly, to any inscription appearing on the flyleaf or elsewhere, even if only penned by a very unfamous former owner. In these instances the buyer is well within his rights to throw a tantrum and return the item.

INTERLEAVED. A book printed with blank pages between the leaves is said to be interleaved. It was occasionally done in the 18th and 19th centuries, almost never today except in limited or other out-of-the-ordinary editions. Usually the interleaved paper is of a different grade (lighter and thinner) than the body of the book, and slightly smaller. It was done to provide protection for illustrations or merely give the volume a haughty appearance. Naturally it resulted in the book being thicker than otherwise, even if tissue was used. It only serves a logical purpose in cases where two engraved plates face each other and there is danger that ink from one will adhere to another.

ITALIC. A style of type first used in 1501 by ALDO MANUTIUS, italic was designed by FRANCESCO GRIFFO. It was based upon the Italian humanistic handwriting of the later 15th century. It was a refreshing change from heavy black gothic and a novel twist on roman, remaining popular more than a century. Afterward it was more or less absorbed into roman and used to set apart words or phrases for emphasis. The name derives from the fact that in other parts of Europe it was called "the type of Italy," or italic. But very soon it had spread elsewhere, particularly into France.

IVORY BINDINGS. Ivory bindings were a great favorite in the Middle Ages, though their high cost restricted them to the most privileged classes. They were seldom executed for monasteries, as was the common run of medieval books, but almost exclusively for the libraries of discriminating private collectors. They did not, of course, consist entirely of ivory, any more than jeweled bindings consisted entirely of jewels. The foundation was wood, the same material used for every grade of binding from the earliest times to the late 15th century, equipped with a stout hide spine which might be of pig or goatskin. The center portion of the front binding board would be gouged away to form a recess, into which was mounted an ivory relief carving, usually representing a religious or mythological scene. The supposition that such bindings must have been intended for churches is incorrect, as devotional subjects are seen in all phases of medieval art. It was very rare that such ivory plaques were actually carved for use in binding. Normally the binders would take them from the lids of old boxes they bought secondhand, or sides of a diptych, which was a good deal cheaper and easier than having an artist sculpt them. Whether the buyers knew or were told the difference is a point to consider. Ivory bindings would sometimes further be embellished with jewels, enamels, or whatever else the binder or his client saw fit. The 12th and 13th centuries saw ivory bindings at their peak; few were produced as late as the 15th century and almost none afterward.

JAPANESE BINDING. Japanese binding is an unusual style of binding which flourished briefly in the 17th century, revived in craft binding afterward. It consists of a plain leather covering, lightly or not at all decorated, with gilded DOUBLURES or liners on the inside covers. It appealed to the puritans but was not a favorite among collectors in general, who wanted more outward show of elegance for their money.

JENSON, NICOLAS. One of the most talented of the incunabula printers, Jenson was responsible for popularizing roman type. According to some ancient legends, he is credited with the invention of printing, based on the fact that his books were of superior quality, but this is obviously a mistake. Not much is recorded of his early life. A French Walloon, he was sent in 1458 by Charles VII to Mainz to become acquainted with the new art of printing, with a view toward using it in France if it seemed worthwhile. What exactly happened at Mainz is not known. Jenson must have visited the offices of Fust and Schoeffer, as they supposedly operated the only press of the day, but whether he merely paid a social call or was hired on as a workman is debatable. In any event the mission did not result in success. Charles VII died and his successor, Louis XI, showed no interest in the project. So France, which could conceivably have boasted a printing works as early as 1459 or 1460, did not attain one until 1470.

Jenson did not print his first book until 1470, at which time he had taken residence in Venice; he played no part in the introduction of typography to France. It was only because of the death of John deSpira, Venice's first printer, that Jenson was able to start in business. DeSpira had held an exclusive patent to be Venice's only printer, which was not to expire until 1474. Influenced by classical ideals, Jenson remodeled the roman letters used by Sweynheym and Pannartz, Italy's pioneer printers. His books served as inspiration for generations of Italian printers and modern type design (including the type in which this is printed) is based upon his work. When Jenson died in 1480 his equipment passed to the Venetian printer ANDREA TORRESANO, whose books consequently much resemble Jenson's.

JEWELED BINDINGS. During the Middle Ages, and even into the early Renaissance, a number of valuable objects were occasionally fixed in book-bindings, including precious and semi-precious jewels. Such bindings were not executed as a matter of routine, but on order of a king or nobleman, or for presentation to someone of rank. They were undoubtedly made from the earliest years of CODEX binding, in the Roman Empire, as the Romans were very fond of incorporating jewels into all sorts of decorations; but as no examples exist we cannot be sure. They followed various styles. Beginning with a binding of heavy wood boards and leather spine, a panel would sometimes be cut from each cover, about half the size of the board and half as deep. Into it would be set delicately carved ivory plaques, surrounded by an array of many-colored jewels. The size of the gems was usually regarded more than their value, which led binders to use polished quartz or agate from time to time; but bindings do exist which were outfitted in what would be a fortune of jewels in today's terms. Jeweled bindings were not destined for an easy life, as they were among the first items plundered when invading troops vaulted the palace walls and smashed into the royal treasury. The king himself was not always their best protector, either. When the privy purse needed fattening, he might steal down at night with a pair of forceps and gently extract a bauble or two. Some existing jeweled bindings have had their jewels replaced with glass. The Morgan

Library in New York has a fine specimen of a single binding board encrusted with jewels, also featuring chased goldwork.

JOHNSON, MARMADUKE. One of the first and most prolific of American colonial printers, Johnson was the first trained printer to operate a press in this country. He set up first at Cambridge, Massachusetts, where his most famous production, the ELIOT INDIAN BIBLE, was issued in 1663. In 1674 he shut down his Cambridge office and began anew in Boston. Any imprint bearing his name is of considerable value.

JUNK. Junk is a dealers' term for odd volumes from sets, cheap books that are damaged, outdated almanacs and yearbooks (unless old enough to be of antiquarian interest), and so forth. Booksellers acquire this material by the ton, as it is often necessary to purchase a large collection or bundled lot to obtain a few choice items. Those who have shops dispose of it in PENNY BOXES; others sell it as waste paper. In buying collections, the value of its discard or junk content is totally discounted, as the cost of transporting it usually exceeds its value. Junk sales are made strictly to the passer-by public, who may want something to read on the subway and are not disturbed if it was once used to swat flies; collectors pretend this class of book does not exist, except occasionally to see if the bookseller has let a rarity slip through.

JUNTA (or GIUNTA). The Juntas were a family of Italian scholar-printers active in the late 15th century and the 16th. Their books are usually small and printed in gothic type. They specialized in religious works.

KNOBLOCHTZER, HEINRICH. A printer at Strasbourg, Germany, Knoblochtzer began to work around 1482. The books of Knoblochtzer (whose name is spelled various ways) are especially notable for their fine decorative initial letters and other ornaments. His edition of Jacopo deCessoli, 1483, contained 15 different woodcuts and is considered one of the most charming illustrated German incunables. His career was completed at Heidelberg.

KOBERGER, ANTON. Koberger was the most prolific and financially successful of the incunabula printers. His offices at Nuremburg, Germany, employed a large number of workers and boasted numerous presses, continually in operation. Koberger's was the first publishing empire in the modern sense of the term, though historians sometimes mistakenly award the distinction to Aldo Manutius. Koberger's books were not, however, aimed at the poorer or middle classes, as were many of Aldus'. They were generally in large format, printed upon fine heavy stock, sturdily bound, and often rubricated by hand—none of which can be said of Aldus' productions. Yet they were rather inexpensive for their day, as compared to most other books, as Koberger's facilities permitted him to buy materials in vast quantities and do much speculation, which was not the case with the average incunabula printer.

Koberger's activity covered a large chunk of the incunabula period, as he began in 1472 and continued into the 16th century. Many of his earlier titles, not printed in such quantity, are very scarce, and it is probable some have even escaped the attention of bibliographers. At the very beginning of his career (he started at the age of 22), he dated but did not sign his books, so a number from the 1472–1475 period remain with questionable attributions. His type was pure gothic throughout, differing in size from one book to another but not much in design, and thus even his later books have a distinctly medieval appearance and charm. Koberger published the works of more contemporary German authors than anyone else, along with many Bibles and other texts. Virtually all the noted German woodcutters and engravers of the time worked for Koberger; ALBRECHT DURER was his godson. In terms of beauty Koberger's books are not inferior to any German incunabula press, with the exception of Fust and Schoeffer, though their enormous production has tended to make bibliographers discount their artistic appeal. A listing of his major works would include the Nuremburg Chronicle of 1493 (the most heavily illustrated incunabula), the Schatz-behalter, German Bible, Sebastian Brant's *Das Narenschiff* (Ship of Fools), etc.

LAMBSKIN. A leather used for binding, lambskin was employed primarily in Germany, Austria, and Switzerland from about 1500 to 1700. It has never been very popular or widely used, as the finish is dull, does not receive gilding successfully, and it become dry and brittle even with good care. It is extremely thin and flimsy, but was sometimes applied over wooden boards and blindstamped by early binders. Here it was at its best, as the stamping stood out better on vellum or pigskin, and just as well as calf. Purists claim it is not exactly the same material as sheepskin, but few collectors are apt to know (or care about) the difference.

LARGE PAPER COPY. During the 18th and 19th centuries, and to some extent before and after, publishers occasionally issued books in two or more editions. This was generally done only in the case of books likely to have appeal to collectors: those by well-known authors, or richly illustrated. The logic was that collectors who could afford to pay a higher price would rather have a better, or at least more attractive (or, at very least, larger) copy than the humble peasants who merely bought the book to read. Usually these special copies were limited and the copy number recorded, but not always. The printing of a portion of the edition on large paper was only one of many hooks to bait the collector (some others being special paper, additional illustrations, leather binding, etc.) If nothing else is said, it can be assumed the type is set exactly as in the cheap version, and that the paper, while larger, is of no finer quality. In other words, the result is nothing more than wider margins, which hardly seems much of an enticement. So-called large paper copies are often copies that simply have survived without being trimmed by the binder, so the proper term would be "tall copy."

LAW CALF. Law calf is a smooth, hard, shiny, almost grainless variety of calf, very thin and somewhat brittle. The name derives from the fact that it was once used to bind legal works. It was also used in trade bindings in the late 18th and early 19th centuries. Law calf bindings have an uncommonly high frequency of weak hinges.

LEAF. The terms "leaf," "page," and "sheet" are a source of confusion to many beginning collectors. A sheet is the unit with which the printer begins when he sets out to print a book. This is then folded to make leaves, and each side of a leaf is a page. Therefore, a description such as "page missing" is fanciful, as there can hardly be only one side of a leaf missing.

Until around 1510 it was normal for leaves to be numbered—in manuscript or type—instead of papers. The bibliographical science of COLLATION is based upon leaves.

LEAFLET. A leaflet is not, or should not be, the same as a pamphlet. Leaflets are normally folded, accordion fashion, out of a single sheet of paper, rather than composed of separate leaves (which a pamphlet is). The common distinction is that anything which depends upon a staple, sewing, or other device to hold it together, is a pamphlet; leaflets must rise or fall on their own strength. Leaflets are commonly issued for advertising or promotional purposes and distributed free of charge, either at street corners, into apartment mailboxes, or other means. But a leaflet should not be confused with a BROADSIDE or flier, which consists of a single **unfolded** leaf. A leaflet must be folded in some way or other to simulate a book.

LEATHER. The earliest leathers used for binding CODEX books must have been those which the Romans had readily at hand and employed in other manufactures, such as goatskin, calf, and, to a lesser degree, pigskin. The use of calfskin was very widespread in Roman craft trades, as it had been in earlier civilizations, for shoes, bags, furniture, jewelry, etc. Calf and VELLUM were the most common binding leathers throughout the Middle Ages. Vellum was also used as writing paper. The usual procedure was to stretch them over WOODEN BOARDS that had been cut to the size of the book. Often leather was used merely to cover the spine, the sides left bare wood. Beginning in the 12th century, BLINDSTAMPING was used as a means of decoration; prior to this the leather had sometimes been painted or inlaid with enamel or gemstones. In the late 15th century GOLD TOOLING for leather was introduced from Persia, where it had long been in use; and from the east also came morocco, a superior grade of goatskin that lent itself well to gilt decoration.

The word leather covers a broad range. There are good leathers and poor, handsome and ugly, smooth and rough, oily and dry, durable and fragile, costly and cheap. Though leather in any form is often valued by collectors over CLOTH bindings, there are few which survive in good condition as long as cloth without periodic oiling. While leather responds—often very unfavorably—to changes in weather and atmospheric conditions, cloth does not, or only to an imperceptible degree. Morocco, available in various grades and finishes, is the highest valued leather. Its surface has a deep richness and warmth, and it can be successfully dyed to almost any color (though it fades, as do all leathers and cloth as well, when continually exposed to direct sunlight). Levant morocco is a high quality variety with deeply textured surface. Turkey morocco has a more subdued grain. Persian morocco (a term not often used any longer) is properly made only from Persian goats and is the finest of the moroccos, often imitated by sheepskin. Venetian morocco is actually not morocco but sheepskin, highly polished, which makes a rather handsome binding but not so enduring. Venetian is also called Paste morocco. Niger morocco is strictly sheepskin, having a coarse finish that resembles levant; often called the poor man's levant. But much good work has been done with it.

The varieties of calf are even more numerous. The natural skin is supple, light to dark brownish in color, and in binding is seldom dyed. It is, however, frequently stained with chemical solution to alter the surface texture and create a false grain. This is perhaps most obvious in Tree calf, where an iron solution is used to penetrate the leather and leave dark, choppy stains along the surface, as in the bark of a tree. Mottled calf is produced by treating with acid or ink, to form a texture that to the untrained eye appears natural. The purpose of these treatments is to liven up the calf, which is rather grainless left to itself; but many of the finest and most handsome calf bindings have been executed with natural-surface calf, lightly polished. The cheapest leathers for bookbinding are roan and skivver (or skiver), which are very thin, drab, and quick to crack at the joints. They were widely used in TRADE BINDINGS in the 18th and early 19th centuries, prior to cloth, and have survived poorly. See LEATHER DRESSING.

LEATHER DRESSING. To retain its strength and appearance, leather must be oiled or dressed from time to time. When first prepared for binding, leather retains a certain moisture or grease content imparted to it from the animal (goat, calf, deer, pig, or whatever). As it ages, this moisture gradually dries out, its lasting qualities depending on the heat and humidity to which it is exposed. When this happens, the surface develops many small veins or cracks, which look like matted hair or lines on a map. If allowed to continue unchecked, it begins to powder; the collector notices little piles of fine, grainy, reddish-brown dust along his shelves, as if someone had sprinkled sand or earth. The leather then begins peeling away, sometimes in tiny pieces, but more often in rather large chunks or strips, which hang by a precarious shred of ligament and then come free upon the last touch. A binding that has started out in fresh, well-oiled condition can reach this state in a few short years if neglected.

Unless one replaces moisture as fast as it disappears, the battle is lost. A treatment every six months is preferable. Instead of attempting to cover his entire library in a short space of time, thus devoting insufficient attention to each volume, the careful collector never thinks of the job as completed. He selects one or more books each week for treatment, depending on the size of the collection, and needs only to remember which have gone longest without care.

There are a number of preparations which can be used, and many which should not be. There are also various polishing techniques. Probably the finest dressing is sold under the name of British Museum Leather Dressing. It is of English manufacture and not widely available in the U.S. An ingredient is neat's foot oil, made from the hoofs of cattle. Though of special value for fine leathers it is seldom included in American preparations. In early days leather was dressed with neat's foot oil alone; now other components are added. If one must resort to concocting his own dressing, a fairly good one can be made from castor oil and lanolin, one part of each. Castor oil is often used straight, as it comes from the pharmacy jar, and is favored by many collectors. Its rejuvenating powers are equal to any, but an objection to castor oil is that it darkens light colors of leather, especially brown morocco. When applied to MOTTLED CALF it reduces the mottling effect. Plain vaseline is sometimes recommended, but tends to dry whitish and remain tacky, though it does a great deal for the leather. Shoe polish should not be used, as it may discolor the binding, as will furniture polish. Any oil made from animal fat, without chemical additives, should also be avoided, as it will turn rancid and attract lice and insects. British-made saddlesoap is suitable for cleaning soiled bindings. It should be applied very lightly, otherwise it will dry white and hard. Afterward the binding must be oiled, as saddlesoap itself is not a sufficient dressing for fine leather.

Whatever dressing is selected it should be applied slowly and worked well into the skin; this is a job that cannot be rushed. Taking a few drops on a piece of cotton wool, it should be rubbed in a circular motion until the cotton is dry, then repeated until the entire binding has been treated. Areas with delicate gilding should only be touched. After standing for a half hour, the binding can be buffed up with a thick cloth.

Vellum cannot be oiled in the standard fashion, as it will not soak up the dressing. It may be cleaned with a solution of one part milk and one part water on a soft cloth.

LENIN STATE LIBRARY. The largest library in the world, the Lenin State Library is located in Moscow. It was of little international importance until after the 1917 revolution, when many noted collections were absorbed into it. It was officially named for Lenin in 1925. The growth in recent years has been phenomenal, far ahead of any western institution, and so rapid that figures on its holdings are soon outdated. It is now believed to contain more than 25 million items. However, in the matter of rare books and manuscripts its holdings are not considered equal to such libraries as the British Museum, Bibliotheque Nationale, or even some of the American university collections.

LENOX, JAMES. Lenox was an American collector (1800–1880), who did more than any other individual to inspire interest in the hobby in the U.S. A businessman and philanthropist, he was also a patron of the arts and gave freely to many artistic causes. At the time Lenox began collecting books, long prior to the Civil War, there were no specialized rare-book dealers or auctioneers in the U.S. and very few collectors. Not only that, there were also few rare books, aside from those printed here. Lenox therefore acquired the vast majority of his treasures from foreign agents, mainly HENRY STEVENS and BERNARD QUARITCH. The class of books in which he was most interested—early printed volumes, manuscripts, and fine printing—were available in quantity in Europe, as many fine libraries were constantly being broken up, so he was able to obtain material in wholesale quantity. Lenox was the first American bibliophile with a taste for European rarities and set the pace for such later collectors as MORGAN, HOE, HUNTINGTON, FOLGER, and others who followed in his footsteps. He brought the first GUTENBERG BIBLE to America, winning it at a tough London auction battle against SIR THOMAS PHILLIPPS in 1847. Unlike some wealthy men whose hobbies are merely a diverting pastime, Lenox had considerable knowledge of his books and approached collecting with a scholar's enthusiasm. The correspondence of Lenox with Henry Stevens, which throws much light on book collecting activities of the mid 19th century, was published by the New York Public Library in 1951. Lenox commissioned a spacious building in New York to house his collection of books and artworks. It was maintained for public use for some years, then in 1895 merged with the Astor and Tilden foundations to become the NEW YORK PUBLIC LIBRARY.

LETTOU, JOHN. English-based incunabula printer, probably the fourth printer in Britain after CAXTON, ROOD, and the SCHOOLMASTER OF ST. ALBANS. He seems to have published very little, concentrating on legal works, and was slim competition to Caxton. Lettou entered the trade at London, 1480, and in 1482 was joined in partnership by WILLIAM MACHLINIA. They printed only five books together, so far as can be learned, although the association lasted several years. Lettou used only gothic type, as did the other English incunabula printers, and never employed commas or CATCHWORDS.

LEVANT. A supple, loose-grained variety of morocco, levant was among the most popular binding materials for fine work in the last century. It can be stained or gilded in virtually any fashion and polished to a mirror finish.

LIBRARY EDITION. "Library edition" was a favorite term of publishers in the 19th and early 20th centuries, used mainly with reference to sets. It was a common practice to issue some classes of books in two or more price ranges, to meet the demands of different tastes and pocketbooks. The library edition was always a grade above the trade or "popular" edition, usually bound in half or three-quarter leather, or at least a better variety of cloth than the ordinary edition. There were also "collectors'" editions, "peoples'" editions, etc.

LIBRARIES. The first libraries were probably collections of clay tablets formed by the Sumerians, Assyrians, Egyptians and other early civilizations. It has been shown that libraries of large scale existed as long ago as 2000 B.C. In 1901, the ruins of a CUNEIFORM library were discovered at Nippur, at the Temple of Bel, which was destroyed circa 1782 B.C. Since the mid 19th century, there have been many discoveries of the remains of royal libraries at ancient Nineveh, which date from the 8th century B.C. and later. Libraries after the year 1000 B.C. were mainly composed of PAPYRUS manuscripts, in SCROLL form. Such was the public library established at Athens by Pisistratus in 540 B.C., and the great library of Ptolemy Philadelphus (284 B.C.). This was called the Alexandrian Library and was one of the foremost treasure houses of the world, but its survival was short; in 47 B.C. Caesar's troops burned it, destroying 400,000 volumes. Nothing comparable was to be seen until the Renaissance.

The first private library was said to be that of Aristotle, but this is almost certainly a mistake; what was probably meant was "the first large library owned by a commoner." The first Roman public library was not founded until 167 B.C., and even then it was secondhand, being outfitted with a collection brought as war spoils from Macedonia. A much better library was at Pergamos in Asia Minor, the city from which the Romans obtained their supplies of writing vellum. It contained 200,000 items and fell to the Romans in 133 B.C. There were many and rather sizable private collections at this time, too. In the 1st century B.C., the grammarian Tyrannion had a collection of some 30,000 scrolls, which must have required vast space for storage.

During the Middle Ages, libraries were largely in the hands of the Christian church. Most books were produced in the monastic scriptoriums, destined for use in the monastery's library. Few monasteries built large collections, as they were concerned almost exclusively with the theological literature and made no attempt to resurrect writings of the classical authors. The Benedictines established a library at Monte Cassino as early as 530 A.D. The first library in Britain was that of Christ Church in Canterbury, 596. Libraries were later founded in Ireland. European university libraries did not become important until the 14th century. The Renaissance sparked collecting interest in both Italy and France, leading to the discovery of many early manuscripts and establishment of public and private libraries. The first library in the U.S. was at Henrico College, Virginia, in 1621, destroyed the following year. It was followed by that of Harvard (1638). New York had a public library in 1700, while Franklin founded a famous subscription library at Philadelphia in 1731. In 1800 came the beginnings of the LIBRARY OF CONGRESS, which grew to become the largest in the country.

LIBRARY OF CONGRESS. America's largest library, the Library of Congress is located in Washington, D.C. A copyright library, it receives without charge two copies of every book published in the U.S. The Library of Congress was founded in 1800 as working library for members of Congress. At first its collections were small and centered upon books of immediate bearing on government, law, or related topics. It was first housed in the Capitol building and destroyed when the Capitol burned in 1814. Its growth was rapid thereafter, as Congress authorized the purchase by the nation of Thomas Jefferson's library and added other notable properties. In 1851, after becoming one of the largest and finest collections in the country, it was again damaged by fire, but this time some 20,000 volumes were saved. The second half of the 19th century was its period of greatest expansion. In 1866 it acquired the library of the neighboring Smithsonian Institution. Yet it remained housed in the Capitol, where it became almost useless due to overcrowding. In 1897 it was moved to its own Renaissance-style marble building, constructed at a cost of more than six million dollars and covering nearly four acres. It was without a copy of the Gutenberg Bible until 1930, when it purchased, by Act of Congress, the hoard of 15th century books offered by the German collector Dr. Otto Vollbehr. A more recent acquisition was the collection of illustrated books formed by Lessing W. Rosenwald. The Library of Congress keeps historic U.S. documents on permanent display. Its collections, including manuscripts and pamphlets, are estimated at well over twenty million pieces. It vies with the Huntington Library in California for the honor of possessing the largest total of INCUNABULA in the U.S.

LIMITATION NOTICE. When a book has been issued in limited edition, the publisher will surely call attention to the fact. It is common, but not mandatory, for the limitation notice to appear on the reverse of the title page. Unless it states the number of copies printed, collectors are skeptical, and where books of value are involved the copy number—written or stamped—should be shown. The reason for numbering each copy is not to serialize the edition but rather as proof that it is no larger than indicated. Limitation notices take on many forms, depending on how the publication was prepared. If all copies are of the same variety—that is, identical in type, paper, binding, etc.—the notice will read something like: "X copies of this edition were printed, of which this is number X." But suppose there was also a trade edition, not limited. Then the notice might read: "Of this edition, X copies were printed on LARGE PAPER (or whatever the case may be), of which this is number X." Things can get far more involved than this, however. There may have been a trade edition, plus a thousand copies on large paper, three hundred of which have added illustrations, one hundred of which are signed by the author and engraver, fifty of which are printed on Japan vellum, twenty of which are bound in full morocco.

LIMITED EDITION. A book whose publication is limited to a pre-set number of copies is a limited edition. After printing, the plates are broken up and no further copies turned out regardless of demand. This differs from an ordinary or trade edition, in which the publisher orders more copies as needed. Limited editions often feature special typefaces, fine paper, or other attractions aimed at collectors. In rare cases they are even hand bound in leather, and may be sold for hundreds of dollars per copy. Many limited editions are in the nature of facsimiles of rare books, intended primarily for libraries. Generally all copies of a limited edition are numbered in series, sometimes signed by the author, binder, illustrator, or others who had a hand in the project. There is no established rule for the number of copies a limited edition may comprise; some are as few as ten or as many as several thousand. But collectors are apt to be unenthusiastic over a limited edition that has had a very large printing. Limited editions are often published by subscription, which means taking advance orders to determine if there is interest. See OUT OF SERIES.

LIMP. When used in relation to bookbindings, limp means the covering material (either leather or cloth) is not supported by boards and is literally as well as figuratively hanging limp. Sometimes scrap papers have been stuffed into the covers to provide some stabilization. Other limp bindings, particularly very early ones, have nothing between the paste down (or cover lining) and the cover. Limp vellum was first used as a trade binding for printed books almost at the outset of typography. It constituted the normal trade binding in Italy, Spain and Portugal from the late 15th to 17 centuries, hanging on in Spain and Portugal even longer. They were commonly equipped with TIES, leather thongs that took the place of clasps. Such bindings were never popular in Germany and Austria, though some were produced in England. In the 19th century limp leather, today imitation leather, was adopted for binding Bibles, travel guides and other volumes that were expected to receive heavy use.

LINDISFARNE GOSPELS.. One of the most famous and historic Anglo-Saxon manuscripts, the Lindisfarne Gospels were written in the early 8th century in the north of England.

LINOLEUM PRINTING. Blocks of linoleum have been widely used in this century as engraving plates, particularly by artists of the French school. The technique is also very popular in America. Linoleum is favored over wood, copper and other materials by some craftsmen because it is softer, more responsive, and can be cut, stippled, or treated in whatever method is desired. The blocks are then used to make print impressions, sometimes in books. Linoleum blocks are a favorite device of pop artists.

LITHOGRAPHY. One of the principal methods of printing in the 19th and 20th centuries, especially suited to the reproduction of line drawings and illustrations. It is based upon surface printing from an impression drawn upon smooth lithographic stone, made from limestone. Its earliest history can be traced to the close of the 18th century, when a forerunner of the process was developed more or less by accident by ALOYS SENEFELDER. He stressed the importance of the chemicals used instead of the surface, but those who sought to improve the invention concentrated on the stone and its possibilities. The story of the various innovations made in lithography during the 19th century is long, as each succeeding craftsman added his contribution. Lithography was used in place of engraving to reproduce prints of a number of 19th century artists, though the majority felt more comfortable in the old medium. Goya did much work in lithography in his later years. It was also used by Delacroix and Daumier, as well as a host of less brilliant artists. The prints of Currier and Ives of New York were printed in lithography, and it was employed for the production of posters. In the 20th century, lithography has become a major art form, a position that could hardly have been foreseen in its beginnings. The first English language book devoted to lithography was *Lithography, or the Art of Making Drawings on Stone for the purpose of being Multipled by Printing* by Bankes, 1813. Senefelder wrote a handbook on the subject in 1818.

LOOSE. When a book is described as loose, the pages are thinking seriously of leaving the binding. In American catalogues "shaken" is more often seen. Most loose books no longer have any connection with their spine but hang only by the joints. As this applies too much strain on the joints, it is not long before the book comes totally free. In cloth bound books, it is usually possible for the collector to perform a successful job of first aid by running a brush filled with glue down the interior of the spine. Elastic bands are used to hold it in place (not too tightly) until dry. But volumes of any value should be handed over to a professional. If a book is totally loose—that is, already come free—it will be listed as "loose in binding."

LOWNDES, WILLIAM THOMAS. A 19th century British bibliographer, Lowndes was the compiler of the lengthy *Bibliographers' Manual of English Literature*, first published in four volumes at London in 1834 and often reprinted, which attempted to record all significant editions of works by British authors and give an indication of their monetary value. Though incomplete and often erroneous, it remained the most ambitious reference work on the subject for many years and is still useful for basic information.

LYONNAISE BINDING. A binding style that grew up in France in the 16th century, named for Lyons but probably did not originate there. The purest form consists of a central medallion or other tool stamped in gilt, with smaller tools at each of the four outer corners, usually accompanied by blind-paneled borders. Sometimes the central tool is the same as those used at the corners. Very often the corner tool was repeated in the spine compartments and the whole binding highly polished. In other specimens the entire ground is covered by small solid diamond or lozenge tools, or dot tools, the delight of French binderies (and, apparently, of their patrons). Lyonnaise bindings were done mostly in calf or morocco, seldom vellum and never pigskin. They were engulfed in the 17th century by a flood of other, generally far more elaborate, styles (see FANFARE).

MACHLINIA (or DeMACHLINIA), WILLIAM. Machlinia was an English incunabula printer, of Belgian origin. In 1482 he went into partnership with JOHN LETTOU and eventually took over the business. By 1490 he dropped from sight, his equipment probably having been acquired by PYNSON.

MADE-UP COPIES. See SOPHISTICATED COPIES.

MAGGS BROTHERS. London rare book dealers, the Maggs brothers were specially known for their long series of sumptuously illustrated catalogues. The business began in 1855, when Uriah Maggs started up a circulating library at 44 Westbourne Terrace North, for which subscribers were charged five shillings per quarter. He also bought and sold secondhand books and took in orders for binding "books and music." After 40 years in the trade he retired in 1894. In 1901 the name was changed to Maggs Brothers, as it was then operated by Uriah's sons, Benjamin and Henry. In that year its headquarters was moved to a large premises in the Strand, which it occupied until 1918. It then moved to Conduit Street and finally, in 1938, to its present address in Berkeley Square.

During the years in Conduit Street, the various rooms of the building were designed to provide suitable settings for the books. There was a medieval manuscript room, furnished in the bare and crude style of a monk's cell, where one could easily imagine a lonely scribe laboring. Then there was an incunabula room, with all books shelved foredges outward in the monastic manner. However, the decision to vacate was wise, as this noble structure was badly injured in air raids during World War II.

MAJUSCULE. Upper-case or capital letters, whether printed or in manuscript are "majuscule."

MALAHIDE PAPERS. For many years scholars and collectors had searched in vain for the papers of Scottish author James Boswell, biographer of Samuel Johnson. Some letters had mysteriously turned up in France around 1840, being used as scrap to wrap goods in a shop. But nothing of substance was found until 1920. In that year a Yale bibliographer named Chauncey B. Tinker placed an inquiry in the London Times, asking if any readers knew the whereabouts of Boswell letters. An anonymous tip told him to try Malahide Castle. This seemed odd, as Malahide Castle was in Ireland, but upon research it was shown that one of Boswell's descendants had married the Lord of the Manor in 1873 and immediately the chase was on. At Malahide Tinker found letters of Boswell to his son Sandy, a few volumes of the now-famous diary, and two large crates of papers from Boswell's ancestral estate that had never even been opened! This was more than he could have hoped but, alas, there seemed no way of acquiring them. Tinker himself was not rich, and it seemed that Lord Talbot, the present resident of Malahide, had no intention of giving them away for research purposes. Once the news was out in the U.S., an antiquarian bookseller offered £50,000 (then $250,000) for the lot but was promptly refused.

The leading collector of Boswell material at the time was A. Edward Newton of Pennsylvania, who was naturally interested in bringing the papers to the U.S., but he had no better luck with Talbot. Finally a friend of Newton's named Colonel Isham succeeded. He had been in the British Army, knew his way around the Isles, and quickly established a friendship with Lord and Lady Talbot. Isham was a collector himself but his primary goal in buying the papers was to turn them over at a profit. After two years of visits, planning, and dickering, he brought the Talbots to the point where they decided they might as well sell. The price was not announced, but was undoubtedly more than the £50,000 already offered and declined. Eventually they went to Yale.

But Malahide, to everyone's surprise, was not finished yielding up treasures. In 1930 a box the Talbots believvd contained sporting equipment was found crammed with manuscripts. In 1937 Isham made an inch by inch search of Malahide and found a number of relics, including a portion of Johnson's diary. Finally, in 1940 two large cases of Boswell papers were discovered. All these finds seem even more remarkable when one considers that the material could only have been in the castle since 1873, a period of little more than half a century, yet had become totally lost and forgotten. The Malahide finds provide detailed insights into Boswell's habits and experiences. All those of consequence have now been published. Another large find of Boswell papers occurred at Fettercairn House, Scotland, in 1930.

MANSION, COLARD. Mansion was the first printer at Bruges, Flanders, but better known as the partner of CAXTON during the latter's residence at Flanders. Mansion is one of the missing links in the history of typography, whose life would tell us much if we could only know the details of it. By some he is depicted as a master printer, who was handed the secrets of the art by LAURENS COSTER, the man Hollanders believed invented printing. Then he meets the simple-minded Caxton, serving in Flanders as representative of a merchant guild, and kindly displays to him the wonders of the invention, not yet seen in Britain. Others tell it quite differently. Here, Mansion is shown as a local laborer whom Caxton chances to take as his apprentice and helper.

The crux of the argument is the question of who taught whom. Over the years there have been waves of opinion in one direction and then another. Some think Caxton learned printing at Cologne and was already skilled before coming to Bruges; others say Mansion was the one who learned at Cologne. Mansion was a calligrapher or writer of manuscripts before becoming involved in printing. The Caxton-Mansion partnership began in 1474. It is believed Caxton designed the first set of types used by the team, basing it upon Mansion's handwriting in a 1471 manuscript. The first books to be printed in English are now strongly thought to have been directed by Caxton, but that the mechanical work of their production was done by Mansion. Undoubtedly their joint efforts were quite successful, but by 1476 the partnership was dissolved. Caxton came to England, while Mansion stayed at Bruges and continued to print. It seems evident Mansion did some printing on his own even during the association, but how much and for how long is debatable. Some contend he was printing at least three years before the partnership, for which a fair case can be made. But even if this is not so, he was almost certainly printing for himself, apart from his work with Caxton, by 1475. The fact that Caxton did **not** print for himself while at Bruges leads one to believe Mansion owned the shop and fixtures, and was in attendance more frequently than Caxton. As soon as Mansion was on his own he began to distinguish himself and produced a number of very handsome volumes, all in gothic letter but well designed and printed. His first dated book was his Boccaccio of 1476, thought to have been his third work, and one of the most desirable of Flemish incunables.

MANUSCRIPT. Anything written by hand is technically called a manuscript, but the term is more properly applied to writings upon PAPER, PAPYRUS, VELLUM, and so forth, rather than stone or clay. It may be in the form of a document, letter, author's manuscript, illuminated book. If the writing is in the author's hand, it is said to be a HOLOGRAPH manuscript. The line between book and autograph collecting is so slim that the two continually overlap and are often considered one and the same hobby. Even a bibliophile who has no particular interest in autographs as such stumbles across INSCRIBED COPIES, or those with MARGINAL NOTES (which might or might not be of value); and if he follows a particular author he will almost certainly venture into the world of manuscripts sooner or later.

The earliest manuscripts were the papyrus and vellum scrolls of the Egyptians and Hebrews, both of which may have originated as early as 3000 B.C. Prior to 1000 B.C., almost all writing was of a legal or clerical nature; popular literature was passed along by word of mouth rather than transcribed. The manuscript played a vital part in the development of Greek and Roman culture. In the Middle Ages, monks wrote ILLUMINATED MANUSCRIPTS on sheets of vellum. With the advent of printing in the 15th century, manuscripts lost stature. But while fewer book manuscripts were produced, there was much more writing done in the way of documents and improvements in postal service which came in the 17th century brought about an increase in personal letter writing. See CALLIGRAPHY, also various manuscript schools.

MANUTIUS, ALDO. It is a curious instance in the history of typography that Aldo Manutius—who was to revolutionize the art—was born in 1450, just as Gutenberg and his workers were bringing printing into the world. Aldo saw the light of day far away from this scene, in sunny Sermonetta, Italy.

During the first several decades of printing, books remained quite expensive. The switch from manuscript copying to printing had cut production costs as much as 90%, but all this meant was that rich people could buy more books, not necessarily that the poor could buy them. Paper was costly and the majority of early incunables were in large folio sizes, requiring the use of considerable paper. Then there was the question of binding, which for folios was not always cheap. So the middle and lower classes, who desperately needed books, were often denied them.

Clearly something was wrong with the way early presses were managed. Enormous expense went into the publication of a book, yet only 200 or 300 copies could be sold, as affluent buyers were not numerous. Aldo, who printed his first book at Venice in 1490, gave much thought to this. At first he worked as others did, issuing expensive sets of such authors as Aristotle and Aristophanes. In their design, they were books of sumptuous beauty, as Aldus—as he was known—had an eye for type and an aesthetic sense foreign to most printers. But for their technical triumph they were commercial failures, because there were not enough wealthy collectors to buy them. Finally he decided to strike off on a new path, one printers had never trod before.

Instead of lavishing huge expense on each edition, trying to outdo the next printer and win the acclaim of princes, Aldus set about to market small, compact, inexpensive books that would have wide appeal. He commissioned FRANCESCO GRIFFO to cast a special type, smaller than had commonly been used in the past. It was based on the sloping Italian humanistic script inscribed by the handwriting of Petrarch. In Italy the type was called Aldino. In other countries it was termed italic, meaning the type that comes from Italy, as the little books were pouring through the continent like a snowstorm. This is how our italic letter got its name, though its use today is merely to place emphasis on certain words.

It was in April, 1501, that the first italic Aldus was born, an edition of the Roman poet Virgil, and from then the rise of the Aldus Press was meteoric. By cutting costs on paper, type, and binding, Aldus was able to sell his books for about a third of what was commonly charged for large-scale editions. Their cost was roughly the same as a modern paperback and their bindings of LIMP vellum a forerunner of this innovation. Soon the Aldine Press was supplying students throughout Europe with all they needed in the way of Greek and Latin texts. There was not a classical author of any substance whom Aldus omitted from his list; most ran through a number of editions. But cheap as they were, the books of Aldus had quality. Aldus was a good scholar and precise workman, and would not permit his name to appear on shoddy work. The Aldine versions of classical writings are generally accepted as authoritative.

Aldus used a mark consisting of a dolphin entwined around an anchor, symbolic of Venice being a city built on water. He died in 1515, the most famous printer-publisher of the time. The press was carried on until 1597 by descendants and others, but its productions toward the close compare unfavorably with those of its glory years. A total of about 900 editions, give or take, were issued.

MARBLED. Marbelizing is a technique of decorating paper, by dipping it into a solution of colors. The effect is a cross between an Easter egg and a slice of freshly cut salami. Although the solutions are generally alike, no two pieces of marbelized decoration are identical; sometimes very interesting patterns are accidentally created, but this is all a matter of chance. Like gold tooling, marbelizing came originally from the near or middle east, where it was practiced at least as early as the first half of the 17th century (perhaps much earlier). It was introduced into Europe later in the 17th century, but early results were disappointing. It did not really become popular until the final quarter of the 18th, when it was widely used for endpapers and covering the sides of half and three-quarters bindings, a service it still performs in hand binderies. For a brief time marbled edges were all the vogue, and are found on many books published from about 1820 to 1870, particularly dictionaries, encyclopedias, and other works of reference. A good job of marbelizing is not unattractive, but too gaudy for the tender tastes of some collectors. When books are rebound, marbled edges should only be applied to volumes issued when the practice was current.

MARGINAL NOTES. Notations—long or short, attractive or ugly—are made in the margins of books by readers. Printed marginal notes are called SIDE NOTES. Collectors look upon them with mixed emotions. If the book is very old and the notes contemporary, and if they could be called scholarly (a favorite word in the hobby), they are tolerated by even the most exacting collector. As early scripts were rather decorative, too, a good measure of 16th or 17th century marginal notes can add much to the appearance of a book. Unfortunately they are often cut into in subsequent bindings. It was a common habit among humanists and university students of the Renaissance to scribble in their books, jotting down information or references that might aid in their study. They were also fond of putting down their own reflections upon the work, and compare the feelings of the author with others, or with their own, which of course was encouraged by their tutors.

When the notes are nothing more than unreadable gibberish, or a grocery list, or something else that cannot (even in the eye of the bookseller or auctioneer) be connected with the book, they are naturally considered a fault, sometimes a serious one. Pencil notes are apt to be erased (see ERASURES) but it will leave a lasting mark. To determine if notes are contemporary, it is necessary to make a study of the history of scripts, but mistakes are still likely. But for minor alterations, script of the last half of the 16th century very much resembled that of the first half of the 17th century in most areas of Europe.

MAZARIN BIBLE. The Gutenberg or 42-line Bible, considered the first book printed from typography, is sometimes called the Mazarin Bible because the French cardinal and statesman owned a particularly famous copy. This specimen bears the rubricator's date of 1456, proving it was issued no later, and is now in the BIBLIOTHEQUE NATIONALE at Paris along with the remainder of his library. Mazarin (1602–1661) had considerable reputation as a bibliophile. Naude, his book hunter, was sent off to roam the continent in search of fine libraries to purchase, price being no object. It was said he often made arrangements with booksellers to purchase volumes by yard measure, rather than take the time to compute individual pieces.

MEARNE, SAMUEL. A legendary English binder of the 17th century, Mearne was the royal binder to Charles II. There is very little known of his life and it is impossible to identify any particular bindings with his shop; experts are hence divided as to whether he deserves the vast credit posterity and tradition have bestowed upon him. The bindings attributed to him are in a sort of English Rococo style, lavish and luxurious but lacking the warmth and bold lines of earlier Italian and French examples. Some leave no fraction of an inch without decoration. A number of the Mearne designs are filled with colored enamel combined with gold, creating bizarre and striking effects of an almost Oriental appearance. At one time Mearne was credited with the invention of the COTTAGE style of binding. He died in 1683.

MENTELIN, JOHANN. Mentelin was the first man to operate a printing office at Strasbourg, Germany, and one of the most sought-after of early incunabula printers. His shop was probably established in 1460; some say 1459. In geographical location, Strasbourg was the next largest city from Mainz, the headquarters of Gutenberg, and it was not surprising that it should receive a press at an early date. There is considerable speculation about the connection of Mentelin with the offices of Fust and Schoeffer at Mainz, where he may have been trained or at least introduced to the art. It is contended by others that Mentelin had an early association with Gutenberg, prior to the printing of the 42-line Bible, and left before Fust took over the business. Some say he could have played a role in the invention of printing, but only as an assistant to Gutenberg. Mentelin is well-known for an undated Latin Bible, excessively rare, printed in an old left-leaning semi-gothic, which he also occasionally used for other books. Among authors he printed was St. Jerome, St. Augustine, St. Isidor, Valerium Maximus, Conrad von Halberstadt. Mentelin had a habit of giving virtually no information in his colophons. The majority mention neither his name, the date, or even the city of Strasbourg. His books run historians a merry chase but are well worthy of study.

MEZZOTINT. A process of engraving upon copper plates, mezzotint was invented in Utrecht by Ludwig van Siegen, whose earliest work is dated 1642. In a short time the technique had been adopted throughout Europe and was especially popular with Italian and British artists. It depends upon the surface of the plate being scratched in preparation, then smoothed down to gain variations in light and tone. Technically it is a separate process from engraving, as engraved lines are not employed in true mezzotint. When they are, the result is called mixed mezzotint. In early days it was called mezzotinto, as most of Europe learned of it from Italy. Most of the earliest mezzotint work was in portraiture. It was afterward widely used in reproductions of paintings, especially in the 18th century. One drawback is that the fine surface of the plate is delicate and wears down after only a small number of impressions have been taken.

MINIATURE. "Miniature" is the name given to the pictures in ILLUMINATED MANUSCRIPTS. It has nothing to do with size. The artists who decorated manuscripts were called **miniators** in Latin, and hence their illustrations miniatures. From a very early time, fine miniatures have been cut from manuscripts and sold as artworks, or framed by the owner of the manuscript. Some manuscripts show evidence of their miniatures having been cut out and later replaced, or others substituted.

MINIATURE BOOKS. There have never been any guidelines for the definition of miniature books, at least none collectors are willing to follow. Usually the designation is applied arbitrarily in each individual case, depending on circumstances. Type sizes made it impossible to produce very small INCUNABLES, so there is generous latitude granted in the matter of early printed miniatures. Most collectors would agree that any 15th century volume measuring four inches or less in height, unless seriously trimmed down in binding, qualified. However, a 17th or 18th century book of four inches is not a miniature in anybody's language, just a common POCKET

EDITION. Even a three-inch book of the 1700s might have trouble making the grade, depending on who is sitting as judge and jury. Almost anything under three inches, of any age, can be safely called miniature, but whether it is worth collecting is another matter. Just as with full-sized volumes, there are good and bad, common and scarce miniatures.

By the latter part of the 17th century a market for miniature editions had arisen, among collectors who wanted them as curiosities (it is doubtful that miniature books, whenever produced, have ever been bought to read). They were particularly common at Leyden, Holland, possibly inspired by the small editions of the Elzevirs. Some of this period are quite attractive and well-printed, with tiny engraved title pages. The works of classical authors were usually chosen as the subject, as they could easily be broken up and arranged to suit any format. Cicero, for one, was squeezed through a number of miniature works, and emerged none the worse for wear. The average size of the miniature of this era was from 2½ to 3 (or slightly over 3) inches tall by 1½ to 2 inches across. Normally they were very thin, consisting of a hundred pages at most, because fat miniatures do not close easily. The majority received initial bindings of vellum boards but, as their sale was mainly to collectors, they are frequently found in sumptuous gilt-tooled morocco, sometimes with a single metal clasp. Miniature editions were also printed to some extent in France in the second half of the 17th century, especially at Lyons. During the 18th century, a good deal of miniature book publishing was done in Britain; the London Almanack is a noted example. During this century there were many attempts at diminutive Bibles, almost all of which were thoroughly unreadable.

In the 19th century, the making of miniature books became nothing more than a contest to see who could design the smallest, regardless of its content, beauty, or quality of materials. Toward this end a number of very tiny volumes were turned out, some measuring an inch or less in height. When it became impossible to reduce the size of type any further, leaving the alternative of printing one letter of a word per page, miniature books that were totally blank came into popularity. The reasoning was that collectors merely wanted them for display anyway, and by doing away with the necessity of printing a text they could be made extremely small. It is thought the smallest book ever printed was the Salmin edition of Galileo, issued at Padua in 1896–97. It was issued uncut, in WRAPPERS, with a portrait of Galileo facing the title page. It measures ⅝ by ⁷⁄₁₆ of an inch but is quite stout. A copy was offered about 1967 by a British bookseller for £60.

MINT CONDITION. Mint condition means, strictly speaking, just as issued by the publisher, without the slightest signs of use. But in bibliography, unlike coin or stamp collection, mild evidences that a book has been read or at least handled are not considered revolting. Mint is seldom applied to books issued before 1900, or those in leather bindings, but each bookseller has his own habit in these matters. As books do not come from a mint, it is all quite out of place.

MINUSCULE. Minuscule was the old term for what we call lower-case or small letters, originally used in connection with manuscripts and then applied to printing. Upper-case letters are known as majuscules. Sometimes minuscule is used to refer to anything of small size: diminutive script in early documents is called minuscule, as are miniature books ("a minuscule edition"). This might be taking bibliophilic license too far.

MISBOUND. In putting together the Signatures or quires for the purpose of sewing, the binding will occasionally mess things up, transposing one quire with another or—rarely—placing one upside down. Binders do not read books to determine the sequence of leaves; rather, they collect the quires according to the signature letters which normally appear at the foot of the first page of the each. Errors are more apt to happen in thick books, where the alphabet has been gone through many times. Where works carrying separate titleplates and different sets of signatures are to be bound in one volume, confusion is that much more likely. This is not a failing that can be blamed entirely upon the craft binder, as it occurs just as often, if not more so, in machine-bound volumes.

MISPRINT. A misprint is generally blamed on the printer, hence the origin of the term, but the fault sometimes rests elsewhere. Wrong words (or spellings) can be copied from proof specimens and the editor, or his blue-pencillers, might deserve responsibility. From a bibliographical point of view, it would seem errors should have enormous value, but it is tricky to deal with them. If an error occurs in only certain copies of an edition, many immediately believe they constitute an earlier, more desirable state. But this is not necessarily so, as the type could have fallen apart while in use, so that early copies are perfect while the error appears in those produced later. There are many ways errors are handled. If the printer notices them before the full run of impressions is completed, he will (or should) attempt a correction. If not, one of two things will happen. If the misprint is of such a nature that it changes the sense of text, or occurs in a proper name or other vital zone, some sort of ERRATA notice is called for. If nothing more than a dropped or inverted letter in a word that is still clearly recognizable, all concerned will put their heads in the sand.

MODERN FIRST EDITIONS. The collecting of "modern firsts" is one of the fastest growing branches of the hobby, at least on a par (on a universal basis) with WESTERN AMERICANA. Yet the term is applied loosely from one collector to another, and one bookseller to another. At one time the definition of modern was any book issued in cloth, but now that would carry us back as far as a century and a half. Some date the modern era at 1900, at least so far as as the publication of an author's major works are concerned, but are willing to stretch back farther for his earlier efforts. There are many exceptions, however; Oscar Wilde, though he did not live beyond the year 1900, is accepted into the circle of modern authors, whereas others of his day (such as Tennyson and Whitman) are not. It is all, of course, a matter of taste, and if one wished to collect Shakespeare, Jonson, and Marlowe under the banner of modern first editions there would be no hunting party set out.

The intrigue of modern firsts consists of several factors, though individual collectors may have other motives: their authors lived in contemporary or near-contemporary times and consequently wrote of our world rather than one far removed; their lives are well chronicled, providing grist for research and study; and, maybe most significant, their works are still common enough to be found on the market without difficulty, and without extraordinary cost. Yet there are some modern firsts which do command high sums, such as Margaret Mitchell's *Gone with the Wind* (1936), depending on the old law of supply and demand. While demand is often strong, the supply in most cases remains large, as initial printings comprised many thousands of copies.

Then there are authors and poets who are not so widely collected as others (the difference, say, between a George Bernard Shaw and a William Saroyan), and who present attractive opportunities. Generally the collector of modern firsts fixes either upon a particular author, school of writing (such as French 1930's), or trend in literary movement. In any event he will usually want not only first editions, but first appearances of magazine and other periodical pieces, manuscripts and letters, and other relevant materials. Collectors of modern firsts have been responsible for putting together almost unbelievable author-bibliographies, searching out youthful writings that the world at large (and possibly the author himself) has long forgotten, including those appearing under pseudonyms.

Collectors of modern first are frequently the butt of criticism for their attention to and love of POINTS which seem meaningless to the outsider: a dropped letter, variant binding, or anything which suggests priority of edition. While bibliographers at large are willing to concede that these considerations are of importance, there is not much sympathy toward those who reject copies because of a half inch tear in the dust jacket. But the whims of collectors make the market, and it's a fact that first editions in undamaged dust jackets have greater sales appeal. There are many dealers who specialize, or trade exclusively in, modern first editions.

MORGAN, J. PIERPONT. Though known better to the world as a collector of art and antiquities, J. Pierpont Morgan (1837–1913) was the leading private book collector in America in his time. He was the son of Julius S. Morgan, an internationally known banker, and inherited his father's fortune. Supplementing it with rail and and steel holdings and vast investments in other industries, he became one of the world's richest men, lavishing huge sums on his hobbies. At his death his art collection, housed primarily in New York's Metropolitan and London's South Kensington museums, was valued at $60,000,000. It would be worth billions today.

As a boy attending school in Switzerland, Morgan bought a few autographs, which formed the beginning of his collection. Later he busily acquired standard sets and popular literature in fine bindings and assembled what was considered one of New York's finest libraries by the Civil War. However, at this point he was far from indulging his interest in rarities. Only when his father passed away in 1890 did he begin collecting in earnest, as he had long said that if any collecting were done in the family, his father had the right to do it (a right he failed to exercise). In those 23 years, from 1890 to 1913, he probably bought more rare books and manuscripts than anyone else in the world, though many other prominent collectors were active. He had agents everywhere and assistants who would handle correspondence from booksellers and read incoming catalogues, all of which he had no time for.

His aim was to build a library in New York that, while small by European standards, would rival the finest Old World libraries in content. His principal interest was illuminated and early text manuscripts and early fine bindings, which were available in large quantities, as a number of old English collections were dispersed. He also purchased significant items in all other branches of the hobby, including modern first editions, broadsides, works on science, travel, natural history, and other subjects. Bibles were well represented in his collection, as he owned first editions of all the major translations, as well as the first Bibles to be printed in America. No less than three Gutenberg Bibles were among his treasures, the most ever possessed by a single collector. He also boasted the largest U.S. holding of volumes from the press of Caxton, the first English printer, as well as the most English incunabula in this country.

For a long while his books were stored in his townhouse on New York's Madison Avenue, but, wishing to leave a suitable home for them, he commissioned the firm of McKim, Mead & White to build a library next door, on East 36th Street. It was opened to the public in 1924 and remains one of the finest rare-book libraries, having made a number of new acquisitions over the years and built further galleries for exhibitions. Morgan Library has also published many useful monographs and books on the history of printing, manuscript illumination, and other specialized topics, as well as guides to its collections.

MOROCCO. Morocco, the finest leather for binding, is made from goatskin. It was introduced to Europe from the east via Spain in the late 15th century and was used for the majority of high-grade work for the next three centuries. See LEATHER.

MORRIS, WILLIAM. An English writer, artist, and crusader for social reform, Morris is known to bibliophiles as a champion of fine printing and designer of type. Late in life he founded and operated the Kelmscott Press, which had as its purpose the rejuvenation of artistic typography. Born in 1834, he set out to be a painter and studied with Rossetti. This not satisfying his creative energies, he operated a furniture and art business which gave birth to the Morris school of design, roughly equal to America's Tiffany. He wrote verse, studied medieval history, spoke in favor of national socialism. He was a friend of many of the publishers, booksellers, and book collectors of the era. As a collector, Morris was mainly interested in incunabula for his own. He sought to use the Kelmscott Press to show that books of the Victorian age were mere shadows of what they could be and poured enormous dedication and cash into the project. Initially he intended printing just as had been done in primitive times, with fresh vellum, homemade ink, and type set by hand. Many problems arose, however. For one reason or another he could not make the ink; vellum stopped coming from Italy because the Vatican had priority to the native supply. The press switched to English vellum, but it was oily and the ink would not take. As a remedy chalk was applied as a ground, but it was discovered that this caused the impressions to wear away with age. Yet the Kelmscott books are among the most attractive of the neo-gothic revival period and are eagerly collected. The Morris edition of Chaucer is held in particular regard. He died in 1896.

Those who take issue with Morris as a type designer argue that he approached the subject as an artist, without giving sufficient thought to the reality that books are meant to be read. Strictly speaking this is probably true. His pages are so heavily embellished with decoration that one is apt to study them as art and ignore the text, just as one often does when confronted with beautiful calligraphy. His critics also level this charge: that he failed to realize 19th century readers were not accustomed to gothic lettering, as was the public of Caxton's time, and found it hard going. But few of the Kelmscott books ever found their way into the possession of common folk.

MOSAIC BINDING. Mosaic bindings are bindings consisting of inlays of colored leather, cut into strips or other shapes and arranged to form decorative patterns. It was a popular style among the rich in the 16th century and even later, most widely practiced in Italy and France. Sometimes the leathers would merely be of contrasting shades or finishes, so the effect was very subtle. Gold leaf was generally used in the gutters between the joinings, to minimize their appearance, as the fit was often imperfect. One must be careful, in purchasing mosaic bindings, that all component parts are original, or, if not, that the seller is aware of the fact and has made allowance in the price.

MOTTLED CALF. Mottled calf bindings are those which have a pattern of dots or splotches on the surface, caused by treating with acid.

MOUNTED. A mounted leaf is one that has been strengthened by pasting on a sheet of fresh, usually rather heavy, paper. The operation is only suitable for leaves printed on one side and therefore used almost exclusively on title pages and endleaves. The only way a leaf of text can be bolstered is by FLOATING, or encasing it in transparent material.

MYDDYLTON, WILLIAM. English printer of the time of Henry VIII, successor to Robert Redman. His shop was located at the sign of the George, next to St. Dunstan's Church, Fleet Street, London. He printed an edition of Froissart's *Cronycles* in 1525 in partnership with PYNSON (Pynson and Redman had been heated rivals). A Henry Middleton, perhaps his son or grandson, appears as printer in the last quarter of the 16th century. William's mark contained two mythological figures and a very clever cipher on his name.

NAME ON TITLE. In the absence of bookplates, owners of books in the 16th and 18th centuries (even into the 19th century) commonly wrote their names on the title page. Many atrocities were innocently committed in this way, as books rare today were of course not when new, so owners did not realize they were sullying sacred ground by scrawling their name wherever they wished. The presence of a signature on the title page does not really hurt the value unless it is large and defacive (written in an oily ink), or run across a portion of printing. Even so the damage is not great: perhaps 5% less in sales potential than if the signature were not present. The real trouble begins when the former owner has decided to **remove** his name before parting with the book, which many did. Some blotted it out in heavy ink; others erased it with a steel scraper; some actually cut out the signature with scissors. None are cause for joy, but a blot, even a bad one, is the least offensive. Scraping done by an unskilled hand usually results in a hole, or at least the removal of some bit of printing; and of course cutting is too terrible. Sometimes the missing piece will be replaced by gluing paper to the reverse side of the title page, but there merely serves aesthetic ends, as all the king's horses cannot put cut paper together to the satisfaction of a critical collector.

NEW YORK PUBLIC LIBRARY. The largest public library in the U.S., the New York Public Library was formed by merger of the Astor, Lenox, and Tilden libraries in 1895. Prior to that time New York possessed only a small network of circulating libraries. The core of the collection was the library of JAMES LENOX, New York's foremost bibliophile of the mid 19th century, who had passed away in 1880 leaving his library intact for public use. It consisted of 86,000 volumes, a large proportion rarities, as well as an art collection. The Astor library, much larger but comprising mainly everyday titles, contained more than a quarter million pieces; the Tilden 20,000. The total endowment which accompanied the three was nearly $3,500,000. In 1901 Andrew Carnegie gave a cash gift of $5,200,000. As yet no building had been constructed to serve as a central headquarters; each of the three libraries remained in separate locations. Searching for a site in "upper" Manhattan, away from the crush of traffic, the trustees decided upon a lot on Fifth Avenue at 42nd Street, which had housed the obsolete Croton Reservoir. The building, in classical revival styles, was opened to the public in 1911. The New York Public Library has since acquired many other notable collections: Arents, tobacco; Gaynor, political science; Rabinowitz, Hebrew books; Berg, English and American Literature, etc. Its Gutenberg Bible, often called the finest in America, came from the Lenox library and was the first copy brought to the U.S. (1847). It is kept on public display in a special room, where one leaf is turned each day.

NEWSPAPERS. Through the Middle Ages news even important news that might decide the fate of kingdoms traveled like a snail on molasses. An event might be weeks old before the people in the street heard of it, if it occurred in another country. There was no source to which the medieval citizen could turn for reliable reports; his own government often knew as little as he. Bits of news and rumor were always drifting through the marketplaces, but such second and third-hand reports were altered in the telling, even if accurate originally. The printing press should have solved the problem easily, and would have but for a number of difficulties. First of all, few of the incunabula printers had royal patronage or large capital behind them. The publishing of a newspaper would have called for a very large operation, not only to collect information but to circulate editions, which was outside the scope of pioneer typography. Even in the early 16th century, when much more money had come into the industry, there was no thought given such a project.

The earliest periodical news source appeared at Strasbourg and Basel in 1566, though it was not published at regular intervals. A paper titled "Avisa" and another called the "Relation" started up in 1609 and were the first true newspapers appearing on an announced schedule. The "Relation" was the work of Strasbourg publisher Johann Carolus, the "Avisa" anonymous. And with the anonymity of "Avisa" a stark reality becomes clear; it was just not very safe to go around publishing reports of news events, if one was not operating under the watchful eye of some royal censor. Just a mere slip of type, a sneeze that placed one letter in the wrong sequence, might create a meaning that would send the printer's office into confiscation and the printer to the stocks.

By 1630 newspapers had appeared in Holland, France, and England. Though basically small enterprises, they managed to collect news from distant points. As ships came and went from the Americas, news would be gathered from those on board, and "foreign correspondents" who sent news by post were an early innovation. The first English newspaper, called a coranto, was the work of Thomas Archer. Its first issue is thought to have been released June 6, 1621, but there is no proof, and not a single specimen of any are known to survive.

Nathaniel Butter became the first titan of the English news media. Beginning in September, 1621, he issued a long series of reports from the continent, but did not concern himself with local British happenings. They were published weekly, or at least supposed to be; some weeks were skipped, and in others several issues appeared to catch up. It was typical of 17th century publishers to turn out their papers only when sufficient news was available; if nothing very exciting occurred or could be learned, labor was saved until it did. A more regular newspaper, and one which more closely resembled the modern counterpart, was the London Gazette, born during the reign of Charles II in 1665 (the plague year). The 18th century saw the development of numerous news journals and magazines, some surviving to the present.

NO DATE. When a date does not appear on the title page or in the COLOPHON but is established from reference works, it is stated in brackets: (1496). If there is strong reason to believe the book appeared at a certain date, but positive evidence is lacking, it appears as (1496?). If the decade of publication is known but not the year, it will be written (149?). The causes for books appearing without a date are numerous and sometimes noteworthy (see DATES). Abbreviated as N.D.

NO PLACE. "No Place" means the title page or colophon does not state the place of publication, nor can the information be obtained from other sources (presuming the cataloguer has made an attempt). If it could, the wording would be: "no place (but Amsterdam...)," or something of that nature. Many early books did not identify the place of printing, for a variety of reasons. Often the printer or publisher wanted to sell part or all of the edition elsewhere and did not want it known to be a foreign product. Or there may have been religious or political problems.

NOTARY, JULIAN. An English incunabula printer, Notary flourished from about 1496 to 1520. He was established at Westminster, also the location of Caxton's office. In terms of technical skill he was a cut above his contemporaries, although England produced no printers of great genius until a slightly later period. Though active a long time he apparently printed very little, far less than Caxton and only a fraction as much as either WYNKYN DeWORDE or PYNSON. His mark comprised a variation of the orb-and-cross with a backwards numeral "4" and the headpiece from a suit of armor. The entire mark, enclosed in a rectangular frame, was drawn as if sprouting from a tree trunk, the significance of which has been bounced about on long winter evenings.

NUNS OF LITTLE GIDDING. An old tradition says that the English convent of Little Gidding produced many of the Elizabethan EMBROI-DERED BINDINGS, but this is now considered nothing more than a hoax.

NUREMBERG CHRONICLE. An encyclopedic reference book published by KOBERGER at Nuremberg, Germany, in 1493. The work of prolific medieval author Hartmann Schedel, it was the most lavish and opulent volume attempted in the incunabula age—and for a good while thereafter. It was printed in gothic letter, in large folio format (about 18 inches tall), with a total of 1,809 woodcut illustrations by the artists WOLGEMUT and PLEYDENWURFF. They were of various sizes, some in the form of maps or town views extending over two pages, others quite small. However, they were not all different. S. C. Cockerell counted 645 different plus 1,164 repetitions. Subjects included Noah's Ark, exotic trees in Eden, monsters, the burning of the Alexandrian library, Henry II and Kunegund holding a model of Bamberg Cathedral, portrait of Maximilian, expulsion of antichrist, map of the ancient world, and so forth. Though long relied upon by historians for their representations of early events and scenes, the illustrations have now been shown to have little factual value, as the same cuts were used again and again to show different cities or emperors. But the Nuremberg Chronicle is still a fascinating and mighty book, the dream of all who collect early illustrated volumes. Though there is no information as to its original cost, it must have sold much higher than the average run of books. The edition was very large, however, so that copies are still not particularly rare. A select few were issued with the woodcuts colored by hand. In its accounts of what was then modern history, it touched upon the invention of printing (credited to Mainz in 1440) and the discovery of the New World.

NUTHEAD, WILLIAM. The first printer in the state of Maryland, Nuthead started in business 1685.

OCTAVO. The standard format in which the majority of books, and almost all novels, are published is called "Octavo." It results from the printer folding his original sheet four times to make eight leaves, or sixteen pages. Each of these eight-leaf sections is called a quire. In binding, the quires of an octavo are sewn into position by threads passing through the connecting folds of leaves four and five. As booksellers describe sizes according to format, it is well to know something of the dimensions in which octavos are found. The **average** is known as Crown 8vo, which measures about 7½ × 5½ inches. Demy is another popular size and works out to roughly 8½ × 6 inches. These terms are based upon the names of various papers, but in common use they are not mentioned; the catalogue merely states small or tall 8vo, which leaves one guessing. These are some of the other sizes.

Foolscap, 6½ by 4½ inches
Post, 7½ by 5½ inches
Imperial, 11 by 7½ inches
The largest sheets of printing paper, Elephant and Atlas, are seldom

used in octavo volumes. Atlas would result in an octavo 13 inches high, which is quite ridiculous.

OFFPRINT. An offprint is an article from a magazine which has been extracted and reprinted—not to be confused with a copy of the original article torn from the issue. So far as collectors are concerned, there is no distinction made regarding time lapse; many offprints are not prepared until the publication in which they appeared has grown long whiskers. The majority of offprints involve articles in medical and scientific journals. It is often the author who pays for the printing, then distributes them free (possibly autographed) to friends or persons he hopes to impress.

ONLY. The word "only" usually appears hiding between brackets ( ) and means something is missing. It will be used in the sense of "sixteen plates (only)," or "eleven volumes (only)." Unless one has access to a good reference library, it will be difficult finding out just how much is lacking, whether one plate or a hundred. If one volume from a set of fifty is present and all the remainder gone, the term seems ludicrous, but is still applied with firm resignation and there is nothing one can do about it. Once the bookseller has said "only," he has discharged all responsibility, whatever the extent of the loss might prove to be. The price usually gives a fair indication.

ORIGINAL BINDING. In the case of early printed books, when TRADE BINDINGS were not uniform (thus making comparison with other copies useless), it is impossible to say with any assurance if a binding is original. If CONTEMPORARY—which is not difficult for an experienced eye to determine—and of a cheap variety such as limp vellum or plain calf, chances are it is original, because an early owner would not likely have had it rebound in as common a style as it was issued. But there can be no proofs, as the removal of one binding and application of a second leaves no outward evidence, unless the leaves have been SHAVED. Early bindings in decorative styles are less apt to be original, as the books were most likely purchased in a trade covering and then sent to be custom bound. But it hardly makes a great deal of difference, as most collectors do not give a groat one way or the other.

ORIGINAL STATE. Supposedly the original state is the state in which the book left the offices of the publisher to begin its life as an article of commerce. It should therefore be complete, undamaged, and in its TRADE BINDING; but there is no guarantee the condition will be absolutely MINT, as very minor faults (such as light foxing) are not thought to count against original state. Original state is of far more concern to collectors of MODERN FIRST EDITIONS than the bibliophilic fraternity at large, which gladly accepts a rebinding if it happens to be a better grade. How much court should be paid to original state is all in the eyes of the beholder. It is a modern, 20th century distinction which collectors of early times did not need to contemplate. But attention to original state had undoubtedly done the hobby well, at least resulting in the preservation of some fine contemporary bindings that might otherwise have perished.

OTTONIAN MANUSCRIPTS. Ottonian was a school of manuscript illumination which flourished briefly, yet brilliantly, for a little more than a century during the middle part of the Dark Ages. Unlike other schools, such as the Carolingian and Romanesque, it was confined to one group of people, the Germans, and never reached beyond German speaking lands. Its beginnings can be traced to the second quarter of the 10th century. At this time the larger monasteries in Germany had acquired recognition for their manuscript production and were slowly evolving a richly nationalistic style to replace the standard Carolingian. The name Ottonian, also applied to German art of the period, derives from the emperors named Otto, who began to rule in 919. Otto I is given credit for the revival of leaning among his countrymen, and a blending of the principal characteristics of Carolingian, Byzantine, and ancient or classical art. Ottonian manuscripts feature rich decoration with heavy use of gold, though there is not a great deal of picture painting. There were centers of manuscript production at Regensburg, Cologne, Fulda, and elsewhere. The influence extended to Switzerland but did not cross into Italy,. By the second half of the 11th century it began to break up, replaced by Romanesque ideals and then gothic. Some of the finest examples of Ottonian manuscripts were made for Germany's princes and kings rather than church use, although produced at monasteries.

OUT OF PRINT. An out of print book is one that can no longer be obtained from the publisher, as all copies in stock have been disposed of and there are no plans for a REPRINT. The common and obvious reason for a book going out of print is that it is no longer (if indeed it ever was) selling. Occasionally a publishing company will go out of business and its titles will then be unobtainable unless the contracts are acquired by another house. As a rule scholarly works remain in print far longer than books intended for general sale. In its strict sense "out of print" means that no copy of the text is currently available from **any** publisher. In other words, the works of Shakespeare cannot be said to be out of print, as modern editions are readily obtained. But in its more accepted meaning, it refers to the work as first published. Thus, the First Folio of Shakespeare (London, 1623) is decidedly out of print.

It is sometimes tricky—and embarrassing—to guess what may or may not still be in print. The respected bookseller makes no claim unless he has the facts in black and white. There have been many cases of antiquarian booksellers offering volumes as "out of print" and even "scarce" that could still be ordered from the publisher, at prices many times the list sum. Publications of museums and learned societies have a knack of hanging on in print a very long time, not from any further supplies being prepared, but because copies sell slowly.

While a book is in print, secondhand copies bring less, usually at least one third less. Once it has been declared out of print, one of two things may happen. If the work is not popular or in demand, it will continue to sell cheaply. If likely to appeal to collectors (especially if a reference work), the fact that it is out of print will almost certainly bring the price higher than the published figure. Later developments depend on supply and demand. It can be assumed that a book described as out of print is not scarce, or the bookseller would have advertised the fact.

OUT OF SERIES. It is general, when publishing a LIMITED EDITION, to issue a few copies "out of series"—that is, over and above the stated limitation number. These are given to the author, the illustrator, used as proof copies, or other similar purposes. It does not affect the limitation of "in series" copies in any way and should not be looked upon with suspicion. If it happened that a hundred out of series copies were issued and distributed on the market, that would constitute a separate, non-limited edition, which would likewise be of no concern.

PAGINATION. The system by which pages in books are numbered is called pagination, and thus the term is applied to these individual numerals. Most medieval manuscripts did not carry any method of numbering. This was also true of printed books in the first 20 years of typography, from about 1450 to 1470, though some had their leaves (rather than pages) numbered by hand. This is known as foliation, or numbering the folios. It was commonly done by means of type in printed books from around 1470. The numbering of pages in the modern fashion arose only after the incunabula period. This is why, in descriptions of early printed books, the number of leaves rather than pages is stated (if one is lucky enough to find a description that goes into such matters). Pagination was further broken down at times, especially in the 17th century, to the numbering of **columns** in books having two columns or more per page. This was done for easy reference, as the location of a certain word in a page containing several thousand is not always like falling off a log.

PALEOGRAPHY. Paleography is the study of manuscripts, especially those of great age, and the various forms of writing which preceded manuscripts. Though confined largely to those who have a collecting passion, it is a rather entertaining pastime and offers ample chances for discovery. Of all pre-Renaissance manuscripts in the world (including letters, charters, legal proceedings, etc., as well as books) only a fraction have been studied by expert paleographers, and a much smaller fraction published. However, it is work which requires dedication, often expense, and little promise of financial reward even if oil is struck. The science of paleography is naturally closely allied with that of CALLIGRAPHY, the study of handwriting. See MANUSCRIPTS, ILLUMINATED MANUSCRIPTS, and entries for individual manuscript schools (GOTHIC, CAROLINGIAN, OTTONIAN, etc.)

PAMPHLET. "Pamphlet" is the standard bibliographical term for what the outside world calls a brochure or booklet; a short, unbound work. Into the first half of the 19th century pamphlets were usually held together by sewing. Afterward they were more often stapled. Pamphlets, if worth keeping, were sometimes bound by their owners, either individually or as a collection. If a collection was made, one can only hope all items included are of similar nature, or the result is a mishmash. Volumes are occasionally found containing three songbooks, seven political pamphlets, a few juvenile primers and perhaps other surprises. The old word for text pamphlets was tract.

PAPER. The earliest "paper," if it can be termed, was made of PAPYRUS by the Egyptians. Next in chronological sequence (for general use, anyway) came vellum, which could hardly be called paper in the modern sense. The first paper manufactured after present methods was introduced in China in the 2nd century A.D. It would have proved an enormous boon to Europe's medieval scribes, but did not become known in the west for many centuries thereafter. The first true European paper seems to have evolved in the 10th century and was made from cotton, but it was unsatisfactory and little attention given it. It is thought rag papers were made in Europe as early as the 12th century, but this is disputed by some historians. There is no question but that Europe had rag papers by the 13th century, and by the 14th century was manufacturing paper in quantity. Still, it was not until the advent in printing of the 15th century that paper was universally accepted for the making of books. Its role up to then had been largely for exercise work, wrapping goods in shops, and so forth.

The variety of papers that have been used in the printing of books are far too numerous to attempt reviewing. They run the gamut from luxurious, silky grades that can scarcely be distinguished from vellum and remain fresh for centuries, to the inferior stock on which newspapers are printed, which bids farewell after a few years of life. The paper used in the incunabula period, and through the first half of the 16th century, were of superior quality, possessing a high rag ingredient. As rag paper came to be more and more costly, the rag content was gradually reduced, but the results were not apparent until the opening years of the 17th century. In examining books of that era, especially those printed in Germany and Austria, one finds the pages turned a uniform shade of harsh brown, almost like intense foxing. These papers do not, however, become brittle, as do modern papers which turn brown. Most English papers of the mid to later 17th century were very thin and grew brown almost immediately, prompting publishers to offer THICK PAPER COPIES to those who could afford them. But the real decline of paper began around 1830, both in Europe and America, and has continued more or less to today. Modern technology has produced a so-called "300-year, acid-free paper" that is extensively used in scholarly reprints but has yet to be adopted in trade publishing. Coated paper used in books illustrated with photo plates is costly, but really undesirable from a collector's view, as it reacts badly to humidity and is ruined by contact with water. Japan vellum is a high grade stock generally used for taking impressions of engravings or lithographs.

PAPYRUS. Papyrus was a plant native to the middle east, used by ancient races in many industries. The Egyptians made shoes, boxes, headdresses, cord, even sailing vessels from papyrus, while it was also boiled and eaten among the common classes. There were hardly any uses to which papyrus (leaf, stalk, or root) was not put at one time or another, and it answered every purpose well. The Egyptians and their neighboring civilizations made writing paper from it by impressing layers of the pith one atop another, moistening them and then leaving in a press to dry. Afterward they were honed with ivory to achieve a fine, smooth, glossy surface. It is thought the initial use of papyrus for writing occurred between 3500 and 4000 B.C. It was written upon with a pointed reed stylus dipped in an archaic form of INK. Egyptians writing with goose quills, such as we see in Hollywood movies, are merely an invention of imagination (or poor research). Most books were in the form of SCROLLS, with the papyrus glued together to form a long continuous roll.

Though far better than anything the Egyptians had previously tried, papyrus was far from the perfect writing material. While it could be made as thick as desired, merely by piling one slice of pith on another, it was not strong. The scribes complained that as they wrote, even if little pressure was used, the point of the stylus would break the surface; and papyrus is something like a nylon stocking, as it has a tendency to run when a puncture has been made. Its keeping qualities were also not of the best. A vegetable, it dried out rapidly and was brittle in no time at all. Today, existing fragments of papyrus manuscripts cannot be handled, even with the utmost care, without causing some damage. The material which the Jews began using in their early centuries—parchment—was much finer, but the Egyptians either did not realize or would not admit it.

Papyrus was adopted by the Greeks and was the paper upon which their classical literature was written. It was then used by the Romans until the 2nd century B.C. when the Egyptians prohibited its exportation. Papyrus continued to be used in Egypt, and even to some extent in Europe, well into the Middle Ages. From early times papyrus was sold in at least four grades: the finest for transcribing books or legal papers, the second for correspondence or ordinary writing, the third for those who could not afford the second, the cheapest for wrapping goods and parcels.

PARCHMENT. While parchment and vellum have come to mean the same in common use, there is really a difference: vellum was the name given to parchment made from the hides of young animals (usually cattle). Any leather prepared for writing is called parchment, regardless of the animal from whence it came. In the matter of bookbindings, parchment is broken down into calfskin, sheepskin, goatskin, pigskin, etc.

PARKE-BERNET GALLERIES. The leading American auctioneers of books and manuscripts, the Parke-Bernet Galleries are located in New York. The firm, which also sells art and other classes of merchandise, was founded in 1938 as the result of a dispute within another organization. Two disgruntled employees of the American Art Association, New York auctioneers, set out to form a competing business. Their names were Hiram Parke and Otto Bernet. Successful almost from the first, Parke-Bernet put the American Art Association out of operation and achieved international prominence in the sales which followed World War II. Some of the well-known libraries it has sold include the Streeter, Hogan, Martin, Newton, Currie, Johnson, Wilmerding. In 1947 it witnessed the record-setting sale of $151,000 of a copy of the BAY PSALM BOOK. It is now administered by SOTHEBY'S of London.

PART ISSUED. In the mid 19th century many novels were issued in parts, in soft wrappers, sold at the equivalent of our newsstands. The motive was to stimulate interest by the low price of each part, which might be less than a shilling, and thus attract buyers who might not care to spend the full price of a book at one toss. The result was very much akin to buying on the installment plan. Generally the total price was higher than charged for regularly published books, however. The final part would include all accessory matter needed for binding, such as title and preliminary leaves. Sometimes the publisher would even supply the binding.

There are many points to be considered when buying a part-issued book in its original parts. The first and most obvious is to check that all parts are present. The original wrappers should be intact, and the binding should (ideally) be furnished by the publisher. A set of the original parts is just as good unbound, to many collectors even better, though they are less apt to have survived well without the protection of a binding. Many popular British authors of the early and mid Victorian era found themselves in parts, including Dickens. It was an honor, as only authors with guaranteed fan appeal were risked in such projects. Purchasers were mainly of the working class.

This is not the only sort of part issued book, however. Properly speaking, any work in more than a single volume, in which the volumes are not published simultaneously, is "part issued." In early times part issuing was confined mainly to encyclopedias and other extensive works of reference, which were frequently the responsibility of a lone compiler working by a flickering candle. Later, more general books were part issued, such as biographies, collections of letters, and diaries, often spread over a very long period of years and handed down from one editor to another.

PASTE ACTION. The endpapers, or PASTE DOWNS, are attached to the insides of the covers by paste. It sometimes happens, owing to the quality of the paste, that it eventually causes them to be discolored. This discoloring is called paste action. Beginners often mistake it for natural paper browning, or even foxing, but it is rarely a serious problem.

PASTE DOWN (or PASTEDOWN). Rather than one, most books have two end or FLYLEAVES at the front and rear. One is the free fly, the other pasted down to the inside of the cover, to hide the binding board and the edges of cloth (or leather). This is called the paste down. In the early years of printing it was common to use any scraps at hand as paste downs. Bookbinders would buy imperfect books to get paper or vellum for this purpose; as a result incunabula and illuminated manuscript leaves are sometimes found doing service as paste downs. Fragments of valuable and unique works have turned up in this fashion.

PAYNE, ROGER. Probably the most famous British bookbinder, Payne lived in the 18th century and successfully revived the binding styles of the late Renaissance, though he did not copy from any particular models. His patterns are based upon smooth, simple, tasteful lines, with a moderate use of gold tools. Compared to the more ornate bindings of the 18th century, Payne's are almost plain. Many bindings identified as his are undoubtedly the product of others, which may be said of almost all legendary binders. In his personal habits Payne was slovenly and unrefined, but this is not evident in his work. He died at the age of 58, in 1797.

PEMBROKE, EARL OF. An English collector, the Earl of Pembroke (1686-1735) was noted for discriminating taste. He gathered a small but exquisite library of rarities, mainly consisting of specimens from the pioneer presses. It was maintained by descendants long after his death, eventually sold in the early part of this century by Sotheby's.

PENNY BOXES. Penny boxes were the trays or boxes outside anti-quarian bookshops, which offered miscellaneous books at inexpensive prices. Though probably of much earlier origin, the practice reached its height in the mid and late 19th century, when the larger dealers were doing such a rapid turnover that it was not profitable to collate or catalogue every incoming volume. At this time penny boxes became the prime hunting ground for BOOK SCOUTS and occasionally yielded up treasures. Even today there are collectors alive who, in their youth, rescued broken incunables or paunchy little Elzevirs from the obscurity of penny boxes. Many collectors of the Victorian age never even bothered entering the shops; they merely went along inspecting the wares of the penny boxes and in this fashion built respectable libraries, in addition to soaking up a good suntan. The nature of bookselling and the quality and number of early books on the market has now altered very much, so the character of selections offered in penny boxes is no longer as rich and intriguing, but still it is a bibliophile with will of stone who can pass one without stopping.

The average penny box in London's Strand or Holywell Street in circa 1890 would contain a variety of odd volumes from sets (as they still do), finely bound works that had become shopworn, scrap albums with family or scenic photographs, bound volumes of Punch or early newspapers, forgotten theological works of the 1600's and 1700's, and maybe outdated editions of popular authors. But if one dug, and knew what to dig for—as few passersby did—he stood a chance of being rewarded for his efforts. Most bookshops were rather small and interior shelf space was limited. If a volume could not be sold for at least a shilling (in some cases two shillings—it varied with the dealer), it simply could not be given valuable room on a shelf. And an awful lot of desirable material fell in the under-one-shilling class, including items that bring as much as $50 today. The more common works of the Aldine Press, for example, brought from about eight to twelve shillings in good condition in 1890. But if the binding happened to be cracked or the pages stained or badly wormed, it was considered suitable only for the penny boxes, where a devotee of the Aldines would be glad to find it. Elzevir printings brought much less. The Pocket Classics for which $20 to $30 is obtained today realized no more than five or six shillings in the very neatest condition. If a flyleaf had departed, or some former owner had splashed ink on the title page, off to the penny boxes it went; and the dealer was happy to see it go, as there were plenty—too many—more where it came from. Almost every library sold in London in Victoria's time, even the shabbiest, overflowed with this sort of thing, and it was an uncommon bookseller who could not lay his hands upon carloads of Elzevirs and Aldines and Gryphii whenever the urge moved him.

Today, while the name "penny box" is retained out of tradition, the prices are usually in the 25¢ to 35¢ range. The books come from a wide range of sources. No bookseller purchases volumes for the purpose of placing them in penny boxes; it would simply be unprofitable. Penny box material is composed of left-overs from large collections or auction lots, which contained items that could be sold for healthier prices. A certain amount is dead stock, books that have been in the shop a very long time and show no signs of finding a buyer. But if a bookseller has better-grade dead stock, he will sell it en bloc to another dealer (at a much reduced figure) or consign it to an auction. Penny boxes have also been called Hotch-Potch boxes.

PEPYS LIBRARY. Though known to the modern public as a diarist, Samuel Pepys (1633-1703) was also a book collector of some standing. His library was bequeathed to Magdalene College, Cambridge, where it was set up in special rooms, in the original cases removed from Pepys' home. It is especially strong in European illuminated manuscripts and fine bindings, as well as English literature. Most of the rarities were collected later in life, after the period covered in the diary.

PERSIAN MINIATURES. The Persians made illuminated manuscripts, just as did the Europeans, and continued making them long after the art died in the west. The prime age of Persian manuscripts occurred from about the 15th to 17th centuries. In terms of ornament and precise attention to detail, they are superior to the best productions of the Italian and Flemish monasteries. Usually in small format and written on thin but tough paper, they contained long series of miniatures, drawn and colored with vigor and accuracy. The scenes and the people who inhabit them are naturally of eastern origin and provide a sharp contrast to European miniatures: a caliph surrounded by his wives, a rich sultan seated on a cushion, a team of elephants, tigers, workers dressed in loincloths and turbans, women with flowing robes and veiled faces. Gold gilt was used just as freely as in Europe. Detail and naturalism in Persian miniatures, even those of early date, are often striking, giving evidence of the long labors that must have been spent on them. They continued to be made until well into the 19th century. Though there is no organized antiquarian book trade in Persia (modern Iran), many fine illuminated manuscripts are found in the shops of antiques and art merchants, occasionally in the street bazaars.

PEWTER BINDING. One of the most curious and attractive sub-types of early bindings, Pewter bindings have a following among specialist collectors. Pewter bindings were most frequently made by the Dutch in the 17th and early 18th centuries. The usual procedure was to begin with velvet over wood, rather than leather. Sheets of lattice-work pewter were then nailed to both sides and sometimes even to the spine, covering almost the entire surface. In some cases clasps and even a chain (purely for ornamental purposes) were added. Or the pewter would be worked into a portrait decoration, or a cluster of cherubs. Often the pewter has been lost from one (or both) covers.

PFISTER, ALBRECHT. Pfister was an early printer of Bamberg, Germany, who published the first books in the German language: Johann von Tepl's *Ackermann aus Bohmen*, and Ulrich Boner's *Edelstein*, both in 1461. Vernacular printing at this early date was an ambitious step, as it meant the books could only be sold locally and not, like those in Latin, across Europe. It also shows that relatively large demand for books existed among the common classes almost at the outset of the incunabula period, as works aimed at scholars were strictly in Latin.

PHILLIPPS, SIR THOMAS. England's premier book collector of the 19th century, along with Lord Spencer, Phillipps has not received popular recognition because his library was neither kept intact or sold en bloc, as were almost all other famous collections, but dispersed piecemeal at distant intervals. He was born in 1792 and started collecting around the time of the Roxburghe sale in 1812. His primary concern at first was manuscripts, particularly those of early monastic origin. All the booksellers of the day were aware of his interests and constantly sent him offerings of material. His zeal was such that he sometimes purchased items of questionable nature from private parties, on the hope they might prove genuine. For nearly fifty years he was one of the most feared competitors at London sales and had an enviable record of obtaining lots in which he was interested. Most times he used an agent but occasionally bid in person. It was not unusual for him to buy half the choicest lots in a sale. Priced and named catalogues of his era show the name Phillipps occurring endlessly, far in excess of any other collector. He was the major purchaser at the Heber sales, the largest collection sold in his lifetime. Later in life he turned heavily to printed books, mainly incunabula, as fine manuscripts became difficult to locate. He died in 1872 at the age of 80. In the century that has followed numerous Phillipps sales have been held and a grand sum of money realized for his material, if one ever took the trouble to figure it up. Of late Phillipps has been held up as a sort of patron saint of collectors who don't know when to stop.

PICKERING, WILLIAM. An English publisher and bookseller of the 19th century, Pickering was the innovator of cloth for trade bindings in 1821. Oddly, this was the very first book he published. His fame extends far beyond this achievement, as he was a student of fine typography and responsible for a rebirth of interest in CASLON types. Following in the footsteps of Aldo Manutius, he published a number of series of scholarly editions in small formats, the most popular being his *Oxford Classics*. Pickering used the same mark as Aldus, a dolphin and anchor, and a Latin motto: "Aldi Discipulus Anglus" (Aldus' English disciple).

PIGSKIN. Unlike footballs, pigskin bindings are literally made from the skins of pigs. Seldom manufactured any longer but for period-style bindings on early printed books, they were quite the thing a few centuries ago. Exactly when the first pigskin bindings were made is another of those bibliophilic facts lost to posterity, but probably not long after the introduction of CODEX books. The toughest of all leathers, pigskin was a common covering for medieval manuscripts, which were costly and required special protection. During the later Middle Ages it was used virtually throughout Europe. However, it did not attain much popularity in Italy and Spain as in the gothic lands. For a time almost every book produced in Germany was bound in pigskin, and it remained in use long after the introduction of printing. Even in the 18th century, pigskin over wooden boards was the usual trade binding for folio books published in Germany and Austria. It was decorated in the same fashion as vellum, with the impression of heated metal tools (see BLINDSTAMPED). Some very decorative examples were produced, though it takes a sensitive heart to fully appreciate them as they are not as flashy as gilded morocco or calf.

There are several ways in which pigskin bindings can be recognized. For one thing they are always more or less rough to the touch, although centuries of handling has sometimes smoothed them. In addition, if one looks closely (depending on how much the surface has been rubbed) he will notice the pores of the skin from which the pig's bristles were extracted in preparing the leather. Pigskin is easily soiled, the grime wedging its way into the recessed areas of blindstamping. Saddlesoap may be used to clean it.

PIRATED EDITION. In the modern sense "pirated" means infringement of copyright; publishing a book (essay, poem, etc.) without permission of the copyright holder. Though piracy is rare today, it was rampant in the early days of publishing. Prior to the establishments of copyright laws some printers worked almost exclusively in pirated editions. Rivalries brought about piracy wars, in which two (or more) printers would pirate everything the other turned out. Recourse to law seldom brought satisfaction, as the skilled pirates took pains to disguise their efforts. The Elzevirs were pirated from left and right, sometimes with their imprint and sometimes not, but they also engaged in piracy themselves. There were few printers who considered themselves below such sport. For this reason it is well to take a long and searching look at the imprints in early books, though the vast majority are genuine.

PLACE NAMES. Those who exclusively collect modern books fail to realize the difficulty in dealing with early versions of place names. Most early printers Latinized everything that was not tied down: their names, the names of the towns where they worked, and so forth. Often this resulted in absurdity, when an obviously Anglo-Saxon name like John Smith became Johanni Smithius. However, there was a historical precedent for most Latinized place names, as the majority of principal European cities (and many small hamlets) had been named by the Romans in their days of conquest. Lyons, France, was known as Lugdunum for a number of centuries before it was called Lyons, and the same can be said of Neapolis (Naples), Hafnia (Copenhagen), Argentorati (Strasbourg), and many others. It was only when national languages took over that place names became the vernaculars we are familiar with today.

This results in wild fun, as many of the Latinized names bear no resemblance whatever to the modern counterpart, while others are dangerously easy to confuse. Lugdunum or Lugduni could well be taken to mean London, and in fact this was embarrassingly done by a west coast bookseller who shall be nameless, while the uninitiated might confound Argentorati with the present country of Argentina (which in early times was Patagonia). Then, there were different ways of Latinizing the same place name. Cologne appears variously as Colonia, Colonia Agrippina, Colonia Claudia, Colonia Ubiorum. But Colonia Munatiana refers to Basel! Most exasperating is that the average reference book, even the average good reference book, gives no help in these matters.

PLANTIN, CHRISTOPHE. An outstanding scholar-printer of the 16th century, Plantin was noted for the beauty of his type and the accuracy of his texts. He was born at Saint-Avertin, near Tours, France, in the springtime of 1520. At an early age his father fled with him to Lyons to avoid the bubonic plague, which took Christophe's mother. Soon afterward the father disappeared and was never heard from again. Christophe was sent as an apprentice to Robert Mace, a printer at Caen, and discovered he had no talent at the trade. In 1546, having established himself as a full-fledged printer, he came to Paris to seek his fortune, as was the custom of French printers. However, the climate in Paris soon proved undesirable for a man of letters, as Henri II issued a decree that heresy—including the publication of writings deemed heretical—would be treated as treason and the offenders executed. Consequently he moved on to Antwerp, Flanders, in 1549, where he rose to fame.

Upon Plantin's coming to Antwerp, the town boasted some 56 commercial printing offices, most of which were quite successful. For the first six years of his residence he operated a leather-goods shop on the outskirts of the city, feeling that the competition in the printing business was too overwhelming. Here he would cover boxes in leather, sell leather trinkets, and bind books. When the shop failed to provide sufficient income he returned to printing.

Having the ability to speak seven languages, Plantin was well equipped to handle any texts and translate when necessary. However, he left most of this work to a group of scholars whom he employed, as the task of type design, printing, and the management of the press occupied most of his time. His contemporaries, who marveled at his dedication, said he never slept. Though he made a considerable fortune, he poured most of it back into the business and lived simply. "I have no other treasures than assiduous work," he once wrote. He was particularly noted for his editions of the Bible in Hebrew and Dutch languages, as well as many versions of the Greek and Latin classics. His type was based on the models of ESTIENNE and TORY.

At one time, when Plantin was on a business mission to Paris, an order was issued against him by the Spanish officials at Antwerp, on the grounds that a tract he printed was offensive. Three of his assistants were arrested and all the stock and equipment of the shop auctioned off. However he managed to make good this loss and was allowed to continue in the city. Late in his life, in 1583, he was lured to Leyden to accept the role of University Printer, leaving the Antwerp office in trusted hands. He stayed two years, working with Louis ELZEVIR as his press supervisor, then returned to Antwerp and died in 1589. The House of Plantin then passed to his son-in-law, Jean Moretus, and the name changed to Plantin-Moretus. It continued to function until 1875, undoubtedly a record for the longevity of a publishing concern, and all this time it occupied the original house in which Plantin himself had lived and worked. The building is now operated as a public museum and contains equipment and furnishings of his time.

PLATES. Plates are those book illustrations (woodcut, engraved, photographic, or any other) which occupy a full page, as opposed to those scattered through the text, which are normally called cuts.

PLEYDENWURFF, WILHELM. Pleydenwurff was the German artist who collaborated with WOLGEMUT on the woodcuts for the NUREMBERG CHRONICLE of 1493.

POCKET EDITION. "Pocket edition" is a term popularly applied to early books of a small size, the exact dimensions of which have never been specified. Usually anything as small as 24mo qualifies (see BOOK SIZES). Many booksellers refrain from using it, as they feel (probably correctly) most customers are not impressed by small books unless tiny enough to qualify as miniature. It is of very early origin. In the incunabula era most volumes were large folios, difficult to carry about and just about impossible to take traveling. When smaller books (such as the Aldus classics) began to appear, they were hailed as volumes that could be placed in the pocket and thus taken anywhere. The modern "pocketbook" or paperback owes its ancestry to such men as Aldus, Gryphus, Elzevir and the rest. Many pocket editions, whose basic aim was to reduce the cost of printing materials, are in type so minute and crowded it cannot be easily read.

POINTS. Points are the characteristics common to any given edition of a book, which set it apart from other editions or impressions. As far as collectors are concerned, only the less obvious features deserve to be called points. Most valuable first editions are known by their points, which could be few or many, such things as dropped letters, misplaced page numerals, a leaf of addenda being common. Descriptions in booksellers' catalogues, especially when rare volumes are offered, usually are concerned with points. In the 20th century there has been such attention to points that the terms "point collecting" and "point maniac" have entered bibliophilic language.

POST-INCUNABULA. The meaning of this term has a knack of changing with the times. It was coined around 1900 and then was used to mean books printed immediately after the close of the incunabula period, from 1501 to about 1510. The collecting of post-incunabula became more popular as incunabula grew increasingly scarcer and too costly for many who admired early printing. Unlike some bibliophilic whims and fancies it has sound historical justification, as many of the 15th century printers remained active after 1500 (WYNKYN DeWORDE, for example, to 1534), a good share still using their original type. In studying incunabula these examples are of interest and often their prices (not in DeWorde's case, though) are modest enough for the collector of less robust pocket.

In a short time those who collected post-incunabula ventured beyond the arbitrary limit of 1510, pointing to the quantity of 15th century presses that survived longer. For some years the limit was 1520, but it has now been extended by some to 1530 and others as far as 1540. This is where the game must end, as there were apparently no incunabula printers who went beyond 1540. Many of the presses did, such as those of Schoeffer and Aldus, but under new direction. And, anyway, things begin getting silly at this point, as the average volume of 1540 bears only faint relationship to incunabula. Even German and English books, which remained gothic for so long, had changed materially in the four decades following the close of the 15th century. To glamorize ordinary 16th century books by the term post-incunabula is really meaningless.

PREFACE. A preface is a note by the author, sometimes running into many thousands of words, placed at the outset of a book, prior to the introduction. Its original intent was to provide the author a chance to get on his knees and beg forgiveness for the evil his book will do, and was called an apologia or apology. In modern times it has become a forum to pour out thanks to old friends who stood by with a whip and did not allow one to quit writing, even when that would have been the humane thing to do; wives and mistresses, who gave moral or other support; creditors who did not knock at crucial moments; museums and libraries which allowed the author to mess up their files; even to the manufacturer of the typewriter. One even bestowed his blessing on a certain brand of underwear, which did not bind or chafe while seated at the desk. These excesses occur because the preface is written after the book is completed, when the author's mind is finally free and he is drunk with joy. The preface is also a vehicle for explaining why the book was written, and once written why it should be read. But except in scholarly works prefaces are of little use as they are almost always ignored.

PRELIMINARY LEAVES. The preliminary leaves are the opening leaves of a book, prior to the body of the text. Usually consists of front free endleaf; additional blank; half-title; title page; preface; and introduction. There may also be a dedication leaf, foreword, leaf of acknowledgments, etc. If paginated, roman numerals are generally used. Even if not paginated, the preliminary leaves are often counted in on the pagination of the text, which begins not at one but a higher number.

PRESENTATION COPY. Unless some word to the contrary is given, the purchaser can expect "presentation copy" to mean a volume inscribed by the author as a gift. It may well be, however, that the recipient (if he can in fact be identified) was totally unknown to the author, and merely sent the copy as an autograph hound. Therefore there would be no association value, though the volume would almost surely be rated higher than a plain. The number of copies of any given book that might be so presented from the author is usually small, as publishers rarely allow an author more than a dozen complimentary copies.

PRESS BOOK. There are many definitions of the term "press book," but most generally it is taken to mean the production of a noted press, such as the Doves, Kelmscott, etc. Such works are valued far more for the fame of the press and its supposed excellence than any literary quality. Works of the early printers are less frequently referred to as press books.

PRESS FIGURES. In the 18th and 19th centuries it was common for a large printing job to be shared among many printers. Each would impress his mark on the quires he produced, to identify them as his, so he could receive proper pay for the work. They were generally on the verso of the leaves, where they cannot easily be confused with SIGNATURE letters. There is still much research to be done on the subject of press figures.

PRESS MARK. A press mark is a number, or combination of letters and numbers, assigned to a book in a library, which indicate its location. The term originates from the old practice of calling bookcases "presses." In books that are refugees from public libraries, the press mark (often called a shelf mark) may be written on a bookplate or other paper pasted to the inner front cover, while volumes from private libraries commonly show the press mark written in pencil on the front free endpaper. Press marks among private collectors are not unusual in Europe, though seldom seen in the

U.S. It is sometimes possible to trace a PROVENANCE via the press mark, but a good dose of fortitude is necessary.

PRINTERS' MARKS. In the pioneer days of typography, most printers used a special mark or symbol in their books as a trademark and protection against piracy. It is almost always found at the conclusion, on the colophon leaf, in incunabula. In books of the 16th and later centuries it may appear on the title page as well as at the rear. It was simply a woodcut device, like a small woodcut illustration, sometimes very plain (bearing only the initials of the printer), in other cases quite decorative. The mark of Fust and Schoeffer, Gutenberg's successors, comprised a pair of shields hung on a tree branch. The most famous mark, that of Caxton, has long puzzled bibliographers. It contains, in addition to his initials, two odd characters which may be numerals. Wynkyn DeWorde, who took over Caxton's business, used a variation of this mark and then later added his own name beneath. Many printers who were active a long time changed their marks a number of times; whether this was done to foil pirateers is difficult to say.

It sometimes happened that one printer, trading on the fame of another, would design a very similar mark, so that at first glance the two could not be distinguished. This was especially true where the mark consisted not of letters but some decorative form, such as an animal or mythological figure. The popularity of the Aldine editions resulted in a number of imitations of their anchor-and-dolphin, maybe substituting an aquatic looking griffin for a dolphin. The olive tree of Robert Estienne was also widely copied. Marks continue to be used by some printing houses, especially those who produce limited editions and other fine printing.

PRINTERS' WASTE. Printers' waste is printed matter which has gone wrong: sheets too heavily or lightly inked, folded, wrinkled, printed off-center, or with typographical or other errors. In incunabula days there was a good deal of this waste, as everything was done by hand—including inking—and mistakes and misjudgments came to even the greatest of the great. At the end of each day the sheets were normally collected and put aside, to be used eventually as stuffings in bindings, or sold to papermills for pulping. But 15th century waste is decidedly not waste today. By placing their fluffs in bindings, early printers preserved evidence of publications which would otherwise be unknown, sometimes enabling bibliographers to put together the history of a press. Modern waste will have no chance to excite historians of future centuries, as it is all pulped or destroyed. Even craft binders no longer make use of it.

PRIVATELY PRINTED. Privately printed books are usually produced at the expense of the author, sometimes in small quantity, for circulation among his friends (or to arouse jealousy in his enemies). It does not necessarily follow that private editions are limited, but generally they are, even if no LIMITATION NOTICE is given. Private printings are seldom actually printed by the author, as the name suggests, but executed by an ordinary commercial printer. The cause for private editions is most often rejection of the manuscript by publishers, or fear of rejection. From a financial standpoint they are rarely a success, as more are given away than sold, but some are carried out with no thought to monetary return. Today there are a number of printers who cater to those who wish to bring out private editions. Works carrying the imprint of vanity or subsidy publishers are not considered privately printed, even though the author pays most or all their cost. Most privately printed books are not registered for copyright.

PRIVATE PRESS. A private press is one which publishes only certain classes of books, often in LIMITED EDITIONS, rather than competing in general trade publishing. Beyond this the definition of what constitutes a private press is very muddy. One often pictures a dedicated lone craftsman, working away in some quiet cellar, turning out books for the pleasure they bring him. While a few private presses operate this way, such an image is more suitable to amateur presses, a totally different ball of wax. Actually some private presses are large operations, involving as much labor and employment as an ordinary commercial publishing house. Well, then, the distinction is that their books are not distributed through the market, is it not? Wrong again. While some private presses sell their works only by mail or subscription, others consign them to general distribution for sale in book-shops. Nor can the line be drawn on the grounds of superiority in materials or workmanship. The average private press book, in fact, could not be distinguished from one regularly published from outward appearance. What might seem the last hope of casting a barrier between them—the handling of freelance manuscripts—also fails, as some private presses do publish such manuscripts. Perhaps all that can safely be said is that private presses take more flings on manuscripts dealing with subjects of interest to the press owner. Many specialize in one field or other, only putting out books when something in their line is available, which could be once in a decade. It has also been said that private press owners are the ones without the ulcers, which may be another method of distinguishing. From their names it is impossible to tell a private from an unprivate press, as Joseph Blough Press could mean anything.

Over the years a number of private presses have gained a reputation for excellence, such as the Golden Cockerel of Robert Gibbings, the Kelms-cott of WILLIAM MORRIS, etc. Their aim has largely been to revive the ideals used to create fine books of the past, and employ craft products and techniques rather than commercial products or processes. To this end some have made, or commissioned, their own types, inks, paper, and bindings, all of which runs into far greater expense than a trade publisher could (or would want to) afford. As a result their books are only available at high prices, which tend to become higher with the passing years. The texts of the most respected private presses are generally items in the public domain, which have been published many times in the past and on which there is no copyright. The popular feeling is that classics merit such treatment more than the average run of books, so the majority of private presses sooner or later have a go at Chaucer, Tolstoy, Voltaire, and the Greeks and Romans (who would undoubtedly marvel to see their efforts so treated).

PRIVILEGE. From the 15th to 17th centuries, it was common for printers to petition the local (usually city) government for an exclusive patent or privilege to print certain books or classes of books. This would normally be done by a printer arriving in a city which had no established presses to discourage or at least reduce competition. Sometimes it carried absolute power and prohibited any other printer working in the city or district, as in the case of John deSpira, the first Venetian printer, who was granted a five-year monopoly in 1469 but did not live it out. The granting of such sweeping privileges was impractical after printing had become a booming trade, especially in the large towns, which would thus cut off a good source of commerce. So for the next 200 years privileges were given which extended only to restricted subject matter—as, for example, Bibles or works of a spiritual nature—or to specific texts. Prior to copyright laws a popular book could easily be pirated by other printers, so the securing of a privilege served a worthwhile purpose. The person or body granting the privilege will generally be recorded at the foot of the title (or, in incunabula, in the COLOPHON), as a privilege was of little use if not prominently displayed. There may be cases of false privileges—those claimed without authority, or attributed to fictitious persons—but so far as I know there has been no research in this area.

PRIZE BINDING. From the 16th to 18th centuries it was common for French universities to offer a sumptuously bound book as a prize for achievement among students. The work selected might be of a humanistic nature, often a product of one of the scholar-printers who were big names on campus. The binding would almost always be in calf or morocco, lavishly gilt, sometimes bearing the monogram of the school stamped in gilt on its covers.

PROOF READING. When books are first set in type, an impression (called a galley proof) is taken, then checked for mistakes before going further. The larger publishing houses employ fulltime proof readers. Yet many books as finally released contain minor goofs that slipped by the proof reader, or which occurred after the final proofs were read. Sometimes the presence or lack of a certain error can distinguish a first from a later impression, and thereby hangs many a tale.

PROVENANCE. The provenance of a book is the history of its ownership. Tracing a provenance is often comparable to drawing up an astrological chart or telling fortunes by tea leaves. In a few cases there will be clear documentation, but generally only if a book has gone from one celebrated library to another (then to another and another) in a succession of auction sales, where it can be checked against the sale catalogues. If a bookseller has, for instance, a volume he knows to have been in the Heber collection, his first step is to locate a copy of the Heber catalogue which gives the names of buyers. If he is lucky, the item was sold in a single lot, not as part of an anonymous bundle. If the buyer was Perkins, he then proceeds to the Perkins catalogue, and there may discover its next purchaser was Hoe, and so forth, working out a neat provenance. But things seldom go this smoothly. More often, the first catalogue will list a buyer whose name is unknown today and cannot be traced. Let us suppose a Mr. Greenside is listed as the successful bidder. He could have been a dealer acting as agent, or a non-dealer acting as agent, which means he did not himself take possession of the book. The next move is to check files of auction catalogues for a period of years after the sale, to discover if the library of a Mr. Greenside ever came up for sale. Most likely it did not; but, even if it did, it might have been included in miscellaneous properties, or disguised as "the property of a gentleman." If the book is something exceptional, there is a good possibility it passed through noted hands, so the bookseller then searches in the catalogues of major sales. But even if a fleeting glimpse is caught of it in 1904, the trail may then be lost until the present. Naturally it is only someone with a well-stocked reference collection who can engage in these antics. Most London dealers resort to the British Museum and those in New York to the New York Public Library, but unless an item has great sales potential the work involved is just not worth the effort.

Bookplates and ownership signatures or inscriptions provide prime evidence of provenance. The problem then is to fill in the gaps. Some medieval manuscripts carry notations of the librarian whose care they were in, then there is a blank period of 400 or 500 years which simply cannot be accounted for. If there is an inscription on the order of "Wyllyame Smythe his booke," this can be assumed to date from the later 16th or 17th centuries.

A distinguished provenance is all too often taken as assurance that the book is in good condition, or at least is not a made-up or otherwise faked copy, but this is fallacious reasoning, as famous libraries have been notorious for containing rank weeds. Although premiums are sometimes obtained on the strength of provenance, there are few clearly justifiable examples. It is equally true that a provenance might sound impressive without being so, if enough names can be strung together. The "Brown-Sherman-Colebart" copy might seem a blockbuster, more so if the names are printed in bold type, but the collector will have a hard time finding references to these supposed titans of the hobby. It is well to beware of all flat statements concerning provenance; they could be intended in all innocence but are easily misunderstood.

PUBLICATION. The omnibus word applied to everything printed, though certain classes of printed matter (such as broadside notices) should not qualify. Publication is generally defined as the sale of printed material, but even this, broad as it may be, is not broad enough. The catalogues issued by booksellers, for example, and normally distributed free, are not copyrighted, and yet deserve to be called publications. Copyright alone cannot be used as a gauge, as a large proportion of circulated material is never copyrighted.

PUBLISHER. Today the accepted understanding of publisher is one who buys literary work from an author, pays all costs of printing and promotion, and divides gross income with the author on a royalty basis.

In the manuscript era (prior to c. 1450) publishers fell into two groups. First there were princes and popes who acted as patrons of the arts, giving money to have transcribed copies made of the works of their favorites. Then there were the church officials who decided what would be written in the scriptoria of their monasteries, thus acting as publishers. But publishing in the modern sense did not begin until the printing press.

In the early years of typography, the printer acted as publisher. He would personally choose books to be printed and pay the expenses. To stay with a sure thing, already popular works were selected more often than new writings. By avoiding contemporary writings, printers cleverly saved themselves royalty costs as well, as Cicero and Pindar and St. Thomas Aquinas were well within public domain. Toward the close of the 15th century, however, the public began to grow weary of so many repeated editions, and original literature was published much more frequently.

Most incunabula printers sold directly from their offices, as can be proven by early woodcuts of printshops as well as circulars and pricelists which were issued. The team of Fust and Schoeffer at Mainz apparently maintained a rather large and noble retail shop; Plantin's, established at Antwerp in the 16th century, was one of the most famous in Europe. The practice continued even later, as the Elzevirs had shops to sell their own editions, but by the 18th century the separate trade of bookselling had become firmly established and most printers assigned their wares to booksellers. There was also foreign distribution of books in the incunabula era. The loose gatherings would be bundled together in barrels, to be sent into a neighboring country for sale. Many printers exchanged consignments and some even exchanged a portion of the printing work.

What arrangements were made with the poor authors is difficult to say. Surely the present standard of 10% from each copy sold had not evolved. Early authors of political pamphlets or books were doubtlessly paid nothing, as their aim was merely to circulate their opinion. Others probably received only as much as the printer-publisher would give at the outset. This was the case in 18th century England, only 200 years ago, so it cannot have been much better in earlier times.

PYNSON, RICHARD. An English incunabula printer, Pynson was the finest of a mediocre lot from a technical standpoint. He was a Frenchman but became a naturalized British subject and eventually gained the title of Royal Printer to Henry VIII. He started in work in 1490 and continued until his death 40 years later. Pynson is credited with introducing roman type to England, though his was a far cry from the humanistic scripts of Italy. He printed works on a wide variety of subjects, including Brant's *Ship of Fools*, Caxton's Chronicles, Sallust, Froissart. There was said to be an intense rivalry over the years between Pynson and Wynkyn DeWorde, Caxton's successor. The office of Pynson developed a number of early English printers, who started there as apprentices or helpers. Pynson published a total of more than 400 books.

QUARITCH, BERNARD. A German-born bibliographer and rare book dealer, Quaritch reigned as "king of the booksellers." His father fought at Waterloo against Napoleon. In Germany he studied Oriental languages and literature and worked for a time for a Berlin bookseller. In 1842, at the age of 23, he came to London and was employed by Henry Bohn, the leading book dealer of the day. Aside from a brief residence in Paris he remained with Bohn until 1847, compiling descriptions for the latter's catalogues. The Bohn catalogue of 1847, successor to the 1841 "Guinea Pig," is said to have largely been the work of Quaritch. In that year, however, he left Bohn to start his own trade, which occasioned the following anecdote. Telling Bohn of his plan, Bohn is said to have chided him for thinking he could compete in the field and remarked, "Don't you know I'm the leading bookseller in London?" To which Quaritch readily replied, "But I intend to be the leading bookseller in the world."

The promise was fulfilled, but the beginnings of Bernard Quaritch & Co. were humble. His first location was in Great Russell Street, as a supplier of new publications, but this was quickly abandoned in favor of a small shop in Castle Street, where he carried on a secondhand business. It was from Castle Street that the famous series of Quaritch catalogues began, continuing without interruption to the present. At first they were printed in large folio size, without wrappers, titled "Quaritch's Cheap Book Circular, Comprising (books) Selling For Cash at Very Reduced Prices." These early specimens are now extremely scarce and are usually only found in British libraries and in the possession of the Quaritch firm today, which maintains extensive historical files.

The Castle Street shop, though it did not witness the buying and selling of rarities on a grand scale, was still very much respected as a literary landmark, just as the homes where great poets and playwrights spent their early years. However, it has since been demolished. In 1860 Quaritch moved to much larger offices in Piccadilly Circus, where he rose to international fame. Attending most auction sales of the day, he purchased a large quantity of choice items, both for stock and on commission for his clients. Those who regularly bought from Quaritch included most of the major collectors of the Victorian age: Robert Hoe, James Lenox, Pierpont Morgan, Lord Carysfort, William Morris, the Earl of Crawford, Duke of Somerset, Henry Huth, the actress Ellen Terry, Oscar Wilde, and a very long list of others. He dealt not only in rare printed books, but manuscripts as well, regularly numbering among his stock dozens of illuminated prayer books and other texts from the Middle Ages, more than could be offered by any other bookseller. His stock of incunabula was generally in excess of a thousand specimens, his early Americana beyond belief by the standards of today. He and his son Alfred bought and sold no less than seven **different** copies of the Gutenberg Bible, a record that can never be approached.

The Quaritch catalogues were monuments of dedication and scholarship. They appeared at regular monthly intervals, though it was his habit to collect the parts (which would be on specialized subjects) from time to time and bind them with an index. He died in 1899, at the age of 80, having worked at his regular post to the end. After spending many years in Grafton Street the business was relocated in Golden Square, Lower John Street, in 1969.

QUARTER BOUND. A binding in which only the spine is of leather, the sides plain or covered boards, is referred to as quarter bound. If cloth or buckram has been used instead of leather, attention should be called to the fact.

QUARTO. A quarto is an intermediate size or format of books, between folio and octavo (see BOOK SIZES). A quarto is, however, a distinct shape, not merely a small folio or a large 8vo. To make a quarto, the original printing sheet is folded over twice. In effect, the second fold accomplishes the same thing as cutting a folio book in half, so that the resulting 4to (as quartos are called) comes off very nearly square. Think of it this way: a sheet of Crown paper measures around 20 by 15 inches when the printer pulls it from his storage rack. If he folds it once to make a folio format, he has a book 15 inches tall by 10 broad. But give it another fold for a 4to, and that 15 inch height is reduced to 7½ inches. So now, instead of being five inches taller than wide, it is only 2½ inches.

Well, you may argue, is that not so with each succeeding fold? No, it is not. The next fold, making an 8vo, results in a book about 7½ by 5 inches, still 2½ inches taller than wide, but the decreased size makes its appearance less squarish.

These are the common sizes in which quartos are discovered:
Foolscap, 8½ by 6½ inches.
Post, 9½ by 7½ inches.
Demy, 11 by 8½ inches.
Royal, 12 by 9½ inches.
Imperial, 15 by 11 inches (almost never used).

When references are found to "tall 4to's," Royal is usually meant. Many cataloguers hesitate to use the actual terms because they are unsure of themselves. When a book has been rebound several times, as is often so with early volumes, the size is apt to be much reduced, owing to the edges being trimmed down on each occasion.

QUIRE. A section of leaves of a book constructed from one large sheet fed into the press, then folded for binding, is a quire. When gathered for binding, the section may be sewn as a unit or broken up if it contains too many leaves (as in the case of pocket or miniature volumes); or it may be combined with another quire, if additional leaves are needed. The deciding factor is strictly the strength and appearance of the binding.

QUOTES. The "quote" is the backbone of the antiquarian book trade. Although offerings are usually made to collectors via a printed catalogue, sales among dealers are carried out by means of quotes. A quote is simply a description of an item for sale, with its price. It has become standard for quotes to be composed on 3×5 or 4×6 index cards, depending on length. The description is typed out as it would appear in a catalogue (in fact catalogue entries are often copied from quote slips). The dealer then rubber-stamps his name and address at the bottom, or the reverse side if too much space has been taken up. Most dealers prepare a quote card or slip for each item of value upon acquiring it, even if they have no immediate intention of sending out the slips; it is simply done to have a record of stock, which can be easily referred to, and from which quotes can be gathered. Some dealers who do not issue lists send these slips to customers for their perusal. With increasing specialization in the hobby, and the difficulty of gathering enough good items to fill a catalogue, the practice is becoming more popular.

To see the quote in action, let's take a hypothetical situation. We will say Dealer A has just purchased a miscellaneous library of 200 volumes. In checking through it he finds 12 worthwhile books on birds, 20 on geology, and 25 on airplanes. Referring to the trade yearbooks, he learns (if he does not already know) the names of dealers who specialize in these subjects. So he sends quotes on the bird books to dealers in natural history material, and so on, until all decent items in the library have been "quoted out." Of course, it may be that there are fifty dealers listed under one heading and only one or two under another; it is then at the discretion of the quoter whether he wishes to solicit them all and, if so, in what rotation. It is common for a 10% discount to be allowed on sales between dealers, as the buyer must add his margin of profit for re-sale. Also, Dealer A wants to get that 10% discount in return the next time he buys from Dealer B, so it is really a sort of mutual co-operation society. Some, however, flatly refuse to grant it and have unpleasant things said behind their backs. Some collectors, when they have books to dispose of, send out quote slips to dealers, hoping they will be mistaken for dealers. To add to the atmosphere they also offer a 10% discount, and sometimes go to the expense of having special stationery printed. Quotes also play a vital role in SEARCH SERVICES.

RAISED BANDS. The humps on the spines of books which have been bound by hand are known as raised bands. They are caused by the cords onto which the quires are sewn, and will be large or small according to the thickness of the cords. Though not originally devised as a means of ornament, raised bands are thought to contribute much to the charm of some early bindings, particularly those in calf or morocco. By dividing the spine into panels they gave rise to the mode of gilding the panels with repetitive tools, so that each panel matches the other (except for the panel or panels which receive lettering labels). In the 16th century single stamps were generally favored for this purpose, featuring such designs as acorns, diamonds, leaves, flowers, etc. But in the 17th century, when more luxurious gilding became the order of the day, spine panels were treated in elaborate fashion, with arabesques, fleur-de-lis, and a variety of geometrical patterns. Sometimes the bands themselves could also be gilded, but more often left plain. The number of bands depends upon the size of the book; an average folio will have four or five, an octavo three or four. Very small books may have only two, while tall folios sometimes seven, eight or more. As cloth bound books are not sewn on cords there are no raised bands, though sometimes they will be artificially created to give the binding a sophisticated appearance. It is possible to craft-bind a book without bands by simply sawing ridges in the leaves for the cords to be recessed, and nothing will show on the spine. But very few collectors favor this sort of binding.

RARITY. Rarity is a word that probably should, for the good of all concerned, be banished from the hobby, as it has resulted in misunderstanding, inflated values, and artificial markets. Of all collecting pursuits, books depend the least upon undiluted rarity, which is all to the good. A stamp or coin which is known in only a single specimen will automatically have value, but not so a book. There are many books printed in small editions, and others of which just a few copies survive, that do not stir the emotions of collectors. Bookmen do not count rarity as an end in itself, which is done to some extent in other hobbies. One will seldom hear a bibliophile remark, "I must try to purchase that book; only five copies are recorded." If the work does not fall within his area of interest, he will not give a second glance to it; if it does, the rarity is only a secondary consideration. There is a natural inclination among collectors to possess things the next collector does not, and here rarity—or ease of obtaining—enters the picture. But with books, it is more than uniqueness of a collection as a whole that appeals to the individual, owning many books that could not easily be brought together again, rather than any thrill over a particular item.

This lack of rarity worship is perhaps better shown by the favor in which rare books are held. The most valuable printed book, the Gutenberg Bible, exists in 47 copies, yet two million dollars is given for one. First editions of Dickens and Mark Twain are quite common, yet bring lofty sums. On the other hand, there are cases of editions limited to 10 or 12 copies which sell for less than $5. Yet rarity is a word that rears its head continually through the pages of catalogues, so the collector must learn to grapple with it.

When something is described as rare, it is very difficult to know just what is meant. How rare? How do you know? And why should I care? Some booksellers seem to define rarity as books they are not familiar with. Others will find a reference in some previous catalogue which stated the item rare and take this as their shield and guardian. The term is so relative that one can seldom fault its use. If ten copies exist, that might constitute rarity; but so could the existence of fifty. One can always argue that a book of which fifty copies exist is rarer than one of which a hundred exist, and this is the sort of logic one runs into. There is really no way of judging rarity. Just because something has not appeared in Book Auction Records in many years means little; of all the zillion of books that have been issued since 1450, there must be many that have missed long runs of B.A.R. and its sister publications. All boiled down, rarity maketh not the book, nor its price, and a collector who buys for rarity foremost is not among the higher order of mankind.

RASTELL, JOHN. An early English printer, Rastell lived and worked in London and is thought to have been married to Sir Thomas More's sister. He passed away in 1536, the business being carried on by his son, William. Neither father or son issued a great many publications, which was customary of the English trade in the first half of the 16th century: of all the workmen who appeared, only DeWorde and Pynson could be termed prolific. This was perhaps owing to the large capital needed to successfully operate as a publisher. The most famous of John Rastell's productions was an edition of the well known *Pastyme of People, or Cronycles of Englond*, which is extremely rare and was issued in facsimile reprint by Dibdin in 1811. Even as long ago as 1888 a copy brought £79 at auction. Rastell's mark comprised a complicated set of symbols, including male and female allegorical figures rising into a star-lit night and two heraldic shields. It bore his name in Latinized style, as Johannes Rastell.

RATDOLT, ERHARD. A printer active at Venice from 1476 to 1485, Ratdolt was a rival of Nicolas Jenson though not his equal as a craftsman. Ratdolt, like many of the early Italian printers, was a German, having migrated to Venice from the medieval city of Augsburg. His books were often embellished with the most attractive woodcuts, done not in the coarse manner of the north but after the fashion of the Renaissance. Many of his books are found in which the plates have been colored by a contemporary hand, sometimes expertly, giving the impression of being printed in colors, which they were not. He was the first printer to use modern title pages.

RAWLINSON, THOMAS. An English bibliophile (1681-1725), Rawlinson was one of the leading collectors of his time. The size of his library was enormous, close to 200,000, in an age when large private libraries were uncommon. It was probably not equal in content, however, to that of ROBERT HARLEY. Rawlinson began selling it four years prior to his death, in 1721. A total of 16 auctions were required to disperse it, not concluding until 1734.

READING COPY. A reading copy is defective in one way or another, not necessarily seriously, but not up to the standards of most collectors. The term originated more than a century ago, when rare books were a good deal more common than today. It was the practice of many wealthy collectors (like Heber) to purchase one copy of a book for display purposes and another for reading. While a fine binding and fresh condition were required for the display copy, the reading copy merely had to be complete enough to read and collectors were happy to find cheaper specimens for the purpose. If really a wreck, it is apt to be called a working copy, but only an occasional bookseller will resort to "poor copy," which in the trade is considered giving up the ship.

REBACKED. Spines take far more wear than the covers of books but unfortunately bookbindings cannot, like suits, be provided with two pairs of pants. So the situation is common where the sides of a fine morocco or calf binding are in good preservation, while the hinges and spines are worn away. Instead of completely rebinding the book, it is usual for merely a new spine and hinges to be added. If done by a competent workman (who will charge a competent price, as this job does not come cheap), the shade and texture of leather will be matched so perfectly that someone unfamiliar with the volume will not immediately notice where the old ends and the new begins. If it is simply a case of ailing hinges, and the spine is whole or nearly so, it can be carefully removed and pasted back over the new spine if the owner is really fond of it. If not, the binder can design a lettering piece that will be in harmony with the age of the binding. Rebacked books are not looked upon as lepers. Most collectors would rather have a sound, rebacked volume than one which is too frail to be safely handled.

REBINDS. In the Victorian age there was an equivalent of today's paperbacks. After a book had run its course in hard cover, the publisher would issue the identical edition (perhaps on cheaper paper) bound in wrappers. Some were sold on the market, in rail stations and the like, while others were bought by the thousand by rebind publishers who slapped cloth bindings on them. The average retail price of rebinds was, in America, 50¢, against an average of 75¢ to $1 for a regularly published book.

RE-CASED. A re-cased book is one that has been removed from, then returned to, its binding (not necessarily the original binding). The reason for removal might have been any of a number of considerations. The owner may have wished to have the leaves WASHED, which is still done. Some of the leaves may have required MOUNTING or FLOATING. The sewing could have become broken. Or—perish the thought—it may be a made-up or SOPHISTICATED copy. Usually the old binding is only salvaged if it happens to be of more than ordinary interest, as it's a delicate operation and not always entirely successful.

RECORDED. Usually the term recorded is used in the sense of "two copies recorded by Jones," meaning that the bibliography cited makes reference to that many specific copies (whose locations are normally given). It should not, but often is, taken by the collector to mean that only this number of copies exist, as precious few bibliographies are so exhaustive as to attempt listing every known specimen of a work.

RECTO. The recto is the upper side of a page or the right-hand page in a book. It occurs endlessly in COLLATIONS ("recto of A1 stained," "ink spots on recto of title," etc.). The opposite of recto is verso, meaning the reverse or left-hand side. This all works very neatly in bound books, but when applied to the autograph hobby it becomes troublesome, as it is very puzzling to say which is the front and back of a loose sheet of paper.

REDMAN, ROBERT. Redman was an English printer of the reign of Henry VIII. Though his books are not of extraordinary quality, Redman is of interest to historians because of his feud with the celebrated incunabula printer PYNSON. He moved into an office that had been used by Pynson, in Fleet Street, London, when the latter decided to shift his headquarters. It seems that Redman's intention was to carry on the business in such fashion that the public would mistake his press for Pynson's and thereby profit from the latter's fame. At once he adopted a mark that was nearly a duplicate of Pynson's, even so far as copying the initials R. P. On several occasions Pynson published denouncements of Redman's practices, but Redman seemed to thrive on the publicity. It is believed there was at one time a close connection between Pynson, Redman and Myddylton, another early printer. It is entirely possible Redman and Myddylton were apprentices in Pynson's shop. Myddylton eventually took over Redman's business. Redman died around 1540, having printed a large number of works, which nevertheless are rare and costly.

REJOINTED. When the joints of a leather binding have splits, and the binding has value, it is customary to have it rejointed. The leather which covers the joints—the point at which the binding boards are attached to the spine—receives heavy wear. Even fine leather regularly dressed will eventually give up the ghost if the volume is in constant use. A split develops, which may extend the whole length of the spine, but if the CORDS remain firm the binding is still said to be tight. Yet it is unsightly and invites complications. In rejointing, the binder finds a leather of the same texture and color (not easy when dealing with a 400-year-old binding), and works a thin strip of it along the joints, beneath the edges that have come free, and glues everything in place. Done by a talented hand rejointing is a thing of beauty; by an amateur it usually succeeds in ruining the binding. At first glance a rejointed may be mistaken for a REBACKED binding.

REMAINDER. A remainder is a book the publisher feels has sold as many copies at the published price as it will likely do, and sells the remaining stock (hence the name) to a distributor at a large reduction. It then appears in bookshops for a fraction of the original price, to the great annoyance of those who paid the full sum. But remaindering is a fact of life with most publishing houses, save those specializing in textbooks and scholarly works. Remainders often represent a considerable loss to the publisher, but at least salvage a portion of the cost, which books that forever sat in a warehouse would fail to do. Just because a book winds up remaindered should not be held against it, as many top sellers end their careers in such fashion. The practice probably dates to the incunabula period, on a much smaller scale than presently.

REMAINDER BINDING. When a publisher decides to sell a book as a REMAINDER to another publisher, a certain number of copies (or the entire stock) may be unbound, because of reluctance to invest in binding before gauging the work's appeal. The second publisher will then apply a cheaper binding than had appeared on copies which previously reached the market. Needless to say, collectors are not very interested in books in remainder bindings.

REMBOITAGE. Remboitage is the act of switching a binding from one book to another. It is almost unknown in America and uncommon in Britain, but on the continent (especially France, Switzerland, and Belgium) it has been done more often than one would care to think. The usual purpose is to unite a binding in good condition with a book in good condition, thus creating a marketable product from what were two beat-up volumes. Sometimes a "name" binding will be spirited off a dull book and replaced on one more apt to draw the interest of collectors. Spotting a good job of remboitage is not easy, if the fit is proper. The majority go undetected. Once in a while one notices a 19th century book in a 16th century binding, but this sort of tomfoolery is, luckily, dying off.

REPAIRS. The collector's concern with repairs falls into two categories: whether to have them performed, and recognizing (and evaluating) them on books he contemplates buying.

There are opposing schools of thought on the first matter. Some will not tamper with a badly damaged book, even if the most elementary repair work would greatly improve its appearance. They will not have a loose cover rejointed, a sagging label glued, or anything else done, period. The other extreme is the collector who is not content with a volume until he has sent it through a complete medical examination and ordered new endleaves, rebacking, mounting, etc., even if these steps were not really necessary. Somewhere between lies the ideal that should be aimed for, but finding it is not a matter of simple formula. Some repairs certainly seem required, even if one has no aesthetic revulsion at the sight of mangled books, as they serve to prolong life and enable the volumes to be used with less fear of accident.

If a page has been torn, without any loss of paper or ragging of edges (called a "clean tear") it can be mended to be unnoticeable. This is done by running a light coating of paste along each edge of the tear, covering with soft tissue paper and leaving between waxed paper to dry. The tissue will pick up some of the paste (hopefully not too much), but this is part of the strategy, as the adhering tissue particles help hide the tear. Superfluous tissue is torn away gently after the paste is dry. If the title or plates of illustrations in a rare book have become worn or frayed, with many small tears and injuries, it is better to have them MOUNTED if the reverse sides are blank, or else FLOATED. For possible remedies against FOXING, see entry on that subject. There is much more that can be done with the binding, and thankfully so, as it usually deteriorates faster than the contents. Both spine and joints can be replaced. In the case of a damaged spine, the original leather can (if desired) be glued back atop the new spine, which conceals the repair. Leather that has been stripped off a cover is more troublesome, but a good binder can make an acceptable job of it. If a binding is in really poor condition, it is well to think of putting it out of its misery and having a new one applied, for several reasons. The cost of a new binding (even if in full leather) is not much more than that of extensive repair work; and, more importantly, a new binding will be stronger and last longer. But a style in keeping with the age and decorum of the book ought to be selected.

Detecting repairs is almost a hobby in itself. In examining a binding one will, of course, look for REJOINTING and REBACKING, and strengthening of the inner hinges; the addition of a new PASTE DOWN, and new free endleaves. The leaves must be checked for mounting, floating, re-margining (all pretty obvious), and WASHING. This in addition to searching for defects that have not been repaired, which are apt to be far more numerous.

REPRINT. A re-issue of something that has been previously published is a reprint. If new material has been added, or old removed, it will be advertised as a "revised edition," or perhaps merely an "enlarged edition." Reprints are often brought out by a secondary publisher, who has acquired the rights, and issues an exact facsimile for those who missed (or couldn't afford) it the first time. A number of houses—such as A. L. Burt and Grosset & Dunlap—have done a major portion of their trade in reprints of works of other publishers, in less expensive editions. Sometimes the cost cut will involve deleting the illustrations and using a humbler grade of paper and binding. If the work has fallen into public domain (lived out its copyright, which in the U.S. is a maximum of 56 years), it is naturally attractive for a reprint publisher. Facsimile reprints of rare books and manuscripts are another story, and often end up as LIMITED EDITIONS with hefty pricetags, but collectors and librarians are very partial to them. The earliest reprints of this nature occurred in the 18th century, but the practice did not hit high gear until the mid 19th century. Today there are few famous rare books that have not been reprinted, the majority more than once. Success depends upon securing a good specimen for photographing, which is sometimes difficult.

REVIEW COPY. The history of review copies, and their method of distribution, has yet to be written. It has been a common procedure of publishers for about two centuries to send or give complimentary copies of new books to editors of magazines and journals. The hope is that the editor will give it over to a contributor to review (the more famous the better), or at least mention that it has been published. However, he is under no obligation to do so. Today many review copies are sent directly to columnists, even at their home addresses if they can be discovered, in the theory that the quickest way to an editor's heart is through his writers. Sometimes a single publication will receive many copies of the same book. The term "review copy"—suggesting a difference from ordinary trade copies—originated from the fact that review books often did not agree, in one way or other, with volumes supplied to shops. Sometimes reviewers were sent copies in wrappers, whereas the trade edition was bound; or differing in the color or style of cloth binding. Occasionally trial or proof copies were consigned for reviewers. The reason was speed; publishers wanted the reviews to appear as quickly as possible, so copies were distributed before the book had assumed its final form. This is rarely done any longer, as publication schedules are now arranged to allow for this sort of thing; also, most of the important reviews appear weekly rather than monthly, as in former days.

Until rather recently review copies were normally stamped to identify them as such, but no longer. Today a small ticket is loosely inserted, begging the recipient to review the book and stating the publication date (which is never mentioned in reviews). Once this has been removed, there is absolutely no difference between a review and trade copy. Usually the reviewer is allowed by the editor to keep the book; this constitutes the only payment among publications with slim budgets. One noted British author spent the last years of his life in near-poverty, living on the proceeds from the sale of books he had reviewed. Reviewers who constantly receive many books make an arrangement with a bookshop to buy them at a flat discount from the list price.

Regarding older review copies, which proclaim themselves as such (sometimes with the warning "not for sale," which makes one stifle a laugh), there is a difference of opinion on the part of collectors. Some think highly of them, as examples of the earliest state; others treat them as dregs. However, it would be unreasonable to demand review copies over normal first editions, as their bibliographical significance is questionable at best.

RINGS. At auction sales, a ring is a group of dealers who have made prior arrangements not to bid against each other, in order to keep prices down. Before the sale a list is drawn up of lots in which each is interested, then one man is designated to bid them in. Afterward, they gather again and divide up the spoils, thereby paying less than in open competition. Auction houses naturally discourage rings, as it results in less profit to them and their consigners. But little can be done, as the existence of a ring is almost impossible to detect. They are more likely to operate at less important sales, where the dealers are buying mostly for stock rather than on order.

RIVIERE, ROBERT. Riviere was a prominent English binder of the 19th century. Born in 1808, he set up shop at Bath in 1829 when only 21 years of age, opening a branch in London in 1840. The quality of his work and the many designs in which he and his workmen were adept brought him patronage from a long list of collectors. Most of his bindings were executed in morocco and follow traditional designs, as opposed to the experimental work carried out by some of his contemporaries. Christie-Miller and the Duke of Devonshire were two of the collectors who placed their books in his care. The firm was taken over by his son at his death in 1882, then eventually was incorporated with the antiquarian bookshop of George Bayntun.

ROBINSON'S OF PALL MALL. A British bookselling firm, Robinson's was founded by William H. Robinson at modest quarters in Nelson Street, Newcastle-upon-Tyne, in 1881. At first it dealt mainly in newly published books, but gradually expanded its antiquarian department. In 1930 this branch of the business had grown to such extent it was necessary to move the secondhand stock to large offices at 16 and 17 Pall Mall, in the heart of London. From then on the Newcastle address was used strictly for the sale of new works. Robinson's was a major buyer at the important sales of its time, providing stiff competition to the longer established London shops. Their catalogues were particularly attractive and distinctive, with all illustrations printed in sepia rather than glossy plates. Robinson's probably did more trade in Americana than any other foreign bookseller.

ROGERS, BRUCE. An American printer and type designer (1870-1957), Rogers was responsible for awakening interest in fine typography. He designed the limited editions of the Riverside Press at Cambridge, Massachusetts (run by Houghton Mifflin) from 1900 to 1911. In Britain he worked with Emery Walker, the former associate of Cobden-Sanderson, and served as advisor to Cambridge University Press. Later he was advisor to Harvard University Press and operated his own Rudge Press at Mount Vernon, New York. Rejecting the intricately detailed pages of WILLIAM MORRIS, he created books that were models of simplicity, stressing nothing more than the beauty of fluid lines. Yet there was great invention in his works, as he used type in ways it was never used before, achieving the most unusual and dramatic effects. A student of printing history, he made use of the principal methods of earlier days in designing his type. He designed the well-known Centaur type, used today for grand editions of the classics, but his greatest accomplishment was doubtlessly the Oxford Lectern Bible. Planned by Oxford University Press as a 20th century equivalent to Gutenberg, it was designed by Rogers in 1929 and published in 1935 at a retail price of 50 guineas (then about $250). The stock was calculated to last until 1985, but was exhausted two decade after publication.

ROMANESQUE MANUSCRIPTS. As many schools of art flourished during the era we call Romanesque, it is not easy to classify manuscripts into one camp or another. Generally the term is not applied to any manuscripts before the 11th century A.D., though Romanesque art dates somewhat prior to this time. The reason is that, basically, earlier manuscripts are more likely to fall into local schools, such as HIBERNO-SAXON, OTTONIAN, etc. In any event this is a problem best left to the advanced specialists.

The Romanesque manuscript school grew, like its predecessors, out of what had gone before, and borrowed elements from a number of sources. It was probably the least regional of manuscript styles, as it reached (simultaneously) into Italy, Greece, The Netherlands, and Britain, to name only a few points on the compass. In the 11th century its principal centers of development were at Arras and Mont Saint Michel. Romanesque were really the first of what we today think of as "illuminated manuscripts," as they made use of the devices that later characterized manuscripts of the dawning years of the Renaissance. The historiated and illuminated border was a feature, for example, as were large scenic illuminations. English examples are considered among the finest, though they were produced in small numbers and are now very scarce. Romanesque manuscripts tended to very large size, such as the great Lambeth and Winchester Bibles. Romanesque faded into gothic first in England and The Netherlands, then Germany and Italy. By the end of the 12th century it had ceased to exist as a separate school. Notable collections are at the British Museum, Bibliotheque Nationale, and Pierpont Morgan Library, though scattered examples are found virtually throughout the world.

ROOD, THEODORIC. An English incunabula printer, Rood was the first printer in Oxford. For many years there was a controversy over whether he or Caxton should be recognized as the first English printer, as a book of Rood's is dated 1468, almost a decade before Caxton came to Westminster. It was felt for a time that Rood might have slipped this work in without knowledge of the world, as an experiment in the new art of typography. It is now agreed the date represents an error for 1478, giving Caxton the nod by two years. Aside from this instance, the career of Rood was not very remarkable. He printed only a few works and has remained an obscure name despite much research.

ROSENBACH, DR. ABRAHAM S. W. Rosenbach was an American antiquarian bookseller (1876-1952). Along with this brother Philip he opened a combination book and antiques shop in Philadelphia in 1903, afterward adding a New York branch. Until 1911 he was relatively unknown, then rose to prominence at the ROBERT HOE sales. From roughly 1920 to his death he was the leading rare-book dealer in the U.S. Customers of the firm included virtually all distinguished collectors of the first half of the century: Pierpont Morgan, Henry Huntington, Owen Young, Henry Folger, Lessing Rosenwald, Arthur Houghton, Louis Silver. Huntington alone spent more than $4,000,000 with Rosenbach. His auction purchases included the Melk Abbey Gutenberg Bible (1926) and the Bay Psalm Book (1947). At the BRITWELL sales in London in the 1920's, the most important collection sold during his career, he bought a majority of the highest priced items. He contributed essays on book collecting to such publications as "The Saturday Evening Post," and wrote a number of books, including *Books and Bidders*, *The Unpublishable Memoirs*, etc. It was said that at the height of his fame, in the 1920's, the stock inventory of The Rosenbach Co. was of more value than Macy's Department Store. Late in life he sold a matchless collection of Shakespeare, which he had been accumulating many years, to the Swiss collector Martin Bodmer for $330,000, a small fraction of its present value. His own library of American children's books was presented to the Free Library of Philadelphia. Following the passing of Philip in 1953, the brothers' Philadelphia home was turned into a foundation and museum.

ROUGH GILT. Rough gilt edges are those that have been gilt without being trimmed. It has never been especially popular, as if represents contrasting styles. The lure of the untrimmed book is that of original state, just as it was bound, and as full a size as possible; whereas gilding can only be looked upon as ornament. Sometimes called "gilt on the rough."

ROXBURGHE, DUKE OF. The Duke of Roxburghe was an English collector. The sale of his library in London, 1812, is considered the spark that generated modern book collecting. The star item was the VALDARFER

BOCCACCIO, which reached £2,260. This sum was astronomical at the time, as nothing approaching it had ever been obtained for a book. Even in terms of modern money it is astounding, if one considers what inflation has done to the purchasing power of currency since 1812. But the impact of the Valdarfer Boccaccio rested mainly in the surprise factor. Paintings and objets d'art had brought good prices on the market, but book sales were never watched by the press as a source of headlines. It was thought that book collectors, unlike art addicts, were sensible people who would mind the value of a shilling, but the Roxburghe sale wiped away this illusion. Greater pandemonium reigned than at any previous auction of any sort. First reports of the price were greeted as a joke. To the average Englishman it was too much to believe: more than a lifetime's wages gone for a book! The sale naturally focused much attention on old and rare books and subsequent sales of importance were well publicized.

The purchaser was the Marquess of Blandford, fifth Duke of Marlborough. When sold from his library in 1819 it failed to realize even half what he had given—only £918 and fifteen shillings. The buyer was Lord Spencer, who had valiantly battled Blandford for it at the Roxburghe sale. This was ascribed to the fact that the book market in general was experiencing a slump. In any case the 1812 record remained for 72 years, during which time several dozen fine libraries, including the Heber, were sold. It was broken only in 1884 at the Syston Park sale, when a copy of the 1459 Fust and Schoeffer Psalter brought £4,950.

ROYAL BINDING. Like other bibliographical terms that promise much, "royal binding" is often misused. Most non-collectors would presume that a royal binding, like a royal footstool or a royal snuffbox, was made expressly for a particular monarch; at least for presentation, if not actually executed at his command. Sadly, this is not so. There are numerous bindings on the market today which bear the arms of kings, queens, popes, and others, yet were never owned or even seen by them. It was a common practice of many early binders to use the armorial bearing of their soverign as a decoration, either as a selling point or safeguard in the event their patriotism might be questioned. Apparently collectors favored this sort of decoration and the royal arms were sufficiently in the pubic domain to permit free use.

The actual number of books bound for royalty and owned by royalty (even if never read or handled) that have passed through the trade could almost fit on the head of a pin. It has been guessed that no book bound for Henry VIII has ever been sold, in spite of many English "royal" bindings of the era that have appeared for sale. Genuine pontifical bindings are probably equally scarce. As such books are not apt to be sold from their original resting places, there is hardly any way they can pass into private collections. Unless contrary evidence is present, royal bindings offered for sale should be looked upon merely as better or worse specimens of the binding craft, sans romanticism.

At one time unscrupulous persons would remove such decorations from the sides of bindings and inlay them on more worthy books. The results of these sorry efforts are still occasionally seen, but hopefully they would no longer fool anyone.

RUBBED. Rubbed is another in the myriad examples of soothing words used to express upsetting sentiments. In the sense of "binding rubbed," it means the leather has been badly scuffed, perhaps (in fact usually) with bits gouged out, leaving the impression that the rubbing has been done by a lovesick mountain goat. Rubbed marks cannot, alas, be erased through oiling, but a well-oiled binding is slightly more apt to resist injury. "Badly rubbed" means prepare for the worst (you will not be disappointed).

RUBRICATOR, RUBRICATED. A rubricator was originally a monastic scribe who added artistic touches to manuscripts, though there were lay rubricators in the medieval manuscript industry as well. In their quest to make their books resemble manuscripts, incunabula printers introduced many of the features common to manuscripts. After the text was printed it was usual for the volume to be placed in the hands of a rubricator, who would go through it with pen and ink, adding headlines, paragraph marks, and flourishes at the beginning of sentences. Sometimes these were done in a solid color, on other occasions a combination of red and green, red and yellow, or (most often) red and blue. A book containing such work is called rubricated. The Germans, Austrians and Swiss were the masters of rubrication, though some fine specimens were turned out in Italy. The practice continued in Germany until about 1510, long after dying out in most other nations. Rubrications were occasionally added later, sometimes much later, than the date of publication, but in most cases are contemporary. They add much to the beauty of incunables.

RUPPELL, BERTOLD. Ruppell was the first printer in Basel in about 1467. He had been employed in the Mainz shop of Gutenberg in the early 1450's and was an established craftsman by the time he came to Basel, relying upon the methods and style he had learned at Gutenberg's hands. His first book at Basel was the EDITIO PRINCEPS of St. Gregory's *Moralia super Job*. Ruppell was also one of the earliest printers to issue a list or catalogue of his works. The number of books he issued was not nearly so numerous as many of his contemporaries, as he was already advanced in age by the time he came to prominence. The name is also spelled Ruppel.

RYLANDS, JOHN. The great rare-book library at Manchester, England bearing the name of John Rylands was formed by Lord Spencer. John Rylands was an English businessman of the Victorian era. When he passed away, his widow set out to build him a lasting memorial. In 1892 she succeeded in purchasing the Spencer collection at Althorp, then the largest and most valuable in Britain, which was brought to Manchester and opened to the public as the John Rylands Library. The transaction was negotiated through Henry Sotheran, the London dealer, and despite all that has passed since this remains the largest sale of rare books in history, in size if not price.

Although acquisitions have since been made, the library as it exists now is not too far from the way Lord Spencer left it, at least regarding the major rarities. It makes no attempt to keep up with the times but retains the flavor of an old private collection. Even in its architecture, strictly gothic and monastic, it appears to belong to another world, saved from the path of time. In total holdings it is small, but almost all its material is of vast significance. The Spencer collection was largely assembled when opportunities for fine acquisitions were frequent. It could not be duplicated today, not even a third of it, had someone the wealth of the world at his fingertips and the luck of the gods smiling upon him. As the Phillipps, Huth, Britwell, Heber, and Syston Park collections were all sold by auction, it is the **only** outstanding British library of the 19th century to be preserved intact.

The collection of English incunabula at the John Rylands Library is perhaps its most outstanding department. Its Caxtons are second only to the British Museum, and its showings of the works of DeWorde, Pynson, and the others are no less remarkable. Lord Spencer also collected foreign books, but of course their showing is not so comprehensive. There are numerous very early manuscripts, including specimens of Babylonian seals and CUNEIFORM writing, PAPYRUS, and early Christian texts, along with many illuminated manuscripts. It has for many years published a journal, containing scholarly articles that are eagerly digested by advanced collectors and librarians, as well as many books, catalogues, guides, and so forth, all of which would be required reading if there were a school for bibliophiles.

SABIN, JOSEPH. An English bookseller (1821-1881), Sabin emigrated to the U.S. at the age of 27 and established himself as the principal American dealer and auctioneer of books and manuscripts. His specialty was Americana, on which he came to be regarded as one of the leading authorities in the field. The final years of his life were occupied in editing his monumental reference work, *Dictionary of Books Relating to America*, which he did not live to complete.

SAINTE-MAURE, LOUIS De. A French 16th century collector, Sainte-Maure followed the lead of GROLIER and employed special workmen to design and execute his bindings, which were considered among the finest ever produced and far scarcer than Grolier's. They are generally tooled in geometrical or architectural motifs.

SCHOOLMASTER OF ST. ALBANS. The schoolmaster was an anonymous English incunabula printer, noted for his edition of *The Boke of Hawking, Hunting and Heraldry*. He started in 1479 or 1480, making him third in chronological order among the English printers behind CAXTON and ROOD. He retired around 1486 and was deceased by 1497, as WYNKYN DeWORDE published a book in that year in which mercy is asked on his soul. Nothing has ever been learned about him and his name remains a mystery, though many guesses have been made. He had probably seen examples of the works of Caxton's press and determined to print his own, for local circulation (Caxton's Westminster and St. Albans were then two different worlds). However, he was undoubtedly faced with financial difficulties and managed to turn out only a small amount of work.

SCHOEFFER, PETER. The longest active and considered by some the foremost genius of the incunabula printers, Schoeffer was deeply involved in the invention of printing but his precise role is unknown. He was from Gernsheim, Germany. In the 1440's he was working as a manuscript rubricator in Paris, when it is supposed Gutenberg was hard at work developing his press. For some reason Schoeffer came to Gutenberg's city of Mainz and was hired by him. Historians believe this may have occurred between

1450 and 1452, which is educated guesswork. But Schoeffer definitely was employed by Gutenberg and his occupation was probably as type designer or pressman. It is obvious he must have done more than sweep down the office, as this duty would not have required someone of his training and abilities. Some have gone so far as to bestow the title of first printer upon Schoeffer. They reason thus: Gutenberg had spent most of his efforts and money on the technical details of constructing a press, but his background included nothing that would qualify him as a designer of type. When all the preliminary details had been finished, they contend, he called in Schoeffer to design and cut the type, and do the printing as well. Without the brilliance of Schoeffer, they conclude, Gutenberg would have had nothing but a useless hunk of machinery. But there is no way, at least with present evidence, of proving or disproving this.

Schoeffer married the daughter of Johann Fust, who had financed Gutenberg's work. In 1455 Fust (no doubt with some prodding from Schoeffer) foreclosed on Gutenberg and took over the business. From then until Fust's death in 1466 the two operated a partnership, though Fust had no knowledge of books or printing and merely handled the business end of the venture. The cutoff date of 1455 solves very few bibliographical problems and creates many more. First there is the question of the 42-line or Gutenberg Bible. Does the fact that the suit was not brought until 1455 mean that the Bible was by then completed? Or that the suit was intended to place the business in Fust and Schoeffer's hands before its completion, so they could claim full credit for its production? Of the books issued by Fust and Schoeffer after the suit, there is no determining what part, if any, Gutenberg had played in them. Their extraordinary technical quality is attributed by some to the hand of Gutenberg. Others feel that Schoeffer had all along been the master of the Gutenberg press.

But no matter, Schoeffer was without doubt one of the great typographical geniuses. In 1457 he and Fust published a Psalter, still regarded as the most attractive book created with type. It was the first dated book, the first book with a COLOPHON, and the first to be printed in more than a single color. It is also considerably rarer than the 42-line Bible. In 1459 a second edition of this Psalter appeared, differing from the 1457 in the number of prayers which follow the Psalms. The Fust and Schoeffer enterprise was extensive for its day. The press offered a variety of titles, all in Latin, and had its pricelists and such for the use of interested parties. After 1466 Schoeffer, who had gained wealth and a fine reputation throughout the continent, continued to print on his own, in an office bustling with apprentices, journeymen, and other workers. The Schoeffer imprint was passed down to a son and then a grandson, the quality of its books remaining high. Schoeffer's type was a stylized gothic, one of the most handsome of its kind. He died in 1502, aged about 80.

SCOTTO, OTTAVIANO. An Italian incunabula printer, Scotto was one of the most active in southern Europe in the 15th century. His empire was nearly comparable to that of Nuremberg's KOBERGER. He began in 1480 at Venice, using a variety of semi-gothic and roman letters. Scotto, or Scotus as he was called, was neither an innovator nor a particularly skilled craftsman, but is noteworthy for the quantity of titles he put before the public and the impetus he gave to Italian publishing. His books were fashioned, in style if not type, after those of JENSON, but lacked the grandeur of the latter's works. It is probable his books were printed in large editions and aimed more or less at the common classes who could afford no better, as they were seldom illustrated or decorated in any manner, and were bound simply. Today they constitute one of the cheapest classes of incunabula, though there are some rarities over which collectors bitterly wrestle. The House of Scotus continued in operation at Venice long into the 16th century, the only essential difference in its books being a total adoption of roman characters. The name is spelled half a dozen ways.

SCRAP PAPER. The uses of scrap paper have played an important part in the history of books, in some cases preserving fragments of books and pamphlets that otherwise would have perished, in others giving evidence of the priority of one edition over another. Scrap paper was used in binding books from a very early time, probably from the beginning of CODEX bindings in the 3rd or 4th century A.D. These books, it is true, were generally covered in wood, but old paper (actually VELLUM) would be used to form the inner hinges. The CORDS on which they were sewn were occasionally fashioned of vellum scraps, rolled thin in the shape of twine. Scrap vellum—and scrap PAPYRUS, too—was sought-after in the Roman Empire for many industrial uses and continually bought and sold by secondhand dealers. Much of it must have been outdated legal documents, letters, school exercises and whatever else could be scrounged up. As the Christian monasteries flourished in the Middle Ages, their scriptoriums produced their own scrap in the form of writing sheets upon which a monk had overturned the inkwell. These were then given over to the monastic bindery. Lay binders bought scrap vellum from dealers.

The introduction of printing in the 15th century brought about a need for far greater supplies of scrap paper. As many printers did their own binding (not by their own hands, but employed workers), they simply used their own waste papers, collected from the shop floor. As many bindings were no longer made of wood, but vellum or calf stiffened with paper, numerous fragments of printing found their way into incunabula and later bindings. Bibliographers investigate all fragments rescued from bindings. It is always possible that, by matching them against the published version (if a specimen exists), some discrepancies will be noticed; and further possible that these will consist not only of an inconsequential mistake, but an instance of change of thought, or fear of censorship.

This explains things for printer-binders, but during the incunabula years the size of editions grew so much that independent binders ended up doing most of the labor. The majority of incunables were bought in loose leaves from the printer, too, so no binding was applied until the book had long left his sight. Consequently the independent binder had great need for waste paper. He could, of course, purchase fresh papers from the mills, but this was too costly. Instead, binders purchased old books, sometimes even illustrated manuscripts, and cut them up. But fate is fickle, and it has frequently happened that the scraps considered worthless have turned out to be more valuable and desirable than the books they were used to bind.

The things which have been pulled from bindings are beyond imagination. Scholars have given up wondering how they got there. A number of leaves from the CONSTANCE MISSAL were so found, now worth a minimum of $10,000 each. So was a collection of early Philadelphia Post Office documents, in the holograph of Franklin.

One more item is worth noting about scrap paper, though in a different way. In the early years of printing, paper was worth a good deal more than today. Binders had agreements with papermills to supply them with scrap for pulping, most of which was obtained by trimming the edges of books far beyond the point of decency.

SCRIPTORIA (or SCRIPTORIUM). A scriptorium was a room set apart in medieval monasteries for the transcribing of books. It was common in the period from about 700 A.D. to several decades after the development of printing for monasteries to operate immense scriptoriums; ealier ones, from the declining years of Rome, were a good deal more modest. Usually the manuscripts produced were not all intended for its own use, but traded amongst monasteries to obtain copies of needed texts. This accounts for Italian manuscripts being bound at German monasteries and vice-versa.

Most scriptoriums operated only by day; artificial light was prohibited. Each monk sat at his easel, with quill pen, bowl of ink, and scraping knife for corrections. At the head of the room a monk would read aloud the text to be transcribed. The scribes were bound by a rule of silence, to prevent someone copying down chance remarks by accident. This went on day after day, year after year, century after century. The work was never finished. When one text was completed another was immediately begun. Writing books was as common a feature of monastic life as eating or chanting hymns. Probably as many as 90% of all illuminated manuscripts were the products of church scribes.

SCRIPTS. See CALLIGRAPHY.

SCROLL. For many centuries prior to the adoption of the present CODEX manner of making books, books were written on scrolls. The Egyptians and Hebrews were the first to use the scrollbook, possibly as long ago as 5,000 years. Prior to this, books had been transcribed on slate, baked clay, tiles, slabs of stone, wax, and other devices. It has traditionally been presumed that PAPYRUS must have come before VELLUM in the history of scrolls, but this is now questioned, and they are judged to be of more or less equal antiquity. The real difference is that vellum was used more extensively by the Hebrew peoples, while the Egyptians preferred their native product, papyrus. At first these manuscript scrolls were quite short, as literature in its modern sense had not emerged and most were merely records of proceedings or legal transactions. A section would be written, then the material rolled to expose the next section, and then the next, until conclusion. The writing was not, as popularly supposed, continuous down the roll; scrolls were read horizontally, not vertically. When one finished reading a scroll, it was necessary to re-wind it, much like a tape recording, to arrive back at the beginning. The tool used to write upon scrolls, whether vellum or papyrus, was usually a metal stylus. The goose quill was not introduced until late in the Roman Empire, or possibly later, depending on which reference book one consults. The ink was greasy and viscous by our standards.

During the years of Greece's glory, scrollbooks began to assume slightly silly dimensions. From humble origins they had grown larger and larger, as the works of classical authors became longer and longer. It was not uncommon for a scroll to measure more than twenty feet when fully extended. Finally, when it was decided something must be done to prevent books becoming too cumbersome to handle, the modern system of division into volumes was devised. For storage, the volumes were tied together with a length of twine and placed in an earthen jar. Large libraries, such as the Alexandrian in Egypt, contained many thousands of these jars, all arranged on shelves. The vast majority of scrollbooks were plain, undecorated texts, but from time to time some illumination was attempted. Scrollbooks ceased to be made in the early Christian period, around the 3rd or 4th century A.D., when it was decided to fold the leaves and bind them between covers.

SEARCH SERVICE. It very seldom happens that a collector, particularly if his tastes are specialized, can walk into a secondhand bookshop and find the titles he needs from its stock. Also, there are many collectors who do not live within hundreds of miles of a well-stocked shop. Therefore, a number of dealers operate what is called a search service, which works in the following manner: The customer presents the title and author (along with publisher and date of issue, if known) of a book to the dealer. The dealer then advertises for it in one of the trade journals, welcoming offerings from other dealers who might have a copy. At this point nothing is said about price unless the customer himself has set a limit. A dealer who has the book sends a QUOTE on it, stating his price. The first dealer then quotes it to his customer, usually at a flat 100% mark-up, and the customer is free to accept or reject. If he accepts, the dealer orders it from the quoter and everyone comes away happy: the two dealers have made a sale and the collector has obtained the book he wanted, which years of personal search might not have flushed out.

If 100% seems a harsh mark-up, one must realize that it is not all profit. First, there is the expense of advertising for the item, then the postage which the first dealer must pay the second, and sometimes incidental expenses besides. On a book whose price to the customer ends up being $10, the dealer running the search has cleared $4 or less. Of course, the profit margin is better on items of higher price. It would not pay to advertise for a single book, unless it were a rather costly one, so most search services collect at least a dozen titles before advertising. Some of the larger services advertise for more than a hundred each week. There is a growing trend today for search services to make a token charge, usually 25¢ or 50¢, to pay the cost of advertising, even if the search ends in failure.

SECONDARY BINDING. Secondary bindings arise from the economics of the publishing business. All publishing projects represent a risk, but there is no point risking more investment than necessary. So when a new book is printed, it is customary (almost universal in the 19th century) to bind only a small quantity, at least until the reviews and initial reaction are in. Subsequent bindings are usually identical, but not always. When they differ, a secondary binding has been born. Collectors will naturally prefer the original.

SECONDHAND. "Secondhand" has survived for at least two centuries as the favorite trade term for old, rare, antiquaian, used or what-have-you books. Under this heading all are reduced to equals, whether Gutenberg Bibles or yesterday's mystery thriller, as all have previous ownership in common. The word is of course euphemistic, as most secondhand volumes have passed through far more than a single pair of hands. Secondhand books are not necessarily out of print. Sometimes a bookseller will have both a secondhand and a new copy of the same work to offer. So long as the title is still available from the publisher, used copies bring quite a bit less than new; afterward it's anybody's ballgame. "Good secondhand condition" means the volume has all the signs of wear and tear one would normally anticipate in a used book, but nothing overly hideous.

SENEFELDER, ALOYS (or ALOIS). Senefelder was a German artist and playwright (1771-1834). In 1796 he was trying to discover a cheap, easy way of duplicating his plays when he invented a process that eventually became LITHOGRAPHY. This turned his attention to the craft of printing, and before long he became one of the most respected printers and book designers of his era. In 1808 he printed the Prayer Book of Maximilian I from the original of 1575, with DURER'S marginal illustrations rendered on stone and reproduced by lithography. Following Senefelder's examples, publishers used the lithographic process for important facsimiles. His famous book on the subject, *Complete Course of Lithography*, appeared first at Munich in 1818 and was translated and reprinted many times.

SHAVED. It is common, when binding a book, for the binder to trim its edges slightly with his knife, to square them off and remove any stains or other surface blemish. Sometimes this operation is performed on a book which has very small margins, so the text (or headlines, or side notes, or page numerals) is touched. Generally, shaved books are created by degrees: they have been bound a number of times and lost that fraction of an inch on each occasion, until finally paydirt was hit. This is why shaving is seen far more in books of the 16th and 17th centuries than those of later date. Occasionally the fault is more than a shave: the entire headlines, or letters of text have vanished. In these cases the book, even if rare, is seldom prized by collectors and can only command a small share of the usual price.

One may well ask: why does it happen? Do binders not have eyes? Fortunately it is no longer a common accident, but, to judge from examples, binders of the 18th and 19th centuries had a merry time slicing up their victims. Perhaps at one time it was considered more desirable to have volumes with neat instead of ragged edges, even if it meant getting a shave in the bargain. When really serious it is called cropping.

SHORT COPY. "Short copy" is one of the numerous terms to denote books that have been seriously cut down by the binder, resulting in their being somewhat smaller in size than normal copies. At the very worst a short copy might have its margins entirely trimmed away, but in no case should any text, side notes or page numerals be touched, unless this is mentioned in the catalogue. If not, grounds for return exist, and the bookseller merits a slap on the backstrip. As some books, particularly in the early days of printing, were issued with extremely large margins, a short copy could be considerably shorter than standard, sometimes two inches or more in a folio volume. Short copies invariably sell at a discount, though the rate of discount lessens in the case of very rare items.

SHORT TITLE. In bibliographies, especially catalogues, the full title of a work is not always given, if it can be easily identified by a shortened version. This is especially true of early books, whose titles were not very distinct from other matter which appeared on the title page and dragged on, sometimes, for hundreds of words.

SHOULDER NOTES. Shoulder notes are SIDE NOTES that are printed toward the top of the page; but in common use they are still called side notes. They suffer, as do all forms of marginalia, from shaving or cropping when the binder cuts too close.

SIDE NOTES. Any matter printed outside the main body of text—such as a running commentary or reference guides—and inserted at the side rather than the foot is a side note. Properly speaking it should refer only to the brief notes inserted by an editor to help the reader sort through the subjects under discussion, but it has taken on an omnibus meaning.

SIGNED BINDING. There are very few examples of medieval signed bindings, and hence we know the names of only a handful of medieval binders. As most books prior to c. 1450 were bound in monasteries, they bear no identification of craftsmen, as the monks seldom felt a need to publicize themselves. Beginning with the use of blindstamped calf and pigskin on printed books, binders would arrange the design so that a pair of blank panels existed on one or both covers, for recording their name and the year of execution. Most such bindings were, however, left blank; others carry only initials plus the date. This has led some authorities to contend that the initials might sometimes, or frequently, be those of the owner rather than the binder, which seems reasonable. But in any event the tracing of unidentified initials at a distance of 450 or more years is no easy task, and very little headway has been made. As far as the gilded bindings of a slightly later era are concerned, the majority are totally unsigned, attributions being strictly on the basis of style or country of origin. Why early binders, especially those of more than usual talent, did not wish to identify themselves is an unanswered question. It was not until the 18th century that binders commonly inserted small printed tickets bearing their names (and sometimes address) on the inside front or rear cover of a custom binding. Later practice has been to stamp the name in ink or gilt, in tiny letters.

SILK-SCREEN PRINTING. Also called Serigraphy, silk-screen printing is a process of stencil printing wherein the stencil is attached to a fine, thin screen of silk mounted on a stretcher like artists' canvas. Ink is worked on the screen and finds its way through open areas to the paper below. It has been popular in the U.S. for book printing, as well as posters, prints, advertisements, calendars, and other work. Various grades of quality can be attained.

SINGLETON. The majority of leaves in a book are connected (the collector's term is CONJUGATE) to another, forming pairs. This results from their being printed on large sheets that are folded down for binding. A singleton is a leaf which is not attached to a connecting leaf, merely sewn in by itself. Unless one knows for sure the book is complete, he ought to look with suspicion on a singleton, as it may indicate a missing leaf. The PRELIMINARY LEAVES will sometimes compose a singleton or two, as they are usually printed last and do not follow the format of the book; but this should not be assumed.

SIZE. A chemical solution applied to paper during its manufacture, which is removed if the book is WASHED and should be replaced by a "size bath." This is far beyond the capability of an amateur and should only be attempted by a qualified expert. Early size preparations were made by boiling ground leather (considered the finest), or fish cartilage.

SKOT, JOHN. Skot was a British printer of the first half of the 16th century. Although he is known to have worked at least from 1521 to 1537, few of his publications are recorded. It is believed the majority must have been issued in small quantities and have totally perished. Yet there is the possibility that much of his work may have been done for other printers and bears their names instead of his own. This was not an uncommon practice. Some printers, to judge from the scanty evidence available, seem to have existed merely to receive overflow jobs from the larger houses, which gladly farmed them out. A good deal of Skot's printings were probably in the form of pamphlets or tracts. One, called "The Rosary," is dated 1537 and can be found in the John Rylands Library at Manchester, England. His mark consisted of a headpiece from an armor suit, with two griffins and a variation of the orb and cross symbol. The name is often spelled Scott.

SLIP. A slip is a piece of printed paper inserted in a volume by the publisher, either loose or pasted down. It could serve any of a number of purposes, as an ERRATA slip, CANCEL, advertisement, etc. When CALLED FOR in a particular edition, its lack will hurt the value, but unless one is familiar with the work he will not be looking for it.

SLOANE, SIR HANS. A British physician, Sloane died in 1753. His library of 50,000 printed books and 2,000 manuscripts was one of the largest and finest of its time. It was purchased by the British government and in 1759 became part of the BRITISH MUSEUM.

SOPHISTICATED COPY. "Sophisticated copy" is a misleading term, which succeeds in fooling nine out of ten beginners because it sounds like something good but is not. "Oh, a **sophisticated** copy," they remark, as if the science of bibliography provided for an opposite—a slum or simple copy. This is not the case; the only sophistication of a sophisticated copy is in the name. It means "made-up." Someone has taken an imperfect copy and completed (or at least improved) it by the addition of leaves from another. Sophisticating was common in the 19th century. It is still done today but not frequently, as collectors are content to settle for replacing missing leaves with loosely inserted photostatic copies.

In cases where two or more editions of a book were virtually identical excluding title page information, sophisticated copies are dangerous because they may include leaves from another impression. Sophisticated copies are more easily detected if the edges have not been trimmed in rebinding, as the inserts will usually be a fraction smaller or larger.

SORG, ANTON. An incunabula printer, Sorg was a pupil of GUNTHER ZAINER at the monastery of Saints Ulric and Afra in Augsburg, he began printing on his own at the monastery in 1475. He became one of the most prominent printers in Germany, issuing finely illustrated books and works in the German language rather than exclusively Latin. In the last decade of his life, up to 1493, he turned out a number of valuable and ambitious works on travel, exploration, and history. Sorg printed the tales of Marco Polo, the adventures of John deMandeville, and Ulrich von Richental's history of the Council of Constance.

SOTHEBY & CO.. Sotheby & Co. are London auctioneers of books and artworks. The firm is well over two centuries old, beginning with Samuel Baker in 1744. It subsequently became Baker, Leigh & Sotheby. From 1861 to 1924 it was called Sotheby, Wilkinson & Hodge, the present name being adopted afterward. Through its salesrooms have passed most of the celebrated book collectors and dealers of the last 200-odd years, as well as hoards of the most valuable manuscripts, printed books, and fine bindings. Libraries dispersed by Sotheby's have included the Britwell, Huth, Dyson Perrins, Holford, Ham House, Pembroke. It has traditionally published two series of catalogues, illustrated and unillustrated, which may be distinguished by their wrappers (the illustrated being in deep green, the unillustrated a cream color). Priced copies of Sotheby catalogues are valued for reference.

SOTHERAN, HENRY. Sotheran was an English bookseller of the 19th century. In 1892 he negotiated the most important transaction in the history of the book trade, the sale of the Spencer library to Mrs. JOHN RYLANDS, thereby preserving it intact. He boasted an extensive clientele of wealthy American collectors, including Pierpont Morgan. The business is still in operation.

SPENCER, LORD. The foremost English collector of printed books during the 19th century, Lord Spencer built a marvelous library at his estate of Althorp, including long series of Caxtons and examples from the presses of other pioneer English printers. Many of the items he owned were unique or nearly so, representing little-known works from Tudor publishers. The collection became the basis of the JOHN RYLANDS Library.

SPRINKLED EDGES. Sprinkling is one of the many ways in which the edges of a book can be decorated, and is probably the most humble, rating far behind gold gilding. It consists of spattering with color, usually red or blue, and is associated with plain bindings in calf, vellum, or even boards. It was practiced from an early date, but when seen on 16th century (or earlier) volumes it is usually in conjunction with a non-contemporary binding. The 18th century was the golden age of sprinkling, and nowhere was it performed more than in France. The Germans and Dutch preferred to have the edges of their books painted solid colors, if decorated at all.

STADTBIBLIOTHEK, MUNICH. The Stadtbibliothek is the Bavarian state library, one of the largest in continental Europe. Its collections are especially rich in early German literature, theology, canon law, and early printed books in general, as well as fine bindings and manuscripts. Many papers of old German monarchs and princes are located here. Among the most treasured material in its collection may be mentioned the following: four books of gospels and a missal that had belonged to Henry II (11th century) and were presented to the cathedral of Bamberg; the Codex Aureus, written in gold ink in 870 at the request of Charles the Bald; prayer book of Duke Albert V of Bavaria; the tournament book of Duke William IV of Bavaria, executed between 1541-1544; Albrecht Durer's prayer book with marginal drawings in his hand, as well as drawings by German artist Lucas Cranach. The assemblage of items relating to the history of Germany, from its very earliest times, is the largest in the world. Many of the more picturesque rarities are kept on public display.

STATIONERS' COMPANY. Stationers' Company is an organization of British printers and publishers, who received a royal charter from Elizabeth I in 1557. In the first 80 years of British printing there had been relatively few restrictions placed upon the trade by the crown. There had been labor problems and minor squabbles but no real censorship. In 1484, after CAXTON had not been in business so much as a decade, Parliament passed a law exempting the printing industry from regulations applying to foreign labor, which was the signal for a flood of continentals to come and try their luck (many printers in Britain prior to 1550 were French or German, but often anglicized their names). In 1534 it was repealed. But this was small potatoes compared to the Stationers' Company, which was intended to provide means by which government control could be exercised over the whole industry. It was by all odds the worst thing that ever happened to British publishing; free expression came to an abrupt halt; printers who had previously engaged in brisk trades cowered in the shadows, relegated to handle only what Her Majesty found acceptable. Slaps on the wrist, at the least, came to those who published controversial religious tracts. Often the books would be confiscated and publicly burned. However, there was no effort to gag popular literature, if it contained nothing offensive to the crown; the writings of Shakespeare were circulated without difficulty.

In conjunction with the Stationers' company existed the Star Chamber, which acted as Royal Censor. The Star Chamber held its hand over the Stationers' Company and would fall with the devastation of an ax upon any printer who dared oppose its rules. Few did; but the Star Chamber was still kept busy overseeing things and drawing up laws. The number of printers who could operate in London was regulated, too; it was set at 22 in 1586, then dropped to 20 in 1662, when the population of the city had enormously increased. The Licensing Act, as it was called, was allowed to die without renewal in 1695, and the British publishing trade breathed freer than it had in a century and a half. Fourteen years later, in Anne's reign, came the first copyright laws.

The Star Chamber hit hardest, though it did not intend to, at the quality of craftsmanship in the printing industry. As only native workers were permitted, there was a lack of new ideas and techniques, and keeping the trade at a fixed number did not help. Many printers had more work than they could execute and the rush was apparent in the results: dropped and misplaced letters, wrong words and punctuation, general sloppy proof reading. There are more atrocities to be discovered in English books of this period than any from the continent, or English works of earlier or later date.

STAVELOT BIBLE. The Stavelot Bible is one of the most celebrated and historically important Romanesque manuscripts, executed in Flanders about 1097, now in the British Museum. Its illuminations are a high quality, employing rich coloration, delicate shading and keen understanding of artistic principles. In the opinion of some it constitutes the most noteworthy surviving example of the Romanesque style, whether in books or otherwise, as almost all Romanesque church painting has perished or been seriously damaged over the years. In one miniature, often reproduced, Christ is depicted seated, holding a book, which happens to have a clasped binding. The scene is surrounded by an optical-illusion border.

S.T.C. Abbreviation for "A Short Title Catalogue of Books printed in England, Scotland and Ireland, and of English books printed abroad, 1475-1640," by Pollard and Redgrave, published in London by the Bibliographical Society, 1926, it instantly became the standard reference work on early British books and is quoted today throughout the trade. It was later carried down to 1700 by Donald Wing of Yale. Other short title catalogues exist, but whenever the initials S.T.C. are used the reference is to Messrs. Pollard and Redgrave.

STENCIL PRINTS. Stencil printing is a process of making prints wherein the designs are cut out of a sheet and the sheet pasted atop another. Ink is then laid in the cut away sections and an impression pulled. It was the forerunner of the modern technique of silk-screening, but was never particularly popular in early times.

STEVENS, HENRY. Stevens was a 19th century Vermont bibliographer and rare-book dealer. He settled in London early in his career and acted as agent for a number of American collectors, in the days when European dealers tended to discount the American market and cultivated native trade. One of his most famous customers was JAMES LENOX, founder of the Lenox Library, who acquired many of his choicest items from or through Stevens. He wrote voluminously, one of his well-known works being his "Catalogue of the American Books in the Library of the British Museum," 1886, an institution with which he did considerable business. On occasion he persuaded libraries—including the B.M.—to trade books with him, a practice usually frowned upon. The firm is still in operation, now known as Henry Stevens, Son & Stiles.

STILTED BINDING. Stilted binding evolved and was popular for a brief period in the 17th century. In consisted of applying oversized covers on small books, usually 12mo's or 24mo's, to make them appear larger and more uniform with other volumes on the shelf; surely one of the most foolish follies ever engaged in by bibliophiles. Collectors who were just as vain but did not wish to incur the extra expense used little blocks of wood to stand their pocket editions upon, or dreamed up other remedies. But why they wished all books to conform in size is a puzzle, as one of the joys of modern collectors is variety. Very often stilted bindings are not pointed out by cataloguers unless the stilting is of grotesque proportions. As oddities they rate in the upper ranks.

SUNDERLAND (CHARLES SPENCER), EARL OF. A son-in-law of the Duke of Marlborough, the Earl of Sunderland (1647-1722) collected a large and choice library, especially strong in English works, numbering more than 20,000 items. It was an unusual circumstance that two of England's leading bibliophiles of the early 18th century, he and ROBERT HARLEY, were both involved in the life of Marlborough—Harley as a political foe. The Sunderland library was kept intact for nearly two hundred years, then sold at auction toward the close of the 19th century, when it created much excitement.

SUPPRESSED BOOKS. This is a broad field as, in its widest and most generally accepted sense, it refers not only to books actually condemned to destruction but those which have been declared unlawful (or irreligious) to own, or read, or sell. The term is seldom applied to modern books which have enjoyed a more or less free circulation: it is reserved for those forcibly removed from bookshops by order of law, cited as pornography in court, or prohibited from import for one reason or other. As these bans and taboos are gradually becoming a thing of the past, books that would have had the added collecting interest of being suppressed now roam both bookshop and library unrestrained.

The most active suppression occurred in the first century of printing, from 1450 to 1550. The Roman Church looked upon the new art as the devil's work and carefully examined every book issued, to determine if it might have a bad influence upon believers. When this was thought to be the case, local church authorities were generally empowered to seize all copies stocked by the printers and their agents and have them burned. Public book burnings were a regular feature of medieval town life. The chore would fall to the hangman, who undoubtedly appreciated a change of pace from his normal duties. It was not only for religious reasons that books were burned, normal duties. It was not only for religious reasons that books were burned, however. There were a number condemned by governments as well, usually on grounds that treason or revolution was preached.

Book burnings were also not restricted to the Dark Ages. There were perhaps more volumes destroyed in Britain in the 17th century than any previous century, including Bastwicke's *Elenchus Religionis Papisticae* (1634), Blount's *King William and Queen Mary, Conquerors* (1692), Pocklington's *Sunday no Sabbath* (1640), Burnet's *Pastoral Letter to the Clergy* (1689), and a good many others. In fact there were instances of books burned as late as the 18th century, which seems extraordinary. It was rare that the operation had any success. A number of copies would almost always escape, sometimes a large number, which were then eagerly bought by the curious (who might otherwise have ignored them). Once in a while books of a perfectly uncontroversial nature were also burned, such as Cowell's *Law Dictionary,* to suit the whim of the local magistrate. There are not many people collecting suppressed books, but it is an interesting topic with endless openings for research and discovery.

SUTRO, ADOLPH. An American tycoon, Sutro was one of the first major U.S. book collectors (1830-1898). His library of 300,000 volumes is thought to have been the largest ever assembled in America. He owned a number of incunables and other early works but in the main the collection was not of high quality. Living in San Francisco, he was well isolated from Europe and there is some wonder over his sources of supply. Eight years after he died, the San Francisco earthquake destroyed most of his books. The Sutro Library, completely rebuilt, is now open to the public and is one of the city's leading reference enters.

SWEYNHEYM & PANNARTZ. Two German printers with the unlikely names of Conrad Sweynheym and Arnold Pannartz have the distinction of being the first to establish a press in Italy. Pannartz came originally from Bohemia and not much is known of him (a statement that, alas, fits about 90% of the incunabula printers). Sweynheym was a resident of Mainz; there is a strong probability he was employed by Fust and Schoeffer. Many of the early printers were fortune hunters who, not content to establish themselves near competition, struck out to foreign lands which knew nothing of the art. So it was with Sweynheym and Pannartz, who trundled their equipment into Italy and were invited to set up at the Abbey of St. Scholastica in Subiaco, 30 miles or so from Rome. In trying to reconstruct events, historians believe the two simply stopped here seeking rest in their journey before carrying on to Rome, but that the monks, learning of their intention, persuaded them to stay. They printed at least four books at Subiaco, all excessively rare. The monks are said to have assisted them in reading proofs and editing, but not in the mechanical work, as this violated their vows. The type they used was a modified gothic, a sort of black letter that had gotten very hip. Afterward they ventured on to Rome, where they became established in 1467. Whether they were truly the first to run a press at Rome is questionable, because ULRICH HAN set up in the same year. As craftsmen the team was superior to Han, further modifying their type to fit the humanistic taste. Their edition of the Epistles of Cicero, 1467, is considered the first appearance of modernized roman letters. They continued to work for some time, printing such authors as St. Augustine, Apuleius, Pliny, Aulus Gellius, Quintilian, Silius Italicus, Ovid, etc. Eventually they ran into financial troubles, having overestimated the Roman appetite for books, and at one time had a stockpile of 12,475 unsold volumes. Finally they petitioned the pope for aid, to save them from bankruptcy.

TABS. There are several component parts of books that are called tabs. The original meaning was small, often colored, shreds of vellum or paper, pasted at the foredge of some early manuscripts and printed books to show where chapters or divisions begin. They were the equivalent of modern thumb indexing, but the tabs got loose and fell off, or else they were handled roughly and ended up tearing the pages. Binding stubs, the little strips of paper that pop up at odd places and look as if a leaf were cut out, are sometimes called tabs. So are the lengths of paper used at the spines of modern bindings in place of CORDS.

THICK PAPER COPY. This was a rather popular device among publishers in the 17th and 18th centuries, particularly in England. As the quality of paper used in trade editions became worse and worse, those who admired books for their physical qualities often did not object to paying for the advantage of thick (or fine) paper.

THREE-QUARTER BINDING. Three-quarter binding is a binding in which the spine and tips of the corners of the covers are in leather, the remainder cloth or boards. The forerunner of the three-quarter was the half-binding, in which only the spine was covered in leather. The idea of tipping the corners arose from a desire on the part of binders to make customers forget they were not receiving full leather. Three-quarter was a common style for fine bindings in England in the 19th century and our own, mainly in calf and morocco.

THUMB INDEX. A thumb index is a convenience feature in some works of reference, such as dictionaries and encyclopedias, in which the place can be found by letters appearing at the FOREDGE. A notch is hollowed out of the paper to allow insertion of a thumb, so that the book opens at the proper spot. Thumb indexing came into use in the 19th century, when reference books grew very thick. The trend today is to publish such works in several volumes, and thumb indexing is on its way out.

TIES. The average binding of the late Middle Ages consisted of wooden boards with a pair of metal clasps that held the covers firmly shut. When limp vellum was substituted for wood, which became common in Italy, Spain and Portugal in the 16th century, clasps could no longer be used because there was no board to nail them to. As a substitute, long leather thongs were supplied that looked very much like the tails of mice, two at the outer edge of each cover. They were supposed to be tied—hence the term—after using the book, but almost never were. Instead, they were more often used as a handle to carry the book around by. Books of the 16th and 17th centuries that survive with four original ties intact are rarities, but unfortunately no one gives a premium for such items. Their absence can be identified by the little slits that once held them. Some booksellers will mention "ties lacking" but usually no notice is taken of the fact.

TIPPED IN. Beginning in the late 1800's, it has been an increasing practice among publishers of art books to "tip in" illustrations rather than print them directly on the pages. It is done by fixing them in place with a few drops of glue. As this operation is rather tricky, unsightly mistakes are not infrequent. Although the target pages are printed with guidelines, these are often missed, so that the illustration is well off-center (sometimes completely inverted). If too much glue is applied, another common occurrence, the plate will buckle. Wrinkles are an indication that the plate was initially laid down wrong and only worked into proper alignment by the exertion of force. If the plates are printed on thick stock some of these dangers will be minimized, but they rarely are.

Publishers claim tipping is done for the benefit of buyers, as it permits illustrations to be removed for framing without injuring the book. The actual reason is that the cost of production is generally far less, as the plates are smaller than page size and permit the book to be printed on a cheap grade of paper. The real argument against tipped-in plates is that they come free in time, especially if the book is much handled, and the loss of just one makes a volume virtually worthless.

TISCHENDORF, CONSTANTINE. Tischendorf was a Russian scholar enshrined in the annals of book collecting for his unexpected discovery of the CODEX SINAITICUS. Believing he might find forgotten copies of early Greek Bibles, Tischendorf made a pilgrimage in 1844 to the Convent of St. Catherine at Mount Sinai. Entering a passageway, he came upon a monk bringing a basket of old parchment leaves to be burned. Examining them he found they were portions of a Greek Old Testament of very primitive date. Although most of the volume had already been burned, he succeeded in salvaging 43 leaves, which he deposited at the Leipzig Library. This fragment is now known as the Codex Frederico-Augustanus. Returning nine years later, in high expectation of locating similar material within the darkened recesses of the convent, he came away empty handed. But he was not to give up so easily. Back again in 1859, filled with new ambition, he sifted through hundreds of manuscript volumes which failed to arouse his interest. Upon preparing to leave, a steward, who knew his taste for early Biblical texts, came to show him a book wrapped in a red cloth cover; it was a 4th century A.D. Greek Bible, comprising both Old and New Testaments. Tischendorf copied some of it that night in his room at the monastery, then begged for the volume as a gift for the Russian Czar. The monks consented, hardly knowing its value or historical significance, and the Codex Sinaiticus went into the library at St. Petersburg. For its later history, see entry.

TISSUE. During the 19th century, and to a much less extent thereafter, it was a practice of some publishers to provide tissue guards next to illustration plates. These were simply sheets of tissue paper, usually slightly smaller than page size, which sometimes carried a printed identification of the plate but more often were blank. On some occasions they were used on all plates in a volume, on others merely the frontispiece. Their purposes were to absorb offset, protect the illustration, and (most important) make the volume appear far more luxurious than it was. Missing tissue, unless it carried some form of printing, is not looked upon as a calamity. Its presence or absence is almost never mentioned in descriptions.

TITLE PAGES. Title pages were rarely supplied to medieval manuscripts. The scribe used the first few lines of text on the opening page to state the subject and author of the book; in English gothic manuscripts the words "here begynnyth..." normally marked the opening of a volume. Title pages were restricted to very elaborate illuminated volumes. They were equally luxurious, with large gold and colored letters and painted decorations, and were placed on the VERSO of the first leaf rather than the RECTO, which is the modern practice. This may have been done for protection. The earliest printed books had nothing resembling a title page but the owner could, if he wished, turn the volume over to an illuminator to design one. The first typographic book to have a title leaf was the *Bul ze Dutsch* of Pope Pius II, printed at Mainz in 1463. It was not a title page as we know it. It merely stated the name of the work, in bold gothic letters on the upper portion of the page, without giving any hint of the place of publication, printer, date, or publisher's blurb; nor was there any printer's mark or device. Nevertheless it was revolutionary for its time, and not for another seven years— until 1470—did the next such title page appear.

The incunabula printers probably never would have adopted the title page if it were not almost a necessity. In the 15th century, bookshops displayed their volumes on racks or open shelves. The majority were unbound GATHERINGS held together with twine, which the purchaser took to his binder to be outfitted to his taste. Without some form of identification on the front leaf it was next to impossible to tell one from another. Prior to the printed title leaf, most booksellers resorted to writing out titles on slips.

For a while that was as far as printers wished to go: to provide a convenience for themselves and their customers. There was no attempt to make the title leaf decorative; the facts relating to the publication of the book remained where they had always been, at the rear, in the COLOPHON. Undoubtedly the title was intended as a discard leaf, to be torn away by the binder, just like modern dust jackets, as incunables very often lack it. It was the Venetian-based printer, ERHARD RATDOLT, who introduced the first full-size decorative title page, in 1476. It appeared on the "Calendarium" of Regiomontanus and was printed in two colors, with a fine Renaissance woodcut border and the date in neat arabic numerals. This also gave it the distinction of first dated title page. When other printers saw it, especially his fellow Italians, they recognized that their volumes were shabby by comparison. By 1490 title pages were more or less standard on Italian books, but took a longer time to catch on in central and northern Europe. Some German and Dutch publications were still without title pages as late as 1520. By this time the majority had adopted them, however, shifting the colophon information from back to front, though many continued to add a colophon or finishing stroke at the conclusion for good measure.

There have been many fads and fashions in title pages. In Italy in the 1490's, and into the early 16th century illustrated titles were in vogue, featuring large panoramic scenes based on subjects from the book. The trend in France at this time was for oversized initial letters, filling almost the whole page, and so embellished with ornament and portraits that they became unrecognizable. This grew out of the manuscript influence, stronger in France—especially Paris—than anywhere else on the continent. Until the 19th century, in some cases later, title pages frequently contained notices of the shops where the book could be purchased.

TOOLING. When used without any further explanation, which it shouldn't be, tooling usually refers to gold gilding on bindings. However, the term is much misused, to such an extent that its true meaning is fast being lost. Properly, tooling is design applied by hand, by the skillful combination of individual tools. Designs applied by a machine, wherein the entire cover is stamped in a single process, are known as blocking, but it is a rare bookseller who makes the distinction and a rare customer who raises a fuss. If blocking seems too foreign a word, the phrase "gilt stamped" serves the same purpose. Tooling in blind is called blindstamping, to avoid confusion.

TORRESANUS, ANDREA. Torresanus was a Venetian incunabula printer. He acquired the types used by NICOLAS JENSON after the latter's passing in 1480, and with them printed volumes that are nearly the equal of Jenson's in beauty and design. Many of his books were decorated with large illuminated initials and marginal ornament, after the fashion of manuscripts. His mark generally appeared in red at the conclusion of his works. When ALDO MANUTIUS died in 1515, Torresanus, who was related to him, was persuaded to carry on the Aldine Press, which he did until his own death in 1529. For three years after this date the press issued nothing, only resuming in 1533. Torresanus was responsible for raising Aldus' son Paulus, called Paolo, who took over the business in 1540.

TORY, GEOFFROI. Tory was a Renaissance printer, author, and designer of type, considered to be one of the most artistic craftsmen of his time. Born in Bourges, France, sometime around 1480, he pursued scholarly interests from an early age. He spent a period of time at Rome, a journey considered mandatory for all aspiring humanists, where he was influenced by the artistic spirit of the city. Back in France in 1504, he produced an edition of Pomponius Mela, which was printed by Gourmont. It caught the notice of local officials, who gave Tory the position of Regent at the College of Plessis, where he was editor for Henri ESTIENNE, first of the outstanding French scholar-printers. After returning again to Italy, he was back in Paris in 1518. As the manuscript industry was still bustling in Paris, long after it had died elsewhere, Tory took up the trade of manuscript illuminator, but soon turned to wood engraving. For a while he operated a bookshop, but made his services as a woodcutter and type designer available to local printers. Those who patronized him were apparently numerous, including the famous Simon deColines. *Champfleury*, a book authored by Tory, is an essential document of Renaissance philosophy and is still published in various translations today. In 1530, at about the age of 50, he was appointed Royal Printer to Francois I, but died three years later. There is some question as to whether he ever printed whole volumes, or was merely involved in their design and layout.

TRADE BINDING. Trade bindings are those applied (or ordered) by the publisher, or in rarer cases bookseller, rather than bindings made to the order of a purchaser. The history of trade bindings is really older than printing, as they were used to some degree on manuscripts. Many IN-CUNABLES, especially the earlier ones, were sold in loose quires so that the purchaser could have them bound in his favorite manner. Some were, however, available in trade bindings, for two good reasons. First, not every buyer wanted to send his books away for a costly job of binding and, secondly, even those who did might care to read them first, which was awkward without a binding. So bindings that were inexpensive yet sturdy and not at all ugly were provided. The purchaser might even have had his choice of plain wooden boards or stamped calf. The majority of rugged, simply decorated bindings we see today on incunabula must have been trade or publishers' bindings, though proving the fact on any individual example is not easy. A large house like KOBERGER'S did much trade binding, as comparison of its books show many of the same tools repeated from one to another.

In the 16th century the average trade binding in Italy and Spain was vellum, usually limp. In its day this was an extremely cheap covering and added little to the production cost of a book. Trade bindings in Germany, Austria, and Holland at the same time were more often composed of stamped vellum or pigskin over wood, with clasps, which could also be applied cheaply.

Many sorts of trade bindings were employed in the 17th century. The most frequent in Britain was plain brown calf or roan. Germany shifted from stamped vellum to calf, usually over hard paperboards, but some German publishers retained their affection for vellum and pigskin (retaining it, in fact, well into the 18th century). Throughout most of the remainder of the continent vellum was used, limp or otherwise, but undecorated. In the 18th century, numerous trade bindings consisted of nothing more than plain boards with a calf spine. With the popularity of cloth for edition binding, which dated from the 1820's, use of leather was gradually abandoned. By this time it was firmly believed by publishers that most buyers had no desire to bind their books in leather, and consequently that buyers would be attracted by a handsome cloth cover. The craze for pictorial cloth lasted until about 1890. Many trade bindings of today, particularly on art books (where the budget has been squeezed dry on illustrations), are composed of half cloth over boards.

TREGASKIS. A family of British booksellers, for many years the Tregaskises operated the Caxton Head shop in London.

TREVERIS, PETER. Treveris was an English printer active in the early part of the 16th century. It is thought he began in the trade about 1514, though this is disputed by some. One of his best known publications was *The Grete herball whiche gyueth parfyt Knowledge*, 1529. His books are in black letter, with a medieval appearance. He did some printing for John Reynes, one of the many booksellers who kept stalls at St. Paul's Churchyard, as well as for Laurence Andrewe of Fleet Street.

TRIAL BINDING. It has been a custom of publishers to make up dummy copies of books prior to publication, to test the format, binding and other features. Sometimes the trial binding will be used for the first few dozen (or maybe few hundred) copies as they come off the press, before someone decides that pink polka-dot buckram is not the ideal covering for a work on the atomic bomb. When the change is made in midstream there will be two versions of the binding in first edition copies. Whether or not collectors prefer the trial binding may depend upon how many were issued, but one thing is sure: copies in trial bindings are always of the earliest state, which usually carries some weight. When two or more bindings are found on the same edition, it is generally impossible, lacking further information, to determine 1) if one is a trial binding, or 2) which came first.

TRINITY COLLEGE LIBRARY. The library of Trinity College in Dublin began when the English Army gave a gift of books after trouncing the Irish in a 1601 battle; by 1604 it had grown to 4,000 volumes. The Trinity College collection of early Irish literature, especially in the field of HIBERNO-SAXON MANUSCRIPTS, is one of the finest. Its glory is the BOOK OF KELLS, regarded as the single most valuable book in the world.

TYPESCRIPT. A typescript is a manuscript produced on a typewriter (or other mechanical writing device) rather than by handwriting. There is no clear distinction, however, between typescripts typed by the author, and thus playing an integral role in the history of the work, or those copied by secretaries or publishing house assistants. The presence of the author's signature at the foot is no indication he actually did, or even supervised, the typing, and in fact is more likely to indicate he did not. Most authors are notoriously poor typists and any work done by them is apt to contain numerous scratch-outs, even if there are no attempts to alter wording. Final copies of manuscripts are seldom typed by the authors themselves, who generally handle nothing more technical than the cork of a spirits bottle after completing a draft. Most authors only stay with the typewriter so long as revision is necessary, which cannot be done by others. In these cases the typescripts will contain manuscript or at least typed changes of sense or wording. These are naturally far more valued than neat, pristine final copies, even if they fail to bear a signature of the author, as one can be 99% certain that penciling was done in his HOLOGRAPH. It sometimes happens that such scripts carry revisions by an agent or editor, but these are vastly in the minority, and any competent individual could easily distinguish the difference.

TYPE SPECIMEN. Books or booklets issued by printing companies to display the varieties of typefaces in their stock are known as type specimen books. The collecting of early specimen books, particularly those of the more well-known houses, has lately become quite popular. Some are mere BROADSIDE sheets, depending on how much type the firm may have or how much expense it cares to engage showing it. The more elaborate specimen books do not merely exhibit the alphabet and numerals in different faces, but show the type at work in short stories, poems, items from newspapers, etc. In the early years of printing it was usual for printers to devote the closing page of their books to a roll-call of their type, which often consisted of nothing more than upper and lower-case letters of the same font.

UNCUT. This does not, as the old-time collector James Lenox found out, mean UNOPENED, but rather that the edges of the leaves have been left rough after separation. Lenox once ordered a book described as uncut from the London dealer Henry Stevens. When it arrived he complained to Stevens that the pages were all open. After Stevens explained the meaning of uncut, Lenox sighed, placed the volume back on his shelves and commented that you learn something new every day. Uncut edges are more often seen on novels than other classes of books and far more on club editions than those released to the general trade. But on the whole they seem not so popular today as in the 1950s. When uncut books are rebound they are sure to lose their virginity, unless the owner gives explicit instructions to the contrary.

UNIQUE. The true bibliographical meaning of unique is that no duplicate copy exists. It can only be safely applied to manuscripts, which are automatically unique, association copies, and other restricted classes of books. When one finds a volume in which 26 political pamphlets of the 18th century have been bound together, it is a pretty safe guess that no exactly alike collection exists. But where regularly published and regularly bound books are concerned, it is always hard to believe that only one specimen is surviving, even though the standard reference sources may record one or none. It is a temptation, when one discovers a work that appears UNRECORDED, to assume it may be unique. Yet this is operating on scanty evidence, as there are many unrecorded books which are not unique. Booksellers get around the problem by the term "possibly unique," which is something like saying "this may be an elephant, but then again it could be a mouse." Of all the items that have ever been offered as "possibly unique," probably less than a tenth actually are.

UNLETTERED. It was not common for the titles of books to appear on spines in trade bindings until the 17th century. In the Middle Ages books were shelved with their spines inward and the title or author would frequently be written in ink on the foredge of the leaves. This practice faded out around the late 15th and early 16th centuries, when books began to be shelved in the modern fashion (though sometimes lying flat rather than standing). Still, binders did not letter the spines unless instructed to. Many owners took the matter in their own hands and scrawled some identifying word on the spine, usually with a soft paintbrush. Some monasteries made vellum title-tickets for their books, but they were generally nailed to the front cover rather than the spine. The early method of professional lettering was by impression with gilt tools, either directly on the spine or, more often, on leather lettering-pieces. The lettering-pieces were then glued to the spine. If there was to be one lettering-piece it would usually go between the first and second RAISED BANDS from the top of the spine; if more than one (if, for instance, the date and place of printing were to be indicated) there were no set styles. The motive of the lettering-piece was to provide a safeguard against mistakes, and allow the stamping to be done on a flat surface rather than the curvature of the spine. Many lettering-pieces seen on old books were added long after binding, including, it would be safe to say, all those on incunabula. Lettering-pieces that include elaborate information are usually later additions. During the 18th and 19th centuries it was inside, to be detached and used on the spine in the event the purchaser had the volume fashionably bound. Missing lettering-pieces are frequent, as the glue dries out and the label is rubbed loose in handling. A bit of glue is all that is necessary to re-attach it, an operation no collector need fear, but the majority of labels are lost upon coming free. There will usually be some revealing evidence, such as traces of crusted glue or a discolored spot whence the label had come, a result of that portion of the leather not being oiled. Missing labels are considered much more of a tragedy when they were applied by the publisher, and are one of the POINTS in a first edition.

UNOPENED. When a book is first bound after coming from the printer, its leaves are still attached one to another along the edges and must be cut apart. This happens because books are not printed in single sheets, as one might think, but in large sheets folded into QUIRES. Economic considerations are not the only cause. A book composed of five hundred loose leaves—in other words, with no conjugates or quires—would be thicker at the spine than the foredge and present a tricky problem in sewing. In books bound for the general trade, the edges will be opened by the bindery, which occasionally misses a few. But in limited or fine editions, copies are commonly sold as bound, for the purchaser to keep as is or open at his discretion. Many collectors prefer unopened copies of second-hand books, as the presence of unopened leaves indicates the volume has received little handling. Once acquired they are often left in this state to increase eventual sales value. This, of course, comes dangerously close to admitting that bibliophiles could as well be illiterates.

Opening an unopened book is a job that cannot be performed carelessly or with the wrong tool. A finger, though God-given, was not intended for this purpose. Anyone who has examined a number of books will have noticed volumes with shredded edges, with large hunks of paper missing from one leaf and a corresponding excess on the next. Though one might imagine some queer animal gnawing away in this fashion, the blame rests entirely with the manner of opening. The fault of the finger is its thickness. An object with a flat blade is needed. If a choice must be made between the two, a kitchen knife is far more preferable to a finger, but kitchen knives are a bit aggressive. The ideal implement is sharp, but not too sharp, and does not have a pointed tip. A paper knife or a bone letter opener will serve well. But selecting the proper instrument is only the beginning. The technique, too, is a matter of concern. The knife should be held at an angle to the page, roughly diagonally, and pulled outward with gentle pressure in short, firm movements. Learning the correct angle takes practice, so it is wise to begin on waste papers. If held too straight it does not cut; if the angle is too severe, it cuts but not evenly. In cases where the angle is right but cutting is still difficult, a tiny amount of grease may be applied to the knife. Of course, if the knife is dull the procedure is doomed to failure, regardless of what steps are taken. When opening page tops, they must be cut all the way to the spine, otherwise tears will result.

UNPRESSED. Unpressed leaves of a book are those that are fresh, crisp, and somewhat rippled, like a caterpillar in motion. The term is sometimes wrongly applied to leaves that have been waterstained. The binding on an unpressed book does not close so flat as one might wish and is sometimes a nuisance on the shelf.

UNRECORDED. When booksellers (and auctioneers) mount their steeds and charge into battle, they would prefer having the word "unrecorded" on their banners to any other. When used without qualification, it is taken to mean that no reference book nor catalogue has ever, in the history of bibliography, contained so much as a note regarding the edition. This presupposes that whoever is making the claim has checked every one, a physical impossibility. In its more accepted sense, unrecorded means the book is not cited by the standard bibliography on the subject. As many of these reference works are long out of print and in need of revision, it often happens that an edition they had failed to mention turns up several times before receiving recognition. Few mortals are infallible and bibliographers are among the most mortal of men. The subject of incunabula proves this out, as omissions can be found—sometimes in legion force—in all the costly, multi-volume works that have appeared.

UNRESERVED SALE. An auction sale at which no reserves are set, meaning that the highest price, regardless of how disappointing, will take each lot is an unreserved sale. The majority of larger auction houses permit reserves. If there are 300 lots in the sale, 290 may be totally unreserved, but the major items are likely to be protected. Auctioneers naturally prefer to operate without reserves, as they are then assured a sale and commission on each lot (assuming, of course, it sells). But, knowing that owners of fine properties would hesitate to launch them into uncertainty, they have little choice but to allow them, though they encourage vendors to make them reasonable. A collection on which a vendor demanded an excessive number of reserves would undoubtedly be unacceptable to the auctioneer. If the reserve is not reached, the lot is said to be "bought in," and is returned to the owner. Reserves are almost never announced before a sale, except in a mail auction where the auctioneer limits bids to certain amounts. Smaller auctions normally operate without reserves.

UNTRIMMED. Edges of a book exactly as opened by the binder, without smoothing down are known as untrimmed. Sometimes they are called uncut or rough edges. When gilt, as they very seldom are, the term "rough gilt" is used.

USED COPY. Not necessarily the same as secondhand, a used copy is one that has been heavily, sometimes mercilessly, used, but it should not lack any pages unless this has been mentioned. Underlining, marginal notes, creased corners, stains, and fingerprints are common features. It is properly applied only to damage resulting from use: foxing or wormholes, for instance, would not qualify.

VALDARFER BOCCACCIO. One of the glories of incunabula, Valdarfer Boccaccio was the work of a Milan printer named Christopher Valdarfer (who published nothing else of monumental stature). A particularly fine copy from the ROXBURGHE library made headlines in 1812 when it sold for £2,260.

VARIANT. A copy which does not match up, in one way or other, with the majority of recorded specimens is a variant. If the accepted reference works call for a certain edition to have a pink trade binding and yours has a green, you have been blessed with a variant. Sometimes a few extra dollars can be raised for a variant, as there are bibliophiles who specialize in just such white elephants. Seldom will a variant prove to be of much value or importance, but they give the hobby an extra touch of mystery.

VARIOUS DATES. This means that books offered in a mixed lot, or volumes from a set, or even works contained in the same book, are not all of the same date. When used in conjunction with an auction lot, the variance could be as sharp as from 1506 to 1970, but volumes of a set seldom differ more than a few decades at most. The greater the range, the less likelihood the component parts will be uniform, or that they were supervised by the same editor or printed by the same house.

VATICAN LIBRARY. The Vatican Library is the Papal library, located at Vatican City in Rome. It contains one of the largest and most important collections of manuscripts in the western world. In addition it boasts priceless hoards of early bookbindings (including those of jewels and gold, as well as other sumptuous designs), incunabula, and collections of coins, medals, and miscellaneous relics. Even in the days of pre-Christian Rome it is likely church leaders were building files of documents and records. The first mention of papal archives occurs in the reign of St. Damasus I (366-384 A.D.). It is believed he ordered the construction of a library, in the

Campus Martinus near the Theater of Pompey. All that survives is an inscribed stone; nothing is known of the collections, though it is understood they were available for public use.

The medieval popes owned libraries which were excellent for their time, though small. Numerous scribes and illuminators were attached to the pope, and in addition he received gifts of fine books from visiting kings and nobles. Nicholas V (1447–1455) was the first Renaissance pope to give serious attention to the Vatican's collections. He conceived the plan of turning the private papal collections into a public library and museum, appointing Giovanni Tortelli the first librarian. At this time it comprised 9,000 bound manuscripts and a far greater number of documents. However, his successors had no interest in the library and sold items from it at will. By the time Sixtus IV—the next bibliophilic pontiff—took the throne in 1471, the library was in a shambles, many of its finest items missing. He set up rooms for the collection in the small Sistine Chapel, newly built and not yet decorated by Michelangelo, and in 1475 gave the job of librarian to Platina. Sixtus also established a program of channeling certain Vatican funds to the library. Thus endowed it grew rapidly, and the increased interest in book collecting brought about by the Renaissance also contributed to its growth. By the early 16th century it had gotten too large for its quarters and various plans were set forth for erecting a special building to house it. This was finally done under Sixtus V, who gave the task to architect Domenico Fontana. When completed it was one of the most ornamental structures in the entire Vatican complex, with marble walls and frescos across the ceilings. Many private and other collections were then added. In 1623 the Elector Maximilian donated the Bibliotheca Palatina of Heidelberg, when Heidelberg fell in the Thirty Years' War. In 1657 came the Bibliotheca Urbinas, founded by the Duke Federigo deMontefeltro; in 1690 the Bibliotheca Reginensis, which had belonged to Queen Christina of Sweden; in 1746 the Bibliotheca Ottoboniana, purchased by Alexander VIII. In 1797 the French stormed the library, making off with 843 manuscripts, but 805 were returned in 1814 (the remainder were from the Palatina of Heidelberg and were given back to that city). The Vatican Library has suffered many misfortunes, including a fire in its bindery in the early 1900's, but survived them well. Among its principal treasures are a 4th century A.D. manuscript of Terence, a 5th century Virgil, and a 5th century Greek New Testament. It also possesses— somewhat out of character—love letters of Henry VIII to Anne Boleyn.

VELLUM. One of the leading actors in the drama of the history of books, vellum has been used as a writing, printing, and binding material for nearly five thousand years. The Hebrews were first to use vellum for the preparation of manuscript scrolls. The Romans adopted it when PAPYRUS could no longer be imported from Egypt. It was superior to papyrus for strength, and it would not dry out and become brittle, but it was also a good deal more costly. When CODEX books took the place of scrolls, vellum had a new career as a covering for their bindings. Many medieval bindings were fashioned of vellum, stretched over oak boards and supplied with clasps, catches, and sometimes metal bosses and cornerpieces. In the 15th century BLINDSTAMPING became popular as a method of decorating vellum bindings. After the craft of gold gilding was introduced from the east at the close of the 15th century, vellum was seldom used for fine bindings as it does not lend itself well to this form of ornament.

Vellum is made from the skins of a variety of animals, but chiefly goats and calves, and differs in texture, quality and color depending upon its source. A very fine, supple vellum is obtained from the skins of unborn animals. Vellum is sometimes mistaken for pigskin, as the two leathers may display similar characteristics when used for binding (pigskin is never employed as writing paper), depending on the sort of vellum and the method of applying it. Vellum has always one smooth side, that which faced the animal, and one rough, which faced outward and from which the hairs grew. If this rough side is placed outward, the resemblance to pigskin is sometimes striking. The place of printing offers a clue, however. If the book was published in the south of Europe, the binding is probably vellum; if in the north, including Germany, pigskin.

Whether used as paper or binding, vellum has a tendency to warp and do all sorts of distressing tricks in a humid climate. The commonly seen damage is vellum covers on books of the 16th and 17th centuries which have curled out airplane wings and are a nuisance to remove and replace on a full shelf. This naturally cannot occur on bindings in which wood has been used, which accounts for early vellum bindings often being better preserved than later ones. In fact, the boards with which many trade bindings of the 17th century were provided were flimsier than today's, no match at all for the free spirit of vellum. When a book has been acquired in this condition there is very little that can be done but rebind it or learn to love it. Most collectors choose the latter. Pasting a sheet of paper inside the cover has been suggested, in the thought it will curl in the opposite direction and carry the cover with it, but in practice this does virtually no good. Pressure will only succeed in cracking both the vellum and binding board.

VELVET BINDING. Velvet was used in the binding of books at least from the late Middle Ages and perhaps earlier. Prior to the introduction of gold tooling in the late 15th century, velvet was one of many materials used for fine bindings: ivory, carved wood, jewels, gold, etc., none of which were ideally adapted to the craft. Although attractive enough when first applied, the plush quickly wore off, leaving bare spots that resembled a skin rash. If handled much, all the plush would vanish and nothing but the discolored undercoat remain, as can be seen in libraries which possess such bindings. They were primarily made in southern Europe, particularly Spain and Portugal, where they continued in vogue until the 17th century. For some reason the majority are in wine-colored rose or dark violet; one will search a great while before finding a green one. Though perhaps eye-catching and luxurious, velvet bindings afforded no opportunity for creative decoration.

VERSO. The reverse side, or back, of a leaf bound in a book is known as the verso.

VINLAND MAP. A manuscript map, supposedly dating from the early 15th century (prior to the voyage of Columbus), showing the east coast of North America, the Vinland map was discovered in 1964.

W.A.F. Often seen in auction, very rarely in retail catalogues, this is a cipher for With All Faults—meaning the book is in pitiable condition and will not be accepted for return under any circumstances. Usually the faults, or at least some of them, are mentioned. The term is only used for volumes the cataloguer is pretty certain the buyer will not like when he sees them, regardless of price.

WANLEY, HUMPHREY. Wanley was an 18th century British librarian who aided in building the collections of Robert and Edward Harley, later acquired by the British Museum. His careful system of keeping records has provided modern readers with interesting insights into book collecting habits and practices of another age.

WANTLIST. The wantlist—a listing of needed books—has become standard in the trade. Wantlists are exchanged from collector to dealer and amongst dealers. Some are temporary and are voided when the items have been acquired; others are permanent, such as a collector's search for "any 19th century furniture catalogues," or books required by a dealer who can use unlimited duplicates. When a dealer receives a wantlist from a customer, he checks it first against his stock and reports on items which may be on hand; or he may advertise for the material, welcoming QUOTES from fellow dealers. Wantlists vary in design and approach with the personality and means of the collector. Some are scratched on a piece of torn notepaper, others professionally printed, but all are invited by booksellers.

WASHED. For many years it has been a habit in France and Belgium, and to a much lesser extent elsewhere, to wash old books that have become soiled. The process involves taking the book apart, gathering by gathering, and dipping the leaves in a specially prepared solution. They are then strung on a clothesline to dry. It is necessary to re-size leaves after washing, as the size (a name given to a chemical in paper) is removed. Inferior grades of paper come away from washing much worse off than before; clean, perhaps, but ruined to all practical purposes. Also, some printing inks will dissolve in water. Washed books have rippled leaves and sometimes a certain odor. Upon recuperation from surgery they are usually RE-CASED. German, British and American bibliophiles have long chosen to accept soiled leaves as a fact of life or, if this requires too much stoicism, to work away at the trouble spots with soft artgum erasers.

WATERMARKS. Marks impressed in paper during the early stages of its manufacture, to identify the quality or maker. The earliest European example dates from 1282. In the 17th century, when papermills were numerous, manufacturers began using a countermark in addition to the regular watermark, giving their name and sometimes place of business. Watermarks constitute an important phase of study. In a COLLATION, the position of a watermark could provide evidence of missing leaves. In fact the tracing of watermarks in each quire constituted the usual method of collation in early days. SOPHISTICATED copies, or forged or facsimile leaves, are likewise occasionally identified by a lack of watermark, or the presence of the wrong watermark. In the first two centuries of printing, paper sizes were known according to the symbol in the watermark, and the names which evolved are still used today. There were such symbols as foolscap (the hat of a jester), crown, post horn (from the horns tooted in olden times by postmen), etc.

WESTERN AMERICANA. One of the quickest growing areas of biblio-philic interest, Western Americana comprises material relating to the American West. Beyond this very loose definition there are no guidelines; the items may be of any nature (books, posters, newspapers, autographs, you name it) or age; nor does it necessarily have to be of western origin. Many of the rarest and most desirable were printed in New York, Boston, Chicago and other dude towns, and are in the nature of guidebooks to the western states, biographies of Indian chiefs or famous outlaws, and so forth. But a number of collectors do concentrate upon early western imprints, often without regard to the subject matter. Here again, as in other fields of bib-liography, it is a question of personal opinion; what seems early to one man might not to another. But generally speaking, any book or other scrap of printing within these limits will have value, provided the condition is rea-sonable:

Arizona, 1890	Nevada, 1890
California, 1860	Oklahoma, 1900
Colorado, 1876	Texas, 1850
Kansas, 1876	Utah, 1860
Montana, 1880	Wyoming, 1890

This does not, of course, imply that all imprints later than these are without value, only that they are not apt to be collected as specimens of pioneer printing. Unlike collectors of early European printing, who hold typographic excellence above other considerations, Western Americana buffs give no attention to the quality of printing. Many frontier printshops were small, makeshift affairs that could not hold to high standards of crafts-manship. They existed merely to serve the local public, by providing a hometown newspaper and any commercial printing that might be required. Many did a brisk trade in handbills and broadsides, passed out on the street or tacked to walls, including the much sought-after reward posters that are now favorites of collectors. The variety of typefaces and symbols left much to be desired, and many of the western presses were not as modern as those in the east and in Europe. But as adversity often produces creativity, so it was in the west. What western printers lacked in hardware they made up in sweat and ingenuity and sound judgment. Many had to act as their own editors, just as the incunabula printers had done four centuries before, and some who had never written in their lives composed prefaces, intro-ductions, and other bits of literature. Compared to other forms of printing there were relatively few books published in the west within the years indicated above, for good and obvious reasons. Authors were few, readers still fewer, and the cost of bringing out a book was far beyond the means of the average printer.

WHITCHURCHE, EDWARD. English printer of the mid 16th century, Whitchurche began his career in 1537, in partnership with RICHARD GRAF-TON. Together they printed the Cromwell Bible of 1539-40, but went their own ways in 1541. Whitchurche is thought to have married the widow of archbishop Cranmer. He printed the *Book of Common Prayer* in 1549, the first edition of Edward VI's prayer book, then the second edition in 1552, both very rare. He also produced a Book of Hours after one used by

Catherine Parr, one of Henry VIII's wives, in 1550, in a tiny 32mo edition. There are various spellings of the name

WHOLESALER'S BINDING. One of the many headaches of collectors of first editions is the existence of wholesalers' bindings. The history of wholesale bindings is not too accurately known, which adds insult to injury. It was probably late in the 18th century that British distributors began to apply their own bindings to books, as they were delivered from the printers. Prior to this time books were either sold in unbound QUIRES or in TRADE BINDINGS. These early trade bindings were not uniform by any means, but at least had the advantage of being ordered by the publisher and thus of equal standing as regards priority. But as soon as wholesalers started commissioning separate bindings, all hades broke loose. There could then be a trade binding and various wholesale bindings on the same edition, depending on how many distributors handled it.

But the trouble really started in earnest when the age of publishers' cloth was ushered in, in the 1820's. Now bindings could be applied cheaper than ever and it was far more attractive for wholesalers—who were becoming a major factor in the book trade—to receive unbound copies at an appropriate discount and commission their own bindings. Here again there were trade and wholesale bindings on an individual edition, and even if they are as different as orange and purple it will defy the most advanced expert to say which is which, as there is generally no evidence in one direction or the other. The fact that fewer purple copies exist means nothing, nor does much else. The only way to settle these questions would be to survey the records of early publishing houses and wholesalers, almost all of which no longer survive. Many books described as in "original cloth" are actually in wholesalers' bindings—which, of course, is the original cloth, if one wishes to be an optimist. The value of a book in a wholesale binding compared to one in the usual trade covering would undoubtedly be somewhat less; but as detection is not apt to be made, no one is the wiser (or poorer). The case of wholesale bindings should serve to show the feeble thread by which much of bibliography hangs.

WIDENER, HARRY ELKINS. An American collector (1884-1912), Widener's basic interest was English literature, of which he accumulated a fine library in his brief life. Limited in funds, he dreamed of the day when he could compete for rarities of the upper class; but it was not to be, as he went down on the Titanic at the age of 28, returning with book purchases from London. His mother donated his library to Harvard University, along with funds to construct a building to house it. The collection has been greatly increased over the years.

WINCHESTER SCHOOL. The Winchester School was the most significant school of manuscript illumination that grew up in England, which was unfortunately short lived and produced comparatively few examples. Though it may have originated at the monastery at Winchester, the style was adopted in monasteries throughout the south of England. Monastic reforms of the 10th century are thought to have given rise to the increased attention to manuscripts, which had been undistinguished in England but for brief periods. The Winchester books were generally large, ponderous folios that took a very long time to complete and must have been handed over from one artist to another along the way. Some are decorated with ambitious miniatures, among the finest of their age, sometimes even considered superior to continental work. The Benedictional of St. Aethelwold in the British Museum is often pointed out as a typical example of the Winchester manner. There is excessive leaf ornament in many Winchester manuscripts, an offshoot of the earlier HIBERNO-SAXON school. Occasionally there was a drastic departure from this style: the miniatures would be drawn in plain pen and ink, without coloration, which scholars are at a loss to explain. By the 12th century the glories of the Winchester school were past and other influences, mainly ROMANESQUE, had taken hold of the English manuscript industry.

WING. The invaluable reference work which bears the name Wing was compiled by Donald Wing of Yale. It consists of a listing of English books, including those published abroad, printed from 1641 to 1700 and gives locations of copies in U.S. libraries. The period was chosen to take up where the Short Title Catalogue (see S.T.C.) leaves off and finish out the 17th century. It is not very thorough in locating copies, however, and the exuberant statement that Wing has found only a single specimen in the U.S. should be taken with reservations. With the hectic acquisitions activity at many institutional libraries, this information is fast outdated anyway.

WOLFE, REYNOLD. Wolfe was an English printer of the 16th century. At one time he held the office of Royal Printer and enjoyed a distinguished career. It is thought he was of continental blood, though probably born in England. He may have been, like PYNSON, a Norman. He began in the trade in 1542 and was active some 31 years, until his death in 1573. Yet the total of works assigned to his press is far less than one would expect, only about two for each year. This is partially the result, it is said, of the long hours he spent in research and other work instead of printing. Naturally, as Royal Printer he had no pitchfork at his back and could take things leisurely. For many years he had in view the publication of a *Universal Cosmography of All Nations*, a vast undertaking which was never executed, but the materials he gathered were used by Holinshed in his chronicles. After his death his widow, Joan, attempted to carry on the business and printed at least three books which she signed with her own name, but the press ceased operation after 1580. His mark was a serpent with a seasick expression entwined around a cross.

WOLGEMUT, MICHAEL. A German artist (1434-1519), Wolgemut was a prominent book illustrator of the incunabula period. He had won fame as a painter in Saxony before experimenting with woodcut, which had been used to produce the BLOCKBOOKS of the 15th century. In the opinion of modern critics his work in woodcut far surpasses his other achievements for its creativity and expression, especially when contrasted with the infancy of the art. Residing in Nuremberg, where he maintained a workshop both for painting and woodcut, he received many commissions from KOBERGER, the leading printer-publisher of that city. Among his most famous book illustrations are those for Hartmann Schedel's *Weltchronik* and the NUREMBERG CHRONICLE, both of which appeared in 1493. Wolgemut"s basic aim was to give woodcutting a character of its own and free it from the reins of the illuminator, who had traditionally been called in to finish the job. In this he succeeded, for the coloration of woodcuts ended with his work and that of ALBRECHT DURER. Durer was apprenticed as a youth to Wolgemut.

WOODEN BOARDS. From the 3rd or 4th century A.D. until little more than 200 years ago, the majority of books issued in western Europe were bound in wooden boards. At first plain bare wood, probably not even sanded or varnished, was used, with a calf or pigskin spine. Later the sides were covered in various undecorated leathers, whatever was handy at the moment, with consideration given mainly to strength and durability rather than beauty. Sometimes the wood would be inlaid with carved ivory or enamel plaques. Iron clasps, bosses, cornerpieces and even chains were added, nailed into the wood. Some medieval bindings were treated virtually as pincushions.

The first European country to abandon wooden boards for bindings was Italy. It is said that ALDO MANUTIUS introduced pasteboards as an inexpensive and less cumbersome substitute, but undoubtedly it was someone else. In any event this occurred toward the close of the 15th century. France and Spain quickly adopted the new technique. At first it was used mainly for small books but soon was applied to all. But a number of countries continued to favor wooden bindings, richly blindstamped, for a good while after. They were used on trade editions in Britain until well into the 16th century, in Germany and eastern Europe until the 18th. Only the increasing expense of leather, wood, and blindstamping caused them to be discontinued.

Most wooden bindings have survived in better condition than others (though the leather may be rubbed or worn). One must be careful in buying such books that the wood is not split, which cannot usually be noticed unless both covers are opened and examined from the inner side. Wooden bindings are desirable to many collectors, as they suggest medieval craftsmanship.

HOW TO USE THIS GUIDE

The price listings in this guide are grouped according to subject. All works of fiction—including drama, poetry, humor, novels and collections of short stories—are found under **Literature,** with the exception of fiction published for children (these works are in a separate section). Non-fiction is divided up into **Americana, Science and Medicine, Sports and Pastimes,** and various other categories (see index). Within each category, the books are listed by author.

In most listings, the author's name is followed by the book title, place of publication, and date, as it appears on the book's title page.

In many cases, old books do not carry a date, or even a place of publication. The lack of a date is indicated by "n.d." The lack of a place of publication appears as "n.p." Sometimes in these instances the place and/or date are known, in which event the listing will read "n.p. (Philadelphia)," or "n.d. (1843)." When the date is merely estimated, it appears as "circa 1843," or, more usually, just "c. 1843." When the place of publication is guessed at, it reads "Philadelphia (?)." When no date or place of publication is given, it means there is no reliable information to base estimates upon.

Whenever a book was published in more than one volume, this is stated in the listing. However, it should be kept in mind that old books are frequently found in rebindings, and that a two-volume set could be bound into one, a six-volume set into three and so forth. By the same token, some thick books issued as a single volume turn up bound into two.

In the case of early books with woodcut or engraved plates, or later volumes with hand-colored aquatints, the number of plates is usually given in the listing, as an aid to collectors in determining whether a volume is complete. It should be needless to advise anyone to **check the plates** before buying such books.

The prices stated are for copies in the original bindings, or, for books of the 17th century and earlier, good contemporary bindings (it is very difficult to determine, in books of that age, whether a binding is original).

To check a price, find the listing for that author, then look through the titles under his name. When the title is found, compare the place and date of publication, as well as any other information that might be given, against your book. If the date is different, you have a different edition and the stated price does not apply.

The prices shown are **fair retail selling prices,** based upon records of sales during the period in which this guide was compiled. They are not dealer buying prices. Generally, a dealer will pay about 50% of these prices for the more valuable books, somewhat less for the common material. Remember that condition is that all-important factor in prices. When a book is damaged or defective, it sells for considerably less than a good copy. A missing leaf can reduce the value of a book by half. By the same token, especially fine copies will often sell higher than the norm, especially if the book is hard to get in fine condition. Any book with aquatints—such as Gould's bird books—is guaranteed to fetch a big premium if all plates are fresh and clean and the binding "tight."

Above all, it should be understood that the prices reflect **past sales,** and make no effort to forecast values in the future.

AMERICANA

PRICE RANGE

☐ **Abbott, C. C.** *Primitive Industry: or Illustrations of the hand-iwork, of the Native Races of the Northern Atlantic Sea-board of America.* Salem, 1881............................. 110.00   135.00

☐ **Abbot, Carlisle S.** *Recollections of a California Pioneer.* N.Y., 1917. 235 pp. Clothbound. 55.00   75.00

☐ **Abbot, Joel.** *Trial of Lieutenant Joel Abbot by the Gen-eral Naval Court Martial.* Boston, 1822. 72 pp. Bound in boards... 38.00   47.00

☐ **Abel, A. H. and Klingberg, Frank J.** *A Sidelight on Anglo-American Relations, 1839–1858.* N.p., 1927. 407 pp. ... 63.00   80.00

☐ **Abernethy, John R.** *In the Camp with Theodore Roosevelt.* Oklahoma City, 1933. 279 pp. With 1 folding plate........ 37.00   47.00

☐ **Abernethy, John R.** *Catch 'Em Alive Jack: the Life and Adventures of an American Pioneer.* N.Y., 1936. 224 pp. 40.00   51.00

☐ **Ackerman, William K.** *Historical Sketch of the Illinois Cen-tral Railroad, together with a Brief Biographical Record of its incorporation and Some of its Early Officers.* Chicago, 1890. 153 pp. Softbound............................... 85.00   110.00

☐ **Adair, James.** *The History of the American Indians.* Lon-don, 1775... 1900.00   2250.00

☐ **Adams, Andy.** *The Log of a Cowboy: A Narrative of the Old Trail Days.* Boston, 1903. 387 pp. Bound in pictorial cloth.. 45.00   56.00

☐ **Adams, Andy.** *The Outlet.* Boston, 1905. 371 pp. Cloth-bound. 37.00   48.00

☐ **Adams, Andy.** *Wells Brothers; the Young Cattle Kings.* N.Y., Riverside Library, n.d. 25.00   32.00

☐ **Adams, Charles F.** *Chapters of Erie, and other Essays.* Boston, 1871. 429 pp.................................. 63.00   83.00

☐ **Adams, James T.** *New England in the Republic 1776–1850.* Boston, 1927. 438 pp............................ 24.00   31.00

☐ **Adams, James T.** *Provincial Society, 1690–1763.* N.Y., 1927. 374 pp.. 24.00   31.00

☐ **Adams, James T.** *Dictionary of American History.* Second edition, revised. N.Y., 1942. Six vols..................... 285.00   290.00

☐ **Adams, James T.** *Album of American History.* N.Y., 1944–1951. Five vols. Clothbound. 170.00   225.00

☐ **Adams, John.** *Correspondence Between the Hon. John Adams and the late William Cunningham, Beginning in 1803 and Ending in 1812.* Boston, 1823. 219 pp........ 58.00   72.00

☐ **Adams, Ramon F.** *Western Words.* Norman, Okl., 1944. 85.00   115.00

☐ **Adams, Ramon F.** *Come an' Get It.* Norman, Okl., 1952. 53.00   69.00

☐ **Adams, Samuel.** *An Appeal to the World; or a Vindication of the Towne of Boston.* 1769............................ 475.00   600.00

☐ **Adams, Samuel.** *An Oration Delivered at the State House, in Philadelphia.* London, 1776. Though Adams' name is on this work it was strictly a fabrication. He never delivered such an address. 285.00   335.00

☐ *Address and Recommendations to the States, by the United States in Congress Assembled.* Boston, 1783............ 285.00   335.00

☐ **Albert, George D.** *History of the County of Westmoreland, Pa.* Philadelphia, 1882................................. 140.00   175.00

PRICE RANGE

☐ **Albert, Col. J. J.** *The Canal Route from the Portage Summit in Ohio to Kearney's Line.* Washington, D.C., 1835. 74 pp. Softbound.. 160.00 195.00

☐ **Albright, Raymond W.** *Two Centuries of Reading, Pa., 1748–1948.* Reading, 1948. Limited to 1,000 copies. 23.00 31.00

☐ **Alexander, John H.** *Mosby's Men.* N.Y., 1907........... 45.00 59.00

☐ **Allaben, Frank.** *John Watts de Peyster.* N.Y., 1908. Two vols.. 35.00 44.00

☐ **Allan, J. T.** *Western Nebraska and the Experiences of its Actual Settlers.* Omaha, 1882. 16 pp. Softbound......... 560.00 685.00

☐ **Allanson, George.** *A Segment of Minnesota History.* Wheaton, Minnesota, n.d. (c. 1911). 20 pp............... 85.00 110.00

☐ **Allen, Albert H.** *Arkansas Imprints, 1821–1876.* N.Y., 1947. 236 pp. Clothbound. 53.00 68.00

☐ **Allen, Ethan.** *A Narrative of Col. Ethan Allen's Captivity.* Walpole, N.H., 1807. Sixth edition...................... 190.00 230.00

☐ **Allen, Col. Ethan.** *Reason, the Only Oracle of Man.* N.Y., 1836. Second edition.................................... 70.00 90.00

☐ **Allen, Gardner W.** *Massachusetts Privateers of the Revolution.* Mass. Historical Society, 1927. 356 pp............. 62.00 83.00

☐ **Allen, George.** *An Appeal to the People of Massachusetts, on the Texas Question.* Boston, 1844. 20 pp. Softbound. 77.00 98.00

☐ **Allen, John H.** *Southwest.* N.Y., 1952.................. 23.00 29.00

☐ **Allen, Paul.** *A History of the American Revolution.* Baltimore, 1822. Two vols. 185.00 230.00

☐ **Allen, Thomas.** *Missouri: Its History, Characteristics, Resources and Present Condition.* Philadelphia, 1876. 29 pp. Softbound... 93.00 118.00

☐ **Allhands, L. L.** *Gringo Builders.* Iowa City, 1931. 284 pp. Privately printed.. 110.00 140.00

☐ **Allhands, J. L.** *Railroads to the Rio.* Saldo, Texas, 1960. 213 pp. Limited to 1,000 copies...................... 40.00 50.00

☐ **Almon, John.** *The Remembrancer; or, Impartial Repository of Public Events. Parts 1 for the Year 1776.......... 105.00 130.00

☐ **Alsop, Richard.** *Narrative of the Adventures and Sufferings of John R. Jewitt...during a Captivity...among the Savages of Nootka Sound.* N.Y., n.d. (c. 1815). 203 pp. With 2 plates. Bound in cloth boards, paper label on spine... 125.00 160.00

☐ **Alter, Cecil.** *James Bridger: Trapper, Frontiersman, Scout and Guide.* Salt Lake City, 1925. 546 pp. With 18 plates. Limited to 1,000 copies, signed and numbered.......... 175.00 235.00

☐ **Ambler, Charles Henry.** *A History of Transportation in the Ohio Valley, with Special Reference to its Waterways.* Glendale, 1932. 465 pp. 80.00 105.00

☐ **Ames, Fisher.** *The Works of Fisher Ames.* Boston, 1809. 519 pp. With a frontispiece portrait. Bound in calf. 50.00 65.00

☐ *An Accurate Version of Historical Truth. Details of the Conspiracy that led to the Overthrow of the Monarchy.* Honolulu, 1897. 80 pp. Softbound........................... 340.00 415.00

☐ *An Act to Amend an Act to Authorize the Sale of the Southern Rail Road Company.* N.p., n.d. (Lansing, 1850). 4 pp. Softbound. 150.00 180.00

PRICE RANGE

☐ **Anderson, Abraham A.** *Experiences and Impressions.* N.Y., 1933. 245 pp. 30.00   38.00

☐ **Anderson, Eva Greenslit.** *Chief Seattle.* Caldwell, Idaho, 1943. 390 pp. 52.00   68.00

☐ **Anderson, George S.** *Report of the Acting Superintendant of the Yellowstone National Park to the Secretary of the Interior.* Washington, D.C., 1895. 24 pp. Softbound. 25.00   32.00

☐ **Anderson, R. A.** *Fighting the Mill Creeks.* Chico, Calif., 1909. 86 pp. Softbound. 75.00   95.00

☐ **Anderson, T. M.** *The Political Conspiracies Preceding the Rebellion, or the True Stories of Sumter and Pickens.* N.Y., 1882. .... 24.00   31.00

☐ **Anderson, Thomas J.** *Life and Letters of Thomas J. Anderson.* N.p., 1904. .... 16.00   21.00

☐ **Andre, Major John.** *An Authentic Narrative of the Causes Which led to the Death of Major Andre.* By Joshua H. Smith. London, 1808. With a map and 2 plates. 230.00   290.00

☐ **Andre's Journal.** *An Authentic Record of the Movements and Engagements of the British Army in America from June, 1777, to November, 1778.* Boston, 1903. Two vols. Quarto, full vellum, boxed, one of ten copies on Japan paper for the Bibliophile Society. 415.00   500.00

☐ **Andrews, C. C.** *Minnesota and Dacotah: in Letters Descriptive of a Tour Through the North-West in the Autumn of 1856.* Washington, D.C., 1857. 215 pp. 140.00   180.00

☐ **Andrews, Charles M.** *The Colonial Period of American History.* New Haven, 1936–38. Four vols. Bound in cloth. 95.00   110.00

☐ **Andrews, Israel D.** *Communication from the Secretary of the Treasury, Transmitting the Report of Israel D. Andrews.* Washington, D.C., 1854. 851 pp. Regarding trade in Canada. 85.00   105.00

☐ **Andrews, William L.** *The Bradford Map.* N.Y., 1893. 115 pp. Clothbound. Limited to 142 copies. 70.00   90.00
This work is sometimes found in full morocco or other deluxe bindings, in which case the value is considerably higher.

☐ **Angle, Paul M.** *The Lincoln Reader.* Rutgers, 1947. ...... 20.00   25.00

☐ **Anspach, Frederick R.** *Sons of the Sires: a History of the Rise, Progress and Destiny of the American Party.* Philadelphia, 1855. 223 pp. Clothbound. 58.00   73.00

☐ **Ansted, David T.** *The Gold–Seeker's Manual.* London, 1849. .... 575.00   715.00

☐ **Armor, William C.** *Lives of the Govenors of Pennsylvania, with a History of the State.* Philadelphia, 1872. .... 20.00   25.00

☐ **Armstrong, M. K.** *History and Resources of Dakota, Montana and Idaho.* N.p., n.d. (1928). 62 pp. Softbound. 37.00   48.00

☐ **Arnold, Benedict.** *The Present State of the American Rebel Army, Navy and Finances.* Edited by Paul Leicester Ford. Brooklyn, 1891. .... 37.00   45.00

☐ **Arnold, Richard D.** *An Oration ... Before the Union and States Rights Association of Chatam County.* Savannah, Georgia, 1835. 21 pp. 105.00   125.00

PRICE RANGE

☐ **Artrip, Louise and Fullen.** *Memoirs of Daniel Fore (Jim Chisholm and the Chisholm Trail).* Booneville, Arkansas, 1949. 89 pp. Softbound.................................... **125.00** **160.00**

☐ *A Sketch of the Life and Public Services of Gen. W.H. Harrison, Candidate of the People.* Washington, D.C., 1840. 16 pp. Softbound... **90.00** **115.00**

☐ **Athearn, Robert G.** *High Country Empire.* N.Y., 1960. ... **22.00** **29.00**

☐ **Atwater, Caleb.** *The Writings of Caleb Atwater.* Columbus, Ohio, 1833. 408 pp. Bound in boards.................... **78.00** **95.00**

☐ **Avary, Myrta Lockett.** *Dixie after the War.* N.Y., 1906. ... **21.00** **27.00**

☐ **Ayer, Edward E.** *Report on Menominee Indian Reservation.* N.p., 1914. 151 pp................................. **53.00** **68.00**

☐ **Babbitt, Charles H.** *Early Days at Council Bluffs.* Washington, D.C., 1916. 96 pp.............................. **65.00** **80.00**

☐ **Babcock, Oliver M.** *The New Conspiracy. The Solid South and Its Bold Purposes. The Lost Cause to be Found Again and Appomattox Avenged.* Philadelphia, 1888. 20 pp. Softbound. **47.00** **62.00**

☐ **Babcock, Sidney H.** *History of Methodism in Oklahoma.* Np, 1935. 440 pp. Identified as "Volume One," but no further volumes were published. **53.00** **68.00**

☐ **Baca, Cabeza.** *We Fed Them Cactus.* Albuquerque, N.M., n.d. (c. 1945). 186 pp. **42.00** **53.00**

☐ **Bacon, Leonard.** *Thirteen Historical Discourses, on the Completion of Two Hundred Years...of the First Church in New Haven.* New Haven, 1939. .... **28.00** **34.00**

☐ **Baegert, Johann Jakob.** *Observations in Lower California.* Berkeley, 1952. 218 pp. **42.00** **57.00**

☐ **Balley, Alfred M.** *Desert River Through Navajo Land.* Article in National Geographic Magazine, August, 1947..... **3.00** **4.00**

☐ **Bailey, James.** *History of the Seventh Day Baptist General Conference.* Toledo, 1866. 322 pp...................... **47.00** **62.00**

☐ **Bailey, James M.** *History of Danbury, Conn., 1684–1896.* N.Y., 1896. .... **230.00** **285.00**

☐ **Bailey, Washington.** *A trip to California in 1853.* N.p., 1915. Softbound. **275.00** **335.00**

☐ **Baird, Charles W.** *History of the Huguenot Emigration to America.* N.Y., 1885. Two vols. **140.00** **175.00**
A reprint was published in 1966, which is now selling for. **35.00** **45.00**

☐ **Baird, Joseph Armstrong.** *California's Pictorial Letter Sheets, 1849–1869.* San Francisco, 1967. 171 pp. A review of letterheads used by California's early business firms. With Facsimilies in a Pocket on the Back Cover.......... **265.00** **325.00**

☐ **Baker, J. C.** *Baptist History of the North Pacific Coast.* Philadelphia, 1912. 472 pp............................. **24.00** **30.00**

☐ **Balch, Edwin S.** *Letters and Papers Relating to the Alaska Frontier.* Philadelphia, 1904. 134 pp. **50.00** **65.00**

☐ **Balch, Thomas W.** *The Alabama Arbitration.* Philadelphia, 1900. .... **21.00** **27.00**

☐ **Baldwin, Alice M.** *The New England Clergy and the American Revolution.* Durham, N.C., 1928. .... **9.00** **12.00**

☐ **Baldwin, Leland D.** *The Keelboat Age on Western Waters.* Pittsburgh, 1941. 268 pp................................. **30.00** **39.00**

PRICE RANGE

☐ **Baldwin, Sara Mullen.** *Nebraskana.* Hebron, Nebraska, 1932. Clothbound. 80.00   100.00

☐ **Baldwin, Simeon E.** *Life and Letters of Simeon Baldwin.* New Haven, n.d. (c. 1920). 503 pp. 20.00   25.00

☐ **Balestier, J. N.** *The Annals of Chicago.* Chicago, 1840. 24 pp. Softbound, rare. The first history of Chicago. 8250.00   10500.00

☐ **Ball, Nicholas.** *The Pioneers of '49.* Boston, 1891. 288 pp. With 7 plates. 95.00   120.00

☐ **Ball, Thomas.** *My Threescore Years and Ten.* Boston, 1892. 379 pp. 13.00   17.00

☐ **Ballou, Robert.** *Early Klickitat Valley Days.* Goldendale, Washington, 1938. 496 pp. Washington State had its famous desperados in the Old West Days, and this book recalls them. 85.00   110.00

☐ **Bancroft, Edward.** *A Narrative of the Objects and Proceedings of Silas Deane, as Commissioner of the United Colonies to France.* Edited by Paul Leicester Ford. Brooklyn, 1891. . . . . 30.00   40.00

☐ **Bancroft, Geo.** *Our Martyr President, Abraham Lincoln.* N.Y., n.d., 1865. . . . . 30.00   40.00

☐ **Bancroft, George.** *Martin Van Buren to the End of his Public Career.* N.Y., 1889. 239 pp. Clothbound. 20.00   25.00

☐ **Bancroft, H. H.** *History of the Native Races of the Pacific Slope.* San Francisco, 1882. Five vols. Maps. 385.00   475.00

☐ **Bancroft, Hubert H.** *Native Races of the U.S.* San Francisco, 1882. Five vols. Bound in half calf. 140.00   175.00

☐ **Bancroft, Hubert H.** *History of Mexico.* San Francisco, 1883–1888. Six vols. Bound in ½ calf. 160.00   200.00

☐ **Bancroft, Hubert H.** *History of Central America.* San Francisco, 1883–1887. Three vols. Bound in half sheepskin. 90.00   115.00

☐ **Bancroft, Hubert H.** *History of Arizona and New Mexico, 1530–1888.* San Francisco, 1889. 829 pp. 60.00   80.00

☐ **Bancroft, Hubert H.** *History of the North Mexican States and Texas.* San Francisco, 1890. Two vols. Bound in half sheepskin. 120.00   150.00

☐ **Bancroft, Hubert H.** *History of Utah.* San Francisco, 1890. 808 pp. Bound in half sheepskin. 48.00   63.00

☐ **Bancroft, Hubert H.** *Essays and Miscellany.* San Francisco, 1890. 764 pp. Half sheep. 30.00   39.00

☐ **Bancroft, Hubert H.** *California Pioneer Register and index, 1542–1848.* Baltimore, 1964. 392 pp. 22.00   28.00

☐ **Bandelier, Adolf F.** *The Gilded Man (El Dorado).* N.Y., 1893. 302 pp. 75.00   100.00

☐ **Bandini, Joseph.** *A Description of Calaifornia in 1828.* Berkeley, 1951. 52 pp. 73.00   95.00

☐ **Banks, Charles E.** *The Planters of the Commonwealth.* Boston, 1930. 231 pp. Limited to 750 copies. 73.00   95.00

☐ **Barbe-Marbois, Marquis de.** *Our Revolutionary Forefathers.* N.Y., 1929. . . . . 9.00   12.00

☐ **Barker, Elliott S.** *Beatty's Cabin.* Albuquerque, 1953. . . . . 21.00   27.00

☐ **Barker, Eugene.** *The Life of Stephen Austin, Founder of Texas.* Austin, 1949. 551 pp. With folding maps. 43.00   55.00

PRICE RANGE

☐ **Barker, Jacob.** *Incidents in the Life of Jacob Barker, of New Orleans, Louisiana, with Historical Facts.* Washington, D.C., 1855. 285 pp. With 2 plates. 48.00   63.00

☐ **Barker, John.** *The British in Boston.* Cambridge, Mass., 1923. . . . .   12.00   16.00

☐ **Barlow, Joel.** *Prospectus of a National Institution to be Established in the United States.* Washington, D.C., 1806. 44 pp. Softbound. The "national institution" was the Smithsonian. 215.00   265.00

☐ **Barnard, Evan G.** *A Rider of the Cherokee Strip.* Boston, 1936. 233 pp. 58.00   73.00

☐ **Barnard, John.** *The Lord Jesus Christ the Only, and Supream (sic) Head of the Church.* Boston, 1738. 34 pp. 80.00   100.00

☐ **Barnard, John.** *The True Divinity of Jesus Christ; evidenced in a Discourse at the Public Lecture in Boston.* Boston, 1761. 38 pp. 50.00   70.00

☐ **Barnes, James.** *Naval Actions of the War of 1812.* N.Y., 1896. 263 pp. 27.00   35.00

☐ **Barney, Mary.** *A Biographical Memoir of the Late Commodore Joshua Barney.* Boston, 1832. 328 pp. Bound in cloth. 57.00   78.00

☐ **Barnhart, John D.** *Henry Hamilton and George Rogers Clark in the American Revolution.* Crawfordsville, Indiana, 1951. 244 pp. 20.00   25.00

☐ **Barns, George C.** *Denver, the Man.* Wilmington, Ohio, 1949. . . . .   32.00   43.00

☐ **Barrett, Ellen C.** *Baja California 1535–1956.* Los Angeles, 1957. 285 pp. Limited to 500 copies. 150.00   190.00

☐ **Barron, S. B.** *The Lone Star defenders; a chronicle of the Third Texas Cavalry, Ross' Brigade.* N.Y., 1908. . . . .   650.00   850.00

☐ **Barry, T. A. and Patten, B. A.** *Men and Memories of San Francisco, in the Spring of '50.* San Francisco, 1873. cloth. 275.00   350.00

☐ **Bartlett, J. R.** *History of the Destruction of His Britannic Majesty's Schooner Gaspee . . . 10th June, 1772.* N.p., 1861. Softbound. 38.00   49.00

☐ **Barton, Rebecca.** *Witness for Freedom.* N.Y., n.d. (1948). 32.00   42.00

☐ **Baskin, R. N.** *Reminiscences of Early Utah.* Salt Lake City, 1914. 252 pp. Clothbound. 65.00   85.00

☐ **Bass, W. W.** *Adventures in the Canyons of the Colorado by Two of its Earliest Explorers, James White and W. W. Hawkins.* Grand Canyon, 1920. 38 pp. Softbound. 250.00   325.00

☐ **Batchelder, Samuel.** *Burgoyne and His Officers in Cambridge 1777–1778.* Cambridge, 1926. 80 pp. Softbound.   15.00   20.00

☐ **Bates, D. B.** *Incidents on Land and Water; or, Four Years on the Pacific Coast.* Boston, 1857. 336 pp. With 4 plates. . . . .   58.00   ˙ 73.00

☐ **Bates, Frederick.** *The Life and Papers of Frederick Bates.* St. Louis, 1926. Two vols. 30.00   38.00

☐ **Bates, James H.** *Notes of a Tour in Mexico and California.* N.Y., 1887. 167 pp. 145.00   185.00

PRICE RANGE

☐ **Battine, Cecil.** *The Crisis of the Confederacy.* N.Y., 1905. . . . . 30.00   39.00

☐ **Baxley, H. Willis.** *What I Saw on the West Coast of South and North America.* N.Y., 1865. 632 pp. Bound in pictorial cloth. 130.00   170.00

☐ **Baxter, James P.** *The Trelawny Papers.* Portland, 1884. 520 pp. Folding maps. 43.00   59.00

☐ **Baxter, James P.** *George Cleeve of Casco Bay, 1630– 1667.* Portland, 1885. 339 pp. With folding map. Soft-bound. 100.00   125.00

☐ **Baxter, James P.** *The British Invasion from the North.* Albany, N.Y., 1887. 412 pp. 105.00   140.00

☐ **Baxter, W. T.** *The House of Hancock: Business in Boston, 1724–1775.* Harvard University Press, 1945. 321 pp. 42.00   58.00

☐ **Bayard, James A.** *Speech of the Hon. James A. Bayard of Delaware, on the Bill Received from the Senate.* Hartford, 1802. 48 pp. Softbound. 35.00   44.00

☐ **Bayard, Samuel.** *A Funeral Oration occasioned by the Death of Gen. George Washington.* New Brunswick, 1880. Softbound. 95.00   115.00

☐ **Bayard, Samuel J.** *A Sketch of the Life of Commodore Robert F. Stockton.* N.Y., 1856. Clothbound. 63.00   82.00

☐ **Baylies, Nicholas.** *Eleazor Wheelock Ripley of the War of 1812.* Des Moines, Iowa, 1890. 191 pp. Clothbound. 32.00   40.00

☐ **Beach, W. W.** *Indian Miscellany; Containing Papers on the History of the American Aborigines.* Albany, N.Y., 1877. 490 pp. 47.00   62.00

☐ **Beardsley, E. Edwards.** *Life and Times of William S. Johnson, first Senator in Congress from Connecticut.* Boston, 1886. 225 pp. 45.00   60.00

☐ **Bechdolt, Frederick.** *When the West Was Young.* N.Y., 1922. 309 pp. 53.00   68.00

☐ **Bechdolt, Frederick.** *Tales of the Old Timers.* N.Y., 1924. 367 pp. Clothbound. 85.00   105.00

☐ **Beebe, Lucius.** *The American West: the Pictorial Epic of a Continent.* N.Y., 1955. 511 pp. 48.00   63.00

☐ **Beecher, Harris H.** *Record of the 114th Regiment, N.Y.S.V.* Norwich, N.Y., 1866. . . . . 27.00   35.00

☐ **Beeson, John.** *A Plea for the Indians.* N.Y., 1858. 143 pp. Softbound. 220.00   275.00

☐ **Belcher, Henry.** *The First American Civil War, First Period 1775–1778.* London, 1911. Two vols. 32.00   39.00

☐ **Belknap, William W.** *Proceedings of the Senate sitting for the Trial of William W. Belnap, Late Secretary of War, on the Articles of Impeachment.* Washington, D.C., 1876. 1,166 pp. Bound in half leather. 90.00   115.00

☐ **Bell, Horace.** *Reminiscences of a Ranger; or, Early Times in Southern California.* Los Angeles, 1881. 457 pp. Bound in cloth. 250.00   325.00

☐ **Bell, Landon C.** *The Old Free State.* Richmond, 1927. Two vols. 37.00   48.00

PRICE RANGE

☐ **Bell, Capt. W. H.** *The Quiddities of an Alaskan trip.* Portland, Ore., 1873. 67 pp. Clothbound (oblong format). A very unusual satirical book about Alaska, with humorous drawings. "Quiddities" was the author's way of saying "bizarre happenings.". 265.00 335.00

☐ **Bell, William S.** *Old Fort Benton.* Helena, Mont., 1909. 31 pp. Softbound. 58.00 73.00

☐ **Belle, Francis P.** *Life and Adventures of the Celebrated Bandit Joaquin Murrieta.* Chicago, 1925. 174 pp. Limited to 975 copies. 70.00 100.00

☐ **Bellinger, E.** *Compilation of Laws Relating to the Powers and Duties of Commissioners of the Poor in South Carolina.* Columbia, S.C., 1859. 110 pp. Softbound. 63.00 75.00

☐ **Benard, John.** *Retrospections of America, 1797–1811.* N.Y., 1887. 380 pp. Clothbound. 53.00 68.00

☐ **Benard, Francis and others.** *Letters to the Ministry.* Boston, 1769. . . . . 180.00 230.00

☐ **Benjamin, Marcus.** *Washington during War time.* Washington, D.C., n.d. (early 1900's). 22.00 28.00

☐ **Bennett, Estelline.** *Old Deadwood Days.* N.Y., 1928. 300 pp. Clothbound. 60.00 80.00

☐ **Bennett, Frank M.** *The Monitor and the Navy Under Steam.* N.Y., 1900. . . . . 18.00 24.00

☐ **Bennett, W. P.** *The First Baby in Camp.* Salt Lake City, 1893. Softbound. 65.00 85.00

☐ **Benson, Adolph B.** *Swedes in America 1638–1938.* New Haven, 1938. 614 pp. 25.00 30.00

☐ **Benson, William S.** *The Merchant Marine.* N.Y., 1923. 183 pp. 12.00 16.00

☐ **Benton, Frank.** *Cowboy Life on the Sidetrack.* Denver, 1903. . . . . 150.00 200.00

☐ **Benton, J. A.** *The California Pilgrim.* Sacramento, 1853. 350.00 450.00

☐ **Benton, J. H.** *What is Government by Injunction?.* Concord, N.H., 1898. 110 pp. Softbound. 42.00 53.00

☐ **Benton, Jesse J.** *Cow by the Tail.* Boston, 1943. 225 pp. 35.00 45.00

☐ **Benton, Josiah Hart.** *Voting in the Field: a Forgotten Chapter of the Civil War.* 332 pp. Limtied to 100 copies. 53.00 68.00

☐ **Benton, Thomas H.** *Thirty Years' View.* N.Y., 1854–56. Two vols. Bound in cloth. 53.00 68.00

☐ **Bernhardt, Joshua.** *The Alaskan Engineering Commission.* N.Y., 1922. 119 pp. 25.00 33.00

☐ **Berquin, Arnaud.** *The family book or children's journal.* Detroit, 1812. Two vols. In French and English, rare. 1900.00 2250.00

☐ **Berthold, Victor M.** *The Pioneer Steamer California, 1848–1849.* Boston, 1932. 106 pp. Limited to 550 copies. 100.00 130.00

☐ **Bertie, Willoughby.** *Thoughts on the Letter of Edmund Burke, Esq.* Lancaster, 1778. . . . . 150.00 190.00

☐ **Beveridge, Albert J.** *The Life of John Marshall.* Cambridge, 1916–1919. Four vols. 65.00 80.00

☐ **Biart, Lucien.** *The Aztecs, Their History, Manners, and Customs.* Chicago, 1887. . . . . 120.00 150.00

PRICE RANGE

☐ **Biddle, Ellen.** *Reminiscences of a Soldier's Wife.* Philadelphia, 1907. 258 pp. 35.00 43.00

☐ **Bidwell, John.** *Echoes of the Past.* Chico, California, n.d. (c. 1900). 91 pp. Softbound............................ 67.00 83.00

☐ **Bidwell, John.** *A Journey to California.* San Francisco, 1937. 48 pp... 135.00 175.00

☐ **Bigelow, John.** *The Life of Samuel J. Tilden.* N.Y., 1895. Two vols. Clothbound. 23.00 29.00

☐ **Bigelow, Timothy.** *An Eulogy on the Life, Character and Services of Brother George Washington, Deceased.* Boston, n.d., 1800. Softbound. 70.00 90.00

☐ **Bingham, Hiram.** *A Residence of Twenty-One Years in the Sandwich Islands.* Hartford, 1849. 616 pp. Bound in half leather.. 80.00 110.00

☐ **Bingham, Hiram, Jr.** *Five Straws Gathered from Revolutionary Fields.* Cambridge, 1901....................... 40.00 50.00

☐ **Bingham, John A.** *Trial of the Conspirators for the Assassination of President Lincoln.* Washington, 1865. 122 pp. Softbound. 45.00 60.00

☐ **Bird, Annie Laurie.** *Boise, the Peace Valley.* Caldwell, Idaho, 1934. 408 pp.. 32.00 39.00

☐ **Bird, M. B.** *The Victorious. A Small Poem on the Assassination of President Lincoln.* Kingston, Jamaica, 1866. .. 87.00 112.00

☐ **Birdsong, James C.** *Brief sketch of the North Carolina State troops in the War between the States.* Raleigh, 1894. .... 68.00 89.00

☐ **Birge, Julius C.** *The Awakening of the Desert.* Boston, 1912. 429 pp. With 25 plates.......................... 50.00 65.00

☐ **Birket, James.** *Some Cursory Remarks Made by James Birket, in his Voyage to North America, 1750–1751.* New Haven, 1916. 73 pp. Bound in boards. Limited to 300 copies. 47.00 63.00

☐ **Birney, William.** *James G. Birney and his Times.* N.Y., 1890. 443 pp. Bound in cloth.......................... 25.00 32.00

☐ **Bishop, Abraham.** *Oration Delivered in Wallingford on the 11th of March 1801 before the Republicans of the State of Connecticut.* New Haven, 1801. 111 pp. Softbound.... 38.00 45.00

☐ **Bishop, Harriet E.** *Floral Home: or, First Years of Minnesota.* N.Y., 1857. 342 pp. With 9 plates. 53.00 69.00

☐ **Bishop, Morris.** *The Odyssey of Cabeza De Vaca.* N.Y., 1933. 306 pp.. 32.00 43.00

☐ **Bishop, Nathaniel H.** *Four Months in a Sneak-Box: a Boat Voyage of 2,600 Miles down the Ohio and Mississippi Rivers.* Boston, 1879. 322 pp. 65.00 85.00

☐ **Bixby-Smith, Sarah.** *Adobe Days.* Cedar Rapids, Iowa, 1925. 208 pp. Bound in boards........................ 70.00 95.00

☐ **Black Hawk.** *The Great Indian Chief of the West.* Cincinnati, 1849.. 210.00 265.00

☐ **Black, Robert.** *The Little Miami Railroad.* Cincinnati, n.d. (c. 1940). 191 pp.. 32.00 39.00

☐ **Blair, E. H..** *Indian Tribes of the Upper Mississippi Valley and Region of the Great Lakes.* Cleveland, 1911. Two vols. 120.00 150.00

PRICE RANGE

☐ **Blair, John.** *A Sermon Delivered in Madison, N.Y., at the Interment of Mr. John Millen, who was Found Near his Father's House Suspended to the Limb of a Tree.* Sangerfield (N.Y.), 1826. 16 pp. Softbound................... 190.00   220.00

☐ **Blair, Walter A.** *A Raft Pilot's Log.* Cleveland, 1930. 328 pp... 52.00   67.00

☐ **Blake, Herbert Cody.** *Blake's Western Stories.* Brooklyn, 1929. 32 pp. Softbound.
In this scarce little book, the author attempted to show that the Old West's legendary characters weren't so legendary if you actually knew them................................ 200.00   250.00

☐ **Blanchard, Leola H.** *Conquest of Southwest Kansas.* Wichita, 1931. 355 pp. 35.00   43.00

☐ **Blanco, Antonio.** *The Journey of the Flame.* Boston, 1933... 20.00   25.00

☐ **Blatchford, John.** *Narrative of Remarkable Occurrences, in the life of John Blatchford, of Cape Ann, Commonwealth of Massachusetts.* New London, 1794.................. 950.00   1200.00

☐ **Bledsoe, Albert T.** *An Essay on Liberty and Slavery.* Philadelphia, 1856. 383 pp. 62.00   83.00

☐ **Bleeker, Leonard.** *The Order Book of Capt. Leonard Bleeker.* N.Y., 1865. Softbound......................... 33.00   39.00

☐ **Block, Eugene B.** *Great Stage Coach Robbers of the West.* N.Y., 1962. .... 18.00   23.00

☐ **Bloomfield, J. K.** *The Oneidas.* N.Y., 1907. .... 32.00   39.00

☐ **Blue, Herbert T. O.** *The Story of Ft. McArthur.* Canton, Ohio, 1933. 180 pp. Softbound.......................... 15.00   20.00

☐ **Bodfish, Harston H.** *Chasing the Bowhead.* Cambridge, Mass., 1936. 281 pp..................................... 42.00   53.00

☐ **Bolles, Albert S.** *The Financial History of the United States, from 1774 to 1789.* N.Y., 1879. 371 pp.................. 55.00   70.00

☐ **Bolton, Herbert E.** *The Colonization of North America, 1492–1783.* N.Y., 1921. 609 pp. 40.00   50.00

☐ **Bolton, Herbert E.** *Anza's California Expeditions.* Berkeley, 1930. Five vols. With folding maps. Bound in cloth. .. 500.00   625.00

☐ **Bolton, Herbert E. and Ross, Mary.** *The Debatable Land.* Berkeley, Calif., 1925. 139 pp. 60.00   80.00

☐ **Bond, Beverley W.** *The Civilization of the Old Northwest.* N.Y., 1934. 543 pp. Clothbound. 37.00   48.00

☐ **Bondy, William.** *The Separation of Governmental Powers.* N.Y., 1893. 129 pp. Softbound. 23.00   30.00

☐ **Bonnin, Gertrude.** *Oklahoma's Poor Rich Indians. An Orgy of Grafting and Exploitation.* Philadelphia, 1924. 39 pp. Softbound. Published by an organization known as "Indian Rights.".. 95.00   120.00

☐ **Bonwick, James.** *The Mormons and the Silver Mines.* London, 1872. 425 pp. Clothbound......................... 90.00   115.00

☐ **Booth, John.** *In memoriam John Booth ... Died in Austin, Nevada, 1884.* Austin, Nevada, 1884. 8 pp. Softbound. .. 25.00   32.00

☐ **Borth, Christy.** *Pioneers of Plenty.* Indianapolis, 1939. 303 pp... 18.00   23.00

☐ **Borup, George.** *A Tenderfoot with Peary.* N.Y., 1911. Folding map. 25.00   32.00

PRICE RANGE

☐ **Boston, Massacre.** *A Fair Account of the Late Unhappy Disturbances at Boston.* London, 1770. The author is unidentified; possibly Francis Maseres. 1925.00 2350.00

☐ **Boston, Massacre.** *Trial of William Wemms, James Hartegan, etc., Soldiers in His Majesty's 29th Regiment of Foot, for the Murder of Crispus Attucks, Samuel Gray, etc.* Boston, 1770. . . . . 1350.00 1675.00

☐ **Boston, Massacre.** *Proceedings of His Majesty's Council of the Province of Massachusetts Bay, Relative to the Deposition of Andrew Oliver, Esq.* Boston, 1770. . . . . 2325.00 2850.00

☐ **Boston, Massacre.** *Short Narrative of the Horrid Massacre in Boston, Perpetrated in Evening of the 5th Day of March 1770.* Boston, 1770. . . . . 1900.00 2375.00

☐ **Boston, Massacre.** *The Boston Gazette and Country Journal. Containing the freshest Advices, Foreign and Domestic.* Boston, 1770. . . . . 650.00 775.00

☐ **Boston, Massacre.** *Innocent Blood Crying to God from the Streets of Boston.* Boston, 1771. . . . . 1375.00 1800.00

☐ **Boston, Massacre.** *The Poem Which the Committee of the Town of Boston Had Voted Unanimously to Be Published With the Late Oration.* Boston, 1772. . . . . 800.00 1075.00

☐ **Botta, Charles.** *History of the War of Independence of the United States of America.* New Haven, 1834. Two vols. 37.00 48.00
Originally published in Italy. Translated from the Italian by George A. Otis.

☐ **Bottolfsen, C. A.** *Little Bits of Los River History.* Arco, Idaho, 1926. 16 pp. Wrappers, laced with buckskin. 63.00 83.00

☐ **Boucher, Jonathan.** *Reminiscences of an American Loyalist, 1783–1789.* Boston, 1925. Boards with paper label, boxed. 40.00 50.00

☐ **Boudinot, Elias.** *Journal, or Historical Recollections of American Events during the Revolutionary War.* Trenton, N.J., 1894. 97 pp. Limited to 315 copies. 37.00 45.00

☐ **Bourke, John G.** *The Snake Dance of the Moquis of Arizona.* N.Y., 1884. With colored and plain plates. 450.00 575.00

☐ **Bowden, Angle Burt.** *Early Schools of Washington Territory.* Seattle, 1935. 631 pp. 26.00 35.00

☐ **Bowditch, Henry I.** *Life and Correspondence of Henry I. Bowditch.* Boston, 1902. Two vols. 22.00 28.00

☐ **Bowen, J. J.** *The Strategy of Robert E. Lee.* N.Y., 1914. 20.00 25.00

☐ **Bower, B. M.** *The Range Dwellers.* N.Y., 1907. Illustrated by Charles M. Russell. 125.00 150.00

☐ **Bower, B. M.** *Cow Country.* Boston, 1921. . . . . 45.00 59.00

☐ **Boyd, Thomas.** *Simon Girty, the White Savage.* N.Y., 1928. 247 pp. 32.00 43.00

☐ **Boyer, Nathalie R.** *A Virginia Gentleman and his Family.* Philadelphia, 1939. 200 pp. Bound in boards. Limited to 300 copies, signed. 27.00 36.00

☐ **Boyle, Esmeralda.** *Biographical Sketches of Distinguished Marylanders.* Baltimore, 1877. 374 pp. Bound in cloth. 43.00 55.00

☐ **Boynton, H. V.** *Sherman's Historical Raid.* Cincinnati, 1875. . . . . 22.00 28.00

PRICE RANGE

☐ **Brackett, R. W.** *A History of the Ranchos of San Diego County, California.* San Diego, 1939. 86 pp. Softbound. . . 65.00 85.00

☐ **Bradbury, Thomas.** *The Ass or the Serpent.* Boston, 1768. Softbound. 85.00 105.00

☐ **Bradlee, Francis B.** *Piracy in the West Indies and its Suppression.* Salem, 1923. . . . . 80.00 105.00

☐ **Brady, Joseph P.** *The Trial of Aaron Burr.* N.Y., 1913. 89 pp. 31.00 42.00
Burr, a U.S. Vice President, shot and killed Alexander Hamilton (George Washington's Secretary of the Treasury) in a duel.

☐ **Bragdon, O. D.** *Facts and Figures, or Useful and Important Information for the People of Louisiana.* New Orleans, 1872. 57 pp. With folding charts and tables. Softbound. 55.00 70.00

☐ **Braman, Milton P.** *The Mexican War.* Danvers, 1847. 36 pp. Softbound. 75.00 100.00

☐ **Bramlette, Gov. T. E.** *Speech to Ratify the Nomination of McClellan and Pendleton.* Frankfort, 1864. 15 pp. Softbound. 145.00 175.00

☐ **Branch, E. Douglas.** *The Hunting of the Buffalo.* N.Y., 1929. 240 pp. 55.00 70.00

☐ **Breakenridge, William M.** *Helldorado.* Boston, 1928. Not first edition. 43.00 55.00

☐ **Brebner, John B.** *The Explorers of North America, 1492– 1806.* N.Y. 1933. 502 pp. 43.00 55.00

☐ **Brebner, John B.** *North Atlantic Triangle.* New Haven, 1945. 385 pp. With maps, some of which are folding. 48.00 62.00

☐ **Breilhan, Carl W.** *Badmen of the Frontier Days.* N.Y., 1957. . . . . 43.00 55.00

☐ **Brewer, William H.** *Up and Down California.* New Haven, 1930. 601 pp. Clothbound. 110.00 140.00

☐ **Brewington, Dorothy and Brewington, M. V.** *The Marine Paintings and Drawings in the Peabody Museum.* Salem, Mass., 1968. 530 pp. Clothbound. 150.00 200.00

☐ **Bridenbaugh, Carl.** *Rebels and Gentlemen. Philadelphia in the Age of Franklin.* N.Y., 1942. 393 pp. 22.00 29.00

☐ **Briggs, Emily Edson.** *The Olivia Letters.* N.Y., 1906. 445 pp. 32.00 40.00

☐ **Briggs, L. Vernon.** *Experiences of a Medical Student in Honolulu, and on the Island of Oahu, 1881.* Boston, 1926. 251 pp. Clothbound. 47.00 63.00

☐ **Brill, Charles J.** *Conquest of the Southern Plains.* Oklahoma City, 1938. 323 pp. 65.00 85.00

☐ **Brinley, Francis.** *Life of William T. Porter.* N.Y., 1860. 273 pp. 25.00 32.00

☐ **Brinton, D. G.** *Ancient Nahuatl Poetry.* Philadelphia, 1887. . . . . 22.00 30.00

☐ **Broke, George.** *With Sack and Stock in Alaska.* London, 1891. 158 pp. 70.00 95.00

☐ **Bromfield, Louis and others.** *Flat Top Ranch.* Norman, Okla., 1957. . . . . 23.00 30.00

PRICE RANGE

☐ **Bronaugh, Warren C.** *The Younger's Fight for Freedom.* Columbia, Mo., 1906. 398 pp. With plates. Tells the story of Bronaugh's efforts to have the notorious Younger Brothers (members of the Cole Younger desperado clan) released from prison. 225.00   300.00

☐ **Bronson, Edgar.** *Reminiscences of a Ranchman.* N.Y., 1908. 314 pp.. 65.00   85.00

☐ **Bronson, Edgar.** *Red Blooded.* N.Y., n.d. (c. 1910). 341 pp. All about the Wild West. 85.00   105.00

☐ **Brooks, Juanita.** *The Mountain Meadows Massacre.* Stanford University Press, n.d. (c. 1950) 243 pp.......... 80.00   105.00

☐ **Bross, William.** *America as a Field for the Exertions of the Christian Scholar.* Chicago, 1866. 55 pp. Softbound...... 47.00   59.00

☐ **Brown, Alexander.** *The First Republic in America.* Boston, 1898. 688 pp... 50.00   70.00

☐ **Brown, John.** *Twenty Five Years a Parson in the Wild West.* Fall River, Mass., 1896. 215 pp. Published by the author. 78.00   105.00

☐ **Brown, Mark H., and Felton, W. R.** *The Frontier Years.* N.Y., 1955. .... 67.00   88.00

☐ **Browne, John Ross.** *Crusoe's Island.* N.Y., 1864. Clothbound. 75.00   90.00

☐ **Brownlow, W. G.** *Message and Inaugural Address.* Nashville, 1865. 23 pp. Softbound............................ 450.00   550.00

☐ **Brownson, O. A.** *An Oration on the Scholar's Mission.* Boston, 1843. 40 pp. Softbound......................... 20.00   25.00

☐ **Brownson, Orestes A.** *The Works of Orestes A. Brownson.* Detroit, 1882–1907. 20 vols. Bound in cloth........ 700.00   850.00

☐ **Bruce, Philip A.** *Social Life in Virginia in the 17th Century.* Lynchburg, 1927. 275 pp. 27.00   35.00

☐ **Bruce, William C.** *Benjamin Franklin, Self-Revealed.* N.Y., 1917. Two vols.. 88.00   112.00

☐ **Bryan, William J.** *Memoirs of William J. Bryan.* Philadelphia, 1925. 560 pp. 21.00   27.00

☐ **Bryan, W. S. and Rose, Robert.** *A History of the Pioneer Families of Missouri.* St. Louis, 1876. 569 pp. Reprinted at Columbia, Mo., 1935. .... 48.00   62.00

☐ **Bryant, Edwin.** *Alcade of St. Francisco.* N.Y. 1848. ..... 215.00   260.00

☐ **Bryce, George.** *The Remarkable History of Hudson's Bay Company.* London, 1900. 502 pp. With 31 maps and plates. 49.00   63.00

☐ **Bryk, Felix.** *Dark Rapture.* N.Y., 1939. .... 32.00   40.00

☐ **Buchanan, James.** *Sketches of the History, Manners and Customs of the North American Indians.* N.Y., 1824. Two vols. (sometimes bound together). 215.00   265.00

☐ **Buchanan, James.** *Execution of Colonel Crabb and Associates.* Washington, D.C., 1858. 84 pp. Softbound...... 245.00   290.00

☐ **Buchanan, James.** *Message of the President of the United States ... in Relation to the Massacre at Mountain' Meadows.* Washington, D.C., 1860. 139 pp. Softbound. 75.00   95.00

☐ **Buck, Solon J.** *Travel and Description 1765–1865.* Springfield, Ill., 1914. 514 pp.................................. 65.00   85.00

PRICE RANGE

☐ **Buckingham, James S.** *America: Historical, Statistical, and Descriptive.* London, 1841. Three vols. With folding map. 115.00   150.00

☐ **Buckley, J. M.** *Two Weeks in the Yosemite and Vicinity.* N.Y., n.d. (c. 1883). 36 pp. Softbound.   48.00   63.00

☐ **Buel, J. W.** *Louisiana and the Fair.* St. Louis, c. 1904–1905. Ten vols. With plates. Bound in ½ leather and boards. 250.00   325.00

☐ **Buffum, G. T.** *Smith of Bear City and Other Frontier Sketches.* N.Y., 1906. 249 pp. 65.00   85.00

☐ **Buley, R. Carlyle.** *The Old Northwest Pioneer Period.* Bloomington, Ind., 1951. Two vols. 65.00   85.00

☐ **Bulfinch, Thomas.** *Oregon and Eldorado.* Boston, 1866. 464 pp. Clothbound. 48.00   63.00

☐ **Burch, L. D.** *Nebraska as it Is.* Chicago, 1878. With folding map. Softbound. 150.00   200.00

☐ **Burder, George.** *The Welch Indians.* Tarrytown, N.Y., 1922. Softbound. 21.00   27.00

☐ **Burke, William M.** *History and Functions of Central Labor Unions.* N.Y., 1899. 127 pp. Softbound. 27.00   34.00

☐ **Burlend, Rebecca.** *A True Picture of Emigration.* London, n.d. (1848). 54 pp. Softbound. 115.00   145.00

☐ **Burnham, L.** *Guide to the Lands of the Union Pacific Railroad Co. in Nebraska.* Omaha, n.d., 1883. . . . .   250.00   325.00

☐ **Burns, Walter Noble.** *The Saga of Billy the Kid.* Garden City, 1926. . . . .   125.00   150.00

☐ **Burns, Walter Noble.** *Tombstone. An Iliad of the Southwest.* N.Y., 1927. . . . .   65.00   85.00

☐ **Burpee, Lawrence J.** *The Search for the Western Sea.* N.Y., 1908. 651 pp. With 6 maps and 51 plates. 110.00   140.00

☐ **Burton, Jonathan.** *Diary and Orderly Book of Sergeant Jonathan Burton of Wilton, N.H., 1775–1776.* Concord, N.Y., 1885. Softbound. 20.00   25.00

☐ **Burton, Richard F.** *The City of Saints, and Across the Rocky Mountains to California.* N.Y., 1862. 574 pp. With 2 maps and 19 plates. 85.00   105.00

☐ **Butler, Frances Anne.** *Journal by Frances Anne Butler.* Philadelphia, 1835. Two vols. 37.00   47.00

☐ **Butterworth, B.** *Commercial Union between Canada and the United States.* N.Y., n.d. (c. 1885). 39 pp. Softbound.   34.00   45.00

☐ **Butterfield, Consul W.** *An Historical Account of the Expedition Against Sandusky under Col. William Crawford in 1782.* Cincinnati, 1873. 404 pp. Bound in cloth. 40.00   50.00

☐ **Butterfield, C. W.** *Washington-Irvine Correspondence.* Madison, Wis., 1882. . . . .   63.00   79.00

☐ **Byington, Cyrus.** *Holisso Anumpa Tosholi. An English and Choctaw Definer; for the Choctaw Academies and Schools.* N.Y., 1852. 252 pp. Bound in boards. English-Indian dictionaries were never too successful, and this one was no exception. Since the Indian languages were strictly oral, they were hard to put into print. 140.00   175.00

☐ *By-laws of the Chicago & Rock Island Rail Road Co..* N.Y., 1858, 10 pp. Softbound. 105.00   140.00

PRICE RANGE

☐ **Cable, George W.** *The Negro Question.* N.Y., 1888. 32 pp. Softbound. 58.00   73.00

☐ **Cable, George W.** *Old Creole Days.* N.Y., 1897. . . . . 30.00   40.00

☐ **Cable, John Ray.** *The Bank of the State of Missouri.* N.Y., 1923. 321 pp. Softbound. 35.00   45.00

☐ **Cadwalader, Gen. John.** *A Reply to Gen. Joseph Reed's Remarks on the Late Publication in the Independent Gazeteer.* Trenton, 1846. 36 pp. Softbound. 37.00   48.00

☐ **Cady, John.** *Arizona's Yesterday, Being the Narrative of John Cady, Pioneer.* (Patagonia, 1915), 127 pp. Softbound. 200.00   265.00

☐ **Calder, Isabel M.** *Colonial Captivities, Marches and Journeys.* N.Y., 1935. 255 pp. With 2 plates. 27.00   34.00

☐ **Caldwell, Joshua W.** *Sketches of the Bench and Bar in Tennessee.* Knoxville, 1898. 402 pp. Bound in cloth. 48.00   63.00

☐ **Calhoun, Arthur W.** *A Social History of the American Family from Colonial Times to the Present.* Cleveland, 1917–1919. Three vols. 72.00   93.00

☐ *California Three Hundred and Fifty Years Ago.* San Francisco, 1888. Cloth. 180.00   230.00

☐ **Calkins, Frank W.** *Frontier sketches.* Chicago, 1893. 134 pp. Bound in cloth. 75.00   100.00

☐ **Call, Daniel.** *Reports of Cases Argued and Adjudged in the Court of Appeals of Virginia.* Richmond, 1801. 588 pp. Bound in full calf. 105.00   135.00

☐ **Calvin, Ross.** *Sky Determines.* N.Y., 1934. 354 pp. 37.00   45.00

☐ **Camden, Quachita County.** *Resources and Advantages with a Description for Those Seeking Homes in the Southwest.* Little Rock, 1883. 16 pp., plus 16 pp. directory of business cards. Softbound. 180.00   230.00

☐ **Campbell, George.** *White and Black: the Outcome of a Visit to the United States.* N.Y., 1879. 420 pp. 43.00   55.00

☐ **Campbell, John F.** *A Short American Tramp in the Fall of 1864.* Edinburgh, 1865. 427 pp. 62.00   83.00

☐ **Campbell, Maria.** *Revolutionary Services and Civil Life of General William Hull.* N.Y., 1848. 482 pp. 34.00   43.00

☐ **Campbell, Tom W.** *Two Fighters and Two Fines.* Little Rock, 1941. . . . . 23.00   31.00

☐ **Canfield, Chauncy L.** *The Diary of a Forty-Niner.* N.Y. and S.F., 1906. 253 pp. 85.00   105.00

☐ **Canning, George.** *A Letter to the Right Honourable Wills Earl of Hillsborough, on the Connection between Great Britain and Her American Colonies.* London, 1768. . . . . . . 115.00   150.00

☐ **Cannon, George Q.** *A Review of the Decision of the Supreme Court of the United States in the Case of George Reynolds vs. the United States.* Salt Lake City, 1879. 57 pp. Softbound. 57.00   72.00

☐ **Canton, Frank M.** *Frontier Trails. The Autobiography of Frank M. Canton.* Boston and N.Y., 1930. 236 pp. 53.00   68.00

☐ **Carey, Charles H.** *History of Oregon.* Chicago, 1922. Three vols. With maps. 130.00   170.00

☐ **Carey, Henry C.** *The Resources of the Union.* Philadelphia, 1866. 26 pp. Softbound. 34.00   43.00

PRICE RANGE

☐ **Carey, Mathew.** *The Olive Branch, or Faults on Both Sides.* Boston, Rowe, 1815. 226 pp. Bound in boards........... 43.00 58.00

☐ **Carleton, James H.** *The Battle of Buena Vista, with the Operations of the "Army of Occupation" for One Month.* N.Y., 1848. 238 pp. 59.00 73.00

☐ **Carlisle, William.** *Bill Carlisle, Lone Bandit.* Illus. by Charles M. Russell. Pasadena, n.d. (c. 1947). 220 pp. 80.00 105.00

☐ **Carpon, E. S.** *History of California, from its Discovery to the Present Time.* Boston, 1854......................... 250.00 325.00

☐ **Carrington, Col. Henry B.** *AB-SA-RA-KA, Land of Massacre.* Philadelphia, 1879............................... 85.00 105.00

☐ **Carroll, Charles.** *Journal of Charles Carroll of Carrollton, During his Visit to Canada in 1776.* Baltimore, 1876. 110 pp. Softbound............................... 37.00 45.00

☐ **Carroll, George R.** *Pioneer Life.* Cedar Rapids, Iowa, 1895. 251 pp...................................... 60.00 80.00

☐ **Carson, Kit.** *Kit Carson's Own Story of His Life.* Taos, N.M., 1926. 138 pp. Softbound...................... 125.00 160.00

☐ **Carstarphen, James E.** *My Trip to California in '49.* Louisiana, Missouri (a town in Missouri), 1914. Softbound. ... 90.00 115.00

☐ **Carter, Robert G.** *The Old Sergeant's Story.* N.Y., 1926. 220 pp. Clothbound. 65.00 85.00

☐ **Cazruthers, Eli W.** *A Sketch of the Life of the Rev. David Caldwell.* Greensborough, N.C., 1842. 302 pp. Bound in half calf...................................... 47.00 62.00

☐ **Caruthers, E. W.** *Revolutionary Incidents.* Philadelphia, 1854... 28.00 34.00

☐ **Carvalho, S. N.** *Incidents of Travel and Adventure in the Far West.* N.Y., 1857. 380 pp........................... 65.00 85.00

☐ **Casey, Charles.** *Two Years on the Farm of Uncle Sam.* London, 1852. 311 pp. 37.00 48.00

☐ **Casey, Robert J.** *The Black Hills and Their Incredible Characters.* Indianapolis, 1949. 383 pp. 27.00 37.00

☐ **Castaneda, Carlos E.** *The Mexican Side of the Texan Revolution.* Dallas, 1928. 391 pp........................... 120.00 150.00

☐ **Catton, Bruce.** *This Hallowed Ground.* Garden City, 1956. .... 12.00 15.00

☐ **Caughey, John Walton.** *McGillivary of the Greeks.* Norman, Oklahoma, 1938. 385 pp. 50.00 65.00

☐ **Chabot, Frederick.** *Texas in 1811.* San Antonio, 1941. 162 pp. Clothbound.................................... 55.00 70.00

☐ **Chadwick, F. E.** *The Graves Papers.* N.Y., 1916. 268 pp. Bound in vellum boards. One of 650 numbered copies. .. 30.00 39.00

☐ **Chaffin, Lorah B.** *Sons of the West.* Caldwell, 1941. 284 pp... 85.00 105.00

☐ **Chamberlain, Joshua L.** *The Passing of the Armies.* N.Y., 1915. .... 32.00 43.00

☐ **Chambers, John.** *The Autobiography of John Chambers.* Iowa City, 1908. 49 pp. Limited to 400 numbered copies. Chambers was the second governor of the Iowa Territory. This book was published by the state's Historical Society. 47.00 63.00

☐ **Channing, Edward** and others. *The Barrington Bernard Correspondence.* Cambridge, Mass., 1912. 306 pp....... 22.00 28.00

PRICE RANGE

☐ **Chapelle, Howard Irving.** *The Baltimore Clipper: Its History and Development.* Salem, 1930. 192 pp............ 160.00 — 210.00

☐ **Chapelle, Howard Irving.** *The History of American Sailing Ships.* N.Y., 1935. 400 pp. With plates, some of them tipped in. Limited to 121 numbered, signed copies. In the original publisher's box.................................. 150.00 — 190.00

☐ **Chapman, Charles E.** *A History of California: the Spanish Period.* N.Y., 1921. 527 pp. With maps. .... 53.00 — 72.00

☐ **Chardon, Francis A.** *Chardon's Journal at Fort Clark, 1834–1839.* Pierce, 1932. 458 pp. .... 58.00 — 79.00

☐ **Chase, Champion S.** *Our Nebraska Farms.* Omaha, 1879. 22 pp. Softbound............................... 73.00 — 100.00

☐ **Chatterton, E. Keble.** *Ship Models.* London, 1923. 53 pp. With 142 colored plates. Bound in cloth. Limited to 1,000 copies....................................... 175.00 — 225.00

☐ **Chauncy, Charles.** *Cornelius' Character. A Sermon Preach'd the Lord's-Day after the Funeral of Mr. Cornelius Thayer.* Boston, 1745................................ 100.00 — 130.00

☐ **Chauncey, Charles.** *A Discourse on "the Good News from a Far Country."* Boston, 1766. .... 375.00 — 450.00

☐ **Cheetham, James.** *A Narrative of the Suppression by Col. Burr, of the History of the Administration of John Adams. By a Citizen of New York,* N.Y., 1802. 72 pp. Bound in ½ calf....................................... 185.00 — 230.00

☐ **Cheeves, Langdon.** *Speech of Hon. Langdon Cheves, in the Southern Convention at Nashville, Tennessee, November 14th, 1850.* Nashville, 1850. 30 pp. Softbound. ...... 75.00 — 100.00
Cheves' speech was an encouragement for southern states to rise up against the North, and thus, is of interest to Civil War collectors—even though it dates 10 years before the war.

☐ *Chicago in Ashes!! Hundreds of millions of dollars' worth of property destroyed. The city in ruins. All ... great business blocks swept away. The conflagration still in progress.* Chicago, 1871. A one sheet broadside, an extra to the Journal newspaper, giving details of the Chicago fire. 800.00 — 1125.00

☐ **Child, Mrs. Lydia M.** *An Appeal in Favor of that Class of Americans called Africans.* N.Y., 1836............... 80.00 — 105.00

☐ **Child, William.** *A History of the Fifth Regiment, New Hampshire Volunteers in the American Civil War, 1861–65.* Bristol, 1893. .... 23.00 — 30.00

☐ **Chipman, N. P.** *Investigation into Indian Affairs before the Committee on Appropriations.* Washington, D.C., 1871. 121 pp. Softbound.. 90.00 — 115.00

☐ **Church, Elihu Dwight.** *Catalogue of Books Relating to the Discovery and Early History of North and South America.* N.Y., 1907. Five vols. Lavishly illustrated. Printed on fine paper. Bound in ½ green morocco. Each volume in a folding morocco-backed box. .... 2200.00 — 2750.00

☐ **Church, Thomas.** *The History of King Philip's War.* Boston, 1865. Two vols. Softbound. Limited to 285 sets. .... 65.00 — 80.00

☐ *Circular Letter from the Congress of the United States ... to Their Constituents.* Boston, 1779. Softbound.......... 290.00 — 340.00

PROCEEDINGS

OF A

BOARD

OF

GENERAL OFFICERS,

HELD BY ORDER OF

. His Excellency Gen. WASHINGTON,

Commander in Chief of the Army of the United States
of AMERICA.

RESPECTING

Major JOHN ANDRÈ,

Adjutant General of the Britiſh Army.

SEPTEMBER 29, 1780.

PHILADELPHIA.
Printed by FRANCIS BAILEY, in Market-Street.
M.DCC.LXXX.

This scarce tract is a cornerstone item for collectors of Revolutionary War material. "His Excellency Gen. Washington" had not yet begun his first term as President when it was published in 1780.

PRICE RANGE

☐ **Cist, Charles.** *Cincinnati in 1841. Its Early Annals and Future Prospects.* Cincinnati, 1841. 300 pp. Illustrated.... | 75.00 | 100.00

☐ **Clappe, Louise A.** *The Shirley Letters from the California Mines.* San Francisco, 1922. 350 pp. With 8 plates. Limited to 450 signed, numbered copies. .... | 200.00 | 250.00

☐ **Clark, Champ.** *Remarks of Champ Clark of Missouri, on Various Topics.* Washington, D.C., 1907. Softbound. ...... | 21.00 | 27.00

☐ **Clark, Ferdinard.** *The American Captives in Havana.* Boston, 1841. 36 pp. Softbound. .... | 80.00 | 105.00

☐ **Clark, John M.** *Social Control of Business.* Chicago, n.d. (1926). 483 pp. .... | 27.00 | 32.00

☐ **Clark, Thomas D.** *The Rampaging Frontier.* Indianapolis, 1939. 350 pp. .... | 42.00 | 53.00

☐ **Clarke, Lewis.** *Narratives of the Sufferings of Lewis and Milton Clarke, Sons of a Soldier of a Revolution, During a Captive of More than Twenty Years Among the Slaveholders of Kentucky.* Boston, 1846. 144 pp. Bound in cloth. .. | 72.00 | 93.00

☐ **Clarke, S. A.** *Pioneer Days of Oregon History.* Cleveland, 1905. Two vols.. | 90.00 | 120.00

☐ **Clay, John.** *My Life on the Range.* N.Y., 1961. (reprint). | 65.00 | 85.00

☐ **Clinch, Bryan J.** *California and its Missions.* San Francisco, 1904. Two vols.................................... | 130.00 | 165.00

☐ **Clinton, Henry.** *Observations on Some Parts of the Answer of Earl Cornwallis to Sir Henry Clinton's Narrative.* London, 1783. With folding table. .... | 260.00 | 335.00

☐ **Clinton, Henry.** *A Letter from Lieut. Gen. Sir Henry Clinton.* London, 1784. .... | 230.00 | 285.00

☐ **Clinton, Henry.** *Observations on Earl Cornwallis' Answer.* Philadelphia, 1866. Clothbound. Limited to 250 copies.... | 52.00 | 65.00

☐ **Coates, Robert M.** *The Outlaw Years.* N.Y., 1930. .... | 45.00 | 60.00

☐ **Coatsworth, Stella S.** *The Loyal people of the North-West.* Chicago, 1869. Collected also as a "pre-fire" Chicago imprint.. | 90.00 | 120.00

☐ **Cockings, George.** *The American War, a Poem.* London, 1781. .... | 700.00 | 850.00

☐ **Cobb, W. Montague.** *The First Negro Medical Society: a History of the Medico-Chirurgical Society of the District of Columbia, 1884–1939.* Washington, D.C., 1939.......... | 43.00 | 56.00

☐ **Coburn, F. W.** *The Battle of Lexington Common.* Lexington, 1921. .... | 15.00 | 20.00

☐ **Codman, John.** *Arnold's Expedition to Quebec.* N.Y., 1903. 371 pp. Large paper copy................................ | 52.00 | 67.00

☐ **Cody, William F.** *Buffalo Bill's Wild West and Congress of Rough Riders of the World.* Chicago, 1893. 64 pp. Softbound. .... | 60.00 | 80.00
This pamphlet was sold at Buffalo Bill's circus. Huge quantities were undoubtedly printed but it has, nonetheless, become a sought-after item.

☐ **Cody, William F.** *True Tales of the Plains.* By Buffalo Bill. N.Y., 1908. 250 pp. .... | 90.00 | 125.00

☐ **Coffin, Charles C.** *Life of Abraham Lincoln.* N.Y., 1893. | 40.00 | 50.00

PRICE RANGE

☐ **Coffin, George.** *A Pioneer Voyage to California and Round the World 1849–52.* Chicago, 1908. 235 pp. With 10 plates. 70.00   90.00

☐ **Coggeshall, George.** *Second Series of Voyages to Various Parts of the World.* N.Y., 1852. 335 pp. 57.00   73.00

☐ **Coghlan, Margaret.** *Memoirs of Mrs. Coghlan, Daughter of the late Major Moncrieffe.* London, 1794. Two vols. . . .   145.00   180.00

☐ **Cohen, A. A.** *An Address on the Railroad Evil and its Remedy Delivered by A. A. Cohen at Platt's Hall, San Francisco.* San Francisco, 1879. 23 pp. Softbound. 70.00   90.00

☐ **Cohen, Octavus R.** *Highly Colored.* N.Y., 1921. . . . .   50.00   65.00

☐ **Coke, Daniel P.** *The Royal Commission on the Losses and Services of American Loyalists, 1783–1785.* Oxford, 1915. One of 25 copies. 265.00   320.00

☐ **Cole, Cornelius.** *Memoirs of Cornelius Cole.* N.Y., 1908. 353 pp. 67.00   88.00
Cornelius Cole went to California in the '49 Rush and ended up becoming a Senator from that state.

☐ **Cole, Gilbert L.** *In the Early Days Along the Overland Trail in Nebraska Territory.* Kansas City, 1905. 125 pp. Clothbound. Privately printed in an edition which, though unnumbered, was apparently very small.   150.00   190.00

☐ **Cole, Harry E.** *Stagecoach and Tavern Tales of the Old Northwest.* Cleveland, 1930. 376 pp. With a folding map.   50.00   65.00

☐ **Colefax, S. and Taylor, J.** *The Mormon Question.* Salt Lake City, 1870. 25 pp. Softbound. 100.00   135.00
A Mormon publication, made in reply to a speech about the Mormons given by Vice President Schuyler Colfax (of the U.S. Grant cabinet).

☐ **Coleman, Emma Lewis.** *New England Captives carried to Canada between 1677 and 1760, during the French and Indian War.* Portland, 1925. Two vols. 77.00   103.00

☐ **Coleman, J. Winston Jr.** *A Bibliography of Kentucky History.* Lexington, 1949. 516 pp. 62.00   83.00

☐ **Coleman, William.** *An Examination of the President's Reply to the New Haven Remonstrance.* N.Y., 1801. 69 pp. Softbound. 55.00   70.00

☐ **Collins, Hubert E.** *Warpath and Cattle Trail.* N.Y., 1928. 296 pp. 57.00   72.00

☐ **Collins, Varnum L.** *The Continental Congress.* Princeton, N.J., 1908. 295 pp. 35.00   45.00

☐ **Collum, Richard S.** *History of the U.S. Marine Corps.* Philadelphia, 1890. 307 pp. With plates. 50.00   65.00

☐ **Colwell, S.** *The South: a Letter from a Friend in the North with Reference to the Effects of Disunion upon Slavery.* Philadelphia, 1856. 46 pp. Softbound. 78.00   100.00

☐ *Complete and Unabridged Edition. Containing the Whole of the Suppressed Evidence. The Trail of the Alleged Assassins and Conspirators at Washington, D.C., May & June, 1865, for the Murder of President Abraham Lincoln.* Philadelphia, n.d., 1865. Softbound. 175.00   225.00

☐ **Cone, Andrew and others.** *Petrolia: a Brief History of the Pennsylvania Petroleum Region.* N.Y., 1870. 652 pp. 160.00   210.00

PRICE RANGE

☐ **Conkey, W. B.** *The Official Guide to the Klondyke country and the Gold Fields of Alaska.* Chicago, 1897. 296 pp. Softbound. 350.00 450.00

☐ **Conklin, E.** *Picturesque Arizona.* N.Y., 1878. 380 pp. 65.00 85.00

☐ **Conkling, Alfred.** *The Life and Letters of Roscoe Conkling.* N.Y., 1889. 709 pp. 24.00 31.00

☐ **Connolly, A. P.** *A Thrilling Narrative of the Minnesota Massacre and the Sioux War of 1862–1863.* Chicago, n.d. (1896). 273 pp. 180.00 235.00

☐ **Cook, Elizabeth C.** *Literary Influences in Colonial Newspapers, 1704–1750.* N.Y., 1912. 279 pp. 40.00 55.00

☐ **Cook, James.** *Fifty Years on the Old Frontier.* Norman, Okla., 1957. . . . . 38.00 49.00

☐ **Cook, John R.** *The Border and the Buffalo.* Topeka, 1907. 352 pp. With plates. Bound in pictorial cloth. 125.00 155.00

☐ **Cooke, John Esten.** *A Life of General Robert E. Lee.* N.Y., 1871. . . . . 16.00 21.00

☐ **Cooke, Philip.** *Exploring Southwestern Trails, 1846–1854.* Glendale, Calif., 1938. 383 pp. 95.00 120.00

☐ **Coolidge, Dane.** *Fighting Men of the West.* N.Y., 1932. 343 pp. 95.00 120.00

☐ **Coolidge, Dane.** *Death Valley Prospectors.* N.Y., 1937. 178 pp. 48.00 62.00

☐ **Coolidge, L. A.** *Klondike and the Yukon Country, a Description of our Alaskan Land of Gold.* Philadelphia, 1897. 251 pp. 95.00 120.00

☐ **Cooper, Alonzo.** *In and Out of Rebel Prisons.* Oswego, N.Y., 1888. . . . . 21.00 27.00

☐ **Copway, G.** *The Traditional History and Characteristic Sketches of the Ojibway Nation.* Boston, 1851. . . . . 85.00 105.00

☐ **Corbett, H. W.** *Oregon: its resources, soil, climate, etc.* Jacksonville, Florida, 1871, rare. 650.00 875.00

☐ **Corlie, Edwin.** *Burro Alley.* N.Y., 1938. . . . . 30.00 39.00

☐ **Corner, William.** *San Antonio de Baxar. A Guide and History.* San Antonio, 1890. 166 pp. Bound in cloth. 110.00 145.00

☐ **Cornwallis, Earl.** *An Answer to that Part of the Narrative of Lieutenant-General Sir Henry Clinton which relates to the Conduct of . . . Earl Cornwallis.* London, 1783. . . . . 170.00 200.00

☐ **Corry, John.** *The Life of George Washington.* N.Y., 1807. First American edition. 140.00 170.00

☐ **Cotton, Josiah.** *Vocabulary of the Massachusetts (or Natick) Indian Language.* Cambridge, 1829. . . . . 45.00 60.00

☐ **Courcy, Henry de.** *The Catholic Church in the United States.* N.Y., 1856. 594 pp. 25.00 35.00

☐ **Cox, Jacob D.** *Military Reminiscences of the Civil War.* N.Y., 1900. Two vols. 83.00 105.00

☐ **Cox, Sanford C.** *Recollections of the Early Settlement of the Wabash Valley.* Lafayette, Ind., 1860. 160 pp. Clothbound. 130.00 170.00

☐ **Crafts, Mrs. E. P. R.** *Pioneer days in the San Bernardino Valley.* Redlands, 1906. . . . . 450.00 575.00

☐ **Crandall, Samuel B.** *Treaties, their Making and Enforcement.* N.Y., 1904. 257 pp. Softbound. 40.00 55.00

PRICE RANGE

☐ **Crane, Leo.** *Indians of the Enchanted Desert.* Boston, 1925. 364 pp. 42.00   57.00

☐ **Crawford, Medorem.** *Journal of Medorem Crawford. An Account of his Trip Across the Plains with the Oregon Pioneers of 1842.* Eugene, 1897. 26 pp. Softbound. 110.00   140.00
Published by the Eugene Star.

☐ **Crawford, Samuel W.** *The Genesis of the Civil War. The Story of Sumter, 1860–1861.* N.Y., 1887. . . . .   20.00   25.00

☐ **Cresswell, Nicholas.** *The Journal of Nicholas Cresswell, 1774–1777.* N.Y., 1924. . . . .   12.00   15.00

☐ **Crichton, Lyle S.** *Law and Order, Ltd. The Rousing Life of Elfego Baca of New Mexico.* Santa Fe, 1928. 219 pp.   125.00   160.00
Despite Elfego Baca's celebrity as a badman, this was the only book written about him. Most western "baddies" were the subject of slews of titles.

☐ **Crittendon, H. H.** *The Crittenden Memoirs.* N.Y., 1936. 542 pp. 100.00   135.00
Crittenden put up the reward which gave Robert Ford the incentive to shoot Jesse James.

☐ **Crofutt, George A.** *Crofutt's Grip-sack Guide of Colorado.* Omaha, Nebraska, 1881. Marked "Volume One." 185 pp.   150.00   195.00

☐ **Croffut, W. A. and others.** *The Military and Civil History of Connecticut During the War of 1861–65.* N.Y., 1868. . .   23.00   30.00

☐ **Crotty, D. G.** *Four Years Campaigning in the Army of the Potomac.* Grand Rapids, Michigan, 1874. . . . .   58.00   73.00

☐ **Crouse, Nellis.** *The Search for the Northwest Passage.* N.Y., 1934. 533 pp. 37.00   48.00

☐ **Crowe, Pat.** *His Story—Confession—and Reformation.* N.Y., 1906. 252 pp. 53.00   69.00

☐ **Crowninshield, Mary B.** *Letters of Mary B. Crowinshield, 1815–1816.* Cambridge, Mass., 1905. 82 pp. Limited to 300 numbered copies. 28.00   36.00

☐ **Cruden, John.** *Report of the Management of the Estates Sequestered in South Carolina, by Order of Lord Cornwallis, in 1780–82.* Brooklyn, 1890. Softbound. 29.00   37.00

☐ **Culbertson, Thaddeus.** *Journal of an Expedition to the Mauvaises Terres and the Upper Missouri in 1850.* Washington, D.C., 1952. 164 pp. With folding maps. Softbound. 40.00   50.00

☐ **Cullen, Countee.** *Color.* N.Y., n.d. (1925). 21.00   27.00

☐ **Cummings, Byron.** *First Inhabitants of Arizona and the Southwest.* Tucson, 1953. 251 pp. 47.00   62.00

☐ **Cummings, Henry.** *Synopsis of the Cruise of the U.S. 'Tuscarora' from the Date of Her Commission to Her Arrival in San Francisco, Cal, Sept. 2nd, 1874.* San Francisco, 1874. 61 pp. Clothbound. 100.00   125.00

☐ **Curti, Merle.** *The Learned Blacksmith.* N.Y., 1937. 241 pp. 18.00   23.00

☐ **Curtis, George William.** *Orations and Addresses of George Williams Curtis.* N.Y., 1894. 3 vols. Clothbound. 33.00   40.00

☐ **Curwen, Samuel.** *The Journal and Letters of Samuel Curwen.* Boston, 1864. . . . .   35.00   45.00

PRICE RANGE

☐ **Cushing, Caleb.** *Outlines of the Life and Public Services, Civil and Military, of William Henry Harrison.* Boston, 1840. 71 pp. Softbound. 33.00   40.00
William Henry Harrison died one month after taking the office of U.S. President, the briefest administration of any President.

☐ **Cushman, H. B.** *History of the Choctaw, Chickasaw and Natchez Indians.* Greenville, 1899. . . . .   125.00   160.00

☐ **Custer, Gen. George Armstrong.** *My Life on the Plains. Or, Personal Experiences with the Indians.* N.Y., 1874. 391 pp. Clothbound. 120.00   155.00

☐ **Cutler, Carl C.** *Story of the American Clipper Ship.* N.Y., n.d., 1930. . . . .   325.00   450.00

☐ **Cutts, J. M.** *The Conquest of California and New Mexico.* Philadelphia, 1847. . . . .   550.00   725.00

☐ **Dabis, W. W. H.** *History of the Battle of the Crooked Billet.* Doylestown, Pa., 1860. Softbound. 63.00   82.00

☐ **Dacus, Joseph.** *A Tour of St. Louis; or, the Inside Life of a Great City.* St. Louis, 1878. 564 pp. 90.00   115.00
St. Louis was considered, at that time, "gateway to the west."

Daggett, David. *Three Letters to Abraham Bishop on His Oration.* Hartford, Hudson, 1800. 36 pp. 31.00   39.00

☐ **Daggett, Stuart.** *Railroad Reorganization.* Cambridge, Mass., n.d., 1908. . . . .   62.00   83.00

☐ **Dahlquist, Laura.** *Meet Jim Bridger.* N.p., 1948. Softbound. 20.00   25.00

☐ **Dallman, William P.** *The Spirit of America as Interpreted in the Works of Charles Sealsfied.* St. Louis, 1935. 125 pp. Softbound. 25.00   32.00

☐ **Dalton, Kit.** *Under the Black Flags.* Memphis, n.d. (1914). Softbound. 37.00   48.00

☐ **Damon, Ethel M.** *Koamalu. A Story of Pioneers on Kauai and of what they built in that island Garden.* Honolulu, 1931. Two vols. Privately printed. 95.00   125.00

☐ **Dana, Charles A.** *Lincoln and his Cabinet.* Cleveland and N.Y., 1896. . . . .   27.00   32.00

☐ **Dana, Samuel W.** *Yale College Subject to the General Assembly.* New Haven, 1784. 44 pp. Softbound. 90.00   120.00

☐ **Daniels, George F.** *The Huguenots in the Nipmuch Country. With an Introduction by Oliver Wendell Holmes.* Boston, 1880. 168 pp. Clothbound. 37.00   48.00

☐ **Davenport, Alfred.** *Camp and Field Life of the Fifth New York Volunteer Infantry.* N.Y., 1879. . . . .   23.00   30.00

☐ **Davenport, Bishop.** *A New Gazetteer, or Geographical Dictionary, or North America and the West Indies.* Baltimore, 1832. 471 pp. Calfbound. 58.00   73.00

☐ **David, Ebenezer.** *A Rhode Island Chaplain in the Revolution.* Providence, 1949. 82 pp. Bound in boards. Limited to 900 copies. 25.00   33.00

☐ **David, Robert B.** *Finn Burnett, Frontiersman. The Life and Adventures of an Indian Fighter.* Glendale, 1937. 378 pp.   135.00   175.00

PRICE RANGE

☐ **Davidson, J. N.** *Muh-he-ka-ne-ok. A history of the Stock-bridge Nation.* Milwaukee, 1893.......................... 37.00   48.00

☐ **Davis, Charles H.** *Report on Interoceanic Canals and Railroads Between the Atlantic and Pacific Oceans.* Washington, D.C., 1867. 37 pp. With 14 folding maps. Bound in cloth........ 43.00   55.00

☐ **Davis, Henry T.** *Solitary Places Made Glad Experiences for 32 Years in Nebraska.* Cincinnati, privately published, 1890. 422 pp........ 75.00   100.00

☐ **Davis, Jefferson.** *The Rise and Fall of the Confederate Government.* N.p., 1881. Two vols. 105.00   135.00

☐ **Davis, John.** *An Eulogy, on General George Washington.* Boston, 1800. 4to. Softbound. 140.00   170.00

☐ **Davis, John.** *Travels of Four Years and a Half in the United States of America during 1798, 1799, 1800, 1801, and 1802.* N.Y., 1909. 429 pp. 35.00   43.00

☐ **Davis, Richard Harding.** *The West from a Car Window.* N.Y., 1904. Illustrated by Frederick Remington. 50.00   65.00

☐ **Davis, Thomas T.** *Speech on Equality of Rights.* Washington, D.C., 1866, 12 pp. Softbound. 32.00   40.00

☐ **Davis, W. H.** *The Spanish Conquest of New Mexico.* Doylestown, Pa., 1869. 438 pp. With a portrait and folding map........ 135.00   170.00

☐ **Davis, W. M.** *Nimrod of the Sea: or, the American Whaleman.* N.Y., 1874. 403 pp............................... 175.00   225.00

☐ **Davis, William H.** *75 Years in California.* San Francisco, 1967. 345 pp........ 85.00   105.00

☐ **Dawson, Nicholas.** *("Cheyenne Dawson"). Narrative of Nicholas Dawson.* San Francisco, 1933. 100 pp. Bound in boards, with a dust jacket. Limited to 500 copies printed at the Grabhorn Press. 200.00   250.00

☐ **Dawson, Sarah M.** *A Confederate Girl's Diary.* Boston, 1913. ...... 16.00   21.00

☐ **Dawson, Thomas F.** *Life and Character of Edward Oliver Wolcott.* N.Y., 1911. Two vols. 30.00   38.00

☐ **Deane, Silas.** *Address to the Free and Independent Citizens of the United States of North-America.* Hartford, 1784. ...... 190.00   230.00

☐ **Debo, Angie.** *Oklahoma: Footloose and Fancy-Free.* Norman, Oklahoma, 1949. 258 pp. 37.00   48.00

☐ **DeChanal, General.** *The American Army in the War of Secession.* Leavenworth, Kan., 1894. .... 22.00   28.00

☐ **Decker, Malcolm.** *Benedict Arnold.* N.Y., 1961. 534 pp. Limited to 750 copies.................................... 35.00   42.00

☐ *Declaration by the Representatives of the United Colonies of North America, Now met in General Congress, Philadelphia, Seting (sic) Forth the Cause and Necessities of Their Taking up Arms.* Philadelphia, 1775................ 380.00   460.00

☐ **Delano, Alonzo.** *California Correspondence.* Sacramento, 1952. 155 pp. Limited to 310 copies..................... 95.00   125.00

☐ **Delaplaine, Edward S.** *The Life of Thomas Johnson.* N.Y., 1927. 517 pp........ 20.00   25.00

PRICE RANGE

☐ **Dellenbaugh, Frederick.** *A Canyon Voyage.* New Haven, 1926. 277 pp. With colored frontispiece.................. 37.00 48.00

☐ **Demilt, A. P.** *The Story of an Old Town. With reminiscences of Early Nebraska.* Omaha, 1902. 173 pp......~........ 80.00 110.00

☐ **Denison, Charles H.** *Rhode Island. A Poem.* San Francisco, 1876. 55 pp. Softbound......................... 32.00 43.00

☐ **Dennett, Tyler.** *John Hay: From Poverty to Politics.* N.Y., 1933. 476 pp.. 22.00 28.00

☐ **DeNormandie, James.** *The Lord Reigneth: A Few Words on Sunday Morning, April 16, 1865, after the Assassination of Abraham Lincoln.* N.p.,n.d., Portsmouth, N.H., 1865. 8 pp. Softbound.. 120.00 150.00

☐ **Depew, Chauncey M.** *One Hundred Years of American Commerce.* N.Y., 1895. Two vols. With colored frontis, portraits. Bound in half calf................................ 110.00 145.00

☐ **DePeyster, John W.** *Personal and Military History of Philip Kearney.* N.Y., 1869. 516 pp. With 5 plates. 35.00 45.00

☐ **Desaussure, Wilmot.** *The Names of the Officers who Served in the South Carolina Regiment of the Continental Establishment... Together with Some Miscellaneous Information... as a Contribution to the History of the War of the Revolution in South Carolina.* Columbia, S.C., 1886. 33 pp. Softbound... 55.00 70.00

☐ **DeVinny, V.** *The Story of a Pioneer. Incidents Pertaining to the Early Settlements of Colorado.* Denver, 1904. 164 pp.. 55.00 70.00

☐ **Devoto, Bernard.** *Across the Wide Missouri.* Boston, 1947. 483 pp... 32.00 43.00

☐ **Dewees, Jacob.** *The Great Future of America and Africa: an Essay Showing our Whole Duty to the Black Man, Consistent with Our Safety and Glory.* Philadelphia, 1854. 236 pp. Bound in full leather. 120.00 150.00

☐ **DeWitt, David M.** *The Impeachment Trial of Andrew Johnson.* N.Y., 1903. 646 pp.................................... 45.00 60.00
Johnson, who succeeded to the Presidency upon Lincoln's death, was the first and only President brought under impeachment proceedings. They were unsuccessful and Johnson served out the remainder of Lincoln's term.

☐ **Dick, Everett.** *The Story of the Frontier. A Social History of the Northern Plains and Rocky Mountains.* N.Y., 1941. 574 pp... 48.00 63.00

☐ **Dickson, Albert Jerome.** *Covered Wagon Days. A Journey Across the Plains in the Sixties.* Cleveland, 1929. 287 pp. With 19 plates and a map.......................... 80.00 105.00

☐ **Dix, Gen. John.** *Speech of the President of the Mississippi & Missouri Railroad Company, at the Celebration at Iowa City, on the Completion of the Road to that Point.* N.Y., 1856. 16 pp. Softbound.................................... 105.00 135.00

☐ **Dix, Morgan.** *Memoirs of John Adams Dix.* N.Y., 1883. Two vols. 27.00 36.00

☐ **Dixon, James.** *Personal Narrative of a Tour Through a part of the United States and Canada.* N.Y., 1849. 431 pp. Clothbound. 68.00 89.00

	PRICE RANGE	
☐ **Dixon, Joseph K.** *The Vanishing Race.* N.Y., 1913......	80.00	105.00
☐ **Dixon, Olive K.** *Life of "Billy" Dixon, Plainsman, Scout and Pioneer.* Dallas, 1941. 251 pp..........................	85.00	110.00
☐ **Dobie, J. Frank.** *Apache Gold and Yaqui Silver.* Boston, 1939. 366 pp. Bound in cloth...........................	90.00	120.00
☐ **Dobie, J. Frank.** *The Longhorns.* Boston, 1941. 388 pp.	53.00	75.00
☐ **Dobie, J. Frank.** *The Ben Lilly Legend.* Boston, 1950. 237 pp...	75.00	100.00
☐ **Dobie, John.** *Journal and Letters from the Mines.* Denver, 1962. 307 pp. Limited to 1,000 copies...................	60.00	75.00
☐ **Dodge, Greenville.** *Biographical Sketch of James Bridger, Mountaineer, Trapper and Guide.* N.Y., 1905. 27 pp. Softbound. With 3 plates, one of which is folding............	130.00	175.00
☐ **Dodge, Col. R. I.** *Our Wild Indians.* Hartford. 1882.......	140.00	180.00
☐ **Dodge, Richard I.** *The Plains of the Great West and their Inhabitants.* N.Y., 1877. 448 pp. Illustrated. With a folding map..	125.00	155.00
☐ **Dodge, Theodore A.** *The Campaign of Chancellorsville.* Boston, n.d., 1881...............................	20.00	25.00
☐ **Dodge, William Sumner.** *Robert Henry Hendershot; or, the Braver Drummer Boy of the Rappannock.* Chicago, 1867.	60.00	75.00
☐ **Dondore, Dorothy Anne.** *The Prairie and the Making of Middle America.* Cedar Rapids, Iowa. 1926. 473 pp......	75.00	100.00
☐ **Donnelly, Ignatius.** *Minnesota. An Address Delivered at the Broadway House, New York.* N.Y., 1857. 15 pp....... Donnelly's address consisted mostly of a pitch to encourage easterners to move to, or invest in, his home town of Nininger, Minnesota. The town—and Donnelly—went broke that same year.	200.00	250.00
☐ **Donoho, M. H.** *Circle-Dot. A True Story of Life 40 Years Ago.* Topeka, 1907, 256 pp..................... "Forty years ago" in Kansas, going back from 1907, was the gunslinger era.	100.00	125.00
☐ **Door, James A.** *Justice to the South.* N.Y., 1856, 12 pp. Softbound.	35.00	44.00
☐ **Dorsey, George A.** *Traditions of the Skidi Pawnee.* Boston and N.Y., 1904.................................	47.00	63.00
☐ **Dorsey, George A.** *The Ponca Sun Dance.* Chicago, 1905. 88 pp. With 35 plates, some colored. Softbound. Published by the Field Museum..................................	47.00	63.00
☐ **Dorsey, Sarah A.** *Recollections of Henry Watkins Allen, Brigadier-General, Confederate States Army, ex-governor of Louisiana.* N.Y., n.d., 1860's.	34.00	41.00
☐ **Douglas, Byrd.** *Steamboatin' on the Cumberland.* Nashville, Tenn. 1961. 407 pp................................	11.00	15.00
☐ **Douglas, David.** *Journal kept by David Douglas, during his Travels in North America, 1823–1827.* N.Y., 1959. 364 pp. Limited to 750 copies..............................	60.00	80.00
☐ **Douglas, Jack.** *Veterans on the March.* N.Y., 1934. 376 pp...	35.00	45.00
☐ **Dover, Cedric.** *Know This of Race.* London, 1939.	35.00	43.00

PRICE RANGE

☐ **Dow, George F.** *Arts and Crafts in New England, 1704–1775.* Topsfield, Mass., 1927. 326 pp................... 110.00   145.00

☐ **Dow, George F.** *Whale Ships and Whaling. A Pictorial History of Whaling during Three Centuries.* N.Y., 1967. With 207 plates. Limtied to 750 copies..................... 225.00   300.00

☐ **Downie, Major William.** *Hunting for Gold.* San Francisco, 1893.. 275.00   350.00

☐ **Doyle, John A.** *The American Colonies previous to the Declaration of Independence.* London, 1869. 219 pp..... 35.00   45.00

☐ *Draft of a Bill for Declaring the Intentions of the Parliament of Great Britain Concerning the Exercise of the Right of Imposing Taxes Within His Majesty's Colonies.* N.Y., 1778.. 2900.00   3675.00

☐ **Drago, Harry Sinclair.** *Outlaws on Horseback.* N.Y., 1964. 320 pp. Limited to 150 numbered and signed copies...... 110.00   150.00

☐ **Drake, Charles D.** *The duties of American citizens. An address delivered before the Franklin Society of St. Louis.* St. Louis, 1837, 28 pp. Softbound....................... 275.00   325.00

☐ **Drake, Daniel.** *Pioneer Education and Life.* Cedar Rapids, Iowa, 1939. 55 pp. Clothbound. Limited to 400 copies.... 30.00   38.00

☐ **Drake, Francis S.** *Tea leaves: Being a Collection of Letters and Documents Relating to the Shipment of Tea to the American Colonies.* Boston, 1884....................... 35.00   48.00

☐ **Drake, J. G.** *Beautiful Isle. Addressed to Dauphine Island, Mobile Point.* Louisville, 1850. 5 pp................... 265.00   325.00

☐ **Draper, Lyman C.** *King's Mountain and Its Heroes.* N.Y., 1929. 612 pp. Limited to 500 copies.................... 48.00   63.00

☐ **Drayton, John.** *Memoir of the American Revolution.* Charleston, 1821. Two vols............................ 375.00   450.00

☐ **Driggs, Howard R.** *The Pony Express Goes Through.* N.Y., 1935. 208 pp... 75.00   100.00

☐ **Driggs, Howard R.** *The Old West Speaks.* N.Y., 1956.... 60.00   80.00

☐ **Dring, Albert G.** *Recollections of the Jersey Prison Ship.* Morrisania, N.Y., 1865. 201 pp. Bound in ½ leather. Limited to 50 copies, signed and numbered................. 130.00   175.00
Actually an early Bronx, N.Y. imprint. Morrisania, then a city in itself, later became part of the Bronx—which in turn became part of New York City.

☐ **Drown, S. D.** *Record and Historical View of Peoria.* Peoria, 1850... 1325.00   1675.00

☐ **Dubois, James T. and Pike, William J.** *The Centennial of Susquehanna County, Pa. 1787–1887.* Washington, D.C., 1888.. 21.00   27.00

☐ **Dubois, W. E. B.** *The World and Africa.* N.Y., 1947. 276 pp.. 37.00   48.00

☐ **Dubose, Samuel.** *A Contribution to the History of the Huguenots of South Carolina.* N.Y., 1887. 176 pp. Softbound... 35.00   45.00

☐ **Dufer, S. M.** *Over the Dead Line or Tracked by Blood-Hounds.* Burlington, Vt., 1902...................... 52.00   68.00

☐ **Duke, Basil.** *History of Morgan's Cavalry.* Cincinnati, 1867... 70.00   90.00

	PRICE RANGE	
☐ **Duke, Basil.** *Reminiscences.* N.Y., 1911................	32.00	38.00
☐ **Dumble, E. T.** *First Annual Report of the Geological Survey of Texas, 1889.* Austin, 1890. 410 pp. With plates, folding maps...	78.00	105.00
☐ **Dumond, Dwight L.** *The Secession Movement, 1860–61.* N.Y., 1931...	15.00	20.00
☐ **Dumond, Dwight L.** *America in Our Time.* N.Y., 1937. 715 pp..	30.00	38.00
☐ **Dunbar, E. E.** *American Pioneering. Jersey City, 1863.* A record of the author's experiences in Arizona from 1855 onward...	700.00	900.00
☐ **Dunbar, Seymour.** *History of Travel in America.* Indianapolis, 1915. Four vols. Large paper edition, limited to 250 numbered and signed sets.............................	275.00	325.00
☐ **Dunn, Jacob Platt Jr.** *Massacres of the Mountains.* N.Y., 1886. 784 pp...	180.00	235.00
☐ **Durand, John.** *New Materials for the History of the American Revolution.* N.Y., 1889. 311 pp. Bound in cloth.	30.00	40.00
☐ **Dustin, Fred.** *The Custer Tragedy.* Ann Arbor, Mich., 1965. 251 pp. With folding maps in rear pocket.	32.00	41.00
☐ **Duval, John C.** *Adventures of Big Foot Wallace, the Texas Ranger and Hunter.* Macon, Georgia, 1870. 309 pp. Bound in cloth.	100.00	130.00
Duval tried to create an instant collectors' item by showing the work to be printed in Macon in 1870. It was actually printed in Austin, Texas around 1900.		
☐ **Duvall, Marius.** *A Navy Surgeon in California, 1846–1847.* San Francisco, 1957. 114 pp. One of 600 copies.........	85.00	105.00
☐ **Duyckinck, E. A.** *Memorial of John Allan.* N.Y., 1864. 39 pp. Limited to 250 copies...............................	22.00	28.00
☐ **Dwight, Margaret.** *A Journey to Ohio in 1810.* New Haven, 1912. 64 pp. Bound in boards...........................	17.00	23.00
☐ **Dyer, Mrs. D. B.** *Fort Reno: or, Picturesque Cheyenne and Arrapahoe Army Life Before the Opening of Oklahoma.* N.Y., 1896. 216 pp.	250.00	325.00
☐ **Eads, H. L.** *Shaker Sermons.* N.p., 1879. 1,222 pp. Bound in cloth.	40.00	50.00
☐ **Early, J. A. (General Confederate States Army).** *Autobiographical Sketch.* Philadelphia, 1912.	70.00	85.00
☐ **Eastman, Mrs. Mary H.** *Aunt Phillis's Cabin; or, Southern Life as It Is.* Philadelphia, 1852. A sort of rebuttal to "Uncle Tom's Cabin"..	80.00	110.00
☐ **Eddy, Richmond.** *History of the 60th Regiment, New York State Volunteers.* Philadelphia, 1864.....................	30.00	37.00
☐ **Edelman, C. O.** *Louisville Citizen Guards March.* Louisville, 1853, 5 pp. Softbound.............................	185.00	230.00
☐ **Edes, Peter.** *A Diary of Peter Edes, the Oldest Printer in the United States.* Bangor, Maine, 1837. Softbound.......	1000.00	1250.00
☐ **Edward, David B.** *The History of Texas.* Cincinnati, 1836. First edition...	1650.00	2175.00

PRICE RANGE

☐ **Edwards, Jennie.** *John N. Edwards: Biography Memoirs, Reminiscences and Recollections.* Kansas City, 1889. 428 pp.. 65.00 85.00
Includes an account of the shooting of Jesse James.

☐ **Edwards, John.** *Shelby and his Men.* Kansas City, 1897... 38.00 48.00

☐ **Edwards, Jonathan.** *A Faithful Narrative of the surprizing Work of God in the Conversion of Many Hundred Souls in Northampton, and the Neighboring Towns and Villages of New Hampshire.* London, 1737......................... 360.00 425.00

☐ **Edwards, Jonathan.** *A History of the Work of Redemption.* N.Y., 1786.. 60.00 80.00

☐ **Eells, Myron.** *History of the Congregational Association of Oregon and Washington Territory.* Portland, 1881. 124 pp. Softbound... 85.00 110.00

☐ **Egan, William.** *Pioneering in the West, 1846–1878.* Richmond, Utah, 1917. 302 pp. With one plate.............. 80.00 105.00

☐ **Egleston, T.** *The Treatment of Fine Gold in the Sands of Snake River.* N.p., 1890, 13 pp. Softbound.............. 135.00 175.00

☐ **Eickemeyer, Carl.** *Among the Pueblo Indians.* N.Y., 1895. 195 pp.. 65.00 85.00

☐ **Eldredge, Zoth S.** *The Beginnings of San Francisco from the Expedition of Anza, 1774, to the City Charter of April 15, 1850.* San Francisco, published by the author, 1912. Two vols. Clothbound................................... 110.00 145.00

☐ **Eldridge, Eleanor.** *Slave Narrative.* Providence, 1842.... 150.00 190.00

☐ **Ellicott, Thomas.** *The Bank of Maryland Conspiracy.* Philadelphia, 1839. 134 pp. Softbound..................... 57.00 72.00

☐ **Elliot, Henry W.** *Report on the Seal Islands of Alaska.* Washington, D.C., 1884. 188 pp. With plates and maps. Bound in ½ leather.................................... 60.00 80.00

☐ **Elliot, Stephen.** *The Farewell Message, and Obituary Notices of Bishop N.H. Cobbs.* Montgomery, 1861, 40 pp. Softbound... 65.00 85.00

☐ **Elliott, Isaac H.** *Records of the Service of Illinois Soldiers in the Black Hawk War 1831–32 and in the Mexican War 1846–48.* Springfield, 1882. 343 pp.................... 72.00 103.00

☐ **Elliott, W. W.** *History of Arizona Territory.* San Francisco, 1884. Folio, cloth with calf spine, 324 pp. Many fine plates, a handsome, rare volume............................ 3500.00 4500.00

☐ **Ellis, J. W.** *Governor's Message to the General Assembly.* Raleigh, 1860. 32 pp. Softbound...................... 280.00 365.00

☐ **Ellis, W. T.** *Memories. My 72 Years in the Romatic County of Yuba, California.* Eugene, Oregon, 1939. 308 pp. Boxed.. 115.00 150.00

☐ **Ellis, William.** *The American Mission in the Sandwich Islands.* Honolulu, 1866............................... 375.00 450.00

☐ **Ellis, William A.** *A Narrative of a Tour Through Hawaii.* Honolulu, 1917. 367 pp. With folding maps............ 90.00 120.00

☐ **Ellison, Robert S.** *Fort Bridger, Wyoming, a Brief History.* Casper, 1931. 60 pp. Softbound...................... 75.00 105.00

PRICE RANGE

☐ **Ellms, Charles.** *The Pirate's Own Book.* Salem, 1924. 470 pp. Clothbound.................................. 45.00   60.00

☐ **Emory, William H.** *Report on the United States—Mexican Boundary Survey 1850–54.* Chicago, n.d. (mid 1960's). 1,566 pp. A reprint of the original 1857 edition. Clothbound. 150.00   190.00

☐ **Erath, George B.** *The Memoirs of Major George B. Erath, 1813–1891.* Waco, Texas, 1956. 105 pp............... 21.00   27.00

☐ **Erskine, Gladys Shaw.** *Broncho Charlie. A Saga of the Saddle.* London, 1934. 316 pp. With 24 plates and maps............................... 80.00   105.00
Broncho Charlie was Charles Miller, an Old West character who was acquainted with a number of celebrated gunslingers.

☐ **Eskew, Garnett L.** *The Pagaent of the Packets: A Book of American Steamboating.* N.Y., 1929. 314 pp.......... 37.00   48.00

☐ **Esmeralsa, Aurora.** *Life and Letters of a 49er's Daughter.* San Francisco, 1929. 371 pp..................... 35.00   43.00

☐ *Estimates for Washington Orange Grove Association.* N.p., n.d. (c. 1880), 9 pp. Softbound...................... 190.00   235.00

☐ **Ethell, Henry C.** *The Rise and Progress of Civilization in the Hairy Nation and the History of Davis County.* Bloomfield, 1883. .... 475.00   600.00

☐ **Everett, Alexander H.** *Defence of the Character and Principles of Mr. Jefferson.* Boston, 1836. 76 pp. Softbound. 27.00   33.00

☐ **Everett, Franklin.** *Memorials of the Grand River Valley.* Chicago, 1878. 545 pp. Clothbound. 120.00   155.00

☐ **Ewell, Alice M.** *A Virginia Scene, or Life in Old Prince William.* Lynchburg, 1931. 228 pp. 13.00   17.00

☐ **Fabour, Alpheus H.** *Old Bill Williams, Mountain Man.* Chapel Hill, N.C., 1936. .... 175.00   235.00

☐ **Fairchild, Henry P.** *Immigration, a World Movement and its American Significance.* N.Y., 1913. 455 pp........... 25.00   35.00

☐ **Fanning, David.** *The Narrative of Colonel David Fanning.* N.Y., 1865. Bound in half morocco.................. 210.00   270.00

☐ **Farnam, Henry W.** *Chapters in the History of Social Legislation in the United States to 1860.* Washington, 1938. 496 pp.................................. 35.00   43.00

☐ **Farnham, Eliza W.** *California indoors and out.* N.Y., 1856. .... 90.00   115.00

☐ **Farnham, Thomas J.** *Life and Adventures in California.* N.Y., 1846, Softbound. 600.00   800.00

☐ **Farnsworth, R. W. C.** *A Southern California Paradise.* Pasadena, 1883. 132 pp. 100.00   125.00

☐ **Farrar, Victor J.** *The Purchase of Alaska.* Washington, 1934. 51 pp. Softbound......................... 27.00   36.00

☐ **Farwell, John W.** *Some Recollections of John W. Farwell.* Chicago, 1911. 230 pp. 20.00   25.00

☐ **Faulkner, Joseph P.** *Eighteen Months on a Greenland Whaler.* N.Y., 1878. 317 pp. Miniature book. 125.00   160.00

☐ **Faunce, Hilda.** *Desert Wife.* Boston, 1934.............. 35.00   43.00

☐ **Faust, Albert.** *The German Element in the United States.* N.Y., 1909. Two vols........................ 30.00   39.00

PRICE RANGE

☐ **Ferguson, Charles D.** *The Experiences of a 49er during 34 Years' Residence in California and Australia.* Cleveland, 1888. 507 pp. 58.00 73.00

☐ **Ferguson, Erna.** *Our Southwest.* N.Y., 1946. . . . . 37.00 48.00

☐ **Ferguson, Henry.** *Journal of Henry Ferguson.* Hartford, 1924. Privately printed, distributed only among members of the family. 100.00 130.00

☐ **Ferris, Benjamin G.** *Utah and the Mormons.* N.Y., 1854. 347 pp. With a portrait and other plates. 68.00 88.00

☐ **Ferris, Jacob.** *The States and Territories of the Great West.* N.Y., 1856. 352 pp. 50.00 65.00

☐ **Ficklen, John R.** *History of Reconstruction in Louisiana.* Baltimore, 1910. . . . . 37.00 45.00

☐ **Field, Edward.** *Revolutionary Defenses in Rhode Island.* Providence, 1896. 161 pp. With maps, 2 of which are folding. 42.00 57.00

☐ **Field, Henry M.** *History of the Atlantic Telegraph.* N.Y., 1866. 364 pp. 85.00 105.00

☐ **Field, Matthew C.** *Prairie & Mountain Sketches.* Norman, Okla. 1957. . . . . 37.00 48.00

☐ **Fillmore, Millard.** *Message transmitting the Constitution of New Mexico.* Washington, D.C., 1850. 18 pp. Softbound. 130.00 165.00

☐ **Finger, Charles J.** *Adventures Under Sapphire Skies.* N.Y., 1931. . . . . 22.00 28.00

☐ **Fish, Carl R.** *The Civil Service.* Cambridge, Mass., 1920. 279 pp. Clothbound. 16.00 20.00

☐ **Fish, H. C.** *The Voice of Our Brother's Blood . . . A Discourse Occasioned by the Summer and Kansas Outrages.* Newark, 1856. 16 pp. Softbound, rare. 850.00 1075.00

☐ **Fish, Stuyvesant.** *The New York Privateers 1756–1763.* N.Y., 1945. 100 pp. Limited to 400 copies. 43.00 54.00
Privateers were privately operated (non-governmental) ships that engaged in acts of piracy against ships of the government's enemies . . . confident that they would not be prosecuted. Privateering was a thriving trade in the 18th century.

☐ **Fisher, Elwood.** *Lecture on the North and the South Delivered before the Young Men's Mercantile Library Association, of Cincinnati, 1849.* Washington, D.C., 1849. 32 pp. Softbound. 35.00 42.00

☐ **Fisher, Rev. H. D.** *The Gun and the Gospel.* Kansas City, 1902. . . . . 58.00 73.00

☐ **Fisher, Sydney G.** *The Struggle for American Independence.* Philadelphia, 1908. Two vols. 25.00 32.00

☐ **Fischer and Abeytia.** *Report as to Socorro County, New Mexico Territory.* Socorro, 1881. 9 pp. Softbound. 1600.00 2000.00

☐ **Fiske, Nathan.** *An Oration Delivered at Brookfield, Nov. 14, 1781. In Celebration of the Capture of Lord Cornwallis and his Whole Army at Yorktown.* Boston, n.d., 1781. 8 pages. 400.00 475.00

☐ **Fite, Emerson David.** *Social and Industrial Conditions in the North during the Civil War.* N.Y., 1910. 318 pp. Clothbound. 30.00 40.00

PRICE RANGE

☐ **Fithian, Philip V.** *Journal and Letters, 1767–1774.* Princeton, 1900. 320 pp. Clothbound. 65.00   80.00

☐ **Fleming, Vivian Minor.** *Campaign of the Army of Northern Virginia including the Jackson Valley Campaign, 1861–65.* Richmond, n.d. (c. 1928). 35.00   45.00

☐ **Fletcher, Daniel C.** *Reminiscences of California and the Civil War.* Ayer, Mass., 1894. . . . .   175.00   235.00

☐ **Fletcher, J.** *American Patriotism Farther Confronted with Reason.* London, 1777. . . . .   100.00   130.00

☐ **Fletcher, John.** *American Patriotism Further Confronted with Reason.* Shrewsbury, England, 1776. 130 pp. Bound in full calf. 95.00   120.00

☐ **Flint, Abel.** *A Discourse delivered at Hartford, Feb. 22, 1800 . . . to the memory of General George Washington.* Hartford, 1800. . . . .   70.00   85.00

☐ **Fobes, James.** *Sketches, Historical and Topographical, of the Floridas; More Particularly of East Florida.* N.Y., 1821. . . . .   1000.00   1275.00

☐ **Fohlin, E. V.** *Salt Lake City Past and Present.* Salt Lake City, published by the author, n.d. (c. 1908). 208 pp. 60.00   75.00

☐ **Foner, Philip S.** *The Fur and Leather Workers Union.* Newark, N.J., 1950. 708 pp. Clothbound. 24.00   31.00

☐ **Foote, Stella.** *Letters from Buffalo Bill.* Billings, Montana, 1954. Softbound. 30.00   39.00

☐ **Forbes, Robert B.** *Notes on Ships of the Past.* Boston, 1885. 156 pp. Softbound. 150.00   200.00

☐ **Ford, Henry J.** *The Scotch-Irish in America.* Princeton, N.J., n.d. 607 pp. 26.00   33.00

☐ **Ford, Paul.** *The Many Sided Franklin.* N.Y., 1899. First edition. 35.00   42.00

☐ **Ford, Paul.** *Bibliography of Benjamin Franklin.* Brooklyn, 1889. Limited to 500 copies. 130.00   170.00

☐ **Ford, Paul Leicester.** *The Origin, Purpose and Result of the Harrisburg Convention of 1788.* Brooklyn, N.Y., 1890. 40 pp. Softbound. Limited to 250 copies. 40.00   50.00

☐ **Ford, Paul Leicester.** *The Sayings of Poor Richard. The Prefaces, Proverbs, and Poems of Benjamin Franklin, originally printed in Poor Richard's Almanacs for 1733–1758.* N.Y., 1890. 288 pp. 53.00   68.00

☐ **Ford, Thomas.** *A History of Illinois, from its Commencement as a State in 1818 to 1847.* Chicago, 1854. 447 pp. Clothbound. 125.00   160.00

☐ **Ford, Worthington C.** *Defences of Philadelphia in 1777.* Brooklyn, N.Y., 1897. 300 pp. Limited to 100 copies. 60.00   75.00

☐ **Ford, Worthington C.** *Family Letters of Samuel Blachley Webb, 1764–1804.* N.Y., privately printed, 1912. 491 pp. Limited to 350 copies. 55.00   70.00

☐ **Fordham, Elias P.** *Personal Narrative of Travels in Virginia, Maryland, Pennsylvania, Ohio, Indiana, Kentucky; and of a Residence in the Illinois Territory, 1817–1818.* Cleveland, 1906. 248 pp. 62.00   82.00

☐ **Foreman, Grant.** *Indian Justice: a Cherokee Murder Trial at Tahlequah in 1840.* Oklahoma City, 1934. 112 pp. 85.00   110.00

THE

PERSONAL NARRATIVE

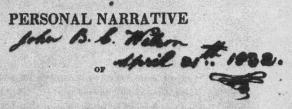

OF

JAMES O. PATTIE,

OF

KENTUCKY,

DURING AN EXPEDITION FROM ST. LOUIS, THROUGH THE VAST REGIONS
BETWEEN THAT PLACE AND THE PACIFIC OCEAN, AND THENCE BACK
THROUGH THE CITY OF MEXICO TO VERA CRUZ, DURING JOURNEY-
INGS OF SIX YEARS; IN WHICH HE AND HIS FATHER, WHO
ACCOMPANIED HIM, SUFFERED UNHEARD OF HARDSHIPS
AND DANGERS, HAD VARIOUS CONFLICTS WITH THE IN-
DIANS, AND WERE MADE CAPTIVES, IN WHICH
CAPTIVITY HIS FATHER DIED; TOGETHER
WITH A DESCRIPTION OF THE COUNTRY,
AND THE VARIOUS NATIONS THROUGH
WHICH THEY PASSED.

———

EDITED BY TIMOTHY FLINT.

———

CINCINNATI:
PRINTED AND PUBLISHED BY JOHN H. WOOD.
1831.

Overland journey narratives (as this type of book is known to collectors) are always in demand, and the early ones—such as Pattie's—can go for really prodigious prices. In this case a well-preserved specimen would run from about $7,500 to $10,000.

PRICE RANGE

☐ **Forrest, Earle R.** *Missions and Pueblos of the Old Southwest.* Cleveland, 1929. 386 pp. Bound in cloth.......... **105.00** **135.00**

☐ **Forrest, Earle R.** *Arizona's Dark and Bloody Ground.* Caldwell, 1936. 370 pp. Clothbound. **95.00** **120.00**

☐ **Fortier, Alice.** *A History of Louisiana.* Paris and New York, 1904. 4 vols., bound in ½ vellum. One of 5 special presentation copies with plates in two states................ **1100.00** **1450.00**

☐ **Foster, James S.** *Outlines of History of the Territory of Dakota and Emigrants' Guide to the Free Lands of the Northwest.* Yankton, 1870. Reprinted 1928. 110 pp. Softbound. **25.00** **32.00**
This price is for the 1928 reprint. The original 1870 edition sells much, much higher..

☐ **Foster, John.** *The Story of a Private Soldier in the Revolution.* N.p., 1902... **9.00** **12.00**

☐ **Foster, Harris.** *The Look of the Old West.* N.Y., 1955..... **37.00** **48.00**

☐ **Fothergill, John A.** *An Account of the Life and Travels in the Work of the Ministry.* London, 1753. 338 pp. Bound in calf... **50.00** **65.00**
Contains much on America.

☐ **Franklin, J. Benjamin.** *A Cheap Trip to the City of the Mormons.* Ipswich, England, n.d. (c. 1860). 33 pp. Softbound. **120.00** **150.00**

☐ **Franklin, Walter S.** *Resolutions, Laws and Ordinances, Relating to the Pay, Half Pay, Commutation of Half Pay, Bounty Lands and Other Promises, Made by Congress to the Officers and Soldiers of the Revolution.* Washington, D.C., 1838. 299 pp....................................... **52.00** **67.00**

☐ **Fraser, J. D.** *The Gold Fever, or Two Years in Alaska. A True Narrative of Actual Events as Experienced by the Author.* N.p., 1923. 100 pp. Softbound.................. **110.00** **135.00**

☐ **Free Trade Convention.** *Journal of the Free Trade Convention, held in Philadelphia.* Philadelphia, 1831. 76 pp. Softbound. **50.00** **60.00**

☐ **Freedley, Edwin T.** *Philadelphia and its Manufactures: a Hand Book.* Philadelphia, 1859. 504 pp. With plates and tables. Clothbound. **75.00** **95.00**

☐ **Freeman, Lewis R.** *The Colorado River.* N.Y., 1923. 451 pp. **53.00** **72.00**

☐ **French, Allen.** *General Gage's Informers: New Material upon Lexington and Concord.* Ann Arbor, Mich., 1832. 207 pp.. **32.00** **40.00**

☐ **French, L. H.** *Seward's Land of Gold.* N.Y., n.d. (c. 1905). 101 pp... **150.00** **195.00**

☐ **Frisbie, Levi.** *An Oration, Delivered at Ipswich, at the Request of a Number of the Inhabitants, on the 29th of April, 1783; on Account of the Happy Restoration of Peace, Between Great Britain and the United States of America.* Boston, 1783... **185.00** **235.00**

☐ **Frost, Donald McKay.** *Notes on General Ashley, the Overland Trail and South Pass.* Worcester, Mass., 1945. 159 pp. With a folding map. Softbound...................... **80.00** **100.00**

PRICE RANGE

☐ **Frost, John.** *History of the State of California.* Auburn, 1853. .... 110.00   140.00

☐ **Fry, Henry.** *The History of North Atlantic Steam Navigation.* N.Y., 1896. 324 pp. With plates, tables and maps. 90.00   115.00

☐ **Fuess, Claude M.** *Daniel Webster.* Boston, 1930. Two vols. 33.00   45.00

☐ **Fugate, Francis.** *The Spanish Heritage of the Southwest.* El Paso, 1952. Limited to 925 copies. 55.00   70.00

☐ **Fuller, Henry C.** *Adventures of Bill Longley, Captured by Sheriff Milton Mast and Deputy Bill Burrows near Keatchie, Louisiana, in 1877.* Nacogdoches, Texas, n.d. (c. 1879). 68 pp. Softbound. 125.00   160.00
Desperado Bill Longley was executed in 1878.

☐ **Fuller, Hiram.** *North and South. By a White Republican.* London, 1863. .... 75.00   95.00

☐ **Fullmer, John S.** *Assassination of Joseph and Hyrum Smith, the Prophet and the Patriarch.* Liverpool (England), 1855. 40 pp. 600.00   725.00

☐ **Fulton, Robert L.** *Epic of the Overland.* San Francisco, 1924: 109 pp. 75.00   100.00

☐ **Furlong, C. W.** *Let'er Buck.* N.Y., 1921. .... 105.00   135.00

☐ **Gale, George.** *Upper Mississippi: or, Historical Sketches of the Moundbuilders, the Indian tribes, and the Progress of Civilization in the North-West.* Chicago, 1867. 460 pp. Clothbound. 225.00   275.00

☐ **Gallagher, William D.** *Facts and Conditions of Progress in the North-West.* Cincinnati, 1850. 88 pp. Softbound. 65.00   85.00

☐ **Gano, Stephen.** *A Sermon on the Death of General George Washington.* Providence, 1800. Softbound. 85.00   110.00

☐ **Gantt, Gen. E. W.** *Address (to the people of Arkansas).* N.p., 1863. 22 pp. Softbound. 325.00   400.00

☐ **Gard, Wayne.** *Sam Bass.* Boston and N.Y., 1936. 262 pp. Clothbound. 125.00   165.00
Sam Bass' fame as an Old West desperado was exceeded by few.

☐ **Gard, Wayne.** *Frontier Justice.* Norman, Okla., 1949. ..... 37.00   48.00

☐ **Garden, Alexander.** *Anecdotes of the Revolutionary War in America.* Charleston, 1822. A second series of Garden's Anecdotes was published in 1828. .... 275.00   325.00

☐ **Garfield, James A.** *The Works of James A. Garfield.* Boston, 1882–83. Two vols. Clothbound. 32.00   40.00
Garfield was not one of our literarily prolific Presidents. He wrote comparatively little and none of his works was widely read.

☐ **Garneau, Joseph.** *Nebraska. Her Resources, Advantages and Development.* Omaha, 1893. 24 pp. Softbound. 275.00   350.00

☐ **Garrard, Lewis H.** *Wah-To-Yah and the Taos Trail.* Oklahoma City, 1927. 320 pp. 115.00   145.00

☐ **Garrett, Patrick Floyd.** *Authentic Life of Billy the Kid.* N.Y., 1927. 233 pp. With colored frontis, plates, a map and other illustrations. Second edition. 95.00   120.00
Patrick F. Garrett, sheriff-turned-author, won lifelong notoriety by gunning down Billy the Kid.

PRICE RANGE

☐ **Garrett, William.** *Reminiscences of Public Men in Alabama.* Atlanta, 1872. 809 pp. Clothbound. 72.00 93.00

☐ **Garrison, A. E.** *Life and Labor of A.E. Garrison. Forty Years in Oregon.* Privately printed, 1943. 130 pp. Softbound. . . . 55.00 70.00

☐ **Garrison, George P.** *Diplomatic Correspondence of the Republic of Texas.* Washington, D.C., 1908–11. Three vols. 135.00 170.00

☐ **Garside, Alston H.** *Cotton Goes to Market.* N.Y., 1934. 411 pp. 26.00 33.00

☐ **Gates, Charles M.** *Messages of the Governors of the Territory of Washington to the Legislative Assembly, 1854–1889.* Seattle, 1940. 297 pp. Softbound. 37.00 45.00

☐ **Gay, Beatrice Grady.** *Into the Setting Sun.* N.p., 1936. . . 42.00 55.00

☐ **Gayarre, Charles.** *History of Louisiana: the Spanish Domination.* N.Y., 1854. 649 pp. 70.00 90.00
Odd volume from a set, but complete in itself.

☐ **Geer, J.** *Beyond the Lines: or a Yankee Prisoner Loose in Dixie.* Philadelphia, 1863. . . . . 20.00 25.00

☐ **Geiser, Samuel Wood.** *Naturalists of the Frontier.* Dallas, 1948. . . . . 32.00 41.00

☐ **George, Todd M.** *Just Memories, and Twelve Years with Cole Younger.* N.p., 1959. 99 pp. 27.00 35.00
Just about everybody who knew outlaw Cole Younger wrote reminiscences of him, sooner or later—this one was MUCH later.

☐ **Gerhard, Fred.** *Illinois as It Is.* Chicago, 1857. 451 pp. With folding maps. 100.00 130.00

☐ **Gibbes, R. W.** *Documentary History of the American Revolution.* N.Y., 1855, three vols. 225.00 275.00

☐ **Gibbs, George.** *A Dictionary of the Chinook Jargon; or, Trade Language of Oregon.* N.Y., 1863. 43 pp. Softbound. 110.00 135.00
Books of this sort seldom improved communications between Indian and white man, but became valuable collectors' items.

☐ **Gibbs, Josiah F.** *The Mountain Meadows Massacre.* Salt Lake City, 1910. 59 pp. Softbound. 55.00 70.00

☐ **Gibson, George R.** *Journal of a Soldier Under Kearny and Doniphan 1846–1847.* Glendale, 1935 371 pp. 37.00 45.00

☐ **Gibson, J. Y.** *The Story of the Zulus.* London, 1911. . . . . . 55.00 75.00

☐ **Giddings, Joshua R.** *The Exiles of Florida; or the Crimes Committed by our Government Against the Maroons, who Fled from South Carolina and Other Slave States, Seeking Protection under Spanish Laws.* Columbus, Ohio, 1858. 338 pp. 65.00 85.00

☐ **Gihon, John H.** *Geary and Kansas.* Philadelphia, 1857. 348 pp. 53.00 69.00

☐ **Gillett, James B.** *Six Years with the Texas Rangers.* Austin, 1921. 332 pp. With 8 plates. 150.00 190.00

☐ **Gillmore, G. A.** *Official Report to the United States Engineer Dept., of the Seige and Reduction of Fort Pulaski, Georgia.* N.Y., 1862. Softbound. 40.00 52.00

PRICE RANGE

☐ **Gilmer, G. R.** *Sketches of Some of the First Settlers of Upper Georgia.* Americus, Ga., 1926. 458 pp. 63.00 80.00

☐ **Gilpin, Thomas.** *Exiles in Virginia.* Philadelphia, 1848. 302 pp. Bound in half morocco. 42.00 58.00

☐ **Gilpin, William.** *The Cosmopolitan Railway.* San Francisco, 1890. 369 pp. 63.00 79.00

☐ **Gleed, Charles S.** *From River to Sea: a Tourists' and Miners' Guide.* Chicago, 1882. 240 pp. With folding colored map. 87.00 112.00

☐ **Glover, Thomas.** *An Account of Virginia.* Oxford, 1904. 31 pp. Reprint of a work originally issued in 1677. Limited to 250 copies. 36.00 44.00

☐ **Gold, Thomas R.** *Address before the Agricultural Society of Oneida.* Utica, 1829. 29 pp. Softbound. 150.00 185.00

☐ **Golder, Frank A.** *John Paul Jones in Russia.* Garden City, N.Y., 1927. 230 pp. Limited to 1,001 copies. In the original publisher's box. 50.00 65.00

☐ **Goodlander, C. W.** *Memoirs and Recollections.* Ft. Scott, Kansas, 1900. .... 170.00 215.00

☐ **Goodwin, John A.** *The Pilgrim Republic. An Historical Review of the Colony of New Plymouth.* Boston, 1888. 662 pp. 15.00 20.00

☐ **Gookin, Daniel.** *Historical Collections of the Indians in New England.* Boston, 1792. .... 1050.00 1375.00

☐ **Goolrick, John T.** *The Life of General Hugh Mercer.* N.Y., 1906. 140 pp. 35.00 42.00

☐ **Gordon, John B.** *Reminiscences of the Civil War.* N.Y., 1904. .... 20.00 25.00

☐ **Gould, Emerson W.** *Fifty Years on the Mississippi.* St. Louis, 1889. 749 pp. Clothbound. 275.00 350.00

☐ **Gould, Nathanial.** *Sketch of the Trade of British America.* London, 1833. 20 pp. Softbound. 32.00 38.00

☐ **Gove, Jesse A.** *The Utah Expedition, 1857–58.* Concord, N.H., 1928. 442 pp. With 5 plates. Limited to 800 copies. 43.00 60.00

☐ **Graham, R. B.** *The Horses of the Conquest.* Norman, Okla., 1949. .... 43.00 60.00

☐ **Graham, W. A.** *The Custer Myth.* Harrisburg, 1955. ...... 175.00 235.00

☐ *Grammar and Vocabulary of the Blackfoot Language.* Ft. Benson, 1882. .... 130.00 160.00

☐ **Grand, W. J.** *Illustrated History of the Union Stockyards.* Chicago, 1901. 362 pp. 67.00 88.00

☐ **Granger, Gideon.** *An Address to the People of New England.* By Algernon Sidney, Washington, D.C., 1808. 38 pp. Softbound. 40.00 55.00

☐ **Grant, Blanche C.** *Taos Indians.* Taos, N.M., 1925. 127 pp. Softbound. 40.00 52.00

☐ **Grant, Bruce.** *How to Make Cowboy Horse Gear.* Cambridge, Maryland, 1953. .... 27.00 35.00

☐ **Grant, Gordon.** *The Life and Adventures of John N. Aariner.* N.Y., 1936. 214 pp. 20.00 25.00

☐ **Grantham, Thomas.** *An Historical Account of Some Memorable Actions Particularly in Virginia.* Richmond, 1882. 71 pp. 47.00 60.00

PRICE RANGE

☐ **Graves, Richard S.** *Oklahoma Outlaws.* Oklahoma City, 1915. 131 pp. Softbound.................................... 100.00   125.00

☐ **Gray, Edward.** *William Gray of Salem.* Boston, 1914. 124 pp. Limited to 500 numbered copies..................... 22.00   28.00

☐ **Gray, Ellis.** *The Design of the institution of the Gospel Ministry.* Boston, 1741. 23 pp. 50.00   65.00

☐ **Graydon, Alexander.** *Memoirs of His Own Time with Reminiscences of the Revolution.* Philadelphia, 1846. 504 pp. 40.00   52.00

☐ *The Great Eastern Gold Mining Company. Map of the Black Hills Lodes.* N.Y., 1880. 7 pp. Softbound................. 275.00   350.00

☐ **Greatorex, Eliza.** *Summer Etchings in Colorado.* N.Y., 1873. 95 pp... 40.00   50.00

☐ **Greeley, Horace.** *An Overland Journey, from New York to San Francisco in the Summer of 1859.* N.Y., 1860. 386 pp. Clothbound. 100.00   130.00
Greeley, responsible for the saying "Go west, young man," was an unsuccessful candidate for the Presidency.

☐ **Green, Lorenzo J.** *Negro in Colonial New England.* Washington, D.C., 1942.. 58.00   73.00

☐ **Greene, George Washington.** *The German Element in the War of American Independence.* N.Y., 1876. .... 20.00   25.00

☐ **Greene, Max.** *The Kansas Region.* N.Y., 1856. With 2 maps. Bound in half morocco.................................. 175.00   235.00

☐ **Greenhow, Robert.** *The History of Oregon and California and the other Territories on the North-West Coast of North America.* Boston, 1844. 482 pp. With a folding map. 105.00   130.00

☐ **Greer, George Cabell.** *Early Virginia Immigrants, 1623–1666.* Richmond, 1912. 376 pp.......................... 60.00   75.00

☐ **Greever, William S.** *Arid Domain.* N.p., 1954. .... 13.00   17.00

☐ **Gregg, Frank M.** *The Founding of a Nation.* Cleveland, 1915. Two vols.. 22.00   28.00

☐ **Gregory, Homer.** *North Pacific Fisheries.* San Francisco, 1939. 322 pp. Clothbound. 32.00   43.00

☐ **Gregory, John.** *Industrial Resources of Wisconsin.* Chicago, 1853. 329 pp.................................... 450.00   575.00

☐ **Grierson, Gen. B. H.** *Annual Report on the Department of Arizona, Bowie and Selden and the Point Loma and Navajo Reservations.* N.p., 1889, 32 pp. Softbound....... 275.00   325.00

☐ **Griffin, Martin.** *Catholics and the American Revolution.* Philadelphia and Ridley Park, Pa., 1907–11. Three vols., privately printed.. 110.00   140.00

☐ **Griffin, Martin I. J.** *Commodore John Barry.* Philadelphia, 1903. 424 pp. Clothbound. Limited to 600 copies......... 30.00   40.00

☐ **Griffis, William Elliot.** *Millard Fillmore, Constructive Statesman.* Ithaca, N.Y., 1915. 159 pp.................. 18.00   23.00
Even in 1915, Millard Fillmore was a forgotten President.

☐ **Griffith, G. W. E.** *My 96 Years in the Great West.* Los Angeles, 1929. .... 68.00   88.00

☐ **Griffith, John.** *A Journal of the Life, Travels, and Labours in the Work of the Ministry of John Griffith.* Philadelphia, 1780. 425 pp. Calfbound.............................. 57.00   73.00

PRICE RANGE

☐ **Grimes, James.** *Message of the Governor, Delivered to the Seventh General Assembly.* Des Moines, 1858. 22 pp. Softbound. **250.00** **315.00**

☐ **Grinnell, George B.** *Beyond the Old Frontier.* N.Y., 1913. 374 pp. **50.00** **65.00**

☐ **Grinnell, George B.** *The Cheyenne Indians. Their History and Ways of Life.* New Haven, 1923. Two vols. **275.00** **325.00**

☐ **Grinnell, Joseph.** *Gold Hunting in Alaska as Told by Joseph Grinnell. Dedicated to Disappointed Gold-Hunters the World Over.* Elgin, Ill., 1901. 96 pp. Clothbound. **130.00** **170.00**

☐ **Guernsey, Charles A.** *Wyoming Cowboy Days.* N.Y., 1936. 288 pp. Clothbound. **55.00** **70.00**

☐ **Gulick, Charles A., Jr.** *Labor Policy of the United States Steel Corporation.* N.Y., 1924. 197 pp. Softbound. **15.00** **20.00**

☐ **Guiley, F. A. and Muss, M.** *Cattle and Stock Feeding.* Tucson, 1893. 10 pp. Softbound......................... **400.00** **500.00**

☐ **Guyer, James S.** *Pioneer Life in West Texas.* Brownwood, Texas, 1938. 185 pp. **75.00** **95.00**

☐ **Hafer, Mary Ann.** *Recollections of a Handcart Pioneer of 1860 with Some Account of Frontier Life in Utah and Nevada.* Denver, privately printed, 1938. 117 pp. With plates. **115.00** **150.00**

☐ **Hagerty, Frank.** *The State of North Dakota.* Aberdeen, S.D., 1889. 90 pp. Softbound...................... **140.00** **185.00**

☐ **Haines, T. L.** *Worth and Wealth. The Art of Getting and Using Money.* Chicago, 1883. 704 pp. **45.00** **60.00**

☐ **Hale, Edward E.** *Kanzas and Nebraska...an Account of the Emigrant Aid Companies and Directions to Emigrants.* Boston, 1854. 256 pp. With folding map. **110.00** **140.00**
It wasn't too unusual, in the 1850's, for Kansas to be spelled "Kanzas."

☐ **Hale, Horatio.** *The Iroquois Book of Rites.* Philadelphia, 1883. Softbound. **85.00** **105.00**

☐ **Haley, J. Evetts.** *The XIT Ranch of Texas.* Chicago, 1929. Rare... **800.00** **1000.00**

☐ **Haley, J. Evetts.** *Charles Goodnight, Cowman and Plainsman.* Boston, 1936. 485 pp. **115.00** **140.00**

☐ **Hall, Fred S.** *Sympathetic Strikes and Sympathetic Lockouts.* N.Y., 1898. 120 pp. Softbound. **23.00** **28.00**

☐ **Hall, James.** *The West: Its Commerce and Navigation.* Cincinnati, 1848. 328 pp............................... **165.00** **215.00**

☐ **Hallenbeck, Cleve.** *Spanish Missions of the Old Southwest.* N.Y., 1926. 184 pp............................... **60.00** **80.00**

☐ **Halsey, Margaret.** *Color Blind: a White Woman Looks at the Negro.* N.Y., 1946. .... **23.00** **29.00**

☐ **Halsey, R. T. H.** *The Boston Port Bill as Pictured by a Contemporary London Cartoonist.* N.Y., 1904. Limited to 328 copies, Grolier Club publication. **130.00** **160.00**

☐ **Hambleton, James A.** *A Biographical Sketch of Henry A. Wise.* Richmond, 1856. 509 pp........................... **55.00** **70.00**

☐ **Hamilton, Holman.** *Zachary Taylor, Soldier in the White House.* Indianapolis, 1951. 496 pp. **15.00** **20.00**

PRICE RANGE

☐ **Hamilton, James A.** *Reminiscences of James A. Hamilton.* N.Y., 1869. 647 pp. 30.00 40.00

☐ **Hamilton, Patrick.** *The Resources of Arizona.* San Francisco, 1884. 414 pp. With a folding map. 80.00 110.00

☐ **Hamilton, William B.** *Thomas Rodney, Revolutionary and Builder of the West.* Duke University Press, 1953. 96 pp. Softbound. 8.00 11.00

☐ **Hamilton, William T.** *My 60 Years on the Plains Trapping, Trading and Indian Fighting.* N.Y., 1905. 244 pp. Illustrated by Charles M. Russell. Clothbound. 165.00 215.00
The Russell illustrations give this volume much of its collector interest.

☐ **Hamilton, Wilson.** *The New Empire and her Representative Men.* Oakland, 1886. .... 160.00 205.00

☐ **Hammond, James H.** *An Address Delivered Before the South Carolina Institute at its Annual Fair.* Charleston, 1849. 54 pp. Softbound. 30.00 40.00

☐ **Hamner, Laura V.** *The No-Gun Man of Texas.* Amarillo, 1935. .... 100.00 130.00

☐ **Hanaford, Mrs. P. A.** *The Young Captain; a Memorial of Capt. Richard C. Berby, 15th Reg. Mass Volunteers, who Fell at Antietam.* Boston, 1865. .... 20.00 25.00

☐ **Hans, Fred M.** *The Great Sioux Nation.* Chicago, n.d. (c. 1907). 575 pp. 65.00 85.00

☐ **Hardenberg, John L.** *The Journal of Lieut. John L. Hardenberg of the Second N.Y. Continental Regiment.* Auburn, N.Y., 1879. .... 80.00 100.00

☐ **Hardin, John Wesley.** *The Life of John Wesley Hardin.* Seguin, Texas, 1896. 144 pp. Softbound. 100.00 135.00

☐ **Harlow, Alvin F.** *Old Bowery Days.* N.Y., 1931. 565 pp. 33.00 42.00
New York City's Bowery, later known as a haven for derelicts, was at one time a theatrical and entertainment center.

☐ **Harlow, Frederick P.** *The Making of a Sailor.* Salem, Mass., 1928. 377 pp. Limited to 97 numbered copies printed on rag paper. 115.00 145.00

☐ **Harmon, S. W.** *Hell on the Border.* Ft. Smith, Arkansas, 1898. 720 pp., with 50 halftone illustrations. The first issue is softbound, in green paper covers. Copies that have been rebound, with the paper covers removed, are worth much less. 1675.00 2150.00

☐ **Harper, M. T. and G. D.** *Old Ranches.* Dallas, 1936. ..... 60.00 75.00

☐ **Harris, Dean.** *By Path and Trail.* Chicago, 1908. 225 pp. 90.00 115.00
Missionary work among the Indians.

☐ **Harris, I. G.** *Message to the General Assembly of Connessee (sic).* Nashville, 1861. 12 pp. Softbound. 550.00 675.00

☐ **Harris, N. Dwight.** *The History of Negro Servitude in Illinois, and of the Slavery Agitation in That State, 1719–1864.* Chicago, 1904. 276 pp. 100.00 135.00

☐ **Harris, Nathaniel E.** *Autobiography.* Macon, n.d., 1925. 17.00 22.00

☐ **Harris, T. M.** *The Assassination of Lincoln. A History of the Great Conspiracy, Trial of the Conspirators etc.* Boston, 1892. 419 pp. 22.00 28.00

PRICE RANGE

☐ **Harris, Townsend.** *The Complete Journal of Townsend Harris.* N.Y., 1930. 616 pp. 20.00   25.00

☐ **Harris, W. R.** *The Catholic Church in Utah.* Salt Lake City, n.d. (c. 1910). 350 pp. 37.00   45.00

☐ **Harris, William H.** *Louisiana: Homes for Farmers, Mechanics, Harvesters and Laboring Men.* Austin, Texas, n.d. (c. 1880). 32 pp. Softbound............................. 75.00   100.00

☐ **Harrison, Benjamin.** *Views of an Ex-President.* Indianapolis, 1901. 532 pp..................................... 9.00   12.00

☐ **Harrison, William Henry.** *The Life of Major General William Henry Harrison.* Philadelphia, 1840. 96 pp. With 4 plates. Bound in boards. 50.00   65.00

☐ **Hart, Albert B.** *Commonwealth History of Massachusetts.* N.Y., 1927–30. 5 vols. Bound in cloth. 105.00   135.00

☐ **Hart, Charles Henry.** *A Biographical Sketch of his Excellency Abraham Lincoln, Late President of the U.S.* Albany, 1870. Boards, limited to 100 copies................ 140.00   180.00

☐ **Hart, Charles Henry.** *Catalogue of the Engraved Portraits of Washington.* N.Y., 1904. 4to, half vellum, Grolier Club publication....................................... 125.00   150.00

☐ **Hart, Francis R.** *Admirals of the Caribbean.* Boston, 1922. 203 pp. Bound in boards with vellum spine. One of 200 copies on large paper. 52.00   67.00

☐ **Haskell, William B.** *Two Years on the Klondike and Alaskan Gold Fields.* Hartford, 1898. 558 pp. 90.00   115.00

☐ **Hastain, E.** *Township plats of the Creek Nation.* Muskogee, 1910. 317 pp. Bound in limp leather................... 450.00   575.00

☐ **Hastings, Frank S.** *A Ranchman's Recollections.* Chicago, 1921. 235 pp. With 14 plates..................... 95.00   125.00

☐ **Hatch, Leonard W.** *Government Industrial Arbitration.* N.Y., 1905. Softbound... 16.00   20.00

☐ **Hatcher, Edmund N.** *The Last Four Weeks of the War.* Columbus, 1892.. 15.00   20.00

☐ **Hawk-Eye Pioneer Association.** *Constitution of the Hawk-Eye Pioneer Association of Des Moines County, Iowa.* Burlington, Iowa, 1858. 54 pp. Softbound. 300.00   375.00

☐ **Hawkins, Christopher.** *The Adventures of Christopher Hawkins, Containing Details of his Captivity, a First and Second Time on the High Seas, in the Revolutionary War, by the British.* N.Y., 1864. Limited to 75 copies........... 110.00   140.00

☐ **Hawkins, John P.** *Memoranda Concerning some Branches of the Hawkins Family and Connections.* Indianapolis, n.d. (c. 1913). 137 pp....................................... 85.00   105.00

☐ **Hawkins, Joseph.** *A History of a Voyage to the Coast of Africa...Containing...Interesting Particulars Concerning the Slave Trade.* Philadelphia, 1797. .... 200.00   265.00

☐ **Hawks, Francis L.** *Narrative of the Expedition of an American Squadron to the China Seas and Japan.* N.Y., 1856. 624 pp. With folding maps.............................. 41.00   52.00

☐ **Hawks, John.** *Orderly Book and Journal of John Hawks.* N.Y., 1911. 92 pp. Clothbound with leather label.......... 35.00   42.00

☐ **Hawley, Walter A.** *The Early Days of Santa Barbara, California.* N.Y., 1910. 105 pp. 60.00   80.00

	PRICE RANGE	

☐ **Hawn, William.** *All Around the Civil War.* N.Y., n.d., 1908. . . . . 20.00 | 25.00

☐ **Haworth, Paul Leland.** *On the Headwaters of the Peace River.* N.Y., 1917. 295 pp. . . . . 27.00 | 37.00

☐ **Hayes, J. D.** *The Niagara Ship Canal.* Buffalo, 1865. 58 pp. Softbound. . . . . 45.00 | 59.00

☐ **Haymond, Creed.** *The Central Pacific Railroad Co.* San Francisco, 1888. 256 pp. Clothbound. . . . . 110.00 | 135.00

☐ **Hayward, Elizabeth.** *John M'Coy, his Life and his Diaries.* N.Y., 1948. 493 pp. . . . . 15.00 | 20.00

☐ **Haywood, John.** *The Civil and Political History of Tennessee.* Knoxville, 1823. . . . . 1450.00 | 1800.00

☐ **Hazard, Blanche Evans.** *Beaumarchais and the American Revolution.* Boston, 1910. 39 pp. Clothbound. . . . . 12.00 | 17.00

☐ **Hazard, Thomas R.** *The Johnny-cake Papers of Shepherd Tom, together with Reminiscences of Narragansett Schools of Former Days.* Boston, 1915. 430 pp. With a folding map. Limited to 600 copies. . . . . 70.00 | 90.00

☐ **Heard, Isaac.** *History of the Sioux War and Massacres of 1862 and 1863.* Illustrated, N.Y., 1863. . . . . 230.00 | 290.00

☐ **Heart, Jonathan.** *Journal of Jonathan Heart, on the March to Fort Pitt, 1785.* Albany, 1885. 94 pp. Limited to 150 copies. . . . . 65.00 | 80.00

☐ **Heath, William.** *Memories of Major-General Heath.* Boston, 1798. . . . . 115.00 | 150.00

☐ **Hebard, George R.** *The Pathbreakers from River to Ocean.* Chicago, 1911. 263 pp. . . . . 13.00 | 17.00

☐ **Heckewelder, John.** *History, Manners, and Customs of the Indian Nations who Once Inhabited Pennsylvania and the Neighboring States.* Philadelphia, 1876. 465 pp. . . . . 110.00 | 145.00

☐ **Heckewelder, John.** *A Narrative of the Mission of the United Brethren among the Delaware and Mohegan Indians.* Cleveland, 1907, large paper copy. . . . . 180.00 | 230.00

☐ **Hedges, James B.** *Building the Canadian West.* N.Y., 1939. . . . . 50.00 | 65.00

☐ **Henderson, Thomas J.** *Official Report of the Trial of the Hon. Albert Jackson, Judge of the Fifteenth Judicial Circuit before the Senate.* Jefferson City, Mo., 1859. 480 pp. Clothbound. . . . . 55.00 | 70.00

☐ **Hendricks, George D.** *The Bad Man of the West.* San Antonio, 1950. . . . . 40.00 | 50.00

☐ **Henry, Patrick.** *Life, Correspondence, and Speeches.* N.Y., 1891. Three vols. . . . . 65.00 | 85.00

☐ **Hensel, W.** *The Christiana Riot and the Treason Trials of 1851.* Lancaster, Pa., 1911. 158 pp. . . . . 30.00 | 36.00

☐ **Henshaw, David.** *Remarks upon the Bank of the United States, being an Examination of the Report of the Committee of Ways and Means.* Boston, 1831. 47 pp. Softbound. . . . . 45.00 | 60.00

☐ **Herbert, Charles.** *A Relic of the Revolution.* Boston, 1857. . . . . 42.00 | 55.00

☐ **Herndon and Welk.** *Abraham Lincoln. The True Story of a Great Life.* N.Y., 1896. Two vols. . . . . 28.00 | 34.00

PRICE RANGE

☐ **Herskovitz, M. J.** *The American Negro.* N.Y., 1930.......　37.00　　48.00
☐ **Heyman, Max L.** *Prudent Soldier: a Biography of Major General E. R. S. Canby, 1817–1873.* Glendale, Calif., 1959. 418 pp..　18.00　　23.00
☐ **Hibben, Paxton.** *The Peerless Leader William Jennings Bryan.* N.Y., 1929. 446 pp. ....　12.00　　16.00
☐ **Highbee, Elias and Thompson, R. B.** *The Petition of the Latter-Day Saints, commonly known as Mormons.* Washington, D.C., 1840. 13 pp. Softbound. ....　250.00　　325.00
☐ **Hill, Jasper S.** *The Letters of A Young Miner. Covering the Adventures of Jasper S. Hill during the California Goldrush, 1848–1852.* San Francisco, 1964. 111 pp. Limited to 475 copies. With a folding map...............................　80.00　　110.00
☐ **Hill, Joseph J.** *The History of Warner's Ranch and its Environs.* Los Angeles, privately printed, 1927. 221 pp. Limited to 1,000 numbered copies. ....　115.00　　140.00
☐ **Hillard, Henry W.** *Speeches and Addresses.* N.Y., 1855. 497 pp..　20.00　　25.00
☐ **Hindle, Brooke.** *The Pursuit of Science in Revolutionary America, 1735–1789.* Chapel Hill, 1956. 410 pp. ....　13.00　　17.00
☐ **Hines, H. K.** *Missionary History of the Pacific Northwest.* Portland, 1899. 510 pp. Clothbound. ....　95.00　　125.00
☐ **Hitchcock, Caroline Hanks.** *Nancy Hanks. The True Story of Abraham Lincoln's Mother.* N.Y., 1899. ....　60.00　　75.00
☐ **Hitchcock, Ethan A.** *A Traveler in Indian Territory.* Cedar Rapids, Iowa, 1930. 270 pp. With folding maps. ....　100.00　　135.00
☐ **Hittell, John S.** *The Resources of California.* San Francisco, 1863. 464 pp. ....　115.00　　145.00
☐ **Hobart, Chauncy.** *Recollections of My Life.* Redwing, Minnesota, 1885. 409 pp. Clothbound......................　65.00　　85.00
☐ **Hodd, J. B.** *Advance and Retreat.* New Orleans, 1880.　30.00　　40.00
☐ **Hodge, Frederick.** *Handbook of American Indians north of Mexico.* Washington, D.C., 1907–10. Two vols. With a folding map. Published by the Smithsonian Institution.....　210.00　　265.00
☐ **Hodge, Hiram.** *Arizona as It Is.* N.Y., 1877. 273 pp. With plates and maps. ....　135.00　　165.00
☐ **Hodgkins, William H.** *The Battle of Fort Stedman, March 25, 1865.* Boston, privately printed, 1889. ....　57.00　　72.00
☐ **Hoff, W. and Schwabach, F.** *North American Railroads.* N.Y., 1906. ....　150.00　　190.00
☐ **Hoffman, William.** *The Monitor.* N.Y., 1863. ....　30.00　　38.00
☐ **Hogaboam, James J.** *The Bean Creek Valley: Incidents of its Early Settlement.* Hudson, 1876. 140 pp. Softbound. ....　75.00　　100.00
The Bean Creek Valley is in Michigan, where this work was published.
☐ **Hohman, Elmo Paul.** *The American Whaleman: a Study of Life and Labor in the Whaling Industry.* N.Y., 1928. 355 pp..　125.00　　160.00
☐ **Holden, Oliver.** *Sacred Dirges, Hymns, and Anthems, commemorative of the Death of General George Washington, the Guardian of this Country and the Friend of Man.* Boston, n.d., 1800. Softbound............................　325.00　　400.00

	PRICE RANGE	

☐ **Holley, Mary Austin.** *Texas.* Lexington, Ky., 1836, 410 pp. **3450.00**   **4175.00**
Second edition of an early Texas guidebook. The first edition, 1833, was the earliest work on Texas in the English language.

☐ **Hollingsworth, John M.** *The Journal of Lieutenant John McHenry Hollingworth of the First New York Volunteers.* San Francisco, 1923. 61 pp. Bound in boards. Limited to 300 copies. **40.00**   **50.00**

☐ **Hollis, Ira.** *The Frigate Constitution.* Boston, 1900. 263 pp. **27.00**   **35.00**

☐ **Hollis, Thomas.** *The True Sentiments of America.* London, 1768. . . . .   **280.00**   **360.00**

☐ **Holmes, Abiel.** *The Annals of America from the Discovery by Columbus to the Year 1826.* Cambridge, Mass., 1829. Two vols. **93.00**   **117.00**

☐ **Holst, Hermann E. von.** *The Constitutional and Political History of the United States.* Chicago, 1889–1892. Eight vols. **130.00**   **160.00**

☐ **Holsters & Heroes.** *An Anthology of Western Stories.* N.Y., 1954. . . . .   **13.00**   **17.00**

☐ **Homes, Dwight O. W.** *The Evolution of the Negro College.* N.Y., 1934. 221 pp. Clothbound. **42.00**   **53.00**

☐ **Hone, Philip.** *The Diary of Philip Hone.* N.Y., 1889. Two vols. **32.00**   **40.00**

☐ **Hooker, William Francis.** *The Prairie Schooner.* Chicago, 1918. 156 pp. Published by the author, who printed only 50 copies (all of which were given away to his friends). . .   **100.00**   **135.00**

☐ **Hopkins, Stephen.** *The Grievances of the American Colonies Candidly Examined.* London, 1766. . . . .   **325.00**   **385.00**

☐ **Horan, James D.** *The Great American West.* N.Y., 1959.   **24.00**   **31.00**

☐ **Horn, Stanley F.** *Invisible Empire: the Story of the Ku Klux Klan.* Boston, 1939. 434 pp. **140.00**   **175.00**

☐ **Horn, Tom.** *Life of Tom Horn, Government Scout and Interpreter. A Vindication.* Denver, 1904. 317 pp. Softbound. **115.00**   **145.00**

☐ **Hornblow, Arthur.** *A History of the Theatre in America.* Philadelphia, 1919. Two vols. **50.00**   **65.00**

☐ **Horne, Melvill.** *Letters on Missions.* Schenectady, 1797.   **190.00**   **225.00**

☐ **Hosmer, James K.** *The Life of Young Sir Henry Vane, Governor of Massachusetts Bay, and the Leader of the long Parliament.* Boston, 1888. 581 pp. **18.00**   **23.00**

☐ **Hough, Emerson.** *The Story of the Outlaw.* N.Y., 1907. Third printing. **100.00**   **130.00**

☐ **Hough, Franklin B.** *History of Durey's Brigade, During the Campaign in Virginia Under Gen. Pope.* Albany, N.Y., 1864. Limited to 300 copies. **60.00**   **80.00**

☐ **Hough, Walter.** *The Moki Snake Dance.* Santa Fe, 1898. 58 pp. Softbound. **100.00**   **135.00**

☐ **House, Albert V.** *Planter Management and Capitalism in Antebellum, Georgia.* N.Y., 1954. 329 pp. **15.00**   **20.00**

PRICE RANGE

☐ **Houston, Andrew J.** *Texas Independence.* Houston, 1938. 300 pp. Limited to 500 numbered, signed copies. Bound in full leather. 140.00   185.00

☐ **Hovgaard, William.** *The Voyages of the Norsemen to America.* N.Y., 1914. 304 pp. 34.00   45.00

☐ **Howar, McHenry.** *Recollections of a Maryland Confederate Soldier.* Baltimore, 1914. Scarce. 120.00   150.00

☐ **Howard, F. K.** *Fourteen Months in American Bastiles.* Baltimore, 1863. . . . . 42.00   55.00

☐ **Howard, Oliver O.** *Autobiography of Oliver O. Howard.* N.Y., 1908, Two vols. 32.00   38.00

☐ **Howard, Oliver O.** *Nez Perce Joseph. An Account of his Ancestors, his Lands, his Confederates, his Enemies, his Murders, his War, his Pursuit and Capture.* Boston, 1881. 274 pp. With plates and folding maps. Bound in cloth. 200.00   250.00

☐ **Howay, F. W. and others.** *British Columbia and the United States.* Toronto, 1942. 408 pp. 36.00   47.00

☐ **Howe, Joseph.** *The Reciprocity Treaty.* Hamilton, 1865. 15 pp. Softbound. 180.00   230.00

☐ **Howe, Mark A.** *The Life and Letters of George Bancroft.* N.Y., 1908. Two vols. 22.00   28.00

☐ **Howe, Octavius T.** *American Ships, 1833–1858.* Salem, 1926. Two vols. Clothbound. 275.00   350.00

☐ **Hower, Ralph.** *The History of an Advertising Agency (N.W. Ayer).* Cambridge, Mass., 1939. 652 pp. 20.00   25.00

☐ **Howison, Robert R.** *A History of Virginia, From its Discovery by Europeans to the Present Time.* Philadelphia, 1846–48. Two vols. Clothbound. 125.00   160.00

☐ **Howland, Henry.** *An Address Delivered Before the Leadville Temperance Club, by the President of the Club.* Leadville, 1880. 16 pp. Softbound. 900.00   1175.00

☐ **Hoyt, E.** *Antiquarian Researchers: Comprising a History of the Indian Wars in the Country Bordering Connecticut River and Parts Adjacent.* Greenfield, Mass., 1824. With engraved folding view. 350.00   425.00

☐ **Hubbard, W.** *A Narrative of the Troubles with the Indians in New England, from the First Planting in the year 1607, to this Present Year 1677.* Boston, printed by John Foster in the year 1677. Small quarto, with map of New England. 40,000.00   55,000.00

☐ **Hudson, James F.** *The Railways and the Republic.* N.Y., 1886. 492 pp. 65.00   85.00

☐ **Huebner, Grover G.** *Agricultural Commerce.* N.Y., 1924. 529 pp. 23.00   29.00

☐ **Hull, John A. T.** *Census of Iowa for 1880.* Des Moines, 1883. 744 pp. Clothbound. 52.00   67.00

☐ **Humphrey, William.** *A Journal Kept by William Humphrey of Capt. Thayer's Company, on a March to Quenec, under the Command of Col. Benedict Arnold, 1775–1776.* Tarrytown, N.Y., 1931. 42 pp. Softbound. 22.00   28.00

☐ **Hunt, Gaillard.** *The Life of James Madison.* N.Y., 1902. 402 pp. 12.00   16.00

PRICE RANGE

☐ **Hunt, J.** *Mormonism: Embracing its Origin, Rise and Progress.* St. Louis, 1844. .... 950.00 1200.00

☐ **Hunter, Alexander.** *Johnny Reb and Billy Yank.* N.Y., 1905. .... 55.00 70.00

☐ **Hunter, J. Marvin.** *Trail Drivers of Texas.* N.Y., 1963. Two vols. In the original publisher's box. 130.00 160.00

☐ **Hunter, Martha T.** *A Memoir of Robert M. T. Hunter.* Washington, D.C. 1903. .... 15.00 20.00

☐ **Hurn, Ethel A.** *Wisconsin Women in the War Between the States.* Wisconsin, n.d., 1911. .... 21.00 27.00

☐ **Hussey, John A.** *The History of Fort Vancouver and its Physical Structure.* Washington State Historical Society, n.d. (c. 1957). 256 pp. With 54 plates. Bound in cloth. Limited to 1,000 numbered copies. 47.00 62.00

☐ **Hutchings, Jere.** *Jere C. Hutchings, a Personal Story.* Detroit, 1938, privately printed. 58.00 73.00

☐ **Hutchins, J. M.** *Scenes of Wonder and Curiosity in California.* San Francisco, 1861.......................... 200.00 250.00

☐ **Hutchinson, Thomas.** *Diary and Letters of.* London, 1883–86. Two vols.. 45.00 60.00

☐ **Hutchinson, W. H.** *A Bar Cross Man.* Norman, Okla., 1956. .... 37.00 48.00

☐ **Huyette, Miles C.** *The Maryland Campaign and the Battle of Antietam.* Buffalo, N.Y., 1915. .... 15.00 20.00

☐ **Hyde, John.** *Wonderland; or the Pacific Northwest and Alaska.* St. Paul, 1888. 96 pp. Softbound. 34.00 43.00

☐ **Hyer, Julien.** *The Land of Beginning Again.* Atlanta, 1952. .... 18.00 23.00

☐ **Ickes, Anna Wilmarth.** *Mesa Land. The History and Romance of the American Southwest.* Boston, 1933. 236 pp.. 27.00 34.00

☐ **Ide, Simeon.** *The Conquest of California.* San Francisco, 1944. 188 pp. Bound in boards. With a colored folding map. Limited to 500 copies................................... 130.00 170.00

☐ **Ide, William B.** *A Biographical Sketch of the Life of William B. Ide: with a Minute and Interesting Account of One of the Largest Emigrating Companies from the East to the Pacific Coast.* N.p., n.d. (Claremont, New Hampshire, 1880). Cloth.. 1000.00 1250.00

☐ **Indian Narratives.** *Containing a Correct and Interesting History of the Indian Wars.* Claremont, 1854. .... 85.00 105.00

☐ **Ingraham, Joseph H.** *The Sunny South. Or, the Southerner at Home.* Philadelphia, 1860. 526 pp. 125.00 160.00

☐ **Innis, Harold A.** *The Cod Fisheries.* New Haven, 1940. 520 pp. Clothbound. 60.00 75.00

☐ **Irby, Richard.** *Historical Sketch of the Nottoway Grays, afterwards Company G., 18th Virginia Regiment.* Richmond, 1878... 55.00 70.00

☐ **Irving, John Treat.** *Indian Sketches, Taken During an Expedition to the Pawnee and other Tribes of American Indian.* London, 1835. Two vols. Bound in boards with paper labels on the spines................................... 175.00 235.00

PRICE RANGE

☐ **Irving, Theodore.** *More than Conquerer.* N.Y., 1873.	12.00	15.00
☐ **Irwin, D. Hanson.** *The Pacific Coast Pulpit.* N.Y., n.d. (1893). 247 pp..	26.00	34.00
☐ **Isbell, F. A.** *Mining and Hunting in the Far West, 1852–1870.* Burlingame, Calif., 1948. Bound in pictorial boards. Limited to 200 copies................................	110.00	145.00
☐ **Ives, Joseph C.** *Report Upon the Colorado River of the West, Explored in 1857 and 1858.* Washington, 1861.....	110.00	145.00
☐ **Izard, Mark W.** *Annual message of Mark W. Izard, Governor of the Territory of Nebraska.* Omaha, 1855. 12 pp. Softbound. One of the first pieces of printing done in Nebraska..	5450.00	6750.00
☐ **Jackson, Albert.** *Official Report of the Trial of Albert Jackson of the State of Missouri.* Jefferson City, Mo., 1859. 480 pp...	47.00	62.00
☐ **Jackson, C. F.** *Inaugural address of C.F. Jackson, to the General Assembly of the State of Missouri.* Jefferson City, 1861. Softbound.	24.00	31.00
☐ **Jackson, Isaac R.** *A Sketch of the Life and Public Service of William Henry Harrison.* N.Y., 1839. 32 pp............. Published when Harrison was being groomed as a Presidential candidate for the following year's election (1840). He ran, won, and died (of natural causes) a month after taking office.	50.00	65.00
☐ **Jackson, Joseph.** *American Colonial Architecture. It's Origin and Development.* Philadelphia, 1924. 228 pp.	21.00	27.00
☐ **Jackson, Joseph Henry.** *Tintypes in Gold. Four Studies in Robbery.* N.Y., 1929.	50.00	62.00
☐ **Jackson, Mary Anna.** *Life and Letters of General Thomas J. Jackson.* N.Y., 1892..................................	38.00	45.00
☐ **Jackson, O. E.** *Idaho Mining Rights. A guide for Miners, Prospectors, and Others Interested in the Rich Mineral Lands of Idaho.* Boise, 1899. 60 pp. Softbound.	180.00	225.00
☐ **Jackson, Sheldon.** *Alaska, and Missions on the North Pacific Coast.* N.Y., 1880. 327 pp.	60.00	75.00
☐ **James, Edward W.** *The Lower Norfolk County (Virginia) Antiquary.* N.Y., 1951. Five vols.	235.00	290.00
☐ **James, Edwin.** *Memoires de John Tanner.* Paris, 1835. French text. Two vols. Bound in ¼ leather............	65.00	80.00
☐ **James, F. Cyril.** *The Growth of Chicago Banks.* N.Y., 1938. Two vols. With plates, many of which are in color.	53.00	67.00
☐ **James, George W.** *The Wonders of the Colorado Desert.* Boston, 1906. Two vols. With many illustrations, some in color..	80.00	110.00
☐ **James, George W.** *What the White Race May Learn from the Indian.* Chicago, 1908.	42.00	53.00
☐ **James, Will.** *Lone Cowboy.* N.Y., 1930.................	70.00	90.00
☐ **Jameson, John F.** *The History of Historical Writing in America.* N.Y., 1961. Limited to 750 copies.	12.00	16.00
☐ **Jarves, James J.** *History of the Hawaiian or Sandwich Islands.* Boston, 1844. 407 pp. With a folding map. Bound in half calf.	130.00	175.00

PRICE RANGE

☐ **Jay, John.** *The Correspondence and Public Papers of John Jay.* N.Y., 1890. Four vols. Bound in half leather, limited to 750 numbered sets. 150.00 180.00

☐ **Jefferson, Thomas.** *Writings of Thomas Jefferson, being his Autobiography, Correspondence, Reports, messages, Addresses, and other Writings, Official and Private.* N.Y., 1853. Nine vols. Bound in cloth. 110.00 140.00

☐ **Jeffrey, William H.** *Richmond Prisons 1861–62.* St. Johnsbury, Vt., n.d., 1893. .... 27.00 36.00

☐ *Jemmy and His Mother: A Tale for Children. And Lucy; or, the Slave Girl of Kentucky.* Cincinnati, 1858. .... 40.00 52.00

☐ **Jennings, N. A.** *A Texas Ranger.* Dallas, 1930. 158 pp. 120.00 150.00

☐ **Jessup, Philip C.** *Elihu Root.* N.Y., 1938. Two vols....... 35.00 42.00

☐ **Jillson, Willard R.** *The Boone Narrative.* Louisville, 1932. 61 pp. Limited to 1,000 copies. 40.00 55.00

☐ **Jillson, Willard R.** *Kentucky History.* Louisville, 1936. 96 pp. Limited to 300 copies. 37.00 48.00

☐ **Johns, Henry T.** *Life with the 49th Massachusetts Volunteers.* Dornbush, Mass., 1864........................ 17.00 22.00

☐ **Johnson, Andrew.** *Proceedings in the Trial of Andrew Johnson.* Washington, D.C., 1868. 1,090 pp. Bound in ½ morocco. 55.00 70.00
The "Watergate affair" of the 1860's.

☐ **Johnson, Kenneth.** *San Francisco as It Is.* Georgetown, Calif., 1964. 285 pp. Bound in boards. Limited to 1,000 copies.. 42.00 55.00

☐ **Johnson, Sidonia V.** *A Short History of Oregon.* Chicago 1904. 329 pp... 95.00 125.00

☐ **Johnston, Abraham R. and others.** *Marching with the Army of the West.* Glendale, 1936. 368 pp. 37.00 45.00

☐ **Johnston, Alexander.** *American Orations.* N.Y., 1899. Four vols. 55.00 70.00

☐ **Johnston, Elizabeth Bryant.** *Original Portraits of Washington.* Boston, 1882, small folio. 50.00 65.00

☐ **Johnston, Frederick.** *Memorials of old Virginia Clerks.* Lynchburg, 1888. 405 pp. 75.00 95.00

☐ **Johnston, Harry P.** *Nathan Hale, 1776. Biography and Memorials.* New Haven, 1914. 296 pp. Limited to 1,000 copies.. 18.00 23.00

☐ **Johnston, Isaac N.** *Four Months in Libby, and the Campaign against Atlanta.* Cincinnati, 1864. Softbound. 65.00 85.00

☐ **Johnston J.** *History of the Towns of Bristol and Bremen.* N.p., 1873. .... 185.00 215.00

☐ **Johnston, James F. W.** *Notes on North America.* Boston, 1851. Two vols. With a folding map. 65.00 80.00

☐ **Johnston, Richard M.** *Life of Alexander H. Stephens.* Philadelphia, 1878... 28.00 34.00

☐ **Johnston, William Preston.** *The Life of Gen. Albert Sidney Johnston.* N.Y., 1878. .... 27.00 35.00

☐ **Jones, C. C.** *Historical Sketch of the Chatham Artillery During the Confederate Struggle for Independence.* Albany, 1867... 80.00 100.00

PRICE RANGE

☐ **Jones, C. C.** *Military Lessons Inculcated on the Coast of Georgia during the Confederate War.* Augusta, Ga., 1883. Softbound. 21.00   27.00

☐ **Jones, C. C.** *The Battle of Honey Hill.* Augusta, 1885. Softbound. 21.00   27.00

☐ **Jones, Charles C.** *Antiquities of the Southern Indians.* N.Y., 1873. .... 175.00   230.00

☐ **Jones, Daniel W.** *Forty Years Among the Indians.* Salt Lake City, 1890. 400 pp. 160.00   190.00

☐ **Jones, David.** *A Journal of Two Visits Made to Some Nations of Indians on the West Side of the River Ohio.* N.Y., 1865. .... 185.00   225.00

☐ **Jones, G. D.** *Life and Adventure in the South Pacific, By a Roving Printer.* N.Y., 1861. .... 190.00   240.00

☐ **Jones, George N.** *Florida Plantation Records from the Papers of George Noble Jones.* St. Louis, 1927. 596 pp. With a folding map. 52.00   68.00

☐ **Jones, Henry M.** *Ships of Kingston: Good-Bye, Fare Ye Well.* Plymouth, Mass., 1926. 130 pp. 43.00   55.00

☐ **Jones, Hugh.** *The Present State of Virginia.* N.Y., 1865. 152 pp. Softbound. 80.00   110.00

☐ **Jones, Ignatius.** *Random Recollections of Albany, from 1800 to 1808.* Albany, 1850. Softbound. 22.00   28.00

☐ **Jones, John Paul.** *The Life, Travels, Voyages, and Daring Engagements of Paul Jones.* Albany, 1813. Miniature format, boards. 125.00   150.00

☐ **Jones, Samuel.** *The Seige of Charleston.* N.Y., 1911..... 75.00   100.00

☐ **Judson, Phoebe.** *A Pioneer's Search for a New Home.* Bellington, Wash., 1925. 309 pp. 210.00   265.00

☐ **Juettner, Otto.** *Daniel Drake and his Followers.* Cincinnati, 1909. 496 pp. 32.00   43.00

☐ **Junkin, George.** *Political Falacies: an Examination of the False Assumptions and Refutation of Sophistical Reasonings which have Brought on the Civil War.* N.Y., 1863. 332 pp. 70.00   90.00

☐ **Kane, Harnett T.** *Deep Delta Country.* N.Y., 1944. Fifth printing. 10.00   14.00

☐ **Kane, Paul.** *Wanderings of an Artist Among the Indians of North America.* Toronto, 1925. 329 pp. 65.00   85.00

☐ **Kautz, August V.** *The Company Clerk. Showings How and When to Make Out all the Returns, Reports, Rolls and other Papers, and What to do With Them.* Philadelphia, 1864. 142 pp. With folding facsimiles. Bound in full leather...... 32.00   40.00

☐ **Keeler, N. E.** *A Trip to Alaska and the Klondike in the Summer of 1905.* Cincinnati, 1906. 115 pp. Softbound.... 75.00   100.00

☐ **Keith, Charles.** *Chronicles of Pennsylvania from the English Revolution to the Peace of Aix-la-Chapelle.* Philadelphia, 1917. Two vols. 43.00   55.00

☐ **Kellogg, Sanford C.** *The Shenandoah Valley and Virginia 1861 to 1865.* N.Y., n.d., 1903. .... 52.00   68.00

☐ **Kelly, Charles.** *The Outlaw Trail. A History of Butch Cassidy and his Wild Bunch.* N.Y., 1959. .... 45.00   60.00

PRICE RANGE

☐ **Kelly, Charles.** *Holy Murder, the Story of Porter Rockwell.* N.Y., n.d. (c. 1935). 313 pp. 95.00 120.00

☐ **Kelly, Leroy Victor.** *The Range Men.* N.Y., 1965. 526 pp. 70.00 90.00

☐ **Kelly, R. P.** *Report and by-laws of the San Jose Gold Mining Company. Adopted March 1, 1851 (error for 1861).* N.p., n.d. (Mesilla, 1861). 16 pp. Softbound, only one copy known to exist. 7000.00 9750.00

☐ **Kelly, Roy W.** *The Shipbuilding Industry.* Boston, 1918. 302 pp. 43.00 55.00

☐ **Kelly, Samuel.** *An Eighteenth Century Seaman.* London, 1925. .... 43.00 55.00

☐ **Kelly, William.** *A Stroll Through the Diggins of California.* London, 1852. 240 pp. Bound in boards. 85.00 110.00

☐ **Kelsey, D. M.** *Our Pioneer Heroes and Their Daring Deeds.* Chicago, 1901. .... 47.00 63.00

☐ **Kemp, Louis W.** *The Signers of the Texas Declaration of Independence.* Salado, Texas, 1959. 398 pp. 57.00 73.00

☐ **Kendall, Amos.** *Autobiography of Amos Kendall.* Boston, 1872. 700 pp. 55.00 70.00

☐ **Kendall, Charles W.** *Private Men-of-War.* N.Y., 1932. ..... 65.00 79.00

☐ **Kenderdine, T. S.** *California Tramp and Later Footprints.* Newtown, Pa., 1888. .... 175.00 230.00

☐ **Kenly, John R.** *Memoirs of a Maryland Volunteer.* Philadelphia, 1873. 521 pp. 27.00 35.00

☐ **Kennedy, E. R.** *The Contest for California in 1861.* Boston, 1912. 361 pp. 26.00 34.00

☐ **Kidder, Frederic.** *The Abenaki Indians.* Portland, 1859. 32.00 39.00

☐ **Kidder, Frederic.** *Military Operations in Eastern Maine and Nova Scotia during the Revolution.* Albany, 1867. .... 30.00 37.00

☐ **Killebrew, J.** *Resources of Montgomery County.* Clarksville, 1870. 60 pp. Softbound. 210.00 265.00

☐ **Killman, E. and Wright T.** *Hugh Roy Cullan.* N.Y., 1954. 21.00 27.00

☐ **King, Clarence.** *Mountaineering in the Sierra Nevada.* Boston, 1872. 292 pp. 80.00 105.00

☐ **King, Frank M.** *Mavericks. The Salty Comments of an Old-Time Cow Puncher.* Pasadena, 1947. 275 pp. Bound in morocco. Limited to 350 copies, numbered and signed. ... 115.00 150.00

☐ **King, T. Butler.** *Report of T. Butler King on California.* Washington, 1850. 72 pp. Softbound. 110.00 145.00

☐ **Kingsbury, Susan M.** *The Record of the Virginia Company of London.* Washington, D.C., 1906–1935. Four vols. 175.00 215.00

☐ **Kinzie, Juliette A.** *Wau-Bun, the Early Days in the Northwest.* N.Y., 1856. 498 pp. With 6 plates. 145.00 185.00

☐ **Kip, Lawrence.** *The Indian Council at Walla Walla.* Eugene, Ore., 1897. 28 pp. Softbound. 37.00 47.00
A reprint of the 1855 edition, which is very rare and costly.

☐ **Kirk, Charles H.** *History of the 15th Pennsylvania Volunteer Cavalry.* Philadelphia, 1906. .... 30.00 37.00

☐ **Kirk, Robert C.** *Twelve Months in the Klondike.* London, 1899. 273 pp. 80.00 110.00

☐ **Kirkpatrick, John E.** *Timothy Flint, Pioneer, Missionary, Author, Editor, 1780–1840.* Cleveland, 1911. 331 pp. 32.00 40.00

PRICE RANGE

☐ **Knauss, James O.** *Territorial Florida Journalism.* Deland, 1926. 250 pp. Limited to 350 copies.................... 100.00 135.00

☐ **Knight, John and Slover, John.** *Indian Atrocities: Narratives of the Perils and Sufferings of Dr. John Knight and John Slover, among the Indians during the Revolutionary War etc.* Cincinnati, 1867. 72 pp. Softbound. 110.00 140.00

☐ **Knorr, F. and Shaw, L.** *Cowboy Dance Tunes.* N.p., 1946. Softbound. 30.00 40.00

☐ **Knower, Daniel.** *The Adventures of a 49er.* Albany,1894. 200.00 275.00

☐ **Knox, Vicesimus.** *Spirit of Despotism.* Morristown, N.J., 1799. 319 pp. Bound in leather......................... 52.00 67.00

☐ **Kohl, J. G.** *Travels in Canada, New York and Pennsylvania.* London, 1861. Two vols. 160.00 200.00
Translation of a work first published in Stuttgart, Germany, in 1856.

☐ **Kouwenhoven, John A.** *Adventures of America, 1857–1900.* N.Y., 1938. .... 25.00 32.00

☐ **Kraitisir, Charles V.** *The Poles in the United States of America.* Philadelphia, 1837. 196 pp. 53.00 65.00

☐ **Krakel, Dean.** *The Saga of Tom Horn.* Laramie, 1954. .... 50.00 63.00

☐ **Kroeber, Alfred.** *Handbook of the Indians of California.* Washington, D.C., 1925. 995 pp. With 73 plates. Bound in cloth. Published by the Smithsonian Institution. 190.00 245.00
A reprint, dated 1953, is now selling for.................. 50.00 65.00

☐ **Kriebel, Howard W.** *The Schwenkfelders in Pennsylvania.* Lancaster, 1904. .... 20.00 25.00

☐ **Kupper, Winifred.** *The Golden Hoof. The Story of the Sheep of the Southwest.* N.Y., 1945........................... 37.00 48.00

☐ **Kurz, Rudolph F.** *The Journal of Rudolph F. Kurz, among Fur Traders etc., 1846–52.* Washington, 1937. 382 pp. With 48 plates. Softbound. 90.00 120.00

☐ **Ladue, Joseph.** *Klondike Facts. A Complete Guide Book to the Great Gold Regions of the Northwest Territories and Alaska.* N.Y., 1897. 205 pp. With 18 maps and plates. Softbound. 200.00 265.00

☐ **LaGrange, Helen.** *Clipper Ships of America and Great Britain, 1833–1869.* N.Y., n.d. (c. 1935). Bound in boards. With 37 colored wood engravings. Limited to 300 numbered and signed copies....................................... 150.00 195.00

☐ **Lake, Simon.** *The Submarine in War and Peace.* Philadelphia, 1918. .... 85.00 105.00

☐ **Lamb, R.** *An Original and Authentic Journal of Occurrences During the late American War.* Dublin, 1809. ...... 105.00 135.00

☐ **Lambert, George W.** *A Trip through the Union Stock Yards and Slaughter Houses.* Chicago, 1892. 29 pp. Softbound. 65.00 85.00

☐ **Lambourne, Alfred.** *The Old Journey. Reminiscences of Pioneer Days.* Salt Lake City, 1897. 53 pp. Bound in ½ cloth... 115.00 150.00

☐ **Lancaster, Joseph.** *Letters on National Subjects.* Washington City (D.C.), 1820. 60 pp. Softbound.............. 40.00 50.00

☐ **Lane, Walter P.** *The Adventures and Recollections of General Walter P. Lane.* Marshall, Texas, 1928. 180 pp. 50.00 65.00

PRICE RANGE

☐ **Langford, Nathaniel P.** *Diary of the Washburn Expedition to the Yellowstone and Firehole Rivers in the year 1870.* N.p., 1905. 122 pp. **60.00** **75.00**

☐ **Langford, W. G.** *Memorial before Congress. Claim for the Lapwau Mission in Idaho Territory.* Washington, 1872. 26 pp. Softbound.. **1100.00** **1450.00**

☐ **Langworthy, Asahel.** *A Biographical Sketch of Colonel Richard M. Johnson of Kentucky.* N.Y., 1843. 46 pp. Softbound. **30.00** **38.00**

☐ **Langworthy, Franklin.** *Scenery of the Plains, Mountains and Mines.* Princeton, 1932............................. **40.00** **50.00**

☐ **Lanham, Charles.** *The Japanese in America.* N.Y., 1872. 352 pp.. **32.00** **40.00**

☐ **Lapham, I. A.** *Wisconsin: Its Geography, History, Geology, and Mineralogy.* Milwaukee, 1846....................... **150.00** **190.00**

☐ **Larkin, Thomas O.** *California in 1846.* San Francisco, 1934. 64 pp. Limited to 550 copies. **145.00** **185.00**

☐ **LaRoche, F.** *En route to the Klondike. A Practical Guide.* Chicago, 1898. Softbound, oblong format............... **350.00** **450.00**

☐ **Lathrop, Elsie.** *Early American Inns and Taverns.* N.Y., 1935. 365 pp. Clothbound. **45.00** **60.00**

☐ **Lathrop, John.** *The Speech of Caunonicus; or an Indian Tradition.* Boston, 1803. .... **85.00** **110.00**

☐ **Latta, Robert R.** *Reminiscences of Pioneer Life.* Kansas City, 1912. 186 pp...................................... **135.00** **175.00**

☐ **Laut, Agnes C.** *The Romance of the Rails.* N.Y., 1929. Two vols. Clothbound. **70.00** **100.00**

☐ **Lawrence, A. B.** *A History of Texas.* N.Y., 1844. The frontispiece is said to be the first engraved view of Austin. **900.00** **1275.00**

☐ **Lawson, Pubius V.** *Bravest of the Brave.* Menasha, Wis., 1904. .... **32.00** **40.00**

☐ **Lechford, Thomas.** *Notebook of Thomas Lechford, from June 27, 1638 to July 29, 1641.* Cambridge, Mass., 1885. 460 pp. Clothbound. **45.00** **60.00**
Thomas Lechford was the only professional lawyer in Massachusetts at the time covered by his notebook.

☐ **LeClerc, Frederick.** *Texas and Its Revolution.* Houston, 1950, 148 pp.. **75.00** **100.00**

☐ **Lee, G. C. and Thorpe, F. M.** *The History of North America.* Philadelphia, 1903–07. 20 vols. Limited to 1,000 sets. **125.00** **165.00**
Despite the ambitiousness of this project, the set did not become popular at the time—nor later with collectors for that matter, as attested by the market value (only $6–$8 per volume)!.

☐ **Lee, Henry.** *Report of a Committee of the Citizens of Boston and Vicinity, Opposed to a Further Increase of Duties on Importations.* Boston, 1827. 196 pp. **37.00** **47.00**
Even after America became self-governing, complaints on duty taxes (which had sparked the "Boston Tea Party") continued.

☐ **Lee, L. P.** *History of the Spirit Lake Massacre, and of Miss Abagail Gardiner's Three Month's Captivity among the Indians.* New Britain, Conn., 1857. 48 pp. Softbound........ **100.00** **130.00**

PRICE RANGE

☐ **Lefors, Joe.** *Wyoming Peace Officer. An Autobiography.* Laramie, Wyoming, 1953. 200 pp. 65.00   85.00

☐ **Leggett, William.** *A Collection of the Political Writings of William Leggett.* N.Y., 1840. Two vols. Clothbound. 26.00   33.00

☐ **Leinhard, Heinrich.** *A Pioneer at Sutter's Fort, 1846–1850.* L.A., 1941. 191 pp. Bound in cloth with leather spine. Published by the Calafia Society. 100.00   135.00

☐ **Leland, Charles G.** *The Algonquin Legends of New England.* Boston, 1884. .... 58.00   73.00

☐ **LeRoy, Bruce.** *H. M. Chittenden: a Western Epic.* Tacoma, 1961. Limited to 1,000 copies. 38.00   48.00

☐ *Letters on the Mission of the Ojibwa Indians.* Boston, 1939. .... 50.00   65.00

☐ **Letts, J. M.** *A Pictorial View of California.* N.Y., 1853. .... 350.00   450.00

☐ **Levy, Babette May.** *Preaching in the First Half Century of New England History.* Hartford, 1945. 215 pp. Clothbound. 16.00   21.00

☐ **Lewis and Clark.** *History of the Expedition of Captains Lewis and Clark, 1804–5–6.* Reprinted from the Edition of 1814 with Introduction and Index by James K. Hosmer. Chicago, 1924. Two vols. 57.00   72.00

☐ **Lewis, Eldad.** *An Eulogy on the Life and Character of his Excellency George Washington.* Pittsfield, 1800. Softbound. 425.00   525.00

☐ **Lewis, George F.** *The Indians Company, 1763–1798: a Study in 18th Century Frontier Land Speculation.* Glendale, 1941. 358 pp. Clothbound. 40.00   52.00

☐ **Leiber, Francis.** *Letters to a Gentleman in Germany, written after a Trip from Philadelphia to Niagara.* Philadelphia, 1834. 356 pp. Bound in boards. 80.00   110.00

☐ **Lieber, Francis.** *Instructions for the Government of Armies of the United States, in the Field.* N.Y., 1863. Softbound. 20.00   25.00

☐ **Lieber, G. Norman.** *The Use of the Army in Aid of the Civil Power.* Washington, D.C., 1898. 86 pp. Bound in half morocco. 20.00   25.00

☐ **Lindsay, David M.** *A Voyage to the Artic in the Whaler Aurora.* Boston, 1911. 223 pp. Bound in cloth. 110.00   140.00

☐ **Linn, William.** *Funeral Eulogy, Occasioned by the Death of General Washington.* N.Y., 1800. Softbound. 72.00   87.00

☐ **Lipps, Oscar H.** *The Navajos.* Cedar Rapids, Iowa, 1909. 136 pp. 40.00   52.00

☐ **Little, George.** *Life on the Ocean.* Baltimore, 1843. .... 125.00   155.00

☐ **Little, James A.** *Jacob Hamblin, a Narrative of (his) Experiences as a Frontiersman.* Salt Lake City, 1881. 140 pp. Clothbound. 80.00   110.00

☐ **Little, Lucius P.** *Ben Hardin: His Times and Contemporaries.* Louisville, 1887. 640 pp. Published by the Louisville Courier (a newspaper). 100.00   135.00

☐ **Littleheart, Oleta.** *The Lure of the Indian Country.* Sulphur, 1908. .... 500.00   625.00

☐ **Lobagola, Bata.** *Lobagola: an African Savage's Own Story.* N.Y., 1930. .... 50.00   65.00

PRICE RANGE

☐ **Lockwood, F. C.** *Life in Old Tucson, 1854–65.* Los Angeles, 1943. . . . . 100.00   135.00

☐ **Lockwood, Frank C.** *Pioneer Days in Arizona.* N.Y., 1932. 387 pp. Clothbound. 125.00   170.00

☐ **Lockwood, George Browning.** *The New Harmony Communities.* Marion, Indiana, 1902. 282 pp. 48.00   62.00

☐ **Logan, Herschel C.** *Buckskin and Satin.* Harrisburg, 1954. . . . . 37.00   48.00

☐ **Long, J.** *Voyages and Travels of an Indian Interpreter and Trader.* London, 1791. Quarto, large paper copy. 1250.00   1675.00

☐ **Long, J. C.** *Lord Jeffery Amherst, a Soldier of the King.* N.Y., 1933. 378 pp. 10.00   14.00

☐ **Long, John.** *Voyages and Travels of an Indian Interpreter and Trader, Describing the Manners and Customs of the North American Indians.* Cleveland, 1904. 329 pp. With a folding map. 70.00   90.00

☐ **Long, Lessel.** *Twelve Months in Andersonville.* Huntington, Indiana, 1886. . . . . 60.00   75.00

☐ **Longstreet, James.** *From Manassas to Appomattox.* Philadelphia, 1896. . . . . 33.00   39.00

☐ **Lord, Benjamin.** *The Important Connection of Time with Eternity.* New London, 1769. 44 pp. 65.00   85.00

☐ **Lord, John.** *Frontier Dust.* Hartford, 1926. 198 pp. Limited to 1,000 copies. 37.00   47.00

☐ **Loring, Charles G.** *Neutral Relations of England and the United States.* N.Y., 1863. Softbound. 21.00   27.00

☐ **Loring, F. W. and Atkinson, C. F.** *Cotton Culture.* Boston, 1869. . . . . 63.00   85.00

☐ *Los Angeles City and County. The Present Condition, Growth, Progress and Advantages of* Los Angeles, 1876. Softbound. 110.00   140.00

☐ *Los Angeles Corral. Brand Book #4.* Los Angeles, 1950. Limited to 400. . . . . 250.00   325.00

☐ **Lossing, Benson J.** *Pictorial Field-Book of the Revolution.* N.Y., n.d. Two vols. 45.00   60.00

☐ **Lovejoy, Joseph C.** *Memoir of the Rev. Elijah P. Lovejoy, who was Murdered in Defence of the Liberty of the Press, at Alton, Illinois, November 7, 1837. With an Introduction by John Quincy Adams.* N.Y., 1838. 382 pp. Clothbound. 80.00   100.00

☐ **Lovell, Solomon.** *The Original Journal of General Solomon Lovell.* Weymouth (Mass.), 1881. . . . . 21.00   27.00

☐ **Lowell, John.** *Peace without Dishonor, War without Hope. Being a Calm and Dispassionate Enquiry into the Question of the Chesapeake and the Necessity and Expediency of War. By a Yankee Farmer.* Boston, 1807. 43 pp. Softbound. 40.00   50.00

☐ **Lowell, John.** *Further Remarks on the Memorial of the Officers of Harvard College. By an Alumnus of that College.* Boston, 1824. 36 pp. Softbound. 28.00   34.00

PRICE RANGE

☐ **Lowell, John.** *Analysis of the Late Correspondence Between our Administration and Great Britain and France with an Attempt to Show What are the Real Causes of the Failure of the Negotiation.* Boston, n.d. (c. 1807). 52 pp. Softbound. 40.00   50.00

☐ **Lowell, Lawrence.** *New England Aviators, 1914–1918.* Boston, 1919. Two vols. Limited to 1,000 sets. 325.00   400.00

☐ **Lubbock, Francis R.** *Six Decades in Texas. Or, Memoirs of Francis R. Lubbock.* Austin, 1900. 685 pp. With 20 plates. 275.00   335.00
A town in Texas was named after the author.

☐ **Lucas, C. L.** *The Milton Loft Tragedy. A Sketch of the Life of Col. Nathan Boone.* Madrid, Iowa, 1905. 24 pp. Softbound. 70.00   90.00

☐ **Ludlow, Noah.** *Dramatic Life as I Found it.* St. Louis, 1880. 733 pp. Clothbound. 375.00   475.00
Scarce early account of theatrical life in the U.S. west and south.

☐ **Ludlow, William.** *Report of a Reconnaissance from Carroll, Montana Territory, on the Upper Missouri, to the Yellowstone National Park and Return...made in 1875.* Washington, D.C., 1876. 155 pp. With 2 plates and 3 folding maps. Bound in cloth. 95.00   120.00

☐ **Lum, D. D.** *Utah and its People.* N.Y., 1882. 47 pp. Softbound. 90.00   115.00

☐ **Lumholtz, Carl.** *New Trails in Mexico.* N.Y., 1912. 411 pp. With folding maps. 110.00   140.00

☐ **Lundy, Benjamin.** *The War of Texas.* Philadelphia, 1836. 56 pp. 850.00   1075.00

☐ **Lyford, C. P.** *The Mormon Problem. An Appeal to the American People.* N.Y., 1886. 323 pp. 55.00   68.00

☐ **Lyman, George D.** *John Marsh, Pioneer.* N.Y., 1930. 394 pp. With 17 plates. Clothbound, boxed, limited to 150 copies signed by the author. 125.00   160.00

☐ **Lynch, Jeremiah.** *Three Years in the Klondike.* London, 1904. 280 pp. 115.00   140.00

☐ **Mably, l'Abbe.** *Remarks Concerning the Government and the Laws of the United States of America.* Dublin, Ireland, 1785. 280 pp. Bound in calf. 70.00   85.00

☐ **MacBride, Thomas Huston.** *In Cabins and Sod-Houses.* Iowa City, 1928. 368 pp. 50.00   65.00

☐ **MacKenzie, Frederic.** *A British Fusilier in Revolutionary Boston.* Cambridge, Mass., 1926. .... 9.00   12.00

☐ **Maclay, Edgar S.** *A History of American Privateers.* N.Y., 1924. 519 pp. 40.00   52.00

☐ **Maclay, Edgar S.** *History of the United States Navy from 1775 to 1902.* N.Y., 1901. Three vols. 55.00   70.00

☐ **MacLean, J. P.** *A Critical Examination of the Evidences Adduced to Establish the Theory of Norse Discovery in America.* Chicago, 1892. 52 pp. Limited to 500 numbered copies. 27.00   35.00

PRICE RANGE

☐ **MacMinn, Edwin.** *On the Frontier with Colonel Antes.* Camden, N.J., 1900. 513 pp. Limited to 1,000 copies..... **25.00** **32.00**

☐ **MacNamara, Daniel G.** *The History of the Ninth Regiment Massachusetts Volunteer Infantry Second Brigade.* Boston, 1899.. **20.00** **25.00**

☐ **Madison, James.** *Letters and Other Writings of James Madison.* N.Y., 1884. Four vols........................ **50.00** **65.00**

☐ **Madison, James.** *Message from the President of the United States Transmitting Communications from the American Ministers at Ghent.* Washington, D.C., 1814. 74 pp. Softbound... **80.00** **100.00**

☐ **Magoffin, Susan S.** *Down the Santa Fe Trail and into Mexico.* New Haven, 1926. 294 pp. With a folding map....... **100.00** **130.00**

☐ **Mahan, Alfred T.** *Report of the Commission to Select a Site for a Navy Yard on the Pacific Coast.* Washington, D.C. 1889. Softbound.................................. **30.00** **37.00**

☐ **Mahan, Captain A. T.** *The Interest of America in Sea Power, Present and Future.* Boston, 1898. 314 pp.............. **37.00** **45.00**

☐ **Majors, Alexander.** *Seventy Years on the Frontier.* Chicago, 1893. 325 pp. Clothbound. **135.00** **165.00**

☐ **Malcolm, M. Vartan.** *The Armenians in America.* Boston, 1919. 142 pp... **13.00** **17.00**

☐ **Manford, Erasmus.** *Twenty-Five Years in the West.* Chicago, 1870. 359 pp. Published by the author............. **115.00** **145.00**

☐ **Manly, William Lewis.** *Death Valley in '49. The Autobiography of a Pioneer, Detailing his Life from a Humble Home in the Green Mountains to the Gold Mines of California.* San Jose, 1894. 498 pp. **275.00** **350.00**

☐ **Mansfield, Edward D.** *Exposition of the Natural Position of Mackinaw City.* Cincinnati, 1857. 48 pp. Softbound. ... **300.00** **375.00**

☐ **Marcy, Randolph B.** *The Prairie Traveler. A Hand-Book for Overland Expeditions.* N.Y., 1859. Reprint edition (c. 1950). 340 pp. Bound in cloth.................................. **27.00** **34.00**
The original 1859 edition is very rare and commands a high price when sold.

☐ **Marcy, Randolph B.** *Border Reminiscences.* N.Y., 1872. **80.00** **110.00**

☐ **Mariette, S. H.** *Annual report of the Surveyor-General of Nevada for 1865.* Carson City, 1866. 83 pp. Softbound. .. **600.00** **800.00**

☐ **Markham, E. R.** *The American Steel Worker.* N.Y., 1903. 343 pp. Clothbound. **32.00** **42.00**

☐ **Marquis, Thomas B.** *Memoirs of a White Crow Indian.* N.Y., 1928. 356 pp. **100.00** **130.00**

☐ **Marquis, Thomas B.** *A Warrior who Fought Custer.* Minneapolis, 1931. 384 pp. With maps..................... **135.00** **160.00**

☐ **Marryat, Frank.** *Mountains and Molehills.* N.Y., 1855. 393 pp. Bound in boards................................... **75.00** **100.00**

☐ **Marsh, Ebenezer G.** *An Oration Delivered at Wethersfield, February 22, 1800, on the Death of General George Washington.* Hartford, 1800. Softbound. **45.00** **60.00**

☐ **Marshall, Albert O.** *Army life, from a Soldier's Journal.* Boston, 1927... **16.00** **21.00**

☐ **Marshall, Thomas M.** *Early Records of Gilpin County, Colorado.* Boulder, 1920. 313 pp. With a folding map........ **32.00** **42.00**

Nevves from *Virginia*.

The loſt Flocke

Triumphant.

With the happy Arriuall of that famous and
worthy Knight Sr. *Thomas Gates*: and the well
reputed & valiant Captaine Mr. *Chri-
ſtopher Newporte*, and others,
into England.

¶ With the maner of their diſtreſſe in the
Iland of Deüils (otherwiſe called *Bermoothawes*)
where they remayned 42. weekes, & builded
two Pynaces, in which they returned
into *Virginia*.

By R. *Rich, Gent.* one of the Voyage.

LONDON
Printed by *Edw: Allde*, and are to be ſolde by *Iohn
Wright* at Chriſt-Church dore. 1610.

Richard Rich's "News from Virginia" was no idle armchair composition.
This is one of the most desirable early publications relating to Virginia,
issued a full decade before the pilgrims landed at Plymouth Rock. The
spelling of "nevves" for "news" on the title is not unusual. $55,000—80,000.

PRICE RANGE

☐ **Martin, Edward Winslow.** *The History of the Great Riots, Being a Full and Authentic Account.* Philadelphia, 1877. 516 pp. With many plates, some folding. **40.00**   **52.00**

☐ **Marvin, Edwin E.** *The Fifth Regiment, Connecticut Volunteers.* Hartford, 1889. . . . .   **20.00**   **25.00**

☐ **Marvin, Winthrop.** *The American Merchant Marine: its History and Romance from 1620 to 1902.* N.Y., 1902. 444 pp. **43.00**   **54.00**

☐ **Marye, George Thomas.** *From '49 to '83 in California and Nevada.* San Francisco, 1923. 212 pp. **70.00**   **90.00**

☐ **Mason, Lieut. James L.** *Memoirs on the Military Resources of the Valley of the Ohio.* Washington, D.C., 1845. 24 pp. Softbound. **30.00**   **40.00**

☐ **Mason, John M.** *An Oration, Commemorative of the Late Major-General Alexander Hamilton, Pronounced Before the New York State Society of the Cincinnati, July 31, 1804.* N.Y., 1804. 40 pp. Softbound. **47.00**   **63.00**
Alexander Hamilton had just been slain in a duel with Aaron Burr. Both men were aspirants to the Presidency.

☐ **Mather, Cotton.** *Memorable Providences, Relating to Witchcrafts and Possessions.* Boston, 1689. . . . .   **9000.00** **11500.00**

☐ **Mather, Cotton.** *The Wonders of the Invisible World . . . the Nature, the Number, and the Operations of the Devils.* Boston, 1693. . . . .   **18000.00** **22500.00**

☐ **Mather, Cotton.** *Pietas in Patriam: the Life of His Excellency Sir William Phips.* London, 1697.   **800.00**   **1100.00**

☐ **Mather, Cotton.** *Magnalia Christi Americana; or, The Ecclesiastical History of New England.* London, 1702. . . . .   **1800.00**   **2600.00**

☐ **Mather, Cotton.** *A Faithful Man. Passages in the Life and Death of Mr. Michael Wigglesworth.* Boston, 1705. . . . . . .   **1800.00**   **2300.00**

☐ **Mather, Cotton.** *Hades Look'd into.* Boston, 1717. . . . . . .   **950.00**   **1275.00**

☐ **Mather, Increase.** *The Order of the Gospel.* Boston, 1700. . . . .   **300.00**   **400.00**

☐ **Mather, Increase.** *A Discourse Proving that the Christian Religion is the Only True Religion.* Boston, 1702. . . . .   **25000.00** **32000.00**

☐ **Mather, Mayor James.** *Regulations for the Port of New Orleans.* New Orleans, 1808, 4 pp. Softbound, rare. **2100.00**   **2650.00**

☐ **Matthews, William.** *American Diaries.* Boston, 1959. 383 pp. **13.00**   **17.00**

☐ **Mattson, H.** *Early Days of Reconstruction in Northeastern Arkansas.* St. Paul, Minn., 1889. 13 pp. Softbound. **47.00**   **62.00**

☐ **Mayhew, Henry.** *The Mormons: or, Latter-Day Saints, with Memoirs of the Life and Death of Joseph Smith, the American Mahomet.* London, 1852. 320 pp. Clothbound. **75.00**   **100.00**

☐ **Mayo, Bernard.** *Henry Clay: Spokesman of the New West.* Boston, 1937. 570 pp. **15.00**   **20.00**

☐ **Mayo, Robert.** *Political Sketches of 8 years in Washington.* Baltimore, 1839. 216 pp. Clothbound. **120.00**   **150.00**

☐ **McAllister, J. T.** *Virginia Militia in the Revolutionary War.* Hot Springs, Ark., 1913. 337 pp. **30.00**   **36.00**

☐ **McBeth, Kate C.** *The Nez Perces since Lewis and Clark.* N.Y., n.d. (c. 1908). 272 pp. **68.00**   **89.00**

PRICE RANGE

☐ **McCaleb, Walter F.** *Bigfoot Wallace.* San Antonio, 1956. 20.00 25.00
☐ **McCall, George A.** *Letters from the Frontiers.* Philadelphia,
1868. 539 pp. Clothbound. 310.00 370.00
☐ **McCarty, John L.** *Maverick Town.* Norman, Okla., 1946. 70.00 90.00
☐ **McClellan, H. B.** *The Life and Campaigns of Major General
J. E. B. Stuart.* Boston and N.Y., 1885. .... 130.00 160.00
☐ **McClintock, Walter.** *Old Indian Trails.* Cambridge, 1923.
336 pp. 80.00 105.00
☐ **McClung, J. W.** *Minnesota as it is in 1870.* St. Paul, 1870.
300 pp. With large folding map and plates. Clothbound..... 100.00 130.00
☐ **McClung, John A.** *Sketches of Western Adventure.* Day-
ton, Ohio, 1847. 315 pp. Bound in full leather. 180.00 230.00
Title page gives the author's name as "M'Clung."
McConnel, J. L. *Western Characters; or, Types of Border
Life in the Western States.* N.Y., 1853. 378 pp. 130.00 170.00
☐ **McCreight, Major I.** *Chief Flying Hawk's Tales: True Stories
of Custer's Last Fight.* N.Y., 1936. 56 pp. Softbound...... 90.00 120.00
☐ **McCreight, Major I.** *Buffalo Bone Days. A Story of the
Buffalo Slaughter on Our Western Plains.* DuBois, Pa., 1950.
85 pp. 32.00 43.00
☐ **McDanield, H. F.** *The Coming Empire. Or, Two Thousand
Miles in Texas on Horseback.* N.Y., 1877. 389 pp. 120.00 160.00
☐ **McDaniel, Ruel.** *Vinegarron.* Kingsport, Tenn., 1936. .... 32.00 42.00
☐ **McGonnigle, Robert.** *When I Went West.* Pittsburg, 1901.
168 pp. Limited to 250 copies. 80.00 105.00
☐ **McGroarty, John S.** *California, its History and Romance.*
Los Angeles, 1911. .... 45.00 60.00
☐ **McIlhany, Edward D.** *Recollections of a 49er.* Kansas City,
1908. 212 pp. 80.00 110.00
☐ **McKenna, James A.** *Black Range Tales.* N.Y., 1936. 301
pp. 5 plates. 80.00 110.00
☐ **McLane, Louis.** *Speech on the Bill Authorizing the People
of Missouri to Form a Constitution.* N.p., 1820. 44 pp.
Softbound. 150.00 180.00
☐ **McMaster, John B.** *History of the United States from the
Revolution to the Civil War.* N.Y., 1883–1913. Eight vols.
Clothbound. 130.00 160.00
☐ **McNamara, John.** *In Perils by my Own Countrymen. Three
Years on the Kansas Border. By a Clergyman of the Epis-
copal Church.* N.Y., 1856. 240 pp. Clothbound. 75.00 95.00
☐ **McNeill, George E.** *The Labor Movement.* N.Y., 1887. 643
pp. 47.00 62.00
☐ **McQuire, Hunter.** *The Confederate Cause and Conduct
in the War Between the States.* Richmond, n.d., 1907. .... 20.00 25.00
☐ **McVaugh, Rogers.** *Edward Palmer.* Norman, 1956. ...... 20.00 25.00
☐ **McWhorter, Lucullus V.** *Tragedy of the Wahk-Shum: Prel-
ude to the Yakima Indian War, 1855–56.* Yakima, Wash.,
1937. 44 pp. Softbound. 90.00 115.00
☐ **Meacham, A. B.** *Wi-Ne-Ma and Her People.* Hartford, 1876.
168 pp. 80.00 100.00
☐ **Meacham, Henry A.** *The Empty Sleeve.* Springfield, n.d.,
1869. Softbound. 34.00 42.00

PRICE RANGE

☐ **Mead, George G.** *With Meade at Gettysburg.* Philadelphia, 1930. .... 20.00 25.00

☐ **Mecklenburg, George.** *The Last of the Old West.* Washington, D.C., 1927... 38.00 47.00

☐ **Meeker, Ezra.** *Pioneer Reminiscences of Puget Sound.* Seattle, Wash., 1905. 554 pp. With 25 plates. 48.00 63.00

☐ **Meline, James F.** *Two Thousand Miles on Horseback.* N.Y., 1867. 317 pp. 80.00 105.00

☐ **Melton, A. B.** *Seventy Years in the Saddle and Then Some.* Kansas City, 1950. 117 pp. Softbound................... 55.00 78.00

☐ **Menaul, John.** *New Mexico and its Claims.* Laguna, 1881, 24 pp. Softbound.................................... 1250.00 1550.00

☐ **Mercer, A. S.** *Washington Territory.* Seattle, 1939. 54 pp. Bound in cloth. Limited to 350 copies.................. 43.00 58.00

☐ **Mercer, Asa Shinn.** *The Banditti of the Plains.* San Francisco, 1935. 136 pp. Bound in boards. 135.00 170.00

☐ **Merriam, George S.** *The Life and Times of Samuel Bowles.* N.Y., 1885. Two vols.................................... 21.00 27.00

☐ **Meriwether, Mrs. Elizabeth A.** *Facts and Falsehoods Concerning the War on the South.* Memphis. n.d., 1904. Softbound. 70.00 90.00

☐ **Milburn, William H.** *The Pioneer Preacher.* N.Y., 1858. .. 14.00 18.00

☐ **Middlebrook, Lewis F.** *History of Maritime Connecticut during the American Revolution.* Salem, Mass., 1925. Two vols. 52.00 67.00

☐ **Miles, Nelson A.** *Personal Recollections and Observations of General Nelson A. Miles.* Chicago, 1897. 591 pp. 36.00 43.00

☐ **Miles, William.** *Journal of the Sufferings and Hardships of Capt. Parker H. French's Overland Expedition to California.* N.Y., 1916. 26 pp. Softbound. Limited to 250 copies.. 37.00 48.00
Originally published in 1851. Of that edition, only 7 copies are known to exist.

☐ **Miller, Alfred Jacob.** *The West of Alfred Jacob Miller.* Norman, Okla., 1951....................................... 55.00 70.00

☐ **Miller, George.** *Correspondence of George Miller, with the Northern Islander.* N.p., n.d. (c. 1900). 50 pp. Softbound. 40.00 50.00

☐ **Miller, H. E.** *History of the town of Savoy.* West Commington, 1865, 22 pp. Softbound........................... 250.00 315.00

☐ **Miller, Lewis B.** *Saddles and Lariats. The Largely True Story of the Bar-Circle Outfit, and of Their Attempt to take a Big Drove of Longhorns from Texas to California.* Boston, 1912. 285 pp.. 190.00 235.00
Note that this was advertised as a LARGELY true tale—which, for yarns about the Old West, was saying something.

☐ **Millet, Samuel.** *A Whaling Voyage in the Bark "Willis."* Boston, 1924. 46 pp. Clothbound. One of 475 copies printed on "American vellum" 80.00 105.00

☐ **Mills, Brig. Gen. Anson.** *My Story.* Washington, published by the author, 1918. 412 pp. Bound in full leather. 55.00 70.00

☐ **Mills, Enos A.** *Wild Life on the Rockies.* Boston, 1909. .. 50.00 65.00

PRICE RANGE

☐ **Milner, Joe E.** *California Joe. With an Account of Custer's Last Fight by Colonel William H. C. Bowen.* Caldwell, Iowa, 1935. 366 pp. 125.00 165.00

☐ **Mitchell, Frederick A.** *Ormsby Macknight Mitchell, astronomer and general.* Boston, 1887. 12.00 15.00

☐ **Mitchell, Samuel A.** *Illinois in 1837.* Philadelphia, 1837. 143 pp. With a folding map. Softbound. 135.00 175.00

☐ **Moellhausen, Henry.** *Norman's Plan of New Orleans and Environs, 1845.* Large colored map which folds into cloth covers. Published at New Orleans in 1845. . . . . 225.00 290.00
⌐ When open the map measures 24″ × 17″.

☐ **Monaghan, Jay.** *Lincoln Bibliography, 1839–1939.* Springfield, 1943. Two vols. 20.00 25.00

☐ **Monroe, James.** *A View of the Conduct of the Executive in Foreign Affairs of the United States.* Philadelphia, 1797. 407 pp. Bound in full calf. 80.00 100.00
An attack by Monroe (early in his political career, well before becoming President) against the policies of George Washington.

☐ **Moody, Claire N.** *Battle of Pea Ridge or Elkhorn Tavern.* Little Rock, Ark., 1956. Softbound. 12.00 16.00

☐ **Moody, James.** *Narrative of the Exertions and Sufferings of Lieut. James Moody.* N.Y., 1865. 98 pp. Bound in ½ leather. Believed to have been printed in only 100 copies. 75.00 95.00

☐ **Moore, Albert B.** *Conscription and Conflict in the Confederacy.* N.Y., 1924. . . . . 35.00 45.00

☐ **Moore, Charles W.** *Timing a Century. History of the Waltham Watch Company.* N.p. (Mass.), 1945. . . . . 25.00 32.00

☐ **Moore, Edward Alexander.** *The Story of a Cannoneer under Stonewall Jackson.* Lynchburg, Va., 1910. . . . . 27.00 35.00

☐ **Moore, Frank.** *The Patriot Preachers of the American Revolution.* N.Y., 1862. . . . . 9.00 12.00

☐ **Moore-Wilson, Minnie.** *The Seminoles of Florida.* Philadelphia, 1896. 126 pp. 55.00 70.00

☐ **Moran, Benjamin.** *The Journals of Benjamin Moran.* Chicago, 1948. Two vols. Clothbound. 26.00 32.00

☐ **Morand, Paul.** *Black Magic.* N.Y., 1929. . . . . 27.00 34.00

☐ **Mordecai, Samuel.** *Richmond in By-gone Days, Being Reminiscences of an Old Citizen.* Richmond, 1856. 321 pp. Clothbound. 75.00 100.00

☐ **Morgan, Appleton.** *The People and the Railways.* N.Y., 1888. 245 pp. 21.00 27.00

☐ **Morgan, Dale L.** *Jedediah Smith and the Opening of the West.* Indianapolis, 1953. 458 pp. 65.00 85.00

☐ **Morgan, Dick.** *Manual of the U.S. Homestead and Townsite Laws.* Guthrie, 1893, 144 pp. Softbound. 500.00 600.00

☐ **Morgan, Lewis H.** *League of the Ho-de-no-san-nee, or Iroquois.* Rochester 1851. With maps and plates. 390.00 460.00

☐ **Morgan, George H.** *Annals of Compromising Memoirs, Incidents and Statistics of Harrisburg, Pa., from its First Settlement.* Harrisburg, 1858. 400 pp. ½ leather. 52.00 67.00

☐ **Morgan, T. R.** *California Sketches.* Towyn, 1898. . . . . 215.00 280.00

PRICE RANGE

☐ **Morgan, William H.** *Personal Reminiscences of the War of 1861–65.* Lynchburg, 1911............................ **27.00** **35.00**

☐ **Morison, Samuel Eliot.** *Builders of the Bay Colony.* Boston, 1930. 365 pp. One of 550 copies on large paper, boxed. **75.00** **95.00**

☐ **Morphis, James.** *History of Texas, From its Discovery and Settlement.* N.Y., 1875. 601 pp. Second edition........... **300.00** **380.00**

☐ **Morrell, W. P.** *The Gold Rushes.* N.Y., 1941. 426 pp. **47.00** **63.00**

☐ **Morrell, Z. N.** *Flowers and Fruits from the Wilderness; or, 36 Years in Texas.* Boston, 1873. 386 pp. Bound in cloth. **115.00** **145.00**

☐ **Morris, Gouveneur.** *The Diary and Letters of Gouveneur Morris.* N.Y., 1888. Two vols. **40.00** **50.00**
Gouveneur Morris was one of America's wealthiest citizens in the 18th century; he put up huge sums of money to finance the Revolution.

☐ **Morris, Gouvenor.** *History of a Volunteer Regiment: 6th N.Y. Volunteers Infantry.* N.Y., 1891...................... **20.00** **25.00**

☐ **Morris, G. P.** *A Life in the West.* Louisville, 1844. 8 pp. Softbound. **200.00** **250.00**

☐ **Morris, Joseph.** *Reminiscences of Joseph Morris.* Columbus, Ohio, 1881. 192 pp. **45.00** **60.00**

☐ **Morris, William G.** *Report Upon the Customs District, Public Service, and Resources of Alaska Territory.* Washington, D.C., 1879. 163 pp. With a folding map.................. **45.00** **60.00**

☐ **Morrison, A. J.** *Travels in Virginia in Revolutionary Times.* Lynchburg, 1922. 138 pp. **20.00** **25.00**

☐ **Morse, Anson Ely.** *The Federalist Party in Massachusetts to the Year 1800.* Princeton, N.J., 1909. 231 pp. **15.00** **20.00**

☐ **Morse, Charles F.** *A Sketch of My Life and a Buffalo Hunt in Nebraska in 1871.* Cambridge, Mass., 1927. 91 pp. ... **80.00** **105.00**

☐ **Morton, J. Sterling and others.** *History of Nebraska from the Earliest Explorations of the Trans-Mississippi region.* Lincoln, 1918. 864 pp. **100.00** **130.00**

☐ **Mosby, John Singleton.** *Mosby's War Reminiscences.* N.Y., n.d., 1887.. **50.00** **65.00**

☐ **Mulford, Prentice.** *California Sketches.* San Francisco, 1935. 105 pp. Limited to 350 copies..................... **90.00** **120.00**

☐ **Mumey, Nolie.** *The Black Ram of Dinwoody Creek.* Denver, 1951. 192 pp. Bound in boards. One of 350 copies numbered and signed by the author...................... **35.00** **45.00**

☐ **Munk, Joseph A.** *Arizona Sketches.* N.Y., 1905. 230 pp.. **50.00** **65.00**

☐ **Murdock, Harold.** *Bunker Hill. Notes and Queries on a Famous Battle.* Boston, 1927. 149 pp. Limited to 500 copies... **18.00** **23.00**

☐ **Murphy, John M.** *Rambles in North-Western America.* London, 1879. 364 pp. With a folding map. Bound in half leather... **75.00** **100.00**

☐ **Murray, Alexander H.** *Journal of the Yukon, 1847–48.* Ottawa, 1910. 138 pp. Softbound............................ **100.00** **130.00**

☐ **Murray, James.** *An Impartial History of the War in America.* New Castle (England), n.d. (c. 1782.). Two vols.......... **175.00** **215.00**

PRICE RANGE

☐ **Murray, James B.** *Autobiography of the Late Col. James B. Murray of New York.* London, privately printed, 1908. 92 pp. With a folding chart. Softbound...................... **25.00** **35.00**

☐ **Murrell, William M.** *Cruise of the Columbia in 1838, 1839, and 1840.* Boston, 1840. 230 pp....................... **47.00** **59.00**

☐ **Mulholland, St. Clair.** *The Story of the 116th Regiment, Pennsylvania Infantry. War of Secession, 1862–65.* Philadelphia, 1899.......................... **20.00** **25.00**

☐ **Musgrove, Richard W.** *Autobiography.* Briston, N.H., 1921. Softbound............................... **34.00** **42.00**

☐ **Myers, J. C.** *Sketches of a Tour Through the Northern and Eastern States, the Canadas and Nova Scotia.* Harrisonburg, Va., 1849. 475 pp. Bound in full leather............ **160.00** **210.00**

☐ **Napton, William B.** *Over the Santa Fe Trail, 1857.* Santa Fe, 1964. 73 pp. Limited to 99 copies. **35.00** **45.00**

☐ **Nasatir, A. P.** *Before Lewis and Clark.* St. Louis, 1952. Two vols. With 5 folding maps. **48.00** **63.00**

☐ **Neff, Andrew Love.** *History of Utah 1847–1869.* Salt Lake City, 1940. 955 pp. Clothbound................. **48.00** **63.00**

☐ **Neihardt, John G.** *Black Elk Speaks: being the Life Story of a Holy Man of the Ogalala Sioux.* N.Y., 1932. 280 pp. **53.00** **68.00**

☐ **Nelson, David T.** *The Diary of Elisabeth Koren, 1853–1855.* Northfield, n.d. (1955). 381 pp. **21.00** **27.00**

☐ **Neville, A. W.** *The Red River Valley Then and Now.* Paris, Texas, 1948. 278 pp...................................... **50.00** **65.00**

☐ **Nevins, Allan.** *Henry White: 30 Years of American Diplomacy.* N.Y., 1930. 518 pp................................ **10.00** **12.00**

☐ **Nevins, Allan.** *Hamilton Fish: the Inner History of the Grant Administration.* N.Y., 1936. 932 pp...................... **15.00** **18.00**

☐ *New Jersey Legislature. Register of the Commissioned Officers and Privates of the N.J. Volunteers.* Jersey City, 1863. .... **60.00** **80.00**

☐ **Newberry, J. S.** *Report on the Properties of the Ramshorn Consolidated Silver Mining Company at Bay Horse, Idaho.* N.Y., n.d., 1881. 16 pp. Softbound...................... **425.00** **525.00**

☐ **Newcomb, Rexford.** *The Old Mission Churches and Historic Houses of California.* Philadelphia, 1925............ **325.00** **400.00**

☐ **Newell, Robert.** *Memoranda: Travels in the Territory of Missouri.* Portland, Ore., 1959. 159 pp. Limited to 1,000 copies. **30.00** **40.00**

☐ **Newlin, William H.** *A History of the 73rd Regiment Illinois Infantry Volunteers.* Springfield, 1890. .... **60.00** **80.00**

☐ **Newmark, Harris.** *Sixty Years in Southern California.* N.Y., 1916. 732 pp... **110.00** **140.00**

☐ **Nibley, Preston.** *Brigham Young, the Man and his Work.* Salt Lake City, 1937. 552 pp................................ **18.00** **24.00**

☐ **Nicholson, John.** *The Tennessee Massacre and its Causes.* Salt Lake City, 1884. 48 pp. Softbound. **130.00** **170.00**

☐ **Nickerson, Grace P.** *The Giant Cactus.* Los Angeles, 1929. .... **13.00** **17.00**

☐ **Nicolay, John G. and Hay, John.** *Abraham Lincoln, A History.* N.Y., 1890. Ten vols............................. **165.00** **200.00**

PRICE RANGE

☐ **Niles, Hezekiah.** *Principles and Acts of the Revolution in America.* N.Y., 1876. 522 pp. Clothbound. 20.00   25.00

☐ **Nix, Everitt Dumas.** *Oklahombres, Particularly the Wilder Ones.* St. Louis, 1929. 280 pp. 65.00   85.00

☐ **Noble, F. H.** *Taxation in Iowa.* N.Y., 1897. 94 pp. Softbound. 26.00   32.00

☐ **Nordhoff, Charles.** *The Communistic Societies of the United States.* N.Y., 1875. 439 pp. Clothbound. 95.00   115.00

☐ **Nordyke, Lewis.** *Great Roundup.* N.Y., 1955. . . . .   30.00   39.00

☐ **Norlie, Olaf M.** *History of the Norwegian People in America.* Minneapolis, 1925. 602 pp. 23.00   30.00

☐ **North, Arthur W.** *The Mother of California.* San Francisco, 1908. 169 pp. 42.00   56.00

☐ **North, Arthur W.** *Camp and Camino in Lower California: a Record of the Adventures of the Author while Exploring Peninsular California.* N.Y., 1910. 356 pp. 48.00   63.00

☐ **North, Lord.** *Correspondence of George III with Lord North from 1768 to 1783.* London, 1867. Two vols. 28.00   35.00

☐ **Northern Pacific Railroad.** *Memorial of the Board of Direction of the Company.* Hartford, 1867. With folding map. Softbound. 200.00   250.00

☐ **Norton, Clifford.** *The Democratic Party in Ante-Bellum North Carolina, 1835–1861.* Chapel Hill, 1930. 276 pp. . .   19.00   24.00

☐ **Norton, L. A.** *Life and Adventures of Col. L. A. Norton, by Himself.* Oakland, Calif., 1887. 492 pp. Bound in cloth. . . .   135.00   180.00

☐ **Norton, Oliver W.** *Strong Vincent and his brigade at Gettysburg.* Chicago, 1909. . . . .   20.00   25.00

☐ **Nourse, Hon. C. C.** *Iowa and the Centennial.* Des Moines, 1876, 42 pp. Softbound. 275.00   350.00

☐ **Noyes, A. J.** *In the Lands of the Chinook.* Helena, Montana, n.d. (c. 1917). 152 pp. 55.00   70.00

☐ **Nye, Elwood L.** *Marching with Custer.* Glendale, Calif., 1964. 53 pp. Limited to 300 copies. 42.00   57.00

☐ **Oates, William C.** *The War between the Union and the Confederacy.* N.Y., 1905. . . . .   90.00   120.00

☐ **Oats, Sergeant.** *Prison life in Dixie.* Chicago, 1880. Author is untraced; may be pen-name of someone who did not wish to reveal identity, or a hoax. In any case, a collector's item. 75.00   100.00

☐ **O'Brien, Harriet.** *Paul Revere's Own Story.* Boston, privately published, 1929. Limited to 500 copies. 16.00   21.00

☐ **O'Conner, Richard.** *Bat Masterson.* N.Y., 1957. . . . .   19.00   25.00

☐ **O'Conner, Richard.** *Wild Bill Hickok.* N.Y., 1959. . . . .   25.00   32.00

☐ **Olcott, Charles S.** *The Life of William McKinley.* Boston, 1916. Two vols. 25.00   32.00

☐ **Olmstead, Frederick Law.** *Journey through Texas.* N.Y., 1857. 516 pp. 135.00   175.00

☐ **Olmstead, Frederick Law.** *Journey in the Seaboard Slave States.* N.Y., 1856. 724 pp. 75.00   100.00

☐ **O'Meara, James.** *Broderick and Gwin.* San Francisco, 1881. 254 pp. 35.00   43.00

PRICE RANGE

☐ **O'Meara, James.** *The Vigilance Committee of 1856, by a Pioneer California Journalist.* San Francisco, 1890. 57 pp. Softbound. 49.00   64.00

☐ **O'Meara, Rev. F.** *Report of a Mission to the Ottahways and Ojibwas, on Lake Huron.* London, 1845–6. Two vols.   85.00   115.00

☐ **O'Neal, James.** *A History of the Amalgamated Ladies' Garment Cutters' Union, Local 10.* N.Y., 1927. 450 pp. . . .   52.00   67.00

☐ **Onken, O. and Wells, W.** *Western Scenery.* Cincinnati, 1851. Usually softbound, rare. 8500.00   10750.00

☐ **Orcutt, Samuel.** *The Indians of the Housatonic and Naugatuck Valleys.* Hartford, 1882. . . . . 35.00   45.00

☐ **Osgood, Rev. David.** *Reflections on the Goodness of God in Supporting the People of the United States Through the Late War, and Giving Them So Advantageous and Honourable a Peace.* Boston, 1784. . . . . 200.00   235.00

☐ **Osgood, Ernest S.** *The Day of the Cattleman.* Minneapolis, 1929. 283 pp. With 14 plates and a map. 100.00   130.00

☐ **Osgood, Ernest S.** *The Field Notes of William Clark, 1803–1805.* New Haven, 1964. 335 pp. 35.00   42.00

☐ **Otero, Miguel Antonio.** *My Life on the Frontier, 1864–1882.* N.Y., 1935. 293 pp. 65.00   85.00

☐ **Otero, Miguel Antonio.** *The Real Billy the Kid.* N.Y., 1936. 200 pp. 100.00   130.00

☐ **Otis, James A.** *Vindication of the British Colonies.* London, 1769. Second edition. 160.00   190.00

☐ **Ottley, Roi.** *New World A-Coming.* Boston, 1943. . . . . 21.00   27.00

☐ **Owen, David D.** *Report of a Geological Survey of Wisconsin, Iowa and Minnesota.* Philadelphia, 1852. Two vols. 638 pp. Clothbound. 63.00   78.00

☐ **Owen, Thomas M.** *Revolutionary Soldiers in Alabama.* Montgomery, 1911. 131 pp. Softbound. 45.00   60.00

☐ **Packman, Ana B.** *Early California Hospitality.* Glendale, 1938. 182 pp. Clothbound. 42.00   56.00

☐ **Paine, Bayard H.** *Pioneers, Indiana and Buffaloes.* Curtis, Nebraska, 1935. . . . . 90.00   115.00

☐ **Paine, Thomas.** *The Political Writings of Thomas Paine.* Boston, 1870. Two vols. 20.00   25.00

☐ **Pairpoint, Alfred.** *Uncle Sam and His Country.* London, 1857. 346 pp. Clothbound. 35.00   42.00

☐ **Page, James W.** *The True Story of the Andersonville Prison.* N.Y., 1908. . . . . 40.00   52.00

☐ **Palmer, John McAuley.** *General Von Steuben.* New Haven, 1937. 434 pp. 15.00   20.00

☐ **Palou, Fray F.** *The Expedition into California.* San Francisco, 1934. 124 pp. Boards with a vellum spine. 124 pp. One of 400 numbered and signed copies. 70.00   90.00

☐ **Pancoast, Henry S.** *The Indian Before the Law.* Philadelphia, 1884. 82 pp. Softbound. 40.00   52.00

☐ **Parrison, Lewis E.** *Message to the General Assembly.* Montgomery, 1865, 16 pp. Softbound. 225.00   265.00

☐ **Parisot, Rev. P. F.** *Reminiscences of a Texas Missionary.* San Antonio, 1899. 227 pp. Clothbound. 48.00   63.00

PRICE RANGE

☐ **Parker, Arthur G.** *The Constitution of the Five Nations.* Albany, 1916. 158 pp. Softbound...................... 23.00   28.00

☐ **Parker, Foxhill A.** *The Battle of Mobile Bay.* Boston, 1878. Has two folding charts in pocket........................ 40.00   52.00

☐ **Parsons, Hubert C.** *A Puritan Outpost.* N.Y., 1937. 546 pp. Clothbound.. 20.00   25.00

☐ **Parton, James.** *Life and Times of Benjamin Franklin.* Boston, 1870. Two vols. 50.00   65.00

☐ **Patten, Lt. Col. G. W.** *Voices of the Border.* N.Y., 1867. 26.00   34.00

☐ **Patterson, Lawson B.** *Twelve Years in the Mines of California.* Cambridge, 1862.................................. 250.00   300.00

☐ **Patterson, Paul.** *Pecos Tails.* Austin, 1967. 101 pp. 11.00   15.00

☐ **Patton, James W.** *Unionism and Reconstruction in Tennessee 1860–1869.* Chapel Hill, N.C., 1934. 267 pp. 20.00   25.00

☐ **Paul, Edward J.** *The Part Borne by Sergeant John White Paul . . . in the Capture of Brigadier General Richard Prescott.* Milwaukee, 1887.............................. 20.00   25.00

☐ **Paul, J. Harland.** *The Last Cruise of the Carnegie.* Baltimore, 1932. 331 pp. 30.00   39.00

☐ **Paul, Rodman W.** *California Gold.* Cambridge, 1947. 380 pp... 43.00   56.00

☐ **Pausch, Capt. George.** *Journal of Captain Pausch, Chief of the Hanau Artillery During the Burgoyne Campaign.* Albany, 1886... 38.00   48.00

☐ **Payne, John H.** *Indian Justice. A Cherokee Murder Trial.* Oklahoma City, 1934. 112 pp. 55.00   70.00

☐ **Peake, Ora B.** *The Colorado Cattle Industry.* Glendale, 1937. 357 pp. Clothbound. 48.00   63.00

☐ **Pearce, T. M.** *Southwest Heritage.* Albuquerque, N.M., 1938. 165 pp. Clothbound. 37.00   48.00

☐ **Pearson, Samuel.** *An Incurable Pioneer.* Ft. Worth, 1928. 287 pp... 36.00   45.00

☐ **Peck, George W.** *Aurifodina: or, Adventures in the Gold Region.* N.Y., 1849. 103 pp. Cloth with leather label on spine.. 120.00   150.00

"Aurifodina" was a word coined by the author, from "aureum," the ancient Roman word for gold.

☐ **Peele, W. J.** *Lives of Distinguished North Carolinians.* Raleigh, 1898. 605 pp. Bound in cloth.................... 80.00   105.00

☐ **Peet, Stephen D.** *The Cliff Dwellers and Pueblos.* Chicago, 1899. .... 75.00   100.00

☐ **Pennington, W.** *Message of the Governor of New Jersey to the Legislature.* Trenton, 1839. 17 pp. Softbound. 165.00   200.00

☐ **Pennsylvania.** *An Historical Review of the Constitution and Government of Pennsylvania.* London, 1759. 444 pp. Bound in calf... 300.00   350.00

Possibly composed by Benjamin Franklin, but his name does not appear in the book and there is no hard evidence to link him with it.

☐ **Pennypacker, Morton.** *The Two Spies: Nathan Hale and Robert Townsend.* Boston, 1930. .... 9.00   12.00

PRICE RANGE

☐ **Percy, Earl.** *Letters of Hugh Earl Percy from Boston and New York, 1774–1776.* Boston, 1902. One of 25 on Japan paper..   60.00   80.00

☐ **Perkins, J. R.** *Trails, Rails, and War.* Indianapolis, 1929. 371 pp. Clothbound.....................................   47.00   58.00

☐ **Perry, G. S.** *Roundup Time.* N.Y., 1943. An anthology, not first edition.....................................   21.00   27.00

☐ **Peters, DeWitt C.** *The Life and Adventures of Kit Carson, the Nestor of the Rocky Mountains.* N.Y., 1858. 534 pp. Bound in ½ leather......................................   180.00   235.00
Nestor was a hero of Greek folklore.

☐ **Peters, Harry T.** *California on Stone.* N.Y., 1935. 227 pp. Clothbound. Limited to 501 copies. Boxed...............   600.00   800.00
Harry T. Peters was best known for his book on Currier and Ives, *America on Stone. California on Stone* is a collection of reproductions of early lithographs, showing the state in the 1800's.

☐ **Peterson, Arnold.** *W. Z. Foster, Renegade or Spy?* N.Y., 1932. 45 pp. Softbound...................................   40.00   50.00

☐ **Peterson, William J.** *Steamboating on the Upper Mississippi.* Iowa City, 1937. 576 pp. Clothbound.............   110.00   140.00

☐ **Peyton, Green.** *America's Heartland.* Norman, Okla., 1948..   23.00   32.00

☐ **Phillips, Catherine C.** *Cornelius Cole: California pioneer and United States Senator.* San Francisco, 1929. 279 pp. With 27 plates. Bound in boards. Boxed. Limited to 250 copies..   100.00   125.00

☐ **Phillips, George W.** *The Mormon Menace. A Discourse before the New West Education Commission.* Worcester, 1885. 16 pp. Softbound.................................   32.00   40.00

☐ **Phillips, James D.** *Salem in the 18th Century.* Boston, 1937. 526 pp. Bound in boards with paper label on spine. Folding map in rear pocket. One of 250 special large-paper copies signed by the author.........................   65.00   80.00

☐ **Pickering, John.** *An Essay on a Uniform Orthography for the Indian Languages of North America.* Cambridge, Mass., 1820. 42 pp. Softbound.................................   90.00   115.00

☐ **Pickering, Timothy.** *Review of the Correspondence between the Hon. John Adams, late president of the United States, and late Wm. Cunningham.* Salem, 1824. 197 pp. Softbound...   35.00   45.00

☐ **Picket, James C.** *The Memory of Pocahontas Vindicated.* Washington, D.C., 1847. 39 pp. Softbound...............   100.00   130.00

☐ **Pierce, Benjamin.** *A History of Harvard University from its Foundation in the Year 1636 to the Period of the American Revolution.* Cambridge, 1833. Bound in boards. 90.00   115.00
In its early years Harvard was a divinity school.

☐ **Pierce, John.** *An Eulogy on George Washington the great and the good. Delivered on the Anniversary of his Birth, at Brookline (Mass.).* Boston, 1800. Softbound...........   70.00   90.00

☐ **Pierce, W. H.** *Thirteen Years of Travel and Exploration in Alaska.* Lawrence, Kansas, 1890. 224 pp. Bound in cloth.   125.00   150.00

PRICE RANGE

☐ **Pike, Zebulon Montgomery.** *The Expeditions of Zebulon M. Pike to the Headwaters of the Mississippi River etc.* N.Y., 1895. Three vols. Clothbound. One of 150 sets printed on large paper. 500.00 600.00
Same, ordinary trade edition. 200.00 275.00

☐ **Pilling, James C.** *Bibliography of the Algonquian Languages.* Washington, D.C., 1891. 614 pp. Softbound. 100.00 130.00

☐ **Pitkin, Timothy.** *A Political and Civil History of the United States of America, from the Year 1763 to the Close of the Administration of President Washington.* New Haven, 1828. Two vols. 45.00 60.00

☐ **Platt, Henry.** *Old Times in Huntington, 1876.* 25.00 33.00

☐ **Poe, John W.** *The Death of Billy the Kid.* Boston, 1933. 60 pp. Clothbound. 85.00 105.00
Said to be one of the more accurate accounts of the famous desperado's death, of which numerous versions (nearly all conflicting) were published.

☐ **Pollard, Edward E.** *The Lost Cause Regained.* N.Y., 1868. .... 40.00 50.00

☐ **Pollack, James.** *Railroad to Oregon.* Washington, D.C., 1848. 77 pp. 130.00 165.00

☐ **Pond, Oscar L.** *Municipal Control of Public Utilities.* N.Y., 1906. 117 pp. Softbound. 19.00 24.00

☐ **Pontgibaud, C. de.** *A French Volunteer of the War of Independence.* N.Y., 1897. .... 9.00 12.00

☐ **Poor, Henry.** *Resumption of the Silver Question.* N.Y., 1878, 249 pp. 80.00 100.00
The "silver question" was whether the U.S. should remain on a bimetallic standard (silver and gold) or switch to a Gold Standard. It was debated for ages, before the short-lived Gold Standard was adopted in 1900.

☐ **Poore, Ben Perley.** *The Life and Public Services of Ambrose E. Burnside.* Providence, 1882. .... 15.00 20.00

☐ **Porsch, Thomas W.** *McCarver and Tacoma.* Seattle, 1906. 198 pp. With 2 plates. 42.00 53.00

☐ **Porter, Eliphalet.** *An Eulogy on George Washington.* Boston, n.d., 1800. Softbound. 95.00 115.00

☐ **Porter, Robert P.** *The West: from the Census of 1880.* Chicago, 1882. 630 pp. Clothbound. 150.00 190.00

☐ **Post, Marie Caroline.** *The Life and Memoirs of Comte Regis de Trobroand.* N.Y., 1910. .... 30.00 40.00

☐ **Potter, Israel.** *Life & Remarkable Adventure of Israel R. Potter. Who was a Soldier in the American Revolution.* Providence, 1824. Herman Melville's novel "Israel Potter" was based on this work. 52.00 67.00

☐ **Poultney, Evan.** *An Appeal to the Creditors of the Bank of Maryland and the Public Generally.* Baltimore, 1835. 58 pp. Softbound. 40.00 50.00

☐ **Powers, Stephen.** *Afoot and Alone.* Hartford, 1884. ...... 50.00 65.00

☐ **Pratt, Julius M.** *Reminiscences.* N.p., 1910. 287 pp. With 9 plates. 80.00 110.00
Undoubtedly published in California.

PRICE RANGE

☐ **Preble, R. Adm. George.** *Chronological History of the Origin and Development of Steam Navigation. 1543–1882.* Philadelphia, 1883. . . . .   70.00   90.00

☐ **Price, Con.** *Memoirs of Old Montana.* Hollywood, Calif., n.d.(c. 1945). 154 pp. 70.00   90.00

☐ **Price, George F.** *Across the Continent with the Fifth Cavalry.* N.Y., 1959. 705 pp. Limited to 750 copies. 43.00   55.00

☐ **Price, Julius M.** *From Euston to Klondike. The Narrative of a Journey through British Columbia and the North-West Territory in the Summer of 1898.* London, 1898. 301 pp. Clothbound. 60.00   75.00

☐ **Price, Richard.** *Observations on the Nature of Civil Liberty.* N.Y., 1776. 107 pp. Softbound. 110.00   140.00
This work has somewhat more value than it would if published in another year: some collectors specialize in American imprints of 1776

☐ **Price, Richard.** *Observations on the Importance of the American Revolution.* London, 1785. . . . .   60.00   80.00

☐ **Priest, Josiah.** *Stories of the Revolution. With an Account of the Lord Child of the Delaware.* Albany, 1833. Folding woodcut frontis. 175.00   225.00

☐ **Prieto, G.** *San Francisco in the Seventies.* San Francisco, 1938. 91 pp. Limited to 650 copies. 95.00   125.00

☐ **Pringle, Henry F.** *The Life and Times of William Howard Taft.* N.Y., 1939. Two vols. 35.00   42.00

☐ **Pritchard, James A.** *The Overland Diary of James A Pritchard.* Denver, 1959. 221 pp. Clothbound. 30.00   40.00

☐ *Proceedings of the Twelve Apostles of the Church of Jesus Christ of Latter-Day Saints.* Liverpool (England), 1845. 16 pp. Softbound. 360.00   435.00

☐ *Proceedings relating to the Northern Pacific Railroad Company's claim to the Mineral Lands of Montana.* Helena, 1890. 28 pp. Softbound. 375.00   450.00

☐ *Prospectus of the Deadwood Gulch Hydraulic Mining Company.* Deadwood, 1882. 12 pp. Two or three copies known to exist. Softbound. 2450.00   2875.00

☐ **Pryor, Roger A.** *Speech of Roger A. Pryor of Virginia, on the Principles and Policy of the Black Republican Party.* Washington, D.C., 1859. 14 pp. Softbound. 53.00   69.00

☐ **Pulszky, Francis and others.** *White, Red and Black: Sketches of Society in the United States.* London, 1853. Three vols., often cloth bound as one 115.00   150.00

☐ **Purcell, Polly J.** *Autobiography and Reminiscences of a Pioneer.* Freewater, Oregon, n.d.(c. 1920). 75.00   100.00

☐ **Putnam, Israel.** *The Two Putmans.* Hartford, 1931. 279 pp. Bound in boards. Boxed. Stated to be a limited edition, but no numeration given. 20.00   25.00

☐ **Pyle, Joseph G.** *The Life of James J. Hill.* N.Y., 1917. Two vols. 20.00   25.00

☐ **Pynchon, William.** *The Diary of William Pynchon of Salem.* Boston, 1890. 349 pp. 65.00   80.00

PRICE RANGE

☐ **Quaife, Milo.** *The Movement for Statehood 1845–1846.* Madison, Wisconsin, 1918. 545 pp. Bound in cloth. 23.00 29.00
Published by the Wisconsin Historical Society.

☐ **Quiett, Glenn C.** *They Built the West.* N.Y., 1934. 569 pp. Clothbound. 42.00 53.00

☐ **Quigley, Dr.** *The Irish Race in California and on the Pacific Coast.* San Francisco, 1878. 548 pp. 53.00 68.00

☐ **Quincy, Josiah.** *Observations on the Act of Parliament . . . Called the Boston Port-Bill.* Boston, 1774. . . . . 215.00 265.00

☐ **Quincy, Josiah.** *Speech on the Bill to Enable the People of the Territory of Orleans to Form a Constitution and State Government.* Baltimore, 1811. 23 pp. Softbound. 215.00 265.00

☐ **Ramsay, David.** *History of the American Revolution.* Philadelphia, 1789. Two vols. 175.00 220.00

☐ **Ramsay, David.** *The Life of George Washington.* N.Y., 1807. . . . . 140.00 170.00

☐ **Raynal, Abbe.** *The Revolution in America.* London, 1781. First English edition of a French work. 100.00 130.00

☐ **Rainey, Thomas.** *Ocean Steam Navigation and the Ocean Post.* N.Y., 1858. . . . . 140.00 180.00

☐ **Ralph, Julian.** *Dixie; or, Southern Scenes and Sketches.* N.Y., 1896. Illustrated by Frederick Remington. 50.00 65.00

☐ **Rand, McNally.** *Official Map of Alaska, including the Klondike District and adjacent gold fields.* Chicago, 1897. 24 × 36 inches, folding to pocket size, gold-stamped covers. 400.00 500.00

☐ **Randall, Emilius O.** *History of Ohio.* N.Y., 1912. Five vols. With maps. Bound in cloth. 275.00 350.00

☐ **Randall, Henry S.** *The Life of Thomas Jefferson.* N.Y., 1858. Three vols. Bound in cloth. 65.00 80.00

☐ **Rankin, Melinda.** *Texas in 1850.* Boston, 1850. 199 pp. 750.00 1000.00

☐ **Raper, Charles Lee.** *North Carolina: A study in English Colonial Government.* N.Y., 1904. 260 pp. Clothbound. 21.00 27.00

☐ **Ray, P. Orman.** *The Repeal of the Missouri Compromise.* Cleveland, 1909. . . . . 42.00 55.00

☐ **Ray, Worth S.** *Austin Colony Pioneers.* Austin, 1949. 378 pp. With maps. 85.00 105.00

☐ **Raymond, Daniel.** *The Missouri Question.* Baltimore, 1819. 39 pp. Softbound. 150.00 190.00

☐ **Raymond, Dora Neill.** *Captain Lee Hall of Texas.* Norman, Oklahoma, 1940. 352 pp. With a folding map. 65.00 85.00

☐ **Rayner, B. L.** *Sketches of the Life, Writings and Opinions of Thomas Jefferson.* N.Y., 1832. 556 pp. 40.00 55.00
Jefferson had died 6 years earlier.

☐ **Reavis, L. U.** *The Commonwealth of Missouri.* London, 1880. 51 pp. Softbound. 105.00 130.00

☐ **Reckett, William.** *Some Account of the Life and Gospel Labours of William Reckett.* Philadelphia, 1784. Bound in calf. 40.00 50.00

☐ *Record of the Service of the 44th Massachusetts Volunteer Militia in North Carolina.* Boston, 1886. . . . . 20.00 25.00

PRICE RANGE

☐ **Redding, J. H.** *Life and Times of Jonathan Bryan.* Savannah, 1901. 97 pp. Clothbound........................... 37.00   48.00
Published by the Savannah Morning News.

☐ **Redpath, James.** *Handbook to Kansas Territory and the Rocky Mountains Gold Region.* N.Y., 1859. 178 pp. Reprint edition published in Denver, 1954. .... 48.00   62.00
The 1859 original edition is rare and valuable.

☐ **Reed, John C.** *The Brothers' War.* Boston, 1906......... 37.00   48.00

☐ **Reeves, Frank.** *A Century of Texas Cattle Brands.* Ft. Worth, n.d.(c. 1935). 80 pp. Softbound. 80.00   105.00

☐ **Reid, A. J.** *The Resources and Manufacturing Capacity of the Lower Fox River Valley.* Appleton, Wisconsin, 1874. 56 pp. Softbound.. 70.00   90.00

☐ **Reid, Arthur.** *Reminiscences of the Revolution, or, Le-Loup's Bloody Trail from Salem to Fort Edward.* Utica, 1859. .... 36.00   46.00

☐ **Reid, Samuel C.** *The Scouting Expeditions of McCulloch's Texas Rangers.* Philadelphia, 1860. 251 pp. 110.00   140.00

☐ **Reidesel, Madame.** *Letters and Memoirs Relating to the War of American Independence.* N.Y., 1827. .... 120.00   150.00

☐ **Renfrow, W. C.** *Oklahoma and the Cherokee Strip.* Chicago, 1893. 16 pp. Softbound, with folding map......... 290.00   345.00

☐ **Reynolds, John.** *The Pioneer History of Illinois.* Belleville, 1852. .... 1650.00   2150.00

☐ **Reynolds, John.** *My Own Times.* Belleville, 1855. 600 pp., polished calf. 2000.00   2500.00

☐ **Rhodes, Eugene Manlove.** *Copper Streak Trail.* Boston, 1922. 318 pp Clothbound............................. 37.00   48.00

☐ **Rhodes, May D.** *Hired Man on Horseback.* Cambridge, 1938. 264 pp...................................... 55.00   70.00

☐ **Rich, Joseph W.** *The Battle of Shiloh.* Iowa City, Iowa, 1911. .... 27.00   35.00

☐ **Richards, Rev. A.** *Zilla Fitz James, the Female Bandit of the Southwest: or, the Horrible Mysterious and Awful Disclosures in the Life of the Creaole Murderess (sic), Zilla Fitz James.* Little Rock, 1852. 31 pp. Softbound.......... 2150.00   2675.00

☐ **Ridings, Sam P.** *The Chisolm Trail: a History of the World's Greatest Cattle Trail.* Guthrie, 1936. 591 pp. Clothbound. 200.00   250.00

☐ **Riedesel, Frederick A. and others.** *Letters and memoirs relating to the War of American Independence.* N.Y., 1827. 323 pp.. 70.00   90.00

☐ **Riggs, Stephen R.** *Mary and I: 40 Years with the Sioux.* Chicago, 1880. 388 pp. Clothbound. 65.00   85.00

☐ **Riley, B. F.** *Alabama as it is.* Atlanta, 1888. 304 pp. with a folding map... 53.00   68.00
Published by the Atlanta Constitution.

☐ **Riley, James.** *An Authentic Narrative of the Loss of the American Brig Commerce.* N.Y., 1817. With folding map and nine plates... 75.00   100.00

PRICE RANGE

☐ **Ripley, Thomas.** *They Died with Their Boots On.* N.Y., 1935. 285 pp. Clothbound. **100.00** **130.00**
The title was seized by Hollywood and used for an Errol Flynn movie, about Custer's last stand. However, Ripley's *They Died with Their Boots On* was mainly about Old West outlaws.

☐ **Ritchie, Thomas.** *The Commonwealth of Virginia vs. Thomas Ritchie, Jr. Tried at the Spring Term of the Chesterfield Superior Court, 1846.* N.Y., 1846. 91 pp. With a folding map. Bound in boards. **80.00** **105.00**
Ritchie was accused of killing an adversary in a duel, near Manchester, Virginia.

☐ **Rives, William C.** *History of the Life and Times of James Madison.* Boston, 1873. 3 vols. **42.00** **55.00**

☐ **Roberts, B. H.** *The Mormon Battalion. Its History and Achievements.* Salt Lake City, 1919. 96 pp. With a folding map. **37.00** **48.00**

☐ **Roberts, O. M.** *A Description of Texas.* St. Louis, 1881. With five double-page maps. **1000.00** **1250.00**

☐ **Robertson, C. F.** *The Attempts made to Separate the West from the American Union.* St. Louis, 1885. 60 pp. Softbound. **25.00** **32.00**

☐ **Robertson, James A.** *True Relation of the Hardships Suffered by Governor Fernando DeSoto and certain Portuguese Gentlemen during the Discovery of the Province of Florida.* Deland, Florida, 1932–33. Two vols. Cloth with vellum spines. Limited to 360 numbered sets. **375.00** **450.00**
Published by the Florida Historical Society.

☐ **Robinson, Charles E.** *A Concise History of the United Society of Believers, called Shakers.* East Canterbury, New Hampshire, 1893. 134 pp. Bound in boards with calf spine. **67.00** **82.00**

☐ **Robinson, John L.** *Whitney's Railroad to the Pacific.* Washington, D.C., 1850, 117 pp. **175.00** **225.00**

☐ **Rock, M. T.** *History of Oklahoma.* Topeka, Kansas, 1890. **750.00** **925.00**

☐ **Rogers, Arthur A.** *English and American Philosophy since 1800. A Critical Survey.* N.Y., 1922. 468 pp. **15.00** **20.00**

☐ **Rogers, Fred B.** *Soldiers of the Overland.* San Francisco, 1938. 290 pp. Bound in boards. Limited to 1,000 copies. **70.00** **90.00**

☐ **Rogers, J. A.** *World's Great Men of Color.* N.Y., 1947. Two vols. **110.00** **140.00**

☐ **Rogers, Robert.** *Ponteach or the Savages of America.* Chicago, 1914, limited to 175 copies. **185.00** **235.00**

☐ **Rollins, Phillip Ashton.** *Gone Haywire. Two Tenderfoots on the Montana Cattle Range in 1886.* N.Y., 1939. 269 pp. **37.00** **48.00**

☐ **Rollinson, John K.** *Wyoming Cattle Trails.* Caldwell, Idaho, 1948. 366 pp. Clothbound. Limited to 1,000 numbered and signed copies. **95.00** **120.00**

☐ **Roosevelt, Theodore.** *Letters of Theodore Roosevelt.* Cambridge, 1951–54. 8 vols. Clothbound. **100.00** **125.00**

PRICE RANGE

☐ **Root, Frank A. and Connelley, William.** *The Overland Stage to California.* Columbus, Ohio, 1950. 630 pp. With a folding map. 75.00 95.00

☐ **Rosa, Joseph G.** *Alias Jack McCall: a Pardon or Death?* Kansas City, 1967. 32 pp. Clothbound. Limited to 250 numbered and signed copies. 27.00 36.00
Jack McCall was executed for the murder of Wild Bill Hickok.

☐ **Ross, Edmund G.** *History of the Impeachment of Andrew Johnson and his Trial by the Senate.* Santa Fe, 1896. 180 pp. Clothbound. 95.00 120.00
Edmund G. Ross was a Senator from Kansas at the time of Johnson's trial. He was among those who voted "not guilty."

☐ **Ross, Fitzgerald.** *A Visit to the Confederate States.* Edinburgh, 1865. . . . . 80.00 100.00

☐ **Rowe, John.** *Letters and diary of John Rowe.* Boston, 1903. . . . . 40.00 50.00

☐ **Rowland, Eron.** *Andrew Jackson's campaign against the British.* N.Y., 1926. 424 pp. 20.00 25.00

☐ **Ruffin, Edmund.** *Agricultural, geological, and descriptive sketches of lower North Carolina.* Raleigh, 1861. . . . . 325.00 400.00

☐ **Ruffin, Frank G.** *Facts, Thoughts and Conclusions in Regard to the Public Debt of Virginia.* Richmond, 1885. 64 pp. Softbound. 10.00 14.00

☐ **Rupp, I. Daniel.** *History of Northhampton, Lehigh, Monroe, Carbon, and Schuykill Counties.* Harrisburg, 1845. . . . . 45.00 57.00

☐ **Russell, Donald L.** *One Hundred and Three Fights and Scrimmages.* Washington, D.C., 1936. 173 pp. Softbound. 75.00 100.00

☐ **Russell, Charles M.** *Trails Plowed Under.* N.Y., 1927. 211 pp. With 10 plates. Clothbound. 110.00 145.00

☐ **Russell, Osborne.** *Journal of a Trapper.* Boise, Idaho, 1921. 149 pp. Clothbound. 85.00 105.00
Russell spent nine years in the Rocky Mountains from 1834 to 1843.

☐ **Ruxton, George F.** *Adventures in Mexico and the Rocky Mountains.* N.Y., 1848. 312 pp. 80.00 100.00

☐ **Sabin, Edwin L.** *Kit Carson Days, 1809–1868.* N.Y., 1935. Two vols. 125.00 150.00

☐ **Sachse, Julius F.** *The German Pietists of Provincial Pennsylvania.* Philadelphia, 1895. Quarto. 70.00 90.00

☐ **Sage, Rufus B.** *Letters and Papers 1836–1847.* Glendale, Calif., 1956. Two vols. Clothbound. 70.00 90.00

☐ **Sakolski, A. M.** *The Finances of American Trade Unions.* Baltimore, 1906. 152 pp. Bound in half morocco. 15.00 20.00

☐ **Sale, Edith T.** *Manors of Virginia in Colonial Times.* Philadelphia, 1909. 309 pp. 42.00 53.00

☐ **Salter, William.** *The Life of James W. Grimes, Governor of Iowa 1854–1858.* N.Y., n.d. 398 pp. Bound in cloth. 21.00 27.00

☐ **Saltonstall, William G.** *Ports of Piscataqua.* Cambridge, 1941. 242 pp. Clothbound. 22.00 27.00

PRICE RANGE

☐ **Sanders, Alvin H.** *Shorthorn Cattle.* Chicago, n.d. (c. 1918).
1,021 pp. Clothbound...................................... 65.00   85.00

☐ **Sanders, Daniel.** *The History of the Indian Wars with the
First Settlers of the U.S.* Montpellier, Vt., 1812. .... 1700.00   2150.00

☐ **Sanderson, Howard K.** *Lynn in the Revolution.* Boston,
1909. Two vols. Clothbound. 22.00   28.00

☐ **Sandoz, Mari.** *The Battle of the Little Bighorn.* N.Y., 1966.
Deluxe edition, bound in half blue morocco, limited to 249
numbered copies signed by the author. 225.00   300.00

☐ **Sargent, Nathan.** *Public Men and Events.* Philadelphia,
1875. Two vols. Clothbound. 15.00   20.00

☐ **Sargent, Winthrop.** *Political Intolerance.* Boston, 1801. 36
pp. Softbound.. 60.00   75.00

☐ **Satterlee, M. P.** *A Detailed Account of the Massacre by
the Dakota Indians of Minnesota in 1862.* Minneapolis, 1923.
128 pp. Softbound....................................... 125.00   155.00

☐ **Savage, James.** *A Genealogical Dictionary of the First
Settlers of New England.* Boston, 1860–1862. Four vols. 220.00   275.00

☐ **Sawtelle, Mrs. M. P.** *The Heroine of '49.* N.p., 1891. .... 25.00   32.00

☐ **Sawyer, Eugene T.** *The Life and Career of Tiburcio Vas-
quez, the California Stage Robber.* Oakland, 1944. 92 pp.
Bound in boards. Limited to 500 copies................. 90.00   115.00

☐ **Schafer, Joseph.** *A History of Agriculture in Wisconsin.*
Madison, 1922. 212 pp. 20.00   25.00

☐ **Schebesta, Paul.** *My Pygmy and Negro Hosts.* London,
n.d.(1936). 42.00   55.00

☐ **Schofield, John M.** *Forty-six Years in the Army.* N.Y., 1897.
577 pp. Clothbound. 28.00   36.00

☐ **Schoolcraft, Henry R.** *Journal of a Tour into the Interior
of Missouri and Arkansas.* London, 1821. 102 pp. With a
folding map.. 175.00   225.00

☐ **Schoolcraft, Henry R.** *Personal Memoirs of a Residence
of 30 Years with the Indian Tribes on the American Frontiers.* Philadelphia, 1851. 703 pp. 225.00   275.00

☐ **Schoonover, T. J.** *Life and Times of Gen. John A. Sutter.*
Sacramento, 1907.. 35.00   45.00

☐ **Schotter, Howard W.** *The Growth and Development of the
Pennsylvania Railroad Company, 1846–1926.* Philadel-
phia, 1927. 518 pp. With a folding map................. 60.00   80.00

☐ **Schpettle, Edwin.** *Sailing Craft.* N.Y., 1928. 786 pp.
Clothbound. 80.00   105.00

☐ **Schultz, James W.** *Lone Bull's Mistake.* Boston, 1918. 208
pp. Clothbound... 42.00   53.00

☐ **Schuricht, Herman.** *History of the German Element in Virginia.* Baltimore, 1898–1900. Two vols. 40.00   50.00

☐ **Schurz, Carl.** *Reminiscences of Carl Schurz.* N.Y., 1907.
Three vols. 30.00   38.00

☐ **Scobee, Barry.** *The Steer Branded Murder.* Fort Davis,
1952. 56 pp. Clothbound................................ 60.00   80.00
Published by the author.

☐ **Scott, Erastus Howe.** *Alaska Days.* Chicago, 1923. 106
pp. Clothbound.. 38.00   47.00

PRICE RANGE

☐ **Scott, Hugh L.** *Some Memoirs of a Soldier.* N.Y., 1928. 673 pp. ... 55.00   70.00

☐ **Scott, James B.** *James Madison's Notes of Debates in the Federal Convention of 1787.* N.Y., 1918. ... 17.00   22.00

☐ **Scott, James K. P.** *The Story of the Battles of Gettysburg.* Harrisburg, Pa., 1927. ... 17.00   22.00

☐ **Scott, Winfield.** *Memoirs of Lieut.-General Scott.* N.Y., 1864. Two vols. Clothbound. ... 28.00   35.00

☐ **Seabury, Samuel.** *Letters of a Westchester, N.Y., farmer 1774–1775.* White Plains, N.Y., 1930. 162 pp. ... 15.00   20.00

☐ **Sears, Rev. Hiram.** *The People's Keepsake; or Funeral Address on the Death of Abraham Lincoln.* Cincinnati, 1885. Wrappers. ... 90.00   120.00

☐ **Secretan, J. H. E.** *To Klondike and Back.* London, 1898. 260 pp. Clothbound. ... 48.00   63.00

☐ **Sedwick, Theodore.** *Thoughts on the Proposed Annexation of Texas to the United States.* N.Y., 1844. 55 pp. Softbound. ... 75.00   100.00

☐ **Segale, Blandina.** *At the End of the Santa Fe Trail.* Milwaukee, 1948. 298 pp. ... 18.00   24.00

☐ **Seger, John H.** *Tradition of the Cheyenne Indians.* Arapaho, n.d.(c. 1905). 11 pp. Softbound. ... 110.00   145.00

☐ **Seidman, Harold.** *Labor Czars. A History of Labor Racketeering.* N.Y., 1938. 317 pp. ... 17.00   23.00

☐ **Severance, Frank H.** *Old Trails on the Niagara Frontier.* Buffalo, 1899. 321 pp. ... 32.00   40.00

☐ **Seville, William P.** *Narrative of the March of Co. A Engineers, from Fort Leavenworth to Fort Bridger, 1858.* Washington, D.C., 1912. 46 pp. Softbound. ... 25.00   32.00

☐ **Sewall, Jonathan M.** *Eulogy on the late General Washington.* Portsmouth, n.d., 1800. Softbound. ... 95.00   115.00

☐ **Sewell, Samuel.** *Diary of Samuel Sewell, 1674–1729.* Boston, 1877–1879. Three vols. ... 100.00   125.00
Published by the Massachusetts Historical Society.

☐ **Sexton, Grover, F.** *The Arizona Sheriff.* N.p., 1925. 47 pp. Softbound. ... 52.00   68.00

☐ **Seybolt, Robert Francis.** *The Town Officials of Colonial Boston, 1634–1775.* Cambridge, 1939. 416 pp. ... 18.00   24.00

☐ **Seyd, Ernest.** *California and its Resources.* London, 1858. ... 550.00   700.00

☐ **Shannon, Fred Albert.** *The Organization and Administration of the Union Army, 1861–1865.* Cleveland, 1928. Two vols. Clothbound. ... 55.00   70.00

☐ **Shaw, James.** *Early Reminiscences of Pioneer Life in Kansas.* Atchinson, Kansas, 1886. 238 pp. ... 90.00   120.00

☐ **Shaw, Luelia.** *True History of Some of the Pioneers of Colorado.* Hitchkiss, Colorado, 1909. 268 pp. Softbound. ... 115.00   150.00

☐ **Shea, John G.** *Perils of the Ocean and Wilderness.* Boston, 1857. 206 pp. ... 30.00   39.00

☐ **Sheldon, Charles.** *The Wilderness of the Pacific Coast Islands.* N.Y., 1912. 246 pp. Clothbound. ... 18.00   24.00

☐ **Shepherd, William R.** *History of Proprietary Government in Pennsylvania.* N.Y., 1896. 601 pp. Clothbound. ... 32.00   41.00

PRICE RANGE

☐ **Sherman, Major Edwin A.** *The Life of the Late Rear-Admiral John Drake Sloat of the United States Navy, who Took Possession of California and Raised the American Flag at Monterey in 1846.* Oakland, 1902. 258 pp. Not first edition. 100.00   125.00

☐ **Sherwell, Samuel.** *Old Recollections of an Old Boy, Including his 1864 Overland Trip.* N.Y., 1923. 271 pp. 90.00   115.00

☐ **Sherwood, George.** *American Colonists in English Records.* Baltimore, 1961. 216 pp. 14.00   19.00

☐ **Shields, R. W.** *Story of the Reno Gang.* Seymour, 1939. 45 pp., Softbound, mimeographed, rare. 325.00   400.00

☐ **Shirley, William.** *Correspondence of William Shirley.* N.Y., 1912. Two vols. 22.00   27.00

☐ **Shoemaker, James.** *Directory of the City of Mankato.* Mankato, 1888. . . . . 400.00   500.00

☐ **Short, John T.** *The North Americans of Antiquity.* N.Y., 1880. . . . . 42.00   53.00

☐ **Shreve, Royal Ornan.** *The Finished Scoundrel: General James Wilkinson, Sometime Commander-in-Chief of the Army of the United States, who made Intrigue a Trade and Treason a Profession.* Indianapolis, 1933. 319 pp. 15.00   20.00

☐ **Shreve, William P.** *The Story of the Third Army Corps Union.* Boston, 1910. . . . . 30.00   37.00

☐ **Shuck, Oscar T.** *History of the Bench and Bar of California.* Los Angeles, 1901. . . . . 85.00   105.00

☐ **Shutter, Maron D. and others.** *Progressive Men of Minnesota.* Minneapolis, 1897. 514 pp. Bound in ½ morocco. 140.00   180.00

☐ **Sibley, Gen. H. H.** *Minnesota Territory.* Washington, D.C., 1852. 6 pp. softbound. 800.00   1075.00

☐ **Siebert, Wilbur H.** *Loyalists in East Florida, 1774–1785.* Deland, 1929. Two vols. Limited to 355 copies. 150.00   190.00

☐ **Silliman, B.** *Report on the United States Reese River Silver Mining Company, situated in Austin, Lander, County.* N.Y., 1865. 24 pp. Softbound. 500.00   650.00

☐ *Silver Mines of Virginia and Austin, Nevada.* Boston, 1865. 19 pp. softbound. 825.00   1100.00

☐ **Simmons, Ezra D.** *The 125th New York State Volunteers. A Regimental History.* N.Y., 1888. . . . . 30.00   39.00

☐ **Simms, James M.** *The First Colored Baptist Church in North America.* Philadelphia, 1888. 264 pp. Bound in cloth. 115.00   150.00
The church in question was located at Savannah, Georgia.

☐ **Simms, Orlando L.** *Gun-Toters I Have Known.* Austin, Texas, 1967. 57 pp. Limited to 750 copies. 18.00   23.00

☐ **Simoce, J. G.** *Simoce's Military Journal.* N.Y., 1844. Boards. 110.00   140.00

☐ **Simpson, George.** *Fur Trade and Empire: George Simpson's Journal.* Cambridge, 1931. 370 pp. With maps in a pocket. 80.00   110.00

☐ **Simpson, Harold B.** *Caines Mill to Appomattox.* Waco, Texas, 1963. Full leather, limited to 50 numbered copies, signed. 160.00   210.00

PRICE RANGE

☐ **Simpson, James H.** *Report of Explorations Across the Great Basin of the Territory of Utah for a Direct Wagon Route from Camp Floyd to Genoa.* Washington, 1876. 518 pp. With 25 maps. Bound in buckram with a morocco label on spine. 175.00   225.00

☐ **Sinclair, James.** *History of Shorthorn Cattle.* London, 1907. 895 pp. Bound in ½ calf. 225.00   285.00

☐ **Singer, Caroline and Baldridge, C. L.** *White Africans and Black.* N.Y., 1929. One of 500 copies signed by the author. 80.00   105.00

☐ **Siringo, Charles A.** *A Lone Star Cowboy.* Santa Fe, 1919. 290 pp. Bound in cloth. 110.00   140.00

☐ **Siringo, Charles A.** *Riatia and Spurs. The Story of a Lifetime Spent in the Saddle as Cowboy and Detective.* Boston, 1927. 276 pp. With 20 plates. 125.00   160.00
The Pinkerton Detective Agency threatened to sue the publishers of this book, claiming it contained references libeling the agency.

☐ **Sites, Clement Moore Lacey.** *Centralized Administration of Liquor Laws in the American Commonwealths.* N.Y., 1899. 164 pp. Softbound. 25.00   32.00
Prohibition was still two decades away.

☐ **Skinner, Roger Sherman.** *The New York State Register, 1830.* N.Y., 1830. . . . . 38.00   45.00

☐ **Slack, W. D.** *Homes in Arkansas! One Million Acres of Choice River Bottom and Upland for Sale by the Little Rock and Ft. Smith Railway Company.* (N.Y., circa 1875). 24 pp., Softbound. 180.00   225.00

☐ **Slade, William.** *An Oration Pronounced at Middlebury, Vermont, on the Anniversary of American Independence, July 4th, 1814.* Middlebury, 1814. 40 pp. Softbound. 30.00   40.00

☐ **Slafter, Edmund F.** *Voyages of the Northmen to America.* Boston, 1877. 162 pp. 40.00   50.00

☐ **Sloan, John and Lafarge, Oliver.** *Introduction to American Indian Art.* N.Y., 1931. Two vols. Softbound. With numerous plates, some of which are tipped in. 85.00   105.00

☐ **Sloan, R. W.** *The Great Contest. The Chief Advocates of Anti-Mormon Measures Reviewed.* Salt Lake City, 1887. 98 pp. Softbound. 80.00   100.00

☐ **Smalley, Eugene V.** *History of the Northern Pacific Railroad.* N.Y., 1883. 437 pp. Large-paper copy, bound in full morocco. 250.00   325.00

☐ **Smedes, W. C.** *Speech upon the Right of a State to Secede from the Union.* Vicksburg, 1860. 40 pp., Softbound. 190.00   230.00

☐ **Smith, Arthur D.** *Old Fuss and Feathers: the Life and Exploits of Lt. General Winfield Scott.* N.Y., 1937. 386 pp. Clothbound. 12.00   16.00

☐ **Smith, Ellen Hart.** *Charles Carroll of Carrollton.* Cambridge, 1945. 340 pp. 12.00   16.00
Charles Carroll, a signer of the Declaration of Independence, outlived all other signers of that document.

PRICE RANGE

☐ **Smith, Gustavus W.** *Company "A" Corps of Engineers.* Willets Point, N.Y., 1896. 70 pp. Softbound.............. **90.00 115.00** Mexican War interest.

☐ **Smith, Jeremiah.** *An Oration on the Death of George Washington.* Exeter, 1800. Softbound................... **120.00 145.00**

☐ **Smith, Capt. John.** *Advertisements for the Unexperienced Planters of New England.* Boston, 1865. 72 pp. With a folding map. Softbound. Limited to 250 copies. .... **35.00 42.00** Reprint of a work which had appeared more than 200 years earlier. Capt. John Smith, the original "planter" of Virginia, gives advice to settlers in New England. He was not fully aware that New England's climate is rather different than Virginia's.

☐ **Smith, Joseph W.** *Visits to Brunswick, Georgia and Travels South.* Boston, 1907. 105 pp. Clothbound. **34.00 42.00**

☐ **Smith, Launa M.** *American Relations with Mexico.* Oklahoma City, 1924. 249 pp. Clothbound................... **17.00 23.00**

☐ **Smith, Morril & Co.** *A True and Comprehensive Narrative of the Discovery and Development of Oil in Beaumont, Texas. The Great Texas Oil Fields, Capacity 6,000,000 Barrels a Day.* Lynn, Mass., n.d. (c. 1902). 16 pp. Softbound. .... **125.00 150.00** Brochure announcing a stock offering. Smith, Morril & Co. was a brokerage house.

☐ **Smith, Oliver.** *Early Indiana Trials and Sketches.* Cincinnati, 1858. 640 pp. Bound in cloth...................... **53.00 68.00**

☐ **Smith, Samuel.** *Memoirs of the Life of Samuel Smith.* Middleborough, Mass., 1853............................... **165.00 200.00**

☐ **Smith, Samuel.** *History of the Province of Pennsylvania.* Philadelphia, 1913. 231 pp........................... **15.00 20.00**

☐ **Smith, Sara S.** *The Founders of the Massachusetts Bay Colony.* Pittsfield, Mass., 1897. 372 pp. Bound in cloth. .. **40.00 50.00**

☐ **Smith, Sol.** *Theatrical Management in the West and South for 30 Years.* N.Y., 1868. 275 pp........................ **135.00 165.00**

☐ **Smith, Theodore C.** *The Liberty and Free Soil Parties in the Northwest.* N.Y., 1897. 353 pp...................... **38.00 48.00**

☐ **Smith, Thomas.** *The Life and Times of Thomas Smith 1745– 1809. A Pennsylvania Member of the Continental Congress.* Philadelphia, 1904.............................. **13.00 17.00**

☐ **Smith, W. C.** *Indiana Miscellany.* Cincinnati, 1867. 304 pp.. **60.00 80.00**

☐ **Smith, W. H.** *The St. Clair Papers.* Cincinnati, 1882. Two vols. **75.00 90.00**

☐ **Smith, William.** *An Oration in the Memory of General Montgomery and the Officers and Soldiers who Fell before Quebec.* Philadelphia, 1776. 44 pp. Softbound.......... **110.00 140.00** Smith went before the Continental Congress and argued that the rebels' cause just wasn't worth a lot of bloodshed. He found few supporters.

☐ **Smith, William.** *The History of the First Discovery and Settlement of Virginia.* N.Y., 1865. 331 pp. Bound in ¾ leather over marbled boards. Limited to 150 copies....... **210.00 270.00**

PRICE RANGE

☐ **Snider, Guy Edward.** *The Taxation of the Gross Receipts of Railways in Wisconsin.* N.Y., 1906. 138 pp. Softbound. — 23.00 · 30.00

☐ **Snowden, Clinton A.** *History of Washington. The Rise and Progress of an American State.* N.Y., 1909. 4 vols. Bound in ½ leather. — 190.00 · 240.00

☐ **Snowden, James Ross.** *A Descriptive of the Medals of Washington.* Philadelphia, 1861. Cloth. — 40.00 · 52.00

☐ **Sola, A. E.** *Klondike: Truth and Facts of the New El Dorado.* London, 1897. 102 pp. Bound in cloth. — 110.00 · 145.00

☐ **Solms-Braunfels, Carl.** *Texas 1844–1845.* Houston, 1936. 141 pp. Limited to 750 copies. — 65.00 · 85.00

☐ **Somerville, E.E.** *The States Through Irish Eyes.* Boston, 1930. 200 pp. — 15.00 · 20.00

☐ **Sowell, A. J.** *Rangers and Pioneers of Texas. With a Concise Account of the Early Settlements, Hardships, Massacres, Battles, and Wars...* San Antonio, 1884. First edition. — 1250.00 · 1575.00

☐ **Sowell, A. J.** *Early Settlers and Indian Fighters of Southwest Texas.* N.Y., 1964. Two vols. Clothbound. — 80.00 · 105.00

☐ **Spargo, John.** *Anthony Haswell: Printer, Patriot, Balladeer.* Rutland, Vt., 1925. 293 pp. Bound in ½ morocco. Limited to 300 copies. — 60.00 · 75.00

☐ **Sparks, A. W.** *The War Between the States as I Saw it.* Tyler, Texas, 1901. Scarce. — 700.00 · 900.00

☐ **Sparks, Edwin E.** *The English Settlement of Illinois.* Cedar Rapids, Iowa, 1907. Clothbound. Limited to 250 copies. — 52.00 · 73.00

☐ **Sparks, William H.** *The Memories of 50 Years, Chiefly Spent in the Southwest.* Philadelphia, 1870. 489 pp. Clothbound. — 57.00 · 78.00

☐ **Spear, Else.** *Fort Phil Kearny, Dakota Territory, 1866–1868.* Sheridan, published by the author, n.d.(c. 1939). 34 pp. Softbound. Limited to 500 numbered copies. — 78.00 · 105.00

☐ **Spears, John R.** *Illustrated Sketches of Death Valley.* Chicago, 1892. — 170.00 · 215.00

☐ **Speed, Thomas.** *The Union Cause in Kentucky, 1860–1865.* N.Y., 1907. 355 pp. Bound in cloth. — 25.00 · 33.00

☐ **Speer, William.** *The Oldest and Newest Empire: China and the United States.* Cincinnati, 1870. 681 pp. Bound in boards with a ½ leather spine. — 42.00 · 53.00

☐ **Spencer, Ichabod S.** *Fugitive Slave Law.* N.Y., 1850. 31 pp., softbound. — 47.00 · 64.00

☐ **Spencer, O. M.** *Indian Captivity. A True Narrative of the Capture of the Rev. O. M. Spencer by the Indians, in the Neighbourhood of Cincinnati.* N.Y., 1842. 160 pp. Illustrated. Bound in boards. — 58.00 · 73.00

☐ **Spotts, David L.** *Campaigning with Custer.* N.Y., 1965. 244 pp. — 37.00 · 48.00
It is said that 800 copies were printed and 500 of them destroyed.

☐ **Sprague, J. T.** *The Treachery in Texas.* N.Y., 1862. Softbound. — 43.00 · 57.00

A very pretty book, and one for which collectors pay a pretty price. The author of The Generall Historie of Virginia, *was Captain John Smith. The three people on the head of the title page are Elizabeth I (who was long deceased by the time this 1724 edition was published), James I (who died the following year), and Prince Charles (who became King Charles in 1625). The publisher was Michael Sparks, here spelled Sparkes.*

PRICE RANGE

☐ **Spring, Agnes Wright.** *The Cheyenne and Black Hills Stage and Express Routes.* Glendale, 1949. 418 pp. Clothbound. 110.00   145.00

☐ **Staab, Franz.** *Chicago Polka.* Chicago, 1855, 5 pp., Softbound. 400.00   475.00

☐ **Stafford, Mrs. M.** *The March of Empire Through Three Decades.* San Francisco, 1884. 189 pp. Bound in cloth.   80.00   105.00

☐ **Stanard, W. G.** *Some Emigrants to Virginia.* Richmond, 1915. 94 pp. Softbound. 21.00   27.00

☐ **Standish, W. H.** *Argument Explaining the Beaubien Title in the Lake Front Lands at Chicago.* Washington, 1878. 67 pp., Softbound. 325.00   400.00

☐ **Stanley, E. J.** *Life of Rev. L. B. Stateler, or 65 Years on the Frontier.* Nashville, 1907. 356 pp. 80.00   105.00

☐ **Stanley, Frank.** *Clay Allison.* Denver, 1956. 236 pp. Autographed copy. 40.00   50.00

☐ **Stansbury, Howard.** *Exploration and Survey of the Valley of the Great Salt Lake of Utah.* Philadelphia, 1852. 487 pp. With 57 plates and 2 maps in a separate folder. Price stated is for a copy with the maps. 100.00   130.00

Without the maps. 50.00   65.00

☐ **Staples, W. R.** *Documentary History of the Destruction of the Gaspee.* Providence, 1845. . . . .   30.00   38.00

☐ **Starr, E. C.** *A History of Cornwall, Conn.* N.p., 1926. . . . . .   175.00   200.00

☐ **Stedman, Charles.** *The History of the Origin, Progress and Termination of the American War.* London, 1794. Two vols., with 15 maps and plans, some folding. 1000.00   1300.00

☐ **Steele, Ashbel.** *Chief of the Pilgrims.* Philadelphia, 1857. 416 pp. 30.00   38.00

☐ **Steele, John.** *Across the Plains in 1850.* Chicago, 1930. 234 pp. Limited to 350 copies. Bound in decorated boards with a cloth spine. Boxed. 140.00   185.00

☐ **Stein, Albert.** *Letter to Samuel J. Peters, President of the New Orleans Chamber of Commerce, in Relation to the Improvement of the Navigation of the Mississippi River.* Philadelphia, 1841. 32 pp. With a folding map. Softbound. 65.00   85.00

☐ **Steiner, Lewis H.** *Report of Lewis H. Steiner, Containing a Diary Kept During the Rebel Occupation of Frederick, Md.* N.Y., 1862. Softbound. 35.00   43.00

☐ **Stenhouse, Thomas B. H.** *The Rocky Mountain Saints.* N.Y., 1873. 761 pp. Clothbound. 63.00   83.00

☐ **Stephens, Alexander H.** *A Constitutional View of the Late War Between the States.* Philadelphia, 1868–70. Two vols. 30.00   38.00

☐ **Stephens, Hazard.** *The Life of Isaac Ingalls Stevens.* Boston, 1900. Two vols. 22.00   26.00

☐ **Sterking, Ada.** *A belle of the fifties.* N.Y., 1905. . . . .   18.00   24.00

☐ **Stevens, Henry.** *Benjamin Franklin's Life and Writings. A Bibliographical Essay on the Stevens Collection of Books and MSS Relating to Dr. Franklin.* London, 1881. . . . .   140.00   170.00

☐ **Stevens, Robert C.** *A History of Chandler, Arizona.* Tucson, 1954. 106 pp. Softbound. 19.00   24.00

PRICE RANGE

☐ **Stewart, Robert Laird.** *History of the 140th Regiment Pennsylvania Volunteers.* Philadelphia, 1912. . . . . 33.00 42.00

☐ **Stifler, James.** *The Religion of Benjamin Franklin.* N.Y., 1925. Limited to 500 copies. 55.00 75.00

☐ **Stiles, Henry R.** *Account of the Interment of the Remains of American Patriots who Perished on Board the British Prison Ships during the American Revolution.* N.Y., 1865. 246 pp. One of 80 copies, numbered and initialed by the author. 32.00 39.00

☐ **Stiles, Robert.** *Four Years Under Marse Robert.* N.Y., 1903. . . . . 17.00 23.00

☐ **Stiller, Charles J.** *Major-General Anthony Wayne and the Pennsylvania Line in the Continental Army.* Philadelphia, 1893. . . . . 28.00 34.00

☐ **Stocking, Abner.** *An Interesting Journal of Abner Stocking, of Chatham, Connecticut, Detailing the Distressing Events of the Expedition against Quebec.* Tarrytown, N.Y., 1921. 36 pp. Softbound. 16.00 21.00

☐ **Stoddard, Solomon.** *Question Whether God is not Angry with the Country for Doing So Little Towards the Conversion of the Indians?* Boston, 1823. . . . . 1875.00 2150.00

☐ **Stoke, Will.** *Episodes of the Early Days in Central and Western Kansas.* Great Bend, Kansas, published by the author, 1926. 197 pp. Clothbound. 95.00 120.00
Stated to be "Volume One," but no further volumes were published.

☐ **Stone, W. L.** *Life of Joseph Brant.* Cooperstown, 1846. Two vols. 110.00 140.00

☐ **Storrs, Richard S.** *The Early American Spirit.* N.Y., 1878. Limited to 150 numbered copies. 28.00 36.00

☐ **Story, Isaac.** *An Eulogy on the Glorious Virtues of the Illustrious Gen. George Washington.* Worcester, 1800. Softbound. 70.00 90.00

☐ **Straley, W.** *Pioneer Sketches of Nebraska and Texas.* Hico, Texas, 1915. 58 pp. Softbound. 110.00 140.00

☐ **Stratton, R. B.** *Life Among the Indians. Or, the Captivity of the Oatman Girls among the Apache and Mohave Indians.* San Francisco, 1935. 209 pp. Bound in boards. . . . 100.00 130.00

☐ **Street, George G.** *Ghe! Wah! Wah! Or, the Modern Montezumas in Mexico.* Rochester, N.Y., 1883. 113 pp. Clothbound. 165.00 215.00

☐ **Streeter, Floyd, B.** *Political Parties in Michigan.* Lansing, 1918. 389 pp. 17.00 23.00

☐ **Strong, Moses M.** *History of the Territory of Wisconsin, from 1836 to 1848.* Madison, 1885. 637 pp. 80.00 105.00

☐ **Strong, Thomas M.** *The History of the Town of Flatbush, in King's County, Long Island.* N.Y., 1842. With map (often lacking). 220.00 275.00

☐ **Struick, Dirk J.** *A Yankee Science in the Making.* Boston, 1948. 430 pp. 15.00 20.00

☐ **Stryker, W. S.** *General Maxwell's Brigade of the New Jersey Continental Line.* Trenton, 1885. 20.00 25.00

PRICE RANGE

☐ **Stuart, Granville.** *Diary and Sketchbook of a Journey to America in 1866.* Los Angeles, 1963. 58 pp. Bound in buckram. 47.00   62.00

☐ **Stuart, John.** *Memoir of Indian Wars, and Other Occurrences.* Richmond, 1833. Softbound. 315.00   390.00

☐ **Stuart, Robert.** *The Discovery of the Oregon Trail.* N.Y., 1935. 392 pp. With 10 maps and portraits. Clothbound. . . 75.00   100.00

☐ **Sturgis, Thomas.** *History of the New York Farmers, 1882–1910.* N.Y., Printed for Private Circulation, 1910. 128 pp. Bound in ½ morocco. 40.00   53.00

☐ **Sturgis, William.** *The Oregon Question.* Boston, 1845. 32 pp. Softbound. 150.00   190.00

☐ **Sullivan, Maurice S.** *Jedediah Smith: Trader and Trail-Breaker.* N.Y., 1936. 233 pp. Clothbound. 32.00   40.00

☐ **Summer, William H.** *Address to the Reader of the Documents Relating to the Galveston & Texas Land Company.* N.Y., 1831. Softbound. 1750.00   2150.00

☐ **Sutherland, Mrs. Redding.** *Five Years Within the Golden Gate.* London, 1868. . . . . 165.00   210.00

☐ **Swallow, G. C.** *Geological Report of the Country Along the Line of the Southwestern Branch of the Pacific Railroad.* St. Louis, 1859. 93 pp. With a folding colored map. Clothbound. 70.00   90.00

☐ **Sweeney, Talbot.** *A Vindication from a Northern Standpoint of Gen. Robert E. Lee.* Richmond, 1890. Softbound. 17.00   23.00

☐ **Swiggett, Howard.** *War Out of Niagara.* N.Y., 1933. 309 pp. 21.00   27.00

☐ **Swisher, Carl B.** *Stephen J. Field, Craftsman of the Law.* Washington, 1930. 473 pp. 26.00   32.00

☐ **Swisher, Jacob A.** *Iowa in Times of War.* Iowa City, 1943. . . . . 16.00   21.00

☐ **Sykes, E. T.** *Walthall's Brigade.* Columbus, n.d., 1905. . . 16.00   21.00

☐ **Symond, Thomas W.** *Report of an Examination of the Upper Columbia River and the Territory in its Vicinity.* Washington, 1882. 133 pp. With folding maps. 25.00   33.00

☐ **Talbot, Theodore.** *The Journals of Theodore Talbot with the Fremont Expedition of 1843.* Portland, Oregon, 1931. 153 pp. 65.00   85.00

☐ **Tallmadge, Benj.** *Memoir of Col. Benjamin Tallmadge.* N.Y., 1858. . . . . 80.00   100.00

☐ **Tansill, Charles C.** *America Goes to War.* Boston, 1938. 731 pp. 15.00   20.00

☐ **Tapley, Harriet S.** *Salem Imprints, 1768–1825.* Salem, Mass., 1927. 512 pp. 25.00   35.00

☐ **Tapley, Rufus P.** *Eulogy of Abraham Lincoln, Sixteenth President of the United States.* Biddeford (Maine), 1865. Wrappers. 55.00   70.00

☐ **Tarbell, Ida M.** *The Life of Abraham Lincoln.* N.Y., 1903. Four vols. 60.00   80.00

☐ **Tarbox, Increase N.** *Sir Walter Raleigh and his Colony in America.* Boston, 1884. 329 pp. Bound in ½ morocco. Limited to 250 copies. 45.00   60.00

PRICE RANGE

☐ **Tarleton, Banastre.** *A History of the Campaigns of 1780 and 1781.* London, 1787.............................. 600.00 750.00

☐ **Taylor, Bayard.** *Eldorado, or, Adventures in the Path of Empire.* N.Y., 1850. Two vols........................... 200.00 250.00

☐ **Taylor, James W.** *Relations between the United States and North-West British America.* Washington, D.C., 1862. 85 pp. With a folding map. Softbound.................... 45.00 55.00

☐ **Taylor, John.** *An Enquiry into the Principles and Tendency of Certain Public Measures.* Philadelphia, 1794. 92 pp. Softbound.. 55.00 70.00

☐ **Taylor, Joseph H.** *Frontier and Indian Life and Kaleidoscope Lives.* Washburn, n.d.(1932). 328 pp. Clothbound. 95.00 125.00

☐ **Taylor, L. H.** *Nevada and her Resources.* Carson City, 1894. 62 pp. With one folding plate and 2 folding maps. Softbound. 130.00 170.00

☐ **Taylor, Nathaniel W.** *Life on a Whaler.* New London, Conn., 1929. 208 pp... 100.00 130.00
Published by the New London Historical Society.

☐ **Taylor, Robert S.** *The Improvement of the Mississippi River.* N.p., 1884. 54 pp. Softbound.......................... 37.00 48.00

☐ **Teakle, Thomas.** *The Spirit Lake Massacre.* Iowa, 1918. 336 pp. Clothbound. 47.00 62.00

☐ **Tenney, Alvan A.** *Social Democracy and Population.* N.Y., 1907. 92 pp. Softbound.................................. 10.00 14.00

☐ **Terrell, John U.** *War for the Colorado River.* Glendale, 1965. Two vols.. 32.00 43.00

☐ **Thacher, Oxenbridge.** *The Sentiments of a British American.* Boston, 1764. .... 325.00 400.00

☐ **Thacher, Peter.** *A Sermon Occasioned by the Death of General George Washington.* Boston, n.d., 1800......... 95.00 115.00

☐ **Thatcher, M.** *The Thatcher Episode.* Salt Lake City,1896. 47 pp. Softbound... 30.00 39.00

☐ **Thian, Raphael P.** *Legislative History of the General Staff of the Army of the United States.* Washington, 1901. 800 pp... 80.00 100.00

☐ **Thomas, B. F.** *Remarks of the Hon. B. F. Thomas of Massachusetts on the Relation of the Seceded States (so called) to the Union.* Boston, 1862. Softbound.................... 25.00 35.00

☐ **Thomas, Benjamin P.** *Russo–American Relations, 1815–1867.* Baltimore, 1930. 185 pp. Softbound. 60.00 80.00
We didn't get along too much better with the czars than we do with the Kremlin.

☐ **Thomas, Lieut.-Col. Frederick.** *The Trail of Lieut. Col. Thomas of the First Regiment of Foot-Guards, on a Charge Exhibited by Lieut. Col. Cosmos Gordon.* London, 1781. 1100.00 1375.00

☐ **Thomas, Isiah.** *The Diary of Isiah Thomas, 1805–1828.* Worcester, Mass., 1909. Two vols. Clothbound........... 73.00 92.00
Isiah Thomas was a printer, publisher, wit and antiquary, who preserved much of the early local history of Massachusetts.

☐ **Thomas, John P.** *South Carolina: In Arms, Arts, and Industries.* N.Y., 1875. 22 pp. Softbound.................. 52.00 67.00

PRICE RANGE

☐ **Thomas, William.** *The Enemies of the Constitution Discovered.* N.Y., 1835. Clothbound. 35.00   48.00

☐ **Thomas, William H.** *On Land and Sea.* Boston,, 1884–5. Two vols. 160.00   200.00

☐ **Thompson, Albert W.** *They Were Open Range Days.* Denver, 1946. 194 pp. 43.00   55.00

☐ **Thompson, C. Mildred.** *Reconstruction in Georgia.* N.Y., 1915. . . . .   57.00   73.00

☐ **Thompson, Charles.** *Evidences in Proof of the Book of Mormon, being a Divinely Inspired Record, Written by the Forefathers of the Natives.* Batavia, 1841. . . . .   780.00   1025.00

☐ **Thompson, James J.** *A History of the Feud Between the Hill and Evans Parties of Garrard County, Ky.* Cincinnati, 1854. 112 pp. Softbound. 120.00   150.00

☐ **Thompson, Robert T.** *Colonel James Neilson. A Business Man of the Early Machine Age in New Jersey, 1784–1862.* New Brunswick, N.J., 1940. 359 pp. Softbound. 15.00   20.00

☐ **Thornwell, J. H.** *Hear the South.* N.Y., 1861. 30 pp. Softbound. 80.00   105.00

☐ **Thorp, Joseph.** *Early Days in the West. Along the Missouri one hundred Years Ago.* Liberty, Mo., 1924. 95 pp. Softbound. 85.00   110.00

☐ **Thorpe, T. B.** *Our Army at Monterey.* Philadelphia, 1847. 204 pp. With 3 plates and a folding map. 115.00   145.00

☐ **Thwaites, Reuben.** *Revolution on the Upper Ohio.* Madison, Wisconsin, 1908. 275 pp. With a folding map. 26.00   36.00

☐ **Tilgham, Zoe A.** *Outlaw Days. A True History of Early Day Oklahoma Characters.* Oklahoma City, 1926. 138 pp. Softbound. 45.00   60.00

☐ **Timothy, Peter.** *Letters of Peter Timothy, to Benjamin Franklin.* Chicago, 1935. 19 pp. Clothbound. Limited to 120 copies. 26.00   34.00

☐ **Tooker, William W.** *John Eliot's First Indian Teacher and Interpreter: Cockenoe-de-Long Island.* N.Y., 1896. 60 pp. Clothbound. Limited to 215 numbered copies. 47.00   63.00
John Eliot, a missionary in Massachusetts in the 1600's, translated the whole Bible into Indian.

☐ **Toulmin, Joshua.** *The American War Lamented.* London, 1776. . . . .   155.00   190.00

☐ **Townsend, George A.** *The Life, Crime and Capture of John Wilkes Booth, with a Full Sketch of the Conspiracy of which he was the Leader, and the Pursuit, Trial and Execution of his Accomplices.* N.Y., 1865. Softbound. 110.00   145.00

☐ **Townsend, R. B.** *The Tenderfoot in New Mexico.* London, 1923. 257 pp. 47.00   63.00

☐ **Tracy, Milton C.** *The Colonizer, a Saga of Stephen F. Austin.* El Paso, 1941. 381 pp. 25.00   32.00

☐ **Treat, Payson J.** *Japan and the United States, 1853–1921.* Boston, 1921. 283 pp. Clothbound. 16.00   21.00

☐ **Trescot, William H.** *A Few Thoughts on the Foreign Policy of the United States.* Charleston, 1849. 24 pp. Softbound. 22.00   27.00

PRICE RANGE

☐ **Trevelyan, George.** *The American Revolution.* London, 1899–1914. Six vols., maps. 85.00   110.00

☐ **Tripler, Eunice.** *Some Notes of Her Personal Recollections.* N.Y., 1910. 184 pp. Clothbound. 170.00   215.00
Eunice Tripler served as an Army surgeon in the Mexican War.

☐ **Trobriand, Regis de.** *Four Years with the Army of the Potomac.* Boston, 1889. . . . . 28.00   35.00

☐ **Truman, Maj. Ben C.** *Semi-Tropical California.* San Francisco, 1874. 204 pp. 47.00   63.00

☐ **Tubbee, Laah C. M. E.** *A Sketch of the Life of Koah Tubbee, alias William Chubbee.* Springfield, Mass., 1848. . . . . 160.00   200.00

☐ **Tucker, Pomeroy.** *Origin, Rise and Progress of Mormonism.* N.Y., 1867. 302 pp. Bound in ½ morocco. 37.00   48.00

☐ **Tuckerman, Henry T.** *America and Her Commentators.* N.Y., 1864. 460 pp. 38.00   48.00

☐ **Tudor, William.** *Letters on the Eastern States.* 356 pp. Bound in boards. 50.00   65.00

☐ **Tuttle, C. R.** *History of Grand Rapids with Biographical Sketches.* Grand Rapids, 1874. . . . . 275.00   325.00

☐ **Tuttle, D. S.** *Reminiscences of a Missionary Bishop.* N.Y., 1906. 498 pp. Clothbound. 38.00   45.00

☐ **Tuttle, Stephen.** *My Services and Losses in Aid of the King's Cause during the American Revolution.* Brooklyn, 1890. . . . . 30.00   38.00

☐ **Twitchell, Ralph E.** *The Leading Facts of New Mexico History.* Cedar Rapids, Iowa, 1911. Two vols. Clothbound. Limited to 1,500 numbered and signed sets. 475.00   600.00
Ralph E. Twitchell asserts in this book that Billy the Kid killed only 9 men—a much lower figure than most historians give.

☐ **Twitchell, Ralph E.** *Old Santa Fe, 1925.* 488 pp. Clothbound. 110.00   140.00

☐ **Tyler, John.** *Observations on the Political Character of President Tyler.* By a native of Maryland. Washington, 1841. 131 pp. Softbound. 20.00   25.00

☐ **Tyler, Samuel.** *Memoir of Roger Brooke Taney.* Baltimore, 1872. 659 pp. Clothbound. 30.00   36.00

☐ **Tyng, Dudley A.** *Reports of Cases Argued and Determined in the Supreme Judicial Court of the Commonwealth of Massachusetts.* Newburyport, Mass., 1807. 268 pp. 40.00   55.00

☐ **U. S. Sanitary Commission.** *Narrative of Privations and Sufferings of U.S. Officers and Soldiers.* Boston, n.d., 1864. Softbound. 23.00   29.00

☐ **Utely, Henry M.** *Michigan as a Province, Territory and State.* N.p., 1906. Four vols. 52.00   68.00

☐ **Vail, Alfred.** *The American Electro-Magnetic Telegraph.* Philadelphia, 1845. 208 pp. Softbound. 140.00   175.00

☐ **Vail, R. W. G.** *The Voice of the Old Frontier.* Philadelphia, 1949. 492 pp. 43.00   55.00

☐ **Valentine, Edward P.** *The Valentine Papers.* Richmond, n.d.(c.1925). 4 vols. Total of 2,768 pp. Clothbound. 190.00   230.00

PRICE RANGE

☐ **Vallandigham, Clement L.** *The Great Civil War in America.* N.Y., n.d., 1863. Softbound...............................   12.00   15.00

☐ **VanBuren, Martin.** *Inquiry into the Origin and Course of Political Parties in the U.S.* N.Y., 1867. 436 pp. 25.00   35.00
This was the first edition, published after VanBuren's death.

☐ **VanCleve, Charlotte.** *Three Score Years and Ten.* Minneapolis, privately published, 1888. 176 pp. Bound in cloth...   65.00   85.00
Charlotte VanCleve claimed to be the first child of European descent born in Wisconsin.

☐ **Van Horne, Thomas B.** *History of the Army of the Cumberland.* Cincinnati, 1875. Two vols. and atlas. 34.00   42.00

☐ **Van Ness, William P.** *The Speeches at Full Length of Mr. Van Ness...on an Indictment for a Libel on Thomas Jefferson.* N.Y., 1804. 78 pp. Softbound. 90.00   115.00

☐ **VanTramp, John C.** *Prairie and Rocky Mountain Adventures of Life in the West.* Columbus, Ohio, 1866. 649 pp. Bound in ½ morocco...................................   80.00   110.00

☐ **Vaughan, George.** *American Hell, Moral and Social.* Washington, D.C., 1883. 8 pp. Softbound................   35.00   43.00

☐ **Vestal, Stanley.** *Kit Carson, Happy Warrior of the Old West.* Cambridge, 1928. 297 pp......................   22.00   28.00

☐ **Victor, Frances Fuller.** *All Over Oregon and Washington.* San Francisco, 1872. 368 pp. Clothbound. 65.00   85.00

☐ **Victory, Beatrice M.** *Benjamin Franklin and Germany.* Philadelphia, 1915. ....   32.00   40.00

☐ **Viele, Mrs. Teresa.** *Following the Drum. A Glimpse of Frontier Life.* N.Y., 1858. 256 pp. Clothbound.............   65.00   85.00

☐ **Vigne, Godfrey T.** *Six Months in America.* London, 1832. 2 vols. With 4 plates. Bound in boards..................   55.00   70.00

☐ **Vignoles, Charles.** *Observations upon the Floridas.* N.Y., 1823. 194 pp..   550.00   675.00

☐ **Voorhees, Luke.** *Personal Recollections of Pioneer Life.* Cheyenne, 1920. 76 pp. Clothbound. Limited to 125 copies. 275.00   350.00

☐ **Wafer, Lionel.** *A New Voyage and Description of the Isthmus of America.* Cleveland, 1903. 212 pp. With folding maps. Limited to 500 numbered copies.................   34.00   42.00

☐ **Wagoner, J. J.** *History of the Cattle Industry in Southern Arizona 1540–1940.* Tucson, 1952. 132 pp. Softbound. ...   37.00   48.00

☐ **Wakeman, Edgar.** *The Log of an Ancient Mariner.* San Francisco, 1878. 378 pp. Clothbound...................   70.00   90.00

☐ **Walcott, Charles F.** *History of the 21st Regiment Massachusetts Volunteers in the War for the Preservation of the Union 1861–65.* Boston, 1882......................   22.00   28.00

☐ **Waldo, S. Putman.** *Biographical Sketches of Distinguished American Naval Heroes in the War of the Revolution.* Hartford, 1823....................................   42.00   50.00

☐ **Wales, W. W.** *The Immigrant's Guide to Minnesota. By an Old Resident.* St. Anthony, 1856. ....   550.00   700.00

☐ **Walker, Aldace F.** *The Vermont Brigade in the Shenandoah Valley, 1864.* Burlington, Vt., 1869. ....   12.00   15.00

PRICE RANGE

☐ **Walker, Francis.** *Double Taxation in the United States.* N.Y., 1895. 134 pp. Softbound. 15.00   20.00
Obviously, complaints about taxes are nothing new.

☐ **Walker, Francis A.** *History of the Second Army Corps in the army of the Potomac.* N.Y., 1886. . . . . 32.00   39.00

☐ **Walker, Franklin.** *A Literary History of Southern California.* Berkeley, 1950. 282 pp. 18.00   24.00

☐ **Walker, R. C.** *Report of the Helena Board of Trade for 1878.* Helena, 1879. 32 pp., printed wrapper. 325.00   400.00

☐ **Walker, Robert J.** *Letter of Robert J. Walker of Mississippi, Relative to the Reannexation of Texas.* Washington, D.C., 1844. 16 pp. Softbound. 37.00   48.00

☐ **Wallace, F. W.** *Wooden Ships and Iron Men: the Story of the Square Rigged Merchant Marine of British North America.* Boston, 1937. 356 pp. 80.00   105.00

☐ **Wallen, H. D.** *Report of H. D. Wallen of his Expedition, in 1859, from Dallas City to Great Salt Lake and back.* Washington, D.C., 1860. 51 pp. With a folding map. 65.00   85.00

☐ **Waller, Henry.** *Speech of Henry Waller, Esq., on the Dred Scott Decision.* Chicago, 1858. 27 pp. Softbound. 110.00   140.00

☐ **Waller, James B.** *The True Doctrine of States Rights with an examination of the Record of the Democratic and Republican Parties.* Chicago, 1880. 83 pp. Softbound. 40.00   50.00

☐ **Wallis, J. L. and Hill, L. L.** *Sixty Years in the Brazos.* N.Y., 1965. 384 pp. 27.00   35.00

☐ **Walther and Taylor.** *The Resources and Advantages of Nebraska.* Omaha, 1871. 27 pp., Softbound. 375.00   475.00

☐ **Ward, Edward.** *Boston, in 1682 and 1699.* Providence, R.I., 1905. 95 pp. Bound in boards. Limited to 100 numbered copies. 27.00   34.00

☐ **Ware, Edith Ellen.** *Political Opinion in Massachusetts during Civil War and Reconstruction.* N.Y., 1916. Softbound. 20.00   25.00

☐ **Ware, Eugene F.** *The Indian War of 1864.* Topeka, 1911. 601 pp. Bound in cloth. 275.00   350.00

☐ **Warfield, Ethelbert Dudley.** *The Kentucky Resolutions of 1798.* N.Y., 1887. 203 pp. 35.00   43.00

☐ **Warren, Charles.** *The Supreme Court in United States History.* Boston, 1923. 3 vols. Clothbound. 45.00   60.00

☐ **Warren, Eliza S.** *Memoirs of the West.* Portland, 1916. 153 pp. With 10 plates. 47.00   63.00

☐ **Warren, Gouveneur K.** *Preliminary Report of Explorations in Nebraska and Dakota.* Washington, D.C., 1875. 125 pp. With a folding map. Softbound. 32.00   42.00

☐ **Warren, Major Gen. Joseph.** *An Eulogy on Major General Joseph Warren, Who Fell in the Action at Charleston.* Boston, 1781. Very rare, only a few copies recorded. 900.00   1200.00

☐ **Warren, Mercy Otis.** *History of the Rise, Progress and Termination of the American Revolution.* Boston, 1805. Three vols. Bound in full calf. 700.00   1000.00

☐ **Washington, George.** *The Diary of George Washington, from 1789 to 1791.* Richmond, 1861. 248 pp. Clothbound. Limited to 150 copies. 50.00   65.00

PRICE RANGE

☐ **Washington, George.** *The Writings of George Washington.* Boston, 1833–37. Twelve vols. Bound in boards with paper labels on the spines. 60.00   75.00
Washington's works were republished so frequently that even an edition this early (the 1830's) isn't worth very much.

☐ **Washington, George.** *Letters from George Washington to Tobias Lear.* Rochester, N.Y., privately printed, 1905. Limited to 300 copies. 40.00   50.00
All the letters were at that time (1905) owned by William K. Bixby, a noted autograph collector from St. Louis.

☐ **Waterhouse, Sylvester.** *The Resources of Missouri.* St. Louis, 1867. 96 pp. Softbound. 65.00   85.00

☐ **Watson, Elkanah.** *Men and Times of the Revolution.* N.Y., 1856. . . . .   17.00   23.00

☐ **Watts, William C.** *Chronicles of a Kentucky Settlement.* N.Y., 1897. 490 pp. Clothbound. 70.00   90.00

☐ **Waugh, Lorenzo.** *Autobiography of Lorenzo Waugh.* Oakland, 1883. 311 pp. Clothbound. 75.00   100.00
Loads of material on early California.

☐ **Webb, James Josiah.** *Adventures in the Santa Fe Trade, 1844–47.* Glendale, Calif., 1931. 301 pp. Clothbound. . . .   75.00   100.00

☐ **Webb, Walter P.** *The Great Plains.* Boston, n.d.(c. 1931). 525 pp. 85.00   110.00

☐ **Webb, Walter P.** *The Texas Rangers.* Boston, 1935. 584 pp. Clothbound. 120.00   150.00

☐ **Weeden, William P.** *Economic and Social History of New England, 1620–1789.* Boston, 1890. Two vols. Clothbound. 50.00   65.00

☐ **Welles, C. M.** *Three Years of Wanderings of a Connecticut Yankee.* N.Y., 1859. 358 pp. Clothbound. 35.00   42.00

☐ **Wellman, Paul I.** *The Tramping Herd.* N.Y., 1939. 433 pp. Clothbound. 50.00   65.00

☐ **Wells, William.** *The Life and Public Services of Samuel Adams.* Boston, 1865. Three vols. Clothbound. 32.00   38.00

☐ **Wertenbaker, Thomas J.** *The Old South.* N.Y., 1942. 364 pp. 28.00   35.00

☐ **West, Nathaniel.** *The Ancestry, Life, and Time of Hon. Henry Hastings Sibley.* St. Paul, 1889. 596 pp. 40.00   55.00

☐ **Westermeir, Clifford P.** *Man, Beast, Dust. The Story of Rodeo.* Denver, 1947. 450 pp. Limited edition. 75.00   100.00

☐ **Weston, W.** *The Cripple Creek Gold District.* Denver, 1896. 9 pp., softbound. 300.00   375.00

☐ **Wharton, Francis.** *The Revolutionary Diplomatic Correspondence of the United States.* Washington, D.C., 1889. Six vols. Bound in full calf. 130.00   160.00

☐ **Wheeler, Homer.** *The Frontier Trail.* Los Angeles, 1923. 334 pp. Clothbound. 90.00   115.00

☐ **Wheeler, John.** *A Discourse Occasioned by the Death of Gen. William Henry Harrison.* Windsor, 1841. . . . .   90.00   115.00

☐ **Whitaker, Fess.** *History of Corporal Fess Whitaker.* Louisville, 1918. . . . .   38.00   46.00

PRICE RANGE

☐ **Whitcomb, James.** *An Act to Provide for the Funded Debt of the State of Indiana, and for the Completion of the Wabash and Erie Canal to Evansville.* N.Y., 1847. 54 pp. . . . . . | 95.00 | 120.00

☐ **White, Horace.** *The Life of Lyman Trumbull.* Boston, 1913. 460 pp. Clothbound. . . . . | 13.00 | 17.00

☐ **White, John E.** *My Old Confederate Address.* Atlanta, 1908. Softbound. . . . . | 13.00 | 17.00

☐ **White, Melvin Johnson.** *The Secession Movement in the United States.* Madison, 1910. 122 pp. Softbound. . . . . | 20.00 | 25.00

☐ **Whitman, C. F.** *History of Norway, Maine.* Norway, 1924. | 90.00 | 120.00

☐ **Whitmer, David.** *An Address to all Believers in Christ.* Richmond, Mo., 1887. 75 pp. Softbound. . . . . | 165.00 | 190.00

☐ **Whitney, Henry C.** *Life on the Circuit with Lincoln.* Boston, n.d., 1892. . . . . | 85.00 | 100.00

☐ **Whittemore, Edwin C.** *History of Waterville, Kennebec Co., Maine.* Waterville, 1902. . . . . | 150.00 | 190.00

☐ **Wilkins, Isaac.** *My Services and Losses in aid of the King's Cause during the American Revolution.* Brooklyn, 1890. Limited to 250 copies. . . . . | 28.00 | 35.00

☐ **Willard, Margaret Wheeler.** *Letters on the American Revolution 1774–1776.* Boston, 1925, with maps. . . . . | 15.00 | 20.00

☐ **Williams, John G.** *Adventures of a 17-Year Old Lad.* Boston, 1894. . . . . | 550.00 | 700.00

☐ **Williams, John Lee.** *The Territory of Florida; or Sketches of the Topography, Civil and Natural History of the Country . . . .* N.Y., 1837. . . . . | 1000.00 | 1250.00

☐ **Williams, Noble.** *Echoes from the Battlefield.* Atlanta, 1902. . . . . | 22.00 | 27.00

☐ **Williamson, James J.** *Prison Life in the Old Capitol.* West Orange, N.J., 1911. . . . . | 32.00 | 43.00

☐ **Wilson, Arabella M.** *Disaster, Struggle, Triumph.* Albany, 1870. . . . . | 20.00 | 25.00

☐ **Wilson, Ephraim.** *Memoirs of the War.* Cleveland, 1893. | 20.00 | 25.00

☐ **Wingate, George W.** *History of the 22nd Regiment of the National Guard of the State of New York.* N.Y., n.d., 1896. . . . . | 28.00 | 34.00

☐ **Wise, Jennings C.** *The Long Arm of Lee.* Lynchburg, 1915. Two vols. . . . . | 60.00 | 75.00

☐ **Wood, C. J.** *Reminiscences of the War.* N.p., n.d., (c. 1890). . . . . | 22.00 | 28.00

☐ **Woods, Rev. James.** *Recollections of Pioneer Work in California.* San Francisco, 1878. . . . . | 165.00 | 220.00

☐ **Wright, Crafts J.** *Official Journal of the Conference Convention held in Washington City, February, 1861.* Washington, 1861. Softbound. . . . . | 57.00 | 72.00

☐ **Wyeth, J. A.** *Life of General Nathan Bedford Forrest.* N.Y., 1899. . . . . | 80.00 | 100.00

☐ **Young, Jesse Bowman.** *The Battle of Gettysburg.* N.Y., 1913. . . . . | 16.00 | 20.00

ART, ANTIQUES, COLLECTING

	PRICE RANGE	
☐ **Adair, John.** *Navajo and Pueblo Silversmiths.* Norman, Oklahoma, 1945.	13.00	17.00
☐ **Adams, Ruth.** *Pennsylvania Dutch Art.* Cleveland, 1950.	5.00	7.00
☐ **Adams-Acton, M.** *Domestic Architecture and Old Furniture.* London, undated, (c. 1930).	80.00	100.00
☐ **Altman, Violet.** *The Book of Buffalo Pottery.* New York, 1969.	35.00	45.00
☐ **Ambler, Louis.** *The Old Halls and Manor Houses of Yorkshire.* London, undated, (c. 1913).	70.00	85.00
☐ **Andren, Erik.** *Swedish Silver.* New York, 1950.	10.00	15.00
☐ **(anonymous).** *Architectural Ornament of All Nations.* London, published by Shaw and Sons, undated, (c. 1850). Large folio, 47 plates, bound in paper covered boards with cloth spine.	75.00	100.00
☐ **Arnason, H. H.** *History of Modern Art.* Englewood Cliffs, 1968.	30.00	40.00
☐ **Ashton, Leigh.** *Samplers, Selected and Described.* London, 1926.	60.00	75.00
☐ **Audsley, W. and G.** *Outlines of Ornament in the Leading Styles.* London, 1881.	90.00	110.00
☐ **Audsley, W. and G.** *Polychromatic Decoration as Applied to Buildings in the Medieval Styles.* London, 1882. With 36 plates in gold and colors.	80.00	100.00
☐ **Ayers, James.** *American Antiques.* New York, 1973.	4.00	6.00
☐ **Ayrton, Michael.** *British Drawings.* London, 1946.	9.00	12.00
☐ **Baccheschi, E.** *The Complete Paintings of Giotto.* New York, 1966.	9.00	12.00
☐ **Bache, Jules S.** *Catalogue of Paintings in the Jules S. Bache Collection.* New York, 1929.	70.00	85.00
☐ **Bailey, C. T. P.** *Knives and Forks.* London, 1927.	100.00	125.00
☐ **Baker, H. S.** *Furniture in the Ancient World.* London, 1966.	25.00	30.00
☐ **Ball, T. S.** *Church Plate of the City of Chester.* Manchester, 1907. Cloth bound with 12 plates.	18.00	23.00
☐ **Bandi, H. G.** *The Art of the Stone Age.* London, 1970. Not first edition.	15.00	20.00
☐ **Barber, Edwin A.** *Majolica of Mexico.* Philadelphia, 1908.	40.00	50.00
☐ **Barsali, I. B.** *European Enamels.* London, 1969.	13.00	17.00
☐ **Batterberry, Michael.** *Art of the Early Renaissance.* New York, 1968.	10.00	15.00
☐ **Battersby, Martin.** *The World of Art Nouveau.* New York, 1968.	18.00	23.00
☐ **Baud-Bovy, Daniel.** *Peasant Art in Switzerland.* London, 1924.	45.00	55.00
☐ **Beardsley, Aubrey.** *The Early Work and the Later Work.* London, 1920. Two volumes.	200.00	250.00
☐ **Beaumont, R.** *Carpets and Rugs.* London, 1924.	90.00	110.00
☐ **Behrman, S. N.** *Duveen.* New York, 1952.	5.00	7.00
☐ **Belcher, J. and M. E. MacCartney.** *Later Renaissance Architecture in England.* London, 1901. Two volumes.	175.00	200.00
☐ **Belknap, E. M.** *Milk Glass.* New York, 1949.	26.00	34.00

PRICE RANGE

☐ **Bemrose, Geoffrey.** *Nineteenth Century English Pottery and Porcelain.* London, 1952.	22.00	28.00
☐ **Bennett, Wendell.** *Ancient Arts of the Andes.* New York, 1954.	18.00	23.00
☐ **Bertram, Anthony.** *Paul Cezanne.* London, 1929.	7.00	10.00
☐ **Bettens, E. D.** *Picture Buying.* New York, undated, (c. 1920).	15.00	20.00
☐ **Beurdeley, Michael.** *The Chinese Collector Through the Centuries.* Rutland, 1966.	45.00	55.00
☐ **Binns, R. W.** *Catalogue of a Collection of Worcester Porcelain in the Museum at the Royal Porcelain Works.* Worcester, England, 1882. Clothbound.	15.00	20.00
☐ **Binyon, Laurence.** *Painting in the Far East.* New York, 1913. Second edition.	110.00	140.00
☐ **Birch, S.** *History of Ancient Pottery.* London, 1858. Two volumes, with 12 colored plates and 207 woodcuts, bound in cloth.	20.00	25.00
☐ **Blacker, J. F.** *The ABC of Collecting Old Continental Pottery.* London, 1913.	20.00	25.00
☐ **Blacker, J. F.** *The ABC of Collecting Old English Pottery.* London, undated, c. 1915.	18.00	23.00
☐ **Blair, Dorothy.** *A History of Glass in Japan.* New York, 1973.	50.00	60.00
☐ **Bles, Joseph.** *Rare English Glasses of the XVII and XVIII Centuries.* London, 1924. Deluxe edition limited to 100 copies, bound in half morocco.	180.00	225.00
☐ **Bliss, Percy.** *A History of Wood Engraving.* London, 1928.	70.00	90.00
☐ **Blunt, Reginald.** *The Cheyne Book of Chelsea China and Pottery.* Boston, 1925.	65.00	85.00
☐ **Boeck, Wilhelm and Jaime Sabartes.** *Pablo Picasso.* New York, 1955.	40.00	50.00
☐ **Boger, L. A.** *Dictionary of World Pottery and Porcelain.* New York, 1971.	18.00	23.00
☐ **Bogolyubov, A. A.** *Carpets of Central Asia.* London, 1973.	80.00	100.00
☐ **Bond, Francis.** *Introduction to English Church Architecture, Eleventh to Sixteenth Century.* London, 1913. Two volumes.	90.00	110.00
☐ **Bonheur, Rosa.** *Reminiscences.* New York, 1910.	35.00	40.00
☐ **Bottomley, William L.** *Spanish Details.* New York, 1924.	50.00	60.00
☐ **Bowes, J. L.** *Japanese Enamels, With Illustrations from Examples in the Bowes Collection.* London, 1886. Clothbound, limited to 200 copies.	110.00	135.00
☐ **Brackett, Oliver.** *English Furniture Illustrated.* London, 1958.	40.00	50.00
☐ **Brankston, A. D.** *Early Ming Wares of Chingtechen.* Peking, 1938. Limited to 650 copies with English text.	130.00	160.00
☐ **Brears, Peter.** *The English Country Pottery.* Rutland, 1971.	20.00	25.00
☐ **Brett, Edwin J.** *A Pictorial and Descriptive Record of the Origin and Development of Arms and Armor.* London, 1894. With 133 plates, bound in half morocco.	400.00	500.00

	PRICE RANGE	
☐ **Brinton, Christian.** *Modern Artists.* New York, 1908.	35.00	45.00
☐ **Britton, J.** *The Architectural Antiquities of Great Britain.* London, 1835. Five volumes, with 365 engraved plates. Not first edition.	250.00	300.00
☐ **Bruce, J. C.** *A Descriptive Catalogue of Antiquities, Chiefly British, at Alnwick Castle.* Newcastle, 1880.	60.00	75.00
☐ **Bruton, Eric.** *Clocks and Watches.* London, 1968.	9.00	12.00
☐ **Buchhein, L. G.** *Picasso, A Pictorial Biography.* New York, 1959.	13.00	17.00
☐ **Buechner, Thomas S.** *Norman Rockwell, Artist and Illustrator.* New York, 1970.	80.00	100.00
☐ **Burgess, Fred W.** *Chats on Old Copper and Brass.* London, 1914.	30.00	35.00
☐ **Burlington Fine Arts Club.** *Exhibition of the Faience of Persia and the Nearer East.* London, 1908. Bound in cloth. . . . . Copies of this work can be found in morocco bindings, with a price about 50% higher.	100.00	125.00
☐ **Burne-Jones, Edward.** *Memorials of Edward Burne-Jones.* New York, 1904. Two volumes.	45.00	55.00
☐ **Burton, W.** *Porcelain, A Sketch of its Nature, Art and Manufacture.* London, 1906. With 50 plates.	9.00	12.00
☐ **Burton, William.** *A General History of Porcelain.* London, 1921.	160.00	200.00
☐ **Bynw, A. and M. Stapley.** *Decorated Wooden Ceilings in Spain.* New York, 1920.	250.00	300.00
☐ **Caldecott, Randolph.** *More Graphic Pictures.* London, 1887.	45.00	55.00
☐ **Camehl, A. W.** *The Blue China Book.* New York, 1916. . .	60.00	75.00
☐ **Candee, Helen C.** *The Tapestry Book.* New York, 1935.	15.00	20.00
☐ **Capart, J.** *Lectures on Egyptian Art.* Chapel Hill, N.C., 1928. Bound in half morocco.	50.00	60.00
☐ **Cary, E. L.** *The Rossettis.* New York, 1903.	20.00	25.00
☐ **Casson, Stanley.** *Some Modern Sculptors.* London, 1928.	15.00	20.00
☐ **Castell, R.** *Villas of the Ancients Illustrated.* London, Printed for the Author, 1728. With nine folding engraved plates, bound in boards with a leather spine.	250.00	300.00
☐ **Cescinsky, H.** *Chinese Furniture.* London, 1922.	90.00	110.00
☐ **Cescinsky, H.** *English Furniture from Gothic to Sheraton.* New York, 1939 Second edition.	75.00	100.00
☐ **Chaffers, William.** *Hall Marks on Gold and Silver Plate.* London, 1922.	65.00	75.00
☐ **Chaffers, W.** *The Keramic Gallery, Containing Illustrations of Rare, Curious and Choice Examples of Pottery and Porcelain.* London, 1907 Second edition. This was no misprint; Chaffers spelled ceramic with a "k" according to early tradition. The word was also pronounced that way, ker-amic, until well into the 1800s.	40.00	50.00
☐ **Chamberlain, Samuel.** *Tudor Homes of England.* New York, 1929.	110.00	140.00
☐ **Charles, C. J.** *Elizabethan Interiors.* New York, undated, c. 1917.	50.00	60.00

PRICE RANGE

☐ **Christensen, E. O.** *Early American Wood Carving.* Cleveland, 1952. . . . .   18.00   23.00

☐ **Church, A. H. and W. Y. Fletcher.** *Some Minor Arts as Practised in England.* New York, 1894. . . . .   60.00   75.00

☐ **Clarke, C..** *Indian Drawings.* London, 1922. . . . .   75.00   95.00

☐ **Clarke, H. G..** *Underglaze Colour Picture Prints on Staffordshire Pottery.* London, 1949. . . . .   100.00   130.00

☐ **Cogniat, R..** *The Century of the Impressionists.* New York, 1967. . . . .   30.00   35.00

☐ **Cole, A. S..** *A Descriptive Catalogue of the Collections of Tapestry and Embroidery in the South Kensington Museum.* London, 1888. . . . .   75.00   100.00
This museum is now known as Victoria and Albert Museum.

☐ **Cole, Timothy.** *Old English Masters.* New York, 1902. . . .   30.00   35.00

☐ **Cook, Sir T. A..** *Twenty Five Great Houses of France.* London, undated c. 1915. . . . .   100.00   130.00

☐ **Cooper, Douglas.** *The Cubist Epoch.* Los Angeles, 1971. . . . .   13.00   17.00

☐ **Cooper, Douglas.** *Henri de Toulouse-Lautrec.* New York, 1969. . . . .   13.00   17.00

☐ **Cornelius, Charles.** *Early American Furniture.* New York, 1926. . . . .   15.00   20.00

☐ **Covell, John.** *Japanese Landscape Painting.* New York, 1962. . . . .   9.00   12.00

☐ **Cox, Warren.** *The Book of Pottery and Porcelain.* New York, 1973 Two volumes. 18.00   23.00

☐ **Cox, Warren.** *Chinese Ivory Sculpture.* New York, 1946.   25.00   30.00

☐ **Craven, Thomas.** *Men of Art.* New York, 1931. . . . .   4.00   6.00

☐ **Craven, Thomas.** *Modern Art.* New York, 1934. . . . .   5.00   7.00

☐ **Cunningham, Alan.** *Lives of the Most Eminent British Painters, Sculptors and Architects.* London, 1829–33. Six volumes. 200.00   250.00

☐ **Curtis, Mattoon.** *The Book of Snuff and Snuff Boxes.* New York, 1935. . . . .   30.00   40.00

☐ **Dabies, George.** *A Collection of Old Chinese Porcelains.* New York, 1913. . . . .   125.00   150.00

☐ **Daix, Pierre.** *Picasso, the Blue and Rose Periods.* Greenwich, 1967. . . . .   50.00   60.00

☐ **Davenport, Cyril.** *Cameos.* London, 1900. . . . .   70.00   85.00

☐ **Davenport, Cyril.** *The English Regalia.* London, 1897. . . . .   100.00   125.00
This refers to all royal trappings, jewels, arms, accessories, etc., used on ceremonial occasions.

☐ **DeRicci, Seymour.** *Louis XVI Furniture.* New York, undated, c. 1910. . . . .   75.00   95.00

☐ **DeWald, E. T.** *Italian Painting 1200–1600.* New York, 1964. . . . .   13.00   17.00

☐ **Dewey, John.** *Art As Experience.* New York, 1934. . . . . . .   13.00   17.00

☐ **Dilke, Lady.** *French Furniture and Decoration in the XVIIth Century.* London, 1901. . . . .   60.00   75.00

☐ **Dillon, Edward.** *Porcelain.* London, 1904. . . . .   90.00   110.00

☐ **Dimand, M. S.** *Handbook of Muhammadan Art.* New York, 1947. . . . .   22.00   27.00

PRICE RANGE

☐ **Dixon, I. L.** *English Porcelain of the Eighteenth Century.* London, 1952. . . . . 8.00   10.00

☐ **Dockstader, F. J.** *Indian Art in North America.* Greenwich, 1961. . . . . 18.00   23.00

☐ **Dollman, F. T. and J. R. Jobbins.** *An Analysis of Ancient Domestic Architecture.* London, undated, mid Victorian. Two volumes. 100.00   125.00

☐ **Dorner, Gerd.** *Mexican Folk Art.* Munich, 1962. . . . . 18.00   23.00

☐ **Downing, A. J.** *The Architecture of Country Houses.* New York, 1852. . . . . 70.00   85.00

☐ **Dreppard, Carl W.** *American Clocks and Clockmakers.* Garden City, 1947. . . . . 22.00   28.00

☐ **Drummond, J.** *Ancient Scottish Weapons.* Edinburgh, 1881. . . . . 175.00   200.00

☐ **d'Ucel, Jeanne.** *Berber Art.* Norman, 1932. . . . . 45.00   55.00
The Berbers are a nomadic tribal people of Africa who have long puzzled anthropologists. They are the only white native tribespeople of Africa and their origins are unknown. It is thought they may have descended from soldiers of Alexander the Great's army.

☐ **Duncan, D. D.** *The Private World of Picasso.* New York, 1958. . . . . 10.00   15.00

☐ **Earle, A. M.** *Two Centuries of Costume in America.* New York, 1903. Two volumes. 80.00   100.00

☐ **Eberlein, H. D. and Abbot McClure.** *The Practical Book of Early American Arts and Crafts.* Philadelphia, 1916. . . . 18.00   23.00

☐ **Eberlein, H. D. and R. W. Ramsdell.** *The Practical Book of Chinaware.* New York, 1925. . . . . 18.00   23.00

☐ **Edwards, Ralph and Margaret Jourdain.** *Georgian Cabinet Makers.* London, 1944. . . . . 90.00   110.00

☐ **Evans, John.** *Ancient Bronze Implements, Weapons and Ornaments of Great Britain and Ireland.* New York, 1881. 85.00   105.00

☐ **Everett, Graham.** *English Caricaturists and Graphic Humorists of the Nineteenth Century.* London, 1886. . . . . 80.00   100.00

☐ **Faggin, Giorgio.** *The Complete Paintings of the Van Eycks.* New York, 1968. . . . . 9.00   12.00

☐ **Feder, Norman.** *American Indian Art.* New York, 1973. . . . 4.00   6.00

☐ **Fermigier, Andre.** *Pierre Bonnard.* New York, 1969. . . . . . . 30.00   40.00

☐ **Fischer, Jacques.** *The French Bronze, 1500–1800.* New York, 1968. . . . . 15.00   20.00

☐ **Fisher, Stanley W.** *English Blue and White Porcelain of the Eighteenth Century.* London, 1947. . . . . 40.00   50.00

☐ **Foley, Edwin.** *The Book of Decorative Furniture.* New York, 1911. . . . . 225.00   275.00

☐ **Forbes-Robertson, John.** *The Great Painters of Christendom.* London, undated, c. 1890. . . . . 70.00   85.00

☐ **Forster, Frank J.** *Country Houses.* New York, 1931. . . . . . . 35.00   40.00

☐ **Foster, J. E. and T. D. Atkinson.** *Catalogue of the Loan Collection of Plate Exhibited in the Fitzwilliam Museum.* Cambridge, England, 1895. Limited to 260 copies. 32.00   40.00

☐ **Foster, J. J.** *Miniature Painters.* London, 1903. Two volumes with 123 plates. 225.00   275.00

☐ **Foster, Joseph.** *Posters of Picasso.* New York, 1957. . . . . 45.00   55.00

PRICE RANGE

☐ **Freeman, Edward A.** *An Essay on the Origin and Development of Window Tracery in England.* Oxford, 1861 ..... 30.00 35.00

☐ **Frothingham, Alice.** *Spanish Glass.* London, 1964. ..... 27.00 33.00

☐ **Fry, Roger.** *Flemish Art, a Critical Survey.* London, 1927. 75.00 100.00

☐ **Fry, Roger.** *Last Lectures.* New York, 1939. .... 40.00 50.00
Flamboyant British art critic Roger Fry came to America in the early 1900s with the intention of becoming director of New York's Metropolitan Museum. He quickly became the darling of the New York art world, but did not achieve his goal. J. P. Morgan, the Metropolitan's chief benefactor, considered Fry too much of a "personality" to be the museum's director, and he was refused the post.

☐ **Furst, Herbert.** *The Modern Woodcut.* London, 1924. .... 40.00 50.00

☐ **Gangoly, O. C.** *South Indian Bronzes.* London, 1915. .... 220.00 265.00

☐ **Garavaglia, N.** *The Complete Paintings of Mantegna.* New York, 1967. .... 9.00 12.00

☐ **Garner, T. and A. Stratton.** *Domestic Architecture of England During the Tudor Period.* New York, 1929. Two volumes. 175.00 225.00

☐ **Gary, Elbert G.** *Notable Paintings and Works of Art, Collection of the Estate of Judge Elbert G. Gary.* New York, 1928. Two volumes. 45.00 55.00

☐ **Gask, N.** *Old Silver Spoons of England, A Practical Guide for Collectors.* London, 1926. With 32 plates. 90.00 110.00

☐ **Gibson, Katharine.** *The Goldsmiths of Florence.* New York, 1929. .... 30.00 35.00

☐ **Glazier, R.** *Historic Textile Fabrics.* London, 1923. .... 110.00 140.00

☐ **Goldscheider, L.** *Five Hundred Self Portraits from Antique Times to the Present Day.* Vienna, 1937. .... 45.00 55.00

☐ **Goldscheider, L.** *Michelangelo.* Greenwich, 1964. .... 22.00 27.00

☐ **Gombrich, E. H.** *The Story of Art.* London, 1950. .... 13.00 17.00

☐ **Goodhue, Bertram G.** *A Book of Architectural and Decorative Drawings.* New York, 1914. .... 50.00 60.00

☐ **Gordon, Jan.** *Modern French Painters.* London, 1929. .. 35.00 45.00

☐ **Gorer, Edgar.** *Catalogue of the Collection of Old Chinese Porcelains Formed by Richard Bennett.* London, 1911. .. 150.00 200.00

☐ **Gorham, Hazel.** *Japanese and Oriental Ceramics.* Rutland, Vermont, 1971. .... 26.00 34.00

☐ **Gotch, J. Alfred.** *Architecture of the Renaissance in England.* London, 1894. Two volumes. 80.00 100.00

☐ **Grandjean. S.** *Empire Furniture, 1800 to 1825.* London, 1966. .... 18.00 23.00

☐ **Grant, Campbell.** *Rock Art of the American Indian.* New York, 1967. .... 15.00 20.00

☐ **Grigson, Geoffrey.** *English Drawing From Samuel Cooper to Gwen John.* London, 1955. .... 17.00 22.00

☐ **Gromont, Georges.** *Italian Renaissance Architecture.* Paris, 1922. Two volumes. 50.00 60.00

☐ **Grose, Francis.** *The Antiquities of England, Wales and Scotland.* London, c. 1790–97. Ten volumes with a total of 814 plates, most of them hand colored. Bound in half morocco. 4500.00 5500.00

PRICE RANGE

☐ **Guinard, Paul.** *El Greco.* New York, 1956. . . . . — 15.00 — 20.00
☐ **Haggar, R. G.** *Staffordshire Chimney Ornaments.* London, 1955. . . . . — 45.00 — 55.00
☐ **Halsey, R. T. H. and E. Tower.** *The Homes of Our Ancestors, as Shown in the American Wing of the Metropolitan Museum.* New York, 1925. . . . . — 22.00 — 27.00
☐ **Hamerton, Philip G.** *The Graphic Arts.* London, 1882. . . . — 70.00 — 85.00
☐ **Hamilton, Sir William.** *Outlines from the Figures and Compositions Upon Greek, Roman and Etruscan Vases.* London, 1814. With 62 engraved plates. — 100.00 — 125.00
☐ **Hammacher, A. M.** *The Evolution of Modern Sculpture.* New York, 1969. . . . . — 60.00 — 75.00
☐ **Hartshorne, A.** *Old English Glasses, An Account of Glass Drinking Vessels in England.* London, 1897. . . . . — 100.00 — 125.00
☐ **Hartwick, A. S.** *Lithography as a Fine Art.* London, 1932. . . . . — 20.00 — 25.00
☐ **Hatton, Thomas.** *Water Colour Without a Master.* London, 1855. . . . . — 75.00 — 100.00
☐ **Havell, E. B.** *Indian Sculpture and Painting.* London, 1911. Two volumes. . . . . — 110.00 — 135.00
☐ **Havelock, C. M.** *Hellenistic Art.* London, 1971. . . . . — 22.00 — 27.00
☐ **Hawkshaw, J. C.** *Japanese Sword Mounts.* London, 1910. Limited to 300 copies, bound in cloth. . . . . — 800.00 — 1000.00
☐ **Hawley, Walter A.** *Oriental Rugs, Antique and Modern.* New York, 1937. . . . . — 110.00 — 140.00
☐ **Hayden, A.** *Royal Copenhagen Porcelain, Its History and Development from the Eighteenth Century to the Present Day.* London, 1911. . . . . — 75.00 — 100.00
☐ **Hayden, A.** *Spode and His Successors.* London, 1925. — 65.00 — 80.00
☐ **Head, Mrs.** *The Lace and Embroidery Collector.* London, 1922. . . . . — 25.00 — 30.00
☐ **Heal, A.** *Signboards of Old London Shops.* London, 1947. Special copy printed on large paper, bound in half morocco. . . . . — 200.00 — 250.00
The author was a prominent collector of antique trade signs, billheads, cards and other items related to early London shops.
☐ **Heal, Sir A.** *London Furniture Makers, 1660–1840.* London, 1953. . . . . — 70.00 — 90.00
☐ **Herberts, K.** *Oriental Lacquer.* London, 1962. With 104 colored plates. . . . . — 110.00 — 135.00
☐ **Hillier, J.** *Japanese Masters of the Color Print.* London, 1954. . . . . — 45.00 — 55.00
☐ **Hind, Arthur M.** *An Introduction to a History of Woodcut.* London, 1935. Two volumes bound in buckram with 480 illustrations. . . . . — 210.00 — 250.00
☐ **Hind, Arthur M.** *Early Italian Engraving.* London, 1938. Three volumes with 487 plates. . . . . — 300.00 — 400.00
☐ **Hobson, R. L.** *Catalogue of the Collection of English Porcelain in the Department of British and Medieval Antiquities of the British Museum.* London, 1905. . . . . — 80.00 — 100.00
☐ **Hodgson, Mrs. W.** *Old English China.* London, 1913. . . . . — 225.00 — 275.00

PRICE RANGE

□ **Hobson, R. L.** *A Catalogue of Chinese Pottery and Porcelain in the Collection of Sir Percival David.* London, 1934. With 180 plates, the majority colored, bound in silk and enclosed in a slipcase 1000.00   1250.00

□ **Hobson, R. L.** *Catalogue of the Leonard Gow Collection of Chinese Porcelain.* London, 1931. Morocco binding 700.00   900.00

□ **Hobson, R. L.** *The Romance of Chinese Art.* Garden City, 1936. . . . . 13.00   17.00

□ **Hobson, R. L.** *Wares of the Ming Dynasty.* London, 1923. Deluxe edition bound in pigskin, limited to 256 signed copies 300.00   400.00

□ **Hoffman, Malvina.** *Sculpture Inside and Out.* New York, undated c. 1939 . . . . 15.00   20.00

□ **Hofstatter, Hans.** *Art of the Late Middle Ages.* New York, 1968. . . . . 22.00   27.00

□ **Holme, Charles.** *Art in Photography.* London, 1905. Soft covered 200.00   250.00

□ **Holme, Charles.** *Modern Etching and Engraving.* London, 1902. Soft covered 50.00   60.00

□ **Homann-Wedeking, E.** *The Art of Archaic Greece.* New York, 1966 . . . . 15.00   20.00

□ **Honey, W. B.** *Dresden China.* London, 1934 . . . . 70.00   90.00

□ **Honour, Hugh.** *Cabinet Makers and Furniture Designers.* London, 1972 . . . . 40.00   50.00

□ **Howe, W. E.** *A History of the Metropolitan Museum of Art.* New York, 1913 . . . . 30.00   40.00

□ **Hughes, Robert.** *The Shock of the New.* New York, 1981. . . . . 20.00   25.00

□ **Humphreys, H. Noel.** *Masterpieces of the Early Printers and Engravers.* London, 1870 . . . . 375.00   450.00

□ **Humphries, Sydney.** *Oriental Carpets, Runners and Rugs.* London, 1910 . . . . 150.00   175.00

□ **Hunter, George L.** *Decorative Furniture.* Philadelphia, 1923. . . . . 140.00   170.00

□ **Hunter, George L.** *Decorative Textiles.* Philadelphia, 1918. . . . . 150.00   175.00

□ **Hunter, George L.** *The Practical Book of Tapestries.* Philadelphia, 1925 . . . . 30.00   40.00

□ **Hurlbutt, Frank.** *Bow Porcelain.* London, 1926 . . . . 60.00   75.00

□ **Hurlbutt, F.** *Old Derby Porcelain and its Artist Workmen.* London, 1925. With 59 plates, bound in half vellum 25.00   30.00

□ **Huyghe, Rene.** *Larousse Encyclopedia of Prehistoric and Ancient Art.* New York, 1962 . . . . 20.00   25.00

□ **Hyde, J. A. L.** *Oriental Lowestoft.* New York, 1936 . . . . 65.00   85.00

□ **Jackson, C. J.** *An Illustrated History of English Plate.* London, 1911. Two volumes with 76 photographic plates about 1,500 other illustrations. Bound in half morocco 300.00   350.00

□ **Jackson, Thomas G.** *Byzantine and Romanesque Architecture.* Cambridge, England, 1920 . . . . 150.00   200.00

□ **Jacobus, John.** *Henri Matisse.* New York, 1972 . . . . 40.00   50.00

□ **Jarves, J. J.** *The Old Masters of Italy.* New York, 1861. Two volumes 75.00   100.00

PRICE RANGE

☐ **Jean, Marcel.** *The History of Surrealist Painting.* New York, 1967. . . . . 26.00 34.00

☐ **Jewitt, L.** *The Wedgewoods.* London, 1865. Bound in gilt stamped cloth. 30.00 40.00

☐ **Jobe, Joseph.** *Great Tapestries.* Lausanne, 1965. . . . . 75.00 100.00

☐ **John, W. D.** *Pontypool and Usk Japanned Wares.* Newport, 1953. . . . . 30.00 40.00

☐ **John, W. D. and W. Baker.** *Old English Lustre Pottery.* Newport, 1951. . . . . 50.00 60.00

☐ **Jonas, F. M.** *Netsuke.* London, 1928. With 55 plates. 275.00 325.00

☐ **Jones, E. A.** *A Catalogue of the Objects in Gold and Silver and the Limoges Enamels in the Collection of the Baroness James de Rothschild.* London, 1912. Limited to 175 copies. 375.00 450.00

☐ **Jones, E. Alfred.** *Catalogue of Plate Belonging to the Duke of Portland.* London, 1935. . . . . 100.00 125.00

☐ **Jones, E. Alfred.** *Old Silver of Europe and America.* Philadelphia, 1928. . . . . 90.00 110.00

☐ **Jones, Owen.** *The Grammar of Ornament.* London, 1868. Bound in half morocco. 250.00 300.00

☐ **Jourdain, Margaret.** *The Decoration and Furniture of English Mansions During the Seventeenth and Eighteenth Centuries.* London, 1909. . . . . 110.00 140.00

☐ **Justice, J.** *Dictionary of Marks and Monograms on Delft Pottery.* London, 1930. . . . . 40.00 50.00

☐ **Katzenbach, L. and W.** *Practical Book of American Wallpaper.* Philadelphia, 1951. . . . . 60.00 80.00

☐ **Kauffman, H. J.** *The American Pewterer.* Camden, 1970. . . . . 15.00 20.00

☐ **Kauffman, Henry.** *Early American Ironware.* Rutland, 1967. . . . . 25.00 30.00

☐ **Kelder, Diane.** *Pageant of the Renaissance.* New York, 1966. . . . . 9.00 12.00

☐ **Kelly, F. M. and R. Schwabe.** *Historic Costume, a Chronicle of Fashion in Western Europe 1490–1790.* London, 1925. With 7 colored and 63 uncolored plates. 12.00 15.00

☐ **Kendrick, A. F.** *English Embroidery.* London, 1904. . . . . . 30.00 37.00

☐ **Kenney, J. T.** *The Hitchcock Chair.* New York, 1971. . . . . 40.00 50.00

☐ **Kerfoot, J. B.** *American Pewter.* New York, undated, c 1960 (reprint of an earlier work). 18.00 23.00

☐ **Kettell, R. H.** *The Pine Furniture of Early New England.* Garden City, 1929. . . . . 125.00 150.00

☐ **King, William.** *Chelsea Porcelain.* London, 1922. . . . . 70.00 90.00

☐ **Kitson, Michael.** *The Complete Paintings of Caravaggio.* New York, 1967. . . . . 9.00 12.00

☐ **Klein, Jerome.** *Cezanne and French Painting.* Philadelphia, 1934. . . . . 9.00 12.00

☐ **Koof, A. J.** *Early Chinese Bronzes.* London, 1924. . . . . . . 100.00 125.00

☐ **Kowalczyk, George.** *Decorative Sculpture.* New York, 1927. . . . . 50.00 65.00

☐ **Krell, P. F.** *The Classics of Painting.* London, undated, c 1880. . . . . 70.00 85.00

PRICE RANGE

☐ **Kuwayama, George.** *Ancient Ritual Bronzes of China.* Los Angeles, 1976. Soft covered. 9.00   12.00

☐ **Laking, Sir Guy.** *The Furniture of Windsor Castle.* London, 1905. Bound in quarter pigskin. 200.00   250.00

☐ **Lamb, Martha.** *The Homes of America.* New York, undated, c. 1879. . . . . 100.00   125.00

☐ **Lane, Arthur.** *English Porcelain Figures of the Eighteenth Century.* New York, 1961. . . . . 18.00   23.00

☐ **Law, Ernest.** *History of Hampton Court Palace.* London, 1888–91. Three volumes. 200.00   275.00

☐ **LeCorbeiller, C.** *European and American Snuff Boxes 1730 to 1830.* London, 1966. . . . . 40.00   50.00

☐ **Leicht, Hermann.** *History of the World's Art.* London, 1952. . . . . 35.00   45.00

☐ **Lejard, Andre.** *French Tapestry.* Paris, 1947. . . . . 30.00   35.00

☐ **Lenygon, Francis.** *Decorations in England from 1660 to 1770.* London, undated. 40.00   50.00

☐ **Lewis, A. B.** *Block Prints from India.* Chicago, 1924. . . . . 13.00   17.00

☐ **Lewis, G. G.** *The Practical Book of Oriental Rugs.* London, 1920. Fifth edition. 100.00   125.00

☐ **Lewis, J. S.** *Old Glass and How to Collect It.* New York, 1925. . . . . 22.00   28.00

☐ **Lipman, Jean.** *American Primitive Painting.* London, 1942. . . . . 70.00   90.00

☐ **Lipman, Jean.** *The Collector in America.* New York, 1971. . . . . 15.00   20.00

☐ **Lockwood, Luke V.** *Colonial Furniture in America.* New York, 1913. Two volumes. 150.00   200.00

☐ **Longman, E. D. and S. Loch.** *Pins and Pincushions.* London, 1911. . . . . 65.00   85.00

☐ **Loran, Erle.** *Cezanne's Composition.* Berkeley, 1963. . . . . 13.00   17.00

☐ **Luebke, Wilhelm.** *Ecclesiastical Art in Germany During the Middle Ages.* Edinburgh, 1873. . . . . 40.00   50.00

☐ **Luxmoore, C. F.** *English Saltglazed Earthenware.* Exeter, 1924. With 89 plates, four of which are colored. Not first edition. 200.00   260.00

☐ **Lynch, B.** *Max Beerbohm in Perspective.* London, 1921. 35.00   45.00

☐ **Lyon, Irving W.** *Colonial Furniture of New England.* Boston, 1892. . . . . 100.00   125.00

☐ **MacFall, Haldane.** *A History of Painting.* Boston, undated, c. 1910. Eight volumes, Milan edition, limited to 100 copies. 500.00   600.00

☐ **Mack, G.** *Gustave Courbet.* New York, 1951. . . . . 13.00   17.00

☐ **Mack, G. and T. Gibson.** *Architectural Details of Southern Spain.* New York, 1928. . . . . 35.00   45.00

☐ **Mackenna, F. S.** *Cookworthy's Plymouth and Bristol Porcelain.* Leigh on Sea, 1946. . . . . 110.00   140.00

☐ **MackIntosh, Sir H.** *Early English Figure Pottery.* London, 1938. . . . . 100.00   125.00

☐ **Macquoid, Percy and Ralph Edwards.** *The Dictionary of English Furniture.* London, 1924–27. Three volumes. 600.00   750.00

☐ **Malan, A. H.** *Famous Homes of Great Britain and Their Stories.* New York, 1900. . . . . 30.00   40.00

PRICE RANGE

☐ **Malone, E.** *The Works of Sir Joshua Reynolds.* London, 1798. Two volumes....................................	75.00	100.00
☐ **Mariacher, Giovanni.** *Italian Blown Glass from Ancient Rome to Venice.* London, 1961.........................	75.00	100.00
☐ **Maskell, Alfred.** *Ivories.* Rutland, Vermont, 1966.........	75.00	95.00
☐ **Maskell, Alfred.** *Wood Sculpture.* New York, 1911.......	50.00	60.00
☐ **May, John.** *Commemorative Pottery 1780–1900.* New York, 1973.	22.00	28.00
☐ **McClellan, Elisabeth.** *History of American Costume.* New York, 1937..	30.00	40.00
☐ **McClelland, Nancy.** *Furnishing the Colonial and Federal House.* Philadelphia, 1947........................	18.00	23.00
☐ **McClinton, Katharine M.** *Antique Collecting for Everyone.* New York, 1951.......................................	13.00	17.00
☐ **McGrew, C. B.** *Italian Doorways.* Cleveland, 1929.	60.00	80.00
☐ **McKearin, George and Helen.** *American Glass.* New York, 1948.	22.00	27.00
☐ **McLaughlin, M. L.** *China Painting.* Cincinnati, 1894......	8.00	10.00
☐ **Meier-Graefe, Julius.** *Modern Art.* New York, 1908. Two volumes.	60.00	75.00
☐ **Mew, Egan.** *Battersea Enamels.* London, 1926...........	55.00	70.00
☐ **Meyer, Karl E.** *The Plundered Past.* New York, 1973.....	9.00	12.00
☐ **Meyrick, Sir Samuel.** *Engraved Illustrations of Ancient Arms and Armour from the Collection at Goodrich Court, Herefordshire.* London, 1830. Two volumes with 151 engraved plates......................................	400.00	500.00
☐ **Millar, O.** *Italian Drawings and Paintings in the Queen's Collection.* London, 1965.	125.00	150.00
☐ **Millard, S. T.** *Opaque Glass.* Topeka, 1941..............	35.00	45.00
☐ **Mitchell, P.** *European Flower Painters.* London, 1973. Bound in half morocco.................................	110.00	135.00
☐ **Monier, P.** *The History of Painting, Architecture, Sculpture, Graving, etc.* London, Printed for T. Bennet, 1699........	200.00	250.00
☐ **Monson-Fitzjohn, G. J.** *Drinking Vessels of Bygone Days.* London, 1927..	45.00	55.00
☐ **Morse, F. C.** *Furniture in the Olden Time.* New York, 1936.	13.00	17.00
☐ **Moses, H.** *A Collection of Antique Vases, Altars, Candelabra etc., From Various Museums and Collections.* London, 1814. With 151 plates, 15 of which are colored......	110.00	135.00
☐ **Mueller, Hans.** *Woodcuts and Wood Engravings.* New York, 1939.	70.00	85.00
☐ **Muentz, Eugene.** *A Short History of Tapestry.* London, 1885.	25.00	30.00
☐ **Mulliner, H. H.** *Decorative Arts in England from 1660 to 1780.* London, 1923. Bound in half vellum..............	45.00	55.00
☐ **Mumford, J. K.** *Oriental Rugs.* New York, 1905. Third edition...	225.00	275.00
☐ **Mutherich, F.** *Carolingian Painting.* New York, 1976.	9.00	12.00
☐ **Nash, Joseph.** *The Mansions of England in the Olden Times.* London, 1869...................................	275.00	350.00
☐ **Naunton, G. H.** *Japanese Sword Fittings.* London, 1912.	600.00	750.00

	PRICE RANGE	
☐ **Nelson, Philip.** *Ancient Painted Glass in England, 1170–1500.* London, 1913.	60.00	75.00
☐ **Nettlefold, F. J.** *The Collection of Bronzes and Castings in Brass and Ormolu Formed by F. J. Nettlefold.* London, 1934.	100.00	125.00
☐ **Neurdenburg, E.** *Old Dutch Pottery and Tiles.* London, 1923.	100.00	125.00
☐ **Nevill, Ralph.** *Old French Line Engravings.* London, 1924.	40.00	50.00
☐ **Newcombe, Rexford.** *Old Kentucky Architecture.* New York, 1940.	75.00	100.00
☐ **Nightingale, J. E.** *Contributions Toward the History of Early English Porcelain.* Salisbury, printed for private circulation, 1881.	80.00	100.00
☐ **Nobili, Riccardo.** *The Gentle Art of Faking.* London, 1922.	30.00	35.00
☐ **Novotny, Fritz.** *Painting and Sculpture in Europe, 1780 to 1880.* New York, 1970.	35.00	45.00
☐ **Oakie, Howard P.** *Old Silver and Old Sheffield Plate.* New York, 1936.	100.00	125.00
☐ **Oertel, Robert.** *Early Italian Painting.* New York, 1966.	26.00	34.00
☐ **Olivar, Marcial.** *The Art Museum of Catalonia.* New York, 1963.	13.00	17.00
☐ **Ormsbee, T. H.** *Early American Furniture Makers.* New York, 1935.	20.00	25.00
☐ **Palmer, Brooks.** *The Book of American Clocks.* New York, 1950.	22.00	27.00
☐ **Parker, J. H.** *Domestic Architecture in England.* Oxford, 1857–59. Four volumes.	80.00	100.00
☐ **Peacock, Edward.** *English Church Furniture.* London, 1866.	25.00	30.00
☐ **Peck, Herbert.** *The Book of Rookwood Pottery.* New York, 1968.	26.00	34.00
☐ **Pennell, Joseph.** *Adventures of an Illustrator.* Boston, 1925.	30.00	35.00
☐ **Pennell, Joseph.** *Etchers and Etching.* New York, 1919. Limited to 100 signed copies.	120.00	150.00
☐ **Penrose, R.** *Picasso, His Life and Work.* New York, 1959.	13.00	17.00
☐ **Perkins, Charles C.** *Tuscan Sculptors.* London, 1864. Two volumes.	110.00	140.00
☐ **Phillips, Duncan.** *A collection in the Making.* New York, undated, c. 1926.	35.00	45.00
☐ **Phillips, F. W.** *A Short Account of Old English Pottery.* London, 1901.	10.00	13.00
☐ **Phillips, John G.** *China Trade Porcelain.* Cambridge, Massachusetts, 1956.	90.00	110.00
☐ **Pijoan, Joseph.** *History of Art.* New York, 1927. Three volumes.	50.00	60.00
☐ **Pilkington, Matthew.** *Dictionary of Painters.* London, 1810.	50.00	60.00
☐ **Piper, John.** *British Romantic Artists.* London, 1942.	9.00	12.00

PRICE RANGE

☐ **Pope, Arthur.** *A Survey of Persian Art From Prehistoric Times to the Present.* Oxford, 1938–58. Six volumes with 1,500 plates. Bound in blue buckram. 1100.00   1300.00

☐ **Pope-Hennessy, John.** *Fra Angelico.* Ithaca, 1974. . . . . . 22.00   28.00

☐ **Porada, Edith.** *The Art of Ancient Iran.* New York, 1965. 15.00   20.00

☐ **Puyvelde, Leo Van.** *The Dutch Drawings in the Collection of His Majesty the King, at Windsor Castle.* London, 1944. . . . . 35.00   45.00

☐ **Pyne, W. H.** *The History of the Royal Residences.* London, 1819. Three volumes, with 100 hand colored aquatints. . . 2000.00   2500.00

☐ **Racinet, Auguste.** *Polychromatic Ornament.* One Hundred Plates in Gold, Silver and Colours, Comprising Upwards of 2,000 Specimens of Ancient, Oriental and Medieval Art, etc. London, 1877. Large folio, half morocco, gilt top. 1000.00   1250.00

☐ **Rackham, Bernard.** *Catalogue of the English Porcelain, Earthenware, Enamels and Glass, collected by Charles and Lady Scribner and Presented to the South Kensington Museum in 1884.* London, 1924–30. Three volumes. 300.00   350.00

☐ **Radnor, Earl of.** *Catalogue of the Pictures in the Collection of the Earl of Radnor.* London, 1909. Two volumes, limited to 200 copies. 200.00   250.00

☐ **Ramsey, S. and J. D. M. Harvey.** *Small Houses of the Late Georgian Period, 1750–1820.* London, 1919–23. Two volumes. 70.00   85.00

☐ **Raynal, M.** *Modern French Painters.* New York, 1934. . . . 15.00   20.00

☐ **Read, Herbert.** *Art and Industry.* London, 1934. . . . . 20.00   25.00

☐ **Reagan, Oliver.** *American Architecture of the Twentieth Century.* New York, undated, c. 1927. 75.00   95.00

☐ **Reau, Louis.** *Fragonard.* Paris, 1938. . . . . 13.00   17.00

☐ **Reitlinger, H. S.** *Old Master Drawings.* London, 1922. . . . 60.00   75.00

☐ **Reitz, S. C.** *Catalogue of an Exhibition of Early Chinese Pottery and Sculpture.* New York, 1916. . . . . 10.00   15.00

☐ **Rhead, G. W.** *History of the Fan.* London, 1910. Limited to 450 copies, with 27 colored and 100 plain plates. 550.00   650.00

☐ **Ritchie, A. C.** *Abstract Painting and Sculpture in America.* New York, 1951. . . . . 15.00   20.00

☐ **Rivoira, G. T.** *Lombardic Architecture.* London, 1910. . . . 120.00   150.00

☐ **Roberts, W.** *Memorials of Christie's, a Record of Art Sales from 1766 to 1896.* London, 1897. Two volumes. 100.00   125.00

☐ **Robertson, Martin.** *Greek Painting.* Geneva, 1959. . . . . . . 40.00   50.00

☐ **Rodier, Paul.** *The Romance of French Weaving.* New York, 1931. . . . . 25.00   30.00

☐ **Rodin, Auguste.** *On Art and Artists.* New York, 1957. . . . 13.00   17.00

☐ **Roditi, E.** *Dialogues on Art.* London, 1960. . . . . 13.00   17.00

☐ **Roth, H. Ling.** *Oriental Silverwork.* London, 1910. . . . . 45.00   55.00

☐ **Rothenstein, W.** *Goya.* New York, 1901. . . . . 7.00   10.00

☐ **Rowlands, Walter.** *Recent English Art.* Boston, 1889. . . . 60.00   75.00

☐ **Russell, C. E.** *English Mezzotint Portraits.* London, 1926. . . . . 200.00   250.00

☐ **Sabartes, Jaime.** *Paintings and Drawings of Picasso.* Paris, 1946. . . . . 10.00   15.00

☐ **Sack, Albert.** *Fine Points of Furniture.* New York, 1955. 22.00   28.00

PRICE RANGE

☐ **Sadleir, Michael.** *Daumier, the Man and the Artist.* London, 1924. . . . . 85.00   110.00
☐ **Saglio, A.** *French Furniture.* London, 1913. . . . . 12.00   16.00
☐ **Salaman, M. C.** *French Color Prints of the XVIII Century.* Philadelphia, 1913. . . . . 60.00   75.00
☐ **Sanborn, Kate.** *Old Time Wall Papers.* New York, 1905.   125.00   150.00
☐ **Schapiro, Meyer.** *Romanesque Art.* New York, 1977. . . . . 15.00   20.00
☐ **Schendel, A. van.** *Camera Studies of Dutch Master Paintings.* Amsterdam, 1949. . . . . 45.00   55.00
☐ **Schug, Albert.** *Art of the Twentieth Century.* New York, 1969. . . . . 22.00   28.00
☐ **Scott, L.** *Renaissance Art in Italy, an Illustrated History.* New York, 1883. . . . . 35.00   45.00
☐ **Scott, Mary W.** *Houses of Old Richmond.* Richmond, 1941. . . . . 75.00   100.00
☐ **Seidlitz, W. von.** *A History of Japanese Colour Prints.* London, 1910. . . . . 100.00   125.00
☐ **Shaw, H.** *Specimens of Ancient Furniture.* London, published by Pickering, 1836. Cloth bound, with 74 plates of which 11 are in color. 125.00   150.00
☐ **Shaw, Richard N.** *Architectural Sketches from the Continent.* London, 1872. . . . . 125.00   175.00
☐ **Shaw, S.** *History of the Staffordshire Potteries.* London, 1829. . . . . 200.00   250.00
☐ **Sheraton, T.** *The Cabinet-Maker and Upholsterer's Drawing Book.* London, 1895. . . . . 60.00   75.00
☐ **Short, Ernest H.** *The Painter in History.* London, 1929. . . 35.00   45.00
☐ **Simpson, F. M.** *History of Architectural Development.* London, 1905–13. Three volumes. 55.00   70.00
☐ **Singleton, E.** *The Furniture of our Forefathers.* London, 1901. Bound in boards with a vellum spine, 346 illustrations. 150.00   200.00
☐ **Siren, O.** *The Walls and Gates of Peking.* London, 1924. Limited to 800 copies. 175.00   225.00
☐ **Sitwell, S.** *Southern Baroque Art.* London, 1931. . . . . 18.00   23.00
☐ **Sloane, Eric.** *A Museum of Early American Tools.* New York, 1964. . . . . 7.00   10.00
☐ **Smith, Alan.** *An Illustrated Guide to Liverpool Herculaneum Pottery, 1796–1840.* New York, 1970. . . . . 30.00   40.00
This was English pottery with designs bsed on artwork from the Italian city of Herculaneum, which was buried by volcanic eruption in 79 A.D.
☐ **Smith, H. C.** *Buckingham Palace, Its Furniture, Decoration etc.* London, 1930. . . . . 22.00   27.00
☐ **Soby, J. T.** *Contemporary Painters.* New York, 1948. . . . . 40.00   50.00
☐ **Solon, M. L.** *A History and Description of the Old French Faience.* London, 1903. . . . . 75.00   100.00
☐ **Soria, Martin S.** *The Paintings of Zubaran.* New York, 1953. . . . . 40.00   50.00
☐ **Spargo, John.** *The ABC of Bennington Pottery Wares.* Bennington, 1938. . . . . 15.00   20.00
☐ **Sparrow, Walter S.** *A Book of British Etching.* London, 1927. . . . . 45.00   55.00

	PRICE RANGE	
☐ **Speaight, Robert.** *The Life of Eric Gill.* London, 1966. . . .	11.00	15.00
☐ **Spearing, H. G.** *Childhood of Art.* New York, 1913.	50.00	60.00
☐ **Speltz, Alexander.** *The Coloured Ornament of All Historical Styles.* Leipzig, 1914–15. Folio, loose in three portfolios.	200.00	250.00
☐ **Spofford, Harriet P.** *Art Decoration Applied to Furniture.* New York, 1877.	55.00	70.00
☐ **Stokes, M.** *Early Christian Architecture in Ireland.* London, 1878.	60.00	75.00
☐ **Stone, Lawrence.** *Sculpture in Britain in the Middle Ages.* New York, 1972.	35.00	45.00
☐ **Stranahan, C. H.** *A History of French Paintings from its Earliest to its Latest Practice.* New York, 1888.	45.00	55.00
☐ **Stratton, Arthur.** *The English Interior, A Review of the Decoration of English Homes from Tudor Times to the XIXth Century.* London, 1920. Folio, bound in half vellum.	75.00	100.00
☐ **Sunderland, John.** *The Complete Paintings of Watteau.* New York, 1968.	9.00	12.00
☐ **Sutton, Denys.** *French Drawings of the Eighteenth Century.* London, 1949.	25.00	30.00
☐ **Swindler, M. H.** *Ancient Painting.* New Haven, 1929.	75.00	100.00
☐ **Symonds, R. W.** *English Furniture from Charles II to George II.* London, 1929. With four colored and 259 uncolored plates.	100.00	125.00
☐ **Symonds, R. W.** *Furniture Making in Seventeenth and Eighteenth Century England.* London, 1955. Bound in half vellum, slipcased.	250.00	300.00
☐ **Symonds, R. W.** *Masterpieces of English Furniture and Clocks.* London, 1940. Limited to 750 copies.	110.00	140.00
☐ **Symonds, R. W.** *Old English Walnut and Lacquer Furniture.* London, 1923.	50.00	60.00
☐ **Taki, Seiichi.** *Japanese Fine Art.* Tokyo, 1931.	50.00	65.00
☐ **Talbot, S.** *The Marvelous Book: An Album Containing One Hundred Studies of Famous Chinese Porcelains.* Shanghai, 1930. Bound in silk.	175.00	200.00
☐ **Taylor, Basil.** *French Painting.* London, 1951.	30.00	35.00
☐ **Taylor, H. H.** *Knowing, Collecting and Restoring Early American Furniture.* Philadelphia, 1930.	13.00	17.00
☐ **Taylor, R. A.** *Leonardo the Florentine.* New York, 1928. . .	4.00	6.00
☐ **Thompson, D. C.** *The Landscapes of Corot.* London, 1914.	60.00	75.00
☐ **Tilley, F.** *Teapots and Tea.* Newport, 1957.	55.00	65.00
☐ **Tomioka, K.** *Ancient Chinese Mirrors from the Collection of the late Kenzo Tomioka.* Kyoto, 1924. Bound in silk. . . .	125.00	150.00
☐ **Tristram, E. W.** *English Wall Painting of the Fourteenth Century.* London, 1955.	22.00	28.00
☐ **Tsuda, Noritake.** *Handbook of Japanese Art.* Tokyo, 1935.	80.00	100.00
☐ **Turner, Laurence.** *Decorative Plasterwork in Great Britain.* London, 1927.	110.00	140.00
☐ **Turner, W.** *The Ceramics of Swansea.* London, 1897.	80.00	100.00
☐ **Uhde, Wilhelm.** *The Impressionists.* Vienna, 1937.	20.00	25.00

PRICE RANGE

☐ **Vaillant, George C.** *Artists and Craftsmen in Ancient Central America.* New York, 1940.	10.00	15.00
☐ **Vallentin, A.** *Leonardo DaVinci.* New York, 1938.	43.00	56.00
☐ **Van Pelt, Garrett.** *Old Architecture of Southern Mexico.* Cleveland, 1926.	80.00	100.00
☐ **Van Tassel, V.** *American Glass.* New York, 1950.	7.00	10.00
☐ **Vayer, Lajos.** *Master Drawings from the Collection of the Budapest Museum of Fine Arts.* New York, 1957.	65.00	85.00
☐ **Waley, Arthur.** *An Introduction to the Study of Chinese Painting.* London, 1923.	60.00	75.00
☐ **Walkowitz, A.** *One Hundred Drawings.* New York, 1925.	50.00	60.00
☐ **Walpole, Horace.** *Anecdotes of Painting in England.* London, 1828. Five volumes.	200.00	300.00
☐ **Walton, Perry.** *The Story of Textiles.* Boston, 1912.	40.00	50.00
☐ **Ware, W. R.** *The Georgian Period.* New York, 1923. Six volumes.	300.00	400.00
☐ **Waring, J. B.** *Masterpieces of Industrial Art and Sculpture at the International Exhibition.* London, 1862. Three volumes.	400.00	500.00
☐ **Warner, Langdon.** *The Craft of the Japanese Sculptor.* New York, 1936.	50.00	60.00
☐ **Waterman, Thomas T.** *The Mansions of Virginia 1706–1776.* Chapel Hill, 1946.	40.00	50.00
☐ **Weighall, Arthur.** *Ancient Egyptian Works of Art.* London, 1924.	60.00	75.00
☐ **Wenham, Edward.** *Domestic Silver of Great Britain and Ireland.* New York, 1935.	40.00	50.00
☐ **Werner, Alfred.** *Amedeo Modigliani.* New York, 1967.	26.00	34.00
☐ **Wheatley, Richard.** *Cathedrals and Abbeys in Great Britain and Ireland.* New York, 1890.	120.00	150.00
☐ **White, Stanford.** *Sketches and Designs.* New York, 1920.	50.00	60.00
☐ **Wilenski, R. H.** *Modern French Painters.* London, 1944.	35.00	45.00
☐ **Wilkinson, Nevile.** *Wilton House Pictures.* London, 1907. Two volumes.	110.00	140.00
☐ **Williamson, G. C.** *The Book of Ivory.* London, 1938.	45.00	55.00
☐ **Williamson, G. C.** *The History of Portrait Miniatures.* London, printed by the Chiswick Press, 1904. Two volumes, printed on handmade paper, bound in half morocco.	375.00	450.00
☐ **Williamson, George C.** *Velazquez.* London, 1901.	7.00	10.00
☐ **Willshire, William H.** *An Introduction to the Study and Collection of Ancient Prints.* London, 1874.	50.00	65.00
This book is very hard to find in well preserved condition, probably because it was extensively used for reference.		
☐ **Wollin, Dr. Nils.** *Modern Swedish Decorative Art.* London, 1931.	10.00	15.00
☐ **Worlidge, T.** *A Select Collection of Drawings From Curious Antique Gems.* London, 1768. Two volumes, large paper edition bound in straight grained morocco.	250.00	300.00
☐ **Wyler, Seymour.** *The Book of Old Silver.* New York, 1949.	18.00	23.00

PRICE RANGE

☐ **Yashiro, Yukio.** *Sandro Botticelli.* London, 1925. Three
    volumes. 130.00   155.00
☐ **Young, J.** *The Ceramic Art.* London, 1879. . . . .   35.00   45.00

BIBLES

No book has been published as frequently as the Bible. Nor is there any book over which so much misunderstanding reigns, so far as collector value goes. Most people believe their "old family Bible" to be valuable and are surprised and disappointed to discover this is seldom the case. It **must** be valuable, they contend, because of its age ("my great-grandfather owned it"), or its size ("I can hardly lift it"), neither of which amounts to much on the antiquarian market. Nor do its sentimental attachments.

Why aren't collectors interested in a Bible 100 years old, when many books of more recent date are valuable? Because bibliophiles concern themselves with the importance of the edition. Having been published and republished, translated, reprinted and facsimilized endlessly through the centuries, few editions of the Bible are bibliographically important. They are simply reissues of reissues, with nothing new or noteworthy to offer.

But do not automatically assume the old family Bible is worthless. It may have a handsome binding or a good series of copperplates, in which event it should bring some kind of price.

The value of common old Bibles rests very much with their bindings. An attractive showy binding in full gilt calf or morocco, well preserved, may lend a value of $50-$100 to a Bible otherwise worth $10. Most large folio Bibles of the 1800's—say fifteen inches tall or larger—fall in that category. Without a good binding their value is not much more than waste paper. The exception is heavily illustrated editions with several dozen (at least) engraved plates, whose value is generally figured at $1 per plate plus a premium if the binding is good.

Small (8vo and 12mo) Bibles later than 1800 are almost uniformly valueless, especially if printed abroad. Miniature Bibles that can qualify as true miniatures, three inches high or less, are of course another matter. There is a market for these, but only at moderate prices. None are worth a fortune.

The fact that a Bible has been in the same family for generations and bears records of births and marriages does not add to its value unless the family is prominent or the volume can be sold to a genealogist for research use.

Listed below are Bibles that **are** of value, including some of great value. This is by no means a complete listing of all valuable editions. As a rough guide, it can be assumed with almost certainty that any Bible printed in continental Europe before 1600, in England before 1700, or in America before 1800, has some value.

As for incunable (15th century) Bibles, the price for a copy with good rubrication (hand painted decoration) is always higher than for a plain copy.

Contemporary bindings well preserved help, too. Many of these Bibles, when rebound in the 18th and 19th centuries, received coverings many times handsomer and flashier than the originals; nevertheless, collectors want them in 15th century bindings when possible.

Latin Bible ("Biblia Latina"). Known as the Gutenberg or 42-line Bible. N.p., n.d. (Mainz, Germany, c. 1454). **$2,225,000.00-$3,000,000.00**

Large folio, about 16 × 12 inches, 643 leaves, usually bound in two, sometimes in three, volumes. Since 1977 two copies have been sold, one for $2,000,000, the other $2,300,000. This is an increase in price of perhaps 500,000% over the first recorded appearance of a Gutenberg Bible in a bookseller's catalogue, when a London dealer named Richardson offered one at a pound sterling in 1750.

Though no longer believed (as it once was) to be the first book printed from moveable type, the Gutenberg Bible was unquestionably the first major undertaking for the printing press. It was preceded by the far rarer **Constance Missal**, two or three years earlier. The value of a complete Constance Missal, if one came on the market today, would approach that of the Gutenberg Bible. It is a much smaller book physically and not as professionally designed.

The Gutenberg Bible carries no identification of printer, place of publication, or date. There is no doubt that it was printed at Mainz (Mayence or, as bibliographers once spelled it, Moguntiae) by Gutenberg and his associates Johannes Fust and Peter Schoeffer. The date can only be estimated. A copy of the Bibliotheque Nationale of Paris has a handwritten date of 1456, placed by a rubicator who added colored initials and marginal decoration, so it must have left the presses by then. Just how much earlier, if any, is hard to say. The experts lean to a dating of 1454. Undoubtedly it was in production several years, being an enormous project. The edition size has been guessed at 300 to 500 copies. Most were printed on paper, some copies on vellum. The vellum copies are more highly prized. None have been sold in many years; the probable current value would be three to four million dollars.

To an untrained eye the Gutenberg Bible looks no different than other "black letter" or gothic-type Bibles of the 15th century. If you think you've found one, count the lines on a page. There should be 42, not including the headline. But some other Bibles had 42-line pages, too.

About all the collector can hope to own are single leaves. These are plentiful but expensive. In 1921 the New York bookseller Gabriel Wells bought an incomplete Gutenberg Bible, consisting of about 600 leaves. Instead of selling it that way he separated the leaves and sold them individually, set into an embossed leather binding by Stikeman and accompanied by an essay by A. Edward Newton, entitled *A Noble Fragment*. The price of this work has climbed meteorically over the years; $200 was the auction price in 1939, today the value is $7,000 or more. Another incomplete copy (more incomplete than Wells') was later broken up by New York's Scribner Bookshop.

Facsimilies of the Gutenberg Bible can also be costly. The best one so far produced (two volumes, Leipzig, 1913–14) sells for $6,000–8,000.

Forty-eight copies of the Gutenberg Bible, some of them consisting of only one volume and most lacking one or more leaves, are known to exist.

The majority are housed in European state libraries but the U.S. owns a fair showing of Gutenberg Bibles. Copies can be seen at the Pierpont Morgan Library, New York (one vellum, one paper, and ½ of a second paper copy); New York Public Library (the Lenox copy, the first Gutenberg Bible owned in America); Yale University (Harkness copy); Harvard University; Princeton University (Scheide copy); Henry E. Huntington Library, San Marino, California (Robert Hoe's vellum copy); Library of Congress (Vollbehr copy); and elsewhere.

PRICE RANGE

- ☐ **Biblia Latina.** Mainz, Johann Fust and Peter Schoeffer, 1462. Copies are on both paper and vellum
  Paper. 20000.00 27500.00
  Vellum. 100000.00 150000.00
- ☐ **Biblia Latina.** N.p., n.d. (Basel, Bernhard Richel, not after 1474). 4750.00 6500.00
- ☐ **Biblia Latina.** Venice, Franciscus Renner de Heilbronn and Nicolaus de Francofordia, 1474. . . . . 4500.00 6000.00
- ☐ **Biblia Latina.** Nuremberg, Johann Sensenschmidt and Andreas Frisner, 1475. . . . . 3750.00 5000.00
- ☐ **Biblia Latina.** Naples, Mathias Moravus, 1476. . . . . 900.00 1200.00
- ☐ **Biblia Latina.** Venice, Nicolaus Jenson, 1476. . . . . 4200.00 5000.00
- ☐ **Biblia Latina.** Nuremberg, Anton Koberger, 1477. . . . . 5000.00 7000.00
- ☐ **Biblia Latina.** Venice, Reynaldus de Novimagio and Theodorus de Reynsburch, 1478. . . . . 1300.00 1600.00
- ☐ **Biblia Latina.** Nuremberg, Anton Koberger, 1478. . . . . 12000.00 15000.00
- ☐ **Biblia Latina.** Venice, Nicolaus Jenson, 1479. . . . . 900.00 1200.00
- ☐ **Biblia Latina.** Cologne, Conrad Winters de Homborch, 1479. . . . . 12500.00 17500.00
- ☐ **Biblia Latina.** Nuremberg, Anton Koberger, 1480. . . . . 10000.00 15000.00
- ☐ **Biblia Latina.** Lyons, Jacques Maillet, 1490. . . . . 800.00 1200.00
- ☐ **Biblia Latina.** Basel, Nicolaus Kessler, 1491. . . . . 700.00 925.00
- ☐ **Biblia Latina.** Venice, Hieronymus de Paganinus, 1492. 700.00 925.00
- ☐ **Biblia Latina.** Venice, Simon Bevilaqua, 1494. . . . . 700.00 925.00
- ☐ **Biblia Latina.** Basel, Johann Froben, 1495. . . . . 3500.00 4750.00
- ☐ **Biblia Latina.** Venice, Hieronymus de Paganinus, 1497. 475.00 650.00
- ☐ **Bible in Bohemian.** Prague, Johann Kamp for Johann Pytlic, etc., 1488. . . . . 22000.00 35000.00
- ☐ **Bible in Bohemian.** Kuttenberg, Martin de Tischniowa, 1489. . . . . 15000.00 20000.00
- ☐ **Bible in French.** Paris, Antoine Verard, n.d. (c. 1498). . . . 45000.00 70000.00
- ☐ **Bible in German.** Strassburg, Heinrich Eggestein, n.d., (Not after 1470). 25000.00 40000.00
- ☐ **Bible in German.** Augsburg, Gunther Zainer, 1475–76. 30000.00 45000.00
- ☐ **Bible in German.** Augsburg, Anton Sorg, 1488. . . . . 12000.00 15000.00
- ☐ **Bible in German.** Nuremberg, Anton Koberger, 1483. . . . . 35000.00 50000.00
- ☐ **Bible in Italian.** Venice, Guilelmus Anima Mia, 1493. . . . . 22000.00 30000.00
- ☐ **Bible in English.** The Bible, that is, the holy Scriptures of the Olde and New Testament, faithfully and truly translated out of Douche and Latyn into Englishe. Issued at Zurich or Cologne, 1535. Black letter, printed in double columns, with woodcuts. Its rarity is legendary, ranking behind only the Gutenberg in its appeal to collectors. Known as the "Coverdale Bible." 250000.00 350000.00

THE
HOLIE BIBLE
FAITHFVLLY TRANS-
LATED INTO ENGLISH,
OVT OF THE AVTHENTICAL
LATIN.

Diligently conferred with the Hebrew, Greeke,
and other Editions in diuers languages.

With ARGVMENTS of the Bookes, and Chapters:
ANNOTATIONS. TABLES: and other helpes,
for better vnderstanding of the text : for discouerie of
CORRVPTIONS in some late translations : and
for clearing CONTROVERSIES in Religion.

BY THE ENGLISH COLLEGE OF DOWAY.

Haurietis aquas in gaudio de fontibus Saluatoris. Isaiæ.12.
You shal draw waters in ioy out of the Sauiours fountaines.

Printed at Doway by LAVRENCE KELLAM,
at the signe of the holie Lambe.

M. DC. IX.

Title page of the first edition of the Roman Catholic Old Testament in
English. It was printed at the city of Douai in France, spelled phonetically
"Doway." It was considered unwise to attempt such a publication in England, where Protestantism had been adopted as the recognized state
religion. The border is composed of repetitive impressions of a standard
design, found in the stock of most printers of that time.

PRICE RANGE

☐ **Bible in English.** *The Matthew Bible.* The Byble, which is all the holy Scripture...1536. Translated into English by Thomas Matthew. Folio.. 60000.00 95000.00

☐ **Bible in English.** *The Taverner Bible.* The most sacred bible, translated into Englyshe...by Richard Taverner. London, John Byddell for Thomas Berthlet, 1539. Folio....... 35000.00 50000.00

☐ **Bible in English.** *The Great Bible.* The Byble in Englyshe, truly translated after the veryte of the Hebrue and Greke textes...Prunted by Rychard Grafton and Edward Whitchurch, Paris and London, 1539. Folio, not really rare, but a complete well-preserved specimen is hard to find....... 5000.00 80000.00

☐ **Bible in English.** London, Grafton, 1541................. 3500.00 5750.00

☐ **Bible in English.** London, E. Whitchurche, 1549......... 8000.00 12000.00

☐ **Bible in English.** London, T. Raynalde and W. Hyll, 1549... 1200.00 1600.00

☐ **Bible in English.** London, J. Daye, 1551................ 1400.00 2000.00

☐ **Bible in English.** London, N. Hyll for J. Wallye, 1551. ... 1000.00 1300.00

☐ **Bible in English.** *With Tyndals Prologues.* London, N. Hyll, 1551... 650.00 900.00

☐ **Bible in English.** London, Grafton, 1553. Quarto, 478 leaves.. 1250.00 1600.00

☐ **Bible in English.** London, E. Whytechurche, 1553....... 1400.00 1800.00

☐ **Bible in English.** *Geneva or Breeches Bible.* Geneva, Rouland Hall, 1560.. 3750.00 5000.00

☐ **Bible in English.** *Cranmer's Version.* London, R. Harrison, 1562... 900.00 1200.00

☐ **Bible in English.** *Cranmer's Version.* Rouen, R. Carmarden, 1566.. 3500.00 4750.00

☐ **Bible in English.** *Bishop's Bible.* London, R. Jugge, 1568... 900.00 1250.00

☐ **Bible in English.** *Cranmer's Version.* London, J. Cawood, 1569. Quarto.. 1750.00 2500.00

☐ **Bible in English.** *Bishop's Bible.* London, R. Jugge, 1572... 1000.00 1300.00

☐ **Bible in English.** *Breeches Bible, with the Book of Common Prayer.* London, Barker, 1578....................... 400.00 600.00

☐ **Bible in English.** *The New Testament (only).* Rheims, John Fogny, 1582.. 2500.00 3500.00

☐ **Bible in English.** London, Barker, 1583................. 400.00 600.00

☐ **Bible in English.** London, Barker, 1594................. 300.00 400.00

☐ **Bible in English.** *The New Testament (only) Translated into English by the English College in Rheims.* Antwerp, Daniel Vervliet, 1600. Second edition of the Roman Catholic version, quarto.. 700.00 1000.00

☐ **Bible in English.** London, Barker, 1606. 8vo............ 95.00 125.00

☐ **Bible in English.** *Breeches Bible.* London, R. Barker, 1608–10. Quarto.. 275.00 350.00

☐ **Bible in English.** London, Barker, 1611. Folio. Prices vary sharply depending on condition......................... 8000.00 25000.00

☐ **Bible in English.** *The New Testament.* London, Barker, 1612. Quarto... 60.00 80.00

☐ **Bible in English.** *King James or Authorized Version.* London, 1613.. 750.00 1000.00

PRICE RANGE

☐ **Bible in English.** *The Holy Bible.* London, Barker, 1615, Quarto... **125.00** **185.00**

☐ **Bible in English.** *New Testament.* Cambridge (England), 1628. .... **130.00** **175.00**

☐ **Bible in English.** *The Holy Bible.* Cambridge (England), 1630. .... **125.00** **160.00**

☐ **Bible in English.** London, Barker and Bill, 1630. Quarto.. **450.00** **650.00**

☐ **Bible in English.** Rouen, J. Cousturier, 1633–35. Three vois., Roman Catholic version......................... **1750.00** **2500.00**

☐ **Bible in English.** Cambridge (England), Buck and Daniel, 1638. .... **800.00** **1200.00**

☐ **Bible in English.** Cambridge (England), R. Daniel, 1648. Miniature. **175.00** **225.00**

☐ **Bible in English.** London, H. Hill and J. Field, 1660...... **325.00** **400.00**

☐ **Bible in English.** London, 1711. 8vo.................... **100.00** **135.00**

☐ **Bible in English.** *The Vinegar Bible.* Oxford, Baskett, 1717. Two vols., large folio. Though an imposing work, it was sloppily proofread, with the result that its critics termed it a "Baskett-full of errors." One of the more glaring, in Luke XX, gained for it the name "Vinegar Bible," that word being mistakenly substituted for "vineyard.". **500.00** **750.00**

☐ **Bible in English.** *Baskett Bible.* in 8vo. Oxford, 1759. Two vols. **120.00** **150.00**

☐ **Bible in English.** *Gill's Bible.* London, 1763. Nine vols., folio. Largest edition of the scriptures published up to that time. **1300.00** **1850.00**

☐ **Bible in English.** *Blayney's Bible.* Oxford, 1769. Thick 4to. **150.00** **200.00**

☐ **Bible in English.** *The Christian's New and Complete Family Bible and Apocrypha, with notes by Bankes.* London, 1780, folio. **90.00** **115.00**

☐ **Bible in English.** *Old and New Testament, illustrated with engravings by Fittler from pictures by the Old Masters.* London, Bensley, 1795. Two vols., 8vo. **120.00** **150.00**

☐ **Bible in English.** *Macklin's Bible, with illustrations by the best English artists.* London, 1800. Six vols., large folio, in a really exquisite binding.......................... **1200.00** **1500.00**

☐ **Bible in English.** *The Oxford Lectern Bible.* Designed by Bruce Rogers. Oxford, 1935. Thick large folio............ **6000.00** **7500.00**

☐ **American Bibles.** *The Eliot Indian Bible.* Cambridge (Massachusetts), 1663. More copies were printed of this book than any other in 17th century America, but it is still scarce on the market because so many have gone into institutional libraries. Extra fine copy. **125,000.00 175,000.00**

☐ **American Bibles.** *Biblia, das ist die Heilige Schrift.* Germantown (Pennsylvania), Christopher Saur (or Sauer), 1743. Thick quarto. Most copies were originally bound in rough leather over thick wooden boards, with clasps, but finding a copy in a well-preserved original binding with clasps intact is not easy... **500.00** **5000.00**

PRICE RANGE

☐ **American Bibles.** *The Holy Bible. Containing the Old and New Testaments.* Philadelphia, R. Aitken, 1782. Two vols., 8vo. **6000.00** **9000.00**
☐ **American Bibles.** Philadelphia, 1790. First American edition of the Douai or Roman Catholic version, two vols. . . . **1750.00** **2500.00**
☐ **American Bibles.** Trenton, N. J., 1791. . . . . **900.00** **1250.00**
☐ **American Bibles.** Philadelphia, 1794. Pocket size. **50.00** **70.00**
☐ **American Bibles.** *The Holy Bible.* Philadelphia, 1798. Two vols, folio. **1750.00** **2250.00**
☐ **American Bibles.** Philadelphia, 1808. Four vols. **1250.00** **1600.00**
☐ **American Bibles.** Windsor, Vermont, 1812. . . . . **750.00** **1000.00**
☐ **American Bibles.** Philadelphia, 1813. Quarto. **300.00** **400.00**
☐ **American Bibles.** Boston, 1817–18. Six vols. **300.00** **375.00**
☐ **American Bibles.** N.Y., 1822. Pocket size. **75.00** **100.00**
☐ **American Bibles.** Brattleboro, Vermont, 1823. . . . . **300.00** **400.00**

BLACK INTEREST

PRICE RANGE

☐ **Bradford, Roark.** *Ol' Man Adam An' His Children.* New York, 1928. Not first edition. **9.00** **12.00**
☐ **Cansler, Charles.** *Three Generations: The Story of a Colored Family of Eastern Tennessee.* 1939. Clothbound, 173 pp. **26.00** **34.00**
☐ **Daniels, Elam.** *An Exposure of Father Divine, the Negro Worshipped by Millions as God.* Orlando, Florida, 1949. Soft covered, 100 pp. **17.00** **23.00**
☐ **Fagan, Myron.** *You Must Decide the Fate of Our Nation.* Hollywood, California, 1967. Soft covered, 36 pp. **4.00** **6.00**
☐ **Freyre, Gilberto.** *The Masters and the Slaves.* New York, 1956. Clothbound, 537 pp. **9.00** **12.00**
☐ **Heywood, Chester D.** *Negro Combat Troops in the World War.* Worcester, Massachusetts, 1928. Clothbound, 310 pp. **47.00** **63.00**
☐ **Huggins, Nathan.** *Black Odyssey.* New York, 1977. Clothbound. **4.00** **5.50**
☐ **Weyl, Nathaniel.** *The Negro in American Civilization.* Washington, D.C., 1960. Clothbound, 360 pp. **12.00** **16.00**
☐ **Woodson, Carter.** *The Negro in Our History.* Washington, D.C., 1927. . . . . **21.00** **26.00**

BOOKBINDINGS

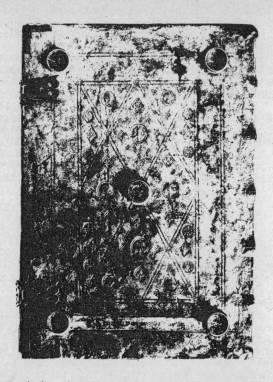

Most incunabula—those books from the dawning years of the printing press—were bulky volumes, with equally bulky bindings. This binding, excellent in Germany in the 1470s, features blindstamped pigskin over stout wooden boards, complemented with a set of metal bosses and metal cornerpieces. A title label (very faded) is pasted between the two upper bosses. $2,750–$3,250

On this VERY old binding—early 17th century—a bishop's hat and crozier adorn the coat-of-arms in the center. Research through heraldry books would tell you that these are the bearings of Antoine deSeve, the Abbot of Isle-le-Barrois, France. The book was printed in Venice in 1604 but bound in France. Later it popped up in an English collection and its location presently unknown. $1,000–$1,300

There were times during the history of bookbinding when MORE automatically meant better—MORE gilding, MORE square inches of leather covered over with ornamentation. This French morocco tour-de-force from the 1620s carries the arms of England's Charles I, the ill-fated monarch who lost his crown and, not long afterward, the head it rested on. In light of its very ornate lavishness, the chances are quite good that it was actually made for the king. $2,500–$3,200

The English were the masters of panel binding. It is very symmetrical and orderly. The material is black morocco, the tooling is in gold, and the spine has extra embellishing, c. 1690. $800–$1,200

It is rare to find a binding on which the owner's label appears. Many collectors had labels made in the 18th century (when this English morocco binding was crafted), but they normally affixed them to the front inner cover. This binding started out plain, and then was gilt-embellished. There are remains of silk ties at the edges. $1,000–$1,500

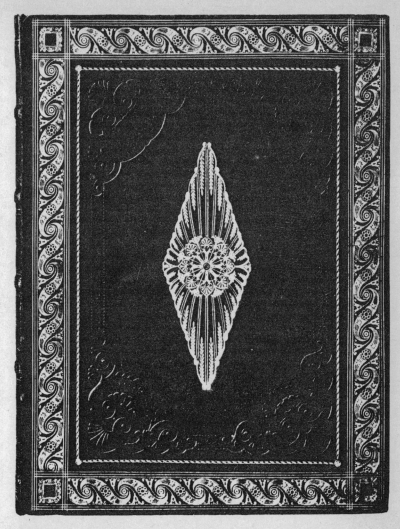

The above binding which features blindstamping and gilt tooling is French and dates from the second quarter of the 19th century. $250–$325

This two-tone inlaid binding (yellow and green morocco) shows the kind of artistic work done in the era of bookbinding's revival as a craft art. It dates c. 1900 and is English workmanship. Even when new, such a book was a deluxe product and not cheap—but not nearly as high as the present value, which is in the range of $600–$800

CHILDREN'S BOOKS

	PRICE RANGE

☐ **Abbott, Jacob.** *Rollo's Correspondence.* Boston, 1841. **115.00 155.00**

☐ **Abbott, Jacob.** *Marco Baul's Travels and Adventures: Erie Canal.* Boston, 1848. Colored frontispiece and four colored plates. **65.00 85.00**

☐ **Abbott, Jacob.** *Rollo at School.* Boston, 1849. **185.00 235.00**

☐ **Adams, Hannah.** *An Abridgement of the History of New England for the Use of Young Persons.* Boston, 1807. Second edition. **20.00 30.00**

☐ **Aikin, Lucy.** *Juvenile Correspondence, or Letters ... for Children of Both Sexes.* Boston, 1822. Calf. **37.00 48.00**

☐ **Alcott, Louisa M.** *Little Women.* Boston, 1869. Second issue. **75.00 95.00**

☐ **Alcott, Louisa M.** *Little Men.* Boston, 1871. **275.00 350.00**

☐ **Alcott, Louisa M.** *Silver Pitchers.* Boston, 1876. **38.00 46.00**

☐ **Alcott, Louisa M.** *Jo's Boys.* Boston, 1886. **38.00 46.00**

☐ **Aldrich, Thomas Bailey.** *The Story of a Bad Boy.* Boston, 1870. **400.00 475.00**

☐ **Aldrich, Thomas Bailey.** *The Story of a Cat.* Boston, 1879. **30.00 38.00**

☐ **Alexander, Caleb.** *The Young Gentleman's and Lady's Instructor.* Boston, 1797. **32.00 40.00**

☐ **Alger, Horatio.** *Adrift in the City.* Philadelphia, n.d. **37.00 45.00**

☐ **Alger, Horatio.** *Ragged Dick.* Boston, 1868. First edition of this classic. Fewer than 12 copies recorded, mostly in well-worn condition. **1450.00 1875.00**

☐ **Alger, Horatio.** *Rufus and Rose.* Boston, 1870. **65.00 85.00**

☐ **Alger, Horatio.** *Tattered Tom; or, the Story of a Street Arab.* Boston, n.d., 1871. First edition but not first printing. **42.00 57.00**

☐ **Andersen, H. C.** *The Marsh King's Daughter and Other Stories.* London, Routledge, n.d. (c. 1870). **9.00 12.00**

☐ **Andersen, H. C.** *The Old Church Bell and Other Stories.* London, Routledge, n.d., c. 1870. **7.00 10.00**

☐ **Andersen, H. C.** *The Story of my Life.* N.Y., 1871. First edition in translation. **75.00 105.00**

☐ **Andersen, H. C.** *Andersen's Stories for the Household.* London, n.d., 1880's. Numerous color plates. **42.00 57.00**

☐ **Andersen, H. C.** *The Snow Queen.* London, Routledge, n.d., c. 1890. **10.00 14.00**

☐ **Andersen, H. C.** *Tales for Children.* London, 1891. **9.00 12.00**

☐ **Andersen, H. C.** *Stories and Fairy Tales.* London, 1893. Two vols. **21.00 26.00**

☐ **Andrews, Jane.** *The Seven Little Sisters Who Live on the Round Ball That Floats in the Air.* Boston, 1861. **235.00 300.00**

☐ **Atherton, Gertrude.** *The Conqueror.* N.Y., 1902. **60.00 80.00**

☐ **Bain, R. Nisbet.** *Cossack Fairy Tales and Folk Tales.* London, 1894. **9.00 12.00**

☐ **Ballantyne, Robert M.** *Ungava: A Tale of Esquimaux Land.* London, 1858. **47.00 63.00**

☐ **Barlow, Jane.** *The Battle of the Frogs and Mice.* London, 1894. **13.00 16.00**

☐ **Barwell, Mrs.** *Little Lessons for Little Learners.* Philadelphia, 1849. First American edition, many fullpage plates. **11.00 14.00**

PRICE RANGE

☐ **Beard, D. C.** *The American Boy's Handy Book.* N.Y., 1882. . . . .   38.00   47.00

☐ **Belson, Mary.** *The Orphan Boy; or, A Journey to Bath.* London, 1812. Two engraved plates. 11.00   15.00

☐ **Bennett C. H.** *Adventures of Young Munchausen.* London, 1865. . . . . 160.00   215.00

☐ **Berquin, M.** *Select Stories for the Instruction and Entertainment of Children.* London, 1802. . . . .   19.00   24.00

☐ **Berquin, M.** *The Blossoms of Morality; Intended for the Amusement and Instruction of Young Ladies and Gentlemen.* London, 1821. Quarter roan, gilt. 13.00   16.00

☐ **Berquin, M.** *The Beauties of the Children's Friend.* Boston, 1827. . . . .   37.00   48.00

☐ **Bible in Miniature.** *Thumb Bible.* Troy, N.Y., 1823. Measures 2 × 1⅝ inches. 160.00   210.00

☐ **Bible Natural History.** Containing a description of Quadrupeds, Birds, Trees, Plants, Insects, etc., mentioned in the Holy Scriptures. London, 1852. . . . .   8.00   11.00

☐ **Bisset, J.** *The Orphan Boy.* A Pathetic Tale, founded on fact. Birmingham, n.d., 1799. Third edition. 21.00   27.00

☐ **Blewitt, Mrs. Octavian.** *The Rose and the Lily.* A Fairy Tale. London, 1877. . . . .   8.00   10.00

☐ **Book of Riddles.** N.Y., 1816. 28pp., softbound. On some copies the wrapper incorrectly reads *"History of Insects."* Rare. 170.00   225.00

☐ **Bouton, Eliz. Gladwin.** *Grandmother's Doll.* N.Y., n.d., 1931. . . . .   50.00   65.00

☐ **Brereton, Captain F. S.** *In the Grip of the Mullah.* A Tale of Adventure in Somaliland. London, 1904. . . . .   9.00   12.00

☐ **Brereton, Captain F. S.** *The Hero of Panama.* A Tale of the Great Canal. London, 1912. . . . .   9.00   12.00

☐ **Browning, Robert.** *The Pied Piper of Hamelin.* London, n.d. 28.00   35.00

☐ **Burnett, Francis H.** *Little Lord Fauntleroy.* N.Y., 1886. . . . 160.00   215.00

☐ **Burnett, Francis H.** *Editha's Burglar.* Boston, 1888. Second issue. 16.00   21.00

☐ **Butterworth, Hezekiah.** *Zig-Zag Journeys in Europe.* Boston, 1880. First edition. 43.00   55.00

☐ **Caldecott, Randolph.** *The House that Jack Built.* London, n.d., 1878. . . . .   30.00   39.00

☐ **Carroll, Lewis (pen-name of Charles L. Dodgson).** *Alice's Adventures in Wonderland.* London, 1865. With 42 illustrations from pen drawings by John Tenniel, red cloth. Extremely rare. The first American edition—New York, 1866—was also bound in red cloth, and is worth $1,750. There are a number of other editions of value, including: Boston, 1869. Green cloth. 230.00   275.00

London, 1907. With illustrations by Arthur Rackham (and of interest mainly on that score). 475.00   600.00

N.Y., 1932. Signed by "Alice" herself (Mrs. Hargreaves). 400.00   475.00

☐ **Carroll, Lewis.** *Phantasmagoria and Other Poems.* London, 1869. Blue cloth. 100.00   130.00

PRICE RANGE

☐ **Carroll, Lewis.** *Through the Looking Glass, and What Alice Found There.* London, 1872. With 50 drawing by Tenniel, red cloth... 350.00 425.00
☐ **Carroll, Lewis.** *The Hunting of the Snark.* London, 1876. 175.00 225.00
☐ **Carroll, Lewis.** *Rhyme? and Reason?* London, 1883. Green cloth.. 80.00 110.00
☐ **Carroll, Lewis.** *A Tangled Tale.* London, 1885. .... 85.00 110.00
☐ **Carroll, Lewis.** *Sylvie and Bruno.* London, 1889......... 120.00 150.00
☐ **Carroll, Lewis.** *Sylvie and Bruno Concluded.* London, 1893. (Physically, "Sylvie and Bruno" was Carroll's biggest work, but failed to achieve half the popularity of "Alice.")........ 120.00 150.00
☐ **Carter, Nicholas ("Nick Carter").** *The Chain of Clues.* N.Y., n.d., 1907... 21.00 27.00
☐ **Champney, Lizzie W.** *Three Vassar Girls Abroad.* Boston, 1883. First edition. The binding should be red cloth. Copies in brown cloth bring somewhat less..................... 130.00 165.00
☐ **Champney, Lizzie W.** *Three Vassar Girls in England.* Boston, 1883. .... 48.00 63.00
☐ *Child's Favorite. A Gift for the Young.* By a Lady, Philadelphia and N.Y., 1847. Ten colored plates.............. 32.00 40.00
☐ *Child's Instructor.* New Haven, 1831..................... 12.00 15.00
☐ *Cinderella or the Little Glass Slipper.* Baltimore, n.d., c. 1850. Softbound. 62.00 78.00
☐ *Cock Robin. The Tragi-Comic History of the Burial of Cock Robin; with the Lamentation of Jenny Wren* ... Philadelphia, 1821. Softbound. 115.00 155.00
☐ **Coolidge, Susan.** *What Katy Did.* Boston, 1873. .... 72.00 93.00
☐ **Cox, Palmer.** *The Brownies, Their Book.* N.Y., n.d., 1887. Second edition.. 125.00 160.00
☐ **Cranch, Christopher P.** *Kobboloozo: A Sequel to the Last of the Huggermuggers.* Boston, 1857. .... 27.00 34.00
☐ **Crowquill, Alfred.** *The Pictorial Grammar.* London, n.d., c. 1840's... 53.00 69.00
☐ **Cupples, Mrs. George.** *A Nice Secret and Other Stories.* London, 1876... 13.00 16.00
☐ *Dame Trot and her Comical Cat. The Adventures of.* Baltimore, n.d., c. 1840's. Softbound, rare................... 140.00 175.00
☐ **Day, Thomas.** *The History of Sandford and Merton: a Work Intended for the Use of Children.* London, 1818. Two vols. 53.00 69.00
☐ **Defoe, Daniel.** *See in "Literature" section.*
☐ **Denslow, W. W.** *Denslow's House that Jack Built.* N.Y., n.d., 1903... 68.00 88.00
☐ **Denslow, W. W.** *Denslow's Simple Simon.* N.Y., n.d., 1904. .... 53.00 68.00
☐ **Denslow, W. W.** *Denslow's Animal Fair.* N.Y., n.d., 1904. 78.00 105.00
☐ **Disney, Walt.** *The Adventures of Mickey Mouse, Book I.* Philadelphia, 1931. The first Mickey Mouse publication. .. 700.00 875.00
☐ **Disney, Walt.** *Who's Afraid of the Big Bad Wolf.* Philadelphia, 1933... 135.00 165.00
☐ **Disney, Walt.** *Donald Duck and his Cat Troubles.* Whitman, Wisconsin, 1945. .... 65.00 85.00

Inftruction with Delight.

A LITTLE PRETTY
POCKET-BOOK,
INTENDED FOR THE
INSTRUCTION and AMUSEMENT
OF
LITTLE MASTER TOMMY,
AND
PRETTY MISS POLLY.
With Two LETTERS from
JACK the GIANT-KILLER;
AS ALSO
A BALL and PINCUSHION;
The Use of which will infallibly make TOMMY
a good Boy, and POLLY a good Girl.
To which is added,
A LITTLE SONG-BOOK,
BEING
A NEW ATTEMPT to teach CHILDREN
the Use of the English Alphabet, by Way
of Diversion.

THE FIRST *WORCESTER* EDITION.

PRINTED at WORCESTER, *Massachusetts*,
By ISAIAH THOMAS,
And SOLD, Wholesale and Retail, at his Book-
Store. MDCCLXXXVII.

This charming little children's book would be a highly desirable collector's item even if it carried a foreign imprint. But as it was printed in Worcester, Massachusetts, by the very celebrated Isaiah Thomas, it carries far greater impact. Thomas was not only a printer/publisher but a pioneer antiquary who preserved many relics of the local New England history. No author is verified for this book.

PRICE RANGE

☐ **Dodge, Mary Mapes.** *Hans Brinker or the Silver Skates.* N.Y., 1874.	57.00	72.00
☐ **Dorset, Catherine Anne.** *Think Before you Speak.* Philadelphia, 1811.	325.00	385.00
☐ **Dwight, Nathaniel.** *Geography of the World by Way of Question and Answer.* Hartford, 1802.	27.00	33.00
☐ **Emerson, Joseph.** *The Evangelical Primer.* Boston, 1814.	18.00	23.00
☐ **Emmet, Rosina.** *Pretty Peggy and Other Ballads.* N.Y., 1880.	25.00	31.00
☐ **Entick, John.** *The Child's Best Instructor in Spelling and Reading.* London, 1773. Sixth edition.	285.00	340.00
☐ *Examples of Goodness Narrated for the Young.* Philadelphia, 1853.	52.00	65.00
☐ *Faithful Fritz.* Troy, N.Y., n.d., 1888?. Colored frontispiece.	23.00	30.00
☐ *Famous Story Book.* Boston, n.d., c. 1890. Colored pictorial boards and frontispiece.	21.00	27.00
☐ **Federer, Charles.** *Yorkshire Chap Books.* London, 1889. Marbled boards with vellum spine.	85.00	105.00
☐ **Field, Eugene.** *Little Willie.* N.p., n.d. Oblong 6½ × 4 inches, softbound.	32.00	39.00
☐ **Field, Rachel.** *Hitty, Her First Hundred Years.* Illustrated by Dorothy P. Lathrop, N.Y., 1929.	63.00	79.00
☐ **Florian, Chevalier de.** *William Tell or Switzerland Delivered.* Translated from the French. Exeter, N.H., 1826.	48.00	62.00
☐ **Frost, John.** *Easy Exercises in Composition: Designed for use of Beginners.* Philadelphia, 1839. First edition.	63.00	78.00
☐ **Goodrich, S. G.** *Stories About Captain John Smith for the Instruction and Amusement of Children.* Hartford, 1829. Rare.	285.00	340.00
☐ **Goodrich, S. G.** *The Life and Adventures of Robinson Crusoe.* A new edition carefully adapted to youth. N.Y., n.d., 1835.	135.00	170.00
☐ **Goodrich, S. G.** *Peter Parley's Geography for Children.* With nine maps and 75 engravings, N.Y., 1839.	30.00	37.00
☐ **Goodrich, S. G.** *Peter Parley's Gift to His Young Friends.* London, n.d., c. 1840.	57.00	73.00
☐ **Goodrich, S. G.** *The Balloon Travels of Robert Merry and His Young Friends.* N.Y., 1855.	62.00	83.00
☐ **Goody Two-Shoes.** *Adventures of.* Albany, n.d., c. 1850. 16 pp. softbound.	85.00	105.00
☐ **Gordon, Pat.** *Geography Anatomiz'd: or, the Geographical Grammar.* London, 1730. 12th edition, with 17 triplefold maps.	95.00	115.00
☐ **Graham, Kenneth.** *Dream Days.* London, n.d. First edition.	47.00	59.00
☐ **Graham, Kenneth.** *The Golden Age.* London, 1900. First edition.	53.00	68.00
☐ **Graham, Kenneth.** *The Wind in the Willows.* N.Y., 1908. First American edition.	75.00	100.00
☐ **Graham, Kenneth.** *Fun o' the Fair.* London, 1929.	37.00	48.00

PRICE RANGE

☐ **Greenaway, Kate.** *Under the Window.* London, n.d., 1878. Boards. 200.00   275.00

☐ **Greenaway, Kate.** *The "Little Folks" Painting Book* (by George Weatherly, illustrated by Kate Greenaway). London, n.d., 1881. Blue cloth. 185.00   235.00

☐ **Greenaway, Kate.** *A Day in a Child's Life.* London, n.d., 1881. Boards. 170.00   215.00

☐ **Greenway, Kate.** *Kate Greenaway's Book of Games.* London, n.d., 1899. Boards. 170.00   215.00

☐ **Greenaway, Kate.** *Kate Greenaway Pictures.* London, 1921. . . . .   250.00   310.00

☐ **Greenwood, James.** *The Philadelphia Vocabulary, English and Latin.* Philadelphia, 1787. First American edition, rare. 350.00   425.00

☐ **Guess Again.** *A New Riddle Book, for the Entertainment of Children.* N.Y., 1834. 22 pp. 34.00   42.00

☐ **Habberton, John.** *Helen's Babies.* Boston, n.d., 1871. Softbound. 37.00   46.00

☐ **Harris, Joel Chandler.** *Uncle Remus, His Songs and His Sayings.* N.Y., 1881. . . . .   550.00   700.00

☐ **Harris, Joel Chandler.** *Daddy Jake the Runaway.* N.Y., n.d., 1899. First edition. Must be in fine condition to command this price. 375.00   450.00

☐ **Harris, Joel Chandler.** *On the Plantation.* N.Y., 1892. . . . .   40.00   55.00

☐ **Harris, Joel Chandler.** *Little Mr. Thimblefinger and his Queer Country.* N.Y., 1894. . . . .   60.00   75.00

☐ **Harris, Joel Chandler.** *The Story of Aaron.* N.Y., 1896. . .   85.00   105.00

☐ **Harris, Joel Chandler.** *Plantation Pagaents.* Boston, 1899. . . . .   105.00   130.00

☐ **Harris, Joel Chandler.** *Told by Uncle Remus.* New Stories of the Old Plantation. N.Y., 1905. First edition. 95.00   115.00

☐ **Headland, Isaac.** *Chinese Mother Goose Rhymes.* N.Y., n.d., 1900. . . . .   95.00   125.00

☐ **Headland, Isaac.** *The Chinese Boy and Girl.* N.Y., n.d., 1901. With photographs and other illustrations. Rhymes and games. 75.00   95.00

☐ **Henry, George Alfred.** *At the Point of the Bayonet.* N.Y., 1901. . . . .   37.00   45.00

☐ **Hering, Jeanie.** *Little Pickles.* London, n.d., c. 1885. . . . . .   27.00   34.00

☐ *Hieroglyphic Bible . . . for the Amusement of Youth.* N.Y., 1858. Illustrated with nearly 500 woodcuts, clothbound. . .   42.00   55.00

☐ *History of Fish.* N.Y., n.d., c. 1820. Softbound, with 15 woodcuts. 42.00   55.00

☐ **Hoffland, Mrs.** *Theodore; or, the Crusaders.* A Tale for Youth. Boston, 1824. With six plates.   63.00   85.00

☐ **Hoffman, Heinrich.** *Slovenly Peter or Cheerful Stories and Funny Pictures.* Philadelphia, n.d. 90.00   115.00

☐ **Holley, Marietta.** *Samantha at Saratoga.* Philadelphia, 1887. Illustrated by Opper, creator of "Happy Hooligan." 30.00   39.00

☐ **Howells, William Dean.** *A Boy's Town.* N.Y., 1890. . . . . . .   25.00   32.00

☐ **Howitt, Mary.** *Our Four-Footed Friends.* London, n.d. 24.00   31.00

☐ *Ill-Natured Boy, The.* New Haven, 1824, softbound. 130.00   175.00

PRICE RANGE

☐ *Instruction and Amusement for the Young.* New Haven, n.d., c. 1830.	35.00	43.00
☐ *Jack the Giant Killer, a Hero.* Banbury (England), n.d., c. 1820. Softbound.	58.00	72.00
☐ **Janeway, James.** *A Token for Children... the Conversion, Holy and Exemplary Lives, and Joyful Deaths of Several Young Children.* Charlestown, 1804.	200.00	250.00
☐ **Kingsley, Charles.** *The Water-Babies.* Boston, 1864. First American edition.	75.00	100.00
☐ **Kingston, W. H. G.** *Round the World.* A Tale for Boys. London, 1859.	32.00	40.00
☐ **Kingston, W. H. G.** *In New Granada or heroes ad patriots.* With 36 engravings. London, 1880. First edition.	41.00	52.00
☐ **Lanier, Sidney.** *The Boy's King Arthur.* N.Y., 1880.	41.00	52.00
☐ **Lear, Edward.** *A Book of Nonsense.* London, 1861.	325.00	400.00
☐ **Lear, Edward.** *Calico Pie.* London, n.d. Boards.	150.00	200.00
☐ **Lear, Edward.** *Nonsense Songs.* London, 1871.	400.00	500.00
☐ **Leech, John.** *Little Tour in Ireland.* London, 1859.	75.00	100.00
☐ **Leigh, Percival.** *The Comic English Grammar.* London, 1856. Upwards of 50 illustrations by John Leech.	42.00	58.00
☐ *Life and Death of Tom Thumb, the Little Giant.* Boston, 1821. Softbound (bound in wallpaper) For a fine copy, which is just about hopeless to find.	550.00	750.00
☐ *Little Ann and Other Stories.* Worcester, n.d., c. 1845.	42.00	53.00
☐ *Little Book of Trades.* New Haven, n.d., c. 1835. 1⅞ inches × 2⅞ inches, softbound.	140.00	175.00
☐ *Little Red Riding Hood.* N.Y., n.d., c. 1855. Softbound.	42.00	57.00
☐ **Lofting, Hugh.** *The Story of Doctor Dolittle.* N.Y., 1923. 12th printing.	21.00	26.00
☐ **Lofting, Hugh.** *Dr. Dolittle's Circus.* N.Y., 1924.	115.00	150.00
☐ **Lofting, Hugh.** *Dr. Dolittle's Garden.* N.Y.	34.00	41.00
☐ **Lofting, Hugh.** *Dr. Dolittle and the Secret Lake.* Philadelphia and N.Y., 1958.	34.00	41.00
☐ **Lulu Tales.** *The Boat Builders, The Little Artist and other stories.* N.Y., 1855. Decorated boards.	19.00	24.00
☐ *Marmaduke Multiply.* N.Y. and Boston, n.d., c. 1840.	70.00	90.00
☐ *Mary's Little Lamb.* Dearborn, Mich., 1928.	26.00	34.00
☐ **May, Sophie.** *Dotty Dimple (Little Prudy Series).* Boston, 1856.	35.00	43.00
☐ *Merry's Book of Travel and Adventure.* N.Y., 1860.	21.00	27.00
☐ *Metamorphosis; or a Transformation of Pictures with Poetical Explanations for the Amusement of Young Person.* N.Y., 1814. Rare.	250.00	325.00
☐ **Milne, A. A.** *Fourteen Songs from When We Were Very Young.* N.Y., 1925. First American edition.	27.00	35.00
☐ **Milne, A. A.** *A Gallery of Children.* Philadelphia, n.d., 1925. First American edition.	63.00	85.00
☐ **Milne, A. A.** *Winnie-the-Pooh.* London, 1926.	250.00	300.00
☐ **Milne. A. A.** *The Ivory Door.* N.Y., 1938. First American edition.	22.00	28.00
☐ **Molesworth, Mrs.** *A Christmas Child.* London, 1880.	20.00	25.00
☐ **Moore, Clement C.** *A Visit from St. Nicholas.* In "The New York Book of Poetry," N.Y., 1837.	115.00	150.00

PRICE RANGE

☐ **Murray, Lindley.** *English Grammar.* Philadelphia, 1829. 19.00 24.00
☐ *New Doll, The.* Or, Grandmama's Gift, London, 1826. . . . . 95.00 120.00
☐ **Newberry, Elizabeth.** *A New History of the Grecian States.* Designed for the use of Young Ladies and Gentlemen. London, 1795. . . . . 125.00 165.00
☐ **New England Primer.** Massachusetts, printed for the purchaser, 1808. . . . . 85.00 105.00
☐ **New England Primer.** New England, printed for the purchaser, n.d., c. 1810. . . . . :.. 225.00 275.00
☐ **New England Primer.** Boston, n.d., c. 1820. . . . . :.. 130.00 160.00
☐ **New England Primer.** Hartford, 1820. . . . . 130.00 160.00
☐ **New England Primer.** Brookfield, Mass., 1822. . . . . 90.00 120.00
☐ **Newell, Peter.** *The Rocket Book.* N.Y., n.d., 1912. One of the earliest books on the subject for children 165.00 210.00
☐ *Night Before Christmas.* London, n.d., c. 1905. Softbound. 25.00 32.00
☐ **Old Ironside.** *The Story of a Shipwreck.* Salem, 1855. . . . 22.00 28.00
☐ **Optic, Oliver.** *The Prisoners of the Cave.* N.Y., n.d., 1915. Softbound. 8.00 10.00
☐ **Otis, James.** *Toby Tyler or Ten Weeks with a Circus.* N.Y., 1881. . . . . 190.00 235.00
☐ **Otis, James.** *Jenny Wren's Boarding House.* Boston, n.d., 1893. First edition. 67.00 88.00
☐ **Otis, James.** *The Cruise of the Comet.* Boston, 1898. . . . 48.00 63.00
☐ **Page, Thomas N.** *Two Little Confederates.* N.Y., 1888. . . 67.00 88.00
☐ **Phillips, E. O.** *Birdie and Her Dog.* London, n.d., c. 1885. . . . . 15.00 20.00
☐ **Pinchard, Mrs.** *The Blind Child or Anecdotes of the Wyndham Family.* London, n.d., c. 1818. . . . . 52.00 67.00
☐ *Poetical Geography.* Cincinnati, 1852. . . . . 32.00 39.00
☐ *Poetry without Fiction for Children Between the Ages of Three and Seven.* By a Mother. Boston, 1825. . . . . 47.00 63.00
☐ **Porter, Eleanor H.** *Polyana.* Boston, 1913. . . . . 180.00 235.00
☐ **Porter, Eleanor H.** *Pollyana Grows Up.* Boston, 1915. . . . 47.00 63.00
☐ **Potter, Beatrix.** *The Tale of Peter Rabbit.* London, n.d., 1901. Boards, limited to 250 copies. 475.00 625.00
☐ **Potter, Beatrix.** *The Tailor of Gloucester.* N.p., n.d., London, 1902. Boards. 300.00 375.00
☐ **Potter, Beatrix.** *The Tale of Benjamin Bunny.* London, 1904. Boards. 115.00 150.00
☐ **Potter, Beatrix.** *The Pie and the Patty-Pan.* London, 1905. Boards. 110.00 140.00
☐ **Potter, Beatrix.** *The Tale of Mrs. Tiggy-Winkle.* London, 1905. Boards. 100.00 130.00
☐ *Prairie Crusoe, The.* Or, *Adventures in the Far West.* Boston, 1866. . . . . 150.00 190.00
☐ *Pride of Peter Prim.* Cooperstown, N.Y., 1838. Softbound. 120.00 150.00
☐ **Ray, Joseph.** *Ray's Arithmetic, First Book . . . For Young Learners.* Cincinnati, n.d., 1857. . . . . 20.00 25.00
☐ **Reiche, Charles C.** *Fifteen Discourses on the Marvelous Works in Nature, Delivered by a Father to His Children.* Philadelphia, 1791. . . . . 175.00 220.00

PRICE RANGE

☐ *Rhymes for the Nursery*. Boston, n.d., 1837.............	25.00	32.00
☐ **Richard, Laura E.** *Captain January*. Boston, 1898. Edition deluxe, signed by author and publisher................	22.00	28.00
☐ **Scudder, Horace E.** *Doings of the Bodley Family in Town and Country*. Boston, 1883. First edition................	53.00	68.00
☐ *Second Book of 100 Pictures*. Philadelphia, n.d., 1862. ..	38.00	47.00
☐ **Sewell, Anna.** *Black Beauty*. Boston, n.d., 1890.........	78.00	102.00
☐ **Shute, Henry A.** *The Real Diary of a Real Boy*. Boston, 1902. First edition..	73.00	92.00
☐ **Sidney, Margaret.** *Five Little Peppers and How They Grew*. Boston, n.d., 1880. First edition but second issue.	32.00	39.00
☐ *Smedley's Venetian History*. N.Y., 1843. Two vols., School District Library series.....................................	21.00	27.00
☐ **Smith, E. Boyd.** *The Story of Noah's Ark*. Boston, 1905. With 26 fullpage colored plates.........................	43.00	52.00
☐ **Smith, Jessie Wilcox.** *The Water Babies*. N.Y., n.d., 1916.	62.00	79.00
☐ **Smith, Joshua.** *The Northmen in New England*. Boston, 1829. Early work on Viking explorations of North America, for children..	80.00	105.00
☐ **Sonvestre.** *Popular Legends of Brittany*. Boston, 1856. With 16 hand colored plates...........................	83.00	110.00
☐ **Southey, Robert.** *The Story of the Three Bears*. Volume IV of "The Doctor." London, 1837. First appearance of this tale. Goldilocks had yet to appear in it..................	90.00	115.00
☐ **Spencer, Otto.** *Dables in Pictures*. Philadelphia, n.d., c. 1860's...	75.00	105.00
☐ **Standish, Burt L.** *Frank Merriwell's Tact*. N.Y., n.d., 1910. Softbound..	13.00	16.00
☐ **Sterndale, Mary.** *Delia's Birthday and Other Interesting Stories for Youth*. Boston, 1821.........................	85.00	105.00
☐ **Stockton, Frank R.** *The Adventures of Captain Horn*. N.Y., 1895.	13.00	16.00
☐ **Stoddard, William Osborn.** *Little Smoke*. N.Y., 1891.....	42.00	55.00
☐ **Taylor, Isaac.** *Scenes in America, for the ... Little Tarry-At-Home Travellers*. London, 1821. 84 hand-colored engravings on 28 plates.....................................	235.00	290.00
☐ **Taylor, Isaac.** *Scenes in Africa for the Amusement and instruction of Little Tarry-At-Home Travellers*. N.Y., 1827.	110.00	145.00
☐ **Taylor, Jane.** *Original Poems*. By Jane Taylor and her Sisters. N.Y., n.d., c. 1850.	23.00	29.00
☐ **Taylor. Jefferys.** *The Little Historians: A new Chronicle of the Affairs of England in Church and State*. London, 1824. Three vols. in one......................................	63.00	78.00
☐ **Thomas, Isaiah, Jr.** *A Bag of Nuts Ready Cracked; or, Instructive Fables, Ingenious Riddles, and Merry Conundrums*. By the Celebrated and Facetious Thomas Thumb, Esq., Worcester, 1798. Second Worcester edition. One of the big rarities among American children's books.........	2150.00	3200.00
☐ **Thomas, Isaiah, Jr.** *The Lilliputian Masquerade*. Worcester, 1802. Third Worcester edition.......................	375.00	450.00
☐ **Thompson, Maurice.** *Alice of Old Vincennes*. Indianapolis, n.d., 1901. First edition...............................	110.00	135.00

	PRICE RANGE	
☐ **Trowbridge, John Townsend.** *Cudjo's Cave.* Boston, 1864....................	170.00	200.00
☐ *True History of a Little Boy who Cheated Himself.* By a Young Naval Officer. London, 1817. Softbound..........	180.00	215.00
☐ *Underhill's New Table-Book; or, Tables of Arithmetic made Easier.* N.Y., n.d., 1845.	27.00	35.00
☐ *Variety; or Stories for Children.* N.Y., 1828.	63.00	82.00
☐ **Watson, Henry C.** *The Yankee Tea-Party; or, Boston in 1773.* Philadelphia, n.d., 1851...........................	19.00	24.00
☐ **Watts, Isaac.** *Divine Songs Attempted in Easy Language for the Use of Children.* London, 1773..................	73.00	89.00
☐ **Webster, Jean.** *Daddy Long Legs.* N.Y., 1912. First edition...	62.00	77.00
☐ **Wiggin, Kate Douglas.** *The Story of Patsy.* Boston, 1890...	21.00	27.00
☐ **Wiggin, Kate Douglas.** *Rebecca of Sunnybrook Farm.* Boston, 1903..	52.00	67.00
☐ **Willard, Samuel.** *The Franklin Primer... Adorned with Elegant Cuts Calculated to Strike a Lasting Impression on the Tender Minds of Children.* Boston, 1803.	175.00	215.00
☐ *Woodbridge and Willard's Geography.* Hartford, 1820....	23.00	28.00
☐ **Worcester, J. E.** *Elements of Geography, Ancient and Modern.* Boston, 1830...................................	25.00	31.00
☐ *Young Child's A.B.C. Or, First Book.* Baltimore, n.d., c. 1816. 13 pp., softbound.	160.00	200.00

CRAFTS AND TRADES

	PRICE RANGE	
☐ **American Mutual Library Association.** *Ladies' Manual of Art for Profit and Pastime, A Self Teacher in All Branches of Decorative Art.* Chicago, 1890........................	32.00	40.00
☐ **American Wood Preservers' Association.** *Handbook on Wood Preservation.* Baltimore, 1916. Clothbound, 73 pp.	14.00	18.00
☐ **American Wool and Cotton Reporer.** *Textile Processess: A Collection of Essays on Processes in Woolen, Worsted and Cotton Manufacturing.* New York, undated..........	14.00	18.00
☐ **(Anonymous).** *A Handbook of Crochet, Useful and Ornamental, Containing New Receipts for Collars, Edgings, Caps, Polkas, Purses, D'Oyleys, etc.* Philadelphia, 1850. Pocket size, clothbound, 64 pp.	35.00	43.00
☐ **(Anonymous).** *A Study in the Development of the American Worsted Manufacture, The Arlington Mills (of) Lawrence, Massachusetts.* Cambridge, 1898. Bound in gilt cloth, 138 pp., illustrated.......................................	21.00	27.00
☐ **(Anonymous).** *The Amateur's Handbook of Practical Information for the Workshop and Laboratory.* New York, 1879. Bound in boards.	14.00	18.00
☐ **(Anonymous).** *The Aneroid Barometer: How to Buy it How to Use it.* London, 1902. Soft covered, 32 pp.............	27.00	34.00

PRICE RANGE

☐ **(Anonymous).** *Architectural Terra Cotta.* New York, 1922. Clothbound, large size...................................... 32.00 42.00

☐ **(Anonymous).** *Arts Revealed, and Universal Guide. Containing Many Rare and Invaluable Recipes and Directions for the Use of Families.* New York, 1860. Clothbound, 135 pp........ 27.00 34.00

☐ **(Anonymous).** *Creosoted Timber, Its Preparation and Uses.* Philadelphia, 1900. Prepared by Norfolk Creosoting Co. Clothbound, 92 pp........................ 14.00 18.00
Has some ads and would rank as a borderline trade catalogue.

☐ **(Anonymous).** *The Decorator's and Renovator's Assistant.* London, 1929. Clothbound, 164 pp. 16.00 21.00

☐ **(Anonymous).** *Dyer and Colour Makers Companion.* N.p., 1886. Clothbound, 104 pp. 19.00 24.00
The spelling "colour" for "color" suggests that this is a British publication.

☐ **(Anonymous).** *Every Man His Own Mechanic, A Complete Guide for Amateurs.* New York and London, 1900. Clothbound... 25.00 33.00

☐ **(Anonymous).** *History and Manufacture of Floor Coverings.* New York, 1899. Bound in silver gilt cloth, 98 pp.... 27.00 36.00

☐ **(Anonymous).** *Humbug: A Look at Some Popular Impositions.* New York, 1859. Bound in soft covers, 94 pp., illustrated.. 32.00 40.00
Includes various business schemes and hoaxes. The word "humbug" was popularized by P. T. Barnum, but this work was definitely not connected with him.

☐ **(Anonymous).** *The Ladies' Guide in Needlework: A Gift for the Industrious.* Philadelphia, 1850. Clothbound, 207 pp........ 28.00 36.00

☐ **(Anonymous).** *Ladies' Work Box Companion: A Hand-Book of Knitting, Netting, Tatting and Berlin Work.* New York, undated, c. 1890. Soft covered, 64 pp.............. 16.00 21.00

☐ **(Anonymous).** *Needle and Brush, Useful and Decorative.* New York, 1889. Clothbound, 308 pp................... 32.00 42.00

☐ **(Anonymous).** *The Painter's, Gilder's, and Varnisher's Manual.* London and New York, 1836 Clothbound, 207 pp. 130.00 160.00

☐ **(Anonymous).** *Pattern Making. A Practical Treatise Embracing the Main Types of Engineering Construction, With Upwards of 370 Illustrations.* London, 1855. Bound in cloth.. 32.00 39.00
Deals with pipes, columns, gears, wheels, turbines, etc..

☐ **(Anonymous).** *Starlight Manual of Knitting and Crocheting.* Boston, 1887. Soft covered, 183 pp................ 25.00 33.00

☐ **(Anonymous).** *The Technical Educator, An Encyclopedia of Technical Education.* London and New York, undated, c. 1890. Three volumes in one. 32.00 43.00

☐ **(Anonymous).** *The Whole Art of Conjuring, or Hocus-Pocus.* Philadelphia, undated, c. 1850–1860. Bound in boards with paper spine, woodcut illustrations........... 185.00 235.00

☐ **(Anonymous).** *Wood Working Tools: How to Use Them. A Manual.* Boston, 1881. Clothbound, 102 pp. 16.00 21.00

PRICE RANGE

☐ **(Anonymous).** *The Young Lady's Book. A Manual of Elegant Recreations, Arts, Sciences, and Accomplishments.* London, 1859. . . . . 25.00   33.00
This is one of the numerous "self help" titles in the Henry G. Bohn line of inexpensive books for the masses.

☐ **(Anonymous).** *The Young Ladies' Journal, A Complete Guide to the Work-Table, With Numerous Illustrations and Colored Designs.* London, 1887. Gilt cloth, 136 pp. 35.00   43.00

☐ **Arnold, L. B.** *American Dairying. A Manual for Butter and Cheese Makers.* Rochester, New York, 1879. Clothbound, 354 pp.. . . . . 33.00   42.00

☐ **Atwater, Mary M.** *The Shuttle Craft Book of American Hand Weaving.* New York, 1947. Clothbound, 281 pp. 35.00   45.00

☐ **Audsley, G.** *The Art of Polychromatic and Decorative Turning.* N.p., 1916. Clothbound, 109 pp. 37.00   48.00

☐ **Bachrach, Max.** *Fur: A Complete Fur Trade Manual.* New York, 1930. Clothbound, 677 pp. 20.00   25.00

☐ **Baker, I.** *Treatise on Masonry Construction.* N.p., 1910. Clothbound 745 pp. 21.00   27.00

☐ **Balderson and Limerick.** *Laundry Manual.* Philadelphia, 1906. Clothbound, 77 pp. 14.00   18.00

☐ **Barker, Alfred.** *An Introduction to the Study of Textile Design.* New York, 1903. Clothbound, 211 pp. 21.00   27.00

☐ **Batty, J.** *Practical Taxidermy.* N.p., 1900. Clothbound, 203 pp. 32.00   43.00

☐ **Bemrose, William.** *Manual of Wood Carving with Practical Instructions for Learners of the Art.* London, undated, c. 1870–1880. Gilt cloth, 50 pp. Tenth edition. 35.00   43.00

☐ **Benjamin, Asher.** *The Practical House Carpenter.* N.p., 1835. Must have 64 plates to be complete. 115.00   145.00

☐ **Bertholiet, C.** *Elements of the Art of Dyeing.* London, 1824. Two volumes, translated from the French. 115.00   145.00

☐ **Bjorling, P. R.** *Briquettes and Patient Fuel, Their Manufacture and Machinery.* London, 1903. . . . . 21.00   27.00

☐ **Black, Rev. John L.** *The Farmer's Every Day Book.* Auburn, N.Y., 1851. Gilt cloth, 654 pp. 21.00   27.00

☐ **Blakelee, George.** *Blakelee's Industrial Cyclopedia.* New York, 1892. Clothbound, 720 pp. 11.00   16.00

☐ **Bottomley, Julia.** *The Milliner's Guide.* New York, n.d., c. 1915–1920. Clothbound, 126 pp. 23.00   31.00

☐ **Bradbury, Fred.** *Calculations in Yarns and Fabrics.* Belfast, Ireland, 1891. Soft covered. 16.00   21.00

☐ **Brainerd and Armstrong.** *Embroidery Lessons.* New London, Connecticut, 1912. Soft covered, 140 pp. 16.00   21.00

☐ **Bramwell, W. C.** *The Wood-Carvers' Vade Mecum.* Boston, 1881. Clothbound, 396 pp. 20.00   25.00

☐ **Brannt, William.** *The Metal Worker's Handy-Book of Receipts and Processes.* Philadelphia, 1903. Gilt Cloth, 538 pp. 20.00   25.00

☐ **Brannt, William.** *The Technico-Chemical Receipt Book.* Philadelphia, 1890. Gilt cloth, 495 pp. 25.00   32.00

☐ **Brayley, Arthur.** *History of the Granite Industry of New England.* Boston, 1913. Two volumes. 40.00   50.00

PRICE RANGE

☐ **Bridgland, A. S.** *The Modern Tailor, Outfitter and Clothier.* London, n.d., c. 1910–1915. Three volumes.............	60.00	80.00
☐ **Brongniart, Alex.** *Coloring and Decoration of Ceramic Ware.* Chicago, 1898. Clothbound, 216 pp.	23.00	30.00
☐ **Brown, William N.** *House Decorating and Painting.* London, 1900. Clothbound, 151 pp..........................	15.00	20.00
☐ **Brown and Sharpe.** *Treatise on Construction and Use of Milling Machines.* Providence, Rhode Island, 1891.......	25.00	33.00
☐ **Brunner, Richard.** *The Manufacture of Lubricants, Shoe Polishes and Leather Dressings.* London, 1906. Clothbound, 176 pp.	13.00	17.00
☐ **Bryn, M. L.** *The Complete Practical Brewer.* Philadelphia, 1876. Clothbound, 199 pp.	60.00	80.00
☐ **Bullock, J.** *Rudiments of the Art of Building.* N.p., 1853. Clothbound, 180 pp.	36.00	47.00
☐ **Burn, Robert S.** *The Illustrated Architectural, Engineering, and Mechanical Drawing-Book.* London, n.d., c. 1870. Clothbound..	25.00	33.00
☐ **Chorlton, William.** *The American Grape Grower's Guide.* New York, 1856. Clothbound, 171 pp.	52.00	67.00
☐ **Clough, Albert.** *The Operation, Care and Repair of Automobiles.* New York, 1907......................	15.00	20.00
☐ **Cobleigh, Rolfe.** *American Agriculturist Hand Book.* N.p., 1910. Soft covered.	9.00	12.00
☐ **Cochrane, Charles H.** *The Wonders of Modern Mechanism.* Philadelphia, 1896. Silver gilt cloth, 402 pp......... Covers all then-recent inventions, such as the automobile, airplane, phonograph, etc..	30.00	40.00
☐ **Crabtree, Jerome.** *Marvels of Modern Mechanism and Their Relation to Social Betterment.* Springfield, Massachusetts, 1901.	20.00	25.00
☐ **Dadd, George.** *The Modern Horse Doctor.* New York, 1859.	23.00	30.00
☐ **Davidson, E.** *Drawing for Stonemasons.* London, n.d., c. 1880–1890. Clothbound, 95 pp.	18.00	23.00
☐ **Davis, Jeanette.** *Elements of Modern Dressmaking for the Amateur and Professional.* London, 1895. Clothbound, 193 pp..	30.00	40.00
☐ **Dearborn, Nathaniel.** *Scrolls, Monograms, Ornaments, Crests for the Use of Artists, Designers, Engravers, and Art Workmen.* Boston, 1869............................	70.00	100.00
☐ **Dipman, Carl.** *The Modern Grocery Store.* New York, 1931. Clothbound, 200 pp. .... About a year after this book was published, America's first self-service supermarket (King Cullen) was opened in New York.	20.00	25.00
☐ **Dixon, Thomas.** *Treatise on the Arrangement, Application, and Use of Slide Rules.* Buttershaw, England, 1881. Clothbound. Second edition....................................	16.00	21.00
☐ **E. M. C. (author identified by initials only).** *The Lady's Knitting Book, Containing Eighty Easy Patterns of Useful and Ornamental Work.* New York, 1879. Pocket size......	23.00	32.00

PRICE RANGE

☐ **Fairham, William.** *Wood Turning.* Philadelphia, n.d., early twentieth century. 14.00   18.00

☐ **FitzGerald, W.** *The Harness Maker's Illustrated Manual.* N.p., 1881. Clothbound, 327 pp. 47.00   63.00

☐ **Flanders, R.** *Gear Cutting Machinery.* N.p., 1909. Clothbound, 319 pp. 14.00   18.00

☐ **Flint, C.** *Milch Cows and Dairy Farming.* N.p., 1874. Clothbound, 452 pp. 25.00   32.00

☐ **Fowler, P. G.** *Fowler's Improved Model, or Dress Making Made Easy.* Chicago, 1853. Soft covered, 8 pp. 47.00   63.00
This is also collectable as a "pre-fire" Chicago imprint.

☐ **Freeman, E.** *An Essay on the Origin and Development of Window Tracery in England.* Oxford, 1851. . . . . 47.00   63.00
Window tracery was the art of decorating windows with lead or wood (usually lead) designs in various styles.

☐ **Fryer, Jane E.** *The Mary Frances Sewing Book.* Philadelphia, 1913. Clothbound, 280 pp. 37.00   48.00

☐ **Gilbert, Alfred.** *Knots and Splices, with Rope Tying Tricks.* New Haven, 1920. Clothbound, 82 pp. 10.00   14.00

☐ **Gillespie, W. M.** *A Manual of the Principles of Road Making.* New York, 1848. . . . . 68.00   87.00
Discusses underground railways (which did not yet exist).

☐ **Gilroy, C.** *The Art of Weaving.* N.p., 1844. Clothbound, 574 pp. 40.00   52.00

☐ **Goodwin, Emma.** *Goodwin's Home Course in Sewing: Practical Instructions in Needlework for Use in the Home.* New York, 1912. Patterns inserted in rear pocket; price is for copy with all seven patterns present and in reasonable condition. 23.00   31.00

☐ **Graham and Emery.** *Audel's Masons and Builders Guide.* N.p., 1924. Four volumes. 19.00   24.00

☐ **Grant, George.** *A Treatise on Gear Wheels.* Boston, 1903. . . . . 14.00   18.00

☐ **Greeley, Horace.** *The Great Industries of the United States.* Hartford, 1872. Calf bound, 1,304 pp. 45.00   58.00
The author was an unsuccessful Presidential candidate.

☐ **Gregory, James J.** *Onion Raising: What Kinds to Raise and the Way to Raise Them.* Salem, Massachusetts, 1875. Soft covered, 34 pp. 11.00   16.00

☐ **Greiner, T.** *Practical Farm Chemistry.* LaSalle, New York, 1891. Clothbound, 163 pp. 14.00   18.00

☐ **Grier, W.** *The Mechanic's Calculator.* N.p., 1839. Clothbound, 308 pp. 27.00   35.00

☐ **Gurley, W. and L. E.** *A Manual of the Principal Instruments Used in American Engineering and Surveying.* Troy, New York, 1878. Gilt cloth binding, 234 pp. 58.00   73.00

☐ **Gurley, W. and L. E.** *A Manual of the Principal Instruments Used in American Engineering and Surveying.* Troy, New York, 1891. Twenty-ninth edition. 32.00   43.00

☐ **Haney, J.** *Soap Maker's Manual.* New York, 1869. Soft covered, 48 pp. 37.00   48.00

PRICE RANGE

☐ **Hapgood, Olive.** *School Needlebook. A Course of Study in Sewing Designed for Use in School.* Boston, 1893. Clothbound, 244 pp. 14.00 18.00

☐ **Hartley, Florence.** *The Ladies' Hand Book of Fancy and Ornamental Work, Comprising Directions and Patterns.* Philadelphia, 1861. Clothbound, 240 pp. 35.00 43.00

☐ **Hasluck, Paul.** House Decoration, Comprising Whitewashing, Paperhanging, etc. Philadelphia, 1914. Clothbound, 160 pp. 16.00 21.00

☐ **Hasluck, Paul N.** *Practical Plumber's Work.* Philadelphia, 1912. .... 11.00 16.00

☐ **Hawney, W.** *The Complete Measurer, or the Whole Art of Measuring. Very Useful for All Tradesmen, Especially Carpenters, Bricklayers, Plasterers, Painters, Joiners, Glassiers, Masons, etc.* Philadelphia, 1807.................... 32.00 43.00

☐ **Heaton, N.** *Outlines of Paint Technology.* London, 1928. Clothbound, 400 pp. 14.00 18.00

☐ **Heller and Co.** *Heller's Guide for Ice Cream Makers.* Chicago, 1918. Clothbound, 154 pp. 23.00 32.00
Contains numerous ads for the company's products and could be classified as a trade catalogue.

☐ *Henderson's American Farmer's Manual, 1890.* New York. Soft covered, 24 pp. 19.00 24.00

☐ **Hess and Bright.** *History and Development of Ball Bearings.* N.p., 1918. Bound in boards, 108 pp. 17.00 23.00

☐ **Hodgson, Fred.** *Easy Lessons in the Art of Practical Wood Carving.* Chicago, 1905................................. 22.00 31.00

☐ **Hodgson, Fred.** *Hodgson's Modern Estimator and Contractor's Guide for Pricing All Builder's Work.* Chicago, 1917. Clothbound, 305 pp. 11.00 16.00

☐ **Hodgson, Fred.** *The Steel Square. A Practical Treatise on the Application of the Steel Square.* N.p., 1916. Clothbound. 18.00 24.00

☐ **Holtzapffel, C.** *Turning and Mechanical Manipulation.* London, 1856. Two volumes.................................. 42.00 54.00

☐ **Hulme, Edward.** *The Birth and Development of Ornament.* London and New York, 1893............................ 16.00 21.00

☐ **Humber, William.** *A Practical Treatise on Cast and Wrought Iron Bridges and Girders.* London, 1857................. 185.00 230.00

☐ **Hurst, George.** *Soaps: A Practical Manual of the Manufacture of Domestic, Toilet and Other Soaps.* London, 1907. Second edition... 14.00 18.00

☐ **Isler, C.** *Well Boring for Water, Brine and Oil.* London and New York, 1902.. 15.00 20.00

☐ **Jack, George.** *Wood Carving Design and Workmanship.* New York, 1903. Boards with cloth spine................. 23.00 31.00

☐ **Jackson, I.** *An Elementary Treatise on Mechanics.* Schenectady, New York, 1854. Clothbound. 16.00 21.00

☐ **Jameson, P. R.** *Weather and Weather Instruments.* Rochester, New York, 1912. Soft cloth binding. 14.00 18.00

☐ **Johnson, John J.** *Directions for Using the Patent Excelsior Tanning Process Patented by John Jay Johnson.* Kalmazoo, Michigan, 1866. Soft covered...................... 12.00 17.00

PRICE RANGE

☐ **Jones, F.** *Thread Cutting Methods.* N.p., 1918. Cloth-bound, 344 pp. 12.00 17.00

☐ **Kelly, Ashmun.** *The Expert Interior Decoration.* N.p., 1921. Privately printed. Second edition. 21.00 28.00

☐ **Kelly, Ashmun.** *The Expert Paper Hanger.* Philadelphia, 1921. Second Edition....................................... 16.00 21.00

☐ **Kentish, Thomas A.** *Treatise on a Box of Instruments and the Slide Rule, for the Use of Guagers, Engineers, Seamen and Students.* Philadelphia, 1877. Clothbound, 228 pp.. 16.00 21.00

☐ **King, Charles A.** *Inside Finishing.* New York, 1912. Cloth-bound, 227 pp. 16.00 21.00
Manual for painters and carpenters.

☐ **Kinsley, Charles.** *The Circle of Useful Knowledge for the Use of Farmers, Mechanics, Merchants, Manufacturers, Surveyors, Housekeepers, etc.* Clinton, Iowa, 1881....... 14.00 18.00
Also of interest as an early Iowa imprint.

☐ **Kinsley, Charles.** *Self-instructor on Lumber Surveying for the Use of Lumber Manufacturers, Surveyors, and Teachers.* Calais, Maine, 1870. Clothbound, 80 pp. 23.00 31.00

☐ **Knight, Edward H.** *Knight's New Mechanical Dictionary.* Boston, 1884. Clothbound, 960 pp. 50.00 65.00

☐ **Koogle, J. D.** *The Farmer's Own Book.* Baltimore, 1857. Clothbound, 226 pp. 50.00 65.00

☐ **Lagenbeck, Karl.** *The Chemistry of Pottery.* Easton, Pennsylvania, 1895. Clothbound, 197 pp. 32.00 43.00
Langenbeck was a director of the prestigious Rookwood Pottery Co..

☐ **Lemos, Pedro.** *Color Cement Handicraft.* Worcester, Massachusetts, 1922. Clothbound, 201 pp.................... 15.00 19.00

☐ **Leslie, Eliza.** *The American Girl's Book.* New York, 1879. Clothbound, 383 pp. 16.00 21.00

☐ **Lieber, Oscar.** *The Assayer's Guide, or Practical Directions to Assayers, Miners and Smelters, for Tests and Assays of the Principal Metals.* Philadelphia, 1875.......... 22.00 30.00

☐ **Lock, C.** *Tobacco Growing, Curing and Manufacturing.* N.p., 1903. Clothbound, 285 pp. 17.00 23.00

☐ **Lukin, Rev. J.** *Amongst Machines: A Description of Various Mechanical Applicances Used in the Manufacture of Wood, Metal and Other Substances.* New York, 1876. Clothbound, 335 pp. 22.00 31.00

☐ **Lyon, R. P.** *Standard Reference Book of the Furniture Trade.* N.p., 1885.. 60.00 80.00

☐ **MacCabe, Frederic.** *The Art of Ventriloquism.* London, n.d., c. 1885–1890. Bound in stiff boards, 110 pp. 28.00 36.00
This was about 40 years before the first internationally known ventriloquist, Edgar Bergen, came on the scene.

☐ **Maginnis, Owen.** *How to Measure Up Woodwork for Buildings.* New York, 1903. .... 14.00 18.00

☐ **Maire, F.** *Modern Painter's Encyclopedia.* Chicago, 1918. Clothbound, 447 pp. 18.00 24.00

☐ **McClure, Abbot.** *Making Floors.* New York, 1915. Cloth-bound, 64 pp.. 16.00 21.00

PRICE RANGE

☐ **McLaren, Walter.** *Spinning Woolen and Worsted.* London, 1884. Clothbound, 256 pp. — 21.00 — 28.00

☐ **Moore, R.** *The Artizan's Guide and Everybody's Assistant, Containing Over Three Thousand New and Valuable Receipts and Tables.* Montreal, 1873. Clothbound, 306 pp. — 21.00 — 28.00

☐ **Moore R.** *The Universal Assistant.* New York, 1880. Clothbound, 1,016 pp. — 26.00 — 35.00

☐ **Nash, E.** *The Farmer's Practical Horse Farriery.* New York, 1859. Clothbound, 198 pp. — 48.00 — 63.00

☐ **Newton, A. V.** *The Saloon Keeper's Companion and Book of Reference for Saloon Keepers, Proprietors of Hotels, and Sporting Men.* Worcester, Massachusetts, 1875. Clothbound, approx. 450 pp. — 48.00 — 63.00

☐ **Noyes, William.** *Handwork in Wood.* Peoria, Illinois, 1915. Clothbound, 231 pp. — 16.00 — 21.00

☐ **Nystrom, John.** *Pocket-Book of Mechanics and Engineering.* Philadelphia, 1864. Pocket size. — 18.00 — 24.00

☐ **Overman and Fresquet.** *The Manufacture of Steel, Containing the Practice and Principles of Working and Making Steel.* Philadelphia, 1891. Clothbound, 285 pp. — 28.00 — 36.00

☐ **Overman and Fresquet.** *The Moulder's and Founder's Pocket Guide.* Philadelphia, 1885. Clothbound, 342 pp. — 28.00 — 36.00

☐ **Owens, C. M.** *Owen's Paint Guide. Easy to Understand.* Chicago, 1926. Clothbound, 74 pp. — 11.00 — 16.00

☐ **Peats, Alfred.** *Designing, Coloring and Uses of Wall Paper.* New York, 1912. Soft covered. — 32.00 — 41.00

☐ **Perrigo, Oscar.** *Change Gear Devices, Showing the Development of the Screw Cutting Lathe.* New York, 1903. Clothbound, 81 pp. — 16.00 — 21.00

☐ **Phin, John.** *The Practical Upholsterer.* New York, 1891. Clothbound, 116 pp. — 23.00 — 31.00

☐ **Plattner and Muspratt.** *The Use of the Blowpipe.* London, 1854. Clothbound, 405 pp. — 18.00 — 24.00

☐ **Pontey, W.** *The Profitable Planter.* Huddersfield, England, 1808. Privately printed. — 43.00 — 58.00

☐ **Poole, B. W.** *The Science of Pattern Construction for Garment Makers.* London, 1927. Clothbound, 439 pp. — 43.00 — 58.00

☐ **Purchase, William.** *Practical Masonry.* London, 1898. — 43.00 — 58.00

☐ **Quinby, M.** *Mysteries of Bee-Keeping Explained, Being A Complete Analysis of the Whole Subject.* New York, 1860. Clothbound, 384 pp. — 21.00 — 27.00

☐ **Richardson, M. T.** *Practical Blacksmithing.* New York, 1890. Clothbound. Three volumes. — 63.00 — 84.00

☐ **Rose, Joshua.** *The Complete Practical Machinist, Embracing Lathe Work, Vice Work, Drills and Drilling, Taps and Dies, etc.* Philadelphia and London, 1883, Clothbound, 441 pp. — 25.00 — 33.00

☐ **Ross, Joseph.** *Waterproofing Engineering for Engineers, Architects, Builders, Roofers and Waterproofers.* New York, 1919. Clothbound, 442 pp. — 14.00 — 18.00

☐ **Ross-Mackenzie, J.** *Brewing and Malting.* New York, 1935. Clothbound, 182 pp. — 23.00 — 31.00

	PRICE RANGE	

☐ **Row, Saundra.** *Geometric Exercises in Paper Folding.* Chicago, 1917. Clothbound, 148 pp. **14.00** **18.00**

☐ **Russell, William.** *Russell on Scientific Horseshoeing for Leveling, and Balancing the Action and Gait of Horses.* Cincinnati, 1895. Clothbound, 279 pp. **52.00** **73.00**

☐ **Sadler, S.** *The Art and Science of Sailmaking.* London, 1892. Clothbound, 137 pp. **27.00** **34.00**

☐ **Schriber, Fritz.** *The Complete Carriage and Wagon Painter.* New York, 1884. Clothbound, 177 pp. **37.00** **48.00**

☐ **Scrimshaw, Steward.** *Bricklaying in Modern Practice.* New York, 1927. Clothbound, 182 pp. **11.00** **16.00**

☐ **Simmonds, Thomas.** *Wood Carving.* London, n.d., early twentieth century. Clothbound, 91 pp. **21.00** **27.00**

☐ **Smead, B.** *Best System of Dying Woolen, Cotton and Silk.* Bennington, Vermont, 1811. . . . . **125.00** **155.00**

☐ **Springsteed, Anne F.** *The Expert Waitress.* New York, 1901. Clothbound, 131 pp. **14.00** **18.00**

☐ **Stephens, Ann S.** *The Ladies' Complete Guide to Fancy Knitting, Crochet and Needlework.* New York, 1854. Clothbound, 117 pp. . . . . : **42.00** **58.00**

☐ **Stephens, W. P.** *Canoe and Boat Building. A Complete Manual.* New York, 1887. Clothbound, 189 pp. **105.00** **135.00**

☐ **Stephenson and Suddards.** A Text Book Dealing With Ornamental Designs for Woven Fabrics. London, 1897. Clothbound, 273 pp. **27.00** **35.00**

☐ **Stokes, J.** *The Cabinet-Maker's and Upholsterer's Companion.* Philadelphia, 1850. Clothbound, 167 pp. **85.00** **105.00**

☐ **Storke, E. G.** *The Family and Householder's Guide.* Auburn, New York, 1859. Clothbound, 238 pp. **42.00** **58.00**

☐ **Strawbridge and Clothier.** *Dictionary of the Stitches Used in Art Needlework.* Philadelphia, 1885. Soft covered, 46 pp. **16.00** **21.00**

☐ **Swift, James.** *The Practical Telegrapher.* New York, 1883. Clothbound, 189 pp. **42.00** **58.00**

☐ **Sylvester, Allen.** *The Modern House-Carpenter's Companion and Builder's Guide..* Boston, 1883. Clothbound, 210 pp. **27.00** **33.00**

☐ **Symonds, William.** *The Practical Gager (sic), or The Young Gager's Assistant, With an Appendix for Maltsters, Distillers, Common Brewers, Victuallers, etc.* London, 1811. Calf bound, 384 pp. **32.00** **43.00**
"Common brewers" was not a slur against brewers; it referred to brewers of so-called "common beer."

☐ **Taylor and Thompson.** *A Treatise on Concrete.* N.p., 1909. Clothbound, 807 pp. **18.00** **23.00**

☐ **Townsend, Gilbert.** *Carpentry and Joinery. A Working Manual of Approved American Practice in the Selection of Lumber, the Framing of Buildings, etc.* Chicago, 1908. Clothbound, 145 pp. **16.00** **21.00**

☐ **Ure, Andrew.** *A Dictionary of Arts, Manufactures and Mines.* New York, 1852. Bound in calf. **67.00** **88.00**

☐ **Usher, J.** *The Modern Machinest.* N. p., 1900. Clothbound, 332 pp. **14.00** **18.00**

PRICE RANGE

☐ **VanDervoort, William H.** *Machine Shop Tools and Shop Practice.* New York, 1918. Clothbound, 552 pp........... **16.00 21.00**

☐ **Vanderwalker, F. N.** *Interior Wall Decoration.* Chicago, 1938. Clothbound, 491 pp. **14.00 18.00**

☐ **Vanderwalker, F. N.** *Painting and Decorating Working Methods. A Text Book for Apprentice, Journeyman, House-painter, Decorator.* New York, 1922..................... **21.00 27.00**

☐ **Vosburgh, H. K.** *Tinsmith's Helper and Pattern Book.* New York, 1901. Clothbound, 120 pp........................ **18.00 25.00**

☐ **Wells and Hooper.** *Modern Cabinet Work, Furniture and Fitments.* London, 1938. Clothbound, 390. With folding plates. **32.00 43.00**

☐ **Whall, C.** *Stained Glass Work, A Text Book for Students and Workers in Glass.* London, 1905. Clothbound, 381 pp... **21.00 27.00**

☐ **Wright, F. B.** *A Practical Handbook of the Distillation of Alcohol from Farm Products.* New York, 1906. Clothbound, 271 pp....................................... **21.00 27.00**

☐ **White, W. F.** *The Practical House, Wagon and Automobile Painter.* Chicago, 1902. Clothbound, 157 pp. **31.00 39.00**
At that time autos were generally available only in basic black, and many owners repainted them.

☐ **Wilton, Countess of.** *The Art of Needlework.* London, 1841. Clothbound, 405 pp. **52.00 67.00**

☐ **Wright, Thomas.** *The Romance of the Lace Pillow.* Olney, England, 1930. Two volumes. **47.00 63.00**

☐ **Young, Charles L.** *Practical Painting and Paper Hanging in All Its Branches.* New York, 1924. Clothbound, 414 pp. **16.00 21.00**

FOOD AND DRINK

PRICE RANGE

☐ **Acton, Eliza.** *The English Bread-Book for Domestic Use. Practical receipts for many varieties of bread, etc.* London, 1857. Clothbound. **48.00 63.00**

☐ **Allen, H. Warner.** *Sherry.* London, 1934. Clothbound..... **15.00 20.00**

☐ **Ames, Richard.** *The Bacchanalian Sessions; or, The Contention of Liquors: With a Farewell to Wine.* By the Author of the Search after Claret. London, for E. Hawkins, 1693. **265.00 335.00**

☐ **Ames, Richard.** *Fatal Friendship. Or, The Drunkard's Misery. Being a Satry against Hard Drinking.* London, for Randal Taylor, 1693. Bound in calf. **240.00 290.00**
"Satry" meant, of course, "satire."

☐ *Archdeacon's Kitchen Cabinet.* Chicago, 1876........... **42.00 58.00**

☐ **Armstrong, John.** *The Young Woman's Guide to Virtue, Economy and Happiness. With a complete and elegant system of Domestic Cookery.* Newcastle (England), n.d. (c. 1819). With engraved frontis, and 10 engraved plates. Calf-bound.. .... **110.00 140.00**
Mainly a handbook for young ladies who intended going into domestic service..

	PRICE RANGE	

☐ **Barrows, Anna.** *Principles of Cookery.* Chicago, 1910. . . | **18.00** | **24.00**

☐ **Bird, William.** *A Practical Guide to French Wines.* Paris, n.d. (c. 1926). With 2 maps. Softbound. . . . . | **14.00** | **19.00**
Intended for English-speaking tourists in Paris.

☐ **Bishop, James.** *A Brief Statement of Facts , in Illustration of the Operation of the New Beer Laws.* London, 1839. 7 pp. Printed in gold type on green paper. . . . . | **80.00** | **105.00**

☐ **Bluher, Dr. P. M.** *International Encyclopaedia of Food and Drink.* Third Edition, Leipzig, 1901. Two vols. Text in English, German and French. Bound in half morocco. . . . . . . | **130.00** | **175.00**

☐ **Blot, Pierre.** *What to Eat and How to Cook it.* N.Y., 1865. | **65.00** | **85.00**

☐ **Blot, Pierre.** *Hand-Book of Practical Cookery.* N.Y., 1868. | **27.00** | **35.00**

☐ **Boyle, Robert.** *Short Memoirs for the Natural Experimental History of Mineral Waters.* London, for Samuel Smith, 1684– 5. Calfbound. . . . . | **450.00** | **600.00**

☐ **Brewer, Samuel Child.** *Every Man His Own Brewer: A small Treatise, explaining the Art and Mystery of Brewing Porter Ale, Twopenny and Table-Beer..* Third Edition, carefully revised. London: Dring and Co., n.d. (c. 1790). Bound in half calf. . . . . | **90.00** | **115.00**

☐ **Briggs, Richard.** *The English Art of Cookery, according to the present practice; being a complete guide to all housekeepers.* Third Edition, London, 1794. With 12 engraved plated. . . . . | **150.00** | **200.00**
The author was a noted tavern cook in his day.

☐ **Brooks, R. O.** *Vinegars and Catsup.* N.Y., 1912. . . . . | **16.00** | **21.00**

☐ **Brown, Susan A.** *The Invalid's Tea-Tray.* Boston, 1885. | **22.00** | **29.00**

☐ **Carnell, P. P.** *A Treatise of Family Wine Making: Calculated for making excellent Wines from the Various Fruits of this United Country.* London, 1814. Bound in boards. . . . . | **180.00** | **235.00**

☐ **Carson, Juliet.** *The American Family Cookbook.* Chicago, 1898. . . . . | **42.00** | **58.00**

☐ **Carter, Charles.** *The Compleat City and Country Cook: or, Accomplished House-Wife.* London: A Bettesworth and C. Hitch, 1732. With 49 copperplate engravings. Calfbound. . . . . | **625.00** | **775.00**

☐ **Clark, Imogen.** *Rhymed Receipts for Any Occasion.* Boston, 1912. . . . . | **21.00** | **28.00**

☐ **Collingwood, Francis** and **Woollams, John.** *The Universal Cook and City and Country Housekeeper. Containing all the various branches of cookery; the different methods of dressing butchers meat, poultry, game and fish; and preparing gravies, cullices, soups and broths; to dress roots and vegetables and to prepare little elegant dishes for suppers or light repasts.* Third Edition. London: Printed by C. Whittingham for J. Scatherd, 1792. With portrait and 13 engraved plates. . . . . | **170.00** | **225.00**

☐ *Cookery for the Many as well as for the "Upper Ten Thousand."* London, 1864. With a colored frontis and 3 colored plates. Half cloth.

PRICE RANGE

☐ **Cooper, A.** *The Complete Distiller. To which are added accurate descriptions of the several Drugs, Plants, Flowers, Fruits, etc., used by Distillers and instructions for choosing the best of each kind.* London: P. Vaillant and R. Griffiths, 1757. . . . . 265.00   335.00

☐ **Cornelius, Mrs.** *The Young Housekeeper's Friend.* Boston and N.Y., 1846. . . . . 135.00   175.00

☐ *Cre-Fydd's Family Fare. The Young Housewife's Daily Assistant on all matters relating Cookery and Housekeeping. Second edition, revised.* London, 1864. Clothbound. 52.00   67.00

☐ **Croly, Mrs. J. C.** *Jennie June's American Cookery Book.* N.Y., 1870. . . . . 47.00   62.00

☐ *Dainty Dishes for Slender Incomes.* N.Y., 1900. . . . . 22.00   30.00

☐ **Darby, Charles.** *Bacchanalia. Or, a Description of a Drunken Club.* London, for Robert Boulter, 1680. Folio. 16 pp. Calfbound. 325.00   425.00

☐ **Decker, John W.** *Cheese Making.* Wisconsin, 1909. . . . . . . 30.00   39.00

☐ *Dining and Its Amenities. By "A Lover of Good Cheer."* N.Y., 1907. . . . . 27.00   35.00

☐ *Experienced American Housekeeper.* Hartford, 1836. With four engraved plates, one of which is a folding plate. Price given is for a sound copy. 135.00   175.00

☐ **Farley, John.** *The London Art of Cookery and Housekeeper's Complete Assistant. Eight Edition.* London: John Fielding, J. Scatcherd, and J. Whitacker, 1796. With portrait and 12 engraved plates, showing menus for every month of the year. 200.00   250.00

☐ **Gillette, Mrs. F. L.** *White House Cook Book.* Chicago, 1889. . . . . 85.00   110.00

☐ **Glasse, Mrs. Hannah.** *The Art of Cookery, made plain and easy, by a Lady.* London, printed for the Author, and sold by Mrs. Ashburn's, a China-shop, the corner of Fleet-Ditch, 1747. Folio. The most valuable cookbook in the English language. But take note that the value is for a FIRST EDITION, published 1747. There were numerous subsequent editions, none of which are worth nearly as much. 14,000.00 19,000.00

☐ **Glasse, Mrs.** *The Art of Cookery made plain and easy . . . in which are included, One Hundred and Fifty new and useful Receipts. New Edition, with all the modern improvements.* London: Longman, 1796. Calfbound. 210.00   265.00

☐ *Good Cook, The.* By a Practical Housekeeper, N.Y., 1853. . . . . 55.00   75.00

☐ **Hackwood, Frederick W.** *Good Cheer. The Romance of Food and Feasting.* London, 1911. With colored frontispiece and 20 plates. Clothbound. 52.00   67.00

☐ **Harrison, Mrs. Sarah.** *The House-Keeper's Pocket-Book: and Compleat Family Cook. Containing above seven hundred curious and uncommon receipts, in Cookery, Pastry, Preserving, Pickling, Candying, Collaring, etc.* London, 1748. Calfbound. 235.00   315.00

PRICE RANGE

☐ **Hasselmore, Anthony.** *The Economist, or New Family Cookery.* London, 1824. With 17 engraved plates, most of them more elaborate than those usually found in cookery books of this era. The title page has an engraving of a peasant girl feeding chickens and watering pigs.......... **215.00 265.00**

☐ **Hassall, A. H.** *Adulterations Detected; or Plain Instructions for the Discovery of Frauds in Food and Medicine.* London, 1857, Clothbound. **75.00 100.00**
A landmark work, which alerted the public to many deceits of the commercial food industry.

☐ **Henderson, Robert.** *An inquiry into the nature and object of the several laws for restraining and regulating the retail sale of Ale, Beer, Wines and Spirits.* London, 1817. 144 pp. **57.00 72.00**
"Retail sale" meant primarily the sale of packaged spirits.

☐ **Henderson, W. A.** *The Housekeeper's Instructor: being a full and clear display of the Art of Cookery in all its branches ... To which is added the Complete Art of Carving.* 12th edition. London, 1805. With engraved frontis, 2 folding plates and 2 other plates. Bound in half calf.................... **110.00 145.00**
Same, 14 edition. London, 1807......................... **87.00 115.00**

☐ **Henderson, W. A.** *Modern Domestic Cookery and Useful Receipt Book.* Boston, 1844. .... **135.00 170.00**

☐ **Heug, H.** *New Book of Designs for Cake-Bakers, etc.* N.p., 1893. .... **30.00 38.00**

☐ **Hill, John.** *An Account of a stone in the possession of the Right Honourable the Earl of Stafford; which on being watered produces excellent mushrooms.* London, 1758. 38 pp. with 2 folding plates. **110.00 140.00**
The remarkable stone apparently had enough moss growing on it to produce fungi, leading unscientific observers to believe that mushrooms were growing from the stone itself.

☐ **Hillard, Thomas M.** *The Art of Carving.* Detroit, n.d. (1899)... **16.00 22.00**

☐ **Hirtzler, Victor.** *The Hotel St. Francis Cook Book.* Chicago, 1919. .... **18.00 24.00**

☐ **Hitchcock, Nevada D.** *The Record War-Time Cook Book.* Philadelphia, 1918....................................... **10.00 13.00**

☐ **Hooper, Mary.** *Handbook for the Breakfast Table. Varied and economical dishes.* London, 1873. 62 pp. Clothbound. **38.00 49.00**
Even the "light" breakfast of 1873 would be deemed heavy—and too bothersome to prepare—by modern standards.

☐ *How to Cook Fish.* Cincinnati, 1886. Softbound. **21.00 27.00**

☐ **King, Chas. H.** *Cakes, Cake Decorations and Desserts.* Philadelphia, 1896....................................... **29.00 38.00**

☐ **Kirwan, A. V.** *Host and Guest.* London, 1864............ **27.00 35.00**

☐ *Kitchen Directory and American Housewife.* N.Y., 1844. Softbound. **75.00 95.00**

☐ **Kitchener, William.** *The Cook's Oracle.* Boston, 1822.... **135.00 170.00**

PRICE RANGE

☐ **Kitchener, William.** *The Cook's Oracle: containing receipts for plain cookery on the most economic plan for private families...containing also a complete system of cookery for catholic families. A new edition.* London, 1827. Bound in boards. 75.00   95.00

☐ **Kittelby, Mary.** *A Collection of above Three Hundred Receipts in Cookery, Physick and Surgery; for the use of all good wives, tender mothers and careful nurses, by several hands. To which is added a second part containing a great number of excellent receipts for preserving and conserving of sweet-meats, etc.* London, 1746. Sixth edition. Calf-bound. 160.00   200.00
The recipes include a drink called "snail water."

☐ **Lambert, Mrs. Almeda.** *Guide for Nut Cookery.* Battle Creek, Michigan, 1899. . . . .   125.00   160.00

☐ **Langdon, Amelie.** *Just for Two. Recipes designed for two Persons.* Minneapolis, 1907. . . . .   12.00   16.00

☐ **Larned, Linda H.** *The New Hostess To-Day.* N.Y., 1917.   16.00   21.00

☐ **Lea, Elizabeth E.** *Domestic Cookery, Useful Receipts etc.* Baltimore, 1853. Fifth edition. 85.00   105.00

☐ **Lebour-Fawssett, Emilie.** *Economical French Cookery for Ladies.* London, 1887. Clothbound. 47.00   62.00

☐ **Lehner, Joseph C.** *World's Fair Menu and Recipe Book.* San Francisco, 1915. . . . .   37.00   48.00

☐ **Lemery, Louis.** *A Treatise of all Sorts of Foods, both Animal and Vegetable; also of Drinkables; Giving an Account how to chuse the best Sort of all Kinds.* London, 1745. Calf-bound. 290.00   365.00

☐ **Leslie, Miss.** *75 Receipts for Pasty, Cakes, and Sweet-meats, by a Lady of Philadelphia.* Boston, n.d. (1828). . . .   185.00   235.00

☐ **Leslie, Miss.** *Directions for Cookery.* Philadelphia, 1863. 59th edition. 21.00   29.00

☐ *Lessons of Thrift published for General Benefit.* By a Member of the Save-All Club. London, 1820. With 12 colored aquatints by Cruikshank. Bound in gilt morocco. Though largely a satirical work, the illustrations give a fairly accurate view of (for example) proceedings in a no-frills chophouse of the era. Theft of tableware was such a problem that knives, forks, etc., were chained to the table. 210.00   275.00

☐ **Lincoln, Mrs.** *Boston Cook Book. What To Do and What Not To Do in Cooking.* Boston, 1884. . . . .   500.00   600.00

☐ **Lincoln, Mrs.** *Carving and Serving.* Boston, 1915. . . . .   20.00   25.00

☐ **Lincoln, Mrs. D. A.** *Boston School Kitchen Textbook.* Boston, 1887. . . . .   27.00   35.00

☐ **Lincoln, Mary.** *The Peerless Cook Book.* Boston, 1901. Softbound. 16.00   21.00

☐ **Lippman, B. F.** *Aunt Betty's Cook Book.* Cincinnati, 1918. . . . .   16.00   22.00

☐ **Llanover, Lady Augusta.** *The First Principles of Good Cookery.* London, 1867. Illustrated. Clothbound. 75.00   95.00

☐ **Lockhart, Marion.** *Standard Cook Book for all Occasions.* N.Y., 1925. . . . .   13.00   18.00

PRICE RANGE

☐ **McCann, Alfred W.** *Thirty Cent Bread.* N.Y., 1917. Bound in boards. 16.00   21.00
Alfred W. McCann hosted the first food-and-cooking radio show.

☐ **MacDougall, A. F.** *Coffee and Waffles.* N.Y., 1927. . . . . . .   13.00   18.00

☐ **MacKenzie, Colin.** *MacKenzie's Five Thousand Receipts.* Philadelphia, 1825. . . . . 160.00   200.00

☐ **Maddocks, Mildred.** *The Pure Food Cook Book.* N.Y., 1914. . . . .   21.00   27.00

☐ **Mann, Mrs. Horace.** *Christianity in the Kitchen.* Boston, 1861. Cover reads "Health and Economy in Cooking.". . . .   72.00   93.00

☐ *Manual for Army Cooks.* Washington, 1896. . . . .   21.00   29.00

☐ **May, Robert.** *The Accomplished Cook; or The Art and Mystery of Cookery. Wherein the whole Art is revealed in a more easie and perfect Method, than hath been publisht in any language. Expert and ready wayes for Dressing of all sorts of Flesh, Fowl, and Fish; the Raising of Pastes; the best Directions for all manner of Kickshaws, and the most Poinant Sauces; with the Tearms of Carving and Serving.* London: R. W. for Nath. Brooke, 1660. Calfbound. . . . 1050.00 1400.00
Contains recipes for snails and baked frogs.

☐ **McKinney, E. and W.** *Aunt Caroline's Dixie-Land Recipes.* Chicago, 1922. . . . .   21.00   29.00

☐ **Mclaren, L. L.** *High Living Recipes from Southern Climes.* San Francisco, 1904. . . . .   95.00   120.00

☐ **Miller, Elizabeth S.** *In the Kitchen.* Boston, 1875. . . . .   27.00   36.00

☐ **Moritz, Mrs. C. F.** and **Kahn, Adele.** *The 20th Century Cook Book.* N.Y., 1898. Fifth edition. 27.00   36.00

☐ **Muckenstrum, Louis.** *Louis' Every Women's Cook Book.* Boston and N.Y., 1910. . . . .   21.00   27.00

☐ **Murrey, Thomas J.** *Valuable Cooking Receipts.* N.Y., 1886. . . . .   25.00   33.00

☐ **Murrey, Thomas J.** *Luncheon.* N.Y., 1888. . . . .   25.00   33.00

☐ **Murrey, Thomas J.** *The Book of Entrees.* N.Y., 1889. . . . .   21.00   27.00

☐ *National Cook Book. By "A Lady of Philadelphia."* Philadelphia, 1855. Fifth edition. Clothbound. 145.00   190.00

☐ **Neely, Flora.** *Hand-Book for the Kitchen and Housekeeper's Guide.* New Rochelle, N.Y., 1910.   21.00   28.00

☐ **Neill, Marion H.** *A Calendar of Dinners with 615 Recipes.* Cincinnati, 1921.
Proctor & Gamble promotional publications. 8.00   11.00

☐ **Neill, Miss E.** *The Every-Day Cook-Book and Encyclopedia of Practical Recipes.* N.Y., 1888. . . . .   27.00   35.00

☐ **Nelson, Harriet S.** *Fruits and their Cookery.* N.Y., 1921.   16.00   21.00

☐ *New Family Receipt-Book, containing 800 Truly Valuable Receipts in various branches of Domestic Economy, selected from the works of British and foreign writers.* London, 1811. Half calf. 85.00   105.00
Same, 1837 edition. 72.00   93.00

☐ **Nichol, Mary E.** *366 Dinners by "M.E.N."* N.Y., 1892. . . . .   21.00   28.00

☐ **Nicholson, Elizabeth.** *What I Know; or, Hints on the daily duties of a Housekeeper.* Philadelphia, 1856. . . . . 135.00   170.00

PRICE RANGE

☐ **Norton, Caroline T.** *The Rocky Mountain Cook Book.* Denver, 1903. . . . . 32.00   41.00
☐ **Nutt, Frederick.** *The Complete Confectioner, or the whole art of confectionary made easy; with receipts for liqueurs, home-made wines, etc.* New Edition, with additions. London, 1809. With 10 plates. Half calf. 160.00   205.00
☐ **Owen, Catherine.** *Culture and Cooking.* N.Y., 1881. . . . . . 32.00   42.00
☐ **Owen, Catherine.** *Choice Cookery.* N.Y., 1889. . . . . 32.00   42.00
☐ **Owens, Mrs. F.** *Cook Book and Useful Household Hints.* Chicago, 1883. . . . . 22.00   29.00
☐ **Panchard, E.** *Meats, Poultry and Game.* N.Y., 1919. . . . . . . 16.00   21.00
☐ **Parloa, Maria.** *The Appledore Cook Book.* Boston, 1878. 27.00   35.00
☐ **Parloa, Maria.** *Choice Receipts.* Dorchester (Mass.), 1895. Softbound. 13.00   18.00
☐ **Paul, Mrs. Sara T.** *Cookery from Experience.* Philadelphia, 1875. . . . . 27.00   35.00
☐ **Parker, T. N.** *Remarks on the Malt Tax: with reference to the debate in the House of Commons on the 10th March, 1835.* Shrewsbury (England), 1835, 34 pp. 27.00   35.00
☐ **Pereira, J.** *A Treatise on Food and Diet.* N.Y., 1843. . . . . . . 47.00   62.00
☐ **Poindexter, Charlotte M.** *Jane Hamilton's Recipes.* Chicago, 1909. . . . . 20.00   25.00
☐ **Poole, H. M.** *Fruits and How to Use Them.* N.Y., 1890. . . 21.00   28.00
☐ **Porter, Ebenezer.** *The Fatal Effects of Ardent Spirits:* A Sermon, by Ebenezer Porter, Late Pastor of the First Church in Washington, Connecticut, and now Professor in the theological Seminary in Andover, Massachusetts. Concord, 1813. Softbound. 95.00   120.00
☐ *Proclamation for restraint of Killing, Dressing and Eating of Flesh in Lent, or on Fish days, appointed by the Law, to be hereafter observed by all sorts of people. Given at Royston the fourteenth day of November, in the seventeenth yeere of Our Reigne (James I).* London: Bonham Norton and John Bill, 1609. Three sheets, unbound. Printed in gothic letter. 110.00   165.00
☐ **Pulte, Mrs. J. H.** *Domestic Cook Book.* Cincinnati, 1888. 30.00   40.00
☐ **Putman, Mrs.** *Receipt Book and Young Housekeeper's Assistant.* Boston, 1849. . . . . 75.00   95.00
☐ **Randolph, Mary.** *The Virginia Housewife, or Methodical Cook.* Washington, 1830. . . . . 525.00   675.00
☐ **Ranhofer, Charles.** *The Epicurean.* N.Y., 1900. . . . . 47.00   62.00
☐ **Reid, T. W.** *The Book of Cheese, being traits and stories of "Ye Olde Cheshire Cheese."* London, 1908. Clothbound gilt. 27.00   35.00
Ye Olde Cheshire Cheese was a noted London coffeehouse, which sponsored the publication of this book.
☐ *Remarks on the Present State of the Distillery of England and Scotland.* London, n.d. (c. 1790). 90 pp. Unbound. Relating to excise duties and the like. 48.00   63.00
☐ **Rees, Mrs. Jennie Day.** *The Complete Cook Book.* Philadelphia, 1900. . . . . 11.00   15.00
☐ **Rice, Louise.** *Dainty Dishes from Foreign Lands.* Chicago, 1911. . . . . 16.00   21.00

PRICE RANGE

☐ **Richards, Ellen H.** *Food Materials and Their Adulterations.* Boston, 1886. ... 47.00 63.00

☐ **Robinson, Mrs. H. M.** *The Practical Cook Book.* N.Y., 1864. ... 52.00 68.00

☐ **Rochfort, Louisa.** *The St. James' Cookery Book.* London, 1894. Clothbound. ... 35.00 45.00

☐ **Ronald, Mary.** *Century Cook Book.* N.Y., 1895 ... 27.00 35.00

☐ **Ronald, Mary.** *Luncheons.* N.Y., 1902. ... 12.00 17.00

☐ **Rorer, Sarah Tyson.** *Danity Dishes.* Philadelphia, 1890. 12.00 17.00

☐ **Rorer, Sarah Tyson.** *How to Cook Vegetables.* Philadelphia, 1893. Softbound. ... 12.00 17.00

☐ **Rorer, Sarah Tyson.** *Mrs. Roger's Cakes, Icings and Fillings.* Philadelphia, 1905. ... 16.00 21.00

☐ **Rouse, Lewis.** *Tunbridge Wells: or, A Directory of the Drinking of those Waters.* Londin, 1725. Unbound. Tunbridge Wells, England, is a well-known source of mineral water. ... 135.00 175.00

☐ **Rundle, Maria Eliza.** *A New System of Domestic Cookery, formed upon principles of economy and adapted to the use of private families.* London, 1807. With frontis and 9 engraved plates, mostly showing carving techniques. One of the earliest English cookbooks aimed at the middle classes. It was a huge success and remained in print for ages. ... 75.00 100.00
Same, 1849 edition (enlarged). ... 43.00 59.00

☐ **Rundell, Maria E.** *A New System of Domestic Cookery.* Boston, 1807. ... 310.00 390.00

☐ **Sala, George A.** *The Thorough Good Cook.* N.Y., 1896. ... 80.00 100.00

☐ **Snaderson, J. M.** and **Parkinson, E.** *The Complete Cook.* Philadelphia, 1846. ... 42.00 58.00

☐ **Scotson-Clark, G. F.** *Eating without Fears.* N.Y., 1923. ... 16.00 21.00

☐ **Scott, Mrs. Anna B.** *Mrs. Scott's North American Seasonal Cook Book.* Philadelphia, 1921 ... 21.00 28.00

☐ **Senn, C. Herman.** *The Book of Sauces.* Chicago, 1915. ... 10.00 14.00

☐ **Shaw, Thomas George.** *The Wine Trade and its History.* London, n.d. (1851). 151 pp. ... 37.00 46.00

☐ **Shillaber, Lydia.** *A New Daily Food. From the Ladies of St. Paul's Church, Morrisania, N.Y., 1885.* ... 27.00 34.00
This book is really more interesting as a piece of regional Americana than as a cookbook. Morrisania, then a town of its own, later became part of the Bronx, N.Y.

☐ **Short, Thomas.** *A Rational Discourse of the Inward Uses of Water. Shrewing it Nature, Choice, and Agreeableness to the Blood; its Operation on the Solids and Fluids, etc.* London: for Samuel Chandler, 1725. ... 225.00 300.00

☐ **Shute, Miss T. S.** *The American Housewife Cook Book.* Philadelphia, 1878. ... 38.00 49.00

☐ **Simpson, John.** *A Complete System of Cookery on a plan entirely new, containing Bills of Fare and directions to dress each dish.* London: W. Stewart, 1806. Bound in half calf. ... 300.00 375.00

Simpson was cook for the Marquis of Buckingham and this work is a compilation of dishes prepared for the Marquis during one full year..

☐ **Smith, Mrs.** *The Female Economist, or a plain system of Cookery for the use of families.* London, 1810. Half calf. — 52.00 — 67.00

☐ **Smith, John.** *Fruits and Farinacea, the proper food of man.* London, 1845. Clothbound. .... — 80.00 — 110.00
"Farinacea" was food made from grains, such as breads and cereals.

☐ **Smith, Mary.** *The Complete House-keeper and Professed Cook. Containing upwards of seven hundred practical and approved receipts. New Edition, with considerable additions and improvements.* Newcastle (England), 1786. Calf-bound. .... — 100.00 — 135.00

☐ **Soyer, Alexis.** *The Modern Housewife or Menegere, comprising nearly one thousand receipts for the economic and judicious preparation of every meal of the day and those of the nursery and sickroom.* London, 1858. With frontis and 5 engraved plates. Clothbound...................... — 77.00 — 102.00

☐ *Specimen authentique des infames speculations aux quelles a donne lieu le Siege de Paris.* Broadside (one sheet, printed on one side only). Paris, 1871............. — 85.00 — 105.00
A remarkable public expose of the black-market prices charged for foodstuffs, during the Siege of Paris in 1870–1871. Food was virtually impossible to obtain at Paris, thereby permitting underground agents to charge high sums, even for the flesh of dogs, cats, rats, and elephants.

☐ **St. Clair, Lady Harriet.** *Dainty Dishes.* Edinburgh, 1866. Clothbound. .... — 47.00 — 62.00

☐ *True Way, The, of Preserving and Candying, and Making Several Sorts of Sweet Meats, according to the Best and Truest Manner. Made Publick for the Benefit of all English Ladies and Gentlewomen; especially for my Scholars.* London: Printed for the Author, 1695. Calfbound............. — 600.00 — 750.00
It is unusual, in a book printed for the author, that the author fails to identify himself—and especially so with a non-controversial subject such as this. That the work was compiled "especially for my Scholars" leads to the conclusion that the author was a school teacher or private instructor.

☐ **Warner, Richard.** *Antiquitates Culinariae; or, Curious Tracts relating to the culinary affairs of the Old English.* London, 1791. With one plate. .... — 275.00 — 350.00

☐ *What One Can do with a Chafing-Dish. By S...A guide for Amateur Cooks.* N.Y., and London, n.d. (1896). Bound in cloth. .... — 37.00 — 48.00

☐ *What to Tell the Cook. Or the Native Cook's Assistant, being a Choice Collection of Recipes for Indian Cookery, Pastry, etc. Seventh edition.* Madras (India), 1901. Clothbound. .... — 25.00 — 32.00
An attempt to solve the communications problem between English natives resident in India and their household help.

☐ **Williams, M. M.** *The Chemistry of Cookery.* London, 1885. Clothbound. .... — 27.00 — 35.00

	PRICE RANGE	
☐ **Worlidge, J.** *Vinetum Britannicum: or, A Treatise of Cider, and such other Wines and Drinks that are extracted from all manner of Fruits growing in this Kingdom.* London, J. C. for Tho. Dring, 1676. Calfbound.	240.00	310.00
☐ **Wrenford, W.** *An Abstract of the Malt Laws, containing all the regulations affecting malsters and dealers in Malt.* London, 1827. 60 pp. Softbound.	35.00	44.00

LITERATURE
(FICTION, DRAMA, POETRY, HUMOR, ESSAYS)

	PRICE RANGE	
☐ **A'Beckett, Gilbert A.** *The Comic History of England.* London, 1857. Three vols., first edition in book form (originally issued in parts).	180.00	230.00
☐ **Addison, Joseph.** *The Free-Holder.* London, 1716.	78.00	105.00
☐ **Addison, Joseph.** *The Old Whig.* London, 1719.	125.00	160.00
☐ **Addison, Joseph.** *The Works of Joseph Addison.* London, 1721. Four vols., portrait.	93.00	125.00
☐ **Addison, Joseph.** *The Works of Joseph Addison.* London, 1811. Six vols.	52.00	67.00
☐ **Ade, George.** *Artie.* Chicago, 1896.	40.00	55.00
☐ **Ade, George.** *Fables in Slang.* Chicago, 1900.	45.00	60.00
☐ **Anderson, Sherwood.** *The American Country Fair.* N.Y., 1930. Softbound, limited edition.	40.00	55.00
☐ **Anderson, Sherwood.** *Perhaps Women.* N.Y., n.d., 1931. Blue cloth with pictorial dust wrapper.	60.00	80.00
☐ **Arnold, Matthew.** *The Strayed Reveler and Other Poems.* London, 1849. Green cloth.	450.00	550.00
☐ **Arnold, Matthew.** *Essays in Criticism.* London, 1865.	70.00	90.00
☐ **Arnold, Matthew.** *Friendship's Garland.* London, 1871.	25.00	32.00
☐ **Arnold, Matthew.** *Alaric at Rome.* London, 1893. Parchment boards.	85.00	110.00
☐ **Auden, W. H.** *The Orators.* London, 1932. Limited edition.	35.00	43.00
☐ **Auden, W. H.** *The Dance of Death.* London, 1933.	100.00	125.00
☐ **Auden, W. H.** *The Group Movement and the Middle Classes.* Oxford, 1934.	20.00	25.00
☐ **Auden, W. H.** *The Dog Beneath the Skin.* London, 1935.	60.00	80.00
☐ **Auden, W. H.** *Look, Stranger.* London, 1936.	60.00	80.00
☐ **Auden, W. H.** *Spain.* London, 1937. Softbound.	20.00	25.00
☐ **Auden, W. H.** *On the Frontier.* London, 1938.	32.00	40.00
☐ **Auden, W. H.** *Another Time.* London, 1940.	25.00	32.00
☐ **Auden, W. H.** *For the Time Being.* London, 1945.	25.00	32.00
☐ **Austen, Jane.** *Sense and Sensibility.* London, 1813. Three vols., second edition.	210.00	265.00
☐ **Austen, Jane.** *Pride and Prejudice.* London, 1817. Two vols., third edition.	155.00	195.00

PRICE RANGE

☐ **Austen, Jane.** *Pride and Prejudice.* London, 1833. Light purple cloth..	27.00	33.00
☐ **Austen, Jane.** *Northanger.* London, 1818.	2500.00	3000.00
☐ **Austen, Jane.** *Mansfield Park.* London, 1833. Light purple cloth..	42.00	57.00
☐ **Austen, Jane.** *The Novels of Jane Austen.* Edinburgh, 1911–12. 12 vols.......................................	130.00	160.00
☐ **Bacon, Francis.** *The Two Bookes of Francis Bacon.* London, 1605...	3250.00	3875.00
☐ **Bacon, Francis.** *A Declaration of the Practices and Treasons Attempted and Committed by Robert, Late Earle of Essex, and His Complices.* London, 1601................	750.00	1000.00
☐ **Bacon, Francis.** *Instauratio Magna.* London, 1620.......	3500.00	4500.00
☐ **Bacon, Francis.** *The History of the Reign of King Henry VII.* London, 1622.	350.00	425.00
☐ **Bacon, Francis.** *Certaine Miscellany Works.* London, 1629...	275.00	350.00
☐ **Bacon, Francis.** *Of the Advancement and Proficience of Learning of the Partitions of Sciences.* Oxford, 1640.	1000.00	1500.00
☐ **Bacon, Francis.** *The Natural and Experimental History of Winds.* London, 1653. First edition in English (translated from Latin)...	750.00	1000.00
☐ **Bacon, Francis.** *The Wisdome of the Ancients.* London, 1669.	75.00	100.00
☐ **Balzac, Honore de.** *Droll Stories.* N.Y., 1932. Three vols.	50.00	65.00
☐ **Beckford, William.** *Vathek.* London, 1815. Frontispiece..	75.00	90.00
☐ **Beecher, Henry Ward.** *Norwood.* N.Y., 1874............	40.00	55.00
☐ **Blake, William.** *Songs of Innocence.* London, 1899. Boards...	40.00	50.00
☐ **Blake, William.** *The Marriage of Heaven and Hell.* London, 1925. Three vols., marbled boards with vellum spines, limited to 1,500 copies. Printed at the Nonesuch Press......	400.00	475.00
☐ **Blake, William.** *The Heresy of Job.* London, n.d.	33.00	42.00
☐ **Boswell, James.** *The Life of Samuel Johnson, LL.D.* London, 1791.	2000.00	2750.00

Two vols., sometimes bound as one or three. Prices vary sharply depending on condition. Copies that have not been frequently rebound and trimmed down are most desirable; uncut specimens are almost impossible to get. There should be a frontispiece (Joshua Reynolds' portrait of Johnson), a facsimile plate of Johnson's handwriting, and the "Round Robin" plate. The original publisher's binding was in boards with a calf spine and paper labels.

A sample of the values of subsequent editions:		
London, 1835. Ten vols............................	135.00	180.00
London, 1846......................................	67.00	88.00
London, 1868. Ten vols............................	43.00	58.00
Philadelphia, 1883. Four vols.......................	22.00	30.00

The first American edition of Boswell's "Life of Johnson" appeared at Boston in 1807. It contains two folding plates and is worth around $350. Other editions of the work are innumerable, having been published almost continuously since first issued and translated into many languages. Most of those after 1850 are of little interest or value, except for extra-illustrated copies and editions edited by Johnsonian scholars. Occasionally, extra-illustrated copies contain original letters by Boswell, Johnson, and members of their circle, and can be very valuable on that account. Buyers are cautioned to examine extra-illustrated copies carefully.

☐ **Boswell, James.** *Journal of a Tour to the Hebrides (with Dr. Samuel Johnson).* London, 1785...................	155.00	190.00
Signed and inscribed...................................	2500.00	3200.00
☐ **Boswell, James.** *Journal of a Tour to the Hebrides.* London, 1816.........	115.00	145.00
☐ **Bronte, Charlotte.** *Jane Eyre.* London, 1847. Three vols.	1100.00	1450.00
☐ **Bronte, Charlotte.** *Shirley.* London, 1849. Three vols.	1650.00	2175.00
☐ **Bronte, Charlotte.** *The Professor.* London, 1857. Two vols.	160.00	200.00
☐ **Bronte, Emily.** *Wuthering Heights.* London, 1847. Three vols. The third volume is titled *Agnes Grey.* Only 1,000 copies were printed, though this was not a "limited edition" in the true sense of the term............................	10500.00	14500.00
☐ **Brooke, Rupert.** *1914 and Other Poems.* London, 1915. Softbound.............................	40.00	55.00
☐ **Brooke, Rupert.** *Lithuania.* Chicago, 1915..............	165.00	190.00
☐ **Brooke, Rupert.** *Letters from America.* London, 1916....	40.00	55.00
☐ **Brooke, Rupert.** *The Old Vicarage.* London, 1916. Softbound.	90.00	115.00
☐ **Brooks, Van Wyck.** *The Confident Years.* N.p., N.Y., 1922.	32.00	38.00
☐ **Brooks, Van Wyck.** *The American Caravan.* N.Y., 1927.	22.00	28.00
☐ **Brooks, Van Wyck.** *Sketches in Criticism.* N.Y., 1932....	30.00	35.00
☐ **Browning, Elizabeth B.** *Two Poems.* London, 1854. Softbound.	42.00	57.00
☐ **Browning, Elizabeth B.** *Aurora Leigh.* N.Y., 1857. First American edition.	42.00	57.00
☐ **Browning, Elizabeth B.** *Poems Before Congress.* London, 1860. Blindstamped cloth.	125.00	155.00
☐ **Browning, Elizabeth B.** *Last Poems.* London, 1862. Purple cloth.............................	63.00	82.00
☐ **Browning, Elizabeth B.** *Psyche Apocalypse.* London, 1876. Softbound.............................	52.00	73.00
☐ **Browning, Elizabeth B.** *Sonnets from the Portuguese.* London, 1887. One of eight copies on vellum.	465.00	580.00
☐ **Browning, Robert.** *Paracelsus.* London, 1835. Boards with paper label.............................	465.00	540.00
☐ **Browning, Robert.** *The Ring and the Book.* London, 1868. Four vols., green cloth.............................	115.00	145.00
☐ **Browning, Robert.** *Balaustion's Adventure.* London, 1871.	16.00	21.00
☐ **Browning, Robert.** *Aristophanes' Apology.* London, 1875.	21.00	27.00

	PRICE RANGE	
☐ **Browning, Robert.** *Dramatic Idyls.* London, 1879........	16.00	21.00
☐ **Browning, Robert.** *Parleyings With Certain People.* London, 1887. Brown cloth..................................	35.00	45.00
☐ **Browning, Robert.** *Men and Women.* London, 1908. Two vols., vellum, limited edition...........................	950.00	1250.00
☐ **Bryant, William C.** *The Embargo.* Boston, 1809. Softbound..	600.00	800.00
☐ **Bryant, William C.** *Poems.* The edition was of 500 or 600 copies, about two-thirds of which were bound in boards, the remainder softbound. Cambridge, 1821.		
In boards...	1450.00	1750.00
Wrappers..	1600.00	1900.00
The softbound copies are much harder to get in good condition.		
☐ **Bryant, William C.** *The Fountain and Other Poems.* N.Y., 1842. Found in either cloth or boarded binding, no appreciable difference in value.	135.00	160.00
☐ **Bryant, William C.** *Letters of a Traveler.* N.Y., 1850. Second edition...	70.00	90.00
☐ **Bryant, William C.** *Hymns.* N.p., n.d., N.Y., 1864.	70.00	90.00
☐ **Bunyan, John.** *The Pilgrim's Progress.* Extremely rare. Only one perfect copy known (formerly in the Holford collection). As long ago as the 1850's it was valued at the equivalent of $250. London, 1678. 8vo, 253 pp...........	25000.00	35000.00
☐ **Bunyan, John.** *The Pilgrim's Progress.* London, 1678. Second edition..	5000.00	7500.00
☐ **Bunyan, John.** *The Pilgrim's Progress.* London, 1764. Pocket size, illustrated with old woodcuts	35.00	43.00
☐ **Bunyan, John.** *The Pilgrim's Progress.* Heptinstall's edition. Two thin vols, often bound as one, illustrated with engravings from pictures by Stothard. London, 1796......	35.00	110.00
☐ **Bunyan, John.** *The Pilgrim's Progress, with Memoir by Dr. Cheever.* With portrait and several hundred woodcuts by Harvey. London, 1857.	34.00	42.00
☐ **Bunyan, John.** *The Pilgrim's Progress, with Original Notes by the Rev. T. Scott.* London, 1857. With line engravings.	47.00	62.00
☐ **Bunyan, John.** *The Pilgrim's Progress, with Preface by the Rev. C. Kingsley.* With 43 engravings and other illustrations by C. Bennett, cloth............................	43.00	54.00
☐ **Bunyan, John.** *The Pilgrim's Progress, with Memoir and Notes by G. Offor.* London, 1860. Woodcuts by J. Gilbert...	13.00	17.00

Next to the Bible, Bunyan's *Pilgrim's Progress* may well have been the best selling book in the English language. So extraordinarily popular did it prove that by 1681, just three years after its first publication, it had reached the seventh edition. By 1702 the 15th edition was published and dozens more followed during the 18th century. In the 19th century, with the work firmly established as a classic and in the public domain (not protected by copyright), publishers brought it out in every conceivable form, in pocket size, in tiny miniature editions, in deluxe editions with luxurious bindings, with illustrations by noted artists, etc. No

THE GOOD

AND

THE BADDE,

OR

Descriptions of the

Worthies, and Vnworthies

of this Age.

WHERE

The Best may see their Graces, and

the worst discerne their Basenesse.

LONDON,

Printed by *George Purslowe* for *Iohn Budge*, and are to be
sold at the great South-dore of Paules,
and at *Britaines Burse*.

1616.

The Good and the Bad *was Nicholas Breton's attempt to let everybody
know who their friends and enemies were. Many books were published
on the greats of their time, but few of them included villains as well.
Obviously, Breton felt that the traditional format needed a little spicing up.*

complete list of these editions has ever been made, or ever likely to be. On the whole, editions after 1750 are of interest only for their illustrations or bindings, or (of course) if put out by one of the private presses. Many of them sell for less today than originally. The lure of "India proofs" is not quite so strong today as in the Victorian age, especially when the artists have become nearly forgotten.

☐ **Burke, Edmund.** *A Philosophical Enquiry into the Origin of our Ideas of the Sublime and Beautiful.* London, 1757. ⸺ 950.00 — 1200.00

☐ **Burke, Edmund.** *A Speech of.* London, 1780. Third edition.. 21.00 — 27.00

☐ **Burke, Edmund.** *Two Letters.* London, 1796. .... 47.00 — 62.00

☐ **Burke, Edmund.** *Speeches in the House of Commons and Westminster Hall.* London, 1816. Four vols.............. 38.00 — 47.00

☐ **Burke, Edmund.** *Correspondence with many Eminent Persons between 1744 and 1797, edited by Earl Fitzwilliam and Sir R. Bourke.* London, 1844. Four vols......... 38.00 — 47.00

☐ **Burke, Edmund.** *Works of the Rt. Hon. Edmund Burke, including his Speeches and his Correspondence.* Eight vols., price varies depending on binding. .... 90.00 — 130.00

☐ **Burns, Robert.** *Poems, Chiefly in the Scottish Dialect.* The "Kilmarnock Burns," one of the famous book rarities. Prices vary sharply according to condition. The preferred state is in the original binding, but copies in morocco, with a miniature of Burns on ivory inlaid into the front cover (or inside the front cover) are also highly desirable. Kilmarnock, Scotland, 1786... 12000.00 — 15000.00

☐ **Burns, Robert.** *Poems, Chiefly in the Scottish Dialect.* Edinburgh, 1787................................... 420.00 — 525.00

☐ **Burns, Robert.** *Poems.* Philadelphia, 1798. .... 105.00 — 150.00

☐ **Burns, Robert.** *Tam O'Shanter.* London, 1825.......... 67.00 — 88.00

☐ **Butler, Samuel.** *Hudibras, in three parts.* London, 1710. Three vols... 68.00 — 87.00

☐ **Butler, Samuel.** *Hudibras, in three parts, with annotations.* The first edition to use Hogarth's illustrations. This was also the edition quoted by Samuel Johnson in his dictionary. London, 1726... 100.00 — 125.00

☐ **Butler, Samuel.** *Hudibras, in three parts, with large annotations and a preface by Zachary Grey, LL.D.* London, 1744. Two vols., illustrated by Hogarth. Often called the "best edition."
Regular copies.. 185.00 — 235.00
Large paper.. 400.00 — 500.00

☐ **Butler, Samuel.** *Hudibras, in three parts.* Pocket edition, with portrait of the author by Nixon. London, 1750........ 30.00 — 38.00

☐ **Butler, Samuel.** *Hudibras, a Poem, in three Cantos, with Notes.* Very lavishly produced edition. One copy (only) was printed on vellum, with cuts on India paper. It was sold at the Earl of Devon's auction in the 1800's for twenty-five pounds sterling. London, 1793. Three vols., quarto (a larger format than usual for this work), limited to 200 copies. The present value: .... 1100.00 — 1625.00

PRICE RANGE

☐ **Butler, Samuel.** *Hudibras, with Dr. Grey's Annotations.* A New Edition, corrected and enlarged. London, 1819. Three vols.

Regular copies.	27.00	34.00
Large paper, with India proofs.	120.00	150.00

☐ **Butler, Samuel.** *Hudibras, with Notes by Dr. Nash.* London, 1847. Two vols., with 60 illustrations.............. 13.00   17.00

☐ **Byron, George Gordon ("Lord Byron").** *Hours of Idleness.* Newark (England), 1807. .... 365.00   415.00

☐ **Byron, George Gordon.** *Childe Harold's Pilgrimage.* London, 1812–18. Three vols. 1800.00   2275.00

☐ **Byron, George Gordon.** *The Bride of Abydos.* London, 1813. .... 400.00   500.00

☐ **Byron, George Gordon.** *Ode to Napoleon Buonaparte.* London, 1814. .... 400.00   500.00

☐ **Byron, George Gordon.** *Lara.* London, 1814. .... 62.00   83.00

☐ **Byron, George Gordon.** *The Prisoner of Chillon and Other Poems.* London, 1816. Softbound. 155.00   200.00

☐ **Byron, George Gordon.** *The Siege of Corinth.* London, 1816. .... 52.00   72.00

☐ **Byron, George Gordon.** *Manfred.* London, 1817. Softbound. 100.00   125.00

☐ **Byron, George Gordon.** *Mazeppa.* London, 1819. Softbound. 200.00   250.00

☐ **Byron, George Gordon.** *Sarsanapalus.* Lodo, 1821. .... 100.00   130.00

☐ **Byron, George Gordon.** *Marino Faliero.* London, 1821. .... 100.00   130.00

☐ **Byron, George Gordon.** *Werner.* London, 1823. .... 150.00   185.00

☐ **Byron, George Gordon.** *The Deformed Transformed.* London, 1824. .... 150.00   185.00

☐ **Cabell, James Branch.** *Jurgen.* N.Y., 1919. .... 40.00   60.00

☐ **Cabell, James Branch.** *Ladies and Gentlemen.* N.Y., 1934. .... 20.00   25.00

☐ **Chaucer, Geoffrey.** *The Workes of Geoffrey Chaucer, with dyvers Workes which were never in print before.* London, Thomas Godfray, 1532. .... 18000.00   25000.00

☐ **Chaucer, Geoffrey.** *Works.* London, John Kyngston for John Wight, 1561. .... 6500.00   9000.00

☐ **Chaucer, Geoffrey.** *Works.* London, George Bishop, 1598. .... 3250.00   4000.00

☐ **Chaucer, Geoffrey.** *Works.* This and the Bishop edition are known as the "Speght Chaucer," having been edited by Thomas Speght. Bishop and Islip were partners in the publication. Both have a full page woodcut, at the beginning, called "The Progenie of Geoffrey Chaucer," with portrait of Chaucer and chart of his ancestors. When this is lacking the price is much lower. London, Adam Islip, 1602. ...... 1200.00   1600.00

☐ **Chaucer, Geoffrey.** *Works.* Based on the Speght Chaucer. London, 1687. .... 375.00   450.00

☐ **Chaucer, Geoffrey.** *Works, both Prose and Poetical, with Three Tales never before printed, and a Glossary by J. Urry.* London, 1721. Large folio. 250.00   300.00

PRICE RANGE

☐ **Chaucer, Geoffrey.** *Canterbury Tales.* London, 1737..... 225.00 265.00
☐ **Cibber, Colley.** *Love in a Riddle.* London, 1729. .... 110.00 140.00
☐ **Cibber, Colley.** *The Non-Juror.* Dublin, 1752............. 22.00 28.00
☐ **Cibber, Colley.** *The Lady's Last Stake.* London, n.d...... 160.00 190.00
☐ **Clemens, Samuel Langhorne.** *"Mark Twain" The Celebrated Jumping Frog of Calaveras County and Other Sketches.* Edited by John Paul. The first issue has traditionally been identified by a page of yellow ads before the title page, and a normal letter "i" in "this" on page 196, last line. An effort is now under way to fix priority on basis of binding. The bindings are in assorted colors, but in some the gold-stamped frog adorning the front cover is at the center, in others at the lower left. It is believed (cautiously) the former represents an earlier or at least scarcer state. N.Y., 1867. .... 2200.00 2750.00
☐ **Clemens, Samuel Langhorne.** *The Innocents Abroad.* Hartford, 1869. Black cloth, without illustration on page 129.. 180.00 235.00
☐ **Clemens, Samuel Langhorne.** *The Gilded Age.* Hartford, 1873.. 520.00 675.00
☐ **Clemens, Samuel Langhorne.** *The Adventures of Tom Sawyer.* London, 1876. Red cloth...................... 385.00 485.00
☐ **Clemens, Samuel Langhorne.** *Tom Sawyer.* The Canadian "first edition" preceded the first U.S. edition. Toronto, 1876. Violet cloth.. 335.00 415.00
☐ **Clemens, Samuel Langhorne.** *Tom Sawyer.* The first issue has versos of the halftitle and preface blank. Copies of the second issue (also carrying Hartford, 1876 imprint) are worth $250–350. Other editions have little value except, perhaps, those of private presses. Hartford, 1876. First American edition. Bindings vary, some in cloth, some leather... 1800.00 2850.00
☐ **Clemens, Samuel Langhorne.** *A Tramp Abroad.* The first state is identified by frontispiece titled "Moses" without giving the artist's name. Hartford, 1880. Black cloth or leather... 675.00 825.00
☐ **Clemens, Samuel Langhorne.** *The Prince and the Pauper.* The ads should be dated November. London, 1881. Red Cloth.. 160.00 210.00
☐ **Clemens, Samuel Langhorne.** *Life on the Mississippi.* First issue is identified by caption on page 443 reading "St. Louis Hotel." It was afterward changed to "St. Charles Hotel." Boston, 1883. Brown cloth.
First state copies.................................... 215.00 270.00
With "St. Charles Hotel". 67.00 88.00
☐ **Clemens, Samuel Langhorne.** *A Connecticut Yankee in King Arthur's Court.* Bindings vary, with none of them worth much more or less than the others. N.Y., 1889. .... 425.00 525.00
☐ **Clemens, Samuel Langhorne.** *The Million Pound Banknote and Other New Stories.* N.Y., 1893. Light beige cloth.. 115.00 145.00

PRICE RANGE

☐ **Clemens, Samuel Langhorne.** *Follow the Equator.* The first issue has only Hartford (not "Hartford and N.Y.") as place of publication. Hartford, 1897. Blue cloth or leather... 115.00 145.00

☐ **Clemens, Samuel Langhorne.** *The Man That Corrupted Hadleyburg and Other Stories.* N.Y., 1900. Red cloth..... 115.00 145.00

☐ **Clemens, Samuel Langhorne.** *A Double-Barrelled Detective Story.* N.Y., 1902. Red cloth..................... 155.00 205.00

☐ **Clemens, Samuel Langhorne.** *Eve's Diary.* N.Y., 1906. Red cloth... 43.00 58.00

☐ **Clemens, Samuel Langhorne.** *A Horse's Tale.* N.Y., 1907. Red cloth... 75.00 100.00

☐ **Clemens, Samuel Langhorne.** *A Horse's Tale.* London, 1907. Red cloth.. 42.00 57.00

☐ **Coleridge, Samuel T.** *Wallenstein.* London, 1800........ 110.00 140.00

☐ **Coleridge, Samuel T.** *Remorse.* London, 1813. Second edition.. 60.00 80.00

☐ **Coleridge, Samuel T.** *Christabel.* London, 1816........ 350.00 425.00

☐ **Coleridge, Samuel T.** *Sibylline.* London, 1817.......... 180.00 240.00

☐ **Coleridge, Samuel T.** *Zapolya.* London, 1817. Soft-bound... 120.00 160.00

☐ **Coleridge, Samuel T.** *Biographia Literaria.* London, 1817. Two vols., boards...................................... 375.00 450.00

☐ **Coleridge, Samuel T.** *The Poems.* London, 1852. Green cloth... 15.00 20.00

☐ **Coleridge, Samuel T.** *Dramatic Works.* London, 1857. Not first edition... 12.00 16.00

☐ **Coleridge, Samuel T.** *Aids to Reflection.* N.Y., 1872..... 22.00 28.00

☐ **Collins, Wilkie.** *A Plot in Private Life.* Leipzig, 1859...... 140.00 180.00

☐ **Collins, Wilkie.** *The Queen of Hearts.* London, 1859. Three vols.. 125.00 160.00

☐ **Collins, Wilkie.** *The Woman in White.* N.Y., 1860........ 350.00 425.00

☐ **Collins, Wilkie.** *The Moonstone.* The first "detective" novel in the English language. London, 1868. Three vols., violet cloth... 1800.00 2300.00

☐ **Collins, Wilkie.** *My Lady's Money.* Leipzig, 1877........ 115.00 145.00

☐ **Cooper, James Fenimore.** *The Spy.* London, 1822. Three vols.. 385.00 485.00

☐ **Cooper, James Fenimore.** *The Pilot.* London, 1824. Three vols.. 120.00 150.00

☐ **Cooper, James Fenimore.** *Lionel Lincoln.* N.Y., 1824–25. Two vols., boards with paper labels................... 200.00 250.00

☐ **Cooper, James Fenimore.** *The Last of the Mohicans.* First issue has page 89 of the first volume misnumbered 93. Philadelphia, 1826. Two vols........................... 7500.00 10000.00

☐ **Cooper, James Fenimore.** *The Prairie.* London, 1827. Three vols.. 180.00 230.00

☐ **Cooper, James Fenimore.** *The Headsman.* London, 1833. Three vols.. 125.00 165.00

☐ **Cooper, James Fenimore.** *The Headsman.* Philadelphia, 1833. Two vols... 385.00 465.00

☐ **Cooper, James Fenimore.** *A Letter to His Countrymen.* N.Y., 1834. Green boards............................. 125.00 160.00

Elaborate woodcut title page from the 1561 edition of Chaucer's Works, printed at London by John Kingston and John Wight. The vinework bears portraits of numerous English sovereigns and nobility, with the then-current king, Edward VI, at the top. The words enclosed in the central panel are, of course, "The Canterbury Tales," here spelled in Old English.

PRICE RANGE

☐ **Cooper, James Fenimore.** *The Monikins.* Philadelphia, 1835. . . . . 100.00 130.00

☐ **Cooper, James Fenimore.** *Gransboerne.* London, 1836. Two vols. 32.00 40.00

☐ **DeLaMare, Walter.** *Memoirs of a Midget.* London, 1921. . . . . 35.00 45.00

☐ **DeLaMare, Walter.** *Come Hither.* London, 1923. . . . . 30.00 38.00

☐ **DeLaMare, Walter.** *Ding Dong Bell.* London, 1924. . . . . . . 35.00 45.00

☐ **DeLaMare, Walter.** *The Captive.* N.Y., 1928. . . . . 30.00 38.00

☐ **DeLaMare, Walter.** *At First Sight.* N.Y., 1928. . . . . 35.00 45.00

☐ **DeLaMare, Walter.** *On the Edge.* London, 1930. . . . . 25.00 33.00

☐ **DeLaMare, Walter.** *Desert Islands.* London, 1930. . . . . 325.00 400.00

☐ **DeLaMare, Walter.** *Seven Short Stories.* London, 1931. Vellum, limited edition. 175.00 225.00

☐ **DeQuincey, Thomas.** *Confessions of an English Opium Eater.* London, 1822. . . . . 475.00 575.00

☐ **DeQuincey, Thomas.** *DeQuincey's Works.* London, 1858– 60. Fourteen vols., cloth. 150.00 175.00

☐ **Dickens, Charles.** *The Posthumous Papers of the Pickwick Club.* Dickens' most valuable book, when found in the original parts. London, 1836–37. 19 parts, green wrappers. 35,000.00 50,000.00

☐ **Dickens, Charles.** *Pickwick.* London, 1837. First book edition, green cloth. 450.00 550.00

☐ **Dickens, Charles.** *Pickwick.* Philadelphia, 1836–7. Five vols., boards. 525.00 650.00

☐ **Dickens, Charles.** *Pickwick.* N.Y., 1838. . . . . 90.00 115.00

☐ **Dickens, Charles.** *Pickwick.* London, 1856. . . . . 55.00 75.00

☐ **Dickens, Charles.** *Oliver Twist.* First issue has the "Fireside" plate in volume three, by Cruikshank. Second issue has "Rose Maylie" plate replacing "Fireside" and is worth $200. The title was then changed to *The Adventures of Oliver Twist,* and instead of being "by Boz," Dickens' penname in the early part of his career, his real name appeared on it. London, 1838. Three vols., brown cloth (dingey looking). 900.00 1150.00

☐ **Dickens, Charles.** *The Adventures of Oliver Twist.* London, 1846. third edition, ten parts, green wrappers. 950.00 1275.00

☐ **Dickens, Charles.** *The Adventures of Oliver Twist.* London, 1846. Hard covers. 275.00 325.00

☐ **Dickens, Charles.** *Nicholas Nickleby.* First issue has misspelling "vister" for "sister," page 123, line 17 of Part Four. London, 1838–39. 19 parts, green wrappers. 475.00 575.00

☐ **Dickens, Charles.** *Nicholas Nickleby.* London, 1839. First book edition. 125.00 175.00

☐ **Dickens, Charles.** *Nicholas Nickleby.* London, 1854. . . . . . 38.00 48.00

☐ **Dickens, Charles.** *Master Humphrey's Clock.* (By "Boz"). The extraordinary length of this set made full runs scarce. Issuing weekly instead of monthly parts was tried as an experiment; it did not prove successful. London, 1840–41. 88 weekly parts, white wrappers. 2100.00 2650.00

PRICE RANGE

☐ **Dickens, Charles.** *Master Humphrey's Clock.* London, 1840–41. Second issue, 19 monthly parts, green wrappers. 650.00   850.00

☐ **Dickens, Charles.** *Master Humphrey's Clock.* London, 1841. Three vols., brown cloth, first book edition. 75.00   95.00

☐ **Dickens, Charles.** *The Uncommercial Traveller.* Ads dated December, 1860. London, 1861. Lilac cloth. 425.00   525.00

☐ **Dickens, Charles.** *Great Expectations.* First issue has ads dated May. London, 1861. Three vols., plum cloth. 6000.00   7750.00

☐ **Dickens, Charles.** *Our Mutual Friend.* London, 1864–65. 19 parts, green wrappers. 650.00   850.00

☐ **Dickens, Charles.** *Our Mutual Friend.* London, 1865. Two vols., brown cloth, first book edition. 80.00   100.00

☐ **Dickens, Charles.** *The Mystery of Edwin Drood.* London, 1870. Six parts, green wrappers. 335.00   400.00

☐ **Dickens, Charles.** *The Mystery of Edwin Drood.* Issued in dust jacket but seldom present. Value with jacket is much higher. London, 1870. Green cloth, first book edition. 215.00   265.00

☐ **Dickens, Charles.** *Works of Charles Dickens, entirely revised by the Author.* Not a very good "reading set," since it lacks Dickens' later works, but highly collectible. London, 1859. Twenty-two vols., cloth. 250.00   310.00

☐ **Dickens, Charles.** *Works.* London, n.d. Seventeen vols., half calf. 300.00   380.00

☐ **Dickens, Charles.** *Works.* London, 1872–74. Sixteen vols., half calf. 475.00   575.00

☐ **Dickens, Charles.** *Works.* "National edition." One of the better "collected works" of Dickens. London, 1906–08. Forty vols., half morocco. 650.00   825.00

☐ **Dickens, Charles.** *Works.* N.Y., 1907. Thirty-six vols., cloth. 375.00   450.00

☐ **Dickens, Charles.** *Works.* London, 1913–14. Twenty-two vols., cloth. 85.00   105.00

☐ **Dickinson, Emily.** *Poems.* Edited by M. L. Todd and T. W. Higginson. Boston, 1890. . . . . 350.00   425.00

☐ **Dickinson, Emily.** *Poems.* London, 1891. First English edition. 350.00   425.00

☐ **Dickinson, Emily.** *Poems.* Second Series. Boston, 1891. Grey cloth, or white with green spine. 130.00   160.00

☐ **Dickinson, Emily.** *Poems.* Third Series. Bindings vary; first state copies have "Roberts Brothers" stamped on spine. Boston, 1891. . . . . 250.00   300.00

☐ **Dos Passos, John.** *Three Soldiers.* N.Y., 1921. Second issue. 30.00   38.00

☐ **Dos Passos, John.** *A Pushcart at the Curb.* N.Y., 1922. . . . . 95.00   120.00

☐ **Dos Passos, John.** *Manhattan Transfer.* N.Y., 1925. . . . . . . 20.00   27.00

☐ **Dos Passos, John.** *The Garbage Man.* N.Y., 1926. . . . . 24.00   31.00

☐ **Dos Passos, John.** *The 42nd Parallel.* N.Y., 1930. . . . . . . 30.00   39.00

☐ **Dos Passos, John.** *The Big Money.* N.Y., n.d., 1936. . . . . 20.00   25.00

☐ **Dos Passos, John.** *Adventures of a Young Man.* N.Y., 1939. . . . . 20.00   25.00

PRICE RANGE

☐ **Dos Passos, John.** *State of the Nation.* Boston, 1944. ...	20.00	25.00
☐ **Douglas, Norman.** *Alone.* London, 1921.	22.00	28.00
☐ **Douglas, Norman.** *Together.* London, 1923.	85.00	100.00
☐ **Douglas, Norman.** *In the Beginning.* Florence, 1927. Boards.	60.00	80.00
☐ **Douglas, Norman.** *How About Europe?* London, 1929.	45.00	60.00
☐ **Dreiser, Theodore.** *Sister Carrie.* N.Y., 1900.............	625.00	825.00
☐ **Dreiser, Theodore.** *Jennie Gerhardt.* N.Y., 1911.	21.00	26.00
☐ **Dreiser, Theodore.** *The Financier.* N.Y., 1912...........	21.00	26.00
☐ **Dreiser, Theodore.** *A Hoosier Holiday.* N.Y., 1916.	82.00	103.00
☐ **Dreiser, Theodore.** *The Hand of the Potter.* N.Y., 1918. Boards with linen spine.................................	63.00	82.00
☐ **Dreiser, Theodore.** *The Color of a Great City.* N.Y., 1923.	30.00	38.00
☐ **Dreiser, Theodore.** *An American Tragedy.* N.Y., 1925. Two vols.	180.00	235.00
☐ **Dreiser, Theodore.** *Chains.* N.Y., 1927.................	21.00	26.00
☐ **Dreiser, Theodore.** *A Gallery of Women.* N.Y., 1929. Two vols.	30.00	39.00
☐ **Dryden, John.** *The Medall.* London, 1682.	275.00	350.00
☐ **Dryden, John.** *Plutarch's Lives.* London, 1683–6. Five vols., frontispiece and other illustrations.	125.00	150.00
☐ **Dryden, John.** *Fables Ancient and Modern.* London, 1700.	175.00	225.00
☐ **Dryden, John.** *The Art of Painting.* London, 1715........	27.00	35.00
☐ **Dryden, John.** *All for Love.* Dublin, 1764...............	27.00	35.00
☐ **Dryden, John.** *Works.* London, 1693. First collected edition, four vols.	475.00	575.00
☐ **Dryden, John.** *Dryden's Dramatic Works, edited by Congreve.* London, 1717. Six vols.........................	225.00	275.00
☐ **Dryden, John.** *Complete Works, with Notes and Life of the Author by Sir Walter Scott.* London, 1821. Eighteen vols., for set in handsome calf or morocco bindings.	650.00	850.00
☐ **Dryden, John.** *Works.* Pickering's "Aldine edition." London, 1832. Five vols...................................	65.00	85.00
☐ **Eliot, George.** *The Mill on the Floss.* Edinburgh, 1860. Three vols...	235.00	290.00
☐ **Eliot, George.** *Silas Marner.* Edinburgh and London, 1861. Brown coarse-grained cloth.	75.00	100.00
☐ **Eliot, George.** *Romola.* London, 1863. Three vols., green cloth..	700.00	900.00
☐ **Eliot, George.** *Felix Holt.* Edinburgh, 1866.............	130.00	165.00
☐ **Eliot, George.** *The Spanish Gypsy.* Edinburgh, 1868.....	47.00	62.00
☐ **Eliot, George.** *Body and Sister.* London, 1869. Softbound.	450.00	550.00
☐ **Eliot, T. S.** *The Sacred Wood.* London, 1920.	60.00	80.00
☐ **Eliot, T. S.** *Marina.* London, n.d. Softbound..............	110.00	150.00
☐ **Eliot, T. S.** *Andrew Marvell.* London, 1922...............	25.00	33.00
☐ **Eliot, T. S.** *Poems.* London, 1925.	80.00	100.00
☐ **Eliot, T. S.** *A Song for Simeon.* London, 1928. Limited edition..	170.00	200.00
☐ **Eliot, T. S.** *Ash Wednesday.* London, 1930.	20.00	25.00

	PRICE RANGE	
☐ **Eliot, T. S.** *Charles Whibley.* London, 1931. Softbound. . .	40.00	55.00
☐ **Eliot, T. S.** *After Strange Gods.* London, 1934.	60.00	80.00
☐ **Eliot, T. S.** *The Rock.* London, 1934		
☐ **Faulkner, William.** *Mosquitoes.* N.Y., 1927. Blue cloth. . . .	1525.00	1950.00
☐ **Faulkner, William.** *Sartoris.* N.Y., n.d., 1929.	615.00	825.00
☐ **Faulkner, William.** *These Thirteen.* N.Y., n.d., 1931.	52.00	67.00
☐ **Faulkner, William.** *Idyll in the Desert.* N.Y., 1931. Limited signed edition.	670.00	835.00
☐ **Faulkner, William.** *Sanctuary.* N.Y., n.d., 1931.	1050.00	1500.00
☐ **Faulkner, William.** *Light in August.* N.Y., n.d., 1932.	120.00	145.00
☐ **Faulkner, William.** *Miss Zliphia Gant.* N.Y., 1932.	620.00	825.00
☐ **Faulkner, William.** *Salmagundi.* Milwaukee, 1932. Softbound, limited edition.	515.00	720.00
☐ **Faulkner, William.** *A Green Bough.* N.Y., 1933.	115.00	145.00
☐ **Faulkner, William.** *Dr. Martino and Other Stories.* N.Y., 1934.	235.00	280.00
☐ **Faulkner, William.** *Pylon.* N.Y., 1935.	125.00	155.00
☐ **Faulkner, William.** *Absalom! Absalom!* N.Y., 1936.	125.00	155.00
☐ **Faulkner, William.** *Hild Palms.* N.Y., 1939.	83.00	102.00
☐ **Faulkner, William.** *The Hamlet.* N.Y., 1940. Black cloth.	230.00	285.00
☐ **Faulkner, William.** *Intruder in the Dust.* N.Y., n.d., 1948.	95.00	125.00
☐ **Faulkner, William.** *Knight's Gambit.* N.Y., n.d., 1949.	620.00	830.00
☐ **Faulkner, William.** *Notes on a Horsethief.* Greenville, 1959. Limited edition.	360.00	485.00
☐ **Faulkner, William.** *Requiem for a Nun.* N.Y., n.d., 1951.	62.00	83.00
☐ **Faulkner, William.** *A Fable.* N.p., n.d., (N.Y., 1954).	43.00	58.00
☐ **Faulkner, William.** *Big Woods.* N.Y., n.d., 1955. Green cloth.	62.00	83.00
☐ **Faulkner, William.** *Jealousy and Episode.* Minneapolis, 1955. Limited edition.	125.00	150.00
☐ **Fielding, Henry.** *The Coffee House Politician.* London, 1730.	160.00	190.00
☐ **Fielding, Henry.** *The Temple Beau.* London, 1730.	230.00	285.00
☐ **Fielding, Henry.** *The Letter Writers.* London, 1731.	230.00	285.00
☐ **Fielding, Henry.** *The Modern Husband.* London, 1732.	210.00	250.00
☐ **Fielding, Henry.** *Don Quixote in England.* London, 1734.	230.00	285.00
☐ **Fielding, Henry.** *The Universal Gallant.* London, 1735. . .	230.00	285.00
☐ **Fielding, Henry.** *Pasquin.* London, 1736.	160.00	190.00
☐ **Fielding, Henry.** *The Wedding Day.* London, 1743.	160.00	200.00
☐ **Fielding, Henry.** *The History of Tom Jones.* London, 1749. Six vols.	300.00	375.00
☐ **Fielding, Henry.** *The History of Tom Jones.* London, 1763. Four vols.	90.00	115.00
☐ **Fielding, Henry.** *The History of Tom Jones.* London, 1831. One-volume edition.	32.00	41.00
☐ **Fielding, Henry.** *The History of Tom Jones.* London, 1831. Two vols.	32.00	41.00

PRICE RANGE

☐ **Fielding, Henry.** *An Inquiry into the Causes of the Late Increase of Robbers.* London, 1751................... 180.00 235.00
☐ **Fielding, Henry.** *Amelia.* London, 1752. Four vols. 600.00 725.00
☐ **Fielding, Henry.** *Amelia.* London, 1763................ 58.00 73.00
☐ **Fielding, Henry.** *A Journal of a Voyage to Lisbon.* London, 1756. .... 85.00 110.00
☐ **Fielding, Henry.** *Joseph Andrews.* London, 1764. Two vols. 650.00 750.00
☐ **Fielding, Henry.** *Works of Henry Fielding.* London, 1766. Twelve vols. 265.00 300.00
☐ **Fielding, Henry.** *Works, with an Essay on his Life and Genius by Murphy.* London, 1821. Ten vols............. 325.00 385.00
☐ **Fielding, Henry.** *Works, with Life by Roscoe.* London, 1856. Illustrated by Cruikshank................................ 160.00 190.00
☐ **Fitzgerald, F. Scott.** *This Side of Paradise.* N.Y., 1920... 380.00 465.00
☐ **Fitzgerald, F. Scott.** *Flappers and Philosophers.* N.Y., 1920. .... 195.00 235.00
☐ **Fitzgerald, F. Scott.** *The Beautiful and the Damned.* N.Y., 1922, without dust jacket........................... 95.00 120.00
☐ **Fitzgerald, F. Scott.** *Tales of the Jazz Age.* N.Y., 1922. ... 365.00 450.00
☐ **Fitzgerald, F. Scott.** *The Vegetable.* N.Y., 1923.......... 285.00 335.00
☐ **Fitzgerald, F. Scott.** *The Great Gatsby.* N.Y., 1925. Green cloth...................................... 180.00 235.00
☐ **Fitzgerald, F. Scott.** *All the Sad Young Men.* N.Y., 1926. 135.00 170.00
☐ **Fitzgerald, F. Scott.** *Taps at Reveille.* N.Y., 1935......... 450.00 525.00
☐ **Fitzgerald, F. Scott.** *The Crack Up.* N.p., N.Y., 1945. Boards....................................... 170.00 210.00
☐ **Ford, F. Madox.** *The Half Moon.* London, 1909. .... 55.00 70.00
☐ **Ford, F. Madox.** *The Panel.* London, 1912.............. 18.00 23.00
☐ **Ford, F. Madox.** *Between St. Dennis and St. George.* London, 1915...................................... 28.00 36.00
☐ **Ford, F. Madox.** *Mister Bosphorus and the Muses.* London, 1923. Signed edition.............................. 175.00 225.00
☐ **Ford, F. Madox.** *A Man Could Stand Up.* London, 1926. .... 30.00 39.00
☐ **Ford, F. Madox.** *Imagist Anthology.* London, 1930. ...... 39.00 48.00
☐ **Ford, F. Madox.** *Return to Yesterday.* London, 1931...... 55.00 70.00
☐ **Ford, F. Madox.** *The Rash Act.* N.Y., 1933.............. 55.00 70.00
☐ **Ford, F. Madox.** *It Was the Nightingale.* London, 1934. ... 28.00 34.00
☐ **Ford, F. Madox.** *Vie Le Roy.* N.Y., 1936. .... 16.00 20.00
☐ **Ford, F. Madox.** *Mightier than the Sword.* London, 1938. 55.00 65.00
☐ **Forster, E. M.** *The Longest Journey.* London, 1907. ...... 62.00 83.00
☐ **Forster, E. M.** *Pharos and Parillon.* N.Y., 1923........... 21.00 27.00
☐ **Forster, E. M.** *A Passage To India.* London, 1924........ 53.00 68.00
☐ **Forster, E. M.** *Anonymity.* London, 1925................ 62.00 83.00
☐ **Forster, E. M.** *The Eternal Moment.* London, 1928. ...... 47.00 68.00
☐ **Forster, E. M.** *Nordic Twilight.* London, 1940. Softbound....................................... 21.00 27.00
☐ **Frost, Robert.** *A Boy's Will.* N.Y., 1915................. 165.00 200.00
☐ **Frost, Robert.** *North of Boston.* N.Y., 1917. Not first edition.. 115.00 140.00
☐ **Frost, Robert.** *Selected Poems.* London, 1923. .... 20.00 25.00
☐ **Frost, Robert.** *New Hampshire.* N.Y., 1923.............. 60.00 75.00

PRICE RANGE

☐ **Frost, Robert.** *West Running Brook.* N.Y., 1928. Signed.	110.00	140.00
☐ **Frost, Robert.** *A Way Out.* N.Y., 1929.	220.00	260.00
☐ **Frost, Robert.** *Education of Poetry.* N.Y., 1931. Softbound.	90.00	120.00
☐ **Frost, Robert.** *A Further Range.* N.Y., 1936.	30.00	38.00
☐ **Frost, Robert.** *From Snow to Snow.* N.Y., 1936.	55.00	70.00
☐ **Frost, Robert.** *A Masque of Reason.* N.Y., 1945.	20.00	25.00
☐ **Gibbon, Edward.** *The History of the Decline and Fall of the Roman Empire.* London, 1776–88. Six vols.	2100.00	2650.00
☐ **Gibbon, Edward.** *Decline and Fall.* London, 1789. Two vols., abridged.	190.00	240.00
☐ **Gibbon, Edward.** *Decline and Fall.* London, 1838. Eight vols.	170.00	225.00
☐ **Gibbon, Edward.** *Decline and Fall.* London, 1846. Six vols.	135.00	170.00
☐ **Gibbon, Edward.** *Decline and Fall.* London, 1855. Eight vols.	135.00	170.00
☐ **Gibbon, Edward.** *The Student's Gibbon.* By Dr. D. W. Smith. London, 1858. With 100 engravings.	32.00	42.00
☐ **Gibbon, Edward.** *Miscellaneous Works, Historical and Critical, with Memoirs of his Life and Writings* ... London, 1796–1815. Three vols.	125.00	155.00
☐ **Gibbon, Edward.** *Miscellaneous Works.* London, 1814. Five vols.	90.00	115.00
☐ **Goldsmith, Oliver.** *Essays.* London, 1765.	200.00	275.00
☐ **Goldsmith, Oliver.** *The Good Natur'd Man.* London, 1768.	300.00	400.00
☐ **Goldsmith, Oliver.** *The Traveller.* London, 1770.	40.00	55.00
☐ **Goldsmith, Oliver.** *She Stoops to Conquer.* Dublin, 1773.	65.00	80.00
☐ **Goldsmith, Oliver.** *The Citizen of the World.* Dublin, 1775. Two vols.	40.00	55.00
☐ **Goldsmith, Oliver.** *A History of England.* London, 1780. Two vols.	25.00	35.00
☐ **Goldsmith, Oliver.** *The Poetical and Dramatic Works of Oliver Goldsmith.* London, 1786. Two vols.	115.00	150.00
☐ **Goldsmith, Oliver.** *Works, with Life.* London, 1812. Four vols.	115.00	150.00
☐ **Goldsmith, Oliver.** *Miscellaneous Works.* London, 1837. Four vols.	150.00	200.00
☐ **Goldsmith, Oliver.** *Works, Essays, Tales, Poems, &c..* London, 1854. Four vols.	70.00	100.00
☐ **Graves, Robert.** *Over the Brazier.* London, 1916. Softbound.	850.00	1100.00
☐ **Graves, Robert.** *On English Poetry.* London, 1922. Boards.	130.00	165.00
☐ **Graves, Robert.** *John Kemp's Wager.* Oxford, 1925.	75.00	100.00
☐ **Graves, Robert.** *Poems.* London, 1927.	140.00	200.00
☐ **Graves, Robert.** *A Pamphlet Against Anthologies.* London, 1928.	140.00	200.00
☐ **Graves, Robert.** *Lawrence and the Arabian Adventure.* N.Y., 1928.	23.00	31.00

VVITS
BEDLAM,

———————— VVhere is had,

Whipping-cheer, to cure the Mad.

The BOOKE.

Those Epigrams *faine would I owe,*
Where euery Word is a Word and a Blow.

Reprofes, where they are Well deseru'd ;
must be Well paide.

At LONDON
Printed by G. ELD, and are to be sould
by *Iames Dauies*, at the Red Crosse
nere Fleete-streete *Conduit.*
1617.

This early jokebook is no laughing matter when it comes to price, as it fetches more than $1,000. Its author was John Davies.

PRICE RANGE

☐ **Graves, Robert.** *Country Sentiment.* London, 1930. .....   100.00   130.00

☐ **Gray, Thomas.** *An Elegy wrote in a Country Church Yard.* London, 1751. The title page has parallel bars, above and below the title, decorated with skull and bones. Only the first issue commands the price stated....................   7000.00   10000.00

☐ **Gray, Thomas.** *Elegy, written in a Country Churchyard.* Illustrated from drawing by Cattermole, Landseer, Westall and others. London, 1839. Cloth, $20. Half morocco, spine gilt, all edges gilt..   100.00   130.00

☐ **Gray, Thomas.** *Elegy, written in a Country Church-yard.* Printed on toned paper, on one side only, with 24 engravings by Birket Foster and others. London, 1855. Full morocco...   150.00   200.00

☐ **Gray, Thomas.** *Elegia Scripta.* London, 1762............   140.00   180.00

☐ **Gray, Thomas.** *Poems by Mr. Gray.* London, 1768.......   130.00   160.00

☐ **Gray, Thomas.** *Gray's Poetical Works.* Edited with introductory Stanza by Moultrie. London, 1845. Cloth.........   17.00   22.00

☐ **Gray, Thomas.** *Gray's Works,* with Life by Mitford. London, 1853. Five vols., Pickering's "Aldine edition," cloth........   38.00   48.00

☐ **Haggard, H. Rider.** *She.* London, 1877. Blue cloth.......   27.00   35.00

☐ **Haggard, H. Rider.** *Allan Quatermain.* London, 1887.....   95.00   120.00

☐ **Haggard, H. Rider.** *Allan's Wife.* London, 1889..........   27.00   35.00

☐ **Haggard, H. Rider.** *Gardener's Year.* N.Y., 1905........   27.00   35.00

☐ **Haggard, H. Rider.** *Child of Storm.* London, 1913. ......   21.00   27.00

☐ **Harte, Bret.** *The Lost Galleon.* San Francisco, 1867......   210.00   290.00

☐ **Harte, Bret.** *The Heathen Chinee.* Chicago, 1870........   155.00   200.00

☐ **Harte, Bret.** *The Luck of Roaring Camp.* Boston, 1870...   60.00   80.00

☐ **Harte, Bret.** *The Queen of the Pirate Isle.* London, n.d., 1887..   400.00   475.00

☐ **Harte, Bret.** *Tales of Trail and Town.* Boston, n.d., 1898. Beige cloth..   30.00   39.00

☐ **Harte, Bret.** *Plain Language from Truthful James.* London, 1924..   48.00   63.00

☐ **Harte, Bret.** *Tales of the Gold Rush.* N.Y., 1944..........   32.00   40.00

☐ **Hawthorne, Nathaniel.** *Twice Told Tales.* Boston, 1837..   500.00   600.00

☐ **Hawthorne, Nathaniel.** *The Scarlet Letter.* Boston, 1850. Blind-stamped cloth....................................   200.00   250.00

☐ **Hawthorne, Nathaniel.** *The House of the Seven Gables.* Boston, 1851. Brown cloth.............................   80.00   100.00

☐ **Hawthorne, Nathaniel.** *The Snow Image.* Boston, 1852..   50.00   65.00

☐ **Hawthorne, Nathaniel.** *The Blithdale Romance.* Boston, 1852..   60.00   80.00

☐ **Hawthorne, Nathaniel.** *Tanglewood Tales.* Boston, 1853. Green cloth...   125.00   165.00

☐ **Hawthorne, Nathaniel.** *The Marble Faun.* Boston, 1860. Two vols., brown cloth..................................   65.00   85.00

☐ **Hawthorne, Nathaniel.** *Our Old Home.* Boston, 1863. ...   65.00   85.00

☐ **Hawthorne, Nathaniel.** *Doctor Grimshaw's Secret.* Boston, 1883...   25.00   32.00

PRICE RANGE

☐ **Hearn, Lafcadio.** *Stray Leaves from Strange Literature.* Boston, 1884. Blue cloth. 150.00   185.00
☐ **Hearn, Lafcadio.** *Some Chinese Ghosts.* Boston, 1887. Red cloth. . . . .⸴ 120.00   150.00
☐ **Hearn, Lafcadio.** *Two Years in the French West Indies.* N.Y., 1890. Green cloth. 85.00   110.00
☐ **Hearn, Lafcadio.** *The Japanese Letters of Lafcadio Hearn.* N.Y., 1910. . . . .   20.00   25.00
☐ **Hearn, Lafcadio.** *Fantastics and Other Fancies.* N.Y., 1914. . . . .   30.00   38.00
☐ **Hearn, Lafcadio.** *Life and Literature.* N.Y., 1924. . . . .   20.00   25.00
☐ **Hearn, Lafcadio.** *Occidental Gleanings.* N.Y., 1925. Two vols. 20.00   25.00
☐ **Hemingway, Ernest.** *The Torrents of Spring.* N.Y., 1926. Dark green cloth. 280.00   335.00
☐ **Hemingway, Ernest.** *The Sun Also Rises.* First state copies have misspelling "stopped" on page 181, line 26. N.Y., 1926. Black cloth. 675.00   825.00
☐ **Hemingway, Ernest.** *Men Without Women.* N.Y., 1927. Weighs 15 to 15½ ounces in the first state. 260.00   320.00
☐ **Hemingway, Ernest.** *Death in the Afternoon.* N.Y., 1932. Black cloth. For fine copy in dust-jacket. 450.00   575.00
☐ **Hemingway, Ernest.** *Winner Take Nothing.* N.Y., 1933. Black cloth. 160.00   210.00
☐ **Hemingway, Ernest.** *God Rest You Merry Gentlemen.* N.Y., 1933. Red cloth. 365.00   435.00
☐ **Hemingway, Ernest.** *Green Hills of Africa.* N.Y., 1935. Green cloth. 115.00   145.00
☐ **Hemingway, Ernest.** *Green Hills of Africa.* London, 1935. First English edition. 95.00   125.00
☐ **Hemingway, Ernest.** *To Have and Have Not.* N.Y., 1937. Black cloth. 115.00   140.00
☐ **Hemingway, Ernest.** *The Spanish Earth.* Cleveland, 1938. Tan cloth. For a first issue copy (limited edition). 425.00   575.00
☐ **Hemingway, Ernest.** *For Whom the Bell Tolls.* N.Y., 1940, light tan cloth. The first state copies are identified by the photographer being unnamed on the dust-jacket. Of course, dust-jackets can be switched, but collectors do not trouble themselves on that score. 185.00   265.00
☐ **Hemingway, Ernest.** *Men at War.* N.Y., n.d., 1942. Black cloth. Hemingway was merely the editor, not writer, of this anthology. 75.00   95.00
☐ **Hemingway, Ernest.** *Across the River and into the Trees.* N.Y., 1950. . . . .   42.00   58.00
☐ **Hemingway, Ernest.** *The Old Man and the Sea.* N.Y., 1952. Blue cloth. 85.00   115.00
☐ **Holmes, Oliver Wendell.** *Dissertations.* Boston, 1836. . . .   80.00   105.00
☐ **Holmes, Oliver Wendell.** *Astraea.* Boston, 1850. Yellow boards. 38.00   50.00
☐ **Holmes, Oliver Wendell.** *The Autocrat of the Breakfast-Table.* Boston, 1858. Brown cloth. 110.00   140.00
☐ **Holmes, Oliver Wendell.** *Songs in Many Keys.* Boston, 1862. . . . .   45.00   55.00

PRICE RANGE

☐ **Holmes, Oliver Wendell.** *Border Lines of Knowledge.* Boston, 1862.. 110.00   140.00

☐ **Holmes, Oliver Wendell.** *The Guardian Angel.* Boston, 1867. .... 20.00   25.00

☐ **Holmes, Oliver Wendell.** *Grandmother's Story of Bunker Hill.* Boston, 1875. .... 40.00   53.00

☐ **Holmes, Oliver Wendell.** *One Hundred Days in Europe.* Boston, 1887.. 20.00   25.00

☐ **Holmes, Oliver Wendell.** *Dorothy Q.* Boston and N.Y., 1893. .... 25.00   33.00

☐ **Housman, A. E.** *Last Poems.* London, 1922............. 53.00   72.00

☐ **Housman, A. E.** *A Fragment Preserved by Oral Tradition.* N.Y., 1930. .... 180.00   235.00

☐ **Housman, A. E.** *A Shropshire Lad.* N.Y., 1932.......... 32.00   40.00

☐ **Housman, A. E.** *The Name and Nature of Poetry.* Cambridge (England), 1933. .... 21.00   27.00

☐ **Housman, A. E.** *More Poems.* London, n.d., 1936. Blue cloth.. 37.00   48.00

☐ **Howe, Julia Ward.** *A Trip to Cuba.* Boston, 1860. .... 12.00   16.00

☐ **Howe, Julia Ward.** *Later Lyrcs.* Boston, 1866. .... 35.00   45.00

☐ **Howe, Julia Ward.** *Is Polite Society Polite?* N.Y., 1895... 20.00   25.00

☐ **Howe, Julia Ward.** *Reminiscences.* N.Y., 1899. .... 12.00   16.00

☐ **Hughes, Thomas.** *Tom Brown's School Days.* Cambridge, 1847. Blue imitation morocco, gilt top.................. 1050.00   1400.00

☐ **Hughes, Thomas.** *Tom Brown's at Oxford.* London, 1861. Three vols. 210.00   285.00

☐ **Hughes, Thomas.** *Gone to Texas.* London, 1884. .... 165.00   210.00

☐ **Hume, David.** *An Enquiry Concerning the Principles of Morals.* London, 1751. .... 1100.00   1375.00

☐ **Hume, David.** *The History of England.* London, 1770. Eight vols., (more if bindings are attractive)................... 60.00   75.00

☐ **Hume, David.** *The History of England.* London, 1816. Eight vols. 70.00   90.00

☐ **Hume, David.** *Hume's Philosophical Works Complete.* London, 1854–56. Four vols........................... 45.00   65.00

☐ **Hunt, Leigh.** *The Indicator.* London, 1820............. 220.00   265.00

☐ **Hunt, Leigh.** *Collected Poems.* London, 1832. Half cloth and boards. 40.00   60.00

☐ **Hunt, Leigh.** *The Palfrey.* London, 1842................. 35.00   42.00

☐ **Hunt, Leigh.** *Wit and Humor.* London, 1846. .... 60.00   75.00

☐ **Hunt, Leigh.** *Men, Women and Books.* London, 1847. Two vols. 42.00   55.00

☐ **Hunt, Leigh.** *A Jar of Honey.* London, 1848. .... 65.00   85.00

☐ **Hunt, Leigh.** *The Town.* London, 1848. Two vols......... 65.00   85.00

☐ **Hunt, Leigh.** *The Old Court Suburb.* London, 1855. Two vols. 80.00   100.00

☐ **Huxley, Aldous.** *Four Poems.* Oxford, 1917. .... 27.00   35.00

☐ **Huxley, Aldous.** *Seven Poems in Wheels.* Oxford, 1919. .... 38.00   47.00

☐ **Huxley, Aldous.** *Limbo.* London, 1920. .... 20.00   25.00

☐ **Huxley, Aldous.** *Crome Yellow.* London, 1921. .... 42.00   58.00

☐ **Huxley, Aldous.** *Mortal Coils.* London, 1922. Blue cloth.. 37.00   48.00

THE

V I C A R

O F

WAKEFIELD:

A T A L E.

Suppofed to be written by HIMSELF.

Sperate miferi, cavete fælices.

V O L. I.

S A L I S B U R Y:

Printed by B. C O L L I N S,

For F. NEWBERY, in Pater-Nofter-Row, London.

M DCC LXVI.

The Vicar of Wakefield, A Tale, *was SUPPOSED to be written by himself. But since its author was Oliver Goldsmith, who was no vicar at all, the supposition was just as fictional as the book. Goldsmith, called "Goldy" by Samuel Johnson, ran off quite a string of literary successes, including* She Stoops to Conquer.

PRICE RANGE

☐ **Huxley, Aldous**. *Antic Hay*. London, 1923.............	42.00	58.00
☐ **Huxley, Aldous**. *Holy Faces*. London, 1929. Limited to 300 copies..	95.00	120.00
☐ **Huxley, Aldous**. *Do What You Will*. London, 1929........	37.00	47.00
☐ **Huxley, Aldous**. *Brief Candles*. N.Y., 1930. One of 842 signed..	160.00	210.00
Ordinary trade edition, unsigned........................	42.00	58.00
☐ **Huxley, Aldous**. *Brave New World*. London, 1932. One of 324 signed...	290.00	360.00
Trade edition, unsigned...............................	115.00	165.00
☐ **Huxley, Aldous**. *Texts and Pretexts*. London, 1932.......	32.00	40.00
☐ **Huxley, Aldous**. *Beyond the Mexique Bay*. N.Y., 1934...	22.00	28.00
☐ **Huxley, Aldous**. *What Are You Going to do About it?* London, 1936...	22.00	28.00
☐ **Huxley, Aldous**. *Eyeless in Gaza*. London, 1936........	37.00	48.00
☐ **Huxley, Aldous**. *Ends and Means*. London, 1937.......	20.00	25.00
☐ **Irving, Washington**. *The Sketch Book of Geoffrey Crayon*. N.Y., 1822. Two vols......................................	60.00	75.00
☐ **Irving, Washington**. *The Beauties of Washington Irving*. London, 1825...	25.00	35.00
☐ **Irving, Washington**. *A Tour on the Prairies*. Philadelphia, 1835..	40.00	55.00
☐ **Irving, Washington**. *The Rocky Mountains*. Philadelphia, 1837. Two vols...	160.00	290.00
☐ **Irving, Washington**. *A History of New York*. Philadelphia, 1838. Two vols...	60.00	80.00
☐ **Irving, Washington**. *Biography and Poetical Remains of the Late Margaret Miller Davidson*. Philadelphia, 1841. Black cloth...	45.00	55.00
☐ **Irving, Washington**. *Works of Washington Irving*. London, 1821–37. Twenty-four vols.	250.00	375.00
☐ **Irving, Washington**. *Works of Washington Irving*. London, 1851–59. Fourteen vols.	175.00	250.00
☐ **Johnson, Samuel**. *Annotations Upon the Plays of Shakespeare*. London, 1787. Six vols.	3500.00	5275.00
☐ **Johnson, Samuel**. *Johnson's Lives of the Poets, edited, with Notes, by P. Cunningham*. London, 1854. Three vols., calf, gilt..	75.00	100.00
☐ **Johnson, Samuel**. *Johnson's Works*. With an Essay on Life and Genius by Murphy. London, 1823. Twelve vols., boards..	140.00	185.00
Full calf, gilt..	250.00	325.00
☐ **Johnson, Samuel**. *Johnson's Works, including Debates in Parliament*. London, 1825. Eleven vols. Pickering's "Oxford Classic" edition, cloth.	140.00	180.00
☐ **Johnson, Samuel**. *Johnson's Works, with Life by Murphy*. London, 1854. Two vols., calf, gilt.	45.00	65.00
☐ **Jones, James**. *From Here to Eternity*. N.Y., 1951........	65.00	85.00
☐ **Joyce, James**. *Chamber Music*. London, 1907.	850.00	1025.00
☐ **Joyce, James**. *Dubliners*. N.Y., n.d., 1914..............	1375.00	1800.00
☐ **Joyce, James**. *Dubliners*. N.Y., 1917..................	225.00	300.00
☐ **Joyce, James**. *Dubliners*. London, 1917.	800.00	1100.00

PRICE RANGE

☐ **Joyce, James.** *Exiles.* London, 1918. Green boards and cloth.. 300.00 375.00

☐ **Joyce, James.** *Exiles.* N.Y., 1918. Boards with buckram spine... 225.00 275.00

☐ **Joyce, James.** *Ulysses.* Paris, 1922. Softbound, blue wrappers, limited to 100 on handmade paper, signed..... 12000.00 15000.00

☐ **Joyce, James.** *Ulysses.* Paris, 1922. Softbound, limited to 150 on Verge d'Arches paper. 3375.00 4150.00

☐ **Joyce, James.** *Anna Livia Plurabelle.* N.Y., 1928. Limited to 850 signed copies. 525.00 725.00

☐ **Joyce, James.** *Collected Poems.* N.Y., 1936. Limited to 750 copies. There was also an edition on vellum, limited to 50 copies, singed by Joyce. These are boxed and worth up to $750.. 185.00 265.00

☐ **Joyce, James.** *Finnegan's Wake.* London, 1939. Limited to 425 on large paper, signed and boxed. 2675.00 3350.00

☐ **Joyce, James.** *Finnegan's Wake.* London, n.d., 1939. First trade edition. 375.00 475.00

☐ **Joyce, James.** *Finnegan's Wake.* N.Y., 1939. Black cloth.. 285.00 340.00

☐ **Joyce, James.** *Stephen Hero.* London, 1914. .... 325.00 410.00

☐ **Keats, John.** *Poems.* London, 1817. Boards, paper label. So scarce that even incomplete copies fetch high prices. 8000.00 12000.00

☐ **Keats, John.** *Endymion.* Boards with paper label. The first issue has one line of errata and two leaves of advertisements at end........................... 2750.00 3750.00

☐ **Keats, John.** *Lamia, Isabella, the Eve of St. Agnes, and Other Poems.* London, 1820. Boards or calf. The first issue should have eight pages of ads at end. 9000.00 12500.00

☐ **Keats, John.** *Keats' Poetical Works, with Memoir by Monckton Milnes.* London, 1854. Cloth. 30.00 40.00
Calf, gilt. 55.00 70.00

☐ **Kipling, Rudyard.** *The Courting of Dinah Shadd.* N.Y., 1890. Softbound.................................... 30.00 40.00

☐ **Lamb, Charles.** *A Tale of Rosamond Gray.* London, 1798. .... 700.00 850.00

☐ **Lamb, Charles A.** *The Adventures of Ulysses.* London, 1808. .... 265.00 315.00

☐ **Lamb, Charles A.** *Specimens of English Dramatic Poets.* London, 1808.. 120.00 150.00

☐ **Lamb, Charles A.** *Elia.* Philadelphia, 1828. Yellow boards with brown cloth spine.............................. 250.00 300.00

☐ **Lamb, Charles A.** *Album Verses.* London, 1830. .... 120.00 150.00

☐ **Lamb, Charles A.** *Satan in Search of a Wife.* London, 1831. .... 250.00 300.00

☐ **Lamb, Charles A.** *Lamb's Works Complete: Poems, Plays, Essays of Elia, Letters, and Final Memorials by Judge Talfourd.* London, 1850. Four vols, cloth.................... 35.00 45.00

☐ **Lamb, Charles A.** *Lamb's Complete Works.* London, 1852. One volume edition, cloth............................. 18.00 23.00

☐ **Lawrence, T. E.** *Seven Pillars of Wisdom.* London, 1926. 8000.00 10000.00

	PRICE RANGE	
☐ **Lawrence, T. E.** *Seven Pillars of Wisdom.* N.Y., 1935.....	28.00	37.00
☐ **Lawrence, T. E.** *The Odyssey of Homer.* London, 1935..	21.00	28.00
☐ **Lawrence, T. E.** *Crusader Castles.* London, 1936. Two vols.	415.00	575.00
☐ **Lawrence, T. E.** *The Diary of T. E. Lawrence.* London, 1937.	800.00	1000.00
☐ **Lawrence, T. E.** *The Private Life of Lawrence of Arabia.* London, 1938–39.	23.00	30.00
☐ **Lawrence, T. E.** *Shaw Ede.* London, 1942................	265.00	315.00
☐ **Lewis, Sinclair.** *Yale Verses.* New Haven, 1909..........	25.00	32.00
☐ **Lewis, Sinclair.** *Our Mr. Wrenn.* N.Y., 1914.............	125.00	160.00
☐ **Lewis, Sinclair.** *Babbitt.* N.Y., n.d., 1922. Blue and orange cloth...	375.00	500.00
☐ **Lewis, Sinclair.** *Elmer Gantry.* N.Y., n.d., 1927..........	45.00	60.00
☐ **Lewis, Sinclair.** *Dodsworth.* N.Y., n.d., 1929.............	33.00	42.00
☐ **Lewis, Sinclair.** *Ann Vickers.* Garden City, 1933.........	33.00	42.00
☐ **Lewis, Sinclair.** *Work of Art.* Garden City, 1934..........	20.00	25.00
☐ **Lewis, Sinclair.** *It Can't Happen Here.* N.Y., 1935.	20.00	25.00
☐ **Lindsay, Vachel.** *The Art of the Moving Picture.* N.Y., 1915.	45.00	60.00
☐ **Lindsay, Vachel.** *The Chinese Nightingale.* N.Y., 1917. Yellow Cloth.	40.00	50.00
☐ **Lindsay, Vachel.** *Collected Poems.* N.Y., 1923..........	20.00	25.00
☐ **Lindsay, Vachel.** *Going to the Sun.* N.Y., 1923..........	20.00	25.00
☐ **Lindsay, Vachel.** *The Candle in the Cabin.* N.Y., 1926. ..	25.00	32.00
☐ **London, Jack.** *The Scarlet Plague.* N.Y., 1915..........	90.00	115.00
☐ **London, Jack.** *The Cry for Justice.* N.Y., 1915..........	40.00	55.00
☐ **Longfellow, Henry Wadsworth.** *Boston Prize Poems.* Boston, 1824. Printed boards.	160.00	190.00
☐ **Longfellow, Henry Wadsworth.** *Hyperion.* N.Y., 1839. Two vols.	110.00	140.00
☐ **Longfellow, Henry Wadsworth.** *The Song of Hiawatha.* Boston, 1855..	90.00	120.00
☐ **Longfellow, Henry Wadsworth.** *The Song of Hiawatha.* London, 1855..	175.00	200.00
☐ **Longfellow, Henry Wadsworth.** *The Song of Hiawatha.* Boston, 1863..	35.00	45.00
☐ **Longfellow, Henry Wadsworth.** *Prose Works.* Boston, 1857. Two vols..	25.00	32.00
☐ **Longfellow, Henry Wadsworth.** *The Courtship of Miles Standish.* Boston, 1858.................................	60.00	75.00
☐ **Longfellow, Henry Wadsworth.** *Tales of a Wayside Inn.* Boston, 1863..	35.00	45.00
☐ **MacLeish, Archibald.** *The Pot of Earth.* Boston, 1925....	140.00	170.00
☐ **MacLeish, Archibald.** *Streets in the Moon.* Boston, 1926.	34.00	43.00
☐ **MacLeish, Archibald.** *Einstein.* Paris, 1929.............	110.00	140.00
☐ **MacLeish, Archibald.** *Frescoes for Mr. Rockefeller's City.* N.Y., 1933. Softbound.	22.00	28.00
☐ **MacLeish, Archibald.** *Conquistador.* London, 1933......	40.00	53.00
☐ **MacLeish, Archibald.** *Panic.* N.Y., 1935.................	24.00	31.00
☐ **MacLeish, Archibald.** *Poems.* London, 1935.	50.00	65.00

PRICE RANGE

☐ **MacLeish, Archibald.** *Air Raid.* N.Y., 1938. . . . . 12.00   18.00
☐ **MacLeish, Archibald.** *America Was Promises.* N.Y., 1939. . . . . 30.00   38.00
☐ **MacLeish, Archibald.** *The Irresponsibles.* N.Y., 1940. . . . 22.00   27.00
☐ **MacLeish, Archibald.** *The American Cause.* N.Y., 1941. 20.00   25.00
☐ **MacLeish, Archibald.** *The American Story.* N.Y., 1944. 20.00   25.00
☐ **Masters, Edgar Lee.** *Spoon River Anthology.* N.Y., 1915. Blue cloth. 180.00   235.00
☐ **Masters, Edgar Lee.** *Children of the Marketplace.* N.Y., 1922. . . . . 16.00   21.00
☐ **Masters, Edgar Lee.** *Mirage.* N.Y., 1924. . . . . 27.00   35.00
☐ **Masters, Edgar Lee.** *Selected Poems.* N.Y., 1925. . . . . . . 21.00   27.00
☐ **Masters, Edgar Lee.** *Jack Kelso.* N.Y., 1928. . . . . 21.00   27.00
☐ **Masters, Edgar Lee.** *Lincoln, the Man.* N.Y., 1931. . . . . . . 25.00   33.00
☐ **Masters, Edgar Lee.** *Poems of People.* N.Y., 1936. . . . . . . 38.00   47.00
☐ **Maugham, William Somerset.** *The Explorer.* London, 1909. . . . . 63.00   78.00
☐ **Maugham, William Somerset.** *Jack Straw.* London, 1924. Softbound. 21.00   27.00
☐ **Maugham, William Somerset.** *Cakes and Ales.* London, n.d. Blue cloth. 37.00   45.00
☐ **Maugham, William Somerset.** *First Person Singular.* London, 1931. . . . . 25.00   32.00
☐ **Maugham, William Somerset.** *For Services Rendered.* London, 1932. . . . . 21.00   27.00
☐ **Maugham, William Somerset.** *Ah King.* London, 1933. Beige buckram. 125.00   165.00
☐ **Maugham, William Somerset.** *Altogether.* London, 1934. . . . . 21.00   27.00
☐ **Maugham, William Somerset.** *The Judgment Seat.* London, 1934. . . . . 72.00   93.00
☐ **Maugham, William Somerset.** *Don Fernando.* London, 1935. . . . . 125.00   155.00
☐ **Maugham, William Somerset.** *Cosmopolitans.* London, 1936. . . . . 21.00   27.00
☐ **Maugham, William Somerset.** *The Hour Before the Dawn.* N.Y., 1942. . . . . 25.00   32.00
☐ **Melville, Herman.** *Narrative of a Four Months' Residence.* London, 1846. . . . . 110.00   135.00
☐ **Melville, Herman.** *Omoo.* N.Y., 1846. . . . . 275.00   340.00
☐ **Melville, Herman.** *Typee.* N.Y., 1846. Two vols., Softbound. 1700.00   2175.00
    Clothbound, in one vol. 1250.00   1675.00
☐ **Melville, Herman.** *Redburn: His First Voyage.* London, 1849. Two vols. Blue cloth. 2800.00   3700.00
☐ **Melville, Herman.** *The Whale.* London, 1851. Three vols. 40,000.00   55,000.00
☐ **Melville, Herman.** *Moby-Dick; or, the Whale.* N.Y., 1851. Prices fluctuate sharply from one sale to another, based mostly on condition. This is not an easy book to get in good condition. 3750.00   8750.00
☐ **Melville, Herman.** *Harper's New Monthly.* N.Y., 1854. . . . 32.00   40.00
☐ **Melville, Herman.** *Israel Potter.* N.Y., 1855. Blue cloth. . . . 110.00   155.00

PRICE RANGE

☐ **Mencken, H. L.** *Prejudices.* N.Y., 1922.	32.00	42.00
☐ **Mencken, H. L.** *To Friends of the American Mercury.* N.Y., 1926. Softbound.	67.00	88.00
☐ **Mencken, H. L.** *Treatise on Right and Wrong.* N.Y., 1934.	27.00	36.00
☐ **Mencken, H. L.** *Happy Days.* N.Y., 1940.	21.00	27.00
☐ **Mencken, H. L.** *Heathen Days.* N.Y., 1943.	21.00	27.00
☐ **Mencken, H. L.** *The American Language.* N.Y., 1945.....	27.00	36.00
☐ **Millay, Edna St. Vincent.** *The Lyric Year.* N.Y., 1912.	70.00	90.00
☐ **Millay, Edna St. Vincent.** *Three Plays.* N.Y., 1926.	17.00	23.00
☐ **Millay, Edna St. Vincent.** *The King's Henchmen.* N.Y., 1927.	70.00	90.00
☐ **Millay, Edna St. Vincent.** *The Buck in the Snow.* N.Y., 1928. Boards with cloth spine.........................	13.00	18.00
☐ **Millay, Edna St. Vincent.** *Huntsman, What Quarry?* N.Y., 1939.	23.00	31.00
☐ **Millay, Edna St. Vincent.** *The Murder of Lidice.* N.Y., 1942.	45.00	60.00
☐ **Miller, Henry.** *The Cosmological Eye.* Norfolk, 1939. Brown Cloth.	75.00	100.00
☐ **Miller, Henry.** *Tropic of Cancer.* N.Y., 1940.	100.00	130.00
☐ **Miller, Henry.** *Wisdom of the Heart.* Norfolk, n.d., 1941..	75.00	100.00
☐ **Miller, Henry.** *Plexus.* Paris, n.d., 1953. Two vols. Softbound.	85.00	110.00
☐ **Miller, Henry.** *The Time of the Assassins.* N.p., n.d. (Norfolk, 1956).	50.00	65.00
☐ **Miller, Henry.** *Quiet Days in Clichy.* Paris, 1956. Softbound.	140.00	170.00
☐ **Milton, John.** *Milton's Poetical Works, with the Notes of various Commentators.* London, 1757. Four vols.	125.00	165.00
☐ **Milton, John.** *Milton's Poetical Works.* Birmingham, 1758. Printed by Baskerville on hot-pressed paper, two vols., large 8vo.......................................	400.00	500.00
☐ **Milton, John.** *Milton's Poetical Works.* London, 1795. Two vols.	65.00	85.00
☐ **Milton, John.** *Milton's Poetical Works, with Life by W. Hayley.* London, Bulmer, 1794. Three vols., folio, profusely illustrated. Depending on binding. This was an expensive set, even on publication.	800.00	1000.00
☐ **Milton, John.** *Milton's Poetical Works.* London, 1801. Six vols.	88.00	112.00
☐ **Milton, John.** *Milton's Poetical Works, with the Notes of various Authors, Life and Illustrations, by Todd.* London, 1826. Six vols......................................	88.00	112.00
☐ **Milton, John.** *Milton's Poetical Works edited with Life by Sir Egerton Brydges.* London, 1835. Six vols. Cloth.	47.00	62.00
☐ **Milton, John.** *Milton's Prose Works, with Life of the Author, interspersed with Translations and critical Remarks by Dr. Symmons.* London, 1806. Seven vols. Calf, gilt.	280.00	360.00
☐ **Milton, John.** *Milton's Prose Works complete, with Preface, Remarks and Notes by J. A. St. John.* London, 1848. Five vols. Cloth.	26.00	36.00

PRICE RANGE

☐ **Mitchell, Margaret.** *Gone with the Wind.* N.Y., 1936. Grey cloth. Carries notice "Published May, 1936." Later editions are of little value. **165.00** **225.00**

☐ **More, Thomas.** *Utopia, written in Latine by Syr Thomas More Knyght, and translated into English by Raphe Robynson.* London, by Abraham Vele, 1551. **3500.00** **5000.00**

☐ **More, Thomas.** *Utopia.* London, 1556. . . . . **2675.00** **3250.00**

☐ **More, Thomas.** *Utopia.* London, 1597. . . . . **1850.00** **2250.00**

☐ **More, Thomas.** *Utopia.* London, 1624. . . . . **300.00** **400.00**

☐ **More, Thomas.** *Utopia.* London, 1639. With portrait of the author. **450.00** **600.00**

☐ **More, Thomas.** *Utopia.* London, 1684. . . . . **400.00** **500.00**

☐ **More, Thomas.** *Utopia.* London, 1685. . . . . **130.00** **175.00**

☐ **More, Thomas.** *Dialogue of Cumfort against Tribulation.* Antwerp, 1573. With portrait, from a rare likeness. **750.00** **1000.00**

☐ **More, Thomas.** *The Workes of Sir Thomas More, Knyght, sometyme Lorde Chancellour of England.* London, 1557. Small thick folio. **6500.00** **10000.00**

☐ **Morley, Christopher.** *The Haunted Bookshop.* Garden City, 1919. . . . . **25.00** **35.00**

☐ **Morley, Christopher.** *Plum Pudding.* N.Y., 1921. . . . . **35.00** **48.00**

☐ **Morley, Christopher.** *The Power of Sympathy.* N.Y., 1923. . . . . **14.00** **19.00**

☐ **Morley, Christopher.** *Hostages to Fortune.* Haverford, Pa., 1925. . . . . **14.00** **19.00**

☐ **Morley, Christopher.** *The Goldfish Under the Ice.* London, 1929. . . . . **9.00** **12.00**

☐ **Morley, Christopher.** *In Modern Dress.* Larchmont, 1929. . . . . **18.00** **23.00**

☐ **Morley, Christopher.** *Max and Moritz.* N.Y., 1932. . . . . **9.00** **12.00**

☐ **Morley, Christopher.** *Effendi.* London, 1934. . . . . **18.00** **23.00**

☐ **Morley, Christopher.** *Footnotes for a Centennial.* N.Y., 1936. . . . . **14.00** **19.00**

☐ **Morley, Christopher.** *Kitty Foyle.* Philadelphia, n.d., 1939. . . . . **14.00** **19.00**

☐ **O'Casey, Sean.** *The Story of the Irish Citizen Army.* Dublin, 1919. . . . . **235.00** **300.00**

☐ **O'Casey, Sean.** *Within the Gates.* London, 1933. . . . . **525.00** **675.00**

☐ **O'Casey, Sean.** *Windfalls.* London, 1934. . . . . **37.00** **47.00**

☐ **O'Casey, Sean.** *Red Roses for Me.* London, 1942. . . . . **32.00** **41.00**

☐ **O'Flaherty, Liam.** *Spring Sowing.* London, 1924. . . . . **37.00** **48.00**

☐ **O'Flaherty, Liam.** *The Informer.* London, 1925. . . . . **210.00** **265.00**

☐ **O'Flaherty, Liam.** *Red Barbara.* London, 1928. . . . . **110.00** **150.00**

☐ **O'Flaherty, Liam.** *The Assassin.* London, 1928. Limited, signed edition. **200.00** **250.00**

☐ **O'Flaherty, Liam.** *Return of the Brute.* London, 1929. . . . . **75.00** **100.00**

☐ **O'Flaherty, Liam.** *The House of Gold.* London, 1929. . . . . . **55.00** **70.00**

☐ **O'Hara, John.** *Appointment for Samarra.* N.Y., 1934. . . . . **275.00** **350.00**

☐ **O'Hara, John.** *Butterfield 8.* N.Y., 1935. . . . . **90.00** **115.00**

☐ **O'Hara, John.** *Files on Parade.* N.Y., 1939. . . . . **25.00** **32.00**

☐ **O'Hara, John.** *Pal Joey.* N.Y., 1940. . . . . **45.00** **60.00**

☐ **O'Hara, John.** *Pipe Night.* N.Y., 1945. . . . . **25.00** **32.00**

PRICE RANGE

☐ **O'Neill, Eugene.** *Before Breakfast.* N.Y., 1916. Softbound. 45.00   60.00
☐ **O'Neill, Eugene.** *The Emperor Jones.* N.Y., n.d., 1921. . . 175.00   225.00
☐ **O'Neill, Eugene.** *The Hairy Ape.* N.Y., n.d., 1922. . . . . 65.00   85.00
☐ **O'Neill, Eugene.** *Strange Interlude.* N.Y., 1928. Limited edition. 130.00   175.00
☐ **O'Neill, Eugene.** *Dynamo.* N.N. 1929. . . . . 50.00   65.00
☐ **O'Neill, Eugene.** *Anna Christie.* N.Y., 1930. Limited signed edition. 175.00   225.00
☐ **O'Neill, Eugene.** *Mourning Becomes Electra. N.Y., 1931.* 40.00   55.00
☐ **O'Neill, Eugene.** *Ah, Wilderness!* N.Y., n.d., 1933. Blue cloth. 35.00   45.00
☐ **O'Neill, Eugene.** *George Pierce Baker.* N.Y., 1939. . . . . . . 130.00   175.00
☐ **Pepys, Samuel.** *Memoirs of Samuel Pepys.* London, 1825. Two vols., quarto, with portraits and other illustrations. First edition of "Pepys' Diary." 1000.00   1500.00
☐ **Pepys, Samuel.** *Pepys' Life, Journals and Correspondence, including his Voyage to Tangier.* London, 1841. Two vols. 115.00   140.00
Pepys' Diary is one of those works published everywhere, in every language. All editions have some value, but the most sought-after are the first edition (1825); first printings of the more notable later edition, such as those prepared by Mynors Bright and Wheatley; and sets in fine bindings.
☐ **Poe, Edgar A.** *Tamerlane and Other Poems.* "By a Bostonian." Boston, 1827. Softbound. 130,000.00 175,000.00
The most valuable American first edition in the field of literature, and the most valuable book of the 19th century excepting Audubon's "Birds of America." Unknown at the time and despairing to find a publisher, Poe brought out the work himself, with predictable results: it failed to sell.
☐ **Poe, Edgar A.** *Al Aaraaf, Tamerlane and Minor Poems.* Baltimore, 1829. Boards. A stitched copy without covers realized $40,000 at auction in 1974. But whether this represents an earlier state is not yet decided. 25000.00   35000.00
☐ **Poe, Edgar A.** *Poems.* N.Y., 1831. This one is tricky. The title page of the first edition states "second edition." Green cloth. 12000.00   18000.00
☐ **Poe, Edgar A.** *The Raven and Other Poems.* N.Y., 1845. Softbound or in cloth. 2750.00   3500.00
☐ **Poe, Edgar A.** *Tales.* N.Y., 1845. Softbound or cloth. 6000.00   8000.00
This price is for a first state copy, identified by the names of Smith and Ludwig, the printers, appearing on the verso of title.
☐ **Pope, Alexander.** *The Rape of the Lock.* London, 1714. Frontispiece. 310.00   415.00
☐ **Pope, Alexander.** *The Rape of the Lock.* London, 1718. 205.00   280.00
☐ **Pope, Alexander.** *The Rape of the Lock.* London, 1798. Duroveray's edition, illustrated. 130.00   155.00
Large paper copies. 235.00   300.00
Large paper copies should have the plates in two states.

	PRICE RANGE	

☐ **Pope, Alexander.** *The Temple of Fame.* London, 1715... | **125.00** | **160.00**

☐ **Pope, Alexander.** *The Dunciad.* An Heroic Poem, in three books, London, 1729. . . . . | **105.00** | **135.00**

☐ **Pope, Alexander.** *The Dunciad.* London, 1743, quarto. . . | **180.00** | **230.00**

☐ **Pope, Alexander.** *An Essay on Man.* London, 1796. . . . . . | **105.00** | **135.00**

☐ **Pope, Alexander.** *An Essay on Man.* Edinburgh, 1806. . . | **100.00** | **130.00**

☐ **Pope, Alexander.** *An Essay on Man, with Warburton's Notes.* London, 1823. . . . . | **27.00** | **36.00**

☐ **Pope, Alexander.** *The Works of Alexander Pope, Esq.* London, 1735–36. Nine vols., small 8vo. The volumes bear imprints of different publishers: volume one, B. Lintot; volume two, L. Gilliver, etc. A supplementary volume, dated 1738, is rarely present. It contains works written by Pope from 1736 to 1738 and bears the imprint of Dodsley. Rather than "volume ten" it is identified as "volume two, part two.". . . . . | **650.00** | **825.00**

☐ **Pope, Alexander.** *The Works of Alexander Pope.* London, Lintot, 1740. Nine vols., thick paper, in a good binding. . . . | **600.00** | **800.00**

☐ **Pope, Alexander.** *The Works of Alexander Pope.* London, 1752. Nine vols. Warburton's second edition. More in a really attractive binding. . . . . | **135.00** | **175.00**

☐ **Pope, Alexander.** *Pope's Works.* London, Knapton and Tonson, 1756. Nine vols. . . . . | **67.00** | **88.00**

☐ **Prior, Matthew.** *Poems on Several Occasions.* London, n.d., c. 1720. Folio. . . . . | **25.00** | **32.00**

☐ **Prior, Matthew.** *Prior's Poetical Works.* London, 1789. Two vols. . . . . | **55.00** | **75.00**

☐ **Prior, Matthew.** *Prior's Poetical Works.* London, 1835. Two vols. Cloth. . . . . | **12.00** | **16.00**

☐ **Richardson, Samuel.** *Pamela.* London, 1741–42. Regarded as the first true novel in the English language. Four vols. . . . . | **2350.00** | **3175.00**

☐ **Richardson, Samuel.** *Clarissa Harlow, or History of a Young Lady.* London, 1810. Eight vols. . . . . | **125.00** | **160.00**

☐ **Richardson, Samuel.** *Richardson's Works, with Life by Mangin.* London, 1811. Nineteen vols. . . . . | **500.00** | **650.00**

☐ **Riley, J. Whitcomb.** *Afterwhiles.* Indianapolis, 1891. . . . . . | **30.00** | **45.00**

☐ **Rossetti, Dante G.** *The Early Italian Poets.* London, 1861. | **115.00** | **145.00**

☐ **Rossetti, Dante G.** *Poems.* London, 1870. Green cloth. | **16.00** | **21.00**

☐ **Rossetti, Dante G.** *Ballads and Sonnets.* London, 1881. Green cloth. . . . . | **32.00** | **42.00**

☐ **Rossetti, Dante G.** *Ballads and Poems.* London, 1893–94. Two vols., vellum, limited edition. . . . . | **625.00** | **825.00**

☐ **Ruskin, John.** *Modern Painters.* London, 1844. . . . . | **55.00** | **75.00**

☐ **Ruskin, John.** *Modern Painters.* London, 1860–67. Five vols. . . . . | **140.00** | **175.00**

☐ **Ruskin, John.** *The Stones of Venice.* London, 1851–53. Three vols. . . . . | **140.00** | **175.00**

☐ **Ruskin, John.** *Lectures on Architecture and Painting.* London, 1854. . . . . | **30.00** | **38.00**

☐ **Ruskin, John.** *The Elements of Drawing.* London, 1857. Green cloth. . . . . | **65.00** | **85.00**

PRICE RANGE

☐ **Ruskin, John.** *The Cambridge School of Art.* Cambridge, 1858. Softbound.	30.00	40.00
☐ **Ruskin, John.** *Essays on Political Economy.* London, 1862.	23.00	31.00
☐ **Ruskin, John.** *The Ethics of the Dust.* London, 1866. Brown cloth.	23.00	31.00
☐ **Ruskin, John.** *The Art of England.* London, 1883–84. Softbound.	55.00	70.00
☐ **Ruskin, John.** *The Art of England.* London, 1887.	20.00	25.00
☐ **Ruskin, John.** *Unto this Last.* London, 1907. Vellum, limited edition.	160.00	220.00
☐ **Saroyan, William.** *The Daring Young Man on the Flying Trapeze and Other Stories.* N.Y., 1934. Purple cloth.	130.00	170.00
☐ **Saroyan, William.** *Inhale and Exhale.* N.Y., n.d., 1936.	25.00	32.00
☐ **Saroyan, William.** *Three Times Three.* Los Angeles, 1936. Semi-soft binding.	130.00	170.00
☐ **Saroyan, William.** *A Christmas Psalm.* San Francisco, n.d. Boards.	125.00	160.00
☐ **Saroyan, William.** *The Trouble with Tigers.* N.Y., 1938.	25.00	32.00
☐ **Saroyan, William.** *A Special Announcement.* N.Y., 1940.	45.00	60.00
☐ **Saroyan, William.** *My Name is Adam.* N.Y., 1940.	28.00	36.00
☐ **Saroyan, William.** *The Beautiful People.* N.Y., 1941.	28.00	36.00
☐ **Saroyan, William.** *Razzle Dazzle.* N.Y., 1942.	28.00	36.00
☐ **Saroyan, William.** *The Human Comedy.* N.Y., 1943.	33.00	42.00
☐ **Saroyan, William.** *Get Away Old Man.* N.Y., 1944.	28.00	36.00
☐ **Saroyan, William.** *Dear Baby.* N.Y., 1944.	28.00	36.00
☐ **Sassoon, Siegfried.** *The Old Huntsman.* London, 1917.	47.00	62.00
☐ **Sassoon, Siegfried.** *Picture Show.* Cambridge, 1919.	475.00	575.00
☐ **Sassoon, Siegfried.** *The Heart's Journey.* N.Y., 1927.	68.00	88.00
☐ **Sassoon, Siegfried.** *Memoirs of a Fox Hunting Man.* London, 1928.	27.00	33.00
☐ **Sassoon, Siegfried.** *Memoirs of an Infantry Officer.* London, 1930.	78.00	105.00
☐ **Sassoon, Siegfried.** *Poems.* London, 1931.	32.00	43.00
☐ **Sassoon, Siegfried.** *Vigils.* London, 1935.	27.00	34.00
☐ **Sassoon, Siegfried.** *Sherstons Progress.* London, 1936.	21.00	27.00
☐ **Sassoon, Siegfried.** *Rhymed Ruminations.* London, 1940.	21.00	27.00
☐ **Sassoon, Siegfried.** *Poems From Italy.* London, 1945.	53.00	72.00
☐ **Scott, Sir Walter.** *Ballads and Lyrical Pieces.* Edinburgh, 1806.	52.00	73.00
☐ **Scott, Sir Walter.** *Marmion.* Edinburgh, 1808.	20.00	25.00
☐ **Scott, Sir Walter.** *Guy Mannering.* Edinburgh, 1815. Three vols.	26.00	35.00
☐ **Scott, Sir Walter.** *The Field of Waterloo.* Edinburgh, 1815.	21.00	27.00
☐ **Scott, Sir Walter.** *The Antiquary.* Edinburgh, 1816. Three vols.	26.00	35.00
☐ **Scott, Sir Walter.** *Tales of My Landlord.* Edinburgh, 1816. Four vols.	52.00	73.00
☐ **Scott, Sir Walter.** *The Abbott.* Edinburgh, 1820. Three vols.	47.00	62.00

PRICE RANGE

☐ **Scott, Sir Walter.** *The Monastery.* Edinburgh, 1820. Three vols. 32.00   40.00

☐ **Scott, Sir Walter.** *Kenilworth.* Edinburgh, 1821. Three vols. 43.00   54.00

☐ **Scott, Sir Walter.** *The Pirate.* London, 1822. Three vols.   220.00   290.00

☐ **Scott, Sir Walter.** *Peveril of the Peak.* Edinburgh, 1822. Four vols. 67.00   88.00

☐ **Scott, Sir Walter.** *St. Ronan's Well.* Edinburgh, 1824. Three vols. 45.00   59.00

☐ **Scott, Sir Walter.** *Woodstock.* Edinburgh, 1826. Three vols. 47.00   63.00

☐ **Scott, Sir Walter.** *Anne of Geierstein.* London, 1829. Three vols. Boards with paper labels. 63.00   83.00

☐ **Scott, Sir Walter.** *The Lady of the Lake.* London, 1863.   140.00   170.00

☐ **Scott, Sir Walter.** *Scott's Waverly Novels.* London, 1836. Forty-eight vols. Illustrated with engravings after Maclise, Melville, etc. In a good leather or half-leather binding. If just one volume is lacking, the value drops by nearly half..... 500.00   675.00

☐ **Scott, Sir Walter.** *Scott's Waverly Novels.* London, 1854. Twenty-five vols. Cloth.................................... 175.00   210.00

☐ **Scott, Sir Walter.** *Scott's Waverly Novels.* London, 1856. Twenty-five vols. Cloth.................................... 175.00   210.00

☐ **Scott, Sir Walter.** *Scott's Poetical Works.* London, 1854. 12 vols. Cloth. 85.00   110.00
Half Morocco, gilt.. 150.00   200.00

☐ **Scott, Sir Walter.** *Scott's Poetical Works.* London, 1860. One volume edition, illustrated, cloth. 14.00   18.00

☐ **Scott, Sir Walter.** *Scott's Works.* London, 1819–23. "Large type library edition." Fifty-one vols., calf, gilt............. 500.00   650.00

☐ **Scott, Sir Walter.** *Scott's Complete Works.* London, 1859. Ninety-eight vols., 12mo, half morocco, gilt.............. 600.00   800.00
Published in boards at L24 10s, (about 125.00).

☐ **Shakespeare, William.** *Shakespeare's Comedies, Histories and Tragedies.* London, Isaac Jaggard and Edward Blount, 1623. Folio. The so-called "first folio" or first collected edition of Shakespeare's writing, including the texts of many plays that had not previously been published. With engraved frontispiece portrait, this book measures about 13 × 9 inches. 52,000.00   77,500.00

☐ **Shakespeare, William.** *Shakespeare's Comedies, Histories and Tragedies.* London, 1632. Folio. The "second folio," a re-issue of the above. Various names of publishers are found on the title page, as the edition was shared among several. Copies bearing the name of William Aspley are said to be the rarest.................................... 26,500.00   37,000.00

☐ **Shakespeare, William.** *Shakespeare's Comedies, Histories and Tragedies.* The third impression. And unto this impression is added seven Playes, never before printed in folio. London, Printed for P.C., 1664. Folio. The "third folio" and the rarest of the famous Four Folios of Shakespeare, presumably because a portion of the publisher's stock burned in the Great Fire of London. This however is unsubstanti-

PRICE RANGE

ated and may be no more than legend. But the book is very
rare. 65,000.00 100,000.00

☐ **Shakespeare, William.** *Shakespeare's Comedies, Histo-*
ries and Tragedies. London, 1685. Folio. The "fourth folio"
and most plentiful of the four, existing in several hundred
copies, but institutional buying has rendered it less common
on the market than it might be. 18,000.00 23,500.00

☐ **Shakespeare, William.** *Shakespeare's Works.* Adorn'd with
Cuts. Revis'd and Corrected, with an Account of the Life
and Writing of the Author, by N. Rowe. London, 1709. Seven
vols., 8vo, first octavo edition. The text is taken from the
1685 Fourth Folio. Sets with the poetry volume (the seventh) lacking sell for much less......................... 2300.00 3100.00

☐ **Shakespeare, William.** *Shakespeare's Works.* Dublin,
Printed by and for Geo. Grierson, in Essex-Street, and for
George Ewing, in Dames-Street, 1726. Eight vols., 12mo,
first Irish edition. The eighth volume, poetry is sometimes
lacking, and this cuts the value......................... 825.00 1050.00

☐ **Shakespeare, William.** *Shakespeare's Works.* Collated with
the Oldest Copies, and Corrected; with Notes, Explanatory
and Critical. London, 1733. Seven vols. 325.00 400.00

☐ **Shakespeare, William.** *Shakespeare's Works.* The Hanmer edition. Oxford, Printed at the Theatre, 1743–6. Six
vols., quarto. The first printing of Sir Thomas Hanmer's
edition, issued under the auspices of the Oxford University
delegates.. 900.00 1075.00

☐ **Shakespeare, William.** *Shakespeare's Works.* By Mr. Pope
and Mr. Warburton. Dublin, 1748. Eight vols., 12mo. 130.00 160.00

☐ **Shakespeare, William.** *The Plays of William Shakespeare.*
With the Corrections and Illustrations of various Commen-
tators; to which are added Notes by Sam. Johnson. London, Printed for J. and R. Tonson, 1765. Eight vols....... 650.00 825.00

☐ **Shakespeare, William.** *The Plays of William Shakespeare.*
Johnson edition. Dublin, 1766. Ten vols. First Irish printing
of the Johnson Shakespeare........................... 425.00 550.00

☐ **Shakespeare, William.** *Twenty of the Plays of Shake-*
speare, being the whole Number printed in Quarto during
his Life-Time, or before the Restoration, Collated where
there are different Copies, and published from the Origi-
nals. By George Steevens, Esq. London, Printed for J. and
R. Tonson, 1766. Four vols., 8vo........................ 235.00 285.00

☐ **Shakespeare, William.** *Shakespeare's Plays.* From the
text of Dr. S. Johnson. Dublin, 1771. Thirteen vols., 12mo.
With portraits of Shakespeare and David Garrick, and other
illustrations. Generally a well-printed edition but some embarrassing errors are found, such as a reference to the
"Pape of Lucrece.". 450.00 525.00

☐ **Shakespeare, William.** *Shakespeare's Plays and Poems.*
London, 1773–77. Nine vols., 8vo, large paper copy. Illus-
trated with portraits and character scenes by Grignion, Izaak
Taylor, etc.. 260.00 315.00

Mᴿ· WILLIAM
SHAKESPEAR'S

Comedies, Hiſtories, and Tragedies.

Publiſhed according to the true Original Copies.

The third Impreſſion.

And unto this Impreſſion is added ſeven Playes, never
before Printed in Folio.

viz.

Pericles Prince of *Tyre.*
The *London Prodigall.*
The Hiſtory of *Thomas* Lᵈ· *Cromwell.*
Sir *John Oldcaſtle* Lord *Cobham.*
The *Puritan Widow.*
A *York-shire* Tragedy.
The Tragedy of *Locrine.*

LONDON, Printed for *P. C.* 1664.

Worth its weight in gold—almost—is the third edition of Shakespeare's plays, known by collectors as the "third folio." This is a rare instance of a later edition being more valuable than the first edition. The date on the title page provides a clue to its scarcity. Two years after this volume was published, a fire destroyed nearly half of the city of London, including (it is said) the warehouse where most copies of the book were stored. Of course, the fact that seven new plays are added to the contents builds collector interest, too—even though most of them are not by Shakespeare.

PRICE RANGE

☐ **Shakespeare, William.** *The Plays of Shakespeare.* London, Printed for C. Bathurst, J. Rivington & Sons, etc., 1785. Ten vols., 8vo... 475.00   575.00

☐ **Shakespeare, William.** *The Plays of William Shakespeare.* With the corrections and illustrations of various Commentators. To which are added, Notes by Samuel Johnson and George Steevens. London, 1793. Fifteen vols., large 8vo. Illustrated with nearly 150 portraits and plates by Harding. Depending on binding.................................... 800.00   1100.00

☐ **Shakespeare, William.** *The Plays and Poems of William Shakespeare.* Corrected from the latest and best London edition, with Notes, by Samuel Johnson, LL.D. To which are added a Glossary and the life of the Author. Philadelphia, Bioren and Madan, 1795–96. Eight vols., 12mo. First American edition of Shakespeare. Some copies are misbound or have sections lacking........................... 2100.00   2650.00

☐ **Shakespeare, William.** *Plays of William Shakespeare.* London, 1797. Six vols. 230.00   280.00

☐ **Shakespeare, William.** *The Plays of Shakespeare, accurately printed from the text of the Corrected Copy left by the late George Steevens.* London, 1803. Ten vols., with oval portrait by C. Warren............................. 275.00   325.00

☐ **Shakespeare, William.** *The Plays of Shakespeare.* From the correct edition of Isaac Reed. London, 1809. Twelve vols., large paper copy, in boards....................... 350.00   425.00

☐ **Shakespeare, William.** *The Plays and Poems of Shakespeare, with the Corrections and Illustrations of Various Commentators; comprehending a Life of the Poet, and an enlarged History of the Stage, by the late Edmond Malone, with a New Glossarial Index.* London, 1821. Twenty-one vols., the Malone "Variorum Edition."................... 900.00   1100.00

☐ **Shakespeare, William.** *Shakespeare's Plays.* London, 1825. Pickering's "Diamond Edition," Nine vols. in miniature size, cloth... 275.00   350.00

☐ **Shakespeare, William.** *Shakespeare's Dramatic Works.* London, 1826. One vol., published by Pickering, printed on India paper, cloth...................................... 16.00   21.00

☐ **Shakespeare, William.** *Shakespeare's Complete Works.* Printed from the text of the most renowned editions. Leipzig, 1837. Quarto, one volume. 16.00   21.00

☐ **Shakespeare, William.** *The Pictorial Edition of the Works of Shakespeare,* edited by Charles Knight. London, n.d., c. 1840. Eight vols., 8vo, with numerous woodcuts.......... 180.00   235.00

☐ **Shakespeare, William.** *The Works of William Shakespeare.* (Edited by Payne Collier.) *The Text formed from an entirely new collation of the old editions. With the various Readings, Notes, a Life of the Poet, and a History of the Early English State.* London, 1844. Eight vols., 8vo. A supplementary volume was issued in 1853, entitled "Note and Emandations to the Text of Shakespeare's Plays, from Early Manuscript Corrections in a Copy of the Folio, 1632." It later proved that these "early manuscript corrections" were

	PRICE RANGE	

forged by Collier, a celebrated Shakespeare collector and respected bibliographer.................................... **130.00** **165.00**

☐ **Shakespeare, William.** *The Doubtful Plays of Shakespeare.* London, 1853. Large 8vo, illustrated............. **83.00** **105.00**

☐ **Shakespeare, William.** *The Dramatic Works of William Shakespeare, the text carefully revised with notes by Samuel Weller Singer. The Life of the Poet and Critical Essays of the Plays by William Watkiss Lloyd.* London, 1856. Ten vols. small 8vo, cloth.......................... **37.00** **48.00**

☐ **Shakespeare, William.** *The Works of William Shakespeare, with copious Notes, Glossary, Life, etc., by Howard Staunton.* London, 1864. Four vols., 8vo, in a good binding... **63.00** **82.00**

☐ **Shakespeare, William.** *The Plays and Poems of William Shakespeare. With the purest Text, and the briefest Notes.* Edited by J. Payne Collier, London, privately printed for Subscribers, 1878. Forty-three parts in eight volumes, softbound (purple wrappers). Only 58 sets printed. **375.00** **475.00**

☐ **Shakespeare, William.** *Works of William Shakespeare.* London, Kegan Paul, 1882. Twelve vols. One of 50 large paper copies, numbered and signed by the printers, bound by Riviere in full crushed levant morocco, uncut, top edges gilt. **350.00** **425.00**

☐ **Shakespeare, William.** *Shakespeare's Comedies, Histories and Tragedies.* Facsimilies of the First Four Folios of 1623, 1632, 1664 and 1685. London, Methuen & Co., 1904–10. Four vols., boards, uncut............................ **700.00** **850.00**
Individual volumes, about $175 each.

PLAYS OF SHAKESPEARE'S PUBLISHED SEPARATELY
(in alphabetical order)

	PRICE RANGE	

☐ **Shakespeare, William.** *Antony and Cleopatra. A Tragedy.* London, Jacob Tonson, 1734. 12mo, frontispiece......... **85.00** **115.00**

☐ **Shakespeare, William.** *Antony and Cleopatra; an historical Play, written by William Shakespeare: fitted for the Stage by abridging only; and now acted, at the Theatre-Royal in Drury-Lane, by his Majesty's Servants.* London, printed for J. and R. Tonson, 1758. Preceded by a poem, said to be by Garrick. **200.00** **275.00**

☐ **Shakespeare, William.** *The Tragedie of Antony and Cleopatra.* London, Doves Press, 1912. .... **500.00** **625.00**

☐ **Shakespeare, William.** *As You Like It.* A Comedy Written by William Shakespeare: Taken from the Manager's Book, at the Theatre-Royal in Drury-Lane. London, printed for R. Butters, n.d., 52 pp................................ **32.00** **43.00**

☐ **Shakespeare, William.** *As You Like It.* Variorum edition, edited by H. H. Furness. Philadelphia, 1890. .... **13.00** **17.00**

PRICE RANGE

☐ **Shakespeare, William.** *As You Like It*. London, 1913. "Edition de luxe," with 40 illustrations in color by Hugh Thomson, vellum, limited to 500 copies.................. 135.00   160.00

☐ **Shakespeare, William.** *The Tragedy of Coriolanus*. London, Doves Press, 1914. Vellum. 275.00   350.00

☐ **Shakespeare, William.** *Cymbeline*. A Tragedy. London, Jacob Tonson, 1734. 12mo. 60.00   80.00

☐ **Shakespeare, William.** *The Tragedy of Hamlet, Prince of Denmark. As it is now Acted at his Highness the Duke of York's Theatre*. London, 1676. .... 1250.00   1675.00

☐ **Shakespeare, William.** *Hamlet, Prince of Denmark*. A Tragedy in Five Acts. London, 1789. Softbound. 65.00   85.00

☐ **Shakespeare, William.** *Hamlet, A Tragedy in Five Acts, as arranged for the Stage by Henry Irving, and presented at The Lyceum Theatre on Monday, December 30th, 1878*. London, 1879. Softbound................................. 3.50   5.00

☐ **Shakespeare, William.** *Julius Caesar, a Tragedy*. London, 1711. 12mo, boards..................................... 75.00   95.00

☐ **Shakespeare, William.** *Julius Caesar, a Tragedy*. London, Jacob Tonson, 1734...................................... 75.00   95.00

☐ **Shakespeare, William.** *King Henry IV*. London, Tonson, 1734. Carries an advertisement warning the public against Walker's edition of Shakespeare's plays. Walker was Tonson's chief competitor for the Shakespeare market. 47.00   62.00

☐ **Shakespeare, William.** *King Henry the Fifth, arranged for Representation at the Princess's Theatre, with Historical and Explanatory Notes by Charles Kean*. Longon, n.d., 1859. .... 18.00   24.00

☐ **Shakespeare, William.** *The Life of Henry VIII, by Mr. William Shakespeare; in which are interspersed Historical Notes, Reflections etc*. Dedicated to Colley Cibber. London, 1758. Six portraits....................................... 53.00   75.00

☐ **Shakespeare, William.** *The Life and Death of King Lear*. London, Tonson, 1734................................... 53.00   75.00

☐ **Shakespeare, William.** *King Lear. A Tragedy. Altered from Shakespeare, by D. Garrick, Esq*. London, n.d., c. 1787. 62 pp...................................... 27.00   36.00

☐ **Shakespeare, William.** *Play of King Richard II. Arranged for representation at The Princess's Theatre, with Historical and Explanatory Notes, by Charles Kean*. London, 1857. Softbound. 8.00   11.00

☐ **Shakespeare, William.** *The Life and Death of Richard III. A Tragedy. With the Landing of the Earl of Richmond, and the Battle of Bosworth Field, being the Last between the Houses of Lancaster and York*. London, printed by R. Walker at Shakespeare's Head in Turn-again Lane, Snow-Hill, 1734. 12mo. One of the pirated editions of Walker, which claimed to be word-for-word as acted at Drury-Lane. Though bogus, they happen to be scarce.............................. 375.00   475.00

☐ **Shakespeare, William.** *Richard the Third. A Tragedy*. Taken from the Manager's Book, at the Theatre-Royal, Covent-Garden. London, sold by Rachael Randall, 1787. .... 30.00   39.00

PRICE RANGE

☐ **Shakespeare, William.** *King Richard the Third. A Historical Play, adapted to the Stage by Colley Cibber: Revised by J. P. Kemble: and now published as it is performed at the Theatre-Royal.* London, 1814........................ **22.00   27.00**

☐ **Shakespeare, William.** *King Richard III. In Five Acts, as arranged for the Stage by Henry Irving from the text of William Shakespeare and presented at The Lyceum Theatre on Saturday, 19th December, 1896.* London, 1896. Wrappers... **10.00   14.00**

☐ **Shakespeare, William.** *The Tragedie of Locrine, the Eldest Son of King Brutus.* London, Tonson, 1734............. **37.00   47.00**

☐ **Shakespeare, William.** *MacBeth, a Tragedy, As it is now Acted at the Theatre Royal.* London, 1695.............. **1200.00   1600.00**

☐ **Shakespeare, William.** *The Tragedy of MacBeth, to which are added, all the original songs never printed in any of the former editions.* London, 1734...................... **37.00   47.00**

☐ **Shakespeare, William.** *MacBeth. A Tragedy.* London, 1786, 41 pp.. **22.00   28.00**

☐ **Shakespeare, William.** *Merchant of Venice. The Excellent History of the Merchant of Venice. With the extreme cruelty of Shylocke the Jew towards the saide Merchant, in cutting a just pound of flesh. And the obtaining of Portia, by the choyse of three Caskets.* Written by W. Shakespeare. London, printed by J. Roberts, 1600. There are some questions whether the date as it appears on the title page is authentic. Alfred W. Pollard, a Shakespeare bibliographer, believed the Roberts edition to date from 1619. .... **8000.00   11250.00**

☐ **Shakespeare, William.** *Merchant of Venice. As altered by Lord Lansdowne, under the title of the Jew of Venice. A Comedy. As it is Acted at the Theatre in Little-Lincolns-Inn-Fields, by his Majesty's Servants.* London, 1701......... **400.00   500.00**

☐ **Shakespeare, William.** *The Merchant of Venice. A Comedy.* London, 1787. 56 pp. **30.00   39.00**

☐ **Shakespeare, William.** *The Merry Wives of Windsor. A Comedy.* London, 1787, 56 pp. **30.00   39.00**

☐ **Shakespeare, William.** *Merry Wives of Windsor.* A facsimile in photo-lithography of the first 4to (1601), together with a reprint of the prompt copy prepared for use at Daly's Theatre. N.Y., 1886...................................... **43.00   54.00**

☐ **Shakespeare, William.** *A Midsommer nights dreame. A it hath beene sundry times publikely acted by the Right Honourable, the Lord Chamberlaine his Servants.* London, printed by James Roberts, 1600. May have actually been published in 1619. .... **6750.00   8250.00**

☐ **Shakespeare, William.** *Midsummer Night's Dream.* London, n.d., 1856. "Kean's Acting Edition".................. **10.00   14.00**

☐ **Shakespeare, William.** *Much Ado About Nothing.* London, Chiswick Press, 1882. Softbound.................... **10.00   14.00**

☐ **Shakespeare, William.** *Othello, the Moor of Venice. A Tragedy. As it hath been divers times acted at the Globe, and at the Black-Friers: and now at the Theatre-Royal, by His Majesties Servants.* London, 1687................... **1275.00   1625.00**

A Midſommer nights dreame.

As it hath beene ſundry times publikely acted, by the Right Honourable, the Lord Chamberlaine his
ſeruants.

VVritten by VVilliam Shakeſpeare.

Printed by Iames Roberts, 1600.

You can't always trust what you find on the title page of an old book. This edition of Shakespeare's Midsummer Night's Dream *claims to have been printed by James Roberts in 1600, which would make it the first edition and place it within Shakespeare's lifetime. Actually, the experts are of the opinion that it was NOT printed by James Roberts but by Isaac Jaggard, who had acquired the rights to Shakespeare's writing after the Bard's death, and that it was actually issued around 1619.*

	PRICE RANGE	
☐ **Shakespeare, William.** *Pericles Prince of Tyre.* London, Tonson, 1734.	37.00	47.00
☐ **Shakespeare, William.** *The Most Excellent and Lamentable Tragedie of Romeo and Juliet. As it hath been sundry times publikely Acted by the Kings Majesties Servants at the Globe. Written by W. Shake-speare. Newly corrected, augmented, and amended.* London, printed by R. Young for John Smethwicke, and are to be sold at his Shop in St. Dunstans Church-yard in Fleetstreet, under the Dyall, 1637.	4000.00	5500.00
☐ **Shakespeare, William.** *Romeo and Juliet. With Alterations, and an additional Scene; by D. Garrick. As it is performed at the Theatre Royal in Drury-Lane.* London, printed for J. Whitworth, n.d., 1780. Should have a frontispiece, though the standard bibliography of Shakespeare's books, by Jaggard, does not mention one.	57.00	72.00
☐ **Shakespeare, William.** *Romeo and Juliet. A Tragedy. Altered from Shakespeare by David Garrick.* Marked with the Variations in the Manager's Book, at the Theatre Royal in Drury-Lane. London, Lowndes, 1784.	37.00	48.00
☐ **Shakespeare, William.** *The first place of the true and honorable historie, of the life of Sir John Old-castle, the good Lord Cobham.* London, printed for T.P., 1600.	2100.00	2675.00
☐ **Shakespeare, William.** *Taming of the Shrew. Catherine and Petruchio: A Comedy, in Three Acts: As it is performed at the Theatre-Royal in Drury-Lane. Alter'd from Shakespeare's Taming of the Shrew.* By David Garrick. London, Tonson, 1756.	37.00	45.00
☐ **Shakespeare, William.** *The Tempest, or The Enchanted Island. A Comedy; As it is now Acted.* London, 1676.....	1050.00	1400.00
☐ **Shakespeare, William.** *The Tempest, or the Enchanted Island. A Comedy, as it is Acted at their Majesties Theatre in Dorset-Garden.* London, 1690.	650.00	825.00
☐ **Shakespeare, William.** *The Tempest. A Comedy.* London, n.d., 1787..	27.00	34.00
☐ **Shakespeare, William.** *Twelfth-Night; or, What You Will. A Comedy in Five Acts.* London, 1884. Softbound..........	10.00	14.00
☐ **Shakespeare, William.** *The Winter's Tale.* London, n.d., 1856. "Kean's Acting Edition"...........................	10.00	14.00

BOOKS ABOUT SHAKESPEARE

	PRICE RANGE	
☐ **Adams, W. H. D.** *A Concordance to the Plays of Shakespeare.* London, 1886.	110.00	140.00
☐ *All About Shakespeare.* London, n.d., 1800's, softbound.	7.00	10.00
☐ *Aphorisms from Shakespeare: arranged according to the Plays, &c.* London, 1812.................................	67.00	82.00
☐ **Arrowsmith, W. R.** *Shakespeare's Editor and Commentators.* London, 1865. Softbound.	32.00	40.00

PRICE RANGE

☐ **Birch, W. J.** *An Inquiry into the Philosophy and Religion of Shakespeare.* London, 1848............................ | 43.00 | 55.00

☐ **Brandes, Georg.** *William Shakespeare.* Paris and Leipzig, 1896.. | 67.00 | 83.00

☐ **Britton, John.** *Remarks on the Life and Writings of William Shakespeare.* London, 1814. 8vo, large and thick paper copy, extra illustrated.................................... | 800.00 | 1050.00

☐ **Butler, Samuel.** *Shakespeare's Sonnets.* London, 1899. | 130.00 | 170.00

☐ **Calmour, Alfred C.** *Fact and Fiction about Shakespeare.* Stratford-on-Avon and London, 1894................... | 37.00 | 48.00

☐ **Campbell, John.** *Shakespeare's Legal Acquirements Considered.* London, 1859........................... | 27.00 | 35.00

☐ **Carr, J. Comyns.** *MacBeth and Lady MacBeth.* London, 1889.. | 21.00 | 27.00

☐ **Chalmers, Geo.** *Another Account of the Incidents from which the title and a part of the Story of Shakespeare's Tempest were Derived.* London, 1815.................. | 42.00 | 53.00

☐ **Coleridge, S. T.** *Note and Lectures upon Shakespeare and some of the Old Poets and Dramatists.* London, 1849. Two vols... | 42.00 | 53.00

☐ **Collier, J. Payne.** *New Facts Regarding the Life of Shakespeare.* London, 1835.............................. | 37.00 | 48.00

☐ **Collier, J. Payne.** *New Particulars Regarding the Works of Shakespeare.* London, 1836........................ | 63.00 | 78.00

☐ **Collier, J. Payne.** *Notes and Emendations to the Text of Shakespeare's Plays.* London, 1853................... | 27.00 | 35.00

☐ **Corbin, John.** *The Elizabethan Hamlet.* London, 1895. .. | 27.00 | 35.00

☐ **Cowden-Clarke, Mrs.** *The Complete Concordance to Shakespeare.* London, 1845........................... | 65.00 | 80.00

☐ **Cowden-Clarke, Charles.** *Shakespeare Characters.* London, 1863.. | 32.00 | 40.00

☐ **Curling, Capt.** *The Forest Youth; or, Shakespeare as he lived.* London, 1853................................... | 26.00 | 33.00

☐ **Daniel, P. A.** *Notes and Conjectural Emendations of certain Doubtful Passages in Shakespeare's Plays.* London, 1870.. | 23.00 | 30.00

☐ **Douce, Francis.** *Illustrations of Shakespeare, and of Ancient Manners.* London, 1807. Two vols., 8vo. Originally bound in boards, with printed labels on covers.......... | 85.00 | 105.00

☐ **Drake, Nathan.** *Memorials of Shakespeare.* London, 1828. Cloth.. | 30.00 | 39.00

☐ **Dyce, Rev. Alexander.** *Remarks on Mr. J. P. Collier's and Mr. C. Knight's Editions of Shakespeare.* London, 1844. | 30.00 | 39.00

☐ **Dyce, Rev. Alexander.** *Strictures on Mr. Collier's New Edition of Shakespeare.* London, 1859. .... | 30.00 | 39.00

☐ **Fairholt, F. W.** *The Home of Shakespeare Illustrated and Described.* London, 1847. With 33 engravings, softbound... | 13.00 | 17.00

☐ **Fleahy, Rev. F. G.** *Shakespeare and Puritanism.* London, n.d., c. 1880. Thin 8vo, 9 pp. Scarce.................. | 25.00 | 33.00

☐ *Footsteps of Shakespeare.* London, 1862.............. | 21.00 | 27.00

☐ **Furnivall, Dr. F. J.** *The Succession of Shakespeare's Works.* London, 1874.. | 8.00 | 11.00

	PRICE RANGE	

☐ **Gervinus, Dr. G.G.** *Shakespeare Commentaries*. London,
1892. Fifth edition. 21.00 27.00

☐ **Grindon, Leo H.** *The Shakespeare Flora*. Manchester, 1883.
Illustrated. 62.00 78.00

☐ **Hall, H. T.** *Shakespearean Statistics*. Cambridge, 1865.
Softbound. 8.00 11.00

☐ **Halliwell, J. O. (later Halliwell-Phillipps).** A Descriptive
Calendar of the Ancient Manuscripts and Records in the
possession of the Corporation of Stratford-upon-Avon . . .
London, 1863. Folio, limited to 75 copies, publishers' bind-
ing, half roan 850.00 1075.00

☐ **Halliwell, J. O.** *An Historical Account of the New Place,
Stratford-upon-Avon, the Last Residence of Shakespeare*.
London, 1864. Folio, woodcut illustrations. Halliwell financed the publication of this work, as with many of his
others, and gave a copy free to anyone who contributed
five British pounds or more to the Shakespeare Fund 225.00 300.00

☐ **Halliwell, J. O.** *A List of Works, illustrative of the Life and
Writings of Shakespeare*. London, 1867. . . . . 35.00 43.00

☐ **Halliwell, J. O.** *Memoranda on the Tragedy of Hamlet*.
London, 1879. . . . . 27.00 34.00

☐ **Halliwell, J. O.** *Outlines of the Life of Shakespeare*. Brigh-
ton, 1881. . . . . 110.00 140.00

☐ **Hamilton, N. E.** *An Inquiry into the Genuineness of the
Manuscript Corrections in Mr. J. Payne Collier's Annotated
Shakespeare*. London, 1860. . . . . 45.00 60.00

☐ **Hamley, Sir. Edward.** *Shakespeare's Funeral and Other
Papers*. Edinburgh and London, 1889. . . . . 21.00 27.00

☐ **Hazlitt, William.** *Characters of Shakespeare's Plays*. Lon-
don, 1817. . . . . 95.00 120.00

☐ **Hazlitt, W. C.** (a different author than the above). *Fairy
Tales, Legends, and Romances, illustrating Shakespeare
and other Early English Writers*. London, 1875. . . . . 32.00 43.00

☐ **Hugo, Victor.** *William Shakespeare*. Paris, 1864. . . . .

☐ **Ingleby, C. N..** *Shakespeare's Centurie of Prayse*. London,
1879. Quarto, large paper copy. 67.00 88.00

☐ **Jackson, Z.** *Shakespeare's Genius Justified*. London,
1819. . . . . 35.00 43.00

☐ **Jephson, Rev. J. M.** *Shakespeare: His Birthplace, Home
and Grave*. London, 1864. Square octavo, with photographic illustrations. The early use of photo plates makes
this volume of interest to collectors of photo-history, too.
The shots were taken the previous year, 1863. . . . . 125.00 150.00

☐ **Jeremiah, John.** *Notes on Shakespeare*. London, 1876.. 27.00 35.00

☐ **Kelsall, Charles.** *The First Sitting of the Committee on the
Proposed Monument to Shakespeare*. Cheltenham, 1823.
A satirical publication. 32.00 40.00

☐ **Kenny, Thomas.** *The Life and Genius of Shakespeare*.
London, 1864. . . . . 18.00 25.00

☐ **Knight, Charles.** *Studies of Shakespeare*. London,
1849. . . . . 18.00 25.00

☐ **Landor, W. S.** *Citation and Examination of William Shake-
speare*. London, 1834. . . . . 150.00 185.00

PRICE RANGE

☐ **Langton, Clare.** *The Light of Shakespeare.* London, 1897. Softbound. .... | 8.00 | 11.00

☐ **Lee, Sir Sidney.** *A Catalogue of Shakespeareana.* London, 1899. Two vols., 4to. The owner of this collection is not identified, but believed to be Marsden Perry. .... | 110.00 | 140.00

☐ **Leyland, John.** *The Shakespeare Country.* London, n.d., late 1800's.. | 10.00 | 14.00

☐ **Maginn, William.** *Shakespeare Papers.* London, 1859. ... | 10.00 | 14.00

☐ **Marshall, Frank A.** *A Study of Hamlet.* London, 1875. ... | 20.00 | 25.00

☐ **Massey, Gerald.** *Shakespeare's Sonnets.* London, 1866. | 8.00 | 11.00

☐ **Montagu, Mrs.** *An Essay on the Writings and Genius of Shakespeare.* London, 1810. Sixth edition. .... | 21.00 | 27.00

☐ **Morgan, Rev. A. A.** *The Mind of Shakespeare.* London, 1860. .... | 13.00 | 17.00

☐ **Neil, Samuel.** *The Home of Shakespeare.* Warwick, n.d., 1800's. Softbound.................................... | 8.00 | 11.00

☐ **Roffe, Alfred.** *The Handbook of Shakespeare Music.* London, 1878... | 32.00 | 40.00

☐ **Rushton, William Lowes.** *Shakespeare's Testamentary Language.* London, 1869. .... | 13.00 | 17.00

☐ **Severn, Emma.** *Anne Hathaway; or Shakespeare in Love.* London, 1845. Three vols., half cloth. .... | 32.00 | 38.00

☐ *Shakespeare's Almanack for 1870.* A Daily Quotation from the Poet's Works. London, 1870. Wrappers, 16 pp. ...... | 2.50 | 3.00

☐ **Singer, Samuel W.** *The Text of Shakespeare Vindicated.* London, 1853... | 13.00 | 16.00

☐ **Skottoew, Augustine.** *The Life of Shakespeare.* London, 1824. Two vols., boards. .... | 47.00 | 68.00

☐ **Smith, C. R.** *Remarks on Shakespeare, His Birth Place, etc.* London, privately printed ("Not Published"), 1868–69... | 32.00 | 40.00

☐ **Symonds, J.A.** *Shakespeare's Predecessors in the English Drama.* London, 1884. .... | 90.00 | 110.00

☐ **Thiselton, A. E.** *Some Textural Notes on the Tragedie of Antony and Cleopatra.* London, printed and published for the Author, 1899. Softbound. .... | 13.00 | 16.00

☐ **Thornbury, G. W.** *Shakespeare's England.* London, 1856. Two vols... | 21.00 | 27.00

☐ **Ulrici, Dr. Herman.** *Shakespeare's Dramatic Art.* London, 1846. .... | 22.00 | 29.00

☐ **Vaughan, Henry H.** *New Readings and New Renderings of Shakespeare's Tragedies.* London, 1886. Three vols., second edition. .... | 16.00 | 21.00

☐ **Walker, William S.** *Shakespeare's Versification and its Apparent Irregularities.* London, 1854. Softbound. .... | 11.00 | 15.00

☐ **Webb, J. Stenson.** *Shakespeare Reference Book.* London, 1898... | 3.50 | 5.00

☐ **Wilkes, George.** *Shakespeare from an American Point of View.* London, 1877................................... | 32.00 | 43.00

☐ **Williams, R. F.** *Shakespeare and his Friends, or the Golden Age of Merrie England.* London, 1838. Three vols., boards... | 25.00 | 33.00

PRICE RANGE

□ **Williams, R. F.** *The Youth of Shakespeare.* London, 1839. Three vols., boards.. 32.00 41.00

□ **Wilson, John.** *Shakespeariana.* London, 1827. Octavo, large paper copy....................................... 85.00 105.00

END OF BOOKS ON SHAKESPEARE

PRICE RANGE

□ **Shelley, Mary W.** *Frankenstein.* London, 1818. Three vols., boards with paper labels. The first "science fiction" novel, and first novel by a woman that was not a love story..... 3250.00 4500.00

□ **Shelley, Mary W.** *Frankenstein.* London, 1831........... 225.00 285.00

□ **Shelley, Percy Bysshe.** *Queen Mab.* London, 1813. Rare, late editions are worth considerably less................. 6500.00 8750.00

□ **Shelley, Percy Bysshe.** *The Revolt of Islam.* London, 1817. Blue boards.. 1200.00 1700.00

□ **Shelley, Percy Bysshe.** *Rosalind and Helen.* London, 1819. Softbound... 700.00 950.00

□ **Shelley, Percy Bysshe.** *Prometheus Unbound.* London, 1820. Extremely rare. The first issue has the spelling "mis-ellaneous" in the table of contents...................... 4000.00 6750.00

□ **Shelley, Percy Bysshe.** *Shelley's Posthumous Poems.* London, 1824... 120.00 160.00

□ **Shelley, Percy Bysshe.** *Shelley's Poetical Works.* London, 1839. Four vols....................................... 40.00 55.00

□ **Shelley, Percy Bysshe.** *Shelley's Poetical Works.* London, 1853. One Vol. 25.00 35.00

□ **Smollett, Tobias.** *The Expedition of Humphrey Clinker.* London, 1771. Three vols............................... 430.00 515.00

□ **Smollett, Tobias.** *Adventures of Peregrine Pickle.* London, 1784. Four vols., seventh edition...................... 47.00 62.00

□ **Smollett, Tobias.** *Smollett's Works Complete.* London, 1797, Eight vols.. 130.00 165.00

□ **Smollett, Tobias.** *Smollett's Works.* Edinburgh, 1811. Six vols... 88.00 115.00

□ **Smollett, Tobias.** *Smollett's Works, with Life by Roscoe.* London, 1858. One vol., cloth........................... 21.00 27.00

□ **Southey, Robert.** *Joan of Arc.* London, 1806. Two vols... 30.00 38.00

□ **Southey, Robert.** *Specimens of the Later English Poets.* London, 1807... 60.00 80.00

□ **Southey, Robert.** *The Life of Nelson.* London, 1813...... 30.00 40.00

□ **Southey, Robert.** *Roderick.* London, 1814.............. 50.00 65.00

□ **Southey, Robert.** *A Tale of Paraguay.* London, 1825..... 30.00 40.00

□ **Southey, Robert.** *Sir Thomas More.* London, 1829. Two vols.. 85.00 110.00

□ **Southey, Robert.** *All for Love.* London, 1829. .... 25.00 160.00

□ **Southey, Robert.** *Southey's Life and Correspondence, edited by Cuthbert Southey.* London, 1849. Six vols., cloth.. 25.00 32.00

□ **Southey, Robert.** *Southey's Letters.* London, 1856. Four vols., cloth... 40.00 53.00

□ **Spenser, Edmund.** *The Faerie Queene.* London, 1596. Two vols., often bound as one. 9000.00 12000.00

PRICE RANGE

☐ **Spenser, Edmund.** *Spencer's Works: Faerie Queen, Shepeard's Calendar, Sonnets, and Poems.* London, 1611. First collected edition, illustrated.....................	1075.00	1500.00
☐ **Spenser, Edmund.** *Spenser's Works in Verse and Prose, with Life and Additions.* London, 1679...................	675.00	850.00
☐ **Spenser, Edmund.** *Spenser's Poetical Works complete, with illustrations of various Commentators, Notes, Life and Glossary by H. J. Todd.* London, 1805. Eight vols........	175.00	225.00
☐ **Spenser, Edmund.** *Spenser's Poetical Works.* London, 1839. Five vols., cloth.	25.00	33.00
☐ **Steele, Richard.** *The Christian Hero.* London, 1701......	30.00	40.00
☐ **Steele, Richard.** *The Crisis.* London, 1714.	60.00	75.00
☐ **Steele, Richard.** *The Roman Ecclesiastical History.* London, 1714..	30.00	40.00
☐ **Steele, Richard.** *An Account of the State of the Roman Catholick Religion.* London, 1715.	35.00	45.00
☐ **Steele, Richard.** *Epistolary Correspondence, including his familiar Letters to his Wife and Daughters.* London, 1809. Two vols., boards.	25.00	32.00
☐ **Steffens, Lincoln.** *The Shame of the Cities.* London, 1904.	12.00	15.00
☐ **Stein, Gertrude.** *Three Lives.* N.Y., 1909.	1250.00	1600.00
☐ **Stein, Gertrude.** *Tender Buttons.* N.Y., 1914.	325.00	450.00
☐ **Stein, Gertrude.** *Geography and Plays.* Boston, n.d., 1922.	110.00	150.00
☐ **Stein, Gertrude.** *The Making of Americans.* Paris, n.d., 1926. Limited to 500....................................	1400.00	1875.00
☐ **Steinbeck, John.** *Bombs Away.* N.Y., 1942. Blue cloth. .	42.00	57.00
☐ **Steinbeck, John.** *Cannery Row.* N.Y., 1945. Cream-yellow cloth...	47.00	63.00
☐ **Steinbeck, John.** *The Wayward Bus.* N.Y., 1947. Brown cloth...	42.00	58.00
☐ **Steinbeck, John.** *A Russian Journal.* N.Y., 1948.........	53.00	70.00
☐ **Steinbeck, John.** *East of Eden.* N.Y., 1952. Green cloth. There was also a limited edition of 1,500 signed copies, now worth around $125.................................	53.00	70.00
☐ **Steinbeck, John.** *The Winter of our Discontent.* N.Y., n.d., 1961.	31.00	39.00
☐ **Swinburne, A. C.** *The Death of John Franklin.* London, 1916. Softbound, limited edition.	95.00	120.00
☐ **Swinburne, A. C.** *Posthumous Poems.* London, 1917. Blue cloth..	20.00	30.00
☐ **Tarkington, Booth.** *Penrod and Sam.* Garden City, 1916.	28.00	35.00
☐ **Tarkington, Booth.** *Seventeen.* N.Y., n.d., 1916..........	40.00	50.00
☐ **Tarkington, Booth.** *The Midlander.* N.Y., 1922...........	22.00	28.00
☐ **Tarkington, Booth.** *Some Old Portraits.* N.Y., 1939.	28.00	35.00
☐ **Tennyson, Alfred.** *Maud.* London, 1855. Green cloth. ...	21.00	27.00
☐ **Tennyson, Alfred.** *Poems.* London, 1857................	105.00	130.00
☐ **Tennyson, Alfred.** *Idylls of the King.* London, 1859. Green cloth..	30.00	39.00
☐ **Tennyson, Alfred.** *Enoch, Arden.* London, 1864.........	30.00	39.00
☐ **Tennyson, Alfred.** *Elaine.* Paris, 1867...................	47.00	63.00

Captain Lemuel Gulliver, of
Redriff Ætat. ſuæ 58.

What good was a novel if you didn't get the feeling that it was for real? Jonathan Swift was determined to have Lemuel Gulliver taken seriously, so he inserted a portrait of him in Gulliver's Travels. This steel engraving shows him at the age of 58, and it was included in the rare first edition published between 1726 and 1727.

	PRICE RANGE	

☐ **Tennyson, Alfred.** *Lucretius.* Cambridge, 1868. . . . . | 260.00 | 315.00
☐ **Tennyson, Alfred.** *Viviane.* Paris, 1868. . . . . | 53.00 | 72.00
☐ **Tennyson, Alfred.** *The New Timon and the Poets.* London, 1876. . . . . | 620.00 | 825.00
☐ **Tennyson, Alfred.** *The Death of Oenone.* London, 1892. | 27.00 | 35.00
☐ **Tennyson, Alfred.** *A Memoir.* London, 1897. . . . . | 32.00 | 43.00
☐ **Thackeray, William M.** *Comic Tales and Sketches.* London, 1841. Two vols. . . . . | 130.00 | 165.00
☐ **Thackeray, William M.** *Mrs. Perkin's Ball.* London, 1847. | 32.00 | 43.00
☐ **Thackeray, William M.** *The Books of Snobs.* London, 1848. . . . . | 210.00 | 290.00
☐ **Thackeray, William M.** *Vanity Fair.* London, 1848. . . . . . . | 385.00 | 515.00
☐ **Thackeray, William M.** *The History of Pendennus.* London, 1849. Two vols. . . . . | 37.00 | 47.00
☐ **Thackeray, William M.** *The Kickleburys.* London, 1850. | 68.00 | 88.00
☐ **Thackeray, William M.** *The History of Henry Esmond.* London, 1852. Three vols. . . . . | 500.00 | 625.00
☐ **Thackeray, William M.** *The Newcomes.* London, 1854. Two vols. . . . . | 21.00 | 26.00
☐ **Thackeray, William M.** *The Rose and the Ring.* London, 1855. . . . . | 210.00 | 265.00
☐ **Thackeray, William M.** *Sketches and Travels in London.* London, 1856. . . . . | 26.00 | 35.00
☐ **Thackeray, William M.** *The Virginians.* London, 1858. Two vols. . . . . | 110.00 | 140.00
☐ **Trollope, Anthony.** *The Fixed Period.* London, 1882. Two vols. . . . . | 120.00 | 150.00
☐ **Trollope, Anthony.** *Kept in the Dark.* London, 1882. Two vols. . . . . | 120.00 | 150.00
☐ **Trollope, Anthony.** *Marion Fay.* London, 1882. Three vols. . . . . | 120.00 | 150.00
☐ **Trollope, Anthony.** *Mr. Scarborough's Family.* London, 1883. Three vols. . . . . | 175.00 | 230.00
☐ **Trollope, Anthony.** *The Landleaguers.* London, 1883. Three vols. . . . . | 120.00 | 150.00
☐ **TWAIN**—See Clemens
☐ **Verne, Jules.** *Around the World in 80 Days.* Boston, 1873. . . . . | 150.00 | 200.00
☐ **Verne, Jules.** *From the Earth to the Moon.* N.Y., 1874. . . . | 80.00 | 110.00
☐ **Whittier, John Greenleaf.** *Poems.* Philadelphia, 1838. . . . | 28.00 | 33.00
☐ **Whittier, John Greenleaf.** *The Patience of Hope.* Boston, 1862. . . . . | 22.00 | 28.00
☐ **Whittier, John Greenleaf.** *The Tent on the Beach.* Boston, 1867. . . . . | 45.00 | 60.00
☐ **Wilder, Thornton.** *The Cabala.* N.Y., 1926. Blue cloth over red. . . . . | 175.00 | 225.00
☐ **Wilder, Thornton.** *The Bridge of San Luis Rey.* N.Y., 1927. . . . . | 100.00 | 130.00
☐ **Wilder, Thornton.** *The Angel That Troubled the Waters.* N.Y., 1928. Limited, signed. . . . . | 38.00 | 48.00
☐ **Wilder, Thornton.** *The Long Christmas Dinner.* N.Y., 1931. . . . . | 38.00 | 48.00

	PRICE RANGE	
☐ **Wilder, Thornton.** *The Ides of March.* N.Y., 1948. Signed.	85.00	110.00
☐ **Williams, Tennessee.** *The Glass Menagerie.* N.Y., 1945.	150.00	180.00
☐ **Williams, Tennessee.** *A Streetcar Named Desire.* N.p., n.d. (Norfolk, 1947)	150.00	180.00
☐ **Williams, Tennessee.** *The Roman Spring of Mrs. Stone.* N.P., n.d. (N.Y., 1950). Limited to 500, signed.	210.00	270.00
☐ **Williams, Tennessee.** *Cat on a Hot Tin Roof.* N.p., n.d., (N.Y., 1955).	50.00	70.00
☐ **Wolfe, Thomas.** *Look Homeward Angel.* N.Y., 1929. Blue cloth. First state has Scribner logo on verso of title.	650.00	775.00
☐ **Wolfe, Thomas.** *Of Time and the River.* N.Y., 1935.	100.00	135.00
☐ **Wolfe, Thomas.** *From Death to Morning.* N.Y., 1935.	100.00	135.00
☐ **Wolfe, Thomas.** *The Face of a Nation.* N.Y., 1939. Cloth.	50.00	70.00
☐ **Wolfe, Thomas.** *You Can't Go Home Again.* N.Y., n.d., 1940.	70.00	90.00
☐ **Wolfe, Thomas.** *The Hills Beyond.* N.Y., n.d., 1941.	110.00	140.00
☐ **Wolfe, Thomas.** *Gentlemen of the Press.* Chicago, n.d., 1942. Limited to 350.	150.00	200.00
☐ **Wolfe, Thomas.** *Mannerhouse.* N.Y., 1948. Limited to 500.	100.00	130.00
☐ **Woolf, Virginia.** *Night and Day.* London, n.d., 1919.	550.00	750.00
☐ **Woolf, Virginia.** *On Being Ill.* London, 1930. Vellum and cloth, limited to 250, signed.	630.00	875.00
☐ **Woolf, Virginia.** *Beau Brummel.* N.Y., 1930. Limited to 550, signed.	265.00	335.00
☐ **Woolf, Virginia.** *Street Haunting.* San Francisco, 1930. Limited to 500, signed.	310.00	385.00
☐ **Woolf, Virginia.** *The Waves.* London, 1931.	190.00	240.00
☐ **Woolf, Virginia.** *The Years.* London, 1937.	240.00	290.00
☐ **Woolf, Virginia.** *Three Guineas.* London, 1937.	115.00	150.00
☐ **Woolf, Virginia.** *Between the Acts.* London, 1941.	70.00	90.00
☐ **Woolf, Virginia.** *A Writer's Diary.* London, 1953.	70.00	90.00
☐ **Woolf, Virginia.** *Hours in a Library.* N.Y., 1957.	70.00	90.00
☐ **Wordsworth, William.** *Poems.* London, 1807. Two vols. The first state is identified by a pair of points: a period after the word "Sonnets" on page 103 of Volume One and the misspelling "fnuction" for "function" on page 98 of Volume Two. The publisher's binding is plain boards with paper label.	1200.00	1500.00
☐ **Wordsworth, William.** *The Excursion.* London, 1814.	275.00	350.00
☐ **Wordsworth, William.** *The River Duddon.* London, 1820. Boarded sides, rough cloth spine.	230.00	300.00
☐ **Wordsworth, William.** *Memorials of a Tour on the Continent.* London, 1882. Boards.	385.00	465.00
☐ **Wordsworth, William.** *The White Doe of Rylstone, or the Fate of the Nortons.* London, 1859.	30.00	40.00
☐ **Wordsworth, William.** *Earlier Poems.* London, 1857.	20.00	25.00
☐ **Wordsworth, William.** *Poetical Works.* London, 1857. Six vols.	25.00	32.00
☐ **Yeats, W. B.** *Stories From Carleton.* London, n.d., 1889. Blue cloth with paper label.	90.00	115.00
☐ **Yeats, W. B.** *The Tables of the Law.* London, 1904.	30.00	38.00

	PRICE RANGE	
☐ **Yeats, W. B.** *The Hour Glass*. London, 1904.	35.00	45.00
☐ **Yeats, W. B.** *The King's Threshold*. London, 1904. Boards with green cloth spine.	90.00	115.00
☐ **Yeats, W. B.** *Plays for an Irish Theatre*. London, 1911. Boards with cloth spine.	175.00	230.00
☐ **Yeats, W. B.** *Four Plays for Dancers*. London, 1921.	120.00	160.00
☐ **Yeats, W. B.** *Essays*. London, 1924.	20.00	25.00
☐ **Yeats, W. B.** *The Winding Stair*. London, 1933.	60.00	80.00
☐ **Yeats, W. B.** *Collected Poems*. London, 1933. Dark red cloth.	12.00	16.00
☐ **Yeats, W. B.** *Dramatis Personae*. London, 1936.	180.00	230.00
☐ **Zola, Emile.** *The Attack on the Mill*. London, 1892.	21.00	27.00
☐ **Zola, Emile.** *Doctor Pascal*. London, 1893.	21.00	27.00

MEDICINE AND SCIENCE

	PRICE RANGE	
☐ **Abbotts, William.** *On Diabetes, Enuresis, and other diseases of a Similar Nature. Seventh edition*. London, 1877. Green cloth binding.	15.00	20.00
☐ **Abercrombie, John.** *Essays and Tracts*. Edinburgh, 1848. 319 pp. Cloth bound.	15.00	20.00
☐ **Abercrombie, John.** *Pathological and Practical Researchers on Diseases of the Stomach, Intestinal Canal, Liver, and other Viscera of the Abdomen*. Edinburgh: Waugh and Innes, 1828. 396 pp.	37.00	48.00
☐ **Abercrombie, John.** *The Philosophy of Moral Feelings*. London, 1833. 244 pp. Bound in cloth with a paper label.	28.00	36.00
☐ **Abernethy, John.** *Surgical Observations on Tumours, and on Lumbar Abcesses*. London, 1811. 222 pp. Bound in half calf.	62.00	83.00
☐ **Abernethy, John.** *The Surgical Works. A New Edition. Two vols*. London, 1816. With one engraved plate. Bound in calf.	32.00	43.00
☐ **Abernethy, John.** *Lectures on Anatomy, Surgery, and Pathology; including Observations on the Nature and Treatment of Local Diseases*. London, 1828. 580 pp. Bound in boards.	27.00	35.00
☐ **Abernethy, John.** *Surgical Observations on the Constitutional Origin and Treatment of Local Diseases; and on Aneurisms*. London, 1825. 346 pp. Bound in boards.	25.00	34.00
☐ **Adams, Joseph.** *Observations on Morbid Poisons, Phagedaena, and Cancer*. London, Printed for J. Johnson, 1795. 328 pp. Bound in boards.	100.00	130.00
☐ **Addison, Thomas.** *Anaemia*. London, 1849. An extract from Vol. VIII of "The London Medical Gazette." Unbound.	73.00	92.00
☐ **Addison, Thomas.** *A Collection of the Published Writings of Thomas Addison. Edited by Dr. Wilks and Dr. Daldy*. London, 1868. 242 pp. With 7 lithographed plates, 3 of them color. Bound in brown cloth.	47.00	62.00

PRICE RANGE

☐ **Agassiz, Louis and Gould, A. A.** *Outlines of Comparative Physiology.* London, 1855. With 390 illustrations in the text and a colored frontis. Bound in cloth........................ 24.00 31.00

☐ **Aikin, John.** *A Manual of Material Medica.* Yarmouth (England), 1785. 194 pp. Bound in boards with calf spine. . . . 21.00 26.00

☐ **Aikin, John.** *A View of the Character and Public Services of the late John Howard.* London, 1792. 248 pp. Bound in half calf.. 21.00 26.00

☐ **Ainslie, Sir Whitelaw.** *Materia Indica; or, some account of those articles which are employed by the Hindoos, and other Eastern Nations, in their Medicine, Arts, and Agriculture.* London, 1826. Two vols. 67.00 83.00

☐ **Albinus, ...** *Tables of the Skeleton and the Muscles of the Human Body.* London, 1749. Plates only (no text). Large folio... 180.00 235.00

☐ **Alley, George.** *Observations on the Hydrargyria; or that vesicular disease arising from the exhibition of Mercury.* London, 1810. 103 pp. With 3 colored plates. Bound in boards... 26.00 34.00

☐ **Allis, Oscar.** *An Inquiry into the Difficulties encountered in the Reproduction of Dislocations of the Hip.* Philadelphia, 1896. 171 pp... 18.00 25.00

☐ **Armstrong, John.** *Facts and Observations Relative to the Fever, commonly called Puerperal.* London, 1819. Second edition. 240 pp. Bound in boards......................... 16.00 22.00

☐ **Armstrong, John.** *Facts, Observations and Practical Illustrations relative to Puerperal Fever etc.* Hartford, Conn., 1823. Three parts in one vol. Total of about 400 pp....... 43.00 58.00

☐ **Arnott, James.** *Cases Illustrative of the Treatment of Obstruction in the Urethra.* London, 1821. 119 pp. With one plate (picturing a dilator). Bound in boards.............. 27.00 35.00

☐ **Arnott, James.** *On the Invention of Local Anaesthesia by Refrigeration.* Extract from "The Medical Times and Gazette," March 30, 1867. 7 pp. Unbound.................. 43.00 59.00

☐ **Asgis, A. J.** *Professional Denistry in American Society.* N.Y., 1941. 260 pp. 12.00 16.00

☐ **Ashton, James.** *The Book of Nature, containing information for Young People who think of Getting Married, on the Philosophy of Procreation and Sexual Intercourse, showing How to Prevent Conception and to Avoid Child-Bearing.* N.Y., 1870. 64 pp. Bound in flexible cloth. One of the earliest American works dealing extensively with birth control... 130.00 165.00

☐ **Austin, William.** *A Treatise on the Origin and Component Parts of the Stone in the Urinary Bladder.* London, 1791. 123 pp. Bound in boards with a cloth spine. 21.00 26.00

☐ **Averill, Charles.** *A Short Treatise on Operative Surgery, describing the principal operations as they are practised in England and France. Designed for the use of students operating on the dead body. Second Edition.* London, 1825. 251 pp. With 4 folding plates. Bound in half calf.......... 21.00 26.00

PRICE RANGE

☐ **Badham, Charles.** *Observations on the Inflammatory Affections on the Mucous Mumbrane of the Bronchaie.* London, 1808. Bound in boards............................ **78.00** **105.00**

☐ **Badham, Charles.** *An Essay on Bronchitis. With a Supplement, containing Remarks on Simple Pulmonary Abcesses.* London, 1814. Second edition. 168 pp. Bound in boards with a paper spine. **42.00** **58.00**

☐ **Bartisch, George.** *Opthalmoduleia.* Dresden (Germany), 1583. Folio. With 88 fullpage woodcuts...................... **8000.00** **11000.00**
A classic pioneer work on eye surgery. The text is in German. Illustrations include surgical instruments, as well as one of a patient **tied to a chair** ready to be operated upon.

☐ **Bary, A. de.** *Lectures on Bacteriology.* Second improved edition. Oxford, 1887, 191 pp. Bound in green cloth, gilt. **6.00** **8.00**

☐ **Baudouin, Charles.** *Suggestion and Autosuggestion.* London, 1922. Bound in blue cloth. **13.00** **18.00**

☐ **Bauer, Julius.** *Constitution and Disease.* N.Y., 1942. 208 pp... **22.00** **28.00**

☐ **Bateman, Thomas and William, Robert.** *Dileneations of Cutaneous Diseases.* London, 1840. With 72 hand-colored plates. **65.00** **85.00**

☐ **Battie, William.** *A Treatise on Madness.* London, 1962. Reprint of a work which originally appeared in 1758. ..... **11.00** **15.00**

☐ **Bayliss, Sir William M.** *Principles of General Physiology.* London, 1915, 850 pp. With 259 illustrations in the text. **55.00** **70.00**

☐ **Beale, Lionel S.** *Illustrations of the Constituents of Urine.* London, 1858. With 35 lithographic plates. **25.00** **35.00**

☐ **Beale, Lionel S.** *On Urine, Urinary Deposits, and Calculi.* London, 1861. 433 pp. Bound in cloth, gilt. **17.00** **23.00**

☐ **Beale, Lionel S.** *On Slight Ailments. Their Nature and Treatment.* Philadelphia, 1880. 353 pp. Clothbound....... **12.00** **15.00**

☐ **Beaman, A. Gaylord.** *A Doctor's Odyssey.* Baltimore, 1935. 340 pp.. **9.00** **12.00**

☐ **Beard, George M.** *A Practical Treatise on Nervous Exhaustion.* N.Y., 1880. 198 pp. Clothbound............... **25.00** **33.00**

☐ **Beaumont, William.** *Infra-Red Irradiation.* London, 1936. 139 pp. Red cloth. **16.00** **22.00**

☐ **Bechhold, Jesse.** *Colloids in Biology and Medicine.* N.Y., 1919. 464 pp. Clothbound. **11.00** **15.00**

☐ **Beclard, P. A.** *Elements of General Anatomy.* Edinburgh, 1830. 399 pp. Bound in boards......................... **27.00** **35.00**

☐ **Beevor, Charles E.** *The Croonian Lectures on Muscular Movements and their representation in the Central Nervous System.* London, 1904. Red cloth binding................ **16.00** **22.00**

☐ **Bell, Benjamin.** *A Treatise on the Theory and Management of Ulcers.* With a dissertation on White Swellings of the Joints. Edinburgh and London, 1784. 491 pp. Bound in sheepskin.. **45.00** **60.00**

☐ **Bell, Benjamin.** *A Treatise on the Hydrocele.* Edinburgh, 1794. 295 pp. With 4 engraved plates. Bound in boards. **60.00** **75.00**

☐ **Bell, Sir Charles.** *A System of Dissections Explaining the Anatomy of the Human Body.* Baltimore, 1814. Two vols.

EXPERIMENTS

AND

OBSERVATIONS

ON

ELECTRICITY,

MADE AT

Philadelphia in *America*,

BY

Mr. BENJAMIN FRANKLIN,

AND

Communicated in feveral Letters to Mr. P. COLLINSON
of *London*, F. R. S.

L O N D O N:

Printed and fold by E. CAVE, at *St. John's Gate*. 1751.
(*Price* 2s. 6d.)

*Historically the most important of all of Benjamin Franklin's writings,
"Experiments and Observations on Electricity" told of his adventures with
kite flying and lightning.*

PRICE RANGE

265 and 264 pp. Bound in calf. Printed on a low grade of paper; all recorded copies are heavily browned.	135.00	175.00
☐ **Bell, Sir Charles.** *A Treatise on the Diseases of the Urethra.* London, 1822. 438 pp. With 5 engraved plates..........	22.00	28.00
☐ **Bell, Sir Charles.** *The Hand: Its Mechanism and Vital Endowments as Evincing Design.* London, 1833. 314 pp. Bound in half calf.......................................	50.00	65.00
☐ **Binz, Carl.** *Lectures on Pharmacology for Practitioners and Students.* London, 1895 and 1897. Two vols. Cloth-bound.	16.00	22.00
☐ **Birkett, John.** *The Diseases of the Breast, and their Treatment.* London, 1850. With 11 plates.	19.00	25.00
☐ **Black, James.** *A Short Inquiry into the Capillary Circulation of the Blood.* London, 1825. 176 pp. Bound in boards. ...	45.00	60.00
☐ **Blacker, C. P.** *The Chances of Morbid Inheritance.* London, 1934. 449 pp. With 3 folding plates.................	22.00	28.00
☐ **Blackmore, Sir Richard A.** *A Treatise of Consumptions and other Distempers belonging to the Breast and Lungs.* London, Printed for John Pemberton, 1724. 223 pp. Bound in calf.	80.00	100.00
☐ **Blair, Patrick.** *Miscellaneous Observations in the Practice of Physick, Anatomy and Surgery.* With New and Curious Remarks in Botany. London, Printed for William Mears, 1718. 149 pp. With 2 engraved plates.	300.00	375.00
☐ **Blake, ... and Lessey, ...** *Cancers Cured without the Use of the Knife. Please Read and Hand to Your Neighbor.* N.Y., 1857. 22 pp. Softbound............................ Classic example of 19th century quackery.	45.00	60.00
☐ **Blandford, G. Fielding.** *Insanity and Treatment.* Lectures on the treatment, Medical and Legal, of Insane Patients. Second edition. Edinburgh, 1877. 476 pp.	16.00	22.00
☐ **Bland-Sutton, J.** *Tumours, Innocent and Malignant.* Chicago, n.d. (1906). 675 pp. Clothbound...................	10.00	15.00
☐ **Bland-Sutton, John.** *Essays on the Position of Abdominal Hysterectomy in London.* London, 1909. 90 pp. With a colored frontis. Bound in flexible leather....................	15.00	20.00
☐ **Blane, Sir Gilbert.** *Elements of Medical Logick, illustrated by Practical Proofs and Examples; including statement of the evidence respecting the contagious nature of the yellow-fever.* London, 1819. 219 pp.	90.00	120.00
☐ **Blumenbach, J. A.** *A Short System of Comparative Anatomy, translated from the German by William Lawrence.* London, 1807. 484 pp. Bound in half calf.	85.00	110.00
☐ **Boerhaave, Hermann.** *De Viribus medicamentorum. Or, A Treatise of the Virtue and Energy of Medicines. Containing An Ample Account of all Medicines Whatsoever.* London, Printed for J. Wilcox, etc., 1720. 328 pp.	230.00	290.00
☐ **Boerhaave, Hermann.** *Aphorisms: Concerning the Knowledge and Cure of Diseases.* London, 1755. 444 pp..	37.00	49.00
☐ **Bolton, Joseph Shaw.** *The Brain in Health and Disease.* London, 1914. 479 pp.	19.00	25.00

PRICE RANGE

☐ **Bottone, S. R.** *Radiography and the X-Rays in Practice and Theory with Constructional and Manipulative Details.* London, 1898. With 47 illustrations. Half calf, gilt. . . . . | 190.00 | 235.00

☐ **Bowman, A. K.** *The Life and Teaching of Sir William Macewen.* London, 1942. 425 pp. . . . . | 19.00 | 25.00

☐ **Boyle, Robert.** *Memoirs for the Natural History of the Humane Blood.* London, Printed for Samuel Smith at the Princes Arms, 1684. Calfbound. . . . . | 1600.00 | 2150.00

☐ **Boyce, Sir Robert.** *Mosquito or Man. The Conquest of the Tropical World.* London, 1909. . . . . | 20.00 | 26.00

☐ **Braithwaite, W.** *The Retrospect of Medicine.* London, 1859. 464 pp. . . . . | 19.00 | 25.00

☐ **Bramwell, Byron.** *Atlas of Clinical Medicine.* Edinburgh, 1892, 1893, 1896. Three vols., folio, with a total of 100 plates, many of them in color. Clothbound. . . . . | 140.00 | 175.00

☐ **Brande, William T.** *A Manual of Pharmacy.* London, 1825. 556 pp. Half calf with red morocco label. . . . . | 21.00 | 27.00

☐ **Brandish, Joseph.** *Observations on the Use of Caustic Alkali.* London, 1811. 48 pp. Boards. . . . . | 12.00 | 17.00

☐ **Bray, George W.** *Recent Advances in Allergy.* Third edition. London, 1937. 517 pp. Green cloth. . . . . | 12.00 | 17.00

☐ **Bright, Richard.** *Clinical Memoirs on Abdominal Tumours and Intumescence.* London, 1861. 326 pp. . . . . | 65.00 | 85.00

☐ **Brock, R. C.** *The Anatomy of the Bronchial Tree. With specific reference to the surgery of lung abcesses.* London, 1946. . . . . | 21.00 | 27.00

☐ **Brodie, Sir B. and Acland, Sir Henry W.** *Biographical Sketch of Sir Benjamin Brodie.* London, 1864. 31 pp. Clothbound. . . . . | 8.00 | 11.00

☐ **Bromfield, William.** *Thoughts Arising from Experience, Concerning Persons Inoculated for the Small-Pox. Relating to The Preparation of the Patients, The Manner of the Operation, the Genuine Nature of the Disease, etc.* London, Printed by H. Woodfall, etc., 1767. 88 pp. . . . . | 110.00 | 135.00

☐ **Bromfield, William.** *Chirurgical Observations and Cases.* London, 1773. Two vols. 352 and 379 pp. With 18 engraved plates. . . . . | 85.00 | 105.00

☐ **Brown, W. Langdon.** *The Sympathetic Nervous System in Disease.* London, 1923. Second edition. 161 pp. . . . . . . | 8.00 | 11.00

☐ **Brown, William.** *Mind, Medicine and Metaphysics.* London, 1936. 294 pp. Blue cloth. . . . . | 9.00 | 12.00

☐ **Browne, John.** *History of a Wound in the Neck, in which the operation of Tying the Common Cartoid Artery was performed with success.* London, n.d. (1817). 10 pp. Unbound. . . . . | 16.00 | 22.00

☐ **Brownlow, John.** *The History and Objects of the foundling Hospital.* London, 1865. Third edition. 164 pp. With 2 engraved plates. Blindstamped cloth binding. . . . . | 32.00 | 43.00

☐ **Bruce, J. M.** *On the Influence of Harvey's Work in the Development of the Doctrine of Infection and Immunity.* London, 1913. 37 pp. Red cloth. . . . . | 8.00 | 11.00

PRICE RANGE

☐ **Brunton, T. Lauder.** *On Disorders of Digestion, their Consequences and Treatment.* London, 1886. 389 pp. Blue cloth, gilt... 19.00   25.00

☐ **Brunton, T. Lauder.** *A Text-Book of Pharmacology, Therapeutics and Materia Medica.* London, 1887. 1,261 pp. Cloth, gilt. 17.00   23.00

☐ **Brunton, T. Lauder.** *Modern Developments of Harvey's Work.* London, 1894. 35 pp. Clothbound. 22.00   28.00

☐ **Brunton, T. Lauder.** *Therapeutics of the Circulation.* London, 1908. 272 pp. Blue cloth, gilt...................... 20.00   26.00

☐ **Buchan, A. P.** *Practical Observations Concerning Sea Bathing. To which are added, Remarks On the Use of the Warm Bath.* London, 1804. 207 pp. Bound in boards. 33.00   42.00

☐ **Buchan, William.** *Domestic medicine; or, the Family Physician.* Edinburgh, 1769. 624 pp. Calf bound............ 250.00   310.00
The book's objective was "an attempt to render the Medical Art more generally useful, by showing people what is in their own power both with respect to the Prevention and Cure of Diseases.".

☐ **Buchanan, Sir George S.** *The Milroy Lectures on International Cooperation in Public Health.* London, 1934. 60 pp... 8.00   11.00

☐ **Buchanan, Thomas.** *Physiological Illustrations of the Organ of Hearing.* London, 1828. 160 pp. With 10 engraved plates. 95.00   120.00
Contains the lengthiest study of ear wax published up to its time.

☐ **Budge, Sir A. E. W.** *The Divine Origin of the Craft of the Herbalist.* London, 1928. 96 pp. Green cloth binding...... 7.00   10.00

☐ **Bullentin, William.** *Bulwarke of Defence Against All Sickness, Soarness, and Wounds that doe dayly assaulte mankind.* Imprinted At London by Thomas Marshe, dwellinge in Fleetestreate, 1579. Second edition. Folio. Woodcuts in the text. 1075.00   1400.00

☐ **Burns, John.** *The Anatomy of the Gravid Uterus. With Practical References relative to Pregnancy and Labour.* Glasgow, 1799. 248 pp. With 2 plates. 190.00   240.00

☐ **Butcher, Richard.** *On Excision of the Knee-Joint.* Dublin, 1855. 60 p. With 3 colored plates. 21.00   27.00

☐ **Butlin, Henry.** *Diseases of the Tongue.* London, Paris and N.Y., 1885. 451 pp. With 8 colored plates............... 25.00   33.00

☐ **Byam, W.** *Trench Fever: A Louse-Borne Disease.* London, 1919. 198 pp. with folding maps and tables (relating to Trench Fever in World War I)............................ 8.00   11.00

☐ **Cadogan, William.** *A Dissertation on the Gout, and all Chronic Diseases.* London, 1771. 100 pp. Bound in quarter calf.. 21.00   27.00

☐ **Cameron, H. C.** *The Nervous Child.* London, 1926. Second edition... 8.00   11.00

☐ **Carmichael, Richard.** *An Essay on the Effects of Carbonate, and other preparations of iron, upon Cancer.* Dublin, 1809. 495 pp. Bound in half calf, morocco label......... 40.00   50.00

PRICE RANGE

☐ **Carpue, Joseph C.** *A Description of the Muscles of the Human Body, as they Appear on Dissection.* London, 1801. With 7 engraved plates, 4 of which are colored. Bound in boards with a paper spine. 140.00 175.00

☐ **Casper, Johann.** *A Handbook of the Practice of Forensic Medicine.* London, 1861–65. Four vols. Clothbound...... 50.00 65.00

☐ **Catlin, George.** *Shut Your Mouth and Save Your Life.* London, 1875. 102 pp., with 29 illustrations................. 11.00 15.00

☐ **Charcot, J. M.** *Clinical Lectures on Senile and Chronic Diseases.* London, 1881. 307 pp. With 6 plates. Bound in cloth, gilt.. 32.00 40.00

☐ **Clutterback, Henry.** *Observations on the Prevention and Treatment of the Epidemic Fever.* London, 1819. Bound in boards.. 45.00 60.00

☐ **Cole, F. J.** *A History of Comparative Anatomy from Aristotle to the 18th Century.* London, 1949. .... 7.00 10.00

☐ **Coley, James M.** *A Practical Treatise on the Remittent Fever of Infants.* London, 1813. 156 pp. Bound in half calf... 55.00 70.00

☐ **Colles, Abraham.** *Selections from the Works of Abraham Colles, Consisting Chiefly of his Practical Observations of the Veneral Disease and on the Use of Mercury.* London, 1881. 431 pp. Clothbound. 15.00 20.00

☐ **Combe, Andrew.** *The Principles of Physiology applied to the Perservation of Health.* Edinburgh, 1834. Second edition. 385 pp. Bound in boards with cloth spine. 35.00 43.00

☐ **Combe, George.** *Elements of Phrenology.* London, 1825. Second edition. 240 pp. With 2 plates. 15.00 20.00

☐ **Comfort, J. W.** *Thomsonian Medical Instructor, containing practical information relating to the Thomsonian medicines, Plants, Barks, and Roots in General Use.* Philadelphia, 1855. 256 pp. Blindstamped cloth................. 12.00 17.00

☐ *Complete Midwife's Practice Enlarged, In the most weighty and high concernments of the Birth of Man. Containing a perfect Directory or Rules for Midwives and Nurses.* Lonson, Printed for Robert Hartford at the Angel in Cornhill, near the Royal Exchange, 1680. 322 pp. With 5 engraved plates.................................... 325.00 425.00

☐ **Compston, H. F. B.** *The Magdalen Hospital.* The story of a Great Charity. London, 1917. With 20 portraits and plates. 11.00 15.00

☐ **Cooke, William.** *A Practical Treatise on Tinea Capitis Contagiosa, and its cure; with an attempt to distinguish this disease from other affections of the scalp.* London, 1810. 259 pp. Bound in boards................................ 25.00 32.00

☐ **Coope, Robert.** *Diseases of the Chest.* Described for Students and Practitioners. Edinburgh, 1945. .... 8.00 11.00

☐ **Cooper, Bransby B.** *A Treatise on Ligaments.* London, 1825. 151 pp. with 13 engraved plates. 55.00 70.00

☐ **Cooper, Bransby B.** *Lectures on Anatomy: Interspread with Practical Remarks.* London, Printed for the Author, 1829–32. Four vols. 310, 308, 300 and 383 pp. Total of 22 plates, with additional illustrations in the text. 60.00 75.00

PRICE RANGE

☐ **Cooper, Sir Astley and Travers, Benjamin.** *Surgical Essays.* London, 1818–1819. Two vols. 264 and 238 pp. With 21 plates, some of which are folding.................... 140.00   170.00

☐ **Cope, Zachary.** *The Royal College of Surgeons of England, A History.* London, n.d. (1959). 360 pp........... 8.00   11.00

☐ **Copeland, Thomas.** *Observations on the Principal Diseases of the Rectum and Anus.* London, 1814. Second edition. 183 pp., plus 24 pp. of publisher's advertisements. Bound in boards... 38.00   49.00

☐ **Corfe, George.** *The Physiognomy of Diseases.* London, 1849. 151 pp., with a colored frontis. Bound in cloth...... 100.00   130.00

☐ **Corfield, W. H.** *The Etiology of Typhoid Fever and Its Prevention.* London, 1902................................... 8.00   11.00

☐ **Cornaro, Lewis.** *Sure Methods of Attaining a Long and Healthful Life: with the means of correcting a Bad Constitution.* London, 1818. Thirty-first edition. 108 pp. Bound in calf with a morocco spine label.
A huge best-seller in its day, originally published in Italian. 18.00   24.00

☐ **Corrigan, D. J.** *Lectures on the Nature and Treatment of Fever.* Dublin, 1853. 104 pp. Clothbound. 24.00   31.00

☐ **Cowper, William.** *The Anatomy of Humane Bodies, with figures drawn after the life by some of the best masters in Europe.* Oxford, Printed at the Theater, For Sam. Smith and Benj. Walford, 1698. Folio With 114 engraved plates. Largely a pirated publication. Cowper stole the text and most of the illustrations from a book by Godfried Bidloo, and didn't even bother to change the title. A "pamphlet war" ensued between the two, and the pamphlets are collectors' items, too.. 425.00   525.00

☐ **Craig, Maurice.** *Psychological Medicine.* London, 1905. 449 pp. With 22 plates. Blue cloth, gilt.................. 19.00   25.00

☐ **Crawfurd, Raymond.** *On Forerunners of Harvey in Antiquity.* London, 1919. 40 pp. Bound in blue cloth.......... 8.00   11.00

☐ **Crookshank, F. G.** *Diagnosis: and Spiritual Healing.* London, 1927. 101 pp. Bound in boards with a cloth spine... 6.00   8.00

☐ **Crosse, John G.** *A Treatise on the Formation, Constituents, and Extractions of the urinary Calculus.* London, 1835. Small folio. 231 pp. with 29 plates, some of which are folding. Bound in green cloth. 80.00   100.00

☐ **Culverwell, Robert J.** *How to Live 100 Years.* London, 1847. 26 pp., bound in stiff paper. 32.00   43.00
Culverwell, a general practitioner, published this work himself.

☐ **Curling, T. B.** *Observations on the Diseases of the Rectum.* Second edition. London, 1855. 129 pp. with 32 pp. of advertisements. Bound in brown cloth...................... 22.00   28.00

☐ **Curry, James.** *Observations on Apparent Death from Drowning, Hanging, suffocation by Noxious Vapours, Fainting-Fits, Intoxication, Lightning, Exposure to Cold etc. And an Account of the Means to be employed for recovery.*

PRICE RANGE

Second edition. London, 1814. 213 pp. with 6 engraved plates. 55.00 70.00

☐ **Curtis, John H.** *An Essay on the Deaf and Dumb.* London, 1834. Second edition. 211 pp. With 2 engraved plates. . . . 43.00 54.00

☐ **Cushing, H.** *Studies in Intracranial Physiology and Surgery.* London, 1926. 146 pp. with 16 illustrations. 48.00 63.00

☐ **Cushing, H.** *From a Surgeon's Journal, 1915–18.* Boston, 1936. 534 pp. 22.00 27.00

☐ **Cushing, Harvey.** *The Life of Sir William Osler.* London, 1940. 1,417 pp. Clothbound. 33.00 43.00

☐ **Dahl, Ludwig.** *Heller's Pathological Chemistry of the Urine, with short and easy directions for its examination.* Dublin and London, 1855. 100 pp., with diagrams in the text. 16.00 22.00

☐ **Dalby, W. B.** *Lectures on Diseases and Injuries of the Ear.* London, 1873. 221 pp. 33.00 43.00

☐ **Darwin, Charles.** *Experiments Establishing a Criterion between Mucaginous and Purulent Matter.* Lichfield (England), Printed for J. Jackson, 1789. 134 pp. 95.00 120.00
This was NOT the Charles Darwin who developed a controversial theory of evolution.

☐ **Davey, James G.** *The Ganglionic Nervous System; its Structure, Functions, and Diseases.* London, 1858. 309 pp. 35.00 45.00

☐ **Davidson, William.** *Observations, Anatomical, Physiological, and Pathological, on the Pulmonary System: with remarks on some of the diseases of the Lungs, viz. Haemorrhage, Wounds, Asthma, Catarrh, Croup, and Consumption.* London, 1795. 226 pp. Bound in boards with a paper spine. 60.00 75.00

☐ **Davies, Frederick.** *The Unity of Medicine.* London, 1870. 302 pp. Bound in red cloth, gilt. 16.00 22.00

☐ **Davy, John.** *Physiological Researches.* London and Edinburgh, 1863. 448 pp. Green cloth. 43.00 58.00

☐ **Dawson, Warren R.** *Magician and Leech. A study in the beginnings of medicine with special reference to ancient Egypt.* London, n.d. 159 pp. Bound in orange cloth. 4.00 6.00

☐ *Declining Birth Rate, The.* Its Causes and Effects. London, 1916. 450 pp. Red cloth. 9.00 12.00

☐ **Denman, Thomas.** *Aphorisms on the Application and Use of the Forceps and Vectis.* London, 1793. Fourth edition. Numbered by the leaf (104 leaves). Bound in boards. 21.00 27.00

☐ **DeStains, V.** *Phonography; or, The Writing of Sounds.* London, 1842. Second edition. 208 pp. With 9 plates. Clothbound. 27.00 35.00
"Phonography" had nothing to do with recorded sound. It was a method of indicating sounds by a special system of notations, along the lines of musical notes.

☐ **Devereus, George.** *A Study of Abortion in Primitive Societies.* London, 1960. 394 pp. 6.00 8.00

☐ **Dewar, Henry.** *Observations on Diarrhoea and Dysentary, as those diseases appeared in the British Army, during the campaign in Egypt, in 1801.* London, 1803. Bound in half calf. 24.00 31.00

PRICE RANGE

☐ **Diday, P.** *A Treatise on Syphillis in New-Born Children and Infants at the Breast.* London, 1859. 272 pp. 27.00   35.00

☐ **Diemerbroeck, Isbrand.** *The Anatomy of Human Bodies, Comprehending the most Modern Discoveries in that Art. To which is added a particular Treatise of the Small-Pox and Measles.* London, Printed for Edward Brewster at the Crane, 1689. Folio. With 16 engraved folding plates. 425.00   550.00

☐ **Dietz, J.** *Master Johann Dietz, Surgeon in the Army of the Great Elector and Barber to the Royal Court.* London, 1923. 315 pp. 9.00   12.00

☐ **Dionis, Pierre.** *A Course of Chirurgical Operations, demonstrated in the Royal Garden at Paris.* London, Printed for Jacob Tonson, 1710. 496 pp. With 61 woodcuts, mostly of surgical instruments. Calfbound. 185.00   235.00

☐ **Dobell, Clifford.** *Antony van Leeuwenhoek and his Little Animals.* N.Y., and London, 1932. 435 pp. Bound in white cloth. 38.00   46.00
The "little animals" were protozoa and bacteria, which Leeuwenhoek was the first to observe under the microscope. The book was published on the 300th anniversary of his birth.

☐ **Dobell, Horace.** *On the Nature, Cause, and Treatment of Tuberculosis.* London, 1866, 84 pp. Clothbound. 16.00   21.00

☐ **Dobell, Horace.** *On Affections of the Heart and in its Neighborhood.* London, 1872. 128 pp. With 3 plates. 28.00   36.00

☐ **Dobell, Horace.** *On Loss of Weight, Blood-Spitting and Lung Disease.* London, 1878. 274 pp. With colored frontis and a large folding table inserted in a pocket at the end. .   32.00   43.00

☐ **Dobson, Matthew.** *A Medical Commentary on Fixed Air.* Third edition, London, 1787. Bound in boards. 38.00   49.00

☐ **Donald, Archibald.** *The Transition. A Retrospect of Gynaecology and Obstetrics.* Manchester (England), 1924. 32 pp. Clothbound. 10.00   14.00

☐ **Donkin, H. B.** *On Inheritance of Mental Characteristics.* London, 1910. 48 pp. Clothbound. 8.00   11.00

☐ **Doolin, William.** *Wayfarers in Medicine.* London, 1949. 284 pp. With 20 plates. 7.00   10.00

☐ **Downie, J. Walter.** *The Early Physicians and Surgeons of the Western Infirmary, Glasgow.* London, Privately Printed, 1923. 148 pp. 16.00   22.00

☐ **Drury, William.** *Eruptive Fevers: Scarlet Fever, Measles, Small-Pox, etc.* London, 1877. 219 pp. Green cloth, gilt.   9.00   12.00

☐ **Duckworth, Sir Dyce.** *The Influence of Character and Right Judgement in Medicine.* London, 1898. 53 pp. 11.00   15.00

☐ **Duffin, Edward D.** *Probationary Essay on Injuries of the head.* Edinburgh, 1822. . . . .   9.00   12.00

☐ **Duncan, Andrew.** *Observations on the Distinguishing Symptoms of Three Different Species of Pulmonary Consumption.* Edinburgh, 1813. 169 pp. Bound in half calf. . . .   37.00   48.00

☐ **Duncan, James M.** *Fecundity, Fertility, Sterility, and Allied Topics.* Edinburgh, 1866. Second edition. 498 pp. Blue cloth binding, gilt. 65.00   80.00

PRICE RANGE

☐ **Duncan, James M.** *On the Mortality of Children, and Maternity Hospitals.* Edinburgh, 1870. 172 pp. Brown cloth binding, gilt. 80.00 105.00

☐ **Dunchenne, D. B.** *Selections from the Clinical Works.* London, 1883. 472 pp. 16.00 22.00

☐ **Dupuytren, Baron.** *On the Injuries and Diseases of Bones.* London, 1847. 458 pp. Clothbound. 32.00 41.00

☐ **Earle, Henry.** *Practical Observations in Surgery.* London, 1823. 229 pp. With 3 plates. Bound in boards. 26.00 34.00

☐ **East, T.** *The Story of Heart Disease.* London, 1958. 148 pp. Clothbound. 4.00 6.00

☐ **Eberle, John.** *A Treatise on the Diseases and Physical Education of Children.* Third edition. Philadelphia, 1841. 555 pp. Calfbound. 65.00 80.00

☐ **Edwards, William F.** *On the Influence of Physical Agents on Life.* London, 1832. 488 pp. Bound in quarter morocco. 325.00 400.00

☐ **Fleming, Sir Alexander.** *Penicillin. Its Practical Application.* London, 1946. 380 pp. 55.00 75.00
Fleming was the discover of penicillin, which, by the time this work appeared, was already being extensively used by the medical profession.

☐ **Flemyng, Malcolm.** *An Introduction to Physiology.* London, Printed for J. Nourse, 1759. 396 pp. 105.00 130.00

☐ **Fletcher, William.** *Notes on the Treatment of Malaria with the Alkaloids of Cinchona.* London, 1923. 91 pp. 9.00 12.00

☐ **Flexner, Abraham.** *Medical Education.* N.Y., 1925. 334 pp. Clothbound. 9.00 12.00

☐ **Flint, Austin, Jr.** *Manual of Chemical Examination of the Urine in Disease.* Third edition. N.Y., 1873. 75 pp. Folding plate at the end. Bound in green cloth. 21.00 27.00

☐ **Flugel, J. C.** *A Hundred Years of Psychology, 1833–1933.* London, 1948. 384 pp. 8.00 11.00

☐ **Flugge, Carl.** *Micro-Organisms with Special Reference to the Ethiology of the Infective Diseases.* London, 1890. 826 pp. Bound in brown cloth, gilt. 32.00 43.00

☐ **Forbes, Sir J.** *Of Nature and Art in the Cure of Disease.* London, 1857. 264 pp. 13.00 18.00

☐ **Forbes, Murray.** *A Treatise upon Gravel and upon Gout, in which their sources and connection are ascertained.* London, 1793. 258 pp. Bound in boards. 32.00 43.00

☐ **Fordyce, George.** *A Dissertation on Simple Fevers or on Fever consisting of one Paroxysm only.* London, Printed for J. Johnson, 1794–99. Two vols. Bound in calf. 69.00 87.00

☐ **Forster, Thomas.** *Medicina Simplex: Or, the Pilgrims Waybook, being an enquiry into the Moral and Physical conditions of a Healthy Life and Happy Old Age, with household prescriptions.* By a Physician. London, 1832. 255 pp. Bound in boards. 21.00 27.00

☐ **Fowler, George B.** *Chemical and Microscopical Analysis of the Urine in Health and Disease.* Third edition. N.Y., 1879. 103 pp. With diagrams. 11.00 16.00

PRICE RANGE

☐ **Fox, Tilbury.** *Eczema: Its Nature and Treatment; and, incidentally, the influence of Constitutional Conditions on Skin Diseases.* London, 1870. Bound in cloth. . . . . | 16.00 | 22.00

☐ **Fox, Tilbury.** *Skin Diseases: Their Description, Pathology, Diagnosis, and Treatment.* Third edition. London, 1873. 532 pp. Clothbound. . . . . | 27.00 | 36.00

☐ **Franklyn, Kenneth.** *A Short History of Physiology.* London and N.Y., 1949. Second edition. 147 pp. . . . . | 9.00 | 12.00

☐ **Frerichs, F. T.** *A Clinical Treatise on Diseases of the Liver.* London, 1860–1861. Two vols. With 3 plates, 2 of which are in color. . . . . | 30.00 | 39.00

☐ **Freud, Sigmund.** *Psychopathology of Everyday Life.* Sixth impression. London, 1920. 342 pp. Bound in red cloth. . . . | 11.00 | 16.00

☐ **Freud, Sigmund.** *Introductory Lectures on Psycho-Analysis.* London, 1929. Revised edition. 393 pp. Blue cloth binding. . . . . | 27.00 | 35.00

☐ **Freud, Sigmund.** *Three Essays on the Theory of Sexuality.* London, 1949. 133 pp. Translation of a work originally in German at Leipzig in 1905. . . . . | 32.00 | 40.00

☐ **Fuller, Francis.** *Medicina Gymnastica: or, A Treatise Concerning the Power of Exercise, With respect to the Animal Oeconomy.* London, Printed for Robert Knaolock, 1718. 271 pp. Calfbound. . . . . | 115.00 | 145.00

☐ **Fulton, J. F.** *Physiology of the Nervous System.* London, 1946. Second edition. . . . . | 11.00 | 15.00

☐ **Fyfe, Andrew.** *A System of the Anatomy of the Human Body.* Second edition. Edinburgh, 1806. Three vols. 187, 206 and 190 pp. With 213 engraved plates, some hand-tinted. Bound in calf. . . . . | 115.00 | 145.00

☐ **Gairdner, Sir William T.** *Reasons for Rejecting the Amended Medical Bill.* Edinburgh, 1856. Unbound. . . . . . . | 8.00 | 11.00

☐ **Gairdner, Sir William T.** *Clinical Medicine Observations Recorded at the Bedside, with Commentaries.* Edinburgh, 1862. 741 pp. Clothbound. . . . . | 16.00 | 21.00

☐ **Galdston, Iago.** *Progress in Medicine. A critical review of the last hundred years.* N.Y. & London, 1940. 347 pp. Black cloth, gilt. . . . . | 15.00 | 20.00

☐ **Galton, Sir Douglas S.** *Observations on the Construction of Healthy Dwellings, Namely Houses, Hospitals, Barracks, Asylums, etc.* Oxford, 1880. 296 pp. With 36 pp. of publishers' advertisements. Bound in brown cloth, gilt. . . . | 75.00 | 95.00

☐ **Gardiner, John.** *An Inquiry into the Nature, Cause, and Cure of Gout, and of Some of the Diseases with Which it is Connected.* Edinburgh, 1792. 242 pp. . . . . | 21.00 | 27.00

☐ **Gardner, John.** *Longevity. The Means of Prolonging Life After Middle Age.* London, 1874. 168 pp. . . . . | 15.00 | 20.00

☐ **Garrison, Fielding H.** *An Introduction to the History of Medicine.* Philadelphia, 1914. 763 pp. Blue cloth binding. | 53.00 | 68.00

☐ **Garrod, Alfred B.** *The Essentials of Materia Medica and Therapeutics.* Ninth edition. London, 1881. 717 pp. . . . . . | 15.00 | 20.00

☐ **Gask, George E. and Ross, J. Patterson.** *The Surgery of the Sympathetic System.* London, 1934. 163 pp. With folding frontis and 13 plates. . . . . | 8.00 | 11.00

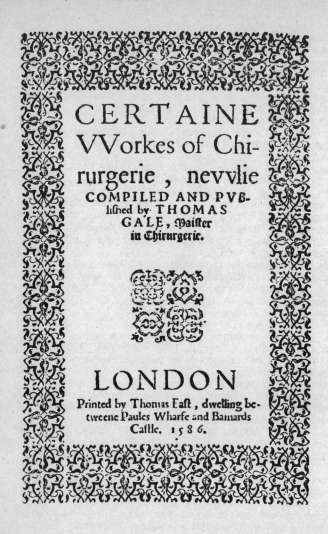

CERTAINE
VVorkes of Chi-
rurgerie , nevvlie
COMPILED AND PVB-
lished by THOMAS
GALE , Maister
in Chirurgerie.

LONDON

Printed by Thomas East , dwelling be-
tweene Paules Wharfe and Bainards
Castle. 1 5 8 6.

Medical works were very seldom published in England in the 16th century: this ranks as one of the first books in the language to deal wholly with medicine ("chirurgerie" was the archaic word for "surgery"). It deals largely with treatment of wounds, especially gunshot wounds. The border is composed of engraved metallic ornaments. $2500–3000

PRICE RANGE

☐ **Gee, Samuel.** *Medical Lectures and Aphorisms.* London, 1915. 408 pp. Clothbound. 10.00   14.00

☐ **Gerster, Arpad G.** *Recollections of a New York Surgeon.* N.Y., 1917. 347 pp. Brown cloth. 11.00   16.00

☐ **Gibson, George Alex.** *The Nervous Affections of the Heart.* Edinburgh and London, 1904. 99 pp.   22.00   31.00

☐ **Glaister, John.** *A Text-Book of Medical Jurisprudence and Toxicology.* Fourth edition. Edinburgh, 1921. 902 pp. Green cloth binding. 11.00   16.00

☐ **Gleig, Rev. G. R.** *Chelsea Hospital, and its Traditions.* London, 1839. 465 pp. 28.00   36.00

☐ **Godlee, Sir R. J.** *Lord Lister.* London, 1918. Second edition. 681 pp. Clothbound. 16.00   22.00

☐ **Gooch, Benjamin.** *The Chirurgical Works of Benjamin Gooch.* London, 1792. Three vols. 460, 422 and 306 pp. With engraved folding plates. Bound in calf. 53.00   68.00

☐ **Gooch, R.** *On Some of the Most Important Diseases Peculiar to Women.* London, 1859. 235 pp. . . . .   16.00   -   22.00

☐ **Goodhart, Sir James F.** *The Passing of Morbid Anatomy.* London, 1912. 33 pp. Clothbound. 11.00   16.00

☐ **Goodhart, J. F. and Still, G. F.** *The Diseases of Children.* London, 1902. Seventh edition. 813 pp. 11.00   16.00

☐ **Gowers, Sir William R.** *Lectures on the Diagnosis of Diseases of the Brain.* London, 1885, 246 pp. 225.00   285.00

☐ **Gowers, Sir William R.** *The Borderland of Epilepsy. Faints, Vagal Attacks, Vertigo, Migraine, Sleep symptoms and their treatment.* London, 1907. 121 pp. 325.00   425.00

☐ **Graham, James.** *The Celestial Beds.* London, 1781. 34 pp. James Graham was a very successful quack doctor who preyed upon public gullibility. His "celestial beds" were elaborate contraptions which he claimed would cure sterility in anyone who slept in them. He also manufactured numerous other worthless devices, for which he charged (and obtained) high prices. 85.00   105.00

☐ **Granville, A. B.** *Further Observations on the Internal Use of the Hydro-Cyanic (Prussic) Acid, in Pulmonary Complaints.* London, 1819. 82 pp. 38.00   48.00
Granville was responsible for introducing iodine into medical use.

☐ **Graves, Robert J.** *Clinical Lectures on the Practice of Medicine.* London, 1884. Two vols. 21.00   27.00

☐ **Gray, Henry.** *Anatomy, Descriptive and Surgical.* London, 1858. 750 pp. 210.00   280.00

☐ **Greenfield, John.** *A Treatise of the Safe, Internal Use of Cantharides in the Practice of Physics.* London, Jeffrey Wale and John Isted, 1706, 363 pp.   125.00   150.00
"John Greenfield" was the assumed name of a Dutchman, Jan Groenveldt.

☐ **Greenhow, Edward H.** *On Diphtheria.* London, 1860. 274 pp. Bound in cloth, gilt. 23.00   31.00

☐ **Greenwood, Major.** *The Medical Dictator.* London, 1936. 213 pp. Bound in brown cloth. 4.00   6.00

PRICE RANGE

☐ **Gregory, John.** *Elements of the Practice of Physick.* Edinburgh, 1788. 249 pp. Half calf binding. 40.00 52.00

☐ **Griesinger, Wilhelm.** *Mental Pathology and Therapeutics.* London, 1867. 530 pp. 40.00 52.00

☐ **Griffin, W. and Griffin, D.** *Medical and Physiological Problems.* Limerick (Ireland), 1839. 114 pp. 21.00 27.00

☐ **Gross, Samuel D.** *A Practical Treatise on Foreign Bodies in the Air-Passages.* Philadelphia, 1854. Bound in cloth. 250.00 325.00

☐ **Gull, William W.** *A Collection of the Published Writings of William Withey Gull.* London, 1894–96. Two vols. With 21 plates, some of them in color. Bound in brown cloth. 43.00 55.00

☐ **Gunewardene, Hugh.** *High Blood Pressure and its Common Sequelae.* London, 1935. 172 pp. with 7 plate. 9.00 12.00

☐ **Guthrie, Douglas.** *A History of Medicine.* London, 1945. 448 pp. with 72 plates. 16.00 22.00

☐ **Guttman, Paul.** *A Handbook of Physical Diagnosis. Comprising the Throat, Thorax, and Abdomen.* London, 1879. 441 pp. 6.00 8.00

☐ **Hahemann, Samuel.** *Organon of Medicine.* Translated from the fifth German edition by R. E. Dudgeon. London, 1849. Bound in cloth. 42.00 55.00

☐ **Halford, W. M.** *The Life of Sir Henry Halford, Bart.* London, 1895. 284 pp. Bound in cloth. 19.00 25.00

☐ **Haldane, J. S..** *Respiration.* New Haven, 1922. 429 pp. With folding tables. Bound in green cloth. 33.00 43.00

☐ **Halford, Sir Henry.** *Essays and Orations read and delivered at The Royal College of Physicians; at which is added An Account of the opening of the Tomb of King Charles I.* London, 1833. Second edition. 173 pp. Bound in half calf. 55.00 70.00

☐ **Hall, Marshall.** *Medical Essays. On the effects of intestinal irritation.* London, 1825. 96 pp. Bound in boards. 55.00 70.00

☐ **Haller, Henry T.** *Memoirs of Albert deHaller, M.D.* Warrington (England), 1783. 161 pp. 21.00 27.00

☐ **Halliday, Andrew.** *Observations on Emphysema; or, The Disease which arises from an affusion of air into the cavity of the Thorax.* London, 1807. Bound in boards. 150.00 190.00

☐ **Hamilton, James.** *Observations on the Utility and Administration of Purgative Medicines in Several Diseases.* Edinburgh, 1805. 320 pp. Bound in half calf. 16.00 22.00

☐ **Hare, Charles J.** *Good Remedies, Out of Fashion.* London, 1883. With folding tables. 15.00 20.00

☐ **Hare, Ronald.** *Pomp and Pestilence: Infections Disease. Its Origin and Conquest.* London, n.d. 224 pp. Book club edition. 3.00 4.00

☐ **Hare, Thomas.** *A View of the Structure, Functions and Disorders of the Stomach and Alimentary Organs of the Human Body.* London, 1821. 300 pp. With 2 plates. London, 1821. . . . . 65.00 85.00

☐ **Harle, Jonathan.** *An Historical Essay on the State of Physick in the Old and New Testament.* London, 1729. 180 pp. Bound in boards. 43.00 55.00

PRICE RANGE

☐ **Harley, George.** *The Urine and its Derangements.* London, 1872. 376 pp. Bound in red cloth........................ 24.00   32.00

☐ **Harrison, Reginald.** *Selected Papers on Stone, Prostate and other Urinary Disorders.* London, 1899. 190 pp. With 16 pp. of publishers' advertisements...................... 24.00   32.00

☐ **Harrison, Robert.** *The Surgical Anatomy of the Arteries of the Human Body. Designed for the use of students in the Dissecting Room.* Dublin, 1829. Two vols. 201 and 195 pp. Bound in boards. 48.00   59.00

☐ **Hart, Bernard.** *The Psychology of Insanity.* Cambridge (England), 1912. Pink cloth. 16.00   21.00

☐ **Hart, James.** *The Diet of the Diseased. Divided into Three Bookes. Wherein is set down at length the whole matter and nature of Diet for those in health, but especially for the sicke; the Aire, and other elements; Meat and Drinke; with divers other things, etc.* London, Printed by John Beale for Robert Allot, 1633. Folio. 411 pp. Calfbound. 1650.00   2175.00

☐ **Hartmann, Franz.** *Occult Science in Medicine.* London, 1893. 100 pp.. 15.00   20.00

☐ **Harty, William.** *Observations on the Simple Dysentery.* London, 1805. 333 pp. Bound in boards with calf spine. 32.00   40.00

☐ **Henoch, Edward.** *Lectures on Children's Diseases.* London, 1889. Two vols. Clothbound...................... 24.00   31.00

☐ **Herbert, S.** *The Unconscious Mind.* London, 1923. 230 pp. 8.00   11.00

☐ **Hewson, William.** *Experimental Inquiries. Containing an Inquiry into the Properties of the Blood.* London, 1780. 218 pp... 225.00   290.00

☐ **Hey, William.** *Practical Observations in Surgery.* London, 1810. Second edition. 578 pp. With 16 engraved plates. Bound in calf... 90.00   115.00

☐ **Hey, William.** *A Treatise on the Puerperal Fever.* Illustrated by Cases. London, 1815, 238 pp. Boards with paper spine. 75.00   100.00

☐ **Hillary, William.** *Observations on the Changes of the Air and the Concomitant Epidemic Diseases, in the Island of Barbadoes. To which is added a Treatise on the Putrid Bilious Fever, Commonly called Yellow Fever.* London, 1766. Second edition. 360 pp. Bound in boards. 185.00   235.00

☐ **Hillier, Thomas.** *Hand-Book of Skin Diseases for Students and Practitioners.* London, 1865. 366 pp. Bound in red cloth.. 9.00   12.00

☐ **Hilton, John.** *Rest and Pain. A Course of lectures on the influence of mechanical and physiological rest in the treatment of accidents and surgical diseases.* London, 1892. Fifth edition. 514 pp. Clothbound...................... 11.00   15.00

☐ **Hinton, James.** *Thoughts on Health, and some of its Conditions.* London, 1871. 293 pp.......................... 10.00   14.00

☐ **Hinton, James.** *The Place of the Physician.* London, 1873. 66 pp. Clothbound................................... 10.00   14.00

☐ **Holden, Luther.** *A Manual of the Dissection of the Human Body.* Second edition. London, 1861. 576 pp. Half calf. ... 25.00   35.00

PRICE RANGE

☐ **Holland, Henry.** *Medical Notes and Reflections.* London, 1839. 628 pp. Blue cloth......................... 53.00 68.00

☐ **Holland, Henry.** *Chapters on Mental Physiology.* London, 1852, 301 pp. Bound in brown cloth.................... 65.00 85.00

☐ **Holmes, Timothy.** *A System of Surgery.* London, 1860–1864. Four vols. 825, 895, 916 and 1,079 pp. Bound in calf with red and black labels on the spines................. 125.00 150.00

☐ **Home, Sir Edward.** *On the Irritability of Nerves.* London, 1800. 22 pp. Bound in boards........................ 21.00 27.00

☐ **Home, Francis.** *Principia Medicinae.* Edinburgh, 1770. Third edition. 340 pp. Bound in sheepskin.............. 21.00 27.00

☐ **Home, Robert.** *The Efficacy and Innocency of Solvents Candidly Examined.* With experiments and cases. London, 1783. 78 pp... 16.00 21.00

☐ **Hone, Campbell R.** *The Life of Dr. John Radcliffe 1652–1714.* London, 1950. 150 pp............................ 9.00 12.00

☐ **Hood, Peter.** *A Treatise on Gout, Rheumatism and the Allied Affections.* Second edition. London, 1879. 431 pp. Brown cloth, gilt....................................... 19.00 25.00

☐ **Hooke, Andrew.** *An Essay on Physick, or, an Attempt to Revive the Practice of the Antients.* London, 1736. 80 pp.. 27.00 36.00

☐ **Hooper, Robert.** *The Morbid Anatomy of the Human Brain.* Illustrated by coloured engravings of the most frequent and important organic diseases to which that viscus is subject. London (privately printed), 1828. Folio. 65 pp. with 65 colored plates.. 1100.00 1450.00

☐ **Howard, Robert.** *A Treatise on Salt, showing its Hurtful Effects on the Body and Mind of Man, and on Animals; its tendency to cause diseases, especially Consumption.* Second edition. London, 1850. 51 pp................... 35.00 45.00
Howard was mistaken in his theory that common table salt caused consumption (tuberculosis), and, in general, his harsh warnings against it later proved unwarranted.

☐ **Howard, Thomas.** *On the Loss of Teeth, and on the Best Means of Restoring Them.* London, 1855. Twenty-first edition. 59 pp. Softbound.................................. 43.00 58.00

☐ **Howship, John.** *A Practical Treatise on the Symptoms, Causes, Discrimination, and Treatment of some of the most important complaints that effect the Secretion and Excretion of The Urine.* London, 1823. First edition. 438 pp. With 4 plates. Bound in boards.............................. 35.00 43.00

☐ **Howship, John.** *Practical Remarks on Discrimination and Appearances of Surgical Disease.* London, 1840, 420 pp.. 32.00 41.00

☐ **Huhner, M.** *A practical Treatise on disorders of the Sexual Function in the Male and Female.* Philadelphia, 1924. Second edition. 326 pp. With 5 diagrams.................... 12.00 17.00

☐ **Hull, John.** *An Essay on Phlegmatia Dolens.* Manchester (England), 1800. 369 pp.............................. 75.00 95.00

☐ **Hull, Robert.** *Essays on Determination of Blood to the Head.* London, 1842. 156 pp. Clothbound. 75.00 95.00

29

PROPOSALS
FOR RAISING

A Colledge of Industry

OF ALL USEFUL

TRADES and Husbandry,
WITH

Profit for the RICH,
A Plentiful Living for the POOR;
AND

A Good Education for YOUTH.
Which will be Advantage to the Government,
by the Increafe of the People,
and their Riches.

By *John Bellers.*

MOTTO,
Industry brings Plenty.

The Sluggard shall be cloathed with Raggs.
He that will not Work, shall not Eat.

London, Printed and Sold by *T. Sowle*, in *White-Hart-Court* in *Gracious-Street.* 1696.

In the late 17th century, English colleges were busily turning out fluent Greek scholars and doctors of philosophy, but the country was suffering from a shortage of carpenters and masons. So John Bellers proposed a "College of Industry," where young men not destined for Aristotle or Cicero could at least learn how to saw a plank of wood. This is a scarce little pamphlet.

PRICE RANGE

☐ **Hunter, John.** *The Natural History of the Human Teeth. Explaining their Structure, Use, Formation, Growth, and Diseases.* London, 1778. With 16 engraved plates. **1125.00** **1550.00**

☐ **Hurst, Sir Arthur.** *Medical Diseases of War.* London, 1941. Second edition. 427 pp. with 8 plates.................... **9.00** **12.00**

☐ **Hutchinson, Benjamin.** *Cases of Neuralgia Spasmodica commonly termed Tic Douloureux successfully treated.* Second edition with additional examples. London, 1822. 189 pp. With 1 engraved plate. Bound in boards. **37.00** **48.00**

☐ **Hutchison, Robert.** *Food and the Principles of Dietetics.* London, 1900. 548 pp. Red cloth....................... **15.00** **20.00**

☐ **Huxham, John.** *An Essay on Fevers. And their Various Kinds.* London, 1750. Second edition. 280 pp. Bound in calf... **43.00** **58.00**
Contains the first use of the word "influenza."

☐ **Ireland, William W.** *Through the Ivory Gate.* Edinburgh, 1889. 320 pp. Blue cloth, gilt........................... **43.00** **58.00**

☐ **Jackson, C.** *Foreign Bodies in the Air and Food Passages.* New Bedford, Mass., 1924. 174 pp. Clothbound......... **37.00** **47.00**

☐ **Jackson, Robert.** *A System of Arrangement and Discipline for the Medical Department of Armies.* London, 1805. 462 pp. Folding tables. Bound in boards................ **32.00** **41.00**

☐ **Jackson, Rowland.** *A Physical Dissertation on Drowning: to which is subjoined, The proper Measures for Recovery and Relief: with an Appendix, containing some methods for the Recovery of those who hang themselves, and of Children supposed to be born dead. By a Physician.* London, 1747. Second edition. 80 pp. With 1 plate........... **100.00** **130.00**

☐ **Jacoby, George W.** *Suggestion and Psychotherapy.* London, 1912. 355 pp. With color plates. **9.00** **12.00**

☐ **Jahr, G. H. G.** *Manual of Homoeopathic Medicine.* London and Paris, 1847. Two vols. 631 and 629 pp. Bound in blue half-calf.. **22.00** **28.00**
Homoeopathic medicine was all the rage in the mid 1800's, in Europe and America. Many manufacturers, not to mention publishers, profited by leading the public to believe it could be its own physicians.

☐ **James, J. H.** *Practical Observations on the Operations for Strangulated Hernia.* London, 1859. 95 pp.............. **25.00** **33.00**

☐ **James, William.** *The Principles of Psychology.* London, 1890. Two vols. 689 and 704 pp. Bound in blue cloth..... **90.00** **115.00**

☐ **Jefferson, J. Cordy.** *A book about Doctors.* London, n.d. 324 pp... **8.00** **11.00**

☐ **Jeffreys, Henry.** *Cases in Surgery, selected from the Records of the Author's Practice at the St. George's and St. Jame's Dispensary.* London, 1820. 237 pp. With 2 plates, one of them in color. Bound in boards. **33.00** **42.00**

☐ **Jenner, Edward.** *An Inquiry into the Causes and Effects of the Variolae Vaccinae.* Undated *reprint* of the 1798 London edition. 78 pp with 4 colored plates. **53.00** **68.00**
This was Jenner's announcement to the world of his development of a vaccine for smallpox. The actual first edition (as opposed to this reprint) is very rare.

PRICE RANGE

☐ **Jenner, Sir Williams.** *Diphtheria: its Symptoms and Treatment.* London, 1861. 107 pp. Clothbound.............. 15.00 20.00

☐ **Jenner, Sir Williams.** *Clinical Lectures and Essays on Rickets, Tuberculosis, Abdominal Tumours and other subjects.* London, 1895. 329 pp............................ 11.00 15.00

☐ **Johnson, Dr. Edward.** *The Domestic Practice of Hydropathy.* London, 1849. 524 pp. Clothbound.............. 18.00 25.00

☐ **Johnson, James.** *A Treatise on Derangements of the Liver, Internal Organs, and the Nervous System.* Third edition. London, 1820. 224 pp................................ 43.00 58.00

☐ **Johnson, James.** *The Economy of Health or the Stream of Human Life from the cradle to the grave.* London, 1838. Third edition. 240 pp. Bound in cloth. 18.00 25.00

☐ **Johnson, Julian and Kirby, Charles K.** *A Handbook of Operative Surgery.* Chicago, 1952. 387 pp.............. 6.00 8.00

☐ **Joll, Cecil A.** *Diseases of the Thyroid Gland.* London, 1932. 682 pp... 53.00 68.00

☐ **Jones, C. Handfield.** *Studies on functional Nervous Disorders.* London, 1870. Second edition. 839 pp. bound in brown cloth. 42.00 57.00

☐ **Labatt, Samuel B.** *An address to the Medical Practitioners of Ireland, on the Subject of Vaccination.* Second edition. Dublin, 1840. 202 pp. With one colored plate........... 58.00 73.00

☐ **LeDran, Henry-Francis.** *Observations in Surgery.* Containing 115 Different Cases, with particular remarks on each. Third edition. London, 1758. 371 pp. With one folding plate... 33.00 41.00

☐ **L'Eppe, Charles M.** *The Method of Educating the Deaf and Dumb.* London, 1801. 230 pp. folding table. Bound in half calf... 85.00 105.00

☐ **LeFevre, Nicolas.** *A Discourse upon Sir Walter Rawleigh's Great Cordial.* London, Printed by J. F. for Octavian Pulleyn Junior, 1664. 110 pp.................................... 650.00 800.00
After being sentenced to death for conspiring to murder James I (the effort failed), Sir Walter Raleigh sought to win a pardon by showing that he possessed remarkable scientific skills—including concoction of the "great cordial." It was to no avail; he was executed.

☐ **Lessius, Leonard.** *Hygiasticon: Or, A Treatise of the Means of Health and Long Life.* London, Printed for the Author, 1742. 126 pp. Bound in boards with a calf spine. 85.00 105.00

☐ **Lewes, Mrs. C. L.** *Dr. Southwood Smith. A Retrospect.* Edinburgh and London, 1898. 169 pp. Bound in blue cloth, gilt. 21.00 27.00

☐ **Lewis, Sir Thomas.** *Clinical Disorders of the Heart Beat. A Handbook for Practitioners and Students.* London, 1925. 6th edition. 131 pp. 10.00 14.00

☐ **Lewis, Sir Thomas.** *Diseases of the Heart.* Described for Practitioners and Students. London, 1933. 297 pp. Clothbound. 19.00 25.00

☐ **Lewis, Sir Thomas.** *The Soldier's Heart and the effort Syndrome.* London, 1940. Second edition. 103 pp. Clothbound. 21.00 27.00

PRICE RANGE

☐ **Lewis, W. Bevan.** *The Human Brain. A Manual for students and Asylum Medical Officers.* London, 1882. 163 pp. With 4 tinted plates. Red cloth. 19.00 25.00

☐ **Lewis, William.** *An Experimental History of the Materia Medica, or of the Natural and Artificial Substances made use of in Medicine.* London, 1768. Second edition, 622 pp. Calfbound. 50.00 65.00

☐ **Limbeck, Rud.** *The Clinical Pathology of the Blood.* London, 1901. Clothbound. 11.00 15.00

☐ **Lister, Lord.** *The Collected Papers of Joseph, Baron Lister.* Oxford, 1909. Two vols. With 14 plates. Clothbound...... 80.00 105.00

☐ **Little, E. M.** *History of the British Medical Association, 1832–1932.* London, 1932. 342 pp...................... 21.00 27.00

☐ **Lloyd, E. A.** *A Treatise on the Nature and Treatment of Scrophula*; describing its connection with diseases of the Spine, Joints, Eyes, Glands & c. London, 1821, 330 pp. Bound in boards. 32.00 43.00

☐ **Lloyd, Wyndham.** *A Hundred Years of Medicine.* London, 1936. 334 pp. Black cloth............................... 11.00 15.00

☐ **Lockwood, Charles B.** *Traumatic Infection.* Edinburgh and London, 1896. 138 pp. Clothbound...................... 7.00 10.00

☐ *London Practice of Physick, The. Wherein the Definition and Symptoms of Diseases, with the Present Method of Cure, are clearly laid down.* London, for G. Robinson, R. Baldwin, and J. Bew, 1778. Third edition. 421 pp. Sheepskin binding. 24.00 31.00

☐ **Louis, P. C.** *Pathological Researched on Phthisis.* London, 1835. 388 pp. Green cloth binding....................... 13.00 18.00

☐ **Lowe, Peter.** *A Discourse of the Whole Art of Chyrurgerie. Wherein is exactly set downe the Definition, Causes, Accidents, Prognostications, and Cures of all sorts of Diseases.* London, Printed by Thomas Purfoot, 1634. 447 pp. Woodcuts in the text.................................... 1075.00 1400.00

☐ **Lucas, A.** *Forensic Chemistry and Scientific Criminal Investigation.* London, 1935. 376 pp. Bound in red cloth.... 11.00 15.00

☐ **Luten, Drew.** *The Clinical Use of Digitalis.* Springfield, 1936. 226 pp. Clothbound................................. 7.00 9.00

☐ **Lyle Cummins, Prof S.** *Tuberculosis in History.* London, 1949, 205 pp.................................... 10.00 14.00

☐ **Macartney, James.** *A Treatise on Inflammation.* London, 1838. 214 pp. With 2 plates. Bound in half calf.......... 38.00 46.00

☐ **MacCormac, Sir William.** *Notes and Recollections of an Ambulance Surgeon.* London, 1871. 155 pp. Clothbound. 12.00 15.00

☐ **Macewan, Sir William.** *Pyogenic Infective Diseases of the Brain and Spinal Cord.* Glasgow, 1893. 354 pp. Bound in green cloth.. 225.00 300.00

A valuable book, because of reputation; considered the most important contribution to knowledge of brain surgery made in the 19th century.

☐ **Macfie, Ronald C.** *Air and Health.* London, n.d. (1909). 345 pp.. 21.00 27.00

FINGER PRINTS

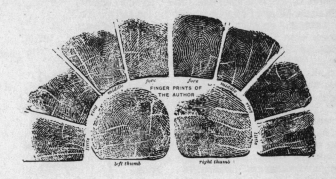

BY

FRANCIS GALTON, F.R.S., ETC.

London

MACMILLAN AND CO.

AND NEW YORK

1892

This was no best-seller, but in terms of long-lasting importance it has to rank as one of the most epochal books ever published. Francis Galton set forth a system by which persons could be identified through their fingerprints.

PRICE RANGE

☐ **MacKenzie, Haweis.** *Sir Morell Mackenzie, Physician and Operator.* London, 1894. 376 pp. Red cloth.............. **15.00 20.00**
"Operator" was the common Scottish term, at that time, for "surgeon" (which, in Britain, refers to all medical doctors).

☐ **MacKenzie, Morell.** *Essay on Growths in the Larynx.* London, 1871. 263 pp. With 5 plates, 2 of which are in color. Bound in cloth. **135.00 170.00**

☐ **MacKenzie, Sir James.** *Principles of Diagnosis and Treatment in Heart Affections.* London, 1916. 264 pp. Bound in red cloth. **21.00 27.00**

☐ **Mackintosh, Sir James.** *Dissertation on the Progress of Ethical Philosophy.* Edinburgh, 1830. 210 pp. Bound in calf. **43.00 59.00**

☐ **Macleod, J. M. H.** *Practical Handbook of the Pathology of the Skin.* London, 1903. 408 pp. With 40 plates, including some in color. Bound in blue cloth, gilt. **8.00 11.00**

☐ **Macmichael, William.** *Is the Cholera Spasmodica of India a Contagious Disease?* London, 1831. 34 pp. **9.00 12.00**

☐ **MacMurray, John.** *Reason and Emotion.* London, 1935. 278 pp. Clothbound. **4.00 6.00**

☐ **Mercier, Charles.** *Sanity and Insanity.* London, 1890. 390 pp. Red cloth binding. **25.00 33.00**

☐ **Metchnikoff, Elsie.** *The Prolongation of Life.* London, 1907. 343 pp. Clothbound. **22.00 28.00**

☐ **Mickle, Julius.** *General Paralysis of the Insane.* Second edition. London, 1866. 466 pp. **25.00 33.00**

☐ **Middleton-Shaw, J. C.** *The Teeth, the Bony Palate and the Mandible in Bantu Races of South Africa.* London, 1931. With 54 illustrations. **22.00 28.00**

☐ **Milligan, William and Wingrave, Wyatt.** *A Practical Handbook of the Diseases of the Ear.* London, 1911. 596 pp. With 6 colored plates. **37.00 45.00**

☐ **Millingen, J. G. V.** *The Army Medical Officer's Manual upon Active Service.* London, 1819. 267 pp. Bound in boards. **23.00 29.00**

☐ **Minot, Charles S.** *Human Embryology.* N.Y., 1892. 815 pp. Clothbound. **26.00 35.00**

☐ **Mitchell, Silas Weir.** *The Relations of Pain to Weather.* Philadelphia, 1877. 25 pp. Softbound. **20.00 26.00**

☐ **Monro, Alexander.** *A Treatise on Comparative Anatomy.* Edinburgh, 1783. 136 pp. **32.00 42.00**

☐ **Monro, Alexander.** *A Description of all the Bursae Mucosae of the Human Body.* Edinburgh, 1788. Folio. With 10 large folding engraved plates. Bound in half calf....... **170.00 210.00**

☐ **Monro, Donald.** *An Account of the Diseases which were most frequent in the British Military Hospitals in Germany, From January 1761 to the Return of the Troops to England in March 1763.* London, 1764. Bound in calf, gilt. **85.00 105.00**

☐ **Moore, George.** *The Use of the Body in Relation to the Mind.* London, 1847. Second edition. 431 pp. Clothbound. **27.00 34.00**

☐ **Moore, Norman.** *The History of the Study of Medicine in the British Isles.* Oxford, 1908. 202 pp. **14.00 19.00**

PRICE RANGE

☐ **Morris, Henry.** *A Treatise on Human Anatomy.* London, 1902. Third revised edition. 1,328 pp. With 846 woodcut illustrations.. 18.00 24.00

☐ **Morris, Malcom.** *Skin Diseases including Their Definition, Symptoms, Diagnosis, and Prognosis.* London, 1879. 288 pp. Brown cloth. 8.00 11.00

☐ **Morrison, J. T.** *William Sands Cox and the Birmingham Medical School.* Birmingham, 1926. 240 pp. Blue cloth binding. 17.00 23.00

☐ **Morrison, John.** *Medicine no Mystery.* London, 1829. 165 pp.. 19.00 25.00

☐ **Morton, William J.** *The invention of Anaesthetic Inhalation.* N.Y.: D. Appleton and Company, 1880. 48 pp. Softbound. 180.00 235.00

☐ **Mosely, Ephraim.** *Teeth, Their Natural History: with the physiology of the human mouth, in regard to Artificial Teeth.* London, 1862. 56 pp. Blue cloth, gilt.................... 25.00 32.00

☐ **Mummery, F. Lockhart.** *The Sigmoidoscope. A Clinical Handbook on the Examination of the Rectum and Pelvic Colon.* London, 1906, 88 pp. Bound in red cloth......... 7.00 10.00

☐ **Munk, William.** *Euthanasia: or, Medical Treatment in aid of an Easy Death.* London, 187. 105 pp................. 17.00 23.00

☐ **Nugent, Christopher.** *An Essay on the Hydrophobia. To which is added The Case of a Person who was bit by a Mad Dog: had the Hydrophobia and was happily cured.* First edition. London, 1753. The person "happily cured" of rabies was undoubtedly bitten by a dog whose madness stemmed from anger only. There is still no effective cure for this affliction. 55.00 70.00

☐ **O'Donoghue, Edward G.** *Bridewell Hospital.* London, 1923. 262 pp... 13.00 17.00
London's Bridewell Hospital, founded in medieval times, was for centuries a unique organization: it combined hospital, prison and schools!

☐ **Olding, William.** *A Course of Practical Chemistry for the Use of Medical Students.* London, 1876. Fifth edition, 262 pp. Brown cloth. 22.00 28.00

☐ **Orffila, M. P.** *A Popular Treatise on the Remedies to be Employed in Cases of Poisoning and Apparent Death, including the means of detecting poisons.* London, 1818. 170 pp. Half calf binding with red morocco label......... 43.00 55.00
"Popular" simply meant it was written for the general public rather than the medical profession. This was not the sort of subject to yield a best-seller.

☐ **Orton, Reginald.** *An Essay on the Epidemic Cholera of India.* London, 1831. Second edition. 488 pp. Clothbound. 22.00 28.00

☐ **Owen, Edmund.** *The Surgical Diseases of Children.* London, 1885. 518 pp. With 4 colored lithographs and 85 black-and-white engravings.................................. 12.00 16.00

☐ **Owen, Sir Richard.** *Lectures on Comparative Anatomy.* London, 1843. 320 pp. Softbound. 21.00 27.00
Clothbound copies have the same value—but are usually in a bit better condition.

PRICE RANGE

☐ **Parker, G.** *The Early History of Surgery in Great Britain.* London, 1920. 204 pp. 7 plates. 12.00   16.00

☐ **Pelt, S. J. Van.** *Hypnotism and its Therapeutic Value in Medicine.* London, 1949. 23 pp. Softbound. 4.00   6.00

☐ **Pemberton, Christopher R.** *A Practical Treatise on Various Diseases of the Abdominal Viscera.* London, 1807. Second edition. 201 pp. With 2 plates. 15.00   20.00

☐ **Philip, A. P. W.** *A Treatise on Indigestion, and its consequences, called Nervous and Bilious Complaints.* London, 1821. 363 pp. Bound in boards. 55.00   70.00

☐ **Playfair, W. S.** *A Treatise on the Science and Practice of Midwifery.* London, 1880. Third edition. Two vols. 403 and 414 pp. With 1 colored plate. 22.00   28.00

☐ **Ploss, H. H., Bartels, Max, and Bartels, Paul.** *Woman: An Historical, Gynaecological and Anthropological Compendium.* London, 1935. Three vols. Clothbound. 400.00   500.00
Actually an important forerunner of the modern fem-lib "women's encyclopedias," far ahead of its time. Most collecting interest in it comes from that sector, rather than collectors of medical works.

☐ **Powell, R. Douglas.** *On Diseases of the Lungs and Pleurae including Consumption.* London, 1886. Third edition. 508 pp. With 2 colored plates. Brown cloth, gilt. 24.00   31.00

☐ **Richardson, B. W.** *Diseases of Modern Life.* N.Y., 1883. 520 pp. Bound in half calf. 18.00   25.00

☐ **Rindfleisch, Eduard.** *A Manual or Pathological History to serve as an introduction to the Study of Morbid Anatomy.* London, 1872. Two vols. 464 and 410 pp. Clothbound. . . .   12.00   16.00

☐ **Riollay, Francis.** *Critical Introduction to the Study of Fevers.* London, 1788. 72 pp. 27.00   35.00

☐ **Rivers, W. H. R.** *Instinct and the Unconscious.* Cambridge (England), 1924. 277 pp. 24.00   31.00

☐ **Riviere, Lazar.** *The Practice of Physick . . . Wherein is plainly set forth, the Nature, Cause, Differences, and Several sorts of Signs; Together with the Cure of all Diseases in the Body.* London, Printed for George Sawbridge, 1678. Sixth edition in English. Folio. 450.00   575.00

☐ **Roberts, William.** *An Essay on Wasting Palsy.* London, 1858. 210 pp. With 4 lithographic plates. Bound in cloth.   53.00   68.00

☐ **Roberts, William.** *A Practical Treatise on Urine and Renal Diseases including Urinary Deposits.* London, 1876. 631 pp. With colored frontis. Bound in black cloth, gilt. 22.00   28.00

☐ **Robertson, John A.** *A Probationary Essay on the Anatomy and Physiology of the Eye.* Edinburgh, 1822. 25 pp. With 1 plate. 11.00   15.00

☐ **Robertson, W. Ford.** *A Text-Book of Pathology in Relation to Mental Diseases.* Edinburgh, 1900. 380 pp. With colored plates. 22.00   28.00

☐ **Robinson, Tom.** *Lectures on Acne, Acne Rosacea, Lichen and Prurigo.* London, 1884. 105 pp. Bound in brown cloth, gilt. 18.00   24.00

A

DISCOURSE

Upon the Institution of

MEDICAL SCHOOLS

In AMERICA;

Delivered at a Public ANNIVERSARY COMMENCE-
MENT, held in the COLLEGE of PHILADELPHIA
May 30 and 31, 1765.

WITH A

PREFACE

Containing, amongst other things,

The AUTHOR's

APOLOGY

For attempting to introduce the regular mode of
practising PHYSIC in PHILADELPHIA :

By JOHN MORGAN M.D.

Fellow of the Royal Society at LONDON; Corre-
spondent of the Royal Academy of Surgery at
PARIS; Member of the Arcadian *Belles Lettres* Society at ROME; Licentiate of the Royal Colleges of
Physicians in LONDON and in EDINBURGH; and
Professor of the Theory and Practice of Medicine
in the College of PHILADELPHIA.

PHILADELPHIA:
Printed and sold by WILLIAM BRADFORD, at the
Corner of *Market* and *Front-Streets*, MDCC,LXV.

---

*John Morgan, a noted British physician, told it like it was in "A Discourse
Upon the Institution of Medical Schools in America," published in Philadelphia in 1765. This work is credited with doing a great deal for improving
the quality of training for American medical students.*

PRICE RANGE

☐ **Rodman, John.** *A Practical Explanation of Cancer in the Female Breast, with the method of Cure.* Paisley (Ireland), 1815. 240 pp. Bound in boards with a paper label on the spine. 38.00   47.00

☐ **Rokitansky, Carl.** *A Manual of Pathological Anatomy.* London, 1849–54. Four vols. 400, 359, 467 and 398 pp. Bound in green cloth. 90.00   115.00

☐ **Romanes, George.** *Mental Evolution in Man.* London, 1888. 452 pp. Bound in red cloth, gilt. 40.00   50.00

☐ **Romer, Frank.** *Modern Bonesetting for the Medical Profession.* London, 1915. 77 pp. with 10 plates. 12.00   16.00

☐ **Ross, Ronald.** *Misquito Brigades and how to Organise them.* London, 1902. 98 pp. Red cloth, gilt. 20.00   26.00
"Misquito brigades" were teams of persons who spread insecticide in malaria-ridden areas.

☐ **Roth, Walter E.** *The Elements of School Hygiene.* London, 1886. 88 pp. Blue cloth. 18.00   24.00

☐ **Rowland, Alexander.** *The Human Hair, Popularly and Physiologically, Improvement and Adornment, and the various modes of its decoration in all countries.* London, 1853. 214 pp. Bound in cloth. 90.00   115.00
Rowland was a cosmetics manufacturer and this book was intended mainly to promote his products.

☐ **Rowland, Richard.** *A Treatise on Neuralgia.* London, 1838. 173 pp. Boards with paper label on spine. 65.00   80.00

☐ **Russel, Alfred E.** *Selected Essays on Syphillis and SmallPox.* London, 1906. 215 pp. Bound in cloth. 6.00   8.00

☐ **Russel, James.** *A Treatise on Scrofula.* Edinburgh, 1808. 144 pp. 12.00   16.00

☐ **Russel, Richard.** *A Dissertation concerning the Use of Sea Water in Diseases of the Glands.* Oxford, 1753. Second edition. 392 pp. Calfbound. 130.00   170.00

☐ **Ryle, John A.** *The Natural History of Diseases.* Oxford, 1936. 438 pp. 11.00   15.00

☐ **Salmon, William.** *Ars Chirurgica. A Compendium of the Theory and Practice of Chirurgery.* London, Printed for J. Dawks, and sold by S. Sprint and G. Conyers, 1699. With engraved frontis (portrait of the author) and 12 engraved plates. 325.00   400.00
Salmon, a jack-of-all-trades, was a physician, astrologer, druggist, and alchemist.

☐ **Salmon, William.** *Praxis Medica. The Practice of Physick. Containing the Names, Places, Signs, Causes, Prognosticks, and Cures, of all the most usual and Popular Diseases afflicting the Bodies of Human Kind.* London, 1716. Third edition, 480 pp. Bound in calf. 95.00   120.00
"Popular diseases" was simply another way of saying "common diseases."

☐ **Sanders, James.** *Treatise on Pulmonary Consumption.* Edinburgh, 1808. 319 pp. Bound in half calf. 32.00   43.00

☐ **Saundby, Robert.** *Lectures on Bright's Disease.* Bristol and London, 1889. 220 pp. With 50 illustrations. 16.00   21.00

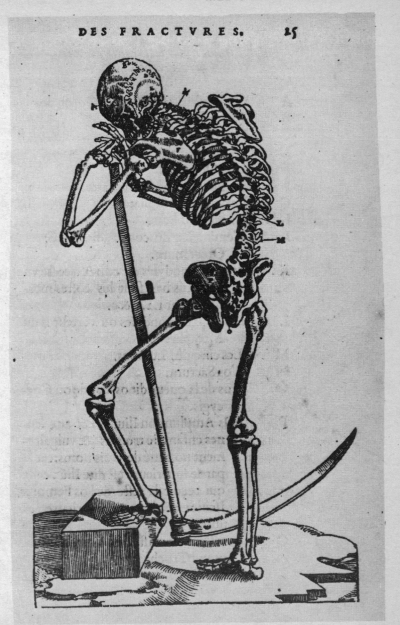

DES FRACTVRES. 25

This woodcut shows common locations of spinal fractures, Father Time with his scythe serves as the model. It's from a 1572 Parisian edition of the writings of the great surgeon Ambrose Pare.

PRICE RANGE

☐ **Saunders, John C.** *A Treatise on Some Practical Points Relating to the Diseases of the Eye.* London, 1811. 216 pp. With 7 colored plates and 1 uncolored. Bound in boards.　35.00　43.00

☐ **Saunders, William.** *Observations on the Hepatitis of Indian.* London, 1809. 82 pp. Softbound. . . . .　22.00　28.00

☐ **Savage, Henry.** *The Surgery, Surgical Pathology and Surgical Anatomy of the Female Pelvic Organs. In a Series of Coloured plates taken from nature.* London, 1876. 81 pp. With 17 colored plates. Bound in brown cloth. . . . .　110.00　140.00

☐ **Saviard, Bart.** *Observations in Surgery.* London, 1740. 289 pp. Bound in boards. . . . .　53.00　68.00
Translation of a French work which appeared in 1702.

☐ **Savoy & Moore.** *On Poisons and the Best means for Preventing Accidents.* London, n.d. (1861). 44 pp. Softbound. . . . .　8.00　11.00

☐ **Schafer, Sir A.** *The Endocrine Organs. An introduction to the study of internal secretion.* London, 1916. 156 pp. With 104 illustrations. . . . .　14.00　18.00

☐ **Scholfield, Alfred.** *Faith Healing.* London, 1892. 128 pp. Published by The Religious Tract Society and containing 16 pages of ads for their other publications. . . . .　17.00　22.00

☐ **Schreber, D. P.** *Memoirs of My Nervous Illness.* London, 1955, 416 pp. . . . .　11.00　15.00
Schreber's was considered one of the classic cases in the history of psychoanalysis.

☐ **South, John Flint.** *A Short Description of the Bones.* London, 1825. 139 pp. Bound in boards. . . . .　22.00　28.00

☐ **Spencer, Herbert.** *The Principles of Psychology.* London, 1855. 620 pp. Brown cloth binding. . . . .　43.00　58.00

☐ **Spiegelberg, Otto.** *A Text Book of Midwifery.* London, 1887–88. Two vols. . . . .　22.00　28.00

☐ **Spurzheim, Johann G.** *Observations on the Deranged Manifestations of the Mind, or Insanity.* London, 1817. 312 pp. With 4 engraved plates. Calfbound. . . . .　100.00　130.00

☐ **Startin, James.** *Two Lectures on Ringworm and other Diseases of the Skin due to vegetoid parasites.* London, 1878. 28 pp. Softbound. . . . .　8.00　11.00

☐ **Stephens, J. W. and Christophers, S. R.** *The Practical Study of Malaria.* London, 1904. 396 pp. Green cloth. . . . . .　22.00　28.00

☐ **Stern, Bernhard J.** *Social Factors in Medical Progress.* N.Y., 1927. 136 pp. . . . .　24.00　31.00

☐ **Sternberg, Dr. M.** *Acromegaly.* London, 1899. 138 pp. Clothbound. . . . .　13.00　17.00

☐ **Still, George F.** *Common Disorders and Diseases of Childhood.* London, 1927. 1,031 pp. Clothbound. . . . .　22.00　28.00

☐ **Stoddart, W. H. B.** *The Mind and its Disorders.* London, 1926. 593 pp. 11 plates, 6 of which are in color. Clothbound. . . . .　20.00　25.00

☐ **Stonhouse, James.** *Every man's Assistant, and the Sick Man's Friend.* Bath (England), 1790. Second edition. 262 pp. Sheepskin binding. . . . .　28.00　35.00

☐ **Strotther, Edward.** *Dr. Radcliffe's Practical Dispensatory.* London, 1721. 464 pp. Calfbound. . . . .　37.00　48.00

PRICE RANGE

☐ **Struve, Christian A.** *Asthenology: or, The Art of Preserving Feeble Life.* London, 1801. 431 pp. Bound in boards. . . . . — 58.00 — 73.00

☐ **Swan, Joseph.** *A Demonstration of the Nerves of the Human Body.* London, 1830. First edition. Folio. With 25 plates. . . . . — 190.00 — 235.00

☐ **Swan, Joseph.** *The Brain in Relation to the Mind.* London, 1854. 113 pp. Blindstamped cloth. . . . . — 150.00 — 190.00

☐ **Swediaur, F. S.** *Practical Observations on Venereal Complaints.* Edinburgh, 1788. 315 pp. Bound in boards. . . . . . — 50.00 — 65.00

☐ **Teale, Thomas P.** *A Treatise on Neuralgic Diseases.* Concord, Mass, n.d. (mid 1800's). 120 pp. Boards with a cloth spine. Printed on low-quality paper, usually found with heavy browning. . . . . — 80.00 — 105.00

☐ **Thoma, Kurt H.** *Oral Anesthesia.* Boston, 1920. Second edition. 185 pp. Blue cloth. — 14.00 — 18.00

☐ **Thompson, Sir H.** *Diet in Relation to Age and Activity.* London, 1886. 94 pp. Clothbound. . . . . — 14.00 — 18.00

☐ **Thompson, Sir H.** *Modern Cremation. Its History and Practice to the Present Date.* London, 1899. Third edition. 187 pp. . . . . — 14.00 — 18.00

☐ **Thompson, Theophilus.** *Annals of Influenza or Epidemic Catarrhal Fever in Great Britain from 1510 to 1837.* London, 1852. 406 pp. Clothbound. . . . . — 75.00 — 95.00

☐ **Thomson, J. Arthur.** *Heredity.* London, 1908. 605 pp. With a number of plates, some in color. . . . . — 22.00 — 28.00

☐ **Thomson, John.** *Lectures on Inflammation.* Edinburgh, 1813. 649 pp. Bound in half calf. . . . . — 70.00 — 85.00

☐ **Tissot, Simon Andre.** *Advice to the People in General, with Regard to their Health: But particularly calculated for those, who are the most unlikely to be provided in time with the best Assistance, in acute Diseases.* London, 1768. Third edition. 620 pp. Calfbound. . . . . — 65.00 — 85.00

☐ **Todd, Robert B.** *The Encyclopaedia of Anatomy and Physiology.* London, 1835–1859. Five vols. Total of about 6,000 pp. . . . . — 380.00 — 460.00
This huge work took twenty-four years to complete and was not finished until just before the compiler's death.

☐ **Topley, W. W. C. and Wilson, G. S.** *The Principles of Bacteriology and Immunity.* London, 1929. Two vols. Total of 1,300 pp. Clothbound. . . . . — 22.00 — 28.00

☐ **Tournefort, Jos.** *Materia Medica or a Description of Simple Medicines generally used in Physick.)* London, 1716. Second edition. 406 pp. Calfbound. . . . . — 30.00 — 39.00

☐ **Tredgold, A. F.** *A Text-Book of Mental Deficiency.* London, 1937. Sixth edition. 556 pp. . . . . — 22.00 — 28.00

☐ **Tully, J. D.** *The History of Plague.* London, 1821. 292 pp. Bound in boards. . . . . — 27.00 — 36.00

☐ **Turnbull, Dennis.** *The New Cancer Treatment.* Cheltenham (England), 1876. Second edition. Bound in green cloth, gilt. . . . . — 17.00 — 23.00

☐ **Turner, G. Grey.** *Inquiries and Diseases of the Oesophagus.* London, 1946. 100 pp. With 8 plates. . . . . — 9.00 — 12.00

PRICE RANGE

☐ **Turton, W.** *A Medical Glossary.* London, 1802. 622 pp.
Bound in half calf.................................... 32.00 43.00

☐ **Tuson, Edward W.** *The Anatomy and Surgery of Inguinal
and Femoral Hernia.* London, 1834. Folio 16 pp. With 3
lifesize colored plates (lithographs). Each plate has several
movable overlays. Boards with cloth spine. The overlays
are often missing. When this is the case, the value is considerably lower than shown............................ 265.00 335.00

☐ **Tweedie, Mrs. A.** *George Harley: The Life of a London
Physician.* London, 1899. 360 pp. Bound in cloth......... 6.00 8.00

☐ **Tyrrell, F.** *A Practical Work on the Diseases of the Eye
and their Treatment.* London, 1840. Two vols. With 9 plates,
8 of them in color. 58.00 73.00

☐ **Upham, Thomas C.** *Outlines of Imperfect and Disordered
Mental Action, 1842.* 399 pp. 58.00 73.00
Same, 1848.. 32.00 43.00

☐ **Ure, Alexander.** *A Practical Compendium of the Materia
Medica.* London, 1838. 239 pp. Green cloth. 15.00 20.00

☐ **Verworn, Max.** *General Physiology. An Outline of the Science of Life.* London, 1899, 615 pp. With 285 illustrations
in the text.. 27.00 36.00

☐ **Voronoff, Serge.** *Rejuvenation by Grafting.* London, n.d.,
(1925). 224 pp. With 38 plates....................... 90.00 110.00

☐ **Wadd, William.** *Cases of Diseased Bladder and Testicle.*
London, 1815. 72 pp. With 21 engraved plates. Bound in
boards.. 43.00 56.00

NATURAL HISTORY

PRICE RANGE

☐ **Adams, A. L.** *Field and Forest Rambles, with Notes and
Observations on the Natural History of Eastern Canada.*
London, 1873.. 115.00 160.00

☐ **Adams, A. L.** *Notes of a Naturalist in the Nile Valley and
Malta.* A Narrative of Exploration and Research. London,
1870. .... 32.00 43.00

☐ **Adams, A. L.** *Travels of a Naturalist in Japan and Man-
churia.* London, 1870................................... 175.00 225.00

☐ **Adams, H. G.** *Humming Birds.* London, n.d., 1856....... 55.00 75.00

☐ **Agassiz, A.** *Three Cruises of the U.S. Coast and Geodetic
Survey Steamer "Blake" in the Gulf of Mexico...1877 to
1880.* Boston and N.Y., 1888. Two vols., with 72 plain and
9 colored plates and maps............................. 225.00 290.00

☐ **Anderson, J.** *Anatomical and Zoological Researches.*
London, 1878. Two vols., large 4to, with map and 85 plates,
50 of them colored, cloth, limited to 250 copies. 2150.00 3200.00

☐ **Anthony, H. E.** *Field Book of North American Mammals.*
N.Y., 1928. .... 10.00 15.00

☐ **Arbuthnott, The Hon. Mrs.** *The Henwife: her own experience in her own Poultry-Yard.* Edinburgh, 1879. Eighth
edition, with 10 hand-colored plates. 120.00 160.00

PRICE RANGE

☐ **Ashton, J.** *Curious Creatures in Zoology.* London, 1890.   50.00   65.00

☐ **Audubon, John J.** *The Birds of America.* London, 1827–38. Issued in 87 parts without binding, usually found bound in four volumes. This is the famous "elephant folio," about 37 inches high. It has 435 hand-colored aquatints........ 425,000.00 550,000.00

☐ The most valuable natural history book *and* the most valuable color-plate book. The same work in a seven-volume octavo edition, N.Y., 1840–44, with 500 hand-colored plates 16250.00 21750.00

☐ **Bailey, F. M.** *Birds of New Mexico.* Washington, D.C., 1928. .... 120.00   160.00

☐ **Bannerman, D. A.** *The Birds of Tropical West Africa.* London, 1930–51. Eight vols., with 75 colored plates 850.00   1075.00

☐ **Bates, H. W.** *The Naturalist of the River Amazons.* London, 1863. Two vols.. 300.00   385.00

☐ **Bates, R. S. P.** *Bird Life in India.* Madras, 1931. With 63 plates. 30.00   40.00

☐ **Bechstein, J. M.** *Chamber of Cage Birds: their Management, Habits, Diseases, Breeding, etc.* London, n.d., 1879. .... 30.00   40.00

☐ **Beddard, F. E.** *Animal Coloration. An Account of the Principle Facts and Theories relating to the Colours and Markings of Animals.* London, 1892. With four colored plates.   65.00   85.00

☐ **Beede, W.** *The Edge of the Jungle.* London, 1922. ......   27.00   35.00

☐ **Bell, T.** *A History of British Quadrupeds.* London, 1837.   24.00   32.00

☐ **Bell, T.** *The Naturalist in Nicaragua.* London, 1874.......   67.00   92.00

☐ **Bennett, J. W.** *A Selection from the most remarkable and interesting Fishes found on the coast of Ceylon.* London, 1830. .... 1150.00   1525.00

☐ **Bent, A. C.** *Life Histories of North American Birds.* Washington, D.C., 1919–58. Twenty vols. 850.00   1075.00

☐ **Bewick, T.** *A History of British Birds.* Newcastle (England), 1805. Two vols... 475.00   625.00

☐ **Bigland, J.** *A Natural History of Animals.* Philadelphia, 1828. With colored vignette title and 11 colored plates.......... 400.00   525.00

☐ **Bingley, W.** *Memoirs of British Quadrupeds.* London, 1809. Two vols., with 71 colored plates, large paper copy....... 675.00   950.00

☐ **Bree, C. R.** *A History of the Birds of Europe.* London, 1875–76. Five vols., with 252 colored plates. 650.00   900.00

☐ **British, Aviary.** *And Bird Keeper's Companion.* Containing copious Directions for propagating the Breed of Canaries. London, n.d., c. 1835. With 18 engraved plates. 37.00   52.00

☐ **Broderip, W. J.** *Leaves from the Note Book of a Naturalist.* London, 1852. .... 15.00   20.00

☐ **Brown, P.** *New Illustrations of Zoology, containing plates of new, curious and nondescript Birds, with a few Quadrupeds, Reptiles and Insects.* London, 1776. With 50 colored plates, text in English and French. 3500.00   4000.00

☐ **Buckland, F. T.** *Curiosities of Natural History.* London, 1888–90. Four vols.. 135.00   175.00

☐ **Buffon, G. C. L. de.** *The History of Singing Birds.* Edinburgh, 1791. With 24 plates............................... 165.00   210.00

PRICE RANGE

☐ **Buller, Sir W. L.** *A History of the Birds of New Zealand.* London, 1873. With 35 handcolored plates............... 1950.00 2575

☐ Second edition, 1888. In two vols., published for subscribers only. 2300.00 2900.00

☐ **Butler, A. G.** *Foreign Finches in Captivity.* London, 1899. Second edition, with 60 colored plates.................. 210.00 265.00

☐ **Calkins, G. N.** *The Smallest Living Things.* N.Y., 1935.... 10.00 15.00

☐ **Chapman, A.** *Bird-Life of the Borders.* London, 1889. ... 15.00 20.00

☐ **Chubb, C.** *The Birds of British Guiana.* London, 1916–21. Two vols., with 20 colored plates...................... 1050.00 1275.00

☐ **Church, J.** *A Cabinet of Quadrupeds.* London, 1805. Two vols., with 84 plates. 95.00 120.00

☐ **Clater, Francis.** *Everyman his own Cattle Doctor.* London, 1811. .... 90.00 115.00

☐ **Collingwood, C.** *Rambles of a Naturalist on the Shores and Waters of the China Sea.* London, 1868............. 115.00 160.00

☐ **Cornish, J.** *A View of the present State of the Salmon and Channel-Fisheries...* London, 1824 .... 12.00 16.00

☐ **Cory, C. B.** *The Birds of the Bahama Islands.* Boston, 1880. With 8 hand-colored plates........................... 800.00 1075.00

☐ **Cottam, C.** *Food Habits of North American Diving Ducks.* Washington, D.C., 1939. .... 33.00 42.00

☐ **Couch, J.** *A History of the Fishes of the British Isles.* London, 1877–78. Four vols., with 252 colored plates........ 325.00 425.00

☐ **Coues and Allen.** *Monograph of North American Rodentia.* Washington, D.C., 1877........................... 80.00 105.00

☐ **Cuvier, G.** *The Animal Kingdom.* London, 1827–35. Sixteen vols., with 8 colored and 787 plain plates........... 575.00 750.00

☐ **Darwin, Charles.** *On the Origin of Species, by means of Natural Selection...* London, 1860. Second edition, "fifth thousand," but still a collector's item.................... 235.00 285.00

☐ **Darwin, Charles.** *The Variation of Animals and Plants under Domestication.* London, 1868. Two vols., first issue of the first edition. 250.00 300.00

☐ **Darwin, Charles.** *The Descent of Man.* London, 1871. Two vols. with a leaf of Postscript, errata on verso of Vol. II title, and Murray's 16 pp. catalogue dated January 1871 at end of each vol. 500.00 625.00

☐ **Darwin, Charles.** *Expression of Emotions in Man and Animals.* London, 1872. First edition, with 7 plates and 21 cuts in the text... 165.00 215.00

☐ **Darwin, Charles.** *Journal of Researches into the Natural History and Geology of the Countries visited during the Voyage round the World of H.M.S. "Beagle."* London, 1902. A new edition. 10.00 15.00

☐ **Day, F.** *The Fishes of Malabar.* London, 1865. With 20 colored plates, bound in half green morocco, spine gilt tooled. 1575.00 2100.00

☐ **DeKaye, J. E.** *Zoology of New York.* Part I: General Introduction and Mammalia. Albany, 1842................... 50.00 65.00

☐ **Distant, W. L.** *A Naturalist in the Transvaal.* London, 1892. With 8 plain and 4 colored plates.................... 110.00 165.00

☐ **Dixon, C.** *Lost and Vanishing Birds.* London, 1898. With 10 plates. 15.00 20.00

PRICE RANGE

☐ **Dobson, R.** *The Birds of the Channel Islands.* London, 1952. . . . . 16.00 21.00

☐ **Donovan, E.** *An Epitome of the Natural History of the Insects of India and the Islands in the Indian Seas.* London, 1800. With 58 colored plates. 3675.00 4750.00

☐ **Dresser, H. E. and Sharpe, R. B.** *A History of the Birds of Europe.* London, 1871–81. Eight vols., large 4to, with 632 hand-colored plates. 13,500.00 16,500.00

☐ **Dresser, H. E. and Sharpe, R. B.** *Eggs of the Birds of Europe.* London, 1905–10. With 106 colored plates. 800.00 1100.00

☐ **Drury, D.** *Illustrations of exciting Entomology.* A new edition. London, 1837. Three vols., with 150 colored plates. 1225.00 1575.00

☐ **Dugmore, A. R.** *The Romance of the Beaver.* Being the History of the Beaver in the Western Hemisphere. London, 1914. With 92 plates. 22.00 28.00

☐ **Duncan, J.** *The National History of Foreign Butterflies.* Edinburgh, 1837. With 30 hand-colored plates. 22.00 28.00

☐ **Edmondston, B. and Saxby, J. M. E.** *The Home of a Naturalist.* London, 1888. . . . . 22.00 28.00

☐ **Elliot, D. G.** *A Monograph of the Felidae or Family of the Cats.* London, 1883. Large folio, with 43 hand-colored plates of lions, tigers, leopards, etc. Issued softbound, but nearly all copies were subsequently bound, usually in morocco or half morocco. 9750.00 12500.00

☐ **Elliot, D. G.** *A Review of the Primates.* N.Y., published by American Museum of Natural History, 1912–13. With 28 colored and 141 plain plates, softbound. 175.00 215.00

☐ **Ellis, R. A.** *Spiderland.* London, 1912. With two colored and 52 plain plates. 16.00 22.00

☐ **Eltringham, H.** *Butterfly Lore.* Oxford, 1923. . . . . 10.00 14.00

☐ **Evans, W. H.** *The Identification of Indian Butterflies.* Madras, 1927. . . . . 27.00 37.00

☐ **Fennell, J. H.** *A Natural History of British and Foreign Quadrupeds.* London, 1841. . . . . 22.00 32.00

☐ **Figuier, L.** *Mammalia. Their various Orders and Habits.* London, n.d., 1870. . . . . 12.00 17.00

☐ **Finn, F.** *The Birds of Calcutta.* Calcutta, 1917. . . . . 10.00 14.00

☐ **Forbes, H. O.** *A Naturalist's Wanderings in the Easter Archipelago.* London, 1885. With colored frontispiece and other illustrations. 105.00 150.00

☐ **Forbush, E. H.** *Portraits of New England Birds.* Boston, 1932. . . . . 90.00 115.00

☐ **Forel, A.** *The Social World of the Ants.* London, 1928. Two vols., with 8 colored plates. 85.00 110.00

☐ **Fraser, L.** *Zoologia Typica, or Figures of new and rare Mammals and Birds described in the Proceedings or exhibited in the Collections of the Zoological Society of London.* London, 1846–9. Large folio, with 70 hand-colored plates. Limited to 250 copies, but only a fraction of that number now exist. 7000.00 9500.00

☐ **Friedmann, H.** *The Cowbirds.* Springfield, Ill., 1929. . . . . . . 27.00 35.00

☐ **Froggatt, W. W.** *Some useful Australian Birds.* Sydney, 1921. . . . . 33.00 42.00

PRICE RANGE

☐ **Frohawk, F. W.** *Varieties of British Butterflies.* London, 1938.	45.00	59.00
☐ **Gabrielson, I. N. and Jewett, S. G.** *Birds of Oregon.* Corvallis, 1940.	28.00	36.00
☐ **Gedney, C. W.** *Foreign Cage Birds.* London, n.d., c. 1882.	34.00	43.00
☐ **Gifford, E. W.** *The Birds of the Galapagos Islands.* California Academy of Sciences, 1913.	36.00	47.00
☐ **Giles, G. M.** *A Handbook of the Gnats or Mosquitoes.* London, 1902.	32.00	41.00
☐ **Gosse, P. H.** *Birds of Jamaica.* London, 1847.	95.00	120.00
☐ **Gosse, P. H.** *A Naturalist's Sojourn in Jamaica.* London, 1851.	115.00	145.00
☐ **Gould, J.** *A Century of Birds from the Himalaya Mountains.* London, 1832. Large folio, with 80 hand-colored plates.	7850.00	10750.00
☐ **Gould, J.** *The Birds of Australia.* London, 1848. Seven vols., large folio, with 600 hand-colored plates.	85,000.00	110,000.00
☐ **Gould, J.** *The Birds of Great Britain.* London, 1873. Five vols., large folio, with 367 colored plates.	28,000.00	39,000.00
☐ **Gray, G. R.** *The Genera of Birds: comprising their Generic Characters*... London, 1844–49. Three vols., folio, with 185 colored plats.	6500.00	8275.00
☐ **Green, J. F.** *Ocean Birds.* London, 1887. With six colored plates.	120.00	150.00
☐ **Greene, W. T.** *Birds I have Kept in Years gone by.* London, 1885. With 16 colored plates.	80.00	110.00
☐ **Grieve, S.** *The Great Auk.* London, 1885. With one plain and two colored plates.	53.00	72.00
☐ **Grosvenor, G. and Wetmore, A.** *The Book of Birds.* Washington, D.C., 1937. Two vols.	130.00	170.00
☐ **Gurney, J. H.** *The Gannet. A Bird with a History.* London, 1913.	47.00	63.00
☐ **Guthrie-Smith, H.** *Bird Life on Island and Shore.* London, 1925. Deals exclusively with birds of New Zealand.	25.00	32.00
☐ **Hachisuka, M.** *The Dodo and kindred Birds.* London, 1953. Limited to 485 copies.	170.00	215.00
☐ **Hamilton, F.** *An Account of the Fishes found in the River Ganges.* Edinburgh, 1822. Two vols., with 39 engraved plates.	1150.00	1675.00
☐ **Harris, Moses.** *The Aurelian; or, Natural History of English Insects; namely Moths and Butterflies.* London, 1778. Large folio, with 45 colored plates, second edition.	10,000.00	13,500.00
☐ **Harting, J. E. and Robert, L. P.** *Glimpses of Bird Life.* London, 1880. With 20 colored plates.	140.00	185.00
☐ **Hartley, G. I.** *The Importance of Bird Life.* N.Y., 1922.	13.00	18.00
☐ **Hayes, W.** *A Natural History of British Birds.* London, 1775. Large folio, with 40 colored plates, 2 folding.	8500.00	10750.00
☐ **Hayes W.** *Portraits of Rare and Curious Birds.* London, 1794–99. Two vols., with 100 hand-colored plates.	12000.00	16250.00
☐ **Henry, G. M.** *Colored Plates of the Birds of Ceylon.* Ceylon, 1927–35. Four parts, usually bound as one volume, with 64 colored plates.	575.00	750.00

PRICE RANGE

☐ **Hewiston, W. C.** *British Oology: being Illustrations of the Eggs of British Birds.* London, n.d., 1831–38. Two vols., with 155 colorful plates.	375.00	475.00
☐ **Hickson, S. J.** *A Naturalist in North Celebes.* A Narrative of Travels in Minahassa... London, 1889.	22.00	32.00
☐ **Hill, J.** *A general Natural History.* London, 1748–52. Three vols., large folio, with folding table and 56 colored plates. Uncolored copies are worth much less.	2100.00	2675.00
☐ **Hoeven, J.** *Handbook of Zoology.* Cambridge (England), 1856–58. Two vols.	23.00	33.00
☐ **Hoffman, R.** *Birds of the Pacific States.* Boston, 1927.	12.00	15.00
☐ **Holder, C. F.** *The Ivory King.* London, n.d., 1886. A history of elephants.	55.00	75.00
☐ **Hollister, N.** *Eastern African Mammals in the U.S. National Museum.* Part III: Primates. Washington, D.C., 1924.	20.00	30.00
☐ **Horsfield, T.** *Zoological Researches in Java.* London, 1824. With 63 colored and eight plain plates.	2425.00	3150.00
☐ **Houghton, W.** *British Fresh-Water Fishes.* London, n.d., 1879. Two vols., with 41 colored plates.	330.00	420.00
☐ **Howard, H. E.** *The British Warblers.* London, 1907–14. Two vols., with 26 maps, 35 colored and 51 plain plates.	425.00	535.00
☐ **Howell, A. H.** *Florida Bird Life.* N.Y., 1932.	80.00	110.00
☐ **Hutton, F. W. and Drummond, J.** *The Animals of New Zealand.* Auckland, 1923.	32.00	48.00
☐ **Jameson, A. P.** *Report on the Diseases of Silkworms in India.* Calcutta, 1922.	12.00	17.00
☐ **Jerdon, T. C.** *The Birds of India.* Calcutta, 1877. Three vols.	43.00	58.00
☐ **Jesse, E.** *Gleanings in Natural History.* London, 1838. Two vols.	135.00	165.00
☐ **Jones, J. M.** *The Naturalist in Bermuda.* London, 1859. With map and 10 illustrations.	27.00	35.00
☐ **Kappel, A. W. and Kirby, W. E.** *British and European Butterflies and Moths.* London, n.d., 1895.	22.00	28.00
☐ **Kearton, R.** *With Nature and a Camera.* London, 1898.	14.00	19.00
☐ **King, W. R.** *The Sportsman and Naturalist in Canada.* London, 1866. With 6 colored plates and 13 wood engravings.	220.00	300.00
☐ **Lankester, Sir E. R.** *Extinct Animals.* London, 1905.	25.00	32.00
☐ **Latham, J.** *A General History of Birds.* London, 1821–28. Eleven vols. (counting the index vol.), with 193 hand-colored plates.	3800.00	4675.00
☐ **Lear, E.** *Illustrations of the Family of Psittacidae, or Parrots.* London, 1832. Large folio, with 42 hand-colored plates.	27,500.00	38,000.00
☐ **Lee, James.** *Coloured Specimens, to illustrate the Natural History of Butterflies.* London, 1806. With 20 hand-colored plates.	2650.00	3175.00
☐ **Lewin, W.** *The Birds of Great Britain.* London, 1789–94. Seven vols. (usually bound in three or four), with 271 colored plates of birds and 52 of eggs.	21,000.00	32,000.00
☐ **Lilford, Lord.** *Coloured Figures of the Birds of the British Islands.* London, 1891–97. Seven vols., with portrait and 421 colored plates.	1550.00	2575.00

PRICE RANGE

☐ **Littler, F. M.** *A Handbook of the Birds of Tasmania.* Tasmania, 1910. . . . . 80.00 110.00
☐ **Low, D.** *On the domesticated Animals of the British Islands.* London, n.d., 1845. . . . . 65.00 85.00
☐ **Lubbock, Sir John.** *Ants, Bees and Wasps.* London, 1886. . . . . 13.00 18.00
☐ **Lydekker, R.** *Animal Portraiture.* London, n.d., 1912. . . . . . 220.00 275.00
☐ **Lyell, J. C.** *Fancy Pigeons.* London, n.d., 1833. . . . . 75.00 105.00
☐ **MacGillivray, W.** *A History of British Birds.* London, 1837–52. Five vols. 200.00 280.00
☐ **Marshall, A. M.** *The Frog.* London, 1912. . . . . 8.00 11.00
☐ **Martin, W. C. L.** *An Introduction to the Study of Birds.* London, 1835. . . . . 60.00 80.00
☐ **Matheson, R.** *Handbook of the Mosquitoes of North America.* Ithaca, N.Y., 1944. . . . . 25.00 33.00
☐ **May, J. B.** *The Hawks of North America.* N.Y., 1935. . . . . . 80.00 105.00
☐ **Meek, F. B.** *A Report on the Invertebrate Cretaceous and Tertiary Fossils of the Upper Missouri Country.* Washington, 1876. . . . . 60.00 80.00
☐ **Meyer, H. L.** *Colored Illustrations of British Birds and their Eggs.* London, 1857. Seven vols., with 322 colored plates of birds. 104 colored plates of eggs and eight uncolored miscellaneous plates. 1925.00 2450.00
☐ **Millais, J. G.** *The Mammals of Great Britain and Ireland.* London, 1904–06. Three vols. 260.00 335.00
☐ **Millais, J. G.** *British Diving Ducks.* London, 1913. Two vols., limited to 450 number copies. 850.00 1175.00
☐ **Miller, G. H.** *A new, complete, and universal Body or System of Natural History.* London, n.d., c. 1785. Large folio, 84 plates. 650.00 875.00
☐ **Mivart, St. George.** *Dogs, Jackals, Wolves, and Foxes.* London, 1890. With 45 hand-colored plates. 550.00 700.00
☐ **Morris, F. O.** *A History of British Birds.* London, 1851–57. Six vols., with 358 colored plates. 1025.00 1350.00
☐ **Mudie, R.** *Gleanings of Nature.* London, 1838. With 14 colored plates. 325.00 425.00
☐ **Murphy, R. C.** *Oceanic Birds of South America.* N.Y., 1936. Two vols., limited to 1,200 copies. 375.00 475.00
☐ The unlimited edition, which is really a reprint, is worth. . . 110.00 140.00
☐ **Newton, A. and Gadow, H.** *A Dictionary of Birds.* London, 1893–96. . . . . 240.00 320.00
☐ **Nott, J. F.** *Wild Animals, photographed and described.* London, 1886. . . . . 80.00 105.00
☐ **Oliver, W.** *New Zealand Birds.* Wellington, 1930. . . . . 75.00 100.00
☐ **Oudemans, A. C.** *The Great Sea-Serpent.* London, 1892. . . . . 40.00 55.00
☐ **Owen, Sir R.** *Memoir on the Gorilla.* London, 1865. . . . . . . 700.00 950.00
☐ **Patterson, A.** *Notes on Pet Monkeys.* London, 1888. . . . . 80.00 105.00
☐ **Peckham, G. W. and E. G.** *On the Instincts and Habits of the Solitary Wasps.* Madison, Wisconsin, 1898. . . . . 27.00 33.00
☐ **Pennant, T.** *British Zoology.* London, 1812. Four vols., with 294 engraved plates. 800.00 1050.00
☐ **Phillips, J. C.** *A Natural History of the Ducks.* Boston and N.Y., 1922–26. Four vols. 5000.00 7000.00

PRICE RANGE

- ☐ **Playfair, R. L. and Gunther, A. C.** *The Fishes of Zanzibar.* London, 1866. . . . .   **750.00**   **1000.00**
- ☐ **Poulton, E. B.** *The Colours of Animals.* London, 1890. . . . .   **9.00**   **12.00**
- ☐ **Poynting, F.** *Eggs of British Birds.* London, 1895–6. With 54 colored plates. **42.00**   **57.00**
- ☐ **Priest, C. D.** *A Guide to the Birds of Southern Rhodesia.* London, 1929. . . . .   **32.00**   **43.00**
- ☐ **Reynolds, J. W.** *The Supernatural in Nature.* London, 1880. Second edition. **14.00**   **19.00**
- ☐ **Richardson, Sir John.** *The Museum of Natural History.* London, n.d., 1868. Two vols., with 150 plates, of which 21 are colored. **120.00**   **160.00**
- ☐ **Ridgway, R.** *The Birds of North and Middle America.* Washington, D.C., 1901–41. Nine vols. **175.00**   **225.00**
- ☐ **Roberts, T. S.** *Bird Portraits in Color.* Minneapolis, 1934.   **25.00**   **35.00**
- ☐ **Rowley, G. D.** *Ornithological Miscellany.* London, 1876–78. Three vols. **1175.00**   **1600.00**
- ☐ **Sanderson, G. P.** *Thirteen Years among the Wild Beasts of India.* London, 1893. . . . .   **21.00**   **32.00**
- ☐ **Saville-Kent, W.** *The Naturalist in Australia.* London, 1897. . . . .   **275.00**   **350.00**
- ☐ **Sclater, P. L.** *Catalogue of a Collection of American Birds.* London, 1862. With 20 colored plates. **950.00**   **1275.00**
- ☐ **Seebohm, H.** *Coloured Figures of the Eggs of British Birds.* Sheffield (England), 1896. . . . .   **21.00**   **32.00**
- ☐ **Seeley, H. G.** *The Fresh-Water Fishes of Europe.* London, 1886. . . . .   **55.00**   **75.00**
- ☐ **Selby, P. J.** *Selby's Illustrations of British Ornithology.* London, 1841. Two vols., atlas folio, 222 plates, all but 4 colored by hand. **28,000.00**   **38,500.00**
- ☐ **Selous, E.** *Birth Watching.* London, 1901. . . . .   **50.00**   **70.00**
- ☐ **Shuckard, W. E.** *British Bees.* London, n.d., 1866. . . . . . .   **13.00**   **18.00**
- ☐ **Sibree, J.** *A Naturalist in Madagascar.* London, 1915. . . .   **110.00**   **155.00**
- ☐ **Slaney, R. A.** *An Outline of the Smaller British Birds.* London, 1833. Designed for the use of "Ladies and Young Persons," both considered dim-witted. **9.00**   **12.00**
- ☐ **Smith, Sir Andrew.** *Illustrations of the Zoology of South Africa.* London, 1838–49. Five vols., with 279 plates. **7750.00**   **11,000.00**
- ☐ **Southwell, T.** *The Seals and Whales of the British Seas.* London, 1818. . . . .   **21.00**   **32.00**
- ☐ **Stanley, E.** *A familiary History of Birds.* London, 1851. . . .   **10.00**   **15.00**
- ☐ **Stark, J.** *Elements of Natural History.* Edinburgh, 1828. Two vols. **25.00**   **32.00**
- ☐ **Staveley, E. F.** *British Spiders.* London, 1866. . . . .   **10.00**   **15.00**
- ☐ **Staveley, E. F.** *British Insects.* London, 1871. . . . .   **8.00**   **11.00**
- ☐ **Stewart, C.** *Elements of Natural History.* London, 1801–02. Two vols. **135.00**   **170.00**
- ☐ **Stone, W.** *Bird Studies at Old Cape May.* Philadelphia, 1937. Two vols. **105.00**   **135.00**
- ☐ **Studer, J. H. and Jasper, T.** *The Birds of North America.* Columbus, Ohio, 1878. Two vols. **350.00**   **425.00**
- ☐ **Swainson, W.** *Zoological Illustrations.* London, 1820–23. Three vols., with 182 colored plates. **2150.00**   **2700.00**

	PRICE RANGE	
☐ **Swammerdam, J.** *The Book of Nature.* London, 1758. With 53 plates.	1575.00	2150.00
☐ **Tanner, J. T.** *The Ivory-billed Woodpecker.* N.Y., 1942.	50.00	70.00
☐ **Taverner, P. A.** *Birds of Eastern Canada.* Ottawa, 1922.	80.00	105.00
☐ **Taverner, P. A.** *Birds of Western Canada.* Ottawa, 1925.	80.00	105.00
☐ **Taylor, A.** *Colouration in Animals and Plants.* London, 1886.	25.00	33.00
☐ **Tegetmeier, W. B.** *Pigeons.* London, 1868. With 16 colored plates.	105.00	145.00
☐ **Thorburn, A.** *British Birds.* London, 1917–18. Four vols.	1350.00	1675.00
☐ **Trimen, R. and Bowker, J. H.** *South-African Butterflies.* London, 1887–89. Three vols.	135.00	175.00
☐ **Waterhouse, G. R.** *A Natural History of the Mammalia.* London, 1846–48.	135.00	175.00
☐ **Waterton, C.** *Essays on Natural History.* London, 1839–58. Three vols.	27.00	35.00
☐ **Watson, J. S.** *The Reasoning Power in Animals.* London, 1870.	12.00	15.00
☐ **Watters, J. H.** *The Natural History of the Birds of Ireland.* Dublin, 1853.	20.00	25.00
☐ **Wheeler, W. M.** *Ants of the American Museum Congo Expedition.* N.Y., 1922. Softbound.	130.00	160.00
☐ **Whitaker, J.** *The Birds of Tunisia.* London, 1905.	500.00	625.00
☐ **Wilson, A.** *American Ornithology.* N.Y. and Philadelphia, 1828–29. Three vols. of text, one vols. in atlas folio with 76 colored plates.	3150.00	3875.00
☐ **Wolf, J.** *Feathered Favorites.* London, 1854, with 12 colored plates.	80.00	105.00

REGIONAL INTEREST

	PRICE RANGE	
☐ **Abbot, William W.** *A Virginia Chronology, 1585–1783.* Williamsburg, 1957. Soft covered, 76 pp.	9.00	12.00
☐ **Baldwin, Leland.** *Pittsburgh: The Story of a City.* Pittsburgh, 1938. Clothbound, 387 pp.	12.00	16.00
☐ **Bemiss, Samuel.** *The Three Chapters of the Virginia Company of London.* Williamsburg, 1957. Soft covered, 128 pp.	9.00	12.00
☐ **Bill, Ledyard.** *A Winter in Florida.* New York, 1869. Clothbound, 222 pp.	75.00	95.00
☐ **Bowie, E. G.** *Across the Years in Prince George's County, Maryland.* Richmond, 1947. Clothbound, 904 pp.	50.00	65.00
☐ **Brown and Williamson.** *A Tour of Historic Louisville.* Louisville, 1965. Soft covered, 48 pp.	3.00	5.00
☐ **Byrd, Sigman.** *Sig Byrd's Houston.* New York, 1955. Clothbound, 250 pp.	20.00	27.00
☐ **Clark, Joe.** *Back Home.* Kingsport, Tennessee, 1965.	10.00	15.00
☐ **Coleman, Kenneth.** *Georgia History in Outline.* Atlanta, 1955. Soft covered, 85 pp.	8.00	11.00

PRICE RANGE

☐ **Corse, Carita.** *Florida, Empire of the Sun.* Tallahassee, 1930. Bound in boards, 160 pp..........................	7.00	10.00
☐ **Couper, Colonel W.** *One Hundred Years at V.M.I.* Richmond, 1939. Four vols..	85.00	105.00
☐ **Cowgill, Flora.** *Never Forgotten: Memories of a Kansas Childhood.* N.p., 1964. Soft covered, 49 pp.	7.00	10.00
☐ **Crabb, Alfred.** *Nashville, Personality of a City.* Indianapolis, 1960..	12.00	16.00
☐ **Craig, James.** *Arts and Crafts in South Carolina, 1699–1840.* Winston-Salem, 1965. Clothbound, 480 pp........	42.00	55.00
☐ **Craven, Wesley.** *The Virginia Company of London.* Williamsburg, 1957. Soft covered, 57 pp...................	9.00	12.00
☐ **Davis, William.** *The Columns of Athens Georgia's Classic City.* Atlanta, 1951. Bound in boards....................	6.00	9.00
☐ **Frey, Laura.** *The Land in the Fork: Pittsburgh 1750–1914.* Philadelphia, 1956......................................	11.00	15.00
☐ **Garwood, Darrell.** *Artist in Iowa (Grant Wood).* New York, 1914. Clothbound, 259 pp.	13.00	17.00
☐ **Goodwyn, Frank.** *Lone-Star Land.* New York, 1955......	17.00	23.00
☐ **Gross, H. W.** *City Guide and Map of St. Louis.* St. Louis, 1946. Soft covered, 89 pp.	7.00	10.00
☐ **Hanson, Joseph.** *The Conquest of the Missouri.* Chicago, 1909. Clothbound, 458 pp.	25.00	33.00
☐ **Harrell, Isaac S.** *Loyalism in Virginia.* Durham, North Carolina, 1926. Clothbound, 203 pp....................	17.00	22.00
☐ **Harris, Bernice K.** *Portulaca.* Garden City, New York, 1941. Clothbound, 335 pp.	10.00	14.00
☐ **Hatch, Charles.** *The First Seventeen Years of Virginia, 1607–1624.* Williamsburg, 1957. Soft covered, 118 pp. ...	9.00	12.00
☐ **Haydn, Ruff.** *Pine Mountain Americans.* New York, 1947. Clothbound, 110 pp.	27.00	35.00
☐ **Hibbard, Addison.** *Stories of the South, Old and New.* Chapel Hill, North Carolina, 1931......................	12.00	16.00
☐ **Houston Press.** *The Houston Press Presents a Pictorial History of Hurricane Clara.* Houston, 1961. Soft covered, 16 pp..	8.00	11.00
☐ **Howison, Robert.** *History of Virginia.* Philadelphia and Richmond, 1846–1848. Two vols.	200.00	250.00
☐ **Kilgore, Ben.** *One Hundred Selected Stories Told in Kentucky.* N.p., n.d., c. 1940–1950. Soft covered, 35 pp.	13.00	18.00
☐ **Knight, Lucian.** *Stone Mountain.* Atlanta, 1923. Clothbound, 277 pp.	12.00	16.00
☐ **Kurtz, Wilbur.** *Atlanta and the Old South.* Atlanta, 1969. Soft covered, 64 pp.	8.00	11.00
☐ **Lee, H. B.** *My Appalachia.* Parsons, West Virginia, 1975. Clothbound, 186 pp.	7.00	10.00
☐ **Lester, John.** *I'll Take New Orleans.* Vieux Carre, Louisiana, 1948...	12.00	16.00
☐ **Liston, T. L.** *The Neglected Educational Heritage of Southern Presbyterians.* Bristol, Tennessee, n.d.	9.00	12.00
☐ **Long, Margaret.** *Louisville Saturday.* New York, 1950. Third Printing.	9.00	12.00
☐ **Lowrey, K.** *Mississippi, An Historical Reader.* Nashville, 1937. Clothbound, 363 pp.	9.00	12.00

	PRICE RANGE	
☐ **Marshall and Evans.** *A Day in Natchez.* Natchez, Mississippi, 1946, Clothbound, 81 pp.	10.00	14.00
☐ **Mims and Payne.** *Southern Prose and Poetry.* New York, 1910. Clothbound.	8.00	11.00
☐ **Mirvish, Robert.** *Texana.* New York, 1954. Bound in boards.	11.00	15.00
☐ **Noel-Hume, Ivor.** *Here Lies Virginia.* New York, 1963. Clothbound, 317 pp.	20.00	25.00
☐ **Norris, Zoe A.** *Twelve Kentucky Colonel Stories.* New York, 1905. Bound in soft leather, 116 pp.	7.00	10.00
☐ **Oliver, Nola.** *Natchez, Symbol of the Old South.* New York, 1940. Clothbound, 102 pp.	7.00	10.00
☐ **Page, Thomas N.** *The Old South.* Chautauqua, New York, 1919. Clothbound, 344 pp.	13.00	18.00
☐ **Saxon, Lyle.** *Fabulous New Orleans.* New York, 1943. Clothbound.	12.00	16.00
☐ **Stoddard, Clarles.** *Over the Rocky Mountains to Alaska.* St. Louis, 1907. Clothbound, 168 pp.	40.00	52.00
☐ **Stokes, Thomas.** *The Savannah.* New York, 1951. Clothbound, 401 pp.	14.00	19.00
☐ **Templeman, Eleanor.** *Arlington Heritage.* Arlington, Virginia, 1966.	9.00	12.00
☐ **Trahey, Jane.** *A Taste of Texas.* New York, 1949. Tenth printing.	9.00	12.00
☐ **Twining, Alfred.** *Down in Dixie.* Scranton, Pennsylvania, 1925. Clothbound, 397 pp.	120.00	145.00
☐ **Vaughn, John.** *Tales of Appalachia.* New York, 1972. Clothbound, 169 pp.	11.00	15.00
☐ **Vincent, Francis.** *History of the State of Delaware.* Philadelphia, 1870. Clothbound, 478 pp.	60.00	80.00
☐ **Waterman, Thomas.** *The Mansions of Virginia, 1706–1776.* Chapel Hill, North Carolina, 1946.	18.00	24.00

SPORTS AND PASTIMES

	PRICE RANGE	
☐ *Across Country.* By "Wanderer." London, 1882. Colored plates G. Bowers.	30.00	40.00
☐ **Adams, John.** *An Analysis of Horsemanship; Teaching the Whole Art of Riding, etc.* London, 1805. Three vols.	105.00	140.00
☐ *Advice to sportsmen, Rural or Metropolitan, Noviciates or Grown Persons.* London, 1809, plates by Rowlandson.	415.00	525.00
☐ **Aiken, Henry.** *The National Sports of Great Britain, with descriptions in English and French.* London, the colored engraved title dated 1820, the printed title 1821. With 50 aquatint plates in colors by Henry Aiken, folio, first issue of the first edition.	7000.00	8750.00
☐ **Aiken, Henry.** *The National Sports of Great Britain.* London, Thomas M'Lean, 1825. Imperial paper copy, but the plates are re-engraved in smaller size than in the 1821 edition.	2325.00	3175.00

PRICE RANGE

☐ **Aiken, Henry.** *A Trip to Melton Mowbray.* London, S. and J. Fuller, n.d., 1822. A set of 14 plates in colors on 12 long narrow strips. Also issued in a cylinder roll, but very rare in that state. 2600.00   3300.00

☐ **Aiken, Henry.** *The British Sportsman's Vade Mecum.* London, T. M'Lean, 1822–25. A collection of 129 plates in colors by Henry Aiken, most of them featuring several sketches. The work is broken down as follows: "Symptoms of Being Amused," title and 41 plates; "Specimens of Riding Near London," title and 15 plates; "Illustrations to Popular Songs," title and 42 plates; "Moments of Fancy," 14 plates; "Involuntary thought," eight plates; "Tutor's Assistant," six plates, folio. 1250.00   1575.00

☐ **Aiken, Henry.** *Characteristic Sketches of Hunting, with Caricatures of Middlesex Sporting.* London, 1826. Twelve colored plates, softbound. Originally the former sold for 15 shillings, the latter 12. To realize the full price, copies in bindings should retain the soft covers. 575.00   725.00

☐ *Annals of Sporting,* by Caleb Quizem, Esq., and his various Correspondents. London, 1809. Plates by Rowlandson. . . 265.00   335.00

☐ **Apperley, C. J.** *Remarks on the Conditions of Hunters, the Choice of Horses and their Management.* London, 1831. 8vo, boards with cloth spine. 32.00   43.00

☐ **Apperley, C. J.** *The Life of a Sportsman.* By "Nimrod." London, 1842. With 36 colored plates by Henry Aiken. . . . 2100.00   3200.00

☐ **Apperley, C. J.** *The Horse and the Hound, their various uses and treatment including practical instructions in Horsemanship and a treatise on Horse-Dealing.* Edinburgh, 1842. Frontis and plates, cloth. 30.00   40.00

☐ **Apperley, C. J.** *The Chase, the Turf, and the Road.* By Nimrod." London, 1843. Second edition, with 11 plates. . . 135.00   170.00

☐ **Apperley, C. J.** *Nimrod Abroad.* London, 1843. Two vols., second edition. 145.00   185.00

☐ **Astley, John.** *The Art of Riding. Set Foorth in a breefe treatise, with a due interpretation of certaine places alledged out of Xenophon*. . . London, 1584. Small 4to. 2250.00   3175.00

☐ **Astley, John.** *The Modern Riding-Master; or, a Key to the Knowledge of the Horse, and Horsemanship; With Several Necessary Rules for Young Horsemen.* London, printed for and sold by the Author at his Riding School, 1775. Woodcuts in the text. 160.00   210.00

☐ **Baden-Powell, Capt. R. S. S.** *Pigsticking or Hog-Hunting.* London, 1889. Dark blue cloth. 48.00   67.00

☐ **Baillie-Grohman, W. A.** *Sport in Art.* London, n.d., c. 1900. Quarto, cloth. 275.00   375.00

☐ **Baily, J.** *Pheasants and Pheasantries.* London, 1883. . . . . 8.00   11.00

☐ **Baker, C.** *Modern Gunsmithing.* North Carolina, 1933. . . . 23.00   32.00

☐ **Baker, E. C. Stuart.** *The Game-Birds of India, Burma and Ceylon.* London, 1921. Two vols., large 8vo. half morocco. 130.00   160.00

☐ **Baker, Ezekiel.** *Remarks on Rifle Guns.* London, 1835. 11th edition, reprinted Huntington, W. Va., n.d. 6.00   8.00

THE

Art of Riding, set foorth in a

breefe treatiſe, with a due interpretation of certeine places alledged out
of *Xenophon*, and *Gryſon*, verie
expert and excellent
Horſſemen:

Wherein alſo the true vſe of the hand by the ſaid
Gryſons rules and precepts is ſpeciallie touched:
and how the Author of this preſent worke hath
put the ſame in practiſe, alſo what profit men
maie reape thereby: without the knowledge
whereof, all the reſidue of the order
of Riding is but vaine.

Laſtlie, is added a ſhort diſcourſe of the Chaine
or *Cauezzan, the Trench, and the Mar-*
tingale: written by a Gentleman of
great skill and long experience in
the ſaid Art.

Imprinted at London, by
Henrie Denham.
1 5 8 4.

According to John Astley, you couldn't survive without a copy of Art of
Riding, published in 1584. Since London moved largely on horseback in
the Elizabethan era, most of its citizens had to learn to ride.

PRICE RANGE

☐ **Baker, Max.** *Sport with Woodpigeons.* London, 1934.....	8.00	11.00
☐ **Barry, W.** *Moorland and Stream.* London, 1871..........	5.00	7.00
☐ **Beckford, Peter.** *Thoughts on Hunting,* in a Series of Familiar Letters to a Friend. Sarum, 1781. Frontis, small quarto.........	320.00	415.00
☐ **Beckford, Peter.** *Thoughts on Hunting.* London, n.d., c. 1825.........	115.00	145.00
☐ *Bedale Hunt, The.* Printed for Private Circulation only. London, 1880. Softbound, rare.....	125.00	160.00
☐ **Beever, John.** *Practical Fly-Fishing.* London, 1893.......	27.00	34.00
☐ **Berenger, Richard.** *The History and Art of Horsemanship.* London, 1771. Two vols........	250.00	325.00
☐ **Berkley, Grantley.** *Reminiscences of a Huntsman.* London, 1854. Colored frontis and three plates, by John Leech.........	130.00	170.00
☐ **Berkeley, Grantley.** *A Month in the Forests of France.* London, 1857. Two colored plates by Leech..........	80.00	105.00
☐ **Bertram, James G.** *Sporting Anecdotes.* London, 1889.	53.00	72.00
☐ **Best, Thomas.** *A Concise Treatise in the Art of Angling.* London, 1807. Engraved frontis.......	85.00	110.00
☐ **Bigelow, Horatio.** *Flying Feathers. A Yankee's Hunting Experiences in the South.* Richmond, Calif., 1937. Limited printing.........	63.00	82.00
☐ **Bigelow, Horatio.** *Gunnerman's Gold. Memories of Fifty Years Afield with a Scatter Gun.* Huntington, W. Va., 1943. 1,000 numbered copies.........	45.00	60.00
☐ **Bilton, W.** *The Angler in Ireland.* London, 1834. Two vols.........	130.00	165.00
☐ **Bindley, Charles.** *The Pocket and the Stud; or, Practical Hints on the Management of the Stable.* By "Harry Hieover," London, 1848.........	14.00	19.00
☐ **Bindley, Charles.** *Sporting Facts and Sporting Fancies.* By "Harry Hieover." London, 1853.........	17.00	22.00
☐ **Bindley, Charles.** *The Sportsman's Friend in a Frost.* By "Harry Hieover." London, 1857.........	14.00	19.00
☐ **Bindley, Charles.** *Stable Talk and Table Talk.* By "Harry Hieover." London, 1845. Two vols.........	25.00	30.00
☐ **Bindley, Charles.** *The Stud.* By "Harry Hieover." London, 1849.........	19.00	24.00
☐ **Bird, T. H.** *A Hundred Grand Nationals.* London, 1937. ...	15.00	20.00
☐ **Blaine D. P.** *An Encyclopedia of Rural Sports, or a Complete Account, historical, practical, and descriptive, of Hunting, Shooting, Fishing, Racing, and other sports.* London, 1840. With 600 word engravings..........	52.00	73.00
☐ **Blakey, Robert.** *Hints on Angling, with suggestions for Angling Excursions in France and Belgium.* London, 1846.........	105.00	135.00
☐ **Blane, William.** *Cynegetica; or, Essays on Sporting: Consisting of Observations on Hare Hunting ... By "William Somerville."* London, 1788. Boards.........	78.00	102.00
☐ **Blew, W. C. A.** *A History of Steeple-Chasing.* London, 1901. With 28 illustrations chiefly drawn by Henry Alken, twelve of which are colored by hand.........	47.00	63.00

PRICE RANGE

☐ **Blome, Richard.** *The Gentlemen's Recreation.* This work is in two parts, generally bound in one volume. The first part, having nothing to do with sports, is an encyclopedia of arts and sciences; the second deals with horsemanship, hawking, hunting, fowling, fishing, and agriculture. There are many fine engraved plates. London, S. Roycroft for the author, 1686. Folio. 1575.00   2150.00

☐ **Blundeville, Thomas.** *The Fower Chiefest Offices Belonging to Horsemanship, that is to say, the Office of the Breeder, of the Rider, of the Keeper, and of the Ferrer. In the first parte whereof is declared the Order of Breeding of Horses. In the second Howe to Break Them and to Make Them Horses of Service, conteyning the Whole Art of Riding, latelye set foorth, etc.* By Tho. Blundevill, of Newton Flotman, in Norff. Imprinted at London by William Seres (Sears), dwellyng at the west ende of Paules churche, at the signe of the Hedgehogg, n.d., c. 1565. Small 4to, black letter, engraved plates of horse-bits. 4100.00   5350.00

☐ **Boner, Charles.** *Chamois Hunting in the Mountains of Bavaria.* London, 1853. . . . . 32.00   42.00

☐ **Boner, Charles.** *Forest Creatures.* London, 1861. . . . . 18.00   24.00

☐ **Bowlker, Charles.** *The Art of Angling, or Complete Fly and Bottom-Fisher.* Ludlow (England), 1814. . . . . 67.00   88.00

☐ **Bracken, Henry.** *Farriery Improved; or, A Complete Treatise on the Art of Farriery. Rules for Breeding and Training of Colts, etc.* London, 1790. Folding plates, 12mo. boards. 95.00   125.00

☐ **Bradley, Cuthbert.** *The Reminiscences of Frank Gillard (Huntsman).* London, 1898. . . . . 21.00   27.00

☐ **Bromley-Davenport, W.** *Sport.* London, 1885. Cloth. 21.00   27.00

☐ **Brookes, R.** *The Art of Angling, Rock and Seafishing.* London, 1740. With 133 woodcuts. 180.00   230.00

☐ **Brown, John J.** *The American Angler's Guide.* N.Y., 1846. Frontispiece and two plates. 67.00   88.00

☐ **Browne, Hablot K.** *The Derby Day.* By "Phiz." London, n.d., printed wrappers. A set of eight illustrations by "Phiz," one of the illustrators of Dickens' works. 75.00   100.00

☐ **Browne, Moses.** *Angling Sports.* London, 1773. Engraved frontis. 67.00   88.00

☐ **Bumstead, John.** *On the Wing.* A Book for Sportsmen. N.Y., 1869. . . . . 25.00   32.00

☐ **Burdon, William.** *The Gentleman's Pocket Farrier; Shewing how to use Your Horse on a Journey, and what Remedies are proper for common Misfortunes that may befall him on the Road.* London, 1730. . . . . 130.00   165.00

☐ **Butler, Thomas.** *The Case of Thomas Butler, Bookseller and Stationer in Pall-Mall, London.* Who was most cruelly treated at Newmarket, October 6, 1753. This qualifies as a sporting item first because Butler was a bookseller specializing in prints of racing horses, second because the work deals with an assault on him at a race track (Guildford Races). London, 1754. . . . . 37.00   47.00

☐ *By-Lanes and Downs of England.* By "Sylvanus." London, 1850. . . . . 20.00   25.00

PRICE RANGE

□ **Careless, John.** *The Old English Squire.* London, 1821.
Large 8vo, with 24 colored plates. **530.00**   **685.00**

□ **Carleton, John William, Capt.** *Recreations in Shooting.*
By "Craven." London, 1846. . . . .   **28.00**   **36.00**

□ **Carleton, J. W.** *Walker's Manly Exercises; Containing
Rowing, Sailing, Riding, and Driving.* By "Craven." London,
1840. Sixth edition. **22.00**   **28.00**

□ **Carroll, W.** *The Angler's Vade-Mecum.* Edinburgh, 1818.
Twelve colored plates. **135.00**   **175.00**

□ **Carruthers, D. and Millais, J. G.** *The Big Game of Asia
and North America.* London, 1915. Large thick 4to, morocco, uncut, top edge gilt, with 118 plates of which eight
are colored. Limited to 600 copies. **210.00**   **270.00**

□ **Chafin, William.** *Anecdotes Respecting Cranbourne
Chase, with a very concise account of it, etc.* Said to be
very rare; a copy sold for $40 as long ago as 1934, in the
midst of the depression. Cranbourne Chase was near Dor-
set. The 1818 second edition is worth around $20. London,
1818. Boards. **295.00**   **365.00**

□ **Cheny, John.** *An Historical List of Horse-Matches Run,
and of Plates and Prizes. Run for in Great Britain and
Ireland in 1748. Containing the names of the owners
of the horses which have run as above and the names
and colours of the horses, also. Etc.* London, 1748
(the roman numerals on the title page mistakenly said
MDCCXLIIVI). **120.00**   **160.00**

□ **Cholmondelay-Pennell, H.** *The Modern Practical Angler.*
London, 1870. Colored frontis, 19 plates, vignettes in
text. **110.00**   **140.00**

□ **Clapham, R.** *Foxhounds and Fox-Hunting.* London, n.d.,
1931. . . . .   **12.00**   **15.00**

□ **Clark, H. Atwood.** *Those were the Days!* London, 1933.   **18.00**   **23.00**

□ **Clark, Roland.** *Pot Luck.* West Hartford, VT., 1945. One
of 150 signed and numbered. **85.00**   **110.00**

□ **Clarke, Charles C.** *The Young Cricketer's Tutor; Comprising Full Directions for Playing the Elegant and Manly Game
of Cricket.* London, 1833. Cloth with paper label. **95.00**   **120.00**

□ **Cockaine, Sir T.** *A Short Treatise of Hunting, 1591.* Oxford
University Press, 1932. Softbound.   **21.00**   **27.00**

□ **Collyns, Charles P.** *Notes on the Chase of the Wild Red
Deer in the Counties of Devon and Somerset.* London,
1862. . . . .   **67.00**   **88.00**

□ **Colquhoun, John.** *The Moor and the Lock.* London, 1841.
Frontispiece and 15 plates. **70.00**   **90.00**

□ *Confessions of a Gamester.* London, 1824. . . . .   **42.00**   **58.00**

□ **Cook, John, Col.** *Observations on Fox-Hunting.* London,
1826. Bound in boards originally. **100.00**   **130.00**

□ **Copperthwaite, R. H.** *The Turf and the Race-Horse.* Lon-
don, 1865. . . . .   **45.00**   **60.00**

□ **Corbet, Henry.** *Tales and Traits of Sporting Life.* London,
1864. . . . .   **43.00**   **58.00**

□ **Corbett, Jim.** *Man-Eaters of Kumaon.* N.Y., 1946. . . . .   **20.00**   **25.00**

PRICE RANGE

☐ **Cornish, C. J.** *Nights with an Old Gunner.* London, 1897. Frontis and 15 plates. 19.00   25.00

☐ **Cotton, Charles.** *The Compleat Gamester: or, instructions how to Play at Billiards, Trucks, Bowls, and Chess.* London, 1674. . . . . 675.00   850.00

☐ **Cox, Nicholas.** *The Gentlemen's Recreation: in Four parts, viz.: Hunting, Hawking, Fowling, Fishing.* London, 1677. Second edition, engraved title and folding engraved plates. 1275.00   1650.00

☐ **Crawfurd, Oswald.** *A Year of Sport and Natural History.* London, 1895. Quarto. 21.00   27.00

☐ **Crawhall, Joseph.** *The Compleatest Angling Booke that Ever was Writ.* Newcastle (England), 1881. Illustrated, limited to 100 copies. 185.00   240.00

☐ **Crealock, Co. H. H.** *The Happy Hunting Ground of Loch Liuchart.* London, n.d. 67.00   87.00

☐ **Crossman, Capt E. C.** *Military and Sporting Rifle Shooting.* North Carolina, 1932. . . . . 21.00   27.00

☐ **Curtis, Capt. Paul A.** *American Game Shooting.* N.Y., 1927. . . . . 14.00   18.00

☐ **Custance, Henry.** *Riding Recollection and Turf Stories.* London, 1894. Second edition. 21.00   27.00

☐ **Daniel, Rev. William.** *Rural Sports.* London, 1801, 1802 and 1813. Three vols., upwards of 70 plates, quarto. 180.00   230.00

☐ **Darrah, Henry Z.** *Sport in the Highlands of Kashmir.* London, 1898. . . . . 33.00   42.00

☐ **Darvill, R.** *A Treatise on the Care, Treatment, and Training of the English Race horse.* London, 1828. Boards with paper label. 45.00   60.00

☐ **Davy, John.** *The Angler in the Lake District.* London, 1857. . . . . 32.00   41.00

☐ **Dawson, Maj. Kenneth.** *Son of a Gun.* London, 1929. . . . . 6.00   8.00

☐ **DeGrey, Thomas.** *The Compleat Horse-Man, and Expert Ferrier.* London, J. L. for Humphrey Moseley, 1656. Don't look for plates; this book was published without illustrations. 290.00   365.00

☐ **DeSainbel, C. V.** *The Posthumous Works of Charles Vial DeSainbel, late Equery to the King and Head of the Royal Veterinary School, etc.* Translated from the French. London, 1795. Frontispiece and folding plates, quarto, first edition. The plates are not of horses, which would probably increase collector interest, but geometrical drawing representing measurements of the Racehorse Eclipse. 340.00   425.00

☐ **Dillin, Capt. John G. W,** *The Kentucky Rifle.* Washington, D.C., 1924. . . . . 70.00   90.00

☐ **Disney, John.** *The Laws of Gaming, Wager, Horse-Racing and Gaming Houses.* London, 1806. Boards. 65.00   85.00

☐ **Dixon, W.** *Kings of the Hunting-Field.* By "Thormanby." London, 1899. . . . . 33.00   42.00

☐ **Dixon, W.** *History of the York and Ainsty Hunt.* Leeds, 1899. Limited to 200 copies. 20.00   25.00

☐ **Dixon, W.** *Kings of the Rod, Rifle and Gun.* By "Thormanby." London, 1901. Two vols. 85.00   105.00

PRICE RANGE

☐ **Dobson, William.** *Kunopaedia, a Practical Essay on breaking or training the English Spaniel or Pointer, with instructions for attaining the Art of Shooting*...London, 1817. Second edition, woodcut frontispiece by Bewick.......... 38.00 50.00

☐ **Dougall, James.** *Shooting.* London, 1881. Second edition..................................... 14.00 19.00

☐ **Dryden, H.** *The Art of Hunting or, Three Hunting Mss.* Northhamptom (England), 1908........................ 32.00 42.00

☐ **Durand, Sir Edward.** *Rifle, Rod and Spear in the East.* London, 1911....................................... 19.00 25.00

☐ **Eardley-Wilmot, Sir John E.** *Reminiscenses of the late Thomas Asheton Smith.* London, 1860. Engraved portrait and seven plates.. 180.00 235.00

☐ **East, Adam.** *Sporting Subjects.* London, n.d., c. 1820. A series of 32 engravings in colors, on eight sheets........ 135.00 170.00

☐ **Edie, George.** *A treatise on English Shooting.* London, 1773. 23 pp.. 70.00 95.00

☐ **Edwards-Moss, John T.** *A Season in Sutherland.* London and New York, 1888..................................... 11.00 15.00

☐ **Egan, Pierce.** *Sporting Anecdotes, original and selected.* London, 1825. With three colored plates and two portraits.. 210.00 265.00

☐ **Egan, Pierce.** *Book of Sports, and Mirror of Life: embracing the Turf, the Chase, the ring, and the Stage*...London, 1832. Woodcut illustrations........................... 115.00 150.00

☐ **Egan, Pierce.** *Pierce Egan's Book of Sports* (a later edition of the above). London, 1847. Illustrations, cloth bound.... 55.00 72.00

☐ **Ellangowan** (pseudonym). *Out of Door Sports in Scotland.* London, 1889.................................. 7.00 10.00

☐ **England, Dick.** *The Life of Dick En-l-d, alias Captain En-l-d; of Turf Memory.* Dick England was a notorious Irish gambler. London, 1792.............................. 265.00 320.00

☐ **Fairfax, T.** *The Complete Sportsman.* London, n.d., 1760. 12 mo, frontispiece...................................... 75.00 95.00

☐ **Fairfax, T.** *The Complete Sportsman.* Differs from the above by having a preface and additional section at the end entitled "Shooting and of Shooting Flying." London, n.d., c. 1764.. 48.00 63.00

☐ **Fairfax-Blakeborough, J.** *The Analysis of the Turf, or the Duties and Difficulties of Racing Officials, Owners, Trainers, Jockeys, Bookmakers and Bettors.* London, 1927.... 12.00 15.00

☐ *Famous Turf Cause, The.* By a Bystander. Account of a trial involving a horserace. York (England), 1791. Softbound.. 68.00 89.00

☐ **Fisher, Arthur.** *Through the Stable and Saddle-Room.* London, 1891.. 7.00 10.00

☐ **Fisher, Maj. Charles H.** *Reminiscences of a Falconer.* London, 1901.. 15.00 20.00

☐ **Fitz-Gerald, George R.** *An Appeal to the Jockey Club.* London, 1775...................................... 33.00 42.00

☐ **Fletcher, J. S.** *The History of the St. Leger Stakes 1776–1901.* London, 1902.................................... 12.00 15.00

☐ **Floyd, William.** *Hints on Dog-Breaking.* London, 1882... 13.00 17.00

PRICE RANGE

☐ **Folkard, H. C.** *The Wild-Fowler.* London, 1875. Engraved frontis and 11 plates. **75.00**   **95.00**

☐ **Forsyth, Lt. James.** *The Sporting Rifle and its Projectiles.* London, 1863. . . . .   **100.00**   **130.00**

☐ 1867 edition. **75.00**   **95.00**

☐ **Francis F.** *Newton Dogvane.* With illustrations by Leech. London, 1859. Three vols., cloth. **95.00**   **120.00**

☐ **Francis and Cooper.** *Sporting Sketches with Pen and Pencil.* London, 1878. . . . .   **7.00**   **10.00**

☐ **Frankland, Robert.** *Eight Representations of Shooting.* Cambridge, 1813. Oblong 8vo, eight colored plates. **900.00**   **1125.00**

☐ **Freeman, G. E and Salvin, F. H.** *Falconry.* London, 1859. 8vo, cloth, published in a very small edition. **130.00**   **170.00**

☐ **Fry, W. H.** *A Complete Treatise on Artificial Fish Breeding.* N.Y., 1866. Two engraved plates. **30.00**   **40.00**

☐ *Fur, Feather and Fin Series.* London, 1894–1905. A set of eleven volumes all bound in pictorial cloth, dealing with aspects of hunting and fishing. The full set. **125.00**   **160.00**

☐ Individual vols. **8.00**   **10.00**

☐ **Gale, Frederick.** *Sports and Recreations in Town and Country.* London, 1888. . . . .   **53.00**   **72.00**

☐ **Gambado, Geoffrey.** *Annals of Horsemanship.* London, 1791. Humorous plates by H. Bunbury, calf. **575.00**   **750.00**

☐ *Game Laws, a New Treatise on the Laws for Preservation of Game.* By a Gentleman of the Middle Temple. London, 1766. Second edition, small 8vo. **23.00**   **30.00**

☐ **Gardiner, J. Smallman.** *The Art and the Pleasure of Hare-Hunting, in six letters to a person of Quality.* London, 1750. Small 8vo. **420.00**   **585.00**

☐ **Gardiner, Richard.** *September.* A Rural Poem, Humbly Inscribed to all Sportsmen. Lynn Regis (England), 1780.   **65.00**   **85.00**

☐ **Garle, Hubert.** *Hunting in the Golden Days.* London, 1896. With humorous plates. **11.00**   **15.00**

☐ **Gathorne-Hardy, A. E.** *Autumns in Argyleshire with Rod and Gun.* London, 1900. Frontis and seven plates. **32.00**   **43.00**

☐ **Gelert,** . . . *A Guide to the Foxhounds and Stag Hounds of England.* London, 1849. Red cloth. **15.00**   **20.00**

☐ **Gerstaecker, Frederick.** *Wild Sports in the Far West.* London, 1854. Frontis and six plates. **42.00**   **58.00**

☐ **Gladstone, Hugh S.** *Record Bags and Shooting Records, together with some account of the Evolution of the Sporting Gun, Marksmanship, and the Speed and weight of Birds.* London, 1930. . . . .   **22.00**   **29.00**

☐ *Golfing. A Handbook to the Royal and Ancient Game.* London, 1887. . . . .   **80.00**   **110.00**

☐ **Gordon, A. L.** *Sporting Verse.* London, 1927. . . . .   **9.00**   **12.00**

☐ **Goodhall, Walter.** *The Sportsman's Pocket Companion.* London: Baily, n.d., c. 1820. 8vo, half morocco, top edge gilt, colored frontis. **275.00**   **325.00**

☐ **Graves.** *A Letter addressed to Lord Ebrington relating to Stag Hunting Establishment of the County of Devon.* Exeter (England), 1814. 22 pp. quarto. **32.00**   **42.00**

PRICE RANGE

☐ **Greatrex, Charles, B.** *Dame Perkins and Her Grey Mare.* London, 1866. With colored plates by "Phiz.".............	**105.00**	**135.00**
☐ **Greener, William.** *Gunnery in 1858.* London, 1858. With five engraved plates.....................................	**200.00**	**275.00**
☐ **Greener, William.** *The Breech-Loader.* London, 1899. Eighth edition...	**100.00**	**150.00**
☐ **Greener, William.** *The Science of Gunnery.* London, 1841. Frontis and plates.....................................	**250.00**	**350.00**
☐ **Greener, William.** *The Gun and its Development.* London, 1910..	**200.00**	**250.00**
☐ **Grimble, Augustus.** *Deer-Stalking.* London, 1886.	**21.00**	**32.00**
☐ **Grimble, Augustus.** *Leaves From a Game Book.* London, 1898. Bound in half vellum, gilt edges.	**34.00**	**43.00**
☐ **H. J.** *The Gentleman's Jockey, and Approved Farrier.* A Collection of writings by a number of authors. The 1674 edition is the third edtion. There was another in 1676, now worth about $200. London, 1674. Engraved frontis.	**315.00**	**390.00**
☐ **Hall, H. B.** *Highland Sports.* London, 1848. Two vols.....	**62.00**	**83.00**
☐ **Hall, H. B.** *The Sportsman and His Dog.* London, 1850. With five engraved plates...............................	**68.00**	**89.00**
☐ **Hall, Robert.** *The Highland Sportsman.* London, 1882. ...	**21.00**	**27.00**
☐ **Hallock, Chas.** *The Sportsman's Gazetter and General Guide.* N.Y., 1878.	**53.00**	**68.00**
☐ **Hamerton, Philip G.** *Chapters on Animals.* London, 1874. Frontis and 19 plates....................................	**34.00**	**48.00**
☐ **Hanger, George.** *To all Sportsmen.* London, 1814........	**67.00**	**83.00**
☐ **Hanger, George.** *To all Sportsmen, A New Edition.* London, n.d., 1816. Uncut, complete with the folding portrait.	**62.00**	**78.00**
☐ **Hansard, George A.** *Trout and Salmon Fishing in Wales.* London, 1834...	**68.00**	**89.00**
☐ **Harcourt, S.** *The Gaming Calendar, to which are added Annals of Gaming* ...London, 1820. 12 mo.	**29.00**	**36.00**
☐ **Hardy, Campbell.** *Sporting Adventures in the New World.* London, 1855. Two vols.	**235.00**	**315.00**
☐ **Hardy, H. F. H.** *English Sport.* London, 1932.............	**20.00**	**25.00**
☐ **Harting, John E.** *Hints on Shore Shooting. With a Chapter on Skinning and Preserving Birds.* London, 1871. Cloth.	**12.00**	**15.00**
☐ **Hawker, Col. Peter.** *Instructions to Young Sportsmen, with directions for the Choice, Care and Management of Guns* ...London, 1814. Very rare in this edition, printed for private circulation...	**1200.00**	**1575.00**
☐ **Hawker, Col. Peter.** *Instructions to Young Sportsmen.* London, 1816. Colored frontis, other plates, original boards.	**335.00**	**415.00**
☐ **Hawker, Col. Peter.** *Instructions to Young Sportsmen.* London, 1825. Fourth edition, boards.	**130.00**	**170.00**
☐ **Hawker, Col. Peter.** *Instructions to Young Sportsmen.* London, 1826. Fifth edition, boards with paper label..........	**90.00**	**120.00**
☐ **Hawker, Col. Peter.** *Instructions to Young Sportsmen.* London, 1844. Ninth edition. Called "the best edition," but far from the most desirable to collectors.	**68.00**	**90.00**
☐ **Hawker, Col. Peter.** *The Diary of Colonel Peter Hawker.* London, 1893..	**165.00**	**215.00**

PRICE RANGE

☐ **Hawley, Jack.** *The Life and Eccentricities of Lionel Scott Pilkington, alias Jack Hawley of Hatfield near Doncaster* ...Doncaster, n.d., c. 1876. Portrait...................... | 15.00 | 20.00

☐ **Hayes, H. Horace.** *Indian Racing Reminiscences.* London, 1883. .... | 12.00 | 16.00

☐ **Hayes, H. Horace.** *Riding and Hunting.* London, 1901. ... | 10.00 | 15.00

☐ **Hazleton, William C.** *Tales of Duck and Goose Shooting.* Springfield, Ill., 1922. .... | 32.00 | 43.00

☐ **Hazleton, William C.** *Classic Hunting Stories.* Chicago, 1940. .... | 30.00 | 39.00

☐ **Herbert, Reginald.** *When Diamonds were Trumps.* London, 1908.. | 17.00 | 23.00

☐ **Herbert, William.** *Frank Forester's Fugitive Sporting Sketches.* Westfield, Wisconsin, 1879. .... | 53.00 | 68.00

☐ **Hinds, John.** *Conversations on Conditioning.* About horses. London, 1829. Colored folding frontis by Alken, boards with paper label... | 115.00 | 160.00

☐ **Hofland, T. C.** *The British Angler's Manual.* London, 1841. Frontis and 13 steel engravings. .... | 80.00 | 105.00

☐ **Hooper, Johnson J.** *Dog and Gun.* N.Y., 1856. Softbound. .... | 55.00 | 80.00

☐ **Hope, Sir William.** *The Compleat Horseman; or, Perfect Farrier.* London, 1706. Second edition, illustrated......... | 335.00 | 415.00

☐ **Hore, J. P.** *The History of the Royal Buckhounds.* London, 1893. .... | 12.00 | 17.00

☐ **Horlock, K. W.** *Letters on the Management of Hounds.* By "Scrutator." London, 1852. Red cloth..................... | 52.00 | 77.00

☐ **Horlock, K. W.** *The Science of Foxhunting.* London, 1868. Half leather. .... | 48.00 | 63.00

☐ *Horse, the. His Beauties and Defects.* By a "Knowing Hand." London, n.d., 1866. 18 colored plates.................... | 75.00 | 95.00

☐ *Horse-Manship of England, the.* A Poem Dedicated to his Grace the Duke of Monmouth. London, 1682. Only two copies known to exist, the authorship is unknown. .... | 1575.00 | 2125.00

☐ *How I Became a Sportsman.* By "Avon." London, 1882. | 9.00 | 12.00

☐ **Howlett, Robert.** *The School of Recreation; or the Gentleman's Tutor to those most Ingenious Exercises of Hunting, Racing, Hawking, Riding, Cock-Fighting, Fowling, Fishing, ect.* London, 1684. 12mo........................... | 450.00 | 525.00

☐ **Howlett, Robert.** *The School of Recreation.* London, 1696. .... | 210.00 | 275.00

☐ **Howlett, Robert.** *The School of Recreation.* London, 1710. .... | 115.00 | 165.00

☐ **Hunt, V.** *The Horse and his Master.* London, 1859....... | 37.00 | 48.00

☐ **Hutchinson, Horace G.** *Shooting.* London, 1903. Two vols. .... | 150.00 | 200.00

☐ **Hutchinson, W. N.** *Dog Breaking.* London, 1848. Cloth. | 38.00 | 50.00

☐ **Jacob, Giles.** *The Compleat Sportsman.* London, 1718. Sheepskin binding...................................... | 325.00 | 400.00

☐ **Jalland, G. H.** *The Sporting Adventures of Mr. Popple.* London, n.d., c. 1890. Humorous colored plates, oblong folio. .... | 32.00 | 40.00

PRICE RANGE

☐ **Jesse, George.** *Researches into the History of the British Dog.* London, 1866. Two vols.	135.00	170.00
☐ **Johnson, T. B.** *The Shooter's Companion.* London, 1819. Illustrated with etchings, boards.	115.00	145.00
☐ **Johnson, T. B.** *The Sportsman's Cyclopedia.* London, 1831. Half calf.	35.00	45.00
☐ **Johnson, T. B.** *The Sportsman's and Gamekeeper's Directory, and complete vermin destroyer.* London, n.d., c. 1820.	32.00	42.00
☐ **Jones, Thomas.** *The Diary of the Quordon Hunt.* Derby, 1816.	45.00	59.00
☐ **Kennedy, Admiral.** *Sporting Sketches in South America.* London, 1892.	15.00	20.00
☐ *King's Majesties Declaration to his Subjects, Concerning Lawfull Sports to be Used.* London, 1618. Small 4to, 11 pp., sewn.	160.00	195.00
☐ **Kinloch, A. A. A.** *Large Game Shooting in Tibet and the North West.* London, 1869–76. Two vols., illustrated with photographs.	55.00	70.00
☐ **Krider, John.** *Krider's Sporting Anecdotes.* Philadelphia, 1853. Stamped cloth.	110.00	135.00
☐ **Lacy, Capt.** *The Modern Shooter.* London, 1842. Engraved plates, cloth.	130.00	170.00
☐ **Lancaster, Charles.** *An Illustrated Treatise on the Art of Shooting.* London, 1889.	60.00	80.00
☐ **Latham, Simon.** *Latham's Falconry; or, the Faulcons Lure and Cure.* London, Thomas Harper, 1633. Illustrated.	1300.00	1750.00
☐ **Lawrence, John.** *The History and Delineation of the Horse.* London, 1809. Plates by Scott.	215.00	265.00
☐ **Lawrence, Richard.** *The Complete Farrier and British Sportsman.* London, 1816. Quarto, with a series of engravings.	130.00	170.00
☐ **Lemon, Mark.** *Tom Moody's Tales.* London, 1864. Illustrated by "Phiz." (H. K. Browne).	55.00	70.00
☐ **Lennox, Lord William.** *Merrie England: its Sports and Pastimes.* London, 1857.	21.00	32.00
☐ **Lennox, Lord William.** *Recreations of a Sportsman.* London, 1862. Two vols.	12.00	16.00
☐ **Lennox, Lord William.** *Pictures of Sporting Life and Character.* London, 1860. Two vols.	20.00	25.00
☐ **Leverson, H. A.** *"Wrinkles," or Hints to Sportsmen and Travellers.* London, 1868.	9.00	12.00
☐ **Lewis, Peter.** *A Fox-Hunter's Anthology.* London, 1934.	9.00	12.00
☐ **Lilford, Lord.** *Lord Lilford on Birds.* London, 1903.	15.00	20.00
☐ *Lion Hunting and Sporting Life in Algeria.* London, 1857. Twelve engravings.	48.00	63.00
☐ **Loder-Symonds, F. C. and Crowdy, E. P.** *A History of the Old Berks Hunt from 1760 to 1904, with a Chapter on Early Foxhunting.* London, 1905.	12.00	15.00
☐ **Love, James.** *Cricket. An Heroic Poem.* London, 1770. Privately printed in a small edition, sewn.	160.00	190.00
☐ **Louth, Rev. R.** *Fox Hunting Sixty Years Ago.* London, 1840.	32.00	41.00

PRICE RANGE

☐ **Lupton, James I.** *The Horse.* London, 1881. . . . . 10.00   14.00

☐ **Luytens, F. M.** *Mr. Spinks and his Hounds.* London, n.d., 1896. . . . . 7.00   10.00

☐ **Lyle, R. C.** *Royal Newmarket.* London, 1940. . . . . 12.00   15.00

☐ **MacKenzie, Osgood.** *A Hundred Years in the Highlands.* London, 1921. . . . . 48.00   63.00

☐ **Malet, Captain.** *Annals of the Road.* London, 1876. Red cloth, gilt. 100.00   130.00

☐ **March, J.** *The Jolly Angler; or Water-Side Companion.* London, n.d., 1833. Frontis. 88.00   115.00

☐ **Markham, Gervase.** *Hunger's Prevention: or, the Whole Art of Fowling by Water and Land.* London, 1655. . . . . 650.00   825.00

☐ **Markham, Gervase.** *Cavelarice, or the English Horseman.* London, 1609. . . . . 525.00   700.00

☐ **Markham, Gervase.** *The Young Sportsman's Instructor in Angling, Fowling, Hawking, etc.* London, n.d., c 1712. Miniature size, rare. 975.00   1250.00

☐ **Markland, Abraham.** *Pterlyphlegia; or, the Art of Shooting Flying.* London, 1735. Second edition. 43.00   58.00

☐ **Mason, Finch.** *Flowers of the Hunt.* London, 1889. . . . . . . 7.00   10.00

☐ **Maude, G. M. A.** *A Tour into Westmoreland and to the Moors.* N.p. (London), 1831. . . . . 32.00   43.00

☐ **Maxwell, W. H.** *Wanderings in the Highlands and Islands.* London, 1844. Two vols. 37.00   48.00

☐ **Mayer, John.** *The Sportsman's Directory.* London, 1819. Engraved frontis and a few diagrams. 115.00   160.00

☐ **Metcalf, John.** *The Life of John Metcalf, commonly called Blind Jack of Knaresborough. With many interesting Anecdotes of his Exploits in Hunting, Card-Playing, etc.* York, 1795. Portrait. 43.00   58.00

☐ **Meynell, H.** *The Meynellian Science: or Fox-Hunting upon System.* Woksop, England, 1851. 16 pp., limp red leather with paper label, rare. 190.00   235.00

☐ **Meyrick, John.** *House Dogs and Sporting Dogs.* London, 1871. . . . . 10.00   14.00

☐ **Millais, Everett.** *The Theory and Practice of Rational Breeding.* London, n.d., c. 1890. . . . . 7.00   10.00

☐ **Millais, J. G.** *British Deer and their Horns.* London, 1897. Folio. 125.00   155.00

☐ **Mills, John.** *The Old English Gentleman, or The Fields and the Woods.* London, 1841. Three vols., half cloth boards, paper labels. 160.00   200.00

☐ **Mills, John.** *The Life of a Foxhound.* London, 1861. Frontis and three plates by John Leech. 58.00   73.00

☐ **Mills, John.** *The Sportsman's Library.* Edinburgh, 1845. Portrait and engravings. 47.00   62.00

☐ *Minor Jockey Club*. . . London, R. Farnham, n.d., 1790's. 32.00   43.00

☐ **Moore, Sir John.** *England's interest: or, the Gentleman's and Farmer's Friend.* London, 1721. 110.00   140.00

☐ **Moreton, Robert.** *On Horse-Breaking.* London, 1877. . . . 10.00   14.00

☐ **Muir, George.** *The Sports of the Field.* Lanark, 1831. . . . . 325.00   425.00

☐ **Muirhead, J. P.** *Winged Words on Chantry's Woodcocks.* London, 1857. Square 8vo, frontis and five plates. 53.00   68.00

PRICE RANGE

☐ **Musters, John Chaworth.** *The Great Run with John Chaworth Musters' Foxhounds.* Nottingham, 1877. . . . . 21.00 27.00

☐ **Napier, Major E.** *Scenes and Sports in Foreign Lands.* London, 1840. Two vols. 19.00 25.00

☐ **Nelson, William.** *The Laws of England.* Concerning Game, etc. London, 1736. Third edition. 125.00 160.00

☐ **Nelson, William.** as above, 1753 edition. 105.00 140.00

☐ **Nelson, William.** as above, 1762 edition. 75.00 95.00

☐ **Nethercote, H. O.** *The Pytchley Hunt; Past and Present.* London, 1888. . . . . 9.00 12.00

☐ **Nettleship, John.** *The Trigger.* London, 1831. Boards or softbound, contains a list of 77 London gunsmiths with their addresses. 225.00 290.00

☐ **Nevill, Ralph.** *Sporting Days and Sporting Ways.* London, 1910. . . . . 7.00 10.00

☐ *New Sporting Almanack.* Edited by "Wildrake." London, 1844. . . . . 63.00 85.00

☐ **Newall, Capt. J. T.** *The Eastern Hunters.* London, 1866. Frontis and five plates. 85.00 115.00

☐ *Nimrod's Songs of the Chase: the best Collection of Hunting Songs ever presented to the lovers of that Sport . . .* London, 1788. . . . . 500.00 625.00

☐ **Oakleigh, Thomas.** *The Oakleigh Shooting Code.* London, 1836. Boards. 53.00 68.00

☐ **O'Connor, R.** *An Introduction to the Field Sports of France.* London, 1846. Cloth. 15.00 20.00

☐ **O'Kelly, Dennis.** *Genuine Memoirs of Dennis O'Kelly, Esq. Commolny (sic) called Count O'Kelly.* O'Kelly was an owner of racehorses, among them the famous horse "Eclipse." The memoirs are mostly humorous. London, 1788. . . . . . . 390.00 465.00

☐ **Orme, E.** *Foreign Field Sports, Fisheries, Sporting Anecdotes and etc.* London, 1819. With 110 colored plates. . . . 1050.00 1325.00

☐ **Paget, J. O.** *Hunting.* London, 1900. 18.00 25.00

☐ **Parr, Remigius.** *A Collection of the Most Famous Horses Belonging to ye Dukes of Somerset, Devonshire, Bolton, Rutland, the Earl of Portmore, and others of ye Nobility and Gentry of England.* Curiously engraved on copper plates, from paintings done after the life of those great artists Wootton, Tillemans and other of the best hands. Printed for John Bowles at ye black horse in Cornhill, n.d., 1739. Oblong folio, marbled paper boards with roan spine. A series of 24 plates. 1575.00 2150.00

☐ **Parsons, Philip.** *Newmarket, or, an Essay on the Turf.* In 1934 an English bookseller offered a specially bound copy of this book at ten pounds and ten shillings, then equivalent to $50. Today that copy would probably be worth as much as $500. London, 1771. Two vols. (often bound as one). 225.00 300.00

☐ **Pennell-Elmhirst, Capt. R. E.** *The Best Season on Record.* London, 1884. . . . . 21.00 27.00

☐ **Pennell-Elmhirst, Capt. R. E.** *Fox-Hound, Forest and Prairie.* London, 1892. Four colored plates. 32.00 42.00

☐ **Pennell-Elmhirst, Capt. R. C.** *The Hunting Countries of England.* London, 1880. Parts 1 and 2 only (of 6). 9.00 12.00

PRICE RANGE

☐ **Pollard, Hugh B. C.** *The Gun Room Guide.* London, 1930. . . . . 175.00 250.00

☐ **Portland, Duke of.** *Memories of Racing and Hunting.* London, 1935. . . . . 22.00 28.00

☐ **Pownall, H.** *Some Particulars Relating to the History of Epsom.* Epsom, 1825. Frontis in color, five plates (uncolored), 8vo. 135.00 165.00

☐ **Proctor, Richard.** *Our Turf, Our Stage and Our Ring.* Manchester, 1862. Softbound (but rarely found that way). For a copy with the original covers. 53.00 67.00

☐ **Pye, Henry James.** *The Sportsman's Dictionary.* This book proved so popular that it went through five editions in the first year of publication. The price stated is for a first edition copy. The others are worth somewhat less. London, 1807. With 17 plates. 80.00 100.00

☐ **Quizem, Caleb (pseudonym).** *Annals of Sporting.* London, 1809. Folding frontis and 27 colored plates, plus vignette on title, 12mo. 265.00 325.00

☐ **Radcliffe, F. P. Delme.** *The Noble Science: a few general ideas on Fox-Hunting for the use of the rising generation of Sportsmen.* London, 1839. Engraved title, seven plates and woodcuts. 100.00 130.00

☐ **Rarey, J. S.** *The Art of Taming Horses.* London, 1858. . . . 63.00 80.00

☐ **Rawstorne, L.** *Gammonia: or, The Art of Preserving Game.* One of the most valuable and earliest books on the subject. London, 1837. With 15 colored plates. 1575.00 2100.00

☐ **Reynard, C. H.** *Hunting Journal of the Holderness Hounds.* Driffield, 1844. Softbound. 53.00 67.00

☐ **Reynardson, C. T.** *Sports and Anecdotes of Bygone Days.* London, 1887. Frontis and five plates, all in color. 90.00 115.00

☐ **Ribblesdale, Lord.** *The Queen's Hounds, and Stag-Hunting Recollections.* London, 1897. . . . . 13.00 17.00

☐ **Rice, James.** *History of the British Turf, from the Earliest Times to the Present Day.* London, 1879. Two vols. 15.00 20.00

☐ **Rice, William.** *Tiger Shooting in India, being an Account of Hunting Experiences on Foot in Rajpootana, during the hot Seasons from 1850 to 1854.* London, 1857. With 12 plates. 265.00 315.00

☐ **Robertson, William.** *Forest Sketches.* Edinburgh, 1865. 9.00 12.00

☐ **Rooper, George.** *Flood, Field and Forest.* London, 1871. Third edition. 6.00 8.00

☐ **Roosevelt, Theodore.** *The Wilderness Hunter.* N.Y., 1899. 4to, cloth, one of 200 signed by the author. 165.00 200.00

☐ **Ross, M. and Somerville, E.** *A Patrick's Day Hunt.* London, n.d., 1902. . . . . 21.00 27.00

☐ **Russell, Lord Charles J. F.** *Some Recollections of the Chase.* Bedford, 1879. . . . . 21.00 27.00

☐ **Russell, F.** *Cross Country Reminiscences.* London, 1887. . . . . 7.00 10.00

☐ **St. John, Charles.** *Natural History and Sport in Moray.* Edinburgh, 1863. . . . . 9.00 12.00

☐ **St. John, Charles.** *A Tour of Sutherlandshire.* London, 1849. Two vols. 21.00 27.00

PRICE RANGE

☐ **St. John, Charles.** *Short Sketches of the Wild Sports and Natural History of the Highlands.* London, 1849 . . . . 8.00   11.00

☐ **Salter, T. F.** *The Angler's Guide.* London, 1815. Colored engraved frontis, two colored plates, six other plates and two maps 125.00   160.00

☐ **Salvin, Francis and Brodrick, William.** *Falconry in the British Isles.* London, 1855. 24 colored illustrations, 4to, cloth 700.00   900.00

☐ **Schwerdt, C. F.** *Hawking, Hunting, Shooting.* Deluxe catalogue of a great private collection of books on sports and related topics. London, 1928–37. Four vols 4000.00   5000.00

☐ **Scott, John.** *The Sportsman's Repository.* London, 1820. With 37 copperplates, 4to 425.00   525.00

☐ **Scrope, William.** *The Art of Deer-Stalking.* London, 1838 . . . . 215.00   280.00

☐ **Sebright, Sir John.** *The Art of Improving the Breeds of Domestic Animals.* London, n.d., 1809. 30 pp 48.00   63.00

☐ **Sebright, Sir John.** *Observations upon Hawking.* London, 1826 . . . . 110.00   140.00

☐ **Selous, F. C. and others.** *The Gun at Home and Abroad.* London, 1914. Limited to 750 numbered copies 300.00   375.00

☐ **Seymour, Richard.** *The Compleat Gamester: in three parts.* About parlor games, including chess. London, 1754. Eighth edition 110.00   145.00

☐ **Shakespeare, Capt. Henry.** *The Wild Sports of India.* London, 1860 . . . . 10.00   14.00

☐ **Sharp, Henry.** *Modern Sporting Gunnery.* London, 1906. 18.00   23.00

☐ **Shirley, E.P.** *Some Account of English Deer Parks,* London, 1867 . . . . 21.00   27.00

☐ *Short Treatise on That Useful Invention, Called the Sportsman's Friend.* By a Gentleman Farmer of Northumberland. Newcastle, n.d., 1801. Softbound, wood engravings by Bewick. 190.00   235.00

☐ **Sidney, S.** *The Book of the Horse.* London, n.d., 1875. 4to, gilt cloth. 135.00   175.00

☐ **Simpson, Charles.** *Trencher and Kennel.* London, 1927. 42.00   50.00

☐ **Smart, Hawley.** *From Post to Finish.* A Novel. London, 1884. Three vols 53.00   69.00

☐ **Smith, Thomas.** *Extracts from the Diary of a Huntsman.* London, 1852 . . . . 27.00   35.00

☐ **Smith, Thomas.** *Sporting Incidents in the Life of Another Tom Smith.* London, 1867 . . . . 33.00   42.00

☐ **Snape, Andrew.** *The Anatomy of An Horse.* London, 1683. With 49 copperplates, folio. Not a bad price-jump; this book sold for $6 in the 1930's. 575.00   750.00

☐ **Sobieski, John and Stuart, C. E.** *Lays of the Deer Forest.* London, 1848. Two vols. 53.00   68.00

☐ *Sporting Guide, and Racing Remembrancer.* Edited by "Judex." June, 1850. 12mo, half roan 15.00   20.00

☐ *Sporting Magazine (The), or Monthly Calendar of the Transactions of the Turf, the Chace, etc.* London, 1792–1870. 156 vols. 6250.00   7750.00

	PRICE RANGE	
☐ *Sporting Reminiscences of Hampshires..* From 1745 to 1862 By "Aesop." London, 1864.	**15.00**	**20.00**
☐ *Sportman's Annual.* This issue deals exclusively with dogs. London, 1836, folio, colored plates, picture boards.	**185.00**	**235.00**
☐ *Sportsman's Cabinet.* All about dogs. London, 1803–4. Two vols., 4to, half calf, engravings.	**275.00**	**325.00**
☐ *Sportsman's Dictionary; or The Gentleman's Companion for Town and Country*...London, 1792. Illustrated with copperplates.	**95.00**	**120.00**
☐ **Stebbing, E. P.** *Jungle By-Ways in India.* London, 1911.	**9.00**	**12.00**
☐ **Stephen, Sir George.** *The Adventures of a Gentleman in Search of a Horse.* London, 1836. Illustrated by Cruikshank, second edition.	**58.00**	**73.00**
☐ **Stringer, Arthur.** *The Experienced Huntsman, or a Collection of Observations upon the Nature and Chace of the Stagg, Buck, Hare, Fox, Martern and Otter.* Belfast, 1714.	**1000.00**	**1275.00**
☐ **Stringhalt.** *Runs with the Lanarkshire and Renfrewshire Fox Hounds.* Glasgow, 1874.	**22.00**	**30.00**
☐ **Strutt, Joseph.** *The Sports and Pastimes of the People of England.* London, 1845. Illustrated with 140 woodcuts in the text, large paper copy, cloth.	**65.00**	**85.00**
☐ **Stubbs, George and Towley, George.** *Review of the Turf from the Year 1750 to the Completion of the Work.* One of the most valuable sporting books. Stubbs published and sold it himself at his "Turf Gallery," an art gallery which displayed, mainly, his oil portraits of famous horses. London, Turf Gallery, 1794. 14 plates.	**2875.00**	**3650.00**
☐ **Surtees, R. S.** *Hawbuck Grange.* London, 1847. Cloth.	**105.00**	**135.00**
☐ **Surtees, R. S.** *Mr. Facey Romford's Hounds.* London, 1864–5. In 12 monthly parts, softbound, illustrated by John Leech and H. K. Brown (two Dickens illustrators)	**1275.00**	**1550.00**
☐ **Surtees, R. S.** *Hillingdon Hall; or, the Cockney Squire.* London, 1888. Colored plates.	**115.00**	**145.00**
☐ **Surtees, Robert S.** *Handley Cross.* London, 1843. Three vols., 8vo, boards.	**130.00**	**165.00**
☐ **Symonds, Rev. B.** *A Treatise on Field Diversions.* Yarmouth, 1824. Boards.	**63.00**	**80.00**
☐ **Sympson, Joseph.** *Twenty-Five Actions of the Manage Horse.* London, 1729. Fourto, 25 engraved plates.	**850.00**	**1075.00**
☐ **Tattersall, George.** *Sporting Architecture.* London, 1841.	**210.00**	**265.00**
☐ **Taylor, Humphrey R.** *The Old Surrey Fox Hounds.* London, 1906.	**12.00**	**15.00**
☐ **Thetford, Lancelot.** *The Perfect Horseman.* London, 1655. Small 8vo, engraved frontis.	**525.00**	**700.00**
☐ *Thirty-Six Hints to Sportsmen.* Okehampton, n.d., c. 1800. Mottled paper, 18 pp.	**65.00**	**85.00**
☐ **Thomas, B.** *The Shooter's Guide; or Sportsman's Companion.* London, 1811. With three plates.	**37.00**	**47.00**
☐ **Thornhill, Richard B.** *The Shooting Directory.* London, 1804. Fourto, boards.	**875.00**	**1100.00**
☐ **Thornton, Col.** *A Sporting Tour Through Various Parts of France in the Year 1802.* London, 1806. Two vols., 4to, large paper copy.	**210.00**	**265.00**

PRICE RANGE

☐ **Tongue, C.** *The Belvoir Hunt.* By "Cecil." London, n.d., c. 1858. Red paper boards. 12.00 15.00

☐ **Tongue (or Tonge), Cornelius.** *Records of the Chase, and Memoirs of celebrated Sportsmen.* London, 1954. With two plates. 21.00 27.00

☐ *Treatise on Greyhounds.* By "A Sportsman." London, 1819. Boards. 105.00 135.00

☐ **Trench, P. C.** *Tiger Hunting.* London, 1836. Large folio, four plates. 210.00 285.00

☐ **Tweedie, Major-Gen. W.** *The Arabian Horse.* London, 1894. Fourto, colored plates, large paper copy. The large paper copies were limited to 100. .... 850.00 1075.00

☐ **Vaughan, L. Lloyd.** *The Description of a Course.* Dolgelgy, 1805. Boards. 35.00 45.00

☐ **Vincent, Rev. Joseph.** *Fowling.* London, 1808. .... 130.00 165.00

☐ **Vyner, Robert T.** *Notitia Venatica: a Treatise on Fox-Hunting.* London, 1841. Royal 8vo, sepia-tinted plates by Alken. 90.00 115.00

☐ **Vyner, Robert T.** as above, 1847 edition. 83.00 105.00

☐ **Vyner, Robert T.** as above, 1871 edition. 21.00 27.00

☐ **Walker, W.** *Angling in the Kuman Lakes.* Calcutta, 1888. 25.00 32.00

☐ **Walter, John.** *Hints to Young Sportsmen.* London, 1870. Cloth. 21.00 27.00

☐ **Walton, Izaak.** *The Compleat Angler.* London, 1661. Third edition, engraved title and 10 small text illustrations. 1150.00 1425.00

☐ **Walton, Izaak.** *The Compleat Angler.* London, 1668. ..... 880.00 1075.00

☐ **Walton, Izaak.** *The Compleat Angler.* London, 1775. Engraved frontis, 14 plates, illustrations in text. 320.00 410.00

☐ **Walton, Izaak.** *The Compleat Angler.* London, 1784. Engraved frontis and 15 plates. 235.00 285.00

☐ **Walton, Izaak.** *The Compleat Angler.* London, 1808. Frontis and 19 plates. 75.00 95.00

☐ **Walton, Izaak.** *The Compleat Angler.* London, 1815. Frontis and 13 plates. 140.00 175.00

☐ **Walton, Izaak.** *The Compleat Angler.* London, 1822. Frontis and 14 plates. This is known as the "Gosden edition," supposedly having been published by Gosden, a bookbinder ("the Sporting Binder"). Some copies are elegantly bound by him in green calf with portrait of Walton on upper cover. These fetch as much as $800, but those in ordinary bindings are in the $40–$60 range.

☐ **Walton, Izaak.** *The Compleat Angler.* London, 1823. Frontis and 13 plates. Considered one of the best editions. 225.00 285.00

☐ **Walton, Izaak.** *The Compleat Angler.* London, 1842. Frontis and 14 plates. 150.00 200.00

☐ **Walton, Izaak.** *The Compleat Angler.* London, 1893. Two vols., with 54 plates. 150.00 195.00

☐ **Warburton, R. E. Egerton.** *Hunting Songs, Ballads, etc.* Chester, 1834. Colored frontis and 13 uncolored plates, cloth. 48.00 63.00

☐ **Warburton, R. E. Egerton.** *Hunting Songs.* London, 1873. .... 15.00 20.00

☐ **Warburton, R. E. Egerton.** *Hunting Songs.* London, 1877. .... 15.00 20.00

PRICE RANGE

☐ **Warburton, R. E. Egerton.** *Four New Songs.* London, 1859.	32.00	38.00
☐ **Watson, Alfred E. T.** *The Turf.* London, 1898.	6.00	8.00
☐ **Watson, John.** *The Confessions of a Poacher.* London, 1890.	6.00	8.00
☐ **Watt, W.** *Remarks on Shooting.* London, 1835. Cloth	35.00	43.00
☐ **Webly, John.** *Memoirs of the Belvoir Hounds.* Grantham, 1867.	32.00	40.00
☐ **White, C.** *English Country Life.* By "Martingale." London, 1843.	12.00	15.00
☐ **White, C.** *Sporting Scenes and Country Characters.* By "Martingale." London, 1840. Floral boards	16.00	21.00
☐ **White, C.** *Turf Characters.* By Martingale. London, 1851.	12.00	15.00
☐ **Whitehead, Charles E.** *The Camp-Fires of the Everglades.* Edinburgh, 1891. Royal 8vo	12.00	15.00
☐ **Whyte, James C.** *History of the British Turf.* London, 1840. Two vols., cloth, illustrated	63.00	83.00
☐ **Willoughby de Broke, Lord.** *Hunting the Fox.* London, 1920.	9.00	12.00
☐ **York, Edward.** *The Master of Game.* London, 1904. Folio, calf.	400.00	525.00
☐ **Zouch, Henry.** *An Account of the Present Daring Practices of Night-Hunters and Poachers.* London, 1783. 8vo, half vellum.	185.00	235.00

TRADE CATALOGUES

Trade catalogues are of a variety of types and styles. All, however, were issued to promote the sale of some kind of product or products. Many thousands have been issued, just in this country alone, so they are anything but rare as a whole. Individually, they can and often do carry a considerable rarity factor. Because of their promotional nature they were normally distributed free of charge. Recipients commonly discarded them after use, and in this fashion the vast majority of specimens were destroyed.

It is not so much the rarity factor, however, which endears old trade catalogues to hobbyists. Rather it is the historical documentation they provide, of the origins and development of various industries and products. For the antiques collector they are of splendid use in assigning dates of manufacture. They are likewise sought by collectors of advertising memorabilia, whose ranks have swelled considerably in recent years. All told the interest in, and active demand for, early trade catalogues has witnessed a sharp increase. Not only are prices a good deal higher than in the 1970s, but the range of collector interest is much wider, encompassing catalogues on virtually all types of products. This is a field (one of not too many remaining in the book hobby) where fresh discoveries can occur. Previously unrecorded trade catalogues still turn up. Also, the opportunity sometimes exists for true bargains, when specimens are found in a bookshop carton marked "your choice, $1 each." The dedicated collector will likewise wish to visit all local sales of antiques and secondhand materials, as trade catalogues are apt to surface among any accumulation of old merchandise.

Trade catalogues can be grouped into several basic categories.

The most prevalent is the manufacturer's catalogue. It illustrated and described the manufacturer's line, either the complete line or (if very extensive) one or more special lines. A large, diversified manufacturer might have issued half a dozen different catalogues simultaneously. There are also examples, however, of large diversified lines being included in huge single catalogues.

The manufacturer's catalogue was normally made available to both the retail trade and the public. It would be restricted to the trade only in cases where the manufacturer did not wish to sell directly to consumers. Of course a problem was presented, when catalogues were going to merchants as well as the general public. If both the retail and wholesale prices were indicated, this would let the public know just how much margin of profit was added, and it was considered undesirable to divulge this information. This was usually solved by placing no prices in the catalogue, but issuing two pricelists in conjunction with it. One went to dealers, the other to consumers. Another technique was to show the retail (or store) prices in the catalogue, but to confine the wholesale prices to a separate list. There was also a third method, less frequently employed but very effective in terms of reducing printing costs. The retail and wholesale prices were both shown, but the wholesale price was disguised in a code. A "stock" number was given, which contained, if you know the secret of reading it, the wholesale price per ten or per 100. For example, an item priced at $1 retail might be accompanied by the stock number 53456. A retailer reading the catalogue knew that the third and fourth digits represented the wholesale price per 100: in this case $45. The remaining digits were meaningless camouflage.

Another type of trade catalogue is the retailer's catalogue. Under this heading fall the catalogues of Sears Roebuck, Montgomery Ward, J.C. Penney and other noted houses. Almost all of the early department stores issued retail catalogues, even if they did most of their selling over the counter. Retail catalogues were likewise issued by many merchants, dealing in sporting goods, toys, clothing, furniture, and other merchandise. In the rare instances where doubt exists over whether a catalogue was issued by a manufacturer or retailer, one need only examine the contents to determine if products of more than one maker are included.

There are also trade catalogues issued by wholesalers, who did neither manufacturing nor selling to the public. These catalogues are well in the minority but if you collect trade catalogues you will encounter them from time to time. Less common still are catalogues issued by lone craftsmen offering their own products. This was not for a want of lone craftsmen; these individuals, very prolific in number, concentrated on local selling to neighborhood customers. Also, most of them were not sufficiently well financed to produce and distribute a catalogue.

Most collectors of trade catalogues specialize by subject. There are, however, those whose interests are regional, and who will collect by point of origin. Another group collects by date and draws the line at 1880, 1900, 1920, or whatever year seems reasonable. There was a time when any dated after 1900 received little attention. Today, with the century approaching a turn, 1900 hardly seems "too recent" to many collectors. Eventually the trade catalogues of today will most likely be regarded as collectible.

Various factors influence the cash value of a trade catalogue. As you will see in the following listings, some are worth a few dollars and others over $100. The aforementioned degree of rarity is only one of the factors. Others to be considered with regard to any particular catalogue are as follows:

AGE. Age is of course an important consideration, from various standpoints. Early catalogues with their rather crude (sometimes extremely crude) woodcut illustrations have a special allure for collectors, as opposed to those illustrated with photographs or high quality line drawings. They demonstrate, for one thing, the free use of exaggeration in early advertising. Products are habitually shown to be larger, sturdier, or more decorative than they actually were. This is not mere supposition but can be easily proven by comparison of the illustrations with surviving examples of the products. In the case of merchandise with carved decor, such as furniture, the carving was shown to be more extensive and in much higher relief than in reality. Exaggeration also extended to illustrations of the ease with which a product could be used.

Beyond this, age can have significance depending on the type of catalogue. In this respect it is necessary to know something of the product's history. Any catalogue offering a newly invented or developed product will have greater value than a later one, even if the later catalogue is larger or more thoroughly illustrated. If it happens to be the first trade catalogue for that product, and if the product in itself has social significance such as the electric fan, washing machine, vacuum cleaner, typewriter, etc., this will be a most desirable and valuable catalogue. It is important to realize that such pioneer catalogues may date later than 1900 and still be of considerable value. If the product was not introduced until after 1900, there can be no earlier catalogues relating to it. Radio company catalogues serve as a prime example, and another group is jukebox catalogues.

If a catalogue is extremely old, prior to the Civil War, it will almost always carry a strong value regardless of its nature or place of origin. Of course the physical condition of the catalogue must be weighed in making an appraisal.

REPUTATION OF PUBLISHER. This can be, and frequently is, a more vital consideration than age. Most companies which issued trade catalogues in the nineteenth and early twentieth centuries have long since vanished and left no lasting memory. Pioneer catalogues of companies still flourishing, especially those of major manufacturers and retailers, tend to be more highly regarded by collectors. There are a variety of reasons for this, not the least of them being the opportunity offered to build up lengthy sets of such catalogues. The early Sears Roebuck catalogues would not be worth as much as they are, if issued by a short-lived organization. Also, Sears was regarded as the leader in its field (general merchandise mail-order) and that too contributes to hobbyist interest and value. The Martinka magic catalogues sell at a premium because Martinka was, likewise, the great name in its industry.

OVERLAPPING COLLECTOR INTEREST. Often unrecognized by the beginning collector of trade catalogues is the fact that strong demand arises from buyers who do not specialize in trade catalogues, and this of course contributes to rising prices. Many firearms collectors, for example, buy early firearms catalogues. This makes for exceptionally high prices on the nineteenth century catalogues of Colt, Smith and Wesson, Remington and other celebrated manufacturers. Toy collectors are very frequently buyers of early toy catalogues; most of the value is in Schoenhut catalogues. This can be said of glassware, porcelain, and many other groups of merchandise.

SIZE. To some degree the size of a trade catalogue does have bearing on its market price. "Size," when used in reference to a trade catalogue, invariably means thickness or number of pages. The linear size as represented in inches is of little account. The larger catalogues normally have more illustrations, and this is an influencing factor. They will generally show a wider range of products or, at the least, carry more detailed text. Thus they are of greater reference value and this translates into cash value. Given two catalogues of the same company, issued at no more than a few years apart, the larger one will almost always outsell the smaller. The only valid exception would occur if the two catalogues dealt with entirely different types of products, in which event the smaller could possibly be the more desirable. Beyond all of this it may be said that large size catalogues have little difficulty bringing good prices, as the buyers feel they are getting a lot for their money.

DEGREE OF SPECIALIZATION. Except in such cases as the Sears Roebuck and Montgomery Ward catalogues, a specialized catalogue is worth more than a general one. It is likewise true that the greater the degree of specialization, the more it will likely be worth. For example, an 1870 catalogue on plumbing fixtures will be more valuable than a catalogue of the same date offering assorted household supplies. But it is not apt to be as valuable as one offering exclusively sink faucets. A catalogue devoted wholly to iceboxes will be more valuable than a sundries catalogue in which some iceboxes are included.

THOROUGHNESS OF TEXT. While the beginning collector is not likely to be concerned on this score, thoroughness of text is a definite factor in the desirability and value of a catalogue. Those who buy early catalogues as reference books, as an adjunct to a collection of antiques or something else, strongly favor those with a descriptive text calling attention to size, materials, specific function of all component parts, patent dates, and so on. Some trade catalogues are remarkable in their detail, but the majority are much more heavily laden with advertising claims, unsolicited testimonials and assorted attempts at persuasion.

PHYSICAL CONDITION. This point applies to all specimens, regardless of their degree of scarcity or other factors. Whether a catalogue is basically expensive or inexpensive, a finely preserved copy will sell higher than one showing extensive wear and tear. The general grade of condition in which trade catalogues are found is low compared to that of most other types of old books. Hence it is unreasonable to demand pristine condition. Of many catalogues there may be no surviving specimens in such a grade of condition. On the other hand, certain defects, such as missing pages or covers, or very severe staining, are certainly objectionable.

There are three essential reasons for the generally mediocre condition of trade catalogues as opposed to other books of the same age:

1. Poor protection. Most trade catalogues are published with soft bindings. This was a major contributing cause to their rapid deterioration.

2. Received use. Unlike a novel which would be read at leisure and handled with some respect, the average trade catalogue received hard use under most unfavorable circumstances. As it was in effect a "tool of the trade," it would often be kept precisely where the products to which it related were kept: amongst tools, supplies of hardware, etc. It was not an item to be stored on the library shelves. A craftsman might want to consult it in the midst of a project. If it was not handy it was useless. And of course the craftsman would be likely to leave it grease smudged. Nor was it unlikely that a user of the catalogue would rip out a page listing an item he selected to order.

3. Free distribution. As trade catalogues were in the vast majority of cases issued gratis, any damage or injuries they received were considered meaningless. For most owners their eventual fate would be to discard them anyway.

Though it is not possible in this limited space to make a comprehensive discussion of condition, it may briefly be said that minor defects are not considered detrimental to their value. These would include: covers which are loose but present, light staining, soiling, pencil or pen notations, wrinkling of some pages or the covers (or both), curling of the covers, staple rust, tears in pages which do not result in loss of text or illustrations. Any catalogue possessing only those defects, and none of a more serious nature, would be ranked as collectible by most hobbyists. The prices as given in the following listings are for specimens in this average grade of condition. The very occasional "near mint" specimen will sell for a higher price. By the same token, one with a major defect such as missing pages or covers will sell for less. Collectors are advised to inspect catalogues for missing pages before purchasing them. The outward appearance of a catalogue does not provide assurance of its completeness. Missing pages did not fall out because of fragility; they were forcibly removed, and it is quite possible that the catalogue could offer no clue of this whatsoever until a page-by-page examination is made.

	PRICE RANGE	
☐ **Abel and Co.** *Arms, Ammunition, Fishing Tackle.* Syracuse, New York, n.d., c. 1880–1890.....................	45.00	57.00
☐ **Albany Hardware and Iron Co.** *Catalogue of Hardware, Cutlery, Tools, Metals and Supplies.* Albany, New York, 1904. Clothbound, 1,231 pp...................................	150.00	200.00
Probably the largest hardware catalogue ever published.		
☐ **Alden Speare's Sons and Co.** *General Mill Supplies, Dyestuffs and Chemicals.* Boston, 1894. Clothbound, 353 pp..	50.00	65.00

PRICE RANGE

☐ **Alteneder and Sons.** *A Catalogue and Price List of Drawing Instruments.* Philadelphia, 1905. Paper boards with cloth spine, 108 pp. 25.00   31.00
Cased sets of drawing instruments, triangles, compasses, dividers.

☐ **Aluminum Shoe Makers.** *Overland Aluminum Shoes.* Racine, Wisconsin, 1923. Soft covered, 32 pp. 18.00   23.00

☐ **American Saw Co.** *Teeth, Circular Saws, Cross Cut Saws, Butcher Saws, Wrenches, Swages, Hand Screw Presses, etc.* Trenton, New Jersey, 1882. Soft covered, 32 pp. 18.00   23.00

☐ **American Horse Goods Co.** *The American Kind.* Detroit, 1910. Paper covers with cloth spine, 108 pp. 45.00   55.00
Saddle, harnesses, racing accessories, veterinary items.

☐ **American Sheet and Tin Plate Co.** *Better Buildings: A Book of Information Relative to the Uses of Formed Metal Roofing and Siding Materials.* Pittsburgh, 1913. Soft covers, 64 pp. 18.00   23.00

☐ **Andrews and Co.** *Illustrated Catalogue of Office Furniture, School Furniture, Church Furniture, Hall Settees, etc.* Chicago, 1873. Soft covered, 96 pp. 70.00   90.00

☐ **Anger's Lumber Co.** *Two Family Homes and Apartments.* Springfield, Massachusetts, n.d., c. 1900–1910. Soft covered, 47 pp. 25.00   32.00

☐ **Annin and Co.** *Fine Flags, The Largest Flag House in the World.* N.p., 1931. Soft covered, 454 pp. 28.00   36.00

☐ **Atlee Burpee and Co.** *Illustrated Catalogue of Reliable Seeds.* Philadelphia, 1879. Soft covered, 16 pp. 59.00   73.00

☐ **Beck, R. and J.** *An Illustrated Catalogue of Microscopes and Accessories Manufactured by R. and J. Beck, London.* Philadelphia, 1884. Soft covered, 120 pp. 60.00   75.00
This is technically an agent's catalogue. It carries the name of W. H. Walmsley and Co. of Philadelphia, which was American agent for the Beck line.

☐ **Bird Neponset Products.** *Pattern Book, Felt Base Rugs and Floor Coverings.* East Walpole, Massachusetts, 1929. Soft covered, 75 pp. 32.00   42.00

☐ **Bliss Brothers.** *Launch Hardware and Supplies.* Boston, 1906. Soft covered, 88 pp. 35.00   43.00
Seafaring accessories.

☐ **Boggs and Buhl.** *Spring and Summer, 1888, Catalogue and Fashion Review.* Alleghany, Pennsylvania, 1888. Soft covered, 72 pp. 45.00   60.00

☐ **Bowman, J. R.** *Bowman's Famous Designs for Fret Sawing.* N.p., 1880. Soft covered, 16 pp. 25.00   33.00

☐ **Braunworth and Co.** *Braunworth Type Book, Showing Monotype and Linotype Faces, Special Characters, Accents, Borders, Ornaments and Complicated Type Setting.* Brooklyn, New York, 1931. .... 24.00   32.00

☐ **Brown Fence and Wire Co.** *Farm and Railway Fencing.* Cleveland, 1908. Soft covered, 56 pp. 15.00   20.00

☐ **Brown Paper Co.** *Makers of the Standard Linen Ledger and Record Papers.* Adams, Massachusetts, 1887 .... 27.00   35.00

PRICE RANGE

☐ **Buchan and Co.** *Soap and Carbolic Acid.* New York, 1870. Soft covered, 20 pp. 21.00 27.00

☐ **Buff and Berger.** *Hand-Book and Illustrated Catalogue of the Engineers' and Surveyors' Instruments Made by Buff and Berger.* Boston, 1892. Soft covers with cloth spine, illustrated. 55.00 70.00

☐ **Caledonia Bean Harvester Works.** *Argricultural Implements.* Caledonia, New York, n.d., c. 1920–1930. Soft covered, 40 pp. 14.00 18.00

☐ **Chadborn and Coldwell Manufacturing Co.** *The Excelsior Lawn Mower for Horse or Hand Power.* Newburgh, New York, n.d., c. 1875–1880. .... 14.00 18.00

☐ **Chase and Sanborn.** *Teas and Coffees. Sole Importers and Distributors of Standard Java.* Boston, n.d., c. 1880–1885. Soft covered, 60 pp. 21.00 27.00

☐ **Cherry Electric Works.** *Catalogue and Price List.* New York, n.d., c. 1890–1900. Soft covered, 28 pp. .... 15.00 20.00 Batteries, coils, phone receivers, electrical machines, dynamos.

☐ **Cincinnati Iron Fence Co.** *Catalogue 35, Iron Fence, Entrance Gates, Guards, Folding Gates.* Cincinnati, n.d., World War I era. Soft covered, 144 pp. 43.00 58.00

☐ **Clark Novelty Co.** *Compressors, Air Tanks, Can Openers, Knives.* Rochester, New York, 1891. Soft covered, 30 pp. 28.00 36.00

☐ **Common Sense Engine Co.** *Illustrated Catalogue for 1881.* Spingfield, Ohio, 1881. Soft covered, 24 pp. 29.00 38.00

☐ **Conners and Sons.** *Compact Specimens of Printing Types, Rules, Inset Corners, Ornaments, Borders, Electrotyped Cuts, Tools, Type Cases, etc.* New York, 1891. .... 90.00 115.00

☐ **Cortland Wagon Co.** *High Grade Carriages.* Cortland, New York, 1902. Soft covered, 80 pp. 49.00 63.00

☐ **Cox, Brothers and Co.** *Catalogue of Canners' Machinery.* Bridgeton, New Jersey, n.d., c. 1890–1900. Soft covered, 23 pp. 28.00 36.00

☐ **Cray Brothers.** *Net Price Catalogue of Carriage and Auto Supplies.* Cleveland, 1915. Soft covered, 512 pp. 23.00 29.00

☐ **Crank and Carrier Manufacturing Co.** *Hardware.* Elmira, New York, 1914. Soft covered, 64 pp. 20.00 25.00

☐ **Crosby Steam Gage and Valve Co.** *New Illustrated Catalogue.* Boston, n.d., c. 1880. Clothbound. 33.00 42.00

☐ **Dannenbaums Sons and Co.** *Latest Styles in Hat and Bonnet Frames. Fall and Winter 1907.* Philadelphia, 1907. Soft covered, 30 pp. 15.00 20.00

☐ **Davidson, R.** *Concrete Pottery and Garden Furniture.* N.p., 1910. .... 27.00 35.00

☐ **Davis Sewing Machine Co.** *Centennial Handbook.* Watertown, New York, 1876. Soft covered, 32 pp. 19.00 24.00

☐ **Day-Brite Reflector Co.** *Day-Brite Reflectors for Stores, Hotels, Banks, Art Galleries, etc. Catalogue 8.* St. Louis, 1929. Soft covered, 56 pp. 14.00 19.00

☐ **Defiance Machine Works.** *Illustrated Descriptive Catalogue of Patent Labor-Saving Wood-Working Machinery.* Defiance, Ohio, 1904. .... 115.00 150.00

PRICE RANGE

☐ **Deutsch and Co.** *Furs, Cloaks.* New York, 1891. Soft covered, 46 pp. Color illustrations. 32.00   41.00

☐ **Devoe and Reynolds Co.** *Priced Catalogue of Artists' Materials and Drawing Materials for Architects and Engineers.* New York, n.d., early twentieth century. Soft covers with cloth spine, 344 pp. 25.00   32.00

☐ **Dodge, Haley and Co.** *Heavy Hardware, Price List.* Boston, 1887. Clothbound, 290 pp. 33.00   43.00
Includes anvils, tackle blocks, axes, hammers, horse shoes, sledges, chisels, etc.

☐ **Domestic Sewing Machine Co.** *Winter Styles, A Domestic Catalogue of Fashions.* New York, 1876. . . . .   18.00   24.00
Catalogue of paper patterns sold by the sewing machine company.

☐ **Domestic Sewing Machine Co.** *Illustrated Catalogue of Domestic Sewing Machines.* New York, n.d., c. 1880. Soft covered, 10 pp. 22.00   28.00

☐ **Edison Lamp Works.** *Price Schedules of Standard Large Edison Mazda Lamps.* Harrison, New Jersey, 1922. Soft covered, 48 pp. 19.00   24.00
A "mazda lamp" was what we call a "light bulb."

☐ **Edwards Manufacturing Co.** *Edwards Metal Roofing, Siding, Ceilings, etc.* Cincinnati, 1913. Soft covered, 123 pp. 14.00   19.00

☐ **Electric Wheel Co.** *Wheel Sense.* Quincy, Illinois, 1909. Soft covered, 14 pp. 14.00   19.00

☐ **Elliot Shaw and Co.** *Catalogue and Price List of Electrical Appliances.* Philadelphia, 1889. Soft covered, 48 pp. 36.00   47.00
Valuable because every item included worked by electricity, including electrical burglar alarms.

☐ **Excelsior Slate Co.** *Illustrated Catalogue of The Excelsior Slate Co., Embracing Enameled Slate Mantels and Other Useful and Ornamental Articles in Slate Work.* New York, 1875. Soft covered. 80.00   105.00

☐ **Evertt and Small.** *Illustrated Catalogue and Price List of Agricultural Implements.* Boston, 1883. Soft covered, 16 pp. 14.00   19.00

☐ **Farley and Loetscher Manufacturing Co.** *Universal Millwork Design Book Number 20.* Dubuque, Iowa, 1920. Clothbound, 396 pp. 38.00   47.00

☐ **Farquhar and Co.** *Catalogue of Seeds, Plants, Bulbs, Garden Requisites, Fertilizers, etc.* Boston, 1888. Soft covered, 96 pp. 21.00   27.00

☐ **Farquhar Co.** *Catalogue of Engines, Boilers and Saw Mills.* York, Pennsylvania, 1895. Soft covered, 149 pp. 25.00   32.00

☐ **Flint Granite Co.** *Cemetery Pillars, Masoleums, Statues, Headstones, etc.* Albany, New York, n.d., c. 1900–1910. Soft covered, 49 pp. 19.00   24.00

☐ **Franvis Kell and Son.** *Catalogue 25 of Iron, Steel, Brass and Bronze Hardware.* New York, 1919. Soft cloth binding, 354 pp. 24.00   31.00
Includes locks, knobs, latches, hooks, pulls, brackets.

PRICE RANGE

☐ **Fuller and Fuller Co.** *Prices Current, Soda Fountain Supplies.* Chicago, n.d., c. 1900–1910. .... 27.00 35.00

☐ **General Gas Light Co.** *The Humphrey Radiantfire.* Kalamazoo, Michigan, n.d., c. 1915–1925. Soft covered, 28 pp. 11.00 16.00

☐ **Glasco Lace Thread Co.** *Glasco Twilled Lace Thread, A New Article for Lace Making.* Glasco, Connecticut, 1890. Soft covered, 64 pp. 25.00 32.00

☐ **Goodeli-Pratt Co.** Greenfield, Massachusetts, 1905. Soft covered, 176 pp. 18.00 23.00

☐ **Goodnow Co.** *Spring Stock of Clothing.* Greenfield, Massachusetts, n.d., late nineteenth century. Soft covered, 16 pp. 22.00 28.00

☐ **Grand Rapids Lithographing Co.** *Check Samples, High Class Color and Commercial Work.* Grand Rapids, Michigan, n.d., c. 1900–1910. Soft covered. 26.00 34.00

☐ **Griffiths, Albert.** *Saws.* Boston, n.d., c. 1880–1890. Soft covered, 4 pp. 11.00 16.00

☐ **Hart Manufacturing Co.** *Advance and Discount Index to the Price List of Hart Manufacturing Co., Manufacturers, Importers, and Dealers in General Hardware.* New York, 1868. Soft covered. 17.00 23.00

☐ **Harvey, H. H.** *Special Illustrated Catalogue of Granite, Marble, Soft Stone Workers, Blacksmiths and Contractors' Hammers and Tools.* Boston, 1901. Soft covered, 140 pp. 58.00 73.00

☐ **Harvey Manufacturing Co.** *Harvey Stylographic Fountain Pens.* Northampton, Massachusetts, 1904. .... 10.00 14.00

☐ **Haughton, Sawyer and Co.** *Army and Navy Outfits.* Boston, n.d., Civil War era. Soft covered. 18.00 23.00

☐ **Herring, Hall, Marvin Safe Co.** *Safes and Related Items.* New York, n.d., c. 1900–1910. Soft covered, 16 pp. 59.00 78.00

☐ **Hervey and Co.** *Condensed Price-List of House Furnishing Goods of Every Description.* Boston, n.d., c. 1885–1890. Soft covered, 48 pp. 26.00 34.00

☐ **Hirshberg, Art Company.** *Catalogue and Price List of Artists' Materials.* Baltimore, n.d., c. 1900. Bound in boards with cloth spine, 292 pp. 24.00 32.00

☐ **Hyman and Oppenheim.** *Coiffures of Style and Quality.* New York, 1918. Soft covered, 78 pp. 33.00 43.00
Wigs for men and women.

☐ **Incandescent Light and Stove Co.** *Make Home Homelike by Using the F-P Home Lighting and Cooking Plant.* Cincinnati, n.d., c. 1905–1915. Soft covered, 36 pp. 10.00 14.00

☐ **Iver Johnson Sporting Goods Co.** Boston, n.d., World War I era. Soft covered, 52 pp. Illustrated.............. 22.00 28.00
Mainly bicycles.

☐ **Jacobson and Co.** *General Catalogue of Architectural Ornaments.* New York, 1929. .... 24.00 32.00

☐ **Jefferson Wood Products Co.** *Universal Millwork Design Book.* Jefferson, Wisconsin, 1920. Clothbound, 396 pp. .. 22.00 28.00

☐ **Johns, W. H.** *Asbestos Liquid Paints.* New York, 1882. Soft covered. 43.00 59.00

PRICE RANGE

☐ **Johnson, S. C.** *Designs of Ornamental Hardwood, Parquetry Floors and Borders.* Racine, Wisconsin, 1890. Soft covered, 22 pp.. 20.00 25.00

☐ **Kakas and Sons.** *Fine Furs.* Boston, 1890. Soft covered, 20 pp.. 20.00 25.00

☐ **Kalamazoo Carriage and Harness Co.** *Surreys, Stanhopes, Buggies, Phaetonettes, Wagons, Accessories, Cutters, Harnesses, Horse Collars.* Kalamazoo, Michigan, n.d., c. 1900–1910. Soft covered, 68 pp.................... 55.00 70.00

☐ **Kelly and Jones Co.** *Illustrated Catalogue and Price List of Hydraulic Fittings, Cast Fittings, etc.* Greensburg, Pennsylvania, 1914. Soft covered, 444 pp. 8.00 11.00

☐ **King Harness Co.** *Price List of Harnesses and Accessories.* Owego, New York, 1905. Soft covered, 100 pp.... 22.00 28.00

☐ **Kirwan Manufacturing Co.** *Catalogue of Cans, Machinery and General Canning House Supplies.* Baltimore, n.d., c. 1890–1900. Soft covered, 174 pp...................... 48.00 63.00

☐ **Kohler Co.** *Planned Plumbing and Heating Catalogue K-39.* Kohler, Wisconsin, 1939. Soft covered, 152 pp. 14.00 18.00

☐ **Landreth and Sons.** *Specialties in Vegetable Garden Seeds.* Philadelphia, 1888. Soft covered, 32 pp.......... 21.00 27.00

☐ **Leroy, W. D.** *Leroy's Mammoth Pictorial 20th Century Up-To-Date Illustrated Catalogue: Conjuring Wonders, Magic, Second Sight Illusions, etc.* Boston, n.d., c. 1905–1910. Soft covered, 212 pp. 43.00 58.00
W. D. Leroy was a member of a famous family of professional magicians.

☐ **Loeser and Co.** *Catalogue of Fine Silver Plate and Sterling Silver.* Brooklyn, New York, n.d., c. 1890–1900. Soft covered, 24 pp. 24.00 31.00

☐ **Louden Machinery Co.** *Illustrated Catalogue of the Louden Hay Tools, Fruits of 24 Years in the Hay Field.* Fairfield, Iowa, 1890. Soft covered. 40 pp........................ 24.00 31.00
"24 Years in the Hay Field" was probably not intended as a pun.

☐ **Lovejoy Tool Co.** *Metal Cutting Tools of the Positive Lock Inserted-Cutter Type.* Springfield, Vermont, 1918. Soft covered, 16 pp. 14.00 19.00

☐ **Lozier and Co.** *Cleveland Safety Bicycles.* Chicago, 1893. Soft covered, 24 pp. 21.00 27.00

☐ **Marshall Field and Co.** *Iron and Steel Bedsteads, Brass Bedsteads, Couches, Cribs, Cots, Springs, Mantel Folding Beds, etc.* Spring, 1910. Chicago. Soft covered, 24 pp. .. 25.00 32.00

☐ **Martinka and Co.** *Illustrated and Descriptive Catalogue of New and Superior Conjuring Wonders.* New York, 1898. Soft covered, 144 pp. 53.00 68.00
Among collectors of magic supplies catalogues, those of Martinka are rated the highest. Compared to some of the company's huge catalogues, this one is small. Prices easily get over $100 on the large ones.

☐ **Mason Electric Co.** *Mason's New Battery System Electric Lighting and Power.* New York, n.d., c. 1890–1895. Soft covered, 28 pp.. 37.00 45.00

PRICE RANGE

The use of dry cell batteries was then in its infancy. At first there were ambitious proposals to use battery power for home and industrial electricity, thereby eliminating power lines and utility bills; but this never came to pass.

☐ **McCormick Machines.** *Unsurpassable, Unapproachable McCormick Harvesting Machine.* Chicago, 1883. Soft covered, 24 pp. 17.00   23.00

This was one of the numerous companies headed by Cyrus McCormick. In the Chicago Fire both he and his neighbor Marshall Field were totally burned out, losing millions of dollars worth of stock, and both continued in business as if the fire had been a minor annoyance.

☐ **McDonald and Morrison Manufacturing Co.** *Iron and Wood Pumps.* Dubuque, Iowa, 1909. Soft covered, 231 pp. 25.00   32.00

☐ **McGraw-Yarbrough Co.** *Catalogue H, Jobbers of Plumbing Supplies.* Richmond, 1915. Soft covered, 336 pp. 14.00   19.00

☐ **McKinney Manufacturing Co.** *Hardware, Catalogue 27.* Pittsburg, 1923. . . . .   16.00   21.00

☐ **Miller Lock Co.** *Champion Locks, Catalogue 9.* Philadelphia, n.d., c. 1885–1895. Soft covered, 16 pp. 22.00   28.00

☐ **Montague and Co.** *Revolution in the Clothing Trade.* Greenfield, Massachusetts, 1860. Soft covered, 16 pp. . . .   23.00   31.00

☐ **Muncie Jobbing and Manufacturing Co.** *Items for Carriage Makers.* Indiana, 1898. Soft covered, 256 pp. 32.00   42.00

☐ **Murray Manufacturing Co.** *Vehicle, Harnesses and Saddles.* Cincinnati, 1899. Soft covered, 130 pp. 43.00   56.00

☐ **Myers and Brother.** *Catalogue and Price List of Pumps, Hay Tools, Cylinders, etc.* Ashland, Ohio, n.d., c. 1900–1910. . . . .   20.00   25.00

☐ **National Enameling and Stamping Co.** *Cooking Ware, Milk Cans, Wash Boilers, Pantry Sets, Well Buckets, etc.* Milwaukee, n.d., c. 1920–1930. . . . .   22.00   28.00

☐ **Neverslip Horseshoe Co.** *Catalogue and Sales Brochure.* Boston, 1885. Soft covered, 48 pp. 16.00   21.00

☐ **New York Iron Roofing and Corrugating Co.** *Iron Roofing.* New York, n.d., c. 1885–1890, 12 pp. 10.00   14.00

☐ **New York Liquid Slate Roofing Co.** *Protect Your Building by Use of Kelly's Patent Liquid Slate Roofing Paint.* New York, n.d., c. 1870–1880. . . . .   22.00   28.00

☐ **Nigara Blue Ribbon Co.** *Wallpaper.* New York, n.d., c. 1920–1930. . . . .   16.00   21.00

☐ **Olney and Warren.** *Catalogue 3, Steam Engines and Boilers.* New York, n.d., c. 1890–1900. Soft covered, 40 pp. 27.00   35.00

☐ **Onondaga Litholite Co.** *Onondaga Cut Cast Stone.* Syracuse, New York, 1925. Soft covered, 47 pp. 19.00   24.00

☐ **Overton Co.** *Artistic Wood Carvings.* South Haven, Michigan, n.d., c. 1920–1930. Soft covered, 62 pp. 22.00   28.00

☐ **Page Woven Wire Fence Co.** *Jubilee Catalogue, Twenty Fifth Season of Page Woven Wire Fence C.* Adrian, Michigan, 1909. Soft covered, 32 pp. 19.00   25.00

PRICE RANGE

☐ **Percival and Co.** *Sterling Silver Bags.* Boston, n.d., c. 1900–1910. Soft covered, 100 pp. 63.00   79.00
These are purses of various types, all made with sterling silver.

☐ **Philadelphia Lawn Mower Co.** *Genuine Philadelphia Lawn Mower.* Philadelphia, 1897. Soft covered, 18 pp. 13.00   17.00

☐ **Piedmont Red Cedar Chest Co.** *Piedmont Old Fashioned Moth Proof Red Cedar Chests.* Statesville, North Caroline, 1921. Soft covered, 48 pp. 16.00   21.00

☐ **Pieffer Brothers.** *Catalogue of Rubber Stamps.* Philadelphia, n.d., c. 1885–1895. Soft covered, 142 pp. 16.00   21.00

☐ **Pike Manufacturing Co.** *Pike Razor Strops.* Pike, New Hampshire, 1925. Soft covered, 16 pp. 20.00   25.00

☐ **Pioneer House.** *Sewing Machines.* New York, 1894. Soft covered, 112 pp. 27.00   35.00
This was not a manufacturer but an agent which handled products of various sewing machine makers.

☐ **Pioneer Iron Works.** *Machinery for Sugar Plantations.* Brooklyn, New York, n.d., c. 1890–1900. Soft covered, 35 pp. 45.00   58.00

☐ **Pittsburgh Plate Glass Co.** *Paints, Varnishes and Brushes.* Pittsburgh, 1923. Clothbound, 196 pp. 19.00   25.00
Also gives a history of these items.

☐ **Planet Junior.** *Farm and Garden Implements.* Philadelphia, 1908. Soft covered, 56 pp. 16.00   21.00

☐ **Pompeian Garden Furniture Co.** *Pompeian Garden Furniture.* New York, 1932. Soft covered, 32 pp. 14.00   24.00
The so-called "Pompeian" style (which was used in interior furnishings, too) was based loosely on items excavated from the city of Pompeii in Italy. The Pompeian Garden Furniture was manufactured in Carrara, Italy.

☐ **Pratt and Whitney.** *Gauges, Reamers, Testing Machines.* Hartford, Connecticut, 1893. Soft covered. 20.00   25.00
This company was also a firearms maker, but none are included in this catalogue.

☐ **Quimby and Co.** *Sportsmen's Goods.* New York, n.d., c. 1885–1890. Soft covered, 27 pp. 27.00   35.00

☐ **Radford, William.** *Radford's Garages and How to Build Them.* Chicago, 1910. Clothbound. 26.00   33.00

☐ **Reading Hardware.** *Illustrated Catalogue and Price List of the Reading Hardware Works, Manufacturers of Building, House Furnishings and Misc. Hardware.* Philadelphia, 1868. Soft cloth binding, 84 pp. 80.00   110.00

☐ **Reading Hardware Co.** *Fine Locks and Builders' Hardware.* Reading, Pennsylvania, 1899. Clothbound, 448 pp. 39.00   49.00

☐ **Risdon-Alcott Turbine Co.** *Descriptive Catalogue.* Mount Holly, New Jersey, n.d., c. 1900–1910. . . . .   19.00   24.00

☐ **Ritchie and Sons.** *Illustrated Catalogue of School Apparatus, Simplified and combined, with Directions for Use.* Brookline, Massachusetts, 1888. Soft covered, 34 pp. 25.00   33.00

☐ **Ritchie and Sons.** *Ritchie's Catalogue of Physical Instruments and School Apparatus.* Boston, 1877. Soft covered, 116 pp. 69.00   88.00

PRICE RANGE

☐ **Roberts and Co.** *Catalogue of Doors, Glazed Sash, Blinds, Mouldings, Fine Stairwork, etc.* Chicago, 1897. Soft covered, 150 pp. 48.00 63.00

☐ **Roes, E. P.** *New Descriptive Catalogue and Price List (seeds). Summer and Fall, 1879.* Cornwall on Hudson, New York, 1879. Soft covered, 24 pp. 20.00 25.00

☐ **Rogers and Brother.** *Price List of the Celebrated Rogers and Brother A-1 Electro Silver Plated Spoons, Forks, Knives, etc.* Waterbury, Connecticut, 1892. Soft covered, 110 pp. 28.00 37.00

☐ **Russell and Co.** *The Russell Steam Road-Roller.* Massillon, Ohio, n.d., c. 1880–1890. Soft covered, 12 pp. 17.00 23.00

☐ **Sackett Electric Co.** *Electric Lamps.* Buffalo, New York, c. 1920–1930. Soft covered, 8 pp. 28.00 36.00

☐ **Sargent George F.** *Rolling Chairs, Carrying Chairs.* New York, 1913. Soft covered. 38.00 49.00
The expression "wheelchair" had not yet come into general use.

☐ **Sargent and Greenleaf Co.** *Catalogue 12, Locks.* Rochester, New York, 1907. .... 35.00 44.00

☐ **Sargent Manufacturing Co.** *Invalid Beds, Commodes, Reclining Chairs, Hospital and Sickroom Accessories.* Muskegon, Michigan, n.d., c. 1890–1900. Soft covered, 8 pp. 16.00 21.00

☐ **Schmidt, W. and E.** *Church Goods, Cummion Ware, Flagons, Baptismal Water Pitchers, Goblets, Communion Plates, Host Boxes, Private Communion Sets, Baptismal Bowls, Candlesticks, etc.* Milwaukee, n.d., c. 1860–1870. Soft covered, 40 pp. 26.00 35.00

☐ **Schoenhut Co.** *Illustrations of Schoenhut's Marvelous Toys, The Humpty Dumpty Circus.* Philadelphia, 1904. Soft covered, 36 pp. 95.00 115.00

☐ **Sheldon and Co.** *Catalogue 20, Industrial, School, and Laboratory Furniture.* Muskegon, Michigan, n.d., c. 1920–1930. Soft covered, 88 pp. 16.00 21.00

☐ **Singer Manufacturing Co.** *Catalogue of Singer Sewing Machines for Family Use.* New York, 1893. Soft covered, 32 pp. 22.00 28.00

☐ **Singer, Wheeler and Wilson.** *Catalogue of Sewing Machines for Family Use.* N.p., 1908. Soft covered, 32 pp. ... 17.00 23.00

☐ **Smith and Holtum Manufacturing Co.** *Cement Tools.* Clinton, Wisconsin, 1910. Soft covered, 24 pp. 11.00 16.00

☐ **Smutz Harness Store, Annual Sale.** Corry, Pennsylvania, 1895. Soft covered, 4 pp. 19.00 24.00

☐ **Stevens and Brothers.** *Fall and Winter Special Catalogue of Charles A. Stevens and Brothers, of Fine Cloaks and Silks.* Chicago, 1897–1898. Soft covered, 40 pp. 22.00 28.00

☐ **Stevens and Brothers.** *Spring Catalogue of Silks, Millinery, Suits, Waists and Skirts, Laces, Grenadines, Black Goods, Ribbons, Underwear, etc.* Chicago, 1898. Soft covered, 48 pp. 16.00 21.00

PRICE RANGE

☐ **Stevens Arms and Tool Co.** *Catalogue Number 50.* Chicopee Falls, Massachusetts, 1902. Soft covered, 128 pp.. 48.00 65.00
Shotguns, pistols, rifles, shooters' accessories, a few auto items.

☐ **Stewart Iron Works Co.** *Stewart's Iron Fence.* Cincinnati, 1914. Soft covered, 80 pp. 17.00 23.00

☐ **Stickley, L. and J. G.** *The Work of L. and J. G. Stickley (furniture).* Fayetteville, North Carolina, n.d., c. 1920–1930. Soft covered, 55 pp. 68.00 87.00

☐ **Technical Supply Co.** *Catalogue of Drawing Materials, Mathematical, Engineering and Scientific Instruments.* Scranton, Pennsylvania, n.d., early twentieth century. Soft covered... 16.00 21.00

☐ **Troemner, Henry.** *Price List of Steel Pivot, Steel and Agate Bearing Scales.* Philadelphia, 1908. Soft covered, 100 pp... 41.00 54.00

☐ **Troy Fire Brickworks.** *Fire Brick.* Troy, New York, 1861. Soft covered.. 27.00 36.00

☐ **Tubbs and Co.** *Penobscot Snowshoes and Accessories.* Norway, Maine, 1931. Soft covered, 19 pp. 14.00 19.00

☐ **Tuck Manufacturing Co.** *Tuck's tools.* Brockton, Massachusetts, n.d., c. 1900–1910. Soft covered, 48 pp........ 14.00 19.00

☐ **U.S. Buggy and Cart Co.** *Manufacturers of Buggies, Phaetons, Carriages, Carts, Wagons.* Cincinnati, 1902.... 24.00 32.00

☐ **Van Nostrand.** *Catalogue of American and Foreign Scientific Books For Sale by D. Van Nostrand, Publisher and Importer.* New York, 1887. Soft covered. 26.00 35.00

☐ **Vermont Marble Co.** *Memorial Designs in Vermont Marble.* Proctor, Vermont, n.d., c. 1910–1920. Soft covered, 287 pp.. 18.00 24.00

☐ **Warren Manufacturing Co.** *Makers of Riegels Paper.* Riegelsville, New Jersey (also other locations), n.d., c. 1900–1910. Soft covered, 36 pp. 27.00 36.00

☐ **Washburn and Moen Manufacturing Co.** *The Brinkerhoff Patent Metallic Fencing, Galvanized, With or Without Barbs.* Worcester, Massachusetts, 1879. Soft covered.......... 24.00 32.00

☐ **Webster, Frank B.** *Naturalist's Supply Depot: Bird Skins.* Boston, 1887. Soft covered, 6 pp....................... 12.00 17.00

☐ **Werner and Pfleiderer.** *Installations and Apparatus for Producing Food.* London, 1893. Soft covered, 52 pp. 53.00 69.00
Kneading and mixing machinery, implements for making spaghetti, macaroni, breads, sausages, etc.

☐ **Western Wheeled Scraper Co.** *Western Machinery For Handling Earth and Stone.* Aurora, Illinois, n.d., c. 1890–1900. .... 36.00 47.00

☐ **Western Wheeled Scraper Co.** *Western Rock Crusher.* Aurora, Illinois, n.d., c. 1890–1900. Soft covoered, 16 pp.. 16.00 21.00

TURN OF THE CENTURY BOOKS

Until a relatively few years ago, "turn of the century books" would not have been considered a recognized category for bibliophiles. Book lovers have long been fond of these works, but they have traditionally taken their place in specialized collections rather than comprising a specialty in themselves. Turn of the century literature, for example, was absorbed into literature collections or special author collections. Today a growing interest has developed in these books as a species unto themselves and one finds collections of turn of the century books in which the subject matter is diverse. Fiction and non-fiction are often included, and a really fine collection will also comprise a selection of the exquisite trade and craft bindings of that era. As book illustration reached a pinnacle at that time, it is natural that illustrated books would be a prime ingredient in such a collection.

The following listings will give a general indication of the types of volumes available to collectors, and the prices one may expect to pay for them. Collectors of turn of the century books are understandably very date conscious. The general rule is to exclude titles published before 1890 or after 1910, but exceptions are made (such as to include writings of authors whose careers, while established in the 1890–1910 era, continued later). Thus we have not held strictly to the 1890–1910 time frame in selecting works to be listed.

While literally any book of this era could be collected as a turn of the century volume, the more advanced or refined hobbyists do impose certain guidelines on their collection. Their primary goal is books that vividly reflect the age in which they were created. Social attitudes expressed in works of fiction stamp them as leading "documents" of the 1890–1910 period. The same may be said of works showing fashions, interior decorations, architecture, or any other changing aspect of daily life. This can also be carried further, to the books themselves as works of design, art and craft. With labor and other production costs low, it was possible for publishers to create very distinctive and handsome books. Many different styles of typeface were used in the publishing industry of 1890–1910, as well as numerous kinds of paper, decorative endleaves, and binding materials. One will find a fair percentage of books from this era printed on finely textured rag-content paper. Though the age of gilt stamped bindings had waned somewhat by 1890, owing to the introduction of dust jackets, many excellent specimens of such bindings can be found on turn of the century editions. These intriguing touches of paper, type and binding give turn of the century books an additional appeal, which likewise is typical of their era. Happily for the average collector, turn of the century books are available in all price ranges. This is a category in which inroads may be made on any budget. The opportunities are frequent, as these books, being fairly modern compared to some groups of collectible books, are offered by virtually every professional dealer. They are even found in abundance outside the antiquarian bookshops, for example in antiques shops and at antiques shows. Estate sales are another fertile source.

PRICE RANGE

☐ **Aristophanes.** *The Eleven Comedies,* completely translated. London, published by the Athenian Society for members only, 1912. Two volumes bound in half green morocco with gilt tops. 60.00 75.00

☐ **Barham, Thomas.** *The Ingoldsby Legends.* With 24 plates by Arthur Rackham. London, 1907. .... 125.00 150.00

☐ **Barrie, J. M.** *Quality Street.* With 22 plates by Hugh Thompson. London, 1901. .... 45.00 60.00

☐ **Bell, Walter.** *Fleet Street in Seven Centuries.* London, 1912. .... 12.00 16.00

☐ **Besant, Walter.** *East London.* London, 1901. With 54 illustrations, bound in half crimson levant morocco. 60.00 75.00

☐ **Blackie, John S.** *Selected Poems.* London, 1896. Bound in blue levant morocco. 50.00 65.00

☐ **Blunt, Wilfred.** *A New Pilgrimage and Other Poems.* London, printed at the Chiswick Press, 1889. Clothbound. ... 20.00 25.00

☐ **Bradbury, Frederick.** *The History of Old Sheffield Plate.* London, 1912. Clothbound. 200.00 260.00

☐ **Broadley, A. M.** *The Boyhood of a Great King. An Account of the Early Years of His Majesty Edward VII.* New York, 1906. Limited to 125 copies bound in mauve morocco, gilt back. 100.00 125.00

☐ **Bronte Sisters.** *The Novels of Charlotte and Emily Bronte,* edited by *Temple Scott.* Thornton Edition. Edinburgh, 1911. Twelve volumes. 150.00 175.00

☐ **Cervantes, Miguel de.** *The History of the Ingenious Gentleman Don Quixote.* Translated by P. A. Motteux. Edinburgh, 1910. Four volumes. 70.00 90.00

☐ **Chaffers, William.** *The Collector's Hand Book of Marks and Monograms on Pottery and Porcelain.* London, 1908. Not first edition. 12.00 16.00

☐ **Chapman, A.** *Unexplored Spain.* London, 1910. .... 40.00 50.00

☐ **Chesterton, G. K.** *A Picture of Tuesday.* London, 1896. 14.00 18.00

☐ **Chesterton, G. K.** *The Ball and the Cross.* London, 1910. .... 18.00 24.00

☐ **Chesterton, G. K.** *Five Types.* London, 1910. Softbound. 18.00 24.00

☐ **Chesterton, G. K.** *Christiana and Her Children.* London, 1914. Boards. 22.00 28.00

☐ **Chesterton, G. K.** *The Man Who Knew Too Much.* London, 1922. .... 30.00 38.00

☐ **Chesterton, G. K.** *Do We Agree?.* London, 1928. .... 16.00 22.00

☐ **Chesterton, G. K.** *The Sword of Wood.* London, 1928. .. 30.00 38.00

☐ **Chesterton, G. K.** *Eyes of Youth.* London, n.d. 15.00 20.00

☐ **Churchill, Sir Winston S.** *London to Ladysmith via Pretoria.* London, 1900. Bound in pictorial cloth. 125.00 150.00
Churchill's experiences in the Boer War.

☐ **Churchill, Sir Winston S.** *The Story of the Malakand Field Force.* London, 1898. Cloth bound. 1600.00 2000.00
This is the scarcest of Churchill's first editions, published long before he had achieved international fame.

☐ **Conrad, Joseph.** *Almayer's Folly.* N.Y., 1895. First American edition. 125.00 160.00

PRICE RANGE

☐ **Conrad, Joseph.** *An Outcast of the Islands.* N.Y., 1896.	12.00	16.00
☐ **Conrad, Joseph.** *The Nigger of the Narcissus.* London, 1898.	360.00	435.00
☐ **Conrad, Joseph.** *Typhoon.* London, 1903. Black cloth. . .	67.00	83.00
☐ **Conrad, Joseph.** *The Secret Agent.* London, 1907.	34.00	43.00
☐ **Conrad, Joseph.** *A Set of Six.* London, 1908.	42.00	57.00
☐ **Conrad, Joseph.** *Under Western Eyes.* London, 1911. . . .	30.00	38.00
☐ **Conrad, Joseph.** *Chance.* London, 1914.	27.00	35.00
☐ **Conrad, Joseph.** *Victory.* London, 1915.	27.00	35.00
☐ **Conrad, Joseph.** *The Shadow Line.* London, 1917.	21.00	27.00
☐ **Conrad, Joseph.** *The Arrow of Gold.* London, 1919.	42.00	58.00
☐ **Conrad, Joseph.** *One More Day.* London, 1919. Limited edition.	34.00	43.00
☐ **Conrad, Joseph.** *The Rescue.* London, 1920.	21.00	28.00
☐ **Conrad, Joseph.** *The Rover.* London, 1923.	21.00	28.00
☐ **Conrad, Joseph.** *Suspence.* London, 1925.	27.00	36.00
☐ **Conrad, Joseph.** *The Sisters.* N.Y., 1928.	27.00	36.00
☐ **Coryat, Thomas.** *Coryat's Crudities.* Glasgow, 1905. Two volumes.	70.00	90.00
☐ **Crisp, Frederick A.** *Armorial China.* London, 1907. Limited to 150 privately printed copies on handmade paper, with 12 colored plates, bound in half vellum.	190.00	235.00
☐ **Darwin, Charles.** *Journal of Researches Into the Natural History and Geology . . . During the Voyage Round the World of H.M.S. Beagle.* London, 1890. With illustrations by R. T. Pritchett, bound in cloth. . . . . Though not the first edition, this was the first to carry illustrations.	20.00	25.00
☐ **Dawber, Guy.** *Old Cottages, Farm Houses and Other Stone Buildings in the Cotswold District.* London, 1905.	40.00	50.00
☐ **DeQuincey, Thomas.** *Collected Writings of Thomas DeQuincey.* London, 1896. Fourteen volumes.	175.00	200.00
☐ **Detmold, Edward J.** (illustrator). *Aesop's Fables.* London, 1909, with 23 colored plates, bound in gilt cloth.	25.00	32.00
☐ **Dobson, Austin.** *The Ballad of Beau Brocade.* Illustrated by Hugh Thompson. London, 1892. Limited to 450 copies.	35.00	45.00
☐ **Doyle, Arthur C.** *Jelland's Voyage.* London, 1892. Softbound.	21.00	29.00
☐ **Doyle, Arthur C.** *The Lost World.* London, n.d.	38.00	47.00
☐ **Doyle, Arthur C.** *The Adventures of Sherlock Holmes.* London, 1892–94. Two vols., blue cloth.	285.00	365.00
☐ **Doyle, Arthur C.** *The Adventures of Sherlock Holmes.* N.Y., n.d., 1892. Blue cloth, not the first issue.	30.00	39.00
☐ **Doyle, Arthur C.** *My Friend the Murderer.* N.Y., n.d., 1893.	30.00	39.00
☐ **Doyle, Arthur C.** *The Memoirs of Sherlock Holmes.* London, 1894. Dark blue cloth.	240.00	290.00
☐ **Doyle, Arthur C.** *The Stark Munro Letters.* London, 1895.	85.00	115.00
☐ **Doyle, Arthur C.** *The Exploits of Brigadier Gerard.* London, 1896.	40.00	52.00
☐ **Doyle, Arthur C.** *The Parasite.* London, 1897.	28.00	36.00

PRICE RANGE

☐ **Doyle, Arthur C.** *The Hound of the Baskervilles.* London, 1902. Red cloth. 550.00 700.00

☐ **Doyle, Arthur C.** *The Return of Sherlock Holmes.* London, 1904. Dark blue cloth. 450.00 550.00

☐ **Doyle, Arthur C.** *Sir Nigel.* London, 1906. . . . . 185.00 230.00

☐ **Doyle, Arthur C.** *The Croxley Master.* N.Y., 1907. . . . . 325.00 400.00

☐ **Doyle, Arthur C.** *Songs of the Road.* London, 1911. . . . . 42.00 54.00

☐ **Doyle, Arthur C.** *The Poison Belt.* N.Y., 1913. . . . . 42.00 54.00

☐ **Doyle, Arthur C.** *The British Campaign.* London, 1916–19. Six vols. 63.00 83.00

☐ **Doyle, Arthur C.** *The Coming of the Fairies.* London, 1922. . . . . 40.00 52.00

☐ **Doyle, Arthur C.** *The Case Book of Sherlock Holmes.* London, n.d., 1927. Red cloth. 115.00 145.00

☐ **Dulac, Edmund.** *Stories From Hans Anderson.* London, 1911. Limited to 750 copies signed by Dulac, bound in vellum. 320.00 375.00

☐ **Evelyn, John.** *The Diary and Correspondence of John Evelyn.* Edited by William Bray, F.S.A. London, 1906. Four volumes. 60.00 75.00

☐ **Fisher, Arthur.** *Outdoor Life in England.* London, 1896. 9.00 12.00

☐ **Flint, William R.** *The Heroes, or Greek Fairy Tales for my Children.* Illustrated by Charles Kingsley. London, published by the Medici Society, 1912. Limited to 500 copies, bound in limp vellum. 300.00 400.00

☐ **Froude, James.** *The English in the West Indies.* London, 1888. Woodcuts by G. Pearson. Bound in gilt calf. 60.00 75.00

☐ **Galsworthy, John.** *The Slaughter of Animals for Food.* London, n.d. 80.00 100.00

☐ **Galsworthy, John.** *The Man of Property.* N.Y., 1906. . . . . 45.00 60.00

☐ **Galsworthy, John.** *Awakening.* London, n.d. 20.00 25.00

☐ **Galsworthy, John.** *Inn of Tranquility.* London, 1912. . . . . . 30.00 40.00

☐ **Galsworthy, John.** *The Dark Flower.* London, 1913. . . . . . 42.00 55.00

☐ **Galsworthy, John.** *In Land.* London, 1918. . . . . 35.00 42.00

☐ **Galsworthy, John.** *Five Tales.* London, 1919. . . . . 20.00 25.00

☐ **Galsworthy, John.** *Another Sheaf.* London, 1919. . . . . 20.00 25.00

☐ **Galsworthy, John.** *The Foundations.* London, 1920. . . . . . 30.00 38.00

☐ **Galsworthy, John.** *The Bells of Peace.* Cambridge, 1921. . . . . 20.00 25.00

☐ **Galsworthy, John.** *The Forsyte Sage.* N.Y., 1922. . . . . . . 30.00 38.00

☐ **Galsworthy, John.** *Caravan.* London, 1924. . . . . 34.00 42.00

☐ **Galsworthy, John.** *The Show.* London, 1925. . . . . 22.00 28.00

☐ **Galsworthy, John.** *Carmen.* London, 1925. . . . . 28.00 34.00

☐ **Galsworthy, John.** *Swan Song.* London, 1928. Signed. 45.00 60.00

☐ **Galsworthy, John.** *A Modern Comedy.* London, 1929. . . 22.00 29.00

☐ **Galsworthy, John.** *Soames and the Flag.* London, 1930. Signed. 22.00 29.00

☐ **Galsworthy, John.** *Flowering Wilderness.* London, 1932. . . . . 28.00 34.00

☐ **Galsworthy, John.** *Author and Critic.* N.Y., 1933. . . . . 27.00 33.00

☐ **Galsworthy, John.** *Glimpses and Reflections.* London, 1937. . . . . 20.00 25.00

PRICE RANGE

☐ **Goldsmith, Oliver.** *She Stoops to Conquer.* London, published by Hodder and Stoughton, undated, c. 1900. With 25 plates by Hugh Thompson, limited to 350 copies signed by the artist. 110.00   140.00

☐ **Green, John R.** *A Short History of the English People.* Illustrated Library Edition. London, 1892. Four volumes bound in half levant morocco, backs gilt. 70.00   85.00

☐ **Greene, Robert.** *The Plays and Poems of Robert Greene.* Oxford, 1905. Two volumes. 65.00   75.00

☐ **Grey, Zane.** *The Last of the Plainsmen.* Toronto, n.d., 1908. . . . .   50.00   70.00

☐ **Grey, Zane.** *Tales of Lonely Trails.* N.Y. and London, n.d., 1922. . . . .   40.00   55.00

☐ **Grey, Zane.** *Under the Toronto Rim.* Toronto and N.Y., n.d., 1926. . . . .   20.00   25.00

☐ **Hagenbeck, Carl.** *Beasts and Men.* London, 1909. With one hundred illustrations. 40.00   50.00

☐ **Hartshorne, Albert.** *Old English Glasses. An Account of Glass Drinking Vessels in England from Early Times to the End of the Eighteenth Century.* New York, 1897. . . . .   225.00   275.00

☐ **Hay, Sir John C.** *The Suppression of Piracy in the China Sea.* London, 1889. With a folding map. 22.00   27.00

☐ **Henley, William E.** *Robert Burns' Life, Genius and Achievement.* Edinburgh, 1898. . . . .   22.00   27.00

☐ **Herbert, Agnes.** *Two Dianas in Alaska.* London, 1909. With 29 plates, bound in cloth. 15.00   20.00
The "two Dianas" were the author and her cousin. This is a non-fiction account of their adventures in the Yukon.

☐ **Hobson, R. L.** *Worcester Porcelain.* London, 1910. Bound in dark blue cloth, gilt design on front cover, gilt top. 200.00   250.00

☐ **Hudson, W. H.** *The Land's End.* London, 1908. . . . .   22.00   27.00

☐ **Humphreys, Sydney.** *Oriental Carpets, Runners and Rugs.* London, 1910. With 24 colored plates, bound in buckram with top edge gilt. 100.00   125.00

☐ **Hunt, William and Reginald Poole.** *The Political History of England.* London, 1906–1910. Twelve volumes, bound in gilt calf. 225.00   275.00

☐ **Jackson, Sir Charles J.** *An Illustrated History of English Plate.* London, 1911. Two volumes, with 76 photographic plates, bound in half green morocco. 750.00   1000.00

☐ **James, Henry.** *Transatlantic Sketches.* Boston, 1875. Green cloth. 230.00   290.00

☐ **James, Henry.** *The American.* Boston, 1877. Green cloth. 130.00   165.00

☐ **James, Henry.** *Confidence.* Boston, 1880. Green cloth. 80.00   100.00

☐ **James, Henry.** *Daisy Miller.* London, 1880. Blue cloth. . . .   21.00   27.00

☐ **James, Henry.** *The Portrait of a Lady.* Boston, 1882. Brown cloth, scarce. 425.00   550.00

☐ **James, Henry.** *A Light Man.* N.Y. 1884. . . . .   21.00   27.00

☐ **James, Henry.** *The Author of Beltraffio.* Boston, 1885. . . .   45.00   57.00

☐ **James, Henry.** *Terminations.* London, 1895. . . . .   21.00   27.00

☐ **James, Henry.** *Embarrassment.* London, 1896. . . . .   32.00   40.00

PRICE RANGE

☐ **James, Henry.** *What Maisie Knew.* Chicago and N.Y.,
1897. . . . . 175.00   230.00
☐ **James, Henry.** *The Awkward Age.* N.Y., 1899. . . . . 21.00   27.00
☐ **James, Henry.** *The Sacred Fount.* N.Y., 1901. Brown
cloth. 77.00   103.00
☐ **James, Henry.** *The Ambassadors.* N.Y., 1903. . . . . 130.00   170.00
☐ **James, Henry.** *The American Scene.* London, 1907. Red
cloth. 63.00   85.00
☐ **Jones, E. Alfred.** *The Gold and Silver of Windsor Castle.*
Letchworth, England, 1911. With 130 plates. 100.00   125.00
☐ **Kennedy, Rankin.** *The Book of the Motor Car. A Compre-
hensive and Authoritative Guide on the Care, Manage-
ment, Maintenance and Construction of the Motor Car and
Motor Cycle.* London, 1913. Three volumes. 400.00   500.00
☐ **Kipling, Rudyard.** *The Jungle Book.* London, 1894. Two
vols., blue cloth. 210.00   265.00
☐ **Kipling, Rudyard.** *Captains Courageous.* London, 1897.
Blue cloth. 52.00   67.00
☐ **Kipling, Rudyard.** *The Day's Work.* London, 1898. . . . . . . 32.00   43.00
☐ **Kipling, Rudyard.** *Stalky & Co.* N.Y., 1899. . . . . 43.00   58.00
☐ **Kipling, Rudyard.** *Stalky & Co.* London, 1899. . . . . 49.00   65.00
☐ **Kipling, Rudyard.** *Barracks Room Ballads.* N.Y., 1899. 21.00   26.00
☐ **Kipling, Rudyard.** *Kim.* London, 1901. . . . . 43.00   58.00
☐ **Kipling, Rudyard.** *Just So Stories.* London, 1920. . . . . 70.00   90.00
☐ **Kipling, Rudyard.** *They.* London, 1905. White cloth. 52.00   67.00
☐ **Kipling, Rudyard.** *Abaft the Funnell.* N.Y., 1909. . . . . 39.00   50.00
☐ **Kipling, Rudyard.** *Limits and Renewals.* London, 1932. 21.00   26.00
☐ **Lamb, Charles and Mary.** *Tales From Shakespeare.* With
18 plates by Arthur Rackham. London, 1909. Limited to
750 copies signed by the artist. 700.00   900.00
☐ **Lawrence, D. H.** *Sons and Lovers.* London, 1913. Dark
blue cloth. 400.00   500.00
☐ **Lawrence, D. H.** *The Prussian Officer.* London, 1914. . . . 85.00   110.00
☐ **Lawrence, D. H.** *Eight Poems.* Chicago, 1914. Soft-
bound. 23.00   31.00
☐ **Lawrence, D. H.** *Look! We Have Come Through!* London,
1914. . . . . 175.00   225.00
☐ **Lawrence, D. H.** *Aaron's Rod.* London, 1922. . . . . 29.00   39.00
☐ **Lawrence, D. H.** *Kangaroo.* N.Y., 1923. . . . . 40.00   52.00
☐ **Lawrence, D. H.** *The Boy in the Bush.* London, 1924. . . . 40.00   52.00
☐ **Lawrence, D. H.** *England, My England.* London, 1924. . . 40.00   52.00
☐ **Lawrence, D. H.** *St. Mawr.* London, n.d., 1925. Brown
cloth. 45.00   58.00
☐ **Lawrence, D. H.** *St. Mawr.* N.Y., 1925. . . . . 23.00   31.00
☐ **Lawrence, D. H.** *Movements in European History.* Oxford,
1925. . . . . 85.00   105.00
☐ **Lawrence, D. H.** *Reflections on the Death of a Porcupine.*
London, 1925. . . . . 45.00   59.00
☐ **Lawrence, D. H.** *David.* London, 1926. . . . . 115.00   160.00
☐ **Lawrence, D. H.** *Lady Chatterley's Lover.* N.p. (Florence,
Italy, 1928). 1175.00   1450.00
☐ **Lawrence, D. H.** *Pansies.* London, 1929. . . . . 300.00   400.00
☐ **Lawrence, D. H.** *Pornography and Obscenity.* London,
1929. . . . . 40.00   52.00

PRICE RANGE

☐ **Lawrence, D. H.** *Mr. Skirmish with Jolly Roger.* N.Y., 1929. Boards. 65.00   85.00

☐ **Lawrence, D. H.** *Birds, Beasts and Flowers.* London, 1930. . . . . 110.00   160.00

☐ **Lawrence, D. H.** *Assorted Articles.* N.Y., 1930. . . . . 37.00   48.00

☐ **Lawrence, D. H.** *The Lovely Lady.* London, 1932. . . . . 37.00   48.00

☐ **Lawrence, D. H.** *The Man Who Died.* London, 1935. . . . . 22.00   28.00

☐ **Lawrence, D. H.** *Phoenix.* London, 1936. Brown cloth. . . . 43.00   54.00

☐ **Lawrence, D. H.** *Amores.* London, n.d. 63.00   85.00

☐ **London, Jack.** *The Call of the Wild.* N.Y., 1903. . . . . 60.00   80.00

☐ **London, Jack.** *The Sea Wolf.* N.Y., 1904. . . . . 475.00   575.00
First state copies have gold lettering on the spine. The second state has spine lettered in white. And is worth. . . . 200.00   250.00

☐ **London, Jack.** *The Faith of Men.* N.Y., 1904. . . . . 150.00   180.00

☐ **London, Jack.** *The Game.* N.Y., 1905. Green cloth. 43.00   58.00

☐ **London, Jack.** *White Fang.* N.Y., 1906. Blue cloth. 22.00   29.00

☐ **London, Jack.** *The Cruise of the Dazzler.* London, n.d., 1906. . . . . 750.00   1000.00

☐ **London, Jack.** *The Road.* N.Y., 1907. . . . . 21.00   27.00

☐ **London, Jack.** *Before Adam.* N.Y., 1907. Brown cloth. . . . 85.00   120.00

☐ **London, Jack.** *Martin, Eden.* N.Y., 1908. . . . . 21.00   27.00

☐ **London, Jack.** *Revolution.* N.Y., 1910. . . . . 110.00   160.00

☐ **London, Jack.** *Burning Daylight.* N.Y., 1910. . . . . 37.00   52.00

☐ **London, Jack.** *Adventure.* N.Y., 1911. . . . . 375.00   475.00

☐ **London, Jack.** *Smoke Bellow.* N.Y., 1912. . . . . 32.00   43.00

☐ **London, Jack.** *Lost Face.* N.Y., 1913. . . . . 21.00   27.00

☐ **London, Jack.** *John Barleycorn.* N.Y., 1913. . . . . 37.00   48.00

☐ **MacQuoid, Percy.** *A History of English Furniture.* London, 1904–08. Four volumes with a total of 60 colored plates. Bound in half green morocco. 500.00   650.00

☐ **Mallory, Sir Thomas.** *Le Morte d'Arthur.* Reprint of the original Caxton edition. London, 1889. Three volumes, bound in blue half morocco. 175.00   225.00
This was the book which originated the legend of King Arthur.

☐ **Marcus Aurelius.** *The Thoughts of the Emperor.* Translated by George Long. London, printed at the Riccardi Press, 1909. With 12 colored plates by Sir W. R. Flint, bound in limp vellum. 100.00   125.00

☐ **Mawson, Thomas.** *Civic Art.* London, 1911. . . . . 140.00   175.00

☐ **Morris, Rev. F. O.** *A History of British Moths.* London, 1903. Four volumes with 132 plates, bound in cloth. Not first edition. 100.00   125.00

☐ **Morris, William.** *The Collected Works of William Morris.* London, 1910–15. Twenty four volumes. 450.00   550.00

☐ **Mummery, A. F.** *My Climbs in the Alps and Caucasus.* London, 1895. . . . . 30.00   37.00

☐ **Petronius.** *Satyricon, a Revised Latin Text with the Earliest English Translation.* London, privately printed by Ralph Straus, 1910. Bound in boards with a vellum spine. 70.00   85.00

☐ **Plutarch's Lives.** *Dryden's Corrected Translation from the Greek, Revised by A. H. Clough.* London, 1893. Five volumes bound in half morocco. 175.00   200.00

PRICE RANGE

☐ **Rabelais, Francois.** *Five Books of the Lives, Heroic Deeds and Sayings of Gargantua and His Son Pantagruel.* London, 1892. Two volumes, bound in full morocco.......... 110.00 135.00

☐ **Robinson, Frederick S.** *English Furniture.* London, 1905. .... 20.00 25.00

☐ **Rothwell, C. F.** *The Printing of Textile Fabrics.* London, 1897. With 86 actual specimens of fabrics included. Bound in cloth. 180.00 225.00

☐ **Ruskin, John.** *Unto This Last.* London, printed at the Doves Press, 1907. Limited to 300 copies, bound in limp vellum. 125.00 150.00

☐ **Shaw, George Bernard.** *An Unsociable Socialist.* London, 1884. .... 335.00 415.00

☐ **Shaw, George Bernard.** *Cashel Byron's Profession.* London, 1886... 32.00 43.00

☐ **Shaw, George Bernard.** *Fabian Essays in Socialism.* London, 1889... 185.00 250.00

☐ **Shaw, George Bernard.** *Love Among the Artists.* Chicago, 1900... 215.00 315.00

☐ **Shaw, George Bernard.** *The Irrational Knot.* London, 1905. .... 110.00 135.00

☐ **Shaw, George Bernard.** *John Bull's Other Island.* London, 1907. .... 42.00 57.00

☐ **Shaw, George Bernard.** *Dramatic Opinions and Essays.* London, 1907. Two vols. 21.00 32.00

☐ **Shaw, George Bernard.** *Misalliance.* London, 1914...... 28.00 36.00

☐ **Shaw, George Bernard.** *Peach Conference Hints.* London, 1919. .... 25.00 33.00

☐ **Shaw, George Bernard.** *Back to Methuselah.* London, 1921... 140.00 170.00

☐ **Shaw, George Bernard.** *Saint Joan.* London, 1924. ..... 37.00 48.00

☐ **Shaw, George Bernard.** *Translations and Tomfooleries.* London, 1926... 28.00 36.00

☐ **Shaw, George Bernard.** *The Intelligent Woman's Guide to Socialism.* London, 1928............................... 265.00 335.00

☐ **Shaw, George Bernard.** *The League of Nations.* London, 1929. Softbound. 35.00 43.00

☐ **Shaw, George Bernard.** *The Applecart.* London, 1930... 13.00 17.00

☐ **Shaw, George Bernard.** *William Morris as I Knew Him.* N.Y., 1936. .... 28.00 35.00

☐ **Shaw, George Bernard.** *Shaw Gives Himself Away.* London, 1939... 135.00 160.00

☐ **Spelman, W. R.** *Lowestoft China.* London, published by Jarrold, 1905. With 97 plates, 24 of which are in color.... 175.00 225.00

☐ **Step, Edward.** *Wild Flowers Month by Month in Their Natural Haunts.* London, 1905. Two volumes with 166 illustrations. 18.00 23.00

☐ **Stevenson, Robert Louis.** *An Inland Voyage.* London, 1878. Blue cloth.. 130.00 160.00

☐ **Stevenson, Robert Louis.** *Travels with a Donkey.* London, 1879. Green cloth.. 265.00 310.00

☐ **Stevenson, Robert Louis.** *New Arabian Nights.* London, 1882. Two vols., green cloth. 240.00 295.00

PRICE RANGE

☐ **Stevenson, Robert Louis.** *Familiar Studies of Men and Books.* London, 1882. Green cloth. 170.00 215.00

☐ **Stevenson, Robert Louis.** *Treasure Island.* London, 1883. The first issue has ads dated July, 1883. It exists in various colors of cloth binding. 700.00 900.00

☐ **Stevenson, Robert Louis.** *Treasure Island.* Boston, 1884. .... 950.00 1150.00

☐ **Stevenson, Robert Louis.** *Treasure Island.* London, 1885. Red cloth. 200.00 250.00

☐ **Stevenson, Robert Louis.** *Prince Otto.* London, 1885. The ads should be dated January. 200.00 250.00

☐ **Stevenson, Robert Louis.** *A Child's Garden of Verses.* London, 1885. Blue cloth. 350.00 425.00

☐ **Stevenson, Robert Louis.** *Kidnapped.* N.p. (London), 1886. .... 290.00 365.00

The first issue has "business" on page 40, line 11, and is always bound in blue cloth. Second issue is worth around. 70.00 90.00

☐ **Stevenson, Robert Louis.** *The Strange Case of Dr. Jekyll and Mr. Hyde.* London, 1886. $175 for a copy in publisher's pink wrappers, $125 for clothbound. The first American edition, also 1886, is scarcer and worth................. 290.00 365.00

☐ **Stevenson, Robert Louis.** *The Merry Men and Other Tales.* London, 1887. The first issue has 32 pages of ads dated September, 1886. .... 67.00 88.00

☐ **Stevenson, Robert Louis.** *The Black Arrow.* London, 1888. Red cloth. 75.00 95.00

☐ **Stevenson, Robert Louis.** *The Master of Ballantrae.* London, 1889. Red cloth. 67.00 90.00

☐ **Stevenson, Robert Louis.** *The South Seas.* London, 1890. .... 650.00 850.00

☐ **Stevenson, Robert Louis.** *A Footnote to History.* London, 1892. .... 37.00 45.00

☐ **Stevenson, Robert Louis.** *Across the Plains.* London, 1892. Buff cloth, limited to 100 on large paper. 185.00 250.00

☐ **Stevenson, Robert Louis.** *St. Ives.* London, 1898. ...... 42.00 53.00

☐ **Stevenson, Robert Louis.** *A Stevenson Medley.* London, 1899. Limited to 300. .... 47.00 60.00

☐ **Straus, Ralph.** *John Baskerville, a Memoir.* Cambridge, printed at the Baskerville Press, 1907. With thirteen plates, bound in half blue crushed morocco, gilt spine and top edge. Limited to 300 copies. 110.00 135.00

☐ **Street, G. S.** *The Ghosts of Piccadilly.* London, 1907. Cloth bound. 12.00 16.00

☐ **Sue, Eugene.** *The Mysteries of Paris.* London, 1903. Six volumes, with a total of 31 etchings. 50.00 65.00

☐ **Swinburne, Algernon.** *The Poetical Works of A. C. Swinburne.* London, 1904. Six volumes. 200.00 250.00

☐ **Synge, John Millington.** *In the Shadow of the Glen.* N.Y., 1904. Softbound. 1200.00 1600.00

☐ **Synge, John Millington.** *The Well of the Saints.* London, 1905. Softbound. 500.00 650.00

☐ **Synge, John Millington.** *The Aran Islands.* Dublin, 1907. .... 170.00 230.00

PRICE RANGE

☐ **Synge, John Millington.** *The Tinker's Wedding.* Dublin, 1907.	400.00	500.00
☐ **Synge, John Millington.** *The Playboy of the Western World.* Dublin, 1907.	500.00	675.00
☐ **Synge, John Millington.** *Diedre of the Sorrows.* Dundrum, 1910. Limited to 250 copies.	350.00	475.00
☐ **Synge, John Millington.** *In Wicklow.* Boston, 1912.	200.00	300.00
☐ **Traherne, Thomas.** *The Poetical Works of Thomas Traherne.* London, 1903.	35.00	45.00
☐ **Tristram, W. O.** *Coaching Days and Coaching Ways.* London, 1888.	75.00	100.00
☐ **Wagner, Richard.** *Parsifal, or The Legend of the Holy Grail.* London, 1912. With 22 colored plates by Willy Pogany.	30.00	37.00
☐ **White, Gilbert.** *The Life and Letters of Gilbert White of Selborne.* London, 1901. Two volumes, bound in half morocco.	40.00	50.00
☐ **Wilde, Oscar.** *The Happy Prince and Other Tales.* London, 1888.	210.00	320.00
☐ **Wilde, Oscar.** *Lord Arthur Savile's Crime.* London, 1891.	160.00	235.00
☐ **Wilde, Oscar.** *Intentions.* London, 1891. Green cloth.	110.00	155.00
☐ **Wilde, Oscar.** *A House of Pomegranates.* London, 1891. White cloth with green spine.	265.00	335.00
☐ **Wilde, Oscar.** *The Picture of Dorian Gray.* London, n.d., 1891. First issued has "and" spelled "nd" on page 208, eighth line from bottom.	320.00	425.00
☐ **Wilde, Oscar.** *Lady Windermere's Fan.* London, 1893.	160.00	215.00
☐ **Wilde, Oscar.** *Phrases and Philosophies.* London, 1894. Softbound.	800.00	1075.00
☐ **Wilde, Oscar.** *The Ballad of Reading Gaol.* By "C.3.3." London, n.d., 1898. For first issue copies, limited to 800 bound in cloth.	210.00	265.00
There was also a deluxe edition limited to 30 on special paper.	1275.00	1550.00
Wilde's name does not appear on the book. He is identified as "C.3.3." his serial number while a prisoner at Reading jail.		
☐ **Wilde, Oscar.** *De Profoundis.* London, n.d., 1905. The first issue has the ads dated February.	80.00	105.00

AUTOGRAPHS—INTRODUCTION

There's a magic about original autographs of celebrities—whether it's the signature of a former President, a novelist, or a movie hero. While many other kinds of celebrity souvenirs exist, autographs top the list in popularity and most times, in cash value. There's good reason why. An expert can authenticate an autograph with little difficulty, while the authenticity of most other celebrity relics is open to question. Also, autographs have established cash values, and are easy to store and display.

Autographs exist of virtually every famous person, going back very far into the past. If you're new to the hobby, you may be amazed by the depth and variety of autographs on the market. The autographs of all American

Presidents and other statesmen are available; so are autographs of the British Prime Ministers, many of the Popes, and most of the kings of Europe since the late Middle Ages. However, there are some celebrities of which no autograph exists, or who are so rare in autographic form that the only surviving specimens are in museum collections. Occasionally, the ambitious swindler will try to sell a fake of such an item, hoping that the buyer's desire to own a rarity will overcome his better judgment. Some really hilarious fakes have come on the market, such as the "original" epistles (or letters) of St. Paul the Apostle. The faker used antique-looking parchment and made every effort to give his product an appearance of vast age—but he wrote the text in English, a language unknown in the time of St. Paul. Another faker offered a portion of the "original" manuscript of a poem by the Greek poet Homer. He overlooked the fact that Homer was blind and dictated or orally told his writings. No serious collector would give such material a second glance; there's just no possibility of it being genuine.

Of autographs that do exist, the most valuable is undoubtedly that of Shakespeare. A total of five genuine signatures of the Bard are known, but all are in museum collections and none have been sold for many, many years. If one came on the market today (which is about as unlikely as the Pacific Ocean drying up), it would probably fetch more than a million dollars. Other collectors' items have brought that much—oil paintings have gone for as high as ten million—and a Shakespeare signature is one of the great collectors' items.

By all rhyme and reason, Shakespeare's autograph shouldn't be that rare. Abundant autographs and manuscripts are in existence, of persons who lived during his time and even earlier. Considering the volume of writing Shakespeare turned out, a fair amount of it should have gotten preserved, even if by nothing more than pure accident. If each of his plays required just 100 manuscript pages to write (a conservative estimate), he penned more than 3,000 pages in his lifetime—not counting his letters, or the signatures he placed on various documents. Yet not a single page of any of his plays, in his handwriting, has been discovered. The five known signatures are all on legal papers—his will, and the deed to a parcel of land. The shortage of Shakespeare signatures is one of the big mysteries of history. And it has, needless to point out, served as a green light for counterfeiters, who always step in to fill voids such as these. Nobody would buy a Shakespeare autograph today, without very careful scrutinizing; but in the 19th century there was a brisk traffic in such fakes, before the collecting public developed a sense of wariness. There's a legend (uncomfirmed) that an ignorant caretaker at Shakespeare's birthplace, in Stratford-on-Avon, discarded large quantities of papers in the late 1700s, which might have included original letters and manuscripts.

The following pages present an introduction to the autograph hobby, with some of the basic steps for beginners, general advice, and price listings for autographs in various fields. Most of the autographs listed are readily available from dealers, or at auction sales. The scarcer ones are not kept "in stock" by the dealers, since there are simply not enough specimens in circulation. If you want to buy a scarce autograph, this might require some searching and possibly contacting a number of dealers, but eventually you will have the chance to buy it.

Keep in mind that the prices are guides only. Autographs VARY IN PRICE more than most collectors' items, because each specimen is usually quite different than another. If the autograph is carried on a letter, its value will hinge on the length and content of the letter. Collecting plain signatures—clipped from letters or other papers—is usually the most inexpensive approach to the hobby. They can make a good collection, but they tend to be harder to authenticate than a whole letter or document.

The values of autographs depend largely on buyer demand. Specimens that aren't particularly scarce can sell for high prices, because of strong demand. Signed photos of, for example, Elvis Presley are not rare, but the prices are always high because collectors are willing to pay dearly for them. Letters of George Washington aren't rare, either, compared to many other historical figures, but competition is overwhelming. Investors are buying this material right along with collectors, so the prices continually rise.

BUILDING AN AUTOGRAPH COLLECTION

It's really better for a collector to start on a small budget. This way, he learns firsthand about the hobby, learns which kinds of autographs appeal most to him and how to buy them, without risking a great deal of money. Too many autograph collectors take a deep financial plunge without the knowledge or experience to spend wisely. Go slow at first, and don't be concerned that your collection is small. The big purchases will come later. Of course, anyone who has been a book collector will accustom himself to the hobby much more quickly than a non-collector. He already knows about reading catalogues, buying from dealers, and probably has a fair sense of historical values versus commercial values.

The first step is to select some area or subject in which to specialize. There is no point in trying to assemble a general collection that has no special direction. This is called in the trade a "mixed" collection. You will discover, when trying to dispose of a mixed collection, that the dealers are either not interested in it, or will offer just a token sum. Be a specialist, and specialize in something realistic. By that I mean, do not attempt to build a George Washington collection if you have a limited budget. Pick a difficult subject if you wish, something that requires research and "digging," but not a class of autographs too expensive for you. But there are ways of getting around this. If your interest is Washington and you cannot afford his autograph material, try collecting letters and documents of his generals (which are quite a bit cheaper), or something of that nature. With almost every big celebrity, it is possible to "collect around" the subject, and you may end up with a very unique collection by doing this.

Get on the mailing lists of autograph dealers to receive their catalogues. You may be asked to pay a subscription fee, but this is only a small sum and a necessary expense. You can't collect without getting catalogues regularly from the dealers. Some writers on the subject have advocated doing business exclusively with one dealer, but by doing this you are sure to miss many good opportunities in the stocks of his competitors. It is true that a dealer will scan other dealers' catalogues for you and report if some item in your special field is offered, but if you buy from one dealer through another dealer, you are likely to pay a higher price. And don't forget the auction houses. Get their catalogues and sale announcements, too.

When writing to a dealer for catalogues, mention your line of interest. This serves a couple of purposes. If you collect medical autographs, he will not send you a catalogue on Old West celebrities. Also, he may be able to offer you items from stock that are not listed in the current catalogues. These may be newly arrived acquisitions, or material from past catalogues that failed to sell. Advanced collectors sometimes give the dealer an order to buy for them any autographs in their field that may be offered by the public. Don't do this if there's a chance you may switch off to another line of collecting.

(For a list of dealers, see the section of dealers' addresses.)

FAKES AND FORGERIES

In the past, autograph collecting was beset with fakes, counterfeits and other questionable material. The old-time dealers (until 1910) did not intentionally deceive, but they took no great pains to keep rotten apples out of their stocks. They sold what came along, in the theory that if they took a chance, their customers should be willing to take a chance. Many old forgeries were not detected until fairly recent times; quite a few pioneer collectors went to their graves believing they owned genuine letters of Washington, Lincoln or other celebrities, when in fact they were fakes. Today, the autograph market is pretty tightly policed. The dealers are careful in what they buy. When they do chance to acquire a fake, they don't try to "pass it along." They absorb the loss, realizing that customer confidence is a lot more profitable in the long run.

Under no circumstances should a beginning collector try his luck at distinguishing genuine autographs from fakes. If you buy from any sources other than responsible dealers, you take a risk. Any autograph offered at a fraction of the normal price should be suspect. Some fakes, it is true, are so amateurish that nobody would be fooled by them; but others are the work of experts. Don't make the mistake of assuming that an inexpensive or common autograph must be genuine, in the theory that a faker would not bother with a $10 or $20 item. Some of the most plentiful faked autographs are inscriptions on photographs of show business personalities. Anyone can buy these pictures without autographs for $1 each, by adding a faked signature the forger can resell them, in quantity, for a tidy profit. And a false signature on a photo of someone like Elvis Presley can turn a $1 purchase into a $200 item.

COLLECTOR TERMINOLOGY

To buy intelligently, one must know the terms and abbreviations used in catalogues. There are much fewer than found in book catalogues, but no less puzzling if one is unfamiliar with them.

HOLOGRAPH LETTER (ALs). A letter entirely in the handwriting of its sender, not merely the signature but the body and address (though the envelope, if present, may not necessarily be in holograph). It is important to note that, all other things being equal, a holograph letter will outsell one in which the body is typed or written by a secretary. Though the typewriter was not in general use until about 1900, people in important positions still had secretaries to transcribe their letters. Most "business" letters of statesmen, from the 19th century and earlier, are secretary written. However, personal letters very often are handwritten, as are letters from the early part of the individual's life, before he could afford a secretary. Expert knowledge is required, sometimes, to distinguish the subject's handwriting from that of the secretary. This is one of the hobby's "stumbling blocks." Many Lincoln letters now proved to be secretary written were once taken to be holographs. In fact it is really only within the past 30–40 years that anyone has bothered about the distinction between holograph and non-holograph letters.

Ls. A letter in which the main body is typed or written out by a secretary.

Ds. Document signed. It is very unusual for documents to be in holograph, regardless of their age or nature. Nearly all are either partly printed or written out by a scribe. However the term HDs (Holograph Document signed) is found occasionally.

Ns. Note signed. The line between a note and a letter is often thin and open to argument. Generally, a note is taken to be a brief message of no more than one or two lines, possibly on the back of a document or letter or something other than a regular sheet of letter paper.

DOCKETED. Notes made by the recipient in the margins, or elsewhere, of a letter.

RECTO. The front side of a letter or document.

VERSO. The reverse side.

WORN AT FOLDS. Any document or other paper item that has been folded in storage for many years and is likely to be weak at the folds, but the term should not be used of specimens ready to fall apart.

SILKED. A fragile autograph overlaid on both sides with thin silk. It is virtually invisible and gives the paper added strength. Still, some collectors consider it tampering and turn thumbs down on silked autographs.

STORAGE AND DISPLAY

For most autograph collections, an album is the best choice for storage. Some hobbyists begin by framing every autograph they acquire, only to discover that they've run out of wall space. Framing is expensive, too. An ordinary scrap album sold in variety stores is suitable. No albums made especially for autographs are on the market. Some collectors prefer "mint sheet" albums, designed for sheets of postage stamps. These have black pages covered in clear acetate that forms a pocket, into which the specimen is inserted. This eliminates the need for hinges or corners to hold items in place. All things considered, though, there is much to be said in favor of the old-fashioned scrap album. Its heavy pages provide protection, and it's easy to keep clean. Acetate draws dust like a magnet. For mounting, photo-corners are good. Philatelic hinges that attach directly to the specimen are undesirable because they leave a mark.

CONDITION STANDARDS FOR AUTOGRAPHS

Autographs, being paper objects, are easily damaged and not always found in the best of condition. However, in the case of autographs which are not rare, the odds of finding well preserved specimens are favorable and there is no reason to settle for a "space filler."

Condition standards for autographs vary with age. Collectors expect, demand might be a better word, that a 20th century specimen should be fresh and clean. A letter ought to look as though it were just written. A photo should still be clear and bright. And so forth. With older autographs, some signs of age have to be allowed, though actual *damage* will usually only be tolerated in really scarce specimens.

The autograph hobby does not have an accepted code for grading specimens, such as exists with stamps and coins. This is probably because for many years collectors were not too condition-conscious. They are becoming more so. So are the dealers.

The following will serve as a general outline of what is meant by the statement of condition in catalogue descriptions.

MINT. Used only of fairly recent specimens, should mean the item is absolutely blemish-free. But "mint" is really not as much cause for ecstasy as "superb." Mint refers only to the physical condition of the paper; a "superb" autograph is one in which the paper is not only flawless but the writing bold and strong.

EXCELLENT. Of 19th century autographs: no paper tears; no stains. There may be light foxing or spotting, not affecting the signature. Of 18th century: good clear writing, not too worn at folds, minor wrinkling or wear at corners, no staining or holes in paper. Of 17th century: clear writing, perhaps some minor staining but not affecting writing, no long tears, only insignificant worming.

VERY GOOD. Of 19th century autographs: lightly stained in margins, the paper may be weak or repaired at folds, but writing should be strong and clear and the signature unaffected by spotting or staining. Of 18th century: shows some signs of wear, a blank corner may be missing, light stains affecting writing but not the signature. Of 17th century: weak at folds, age-marked or stained but the writing should still be reasonably clear.

GOOD. Of 19th century autographs: repaired; writing faded. Of 18th century: stained, perhaps touching but not obliterating the signature, long tears affecting writing. Of 17th century: a portion of the item may be missing, the writing may be faded, the signature stained.

But remember, the rarer the autograph, the less its value will be affected by defects. If a newly discovered letter by Beethoven or DaVinci came on the market, buyers would not care very much about staining or soiling.

HOW TO USE THE AUTOGRAPH PRICE GUIDE

In the following pages are listed many celebrities in various fields, grouped by category. Next to each name are prices for typical autograph specimens, such as ALs, Ls, signed photo, manuscript page or mss. (in the case of authors), document, and plain signature. An ALs (autograph letter signed) is a letter entirely in the sender's handwriting, while an Ls (letter signed) is one written by a secretary which merely carries the sender's signature.

The listing of Presidents gives prices in more categories than do the other listings, because more types of autograph material exists and is sold frequently enough for firm markets to be established.

It is of course impossible to include every world celebrity in this book. For autographs of some of those omitted, see the first edition of "Official Guide to Old Books and Autographs." New names will be added to each revised edition.

PRICE RANGES. The price range ($300–$500), means that autograph specimens have been known to sell within that range during the period over which this guide was compiled, or, in the case of very rare autographs, are estimated to be worth the sums shown. As with any collectors' item, prices change, so these figures should not be taken as anything more than rough guides, or, maybe better, as a record of the prices at which autographs have been selling, not what they will be selling for in six months or a year. This is not a book of price forecasts.

Bear in mind that the individual specimen makes the price. A really exceptional specimen will usually beat the prices shown. There is no doubt that a great Lincoln or Washington letter could easily bring $50,000. By the same token, any autograph in less than good condition may sell below the stated price, so may, in fact, a perfectly well preserved letter that just happens to contain a dull message. Remember that collectors are not fond of pencil writing; deduct 10% to 30% from these prices for autographs in pencil. "Good condition" does not only refer to tears and stains, but to the writing itself. A letter in which the writing has faded is considered in poor condition. It may be worth half the usual price.

The *length* of a holograph letter also counts. You can add at least $1,000 for each page of a lengthy letter by Washington, Jefferson or Lincoln.

OMITTED PRICES. In some instances it will be obvious why prices are omitted, for a signed photo of John Adams, for example, who lived prior to the age of photography. Otherwise, the lack of a price indicates that no pricing information is available, or that no specimens of that type are known to exist. Absence of a price is not necessarily an indication of rarity.

AMERICAN PRESIDENTS' AUTOGRAPHS

	Als	Ls Document	Signed Photo	Plain Signature
☐ Washington, George.	10000.00- 35,000.00	1800.00- 9500.00	1500.00- 4000.00	450.00- 650.00
☐ Adams, John	4000.00- 7000.00	1250.00- 4000.00	1000.00- 2500.00	300.00- 400.00
☐ Jefferson, Thomas.	7500.00- 30,000.00	2000.00- 8000.00	1200.00- 3000.00	400.00- 500.00
☐ Madison, James	1000.00- 3000.00	500.00- 1400.00	200.00- 800.00	100.00- 150.00
☐ Monroe, James	1000.00- 1500.00	450.00- 1200.00	150.00- 300.00	75.00- 100.00
☐ Adams, John Q.	750.00- 1500.00	450.00- 1200.00	150.00- 300.00	80.00- 125.00
☐ Jackson, Andrew	1750.00- 3000.00	700.00- 2000.00	400.00- 650.00	200.00- 300.00
☐ Van Buren, Martin	500.00- 1000.00	300.00- 600.00	150.00- 200.00	65.00- 85.00
☐ Harrison, William H.	1000.00- 1500.00	350.00- 1000.00	350.00- 475.00	80.00- 100.00
☐ Tyler, John.	600.00- 1000.00	350.00- 600.00	150.00- 200.00	60.00- 75.00
☐ Polk, James K.	500.00- 1000.00	350.00- 600.00	150.00- 200.00	60.00- 70.00
☐ Taylor, Zachary	750.00- 2000.00	350.00- 1100.00	275.00- 600.00	60.00- 100.00
☐ Fillmore, Millard	275.00- 400.00	175.00- 300.00	100.00- 200.00	50.00- 60.00
☐ Pierce, Franklin.	250.00- 400.00	175.00- 275.00	100.00- 200.00	50.00- 60.00
☐ Buchanan, James	250.00- 400.00	175.00- 275.00	100.00- 200.00	50.00- 60.00
☐ Lincoln, Abraham.	5000.00- 25,000.00	2000.00- 12,000.00	750.00- 2500.00	4000.00- 7000.00	500.00- 350.00
☐ Johnson, Andrew.	1000.00- 2200.00	400.00- 1000.00	150.00- 200.00	1800.00- 2500.00	50.00- 60.00
☐ Grant, U. S.	750.00- 1200.00	400.00- 750.00	85.00- 150.00	100.00- 175.00	40.00- 45.00
☐ Hayes, R. B.	250.00- 500.00	150.00- 150.00	65.00- 65.00	250.00- 300.00	30.00- 38.00
☐ Garfield, James.	350.00- 600.00	200.00- 350.00	100.00- 90.00	350.00- 700.00	38.00- 50.00
☐ Arthur, Chester A.	200.00- 300.00	120.00- 250.00	60.00- 85.00	850.00- 1200.00	30.00- 38.00
☐ Cleveland, Grover	175.00- 250.00	80.00- 120.00	50.00- 70.00	100.00- 200.00	26.00- 32.00
☐ Harrison, Benjamin	300.00- 400.00	145.00- 175.00	65.00- 85.00	325.00- 450.00	28.00- 32.00
☐ McKinley, William.	500.00- 750.00	190.00- 300.00	95.00- 140.00	175.00- 225.00	38.00- 42.00
☐ Roosevelt, Theodore.	300.00- 750.00	100.00- 190.00	60.00- 60.00	100.00- 400.00	32.00- 38.00

I have no passion or resentment to gratify; but I am anxious to know, Early in my term, whether I am to be a registering clerk or President — Thanking you for your several favors, & hoping to hear from you whenever it pleases you to write, I am

Very Truly I am

J. A. Garfield.

Hon
Edwards Pierrepont
N.Y.

A genuine rarity. This is an excerpt of a letter written by James Garfield while President. Next to William Henry Harrison, who served only a month, Garfield had the shortest Presidency (four months).

One of the most sought after signatures of modern Presidents: John F. Kennedy's with a complimentary close from a letter. Almost all of Kennedy's official correspondence, both as Senator and President, was signed by an automatic writing device called the "autopen."

	Als	Ls	Document	Signed Photo	Plain Signature
☐ Taft, William H.	150.00-200.00	90.00-100.00	45.00-50.00	150.00-180.00	28.00-35.00
☐ Wilson, Woodrow.	500.00-700.00	140.00-190.00	60.00-70.00	160.00-220.00	38.00-45.00
☐ Harding, Warren G.	700.00-900.00	250.00-350.00	60.00-75.00	110.00-140.00	28.00-35.00
☐ Coolidge, Calvin.	475.00-700.00	140.00-180.00	75.00-70.00	75.00-100.00	28.00-35.00
☐ Hoover, Herbert.	4000.00-6000.00	150.00-190.00	45.00-60.00	150.00-200.00	28.00-35.00
☐ Roosevelt, Franklin.	600.00-1000.00	100.00-265.00	95.00-150.00	120.00-180.00	33.00-39.00
☐ Truman, Harry.	1200.00-2000.00	140.00-350.00	80.00-120.00	150.00-180.00	39.00-45.00
☐ Eisenhower, Dwight.	1000.00-1500.00	200.00-275.00	80.00-100.00	200.00-300.00	28.00-35.00
☐ Kennedy, John F.	1500.00-4000.00	450.00-900.00	175.00-350.00	500.00-1000.00	100.00-150.00
☐ Johnson, Lyndon B.	1300.00-1800.00	300.00-500.00	80.00-100.00	140.00-190.00	35.00-48.00
☐ Nixon, Richard M.	4500.00-6500.00	450.00-800.00	150.00-190.00	250.00-375.00	75.00-100.00

	Als	Ls	Document	Signed Photo	Plain Signature
☐ Ford, Gerald.	700.00- 1000.00	250.00- 400.00	80.00- 110.00	140.00- 190.00	28.00- 35.00
☐ Carter, James.	700.00- 1000.00	200.00- 350.00	70.00- 90.00	120.00- 150.00	25.00- 35.00
☐ Reagan, Ronald.	1000.00- 1500.00	175.00- 250.00	85.00- 125.00	70.00- 100.00	25.00- 30.00

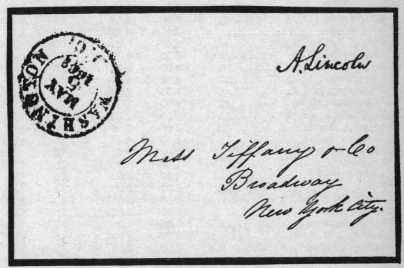

A valuable signature and interesting association item: Abraham Lincoln's free frank on an envelope addressed to the leading specialty shop of its day, Messrs. Tiffany and Co. The address is not in Lincoln's handwriting but in that of his wife, Mary. Quite obviously this was not "official business," but the franking privilege was good regardless. It dates to 1862.

ENTERTAINMENT FIGURES

	8 × 10 Black and White Photo Signed		Plain Signature	
☐ Abel, Walter	2.50-	3.50	.75-	1.00
☐ Adams, Don.....................	2.00-	3.00	.75-	1.00
☐ Adams, Edie	3.00-	4.00	.75-	1.00
☐ Adams, Joey.....................	2.50-	3.50	.75-	1.00
☐ Agar, John	2.00-	3.00	.75-	1.00
☐ Aherne, Brian	3.00-	4.00	.75-	1.00
☐ Aimee, Anouk...................	4.00-	6.00	.75-	1.00
☐ Akins, Claude	2.00-	3.00	.75-	1.00
☐ Albert, Eddie	2.00-	3.00	.75-	1.00
☐ Albertson, Jack	10.00-	15.00	1.00-	1.75

	8 × 10 Black and White Photo Signed		Plain Signature	
☐ Albright, Lola	1.50-	2.50	.75-	1.00
☐ Alda, Alan......................	10.00-	15.00	2.00-	3.00
☐ Alda, Robert	2.00-	3.00	.75-	1.00
☐ Allen, Fred	40.00-	60.00	5.00-	8.00
☐ Allen, Gracie	50.00-	75.00	5.00-	8.00
☐ Allen, Steve	1.50-	2.50	.75-	1.00
☐ Allen, Woody...................	5.00-	8.00	1.50-	2.75
☐ Allison, Fran	2.00-	3.00	.75-	1.00
☐ Allyson, June	3.00-	4.50	.75-	1.00
☐ Altman, Robert.................	5.00-	7.00	1.00-	1.50
☐ Ameche, Don....................	3.00-	4.00	.75-	1.00
☐ Ames, Ed	2.00-	3.00	.75-	1.00
☐ Ames, Leon	3.00-	4.00	.75-	1.00
☐ Ames, Nancy...................	1.50-	2.50	.75-	1.00
☐ Amsterdam, Morey	2.00-	3.00	.75-	1.00
☐ Anderson, Lynn.................	3.00-	4.00	.75-	1.00
☐ Andress, Ursula................	4.00-	7.00	.75-	1.00
☐ Andrews, Julie	2.00-	3.00	.75-	1.00
☐ Ansara, Michael................	2.00-	3.00	.75-	1.00
☐ Arden, Eve	3.00-	4.00	.75-	1.00
☐ Arkin, Alan.....................	4.00-	6.00	.75-	1.00
☐ Arnaz, Desi.....................	5.00-	8.00	.75-	1.00
☐ Arnaz, Lucie	2.00-	3.00	1.00-	1.75
☐ Arness, James	2.00-	3.00	.75-	1.00
☐ Arthur, Beatrice	3.00-	4.00	.75-	1.00
☐ Arthur, Jean....................	3.00-	4.00	.75-	1.00
☐ Ashley, Elizabeth..............	2.00-	3.00	.75-	1.00
☐ Astin, John.....................	1.50-	2.50	.75-	1.00
☐ Aumont, Jean-Pierre	2.00-	3.00	.75-	1.00
☐ Ayers, Lew.....................	4.00-	6.00	.75-	1.00
☐ Aznavour, Charles..............	2.00-	3.00	.75-	1.00
☐ Bacall, Lauren..................	9.00-	15.00	1.50-	2.75
☐ Backus, Jim....................	2.00-	3.00	.75-	1.00
☐ Baer, Max, Jr...................	1.50-	2.50	.75-	1.00
☐ Bailey, Pearl...................	5.00-	8.00	1.00-	1.50
☐ Bain, Barbara	2.00-	3.00	.75-	1.00
☐ Baker, Carroll	5.00-	8.00	.75-	1.00
☐ Baker, Diane	2.00-	3.00	.75-	1.00
☐ Baker, Stanley..................	2.00-	3.00	.75-	1.00
☐ Ball, Lucille	6.00-	9.00	.75-	1.00
☐ Ballard, Kaye...................	2.50-	3.50	.75-	1.00
☐ Balsam, Martin	2.00-	3.00	.75-	1.00
☐ Bancroft, Anne.................	4.00-	6.00	.75-	1.00
☐ Bardot, Brigitte................	15.00-	20.00	2.00-	3.00
☐ Bari, Lynn......................	2.00-	3.00	.75-	1.00
☐ Barrie, Wendy	2.00-	3.00	.75-	1.00
☐ Barry, Gene	3.00-	400	.75-	1.00
☐ Barry, Jack.....................	1.50-	2.50	.75-	1.00
☐ Bartholomew, Freddie	4.00-	6.00	.75-	1.00
☐ Bates, Alan.....................	4.00-	6.00	.75-	1.00
☐ Baxter, Anne	2.00-	3.00	.75-	1.00
☐ Bean, Orson	2.00-	3.00	.75-	1.00

	8 × 10 Black and White Photo Signed		Plain Signature	
☐ Beatty, Warren	5.00-	7.00	1.00-	1.50
☐ Becker, Sandy	1.50-	2.50	.75-	1.00
☐ Bel Geddes, Barbara	2.00-	3.00	.75-	1.00
☐ Bellamy, Ralph	3.00-	4.00	.75-	1.00
☐ Belmondo, Jean-Paul	2.00-	3.00	.75-	1.00
☐ Belushi, John	175.00	250.00	25.00-	35.00
☐ Benjamin, Dick	2.00-	3.00	.75-	1.00
☐ Benny, Jack	40.00-	50.00	5.00-	8.00
☐ Bergen, Candice	4.00-	6.00	.75-	1.00
☐ Bergen, Polly	2.00-	3.00	.75-	1.00
☐ Berger, Senta	2.00-	3.00	.75-	1.00
☐ Bergman, Ingmar	10.00-	15.00	1.00-	1.50
☐ Bergman, Ingrid	60.00-	80.00	6.00-	9.00
☐ Berle, Milton	5.00-	8.00	1.00-	1.50
☐ Berman, Shelley	2.00-	3.00	.75-	1.00
☐ Bernardi, Hershel	2.00-	3.00	.75-	1.00
☐ Berry, Ken	1.50-	2.50	.75-	1.00
☐ Bessell, Ted	2.00-	3.00	.75-	1.00
☐ Bikel, Theodore	4.00-	6.00	.75-	1.00
☐ Bishop, Joey	2.00-	3.00	.75-	1.00
☐ Bisset, Jacqueline	3.00-	4.00	.75-	1.00
☐ Bixby, Bill	3.00-	4.00	.75-	1.00
☐ Black, Karen	2.00-	3.00	.75-	1.00
☐ Blaine, Vivian	3.00-	4.00	.75-	1.00
☐ Blair, Janet	2.00-	3.00	.75-	1.00
☐ Blair, Linda	5.00-	8.00	1.00-	1.75
☐ Blake, Amanda	2.00-	3.00	.75-	1.00
☐ Blakely, Susan	3.00-	4.00	.75-	1.00
☐ Blondell, Joan	2.00-	3.00	.75-	1.00
☐ Bloom, Claire	6.00-	9.00	1.00-	1.50
☐ Blyth, Ann	2.00-	3.00	.75-	1.00
☐ Bogarde, Dirk	3.00-	4.00	.75-	1.00
☐ Bogart, Humphrey	125.00	175.00	12.00-	17.00
☐ Bogdanovich, Peter	10.00-	15.00	1.00-	1.50
☐ Boone, Richard	10.00-	15.00	1.00-	1.50
☐ Booth, Shirley	5.00-	7.00	1.00-	1.50
☐ Borge, Victor	3.00-	4.00	.75-	1.00
☐ Borgnine, Ernest	3.00-	4.00	.75-	1.00
☐ Bosley, Tom	2.00-	3.00	.75-	1.00
☐ Bowman, Lee	2.00-	3.00	.75-	1.00
☐ Boyer, Charles	10.00-	15.00	1.00-	1.75
☐ Boyle, Peter	3.00-	4.00	.75-	1.00
☐ Bracken, Eddie	2.00-	3.00	.75-	1.00
☐ Brand, Neville	1.50-	2.50	.75-	1.00
☐ Brando, Marlon	20.00-	30.00	3.00-	5.00
☐ Brasselle, Keefe	2.00-	3.00	.75-	1.00
☐ Brazzi, Rossano	2.00-	3.00	.75-	1.00
☐ Brenner, David	2.00-	3.00	.75-	1.00
☐ Brent, George	3.00-	4.00	.75-	1.00
☐ Bridges, Beau	2.00-	3.00	.75-	1.00
☐ Britton, Barbara	2.00-	3.00	.75-	1.00
☐ Brolin, James	2.00-	3.00	.75-	1.00

	8 × 10 Black and White Photo Signed		Plain Signature	
☐ Bronson, Charles	4.00-	6.00	.75-	1.00
☐ Brooks, Mel	5.00-	7.00	.75-	1.00
☐ Brown, Vanessa.................	2.00-	3.00	.75-	1.00
☐ Bruce, Carol	2.00-	3.00	.75-	1.00
☐ Bruce, Virginia	2.00-	3.00	.75-	1.00
☐ Brynner, Yul	3.00-	4.00	.75-	1.00
☐ Buchanan, Edgar...............	2.00-	3.00	.75-	1.00
☐ Bucholz, Horst	2.00-	3.00	.75-	1.00
☐ Bujold, Genevieve..............	3.00-	4.00	.75-	1.00
☐ Buono, Victor	4.00-	7.00	1.00-	1.75
☐ Burke, Paul	2.00-	3.00	.75-	1.00
☐ Burnett, Carol	3.00-	4.00	.75-	1.00
☐ Burr, Raymond	3.00-	4.00	.75-	1.00
☐ Burstyn, Ellen	4.00-	6.00	.75-	1.00
☐ Burton, Richard	40.00	60.00	5.00	8.00
☐ Buttons, Red..................	2.00-	3.00	.75-	1.00
☐ Buzzi, Ruth....................	2.00-	3.00	.75-	1.00
☐ Caan, James	5.00-	7.00	1.00-	1.50
☐ Cabot, Sebastian	3.50-	6.00	.75-	1.00
☐ Caesar, Sid	3.00-	4.00	.75-	1.00
☐ Cagney, James	15.00-	25.00	3.00-	5.00
☐ Caine, Michael	3.00-	4.00	.75-	1.00
☐ Caldwell, Sarah	3.00-	4.00	.75-	1.00
☐ Caldwell, Zoe..................	4.00-	6.00	.75-	1.00
☐ Calhoun, Rory.................	2.00-	3.00	.75-	1.00
☐ Callan, Michael................	2.00-	3.00	.75-	1.00
☐ Calvet, Corinne................	2.00-	3.00	.75-	1.00
☐ Cameron, Rod.................	2.00-	3.00	.75-	1.00
☐ Cannon, Dyan.................	2.00-	3.00	.75-	1.00
☐ Cantinflas....................	7.00-	10.00	1.00-	1.50
☐ Cantor, Eddie..................	40.00-	60.00	8.00-	11.00
☐ Cardinale, Claudia.............	6.00-	8.00	1.00-	1.50
☐ Carey, MacDonald	2.00-	3.00	.75-	1.00
☐ Carlisle, Kitty..................	5.50-	2.50	.75-	1.00
☐ Carlson, Richard	2.00-	3.00	.75-	1.00
☐ Carne, Judy	2.00-	3.00	.75-	1.00
☐ Carney, Art...................	3.00-	4.00	.75-	1.00
☐ Caron, Leslie..................	4.00-	6.00	.75-	1.00
☐ Carradine, David	7.00-	10.00	1.00-	1.50
☐ Carradine, John...............	3.00-	4.00	.75-	1.00
☐ Carroll, Madeleine.............	5.00-	7.00	1.00-	1.50
☐ Carroll, Pat...................	1.50-	2.50	.75-	1.00
☐ Carson, Joanna	7.00-	10.00	1.00-	1.50
☐ Carson, Johnny	4.00-	6.00	1.00-	1.50
☐ Carter, Jack	1.50-	2.50	.75-	1.00
☐ Caruso, Enrico	180.00	260.00	20.00-	35.00
☐ Cass, Peggy	1.50-	2.50	.75-	1.00
☐ Cassavetes, John	2.00-	3.00	.75-	1.00
☐ Cavett, Dick...................	2.00-	3.00	.75-	1.00
☐ Chamberlain, Richard	4.00-	6.00	.75-	1.00
☐ Chaney, Lon..................	60.00-	80.00	10.00-	15.00
☐ Chaplin, Charles	75.00-	100.00	6.00-	10.00

	8×10 Black and White Photo Signed		Plain Signature	
☐ Charisse, Cyd	4.00	6.00	.75-	1.00
☐ Chase, Chevy	3.00-	4.00	.75-	1.00
☐ Christian, Linda	3.00-	4.00	.75-	1.00
☐ Christie, Julie	5.00-	7.00	1.00-	1.50
☐ Christy, June	2.00-	3.00	.75-	1.00
☐ Cilento, Diane	4.00-	6.00	.75-	1.00
☐ Clark, Dane	2.00-	3.00	.75-	1.00
☐ Coburn, James	3.00-	4.00	.75-	1.00
☐ Coca, Imogene	5.00-	7.00	.75-	1.00
☐ Coco, James	2.00-	3.00	.75-	1.00
☐ Cohan, George M	50.00-	70.00	10.00-	15.00
☐ Cohen, Myron	2.00-	3.00	.75-	1.00
☐ Colbert, Claudette	10.00-	15.00	2.00-	3.00
☐ Collins, Joan	2.00-	3.00	.75-	1.00
☐ Connor, Nadine	2.00-	3.00	.75-	1.00
☐ Connery, Sean	3.00-	4.00	.75-	1.00
☐ Connors, Chuck	3.00-	4.00	.75-	1.00
☐ Connors, Michael	2.00-	3.00	.75-	1.00
☐ Conrad, Michael	2.00-	3.00	.75-	1.00
☐ Conrad, Robert	2.50-	3.50	.75-	1.00
☐ Conreid, Hans	3.00-	5.00	.75-	1.00
☐ Constantine, Michael	2.00-	3.00	.75-	1.00
☐ Converse, Frank	2.00-	3.00	.75-	1.00
☐ Conway, Tim	1.50-	2.50	.75-	1.00
☐ Coogan, Jackie	4.00-	6.00	.75-	1.00
☐ Cook, Barbara	2.00-	3.00	.75-	1.00
☐ Cooper, Gary	40.00-	60.00	3.00-	5.00
☐ Cooper, Jackie	3.00-	4.00	.75-	1.00
☐ Corby, Ellen	2.00-	3.00	.75-	1.00
☐ Corey, Jeff	3.00-	4.00	.75-	1.00
☐ Cosby, Bill	2.00-	3.00	.75-	1.00
☐ Crabbe, Buster	15.00-	25.00	2.00-	3.50
☐ Crain, Jeanne	3.00-	4.00	.75-	1.00
☐ Crane, Bob	2.00-	3.00	.75-	1.00
☐ Crawford, Broderick	5.00-	7.00	.75-	1.00
☐ Crawford, Joan	75.00-	110.00	12.00-	18.00
☐ Crenna, Richard	2.00-	3.00	.75-	1.00
☐ Cristal, Linda	3.00-	4.00	.75-	1.00
☐ Cronyn, Hume	3.00-	4.00	.75-	1.00
☐ Crowley, Pat	2.00-	3.00	.75-	1.00
☐ Cullen, Bill	2.50-	1.50	.75-	1.00
☐ Culp, Robert	2.00-	3.00	.75-	1.00
☐ Cummings, Robert	2.00-	3.00	.75-	1.00
☐ Curtis, Ken	2.00-	3.00	.75-	1.00
☐ Cushing, Peter	3.00-	4.00	.75-	1.00
☐ Dahl, Arlene	2.00-	3.00	.75-	1.00
☐ Dailey, Dan	3.00-	4.00	.75-	1.00
☐ Dalton, Abby	2.00-	3.00	.75-	1.00
☐ Daly, James	3.00-	4.00	.75-	1.00
☐ Daly, John	2.00-	3.00	.75-	1.00
☐ Dana, Bill	2.00-	3.00	.75-	1.00
☐ Dangerfield, Rodney	2.00-	3.00	.75-	1.00

	8 × 10 Black and White Photo Signed		Plain Signature	
☐ Danner, Blythe	3.00-	4.00	.75-	1.00
☐ Danton, Ray	2.00-	3.00	.75-	1.00
☐ Darby, Kim	2.00-	3.00	.75-	1.00
☐ Darcel, Denise	2.00-	3.00	.75-	1.00
☐ Darren, James	3.00-	4.00	.75-	1.00
☐ DaSilva, Howard	2.00-	3.00	.75-	1.00
☐ Davis, Bette	15.00-	20.00	3.00-	5.00
☐ Davis, Ossie	3.00-	4.00	.75-	1.00
☐ Day, Dennis	2.00-	3.00	.75-	1.00
☐ Day, Laraine	2.00-	3.00	.75-	1.00
☐ Dean, James	175.00-	250.00	20.00-	30.00
☐ DeCamp, Rosemary	2.00-	3.00	.75-	1.00
☐ Dee, Sandra	3.00-	4.00	.75-	1.00
☐ DeHaven, Gloria	2.00-	3.00	.75-	1.00
☐ DeHaviland, Olivia	10.00-	15.00	1.50-	2.00
☐ Dell, Gabriel	2.00-	3.00	.75-	1.00
☐ Delon, Alain	4.00-	6.00	.75-	1.00
☐ DeLuise, Dom	2.00-	3.00	.75-	1.00
☐ Deneuve, Catherine	4.00-	6.00	.75-	1.00
☐ DeNiro, Robert	7.00-	10.00	1.00-	1.50
☐ Dennis, Sandy	5.00-	7.00	.75-	1.00
☐ Denver, Bob	3.00-	4.00	.75-	1.00
☐ Derek, Bo	10.00-	15.00	2.00-	3.00
☐ Derek, John	5.00-	7.00	1.00-	1.50
☐ Dern, Bruce	2.00-	3.00	.75-	1.00
☐ Dewhurst, Colleen	5.00-	7.00	.75-	1.00
☐ Dey, Susan	2.00-	3.00	.75-	1.00
☐ Dickinson, Angie	3.00-	4.00	.75-	1.00
☐ Dietrich, Marlene	17.00-	30.00	4.00-	7.00
☐ Diller, Phyllis	2.00-	3.00	.75-	1.00
☐ Dillman, Bradford	2.00-	3.00	.75-	1.00
☐ Donahue, Troy	3.00-	4.00	.75-	1.00
☐ Douglas, Donna	2.00-	3.00	.75-	1.00
☐ Douglas, Kirk	3.00-	4.00	.75-	1.00
☐ Douglas, Mike	4.00-	6.00	.75-	1.00
☐ Downs, Hugh	2.00-	3.00	.75-	1.00
☐ Drake, Alfred	3.00-	4.00	.75-	1.00
☐ Drew, Ellen	2.00-	3.00	.75-	1.00
☐ Dreyfuss, Richard	5.00-	7.00	.75-	1.00
☐ Dru, Joanne	2.00-	3.00	.75-	1.00
☐ Drury, James	2.00-	3.00	.75-	1.00
☐ Duff, Howard	2.00-	3.00	.75-	1.00
☐ Duke, Patty	3.00-	4.00	.75-	1.00
☐ Dunaway, Faye	5.00-	7.00	1.00-	1.50
☐ Duncan, Sandy	2.00-	3.00	.75-	1.00
☐ Dunne, Irene	4.00-	6.00	.75-	1.00
☐ Dunnock, Mildred	3.00-	4.00	.75-	1.00
☐ Durante, Jimmy	9.00-	14.00	1.50-	3.00
☐ Durbin, Deanna	8.00-	10.00	1.50-	2.50
☐ Duvall, Robert	7.00-	10.00	1.00-	1.50
☐ Eastwood, Clint	10.00-	15.00	1.00-	1.50
☐ Eaton, Shirley	2.00-	3.00	.75-	1.00

	8 × 10 Black and White Photo Signed		Plain Signature	
☐ Ebsen, Buddy...................	2.00-	3.00	.75-	1.00
☐ Eden, Barbara..................	3.00-	4.00	.75-	1.00
☐ Edwards, Ralph	1.50-	2.50	.75-	1.00
☐ Edwards, Vincent	3.00-	4.00	.75-	1.00
☐ Egan, Richard..................	3.00-	4.00	.75-	1.00
☐ Eggar, Samantha	4.00-	6.00	.75-	1.00
☐ Ekberg, Anita	5.00-	7.00	1.00-	1.50
☐ Elliott, Bob....................	1.50-	2.50	.75-	1.00
☐ Emerson, Faye	2.00-	3.00	.75-	1.00
☐ Etting, Ruth	6.00-	8.00	1.00-	1.50
☐ Ewell, Tom	2.00-	3.00	.75-	1.00
☐ Fabares, Shelley	2.00-	3.00	.75-	1.00
☐ Fabray, Nanette	2.00-	3.00	.75-	1.00
☐ Falk, Peter	4.00-	6.00	.75-	1.00
☐ Falkenburg, Jinx	2.00-	3.00	.75-	1.00
☐ Farber, Barry	1.50-	2.50	.75-	1.00
☐ Farentino, James..............	3.00-	4.00	.75-	1.00
☐ Farr, Felicia	2.00-	3.00	.75-	1.00
☐ Farrow, Mia....................	7.00-	10.00	1.00-	1.50
☐ Fawcett, Farrah	8.00-	12.00	1.50-	2.50
☐ Faye, Alice	2.00-	3.00	.75-	1.00
☐ Feldman, Marty.................	7.00-	10.00	1.00-	1.50
☐ Feldon, Barbara	2.00-	3.00	.75-	1.00
☐ Fellini, Federico	10.00-	16.00	2.00-	3.50
☐ Fellows, Edith.................	2.00-	3.00	.75-	1.00
☐ Ferrer, Jose	3.00-	4.00	.75-	1.00
☐ Ferrer, Mel	3.00-	4.00	.75-	1.00
☐ Ferris, Barbara................	5.00-	7.00	.75-	1.00
☐ Field, Sally	1.50-	2.50	.75-	1.00
☐ Finney, Albert	3.00-	4.00	.75-	1.00
☐ Fisher, Carrie..................	6.00-	8.00	.75-	1.00
☐ Fitzgerald, Geraldine	4.00-	6.00	.75-	1.00
☐ Fleming, Rhonda...............	3.00-	4.00	.75-	1.00
☐ Fletcher, Louise	2.00-	3.00	.75-	1.00
☐ Foch, Nina	2.00-	3.00	.75-	1.00
☐ Fonda, Henry...................	25.00-	32.00	2.00-	3.00
☐ Fonda, Jane....................	7.00-	10.00	1.00	1.50
☐ Fonda, Peter	5.00-	7.00	.75-	1.00
☐ Fontaine, Frank	2.00-	3.00	.75-	1.00
☐ Fontaine, Joan	5.00-	7.00	.75-	1.00
☐ Fontanne, Lynn	12.00-	20.00	2.50-	4.00
☐ Foran, Dick....................	2.00-	3.00	.75-	1.00
☐ Ford, Glenn	4.00-	6.00	.75-	1.00
☐ Forrest, Steve	2.00-	3.00	.75-	1.00
☐ Forsythe, John.................	2.00-	3.00	.75-	1.00
☐ Fosse, Bob....................	2.00-	3.00	.75-	1.00
☐ Foster, Phil....................	1.50-	2.50	.75-	1.00
☐ Foxx, Redd....................	2.50-	4.00	.75-	1.00
☐ Franciosa, Tony	2.00-	3.00	.75-	1.00
☐ Francis, Arlene.................	2.00-	3.00	.75-	1.00
☐ Franciscus, James	2.00-	3.00	.75-	1.00
☐ Frost, David...................	2.00-	3.00	.75-	1.00

	8 × 10 Black and White Photo Signed		Plain Signature	
☐ Frye, David......................	4.00-	6.00	.75-	1.00
☐ Funt, Allen	1.50-	2.50	.75-	1.00
☐ Gabel, Martin...................	2.00	3.00	.75-	1.00
☐ Gable, Clark....................	275.00-	375.00	85.00-	125.00
☐ Gabor, Eva	3.00-	4.00	.75-	1.00
☐ Gabor, Zsa Zsa	3.00-	4.00	.75-	1.00
☐ Gam, Rita	2.00-	3.00	.75-	1.00
☐ Garbo, Greta	350.00-	450.00	175.00-	225.00
☐ Gardenia, Vincent	2.00-	3.00	.75-	1.00
☐ Gardner, Ava	8.00-	10.00	1.00-	1.50
☐ Garland, Beverly	2.00-	3.00	.75-	1.00
☐ Garner, James...................	2.50-	4.00	.75-	1.00
☐ Garner, Peggy Ann	2.00-	3.00	.75-	1.00
☐ Garrett, Betty..................	2.00-	3.00	.75-	1.00
☐ Garroway, Dave	18.00-	25.00	2.00-	3.00
☐ Garson, Greer	6.00-	8.00	1.00-	1.50
☐ Gary, John	2.00-	3.00	.75-	1.00
☐ Gavin, John	3.00-	4.00	.75-	1.00
☐ Gaynor, Janet	7.00-	10.00	1.00-	1.50
☐ Gaynor, Mitzi	2.00-	3.00	.75-	1.00
☐ Gazzara, Ben...................	2.00-	3.00	.75-	1.00
☐ Geeson, Judy	2.00-	3.00	.75-	1.00
☐ Gentry, Bobby..................	4.00-	6.00	.75-	1.00
☐ Gere, Richard	7.00-	10.00	1.00-	1.50
☐ Ghostley, Alice.................	3.00-	4.00	.75-	1.00
☐ Gielgud, John	7.00-	10.00	1.00-	1.50
☐ Gilford, Jack	3.00-	4.00	.75-	1.00
☐ Gillette, Anita	2.00-	3.00	.75-	1.00
☐ Gingold, Hermione	3.00-	4.00	.75-	1.00
☐ Gleason, Jackie	3.00-	4.00	.75-	1.00
☐ Gobel, George	4.00-	6.00	.75-	1.00
☐ Goddard, Paulette...............	6.00-	8.00	1.00-	1.50
☐ Godfrey, Arthur.................	10.00-	15.00	2.00-	3.00
☐ Goodman, Dody.................	2.00-	3.00	.75-	1.00
☐ Gordon, Gale...................	2.00-	3.00	.75-	1.00
☐ Gordon, Ruth	4.00-	6.00	.75-	1.00
☐ Gorshin, Frank	2.00-	3.00	.75-	1.00
☐ Gould, Elliot...................	3.00-	4.00	.75-	1.00
☐ Goulding, Ray..................	1.50-	2.50	.75-	1.00
☐ Goulet, Robert	2.00-	3.00	.75-	1.00
☐ Graham, Martha.................	10.00-	15.00	1.00-	1.50
☐ Granger, Farley.................	2.00-	3.00	.75-	1.00
☐ Granger, Stewart	2.00-	3.00	.75-	1.00
☐ Grant, Cary....................	10.00-	15.00	1.50-	2.50
☐ Grant, Lee.....................	2.00-	3.00	.75-	1.00
☐ Granville, Bonita	2.00-	3.00	.75-	1.00
☐ Graves, Peter	2.00-	3.00	.75-	1.00
☐ Gray, Delores..................	2.00-	3.00	.75-	1.00
☐ Grayson, Kathryn	2.00-	3.00	.75-	1.00
☐ Greene, Lorne..................	3.00-	4.00	.75-	1.00
☐ Greer, Jane....................	2.00-	3.00	.75-	1.00
☐ Grey, Joel	3.00-	4.00	.75-	1.00

San Francisco
Mon. Aug. 22, 1938

Dear Mr. Winchell

This is just a note to tell you how much I appreciate the lovely things you said about me, both in your column and on your radio program.

They mean so much to a person who is just getting started like me.

I hope I will always live up to your praises, and deserve them

I'm Sincerely yours

OXOXOXOX P.S. PARDON AWFULL WRITING PLEASE!

Great prize for any collector of show business autographs: holograph letter signed by Judy Garland, written to columnist Walter Winchell. She was only fifteen at the time and had not yet starred in "The Wizard of Oz." The postscript asks Winchell to pardon the awful writing.

	8 × 10 Black and White Photo Signed		Plain Signature	
☐ Griffin, Merv......................	4.00-	6.00	.75-	1.00
☐ Griffith, Andy....................	3.00-	4.00	.75-	1.00
☐ Grimes, Tammy	3.00-	4.00	.75-	1.00
☐ Grizzard, George...............	2.00-	3.00	.75-	1.00
☐ Guardino, Harry	2.00-	3.00	.75-	1.00
☐ Guinness, Alec..................	10.00-	15.00	2.00-	3.00
☐ Gunn, Moses....................	2.00-	3.00	.75-	1.00
☐ Hackett, Buddy..................	2.00-	3.00	.75-	1.00
☐ Hackett, Joan	2.00-	3.00	.75-	1.00
☐ Hackman, Gene	2.00-	3.00	.75-	1.00
☐ Hagen, Uta.....................	3.00-	4.00	.75-	1.00
☐ Hagman, Larry..................	9.00-	12.00	1.00-	1.75
☐ Hale, Barbara	2.00-	3.00	.75-	1.00
☐ Hall, Monty.....................	1.50-	2.50	.75-	1.00
☐ Hampshire, Susan..............	5.00-	7.00	.75-	1.00
☐ Harlow, Jean	300.00-	400.00	35.00-	45.00
☐ Harrington, Pat, Jr	2.00-	3.00	.75-	1.00
☐ Harris, Barbara.................	4.00-	6.00	.75-	1.00
☐ Harris, Julie....................	5.00-	7.00	.75-	1.00
☐ Harris, Phil.....................	3.00-	4.00	.75-	1.00
☐ Harris, Richard.................	5.00-	7.00	.75-	1.00
☐ Harris, Rosemary...............	3.00-	4.00	.75-	1.00
☐ Harrison, George...............	110.00-	160.00	28.00-	38.00
☐ Harrison, Noel..................	2.00-	3.00	.75-	1.00
☐ Harrison, Rex	3.00-	4.00	.75-	1.00
☐ Hartman, David.................	2.00-	3.00	.75-	1.00
☐ Hasso, Signe...................	2.00-	3.00	.75-	1.00
☐ Haver, June	3.00-	4.00	.75-	1.00
☐ Havoc, June....................	4.00-	6.00	.75-	1.00
☐ Hawn, Goldie...................	4.00-	6.00	.75-	1.00
☐ Haworth, Jill	2.00-	3.00	.75-	1.00
☐ Hayden, Sterling	2.00-	3.00	.75-	1.00
☐ Hayes, Helen...................	5.00-	7.00	1.00-	1.50
☐ Hayworth, Rita	10.00-	15.00	2.00-	3.00
☐ Healy, Mary.....................	2.00-	3.00	.75-	1.00
☐ Heatherton, Joey................	3.00-	4.00	.75-	1.00
☐ Heckart, Eileen.................	2.00-	3.00	.75-	1.00
☐ Hemmings, David	2.00-	3.00	.75-	1.00
☐ Henderson, Forence............	2.00-	3.00	.75-	1.00
☐ Henry, Pat.....................	4.00-	7.00	1.00-	1.75
☐ Hepburn, Audrey...............	3.00-	4.00	.75-	1.00
☐ Hepburn, Katherine	15.00-	28.00	2.00-	4.00
☐ Heston, Charlton	6.00-	8.00	1.00-	1.50
☐ Heywood, Anne	2.00-	3.00	.75-	1.00
☐ Hickman, Daryl.................	2.00-	3.00	.75-	1.00
☐ Hickman, Dwayne	2.00-	3.00	.75-	1.00
☐ Hill, Arthur	2.00-	3.00	.75-	1.00
☐ Hiller, Wendy	3.00-	4.00	.75-	1.00
☐ Hines, Mimi	2.00-	3.00	.75-	1.00
☐ Hingle, Pat	2.00-	3.00	.75-	1.00
☐ Hitchcock, Alfred................	15.00-	23.00	1.00-	1.75
☐ Hoffman, Dustin................	5.00-	7.00	.75-	1.00

	8 × 10 Black and White Photo Signed		Plain Signature	
☐ Holbrook, Hal	3.00-	4.00	.75-	1.00
☐ Holden, William	30.00-	45.00	.75-	1.00
☐ Holder, Geoffrey................	2.00-	3.00	.75-	1.00
☐ Holliman, Earl	2.00-	3.00	.75-	1.00
☐ Holly, Buddy	150.00-	200.00	20.00-	30.00
☐ Holm, Celeste	3.00-	4.00	.75-	1.00
☐ Hooks, Robert..................	2.00-	3.00	.75-	1.00
☐ Hope, Bob	4.00-	6.00	1.00-	1.50
☐ Hopkins, Anthony..............	5.00-	7.00	.75-	1.00
☐ Horton, Robert	2.00-	3.00	.75-	1.00
☐ Howard, Trevor.................	3.00-	4.00	.75-	1.00
☐ Howes, Sally Ann	3.00-	4.00	.75-	1.00
☐ Hudson, Rock..................	5.00-	7.00	.75-	1.00
☐ Hunt, Lois......................	2.00-	3.00	.75-	1.00
☐ Hunt, Marsha..................	2.00-	3.00	.75-	1.00
☐ Hunter, Kim	3.00-	4.00	.75-	1.00
☐ Huston, John...................	8.00-	10.00	1.00-	1.50
☐ Huston, Walter	20.00-	35.00	3.00-	5.00
☐ Hutton, Betty...................	4.00-	6.00	.75-	1.00
☐ Hutton, Lauren.................	2.00-	3.00	.75-	1.00
☐ Hyde-White, Wilfrid.............	3.00-	4.00	.75-	1.00
☐ Hyer, Martha	2.00-	3.00	.75-	1.00
☐ Hyman, Earl...................	2.00-	3.00	.75-	1.00
☐ Ingels, Marty	2.00-	3.00	.75-	1.00
☐ Ireland, John...................	2.00-	3.00	.75-	1.00
☐ Ives, Burl.....................	3.00-	4.00	.75-	1.00
☐ Jackson, Anne	4.00-	6.00	.75-	1.00
☐ Jackson, Glenda	5.00-	7.00	.75-	1.00
☐ Jackson, Kate..................	3.00-	4.00	.75-	1.00
☐ Jaffe, Sam	3.00-	4.00	.75-	1.00
☐ Jagger, Dean...................	2.00-	3.00	.75-	1.00
☐ Janssen, David.................	15.00-	20.00	2.00-	3.00
☐ Jason, Rick	2.00-	3.00	.75-	1.00
☐ Jeffreys, Anne	2.00-	3.00	.75-	1.00
☐ Jeffries, Fran..................	3.00-	4.00	.75-	1.00
☐ Jepson, Helen..................	2.00-	3.00	.75-	1.00
☐ Jessel, George	10.00-	15.00	1.00-	1.75
☐ Johns, Glynis	2.00-	3.00	.75-	1.00
☐ Johnson, Van	3.00-	4.00	.75-	1.00
☐ Jolson, Al	60.00-	80.00	10.00-	15.00
☐ Jones, Allan...................	2.00-	3.00	.75-	1.00
☐ Jones, Carolyn.................	2.00-	3.00	.75-	1.00
☐ Jones, Dean....................	2.00-	3.00	.75-	1.00
☐ Jones, Jack	2.00-	3.00	.75-	1.00
☐ Jones, Jennifer.................	6.00-	8.00	1.00-	1.50
☐ Jones, Shirley..................	3.00-	4.00	.75-	1.00
☐ Joplin, Janis	125.00-	175.00	20.00-	30.00
☐ Joslyn, Allyn	2.00-	3.00	.75-	1.00
☐ Kahn, Madeline.................	6.00-	8.00	1.00-	1.50
☐ Kaplan, Gabe..................	3.00-	4.00	.75-	1.00
☐ Kasznar, Kurt..................	5.00-	7.00	.75-	1.00
☐ Kaye, Danny	9.00-	6.00	1.00-	1.50

	8 × 10 Black and White Photo Signed		Plain Signature	
☐ Kazan, Elia	8.00-	10.00	1.50-	2.50
☐ Keach, Stacy	4.00-	6.00	.75-	1.00
☐ Keaton, Diane	5.00-	7.00	.75-	1.00
☐ Keel, Howard	3.00-	4.00	.75-	1.00
☐ Keeler, Ruby	8.00-	10.00	1.00-	1.50
☐ Keeshan, Bob	2.00-	3.00	.75-	1.00
☐ Keith, Brian	3.00-	4.00	.75-	1.00
☐ Kellerman, Sally	5.00-	7.00	.75-	1.00
☐ Kelly, Grace	150.00-	225.00	5.00-	8.00
☐ Kelly, Jack	2.00-	3.00	.75-	1.00
☐ Kennedy, Arthur	2.00-	3.00	.75-	1.00
☐ Kennedy, George	2.00-	3.00	.75-	1.00
☐ Kerr, Deborah	4.00-	6.00	.75-	1.00
☐ Keyes, Evelyn	2.00-	3.00	.75-	1.00
☐ Kiley, Richard	3.00-	4.00	.75-	1.00
☐ King, Alan	2.00-	3.00	.75-	1.00
☐ King, Henry	2.00-	3.00	.75-	1.00
☐ Kirby, Durward	2.00-	3.00	.75-	1.00
☐ Kirk, Lisa	2.00-	3.00	.75-	1.00
☐ Kirk, Phyllis	2.00-	3.00	.75-	1.00
☐ Klugman, Jack	4.00-	6.00	.75-	1.00
☐ Knotts, Don	2.00-	3.00	.75-	1.00
☐ Knowles, Patric	2.00-	3.00	.75-	1.00
☐ Korman, Harvey	2.00-	3.00	.75-	1.00
☐ Kramer, Stanley	7.00-	9.00	1.00-	1.50
☐ Kristofferson, Kris	6.00-	8.00	.75-	1.00
☐ Kubrick, Stanley	10.00-	15.00	1.00-	1.50
☐ Kwan, Nancy	2.00-	3.00	.75-	1.00
☐ Lamarr, Hedy	30.00-	50.00	4.00-	7.00
☐ Lamas, Fernando	9.00-	12.00	1.00-	2.00
☐ Lancaster, Burt	8.00-	10.00	1.00-	1.50
☐ Lanchester, Elsa	4.00-	6.00	.75-	1.00
☐ Landau, Martin	3.00-	4.00	.75-	1.00
☐ Landon, Michael	3.00-	4.00	.75-	1.00
☐ Lane, Abbe	2.00-	3.00	.75-	1.00
☐ Lane, Priscilla	6.00-	8.00	.75-	1.00
☐ Lange, Hope	2.00-	3.00	.75-	1.00
☐ Langella, Frank	4.00-	6.00	.75-	1.00
☐ Langford, Frances	4.00-	6.00	.75-	1.00
☐ Lansbury, Angela	2.00-	3.00	.75-	1.00
☐ Lansing, Robert	2.00-	3.00	.75-	1.00
☐ Lasser, Louise	5.00-	7.00	.75-	1.00
☐ Laurie, Piper	2.00-	3.00	.75-	1.00
☐ Lavin, Linda	4.00-	5.00	.75-	1.00
☐ Lawford, Peter	4.00-	6.00	.75-	1.00
☐ Lawrence, Vicki	2.00-	3.00	.75-	1.00
☐ Leachman, Cloris	3.00-	4.00	.75-	1.00
☐ Learned, Michael	3.00-	4.00	.75-	1.00
☐ Lee, Bruce	75.00-	100.00	25.00-	35.00
☐ Lee, Christopher	3.00-	4.00	.75-	1.00
☐ Lee, Pinky	2.00-	3.00	.75-	1.00
☐ Leigh, Janet	4.00-	6.00	.75-	1.00
☐ Lembeck, Harvey	2.00-	3.00	.75-	1.00

	8 × 10 Black and White Photo Signed		Plain Signature	
☐ Lemmon, Jack	6.00-	8.00	1.00-	1.50
☐ Lennon, John	250.00-	350.00	35.00	50.00
☐ Leslie, Joan	2.00-	3.00	.75-	1.00
☐ Lester, Jerry	2.00-	3.00	.75-	1.00
☐ Levene, Sam	2.00-	3.00	.75-	1.00
☐ Lewis, Jerry	2.00-	3.00	.75-	1.00
☐ Lewis, Monica	2.00-	3.00	.75-	1.00
☐ Lewis, Robert Q	2.00-	3.00	.75-	1.00
☐ Lewis, Shari	3.00-	4.00	.75-	1.00
☐ Liberace	8.00-	11.00	1.00-	2.00
☐ Lillie, Beatrice	10.00-	15.00	1.00-	1.50-
☐ Lincoln, Abbey	2.00-	3.00	.75-	1.00
☐ Linden, Hal	3.00-	4.00	.75-	1.00
☐ Lindfors, Viveca	2.00-	3.00	.75-	1.00
☐ Linkletter, Art	2.00-	3.00	.75-	1.00
☐ Lipton, Peggy	2.00-	3.00	.75-	1.00
☐ Lisi, Virna	5.00-	7.00	.75-	1.00
☐ Little, Rich	2.00-	3.00	.75-	1.00
☐ Lockhart, June	2.00-	3.00	.75-	1.00
☐ Loden, Barbara	3.00-	4.00	.75-	1.00
☐ Logan, Joshua	8.00-	10.00	1.00-	1.50
☐ Lollobrigida, Gina	10.00-	15.00	1.00-	1.50
☐ Lom, Herbert	2.00-	3.00	.75-	1.00
☐ Lombard, Carole	100.00-	150.00	9.00-	14.00
☐ Longet, Claudine	8.00-	10.00	1.00-	1.50
☐ Loren, Sophia	17.00-	23.00	2.00-	3.00
☐ Loudon, Dorothy	2.00-	3.00	.75-	1.00
☐ Louise, Tina	2.00-	3.00	.75-	1.00
☐ Loy, Myrna	10.00-	15.00	1.00-	1.50
☐ Lunt, Alfred	12.00-	20.00	2.00-	4.00
☐ Lupino, Ida	4.00-	6.00	.75-	1.00
☐ Lynde, Paul	7.00-	10.00	1.00-	1.75
☐ Lynley, Carol	2.00-	3.00	.75-	1.00
☐ Lynn, Jeffrey	2.00-	3.00	.75-	1.00
☐ Lyon, Sue	2.00-	3.00	.75-	1.00
☐ MacGraw, Ali	8.00-	10.00	1.00-	1.50
☐ MacKenzie, Gizele	2.00-	3.00	.75-	1.00
☐ MacLaine, Shirley	10.00-	15.00	1.00-	1.50
☐ MacMurray, Fred	8.00-	10.00	1.00-	1.50
☐ MacRae, Gordon	2.00-	3.00	.75-	1.00
☐ MacRae, Sheila	2.00-	3.00	.75-	1.00
☐ Macy, Bill	2.00-	3.00	.75-	1.00
☐ Majors, Lee	5.00-	7.00	.75-	1.00
☐ Malden, Karl	2.00-	3.00	.75-	1.00
☐ Malone, Dorothy	2.00-	3.00	.75-	1.00
☐ Marceau, Marcel	15.00-	20.00	2.00-	3.00
☐ Margolin, Janet	2.00-	3.00	.75-	1.00
☐ Marlowe, Hugh	2.00-	3.00	.75-	1.00
☐ Marsh, Jean	3.00-	4.00	.75-	1.00
☐ Marshall, E.G.	3.00-	4.00	.75-	1.00
☐ Martin, Dick	2.00-	3.00	.75-	1.00
☐ Martin, Ross	2.00-	3.00	.75-	1.00

	8 × 10 Black and White Photo Signed		Plain Signature	
☐ Marx, Groucho	40.00–	55.00	5.00–	8.00
☐ Marvin, Lee	4.00–	6.00	.75–	1.00
☐ Mason, Jackie	2.00–	3.00	.75–	1.00
☐ Mason, James	3.00–	4.00	.75–	1.00
☐ Mason, Pamela	2.00–	3.00	.75–	1.00
☐ Massey, Raymond	4.00–	6.00	.75–	1.00
☐ Matthau, Walter	4.00–	6.00	.75–	1.00
☐ Mature, Victor	3.00–	4.00	.75–	1.00
☐ May, Elaine	4.00–	6.00	.75–	1.00
☐ Mayehoff, Eddie	2.00–	3.00	.75–	1.00
☐ Mayo, Virginia	2.00–	3.00	.75–	1.00
☐ McArdle, Andrea	4.00–	6.00	.75–	1.00
☐ McBride, Patricia	2.00–	3.00	.75–	1.00
☐ McCallum, Daivd	3.00–	4.00	.75–	1.00
☐ McCambridge, Mercedes	2.00–	3.00	.75–	1.00
☐ McCartney, Paul	175.00–	225.00	25.00–	35.00
☐ McClure, Doug	2.00–	3.00	.75–	1.00
☐ McCord, Kent	2.00–	3.00	.75–	1.00
☐ McCrea, Joel	5.00–	8.00	1.00–	2.00
☐ McDowall, Roddy	3.00–	4.00	.75–	1.00
☐ McFarland, George	5.00–	7.00	.75–	1.00
☐ McGavin, Darren	2.00–	3.00	.75–	1.00
☐ McGoohan, Patrick	4.00–	6.00	.75–	1.00
☐ McIntire, John	3.00–	4.00	.75–	1.00
☐ McKenna, Siobhan	5.00–	7.00	.75–	1.00
☐ McMahon, Ed	1.50–	2.50	.75–	1.00
☐ McQueen, Steve	25.00–	35.00	5.00–	8.00
☐ Meadows, Audrey	2.00–	3.00	.75–	1.00
☐ Meadows, Jayne	2.00–	3.00	.75–	1.00
☐ Meara, Anne	2.00–	3.00	.75–	1.00
☐ Medford, Kay	2.00–	3.00	.75–	1.00
☐ Meeker, Ralph	2.00–	3.00	.75–	1.00
☐ Melton, Sid	2.00–	3.00	.75–	1.00
☐ Mercouri, Melina	5.00–	7.00	1.00–	1.50
☐ Meredith, Burgess	5.00–	7.00	1.00–	1.50
☐ Merkel, Una	4.00–	6.00	.75–	1.00
☐ Merrick, David	6.00–	8.00	1.00–	1.50
☐ Merrill, Dina	4.00–	6.00	.75–	1.00
☐ Merrill, Gary	3.00–	4.00	.75–	1.00
☐ Midler, Bette	7.00–	10.00	1.00–	1.50
☐ Miles, Sarah	6.00–	8.00	1.00–	1.50
☐ Miles, Vera	2.00–	3.00	.75–	1.00
☐ Milland, Ray	4.00–	6.00	.75–	1.00
☐ Miller, Ann	3.00–	4.00	.75–	1.00
☐ Miller, Jason	2.00–	3.00	.75–	1.00
☐ Mills, Hayley	2.00–	3.00	.75–	1.00
☐ Mills, John	2.00–	3.00	.75–	1.00
☐ Mills, Juliet	2.00–	3.00	.75–	1.00
☐ Miner, Martin	2.00–	3.00	.75–	1.00
☐ Mimieux, Yvette	3.00–	4.00	.75–	1.00
☐ Mitchell, Cameron	2.00–	3.00	.75–	1.00
☐ Mitchum, Robert	4.00–	6.00	.75–	1.00

	8 × 10 Black and White Photo Signed		Plain Signature	
☐ Monroe, Marilyn.................	275.00-	350.00	25.00	35.00
☐ Montalban, Ricardo	2.00-	3.00	.75-	1.00
☐ Montand, Yves.................	3.00-	4.00	.75-	1.00
☐ Montgomery, Elizabeth	2.00-	3.00	.75-	1.00
☐ Montgomery, George............	2.00-	3.00	.75-	1.00
☐ Montgomery, Robert.............	2.00-	3.00	.75-	1.00
☐ Moore, Garry	2.00-	3.00	.75-	1.00
☐ Moore, Mary Tyler..............	3.00-	4.00	.75-	1.00
☐ Moore, Roger	5.00-	7.00	1.00-	1.50
☐ Moore, Terry	2.00-	3.00	.75-	1.00
☐ Moreau, Jeanne	3.00-	4.00	.75-	1.00
☐ Morena, Rita	3.00-	4.00	.75-	1.00
☐ Morgan, Dennis	2.00-	3.00	.75-	1.00
☐ Morgan, Henry	3.00-	4.00	.75-	1.00
☐ Morley, Robert	2.00-	3.00	.75-	1.00
☐ Morris, Greg	2.00-	3.00	.75-	1.00
☐ Morris, Howard.................	2.00-	3.00	.75-	1.00
☐ Morrow, Vic	2.00-	3.00	.75-	1.00
☐ Morse, Robert..................	2.00-	3.00	.75-	1.00
☐ Mostel, Zero...................	12.00-	17.00	1.50-	2.50
☐ Muir, Jean	2.00-	3.00	.75-	1.00
☐ Mulhare, Edward	2.00-	3.00	.75-	1.00
☐ Murphy, George	12.00-	18.00	2.00-	3.00
☐ Murray, Anne..................	3.00-	4.00	.75-	1.00
☐ Murray, Arthur.................	5.00-	7.00	.75-	1.00
☐ Murray, Don	2.00-	3.00	.75-	1.00
☐ Murray, Jan	2.00-	3.00	.75-	1.00
☐ Murray, Ken	4.00-	6.00	.75-	1.00
☐ Nabors, Jim	2.00-	3.00	.75-	1.00
☐ Natwick, Mildred	3.00-	4.00	.75-	1.00
☐ Neal, Patricia..................	8.00-	10.00	1.00-	1.50
☐ Nelson, Barry	2.00-	3.00	.75-	1.00
☐ Nelson, David	2.00-	3.00	.75-	1.00
☐ Nelson, Gene..................	2.00-	3.00	.75-	1.00
☐ Newhart, Bob	2.00-	3.00	.75-	1.00
☐ Newman, Barry.................	2.00-	3.00	.75-	1.00
☐ Newman, Paul..................	10.00-	15.00	1.00-	1.50
☐ Newman, Phyllis	2.00-	3.00	.75-	1.00
☐ Newmar, Julie	3.00-	4.00	.75-	1.00
☐ Nicholas, Mike	8.00-	10.00	1.00-	1.50
☐ Nicholson, Jack................	7.00-	9.00	1.00-	1.50
☐ Nimoy, Leonard	10.00-	15.00	1.50-	2.75
☐ Niven, David	20.00-	30.00	3.00-	5.00
☐ Nolan, Kathy	2.00-	3.00	.75-	1.00
☐ Nolan, Lloyd	3.00-	4.00	.75-	1.00
☐ Nolte, Nick	2.00-	3.00	.75-	1.00
☐ North J. Ringling...............	6.00-	8.00	1.00-	1.50
☐ North, Sheree	2.00-	3.00	.75-	1.00
☐ Novak, Kim....................	5.00-	7.00	1.00-	1.50
☐ Nugent, Elliot	2.00-	3.00	.75-	1.00
☐ Nuyen, France	2.00-	3.00	.75-	1.00
☐ Oakie, Jack	4.00-	6.00	.75-	1.00

	8 × 10 Black and White Photo Signed		Plain Signature	
☐ Oberon, Merle...................	6.00-	8.00	.75-	1.00
☐ O'Brian, Hugh..................	2.00-	3.00	.75-	1.00
☐ O'Brien, Edmund...............	2.00-	3.00	.75-	1.00
☐ O'Brien, Margaret	3.00-	4.00	.75-	1.00
☐ O'Connell, Helen	3.00-	4.00	.75-	1.00
☐ O'Connor, Carroll..............	4.00-	6.00	.75-	1.00
☐ O'Hara, Jill	2.00-	3.00	.75-	1.00
☐ O'Hara, Maureen	3.00-	4.00	.75-	1.00
☐ O'Herilhy, Dan..................	2.00-	3.00	.75-	1.00
☐ Olivier, Laurence	12.00-	18.00	2.00-	3.00
☐ O'Neal, Patrick	2.00-	3.00	.75-	1.00
☐ O'Neal, Ryan	4.00-	5.00	.75-	1.00
☐ O'Neal, Tatum	6.00-	8.00	.75-	1.00
☐ Orbach, Jerry	3.00-	4.00	.75-	1.00
☐ Osmond, Donny.................	2.00-	3.00	.75-	1.00
☐ Osmond, Marie.................	3.00-	5.00	.75-	1.00
☐ O'Sullivan, Maureen............	3.00-	4.00	.75-	1.00
☐ O'Toole, Peter	5.00-	7.00	.75-	1.00
☐ Owens, Gary	2.00-	3.00	.75-	1.00
☐ Paar, Jack......................	2.00-	3.00	.75-	1.00
☐ Pacino, Al	7.00-	9.00	1.00-	1.50
☐ Page, Geraldine	3.00-	4.00	.75-	1.00
☐ Paige, Janis....................	2.00-	3.00	.75-	1.00
☐ Palance, Jack	3.00-	4.00	.75-	1.00
☐ Palmer, Betsy	2.00-	3.00	.75-	1.00
☐ Papp, Joseph	5.00-	7.00	.75-	1.00
☐ Parker, Eleanor.................	5.00-	7.00	.75-	1.00
☐ Parker, Fess....................	4.00-	6.00	.75-	1.00
☐ Parker, Suzy....................	2.00-	3.00	.75-	1.00
☐ Parkins, Barbara	2.00	3.00	.75-	1.00
☐ Parks, Bert.....................	2.00-	3.00	.75-	1.00
☐ Parsons, Estelle................	3.00-	4.00	.75-	1.00
☐ Parton, Dolly	8.00-	11.00	1.00-	1.75
☐ Payne, John....................	3.00-	4.00	.75-	1.00
☐ Pearl, Jack	3.00-	4.00	.75-	1.00
☐ Pearl, Minnie	4.00-	6.00	.75-	1.00
☐ Peck, Gregory..................	8.00-	11.00	1.00-	1.50
☐ Peppard, George	3.00-	4.00	.75-	1.00
☐ Perkins, Anthony...............	2.00-	3.00	.75-	1.00
☐ Perrine, Valerie.................	5.00-	7.00	.75-	1.00
☐ Peters, Brock	2.00-	3.00	.75-	1.00
☐ Peters, Jean....................	2.00-	3.00	.75-	1.00
☐ Pickford, Mary	15.00-	20.00	2.00-	3.00
☐ Picon, Molly....................	3.00-	4.00	.75-	1.00
☐ Pidgeon, Walter	3.00-	4.00	.75-	1.00
☐ Pleasance, Donald	5.00-	7.00	.75-	1.00
☐ Pleshette, Suzanne.............	3.00-	4.00	.75-	1.00
☐ Plimpton, George	3.00-	4.00	.75-	1.00
☐ Plowright, Joan	2.00-	3.00	.75-	1.00
☐ Plummer, Christopher	5.00-	7.00	.75-	1.00
☐ Poitier, Sidney..................	5.00-	7.00	1.00-	1.50
☐ Polanski, Roman	10.00-	15.00	1.50-	2.50

	8 × 10 Black and White Photo Signed		Plain Signature	
☐ Pollard, Michael	4.00-	5.00	.75-	1.00
☐ Ponti, Carlo	10.00-	16.00	.75-	1.00
☐ Poston, Tom	2.00-	3.00	.75-	1.00
☐ Powell, Eleanor	25.00	35.00	4.00-	7.00
☐ Powell, Jane	2.00-	3.00	.75-	1.00
☐ Powell, William	10.00-	15.00	1.00-	1.50
☐ Powers, Stephanie	2.00-	3.00	.75-	1.00
☐ Preminger, Otto	8.00-	10.00	1.00-	2.00
☐ Prentiss, Paula	3.00-	4.00	.75-	1.00
☐ Presley, Elvis	325.00-	425.00	30.00-	40.00
☐ Preston, Robert	3.00-	4.00	.75-	1.00
☐ Prinz, Freddie	50.00-	70.00	8.00-	11.00
☐ Provine, Dorothy	2.00-	3.00	.75-	1.00
☐ Prowse, Juliet	3.00-	4.00	.75-	1.00
☐ Pryor, Richard	10.00-	15.00	1.00-	1.75
☐ Quayle, Anthony	3.00-	4.00	.75-	1.00
☐ Quinn, Anthony	6.00-	8.00	1.00-	1.50
☐ Raft, George	8.00-	10.00	1.00-	2.00
☐ Rainer, Luise	10.00-	15.00	1.00-	1.50
☐ Raitt, John	3.00-	4.00	.75-	1.00
☐ Randall, Tony	2.00-	3.00	.75-	1.00
☐ Ray, Aldo	2.00-	3.00	.75-	1.00
☐ Rayburn, Gene	2.00-	3.00	.75-	1.00
☐ Raye, Martha	6.00-	8.00	1.00-	1.50
☐ Raymond, Gene	3.00-	4.00	.75-	1.00
☐ Redford, Robert	6.00-	8.00	1.00-	1.50
☐ Redgrave, Lynn	5.00-	7.00	.75-	1.00
☐ Redgrave, Michael	6.00-	8.00	1.00-	1.50
☐ Redgrave, Vanessa	10.00-	15.00	2.00-	3.00
☐ Reed, Donna	2.00-	3.00	.75-	1.00
☐ Reed, Rex	1.50-	2.50	.75-	1.00
☐ Reilly, Charles Nelson	2.00-	3.00	.75-	1.00
☐ Reiner, Carl	3.00-	4.00	.75-	1.00
☐ Reiner, Rob	4.00-	5.00	.75-	1.00
☐ Remick, Lee	3.00-	4.00	.75-	1.00
☐ Renoldo, Duncan	8.00-	11.00	1.00-	1.50
☐ Reynolds, Burt	10.00-	15.00	2.00-	3.50
☐ Reynolds, Marjorie	2.00-	3.00	.75-	1.00
☐ Rich, Irene	3.00-	4.00	.75-	1.00
☐ Richardson, Ralph	10.00-	15.00	1.00-	1.50
☐ Rickles, Don	2.00-	3.00	.75-	1.00
☐ Rigg, Diana	6.00-	8.00	.75-	1.00
☐ Ritchard, Cyril	8.00-	10.00	1.00-	1.50
☐ Rivera, Chita	2.00-	3.00	.75-	1.00
☐ Robards, Jason Jr	5.00-	7.00	.75-	1.00
☐ Robertson, Cliff	2.00-	3.00	.75-	1.00
☐ Robertson, Dale	2.00-	3.00	.75-	1.00
☐ Rogers, Ginger	8.00-	10.00	1.00-	1.50
☐ Roland, Gilbert	10.00-	15.00	2.00-	3.00
☐ Roman, Ruth	2.00-	3.00	.75-	1.00
☐ Romero, Cesar	2.00-	3.00	.75-	1.00
☐ Rooney, Mickey	3.00-	4.00	.75-	1.00

	8 × 10 Black and White Photo Signed		Plain Signature	
☐ Ross, Katharine	2.00-	3.00	.75-	1.00
☐ Roth, Lillian	8.00-	10.00	1.00-	1.50
☐ Roundtree, Richard	2.00-	3.00	.75-	1.00
☐ Rowan, Dan	3.00-	4.00	.75-	1.00
☐ Rowlands, Gena	2.00-	3.00	.75-	1.00
☐ Rule, Janice	2.00-	3.00	.75-	1.00
☐ Rush, Barbara	3.00-	4.00	.75-	1.00
☐ Russell, Jane	5.00-	7.00	.75-	1.00
☐ Russell, Ken	5.00-	7.00	.75-	1.00
☐ Sahl, Mort	2.00-	3.00	.75-	1.00
☐ Saint, Eva Marie	4.00-	6.00	.75-	1.00
☐ St. James, Susan	2.00-	3.00	.75-	1.00
☐ St. John, Jill	3.00-	4.00	.75-	1.00
☐ Sainte-Marie, Buffy	6.00-	8.00	.75-	1.00
☐ Sales, Soupy	2.00-	3.00	.75-	1.00
☐ Sand, Paul	2.00-	3.00	.75-	1.00
☐ Sarrazin, Michael	6.00-	8.00	.75-	1.00
☐ Savalas, Telly	5.00-	7.00	.75-	1.00
☐ Saxon, John	2.00-	3.00	.75-	1.00
☐ Schell, Maria	3.00-	4.00	.75-	1.00
☐ Schneider, Romy	3.00-	4.00	.75-	1.00
☐ Scofield, Paul	5.00-	7.00	.75-	1.00
☐ Scott, George C	10.00-	15.00	1.00-	1.50
☐ Scott, Hazel	2.00-	3.00	.75-	1.00
☐ Scott, Martha	2.00-	3.00	.75-	1.00
☐ Scott, Randolph	4.00-	6.00	.75-	1.00
☐ Scourby, Alexander	3.00-	4.00	.75-	1.00
☐ Seberg, Jean	2.00-	3.00	.75-	1.00
☐ Segal, George	3.00-	4.00	.75-	1.00
☐ Sellers, Peter	15.00-	20.00	3.00-	5.00
☐ Shariff, Omar	6.00-	8.00	.75-	1.00
☐ Shatner, William	3.00-	4.00	.75-	1.00
☐ Shaw, Robert	2.00-	3.00	.75-	1.00
☐ Shearer, Norma	8.00-	10.00	1.00-	1.50
☐ Shepherd, Cybil	6.00-	8.00	.75-	1.00
☐ Shields, Brooke	40.00-	50.00	5.00-	8.00
☐ Signoret, Simone	3.00-	4.00	.75-	1.00
☐ Silvers, Phil	3.00-	4.00	.75-	1.00
☐ Simmons, Jean	2.00-	3.00	.75-	1.00
☐ Skleton, Red	4.00-	6.00	.75-	1.00
☐ Skinner, Cornelia Otis	8.00-	10.00	1.00-	1.50
☐ Slezak, Walter	10.00-	15.00	1.00-	1.50
☐ Smith, Alexis	2.00-	3.00	.75-	1.00
☐ Smith, Maggie	4.00-	6.00	.75-	1.00
☐ Snodgrass, Carrie	2.00-	3.00	.75-	1.00
☐ Sommer, Eike	8.00-	10.00	1.00-	1.50
☐ Sorvino, Paul	6.00-	8.00	.75-	1.00
☐ Sothern, Ann	3.00-	4.00	.75-	1.00
☐ Spacek, Sissy	2.00-	3.00	.75-	1.00
☐ Stack, Robert	3.00-	4.00	.75-	1.00
☐ Stallone, Sylvester	12.00-	17.00	1.50-	2.50
☐ Stamp, Terence	3.00-	4.00	.75-	1.00
☐ Stang, Arnold	2.00-	3.00	.75-	1.00

	8 × 10 Black and White Photo Signed		Plain Signature	
☐ Stanley, Kim......................	3.00-	4.00	.75-	1.00
☐ Stanwyck, Barbara	5.00-	7.00	.75-	1.00
☐ Stapleton, Maureen..............	3.00-	4.00	.75-	1.00
☐ Stark, Koo	75.00-	100.00	15.00-	20.00
☐ Starr, Ringo	100.00-	150.00	15.00-	25.00
☐ Steiger, Rod.....................	5.00-	7.00	.75-	1.00
☐ Sterling, Jan	2.00-	3.00	.75-	1.00
☐ Sterling, Robert	2.00-	3.00	.75-	1.00
☐ Stevens, Connie.................	2.00-	3.00	.75-	1.00
☐ Stevens, Mark...................	2.00-	3.00	.75-	1.00
☐ Stevens, Stella	3.00-	4.00	.75-	1.00
☐ Stewart, James..................	7.00-	10.00	1.00-	1.50
☐ Stickney, Dorothy	3.00-	4.00	.75-	1.00
☐ Stockwell, Dean.................	2.00-	3.00	.75-	1.00
☐ Stone, Carol....................	2.00-	3.00	.75-	1.00
☐ Stone, Milburn	4.00-	7.00	1.00-	1.75
☐ Storch, Larry....................	2.00-	3.00	.75-	1.00
☐ Strasberg, Lee	15.00-	20.00	2.00-	3.00
☐ Strasberg, Susan...............	3.00-	4.00	.75-	1.00
☐ Stritch, Elaine..................	2.00-	3.00	.75-	1.00
☐ Strode, Woody	2.00-	3.00	.75-	1.00
☐ Struthers, Sally.................	6.00-	8.00	1.00-	1.50
☐ Sullivan, Barry	2.00-	3.00	.75-	1.00
☐ Sutherland, Donald..............	6.00-	8.00	1.00-	1.50
☐ Swanson, Gloria	18.00-	30.00	3.00-	5.00
☐ Swift, Loretta...................	9.00-	15.00	1.50-	2.75
☐ Talbot, Nita.....................	2.00-	3.00	.75-	1.00
☐ Tamblyn, Russ	2.00-	3.00	.75-	1.00
☐ Tandy, Jessica	4.00-	5.00	.75-	1.00
☐ Tate, Sharon	125.00-	175.00	10.00-	15.00
☐ Taylor, Elizabeth................	25.00-	35.00	3.00-	5.00
☐ Taylor, Kent	2.00-	3.00	.75-	1.00
☐ Taylor, Rod.....................	2.00-	3.00	.75-	1.00
☐ Temple, Shirley..................	10.00-	15.00	1.50-	2.50
☐ Terry-Thomas	2.00-	3.00	.75-	1.00
☐ Thaxter, Phyllis.................	2.00-	3.00	.75-	1.00
☐ Thinnes, Roy....................	2.00-	3.00	.75-	1.00
☐ Thomas, Danny	3.00-	4.00	.75-	1.00
☐ Thomas, Marlo	4.00-	5.00	.75-	1.00
☐ Thomas, Richard................	3.00-	4.00	.75-	1.00
☐ Tierney, Gene	4.00-	5.00	.75-	1.00
☐ Tiffin, Pamela	2.00-	3.00	.75-	1.00
☐ Todd, Richard	2.00-	3.00	.75-	1.00
☐ Tomlin, Lily.....................	3.00-	4.00	.75-	1.00
☐ Tompkins, Angel	3.00-	4.00	.75-	1.00
☐ Toomey, Regis	2.00-	3.00	.75-	1.00
☐ Torn, Rip	2.00-	3.00	.75-	1.00
☐ Totter, Audrey	2.00-	3.00	.75-	1.00
☐ Tracy, Arthur	3.00-	4.00	.75-	1.00
☐ Travolta, John...................	12.00-	17.00	2.00-	3.00
☐ Trevor, Claire...................	3.00-	4.00	.75-	1.00
☐ Tucker, Forrest	2.00-	3.00	.75-	1.00
☐ Turner, Lana....................	10.00-	15.00	1.50-	2.50

	8 × 10 Black and White Photo Signed		Plain Signature	
☐ Twiggy.........................	30.00-	40.00	4.00-	6.00
☐ Tyrell, Susan....................	2.00-	3.00	.75-	1.00
☐ Tyson, Cicely	3.00-	4.00	.75-	1.00
☐ Uggams, Leslie.................	2.00-	3.00	.75-	1.00
☐ Ullman, Liv.....................	8.00-	10.00	1.00-	1.50
☐ Ustinov, Peter	3.00-	4.00	.75-	1.00
☐ Vaccaro, Brenda	2.00-	3.00	.75-	1.00
☐ Valentino, Rudolph..............	250.00-	350.00	25.00-	35.00
☐ Vance, Vivian...................	4.00-	5.00	.75-	1.00
☐ Van Cleef, Lee..................	6.00-	8.00	.75-	1.00
☐ Vandervere, Trish	3.00-	4.00	.75-	1.00
☐ Van Doren, Mamie...............	3.00-	4.00	.75-	1.00
☐ Van Dyke, Dick.................	4.00-	6.00	.75-	1.00
☐ Van Fleet, Jo...................	2.00-	3.00	.75-	1.00
☐ Van Vooren, Monique	3.00-	4.00	.75-	1.00
☐ Varnay, Astrid	6.00-	8.00	1.00-	1.50
☐ Vaughn, Robert	3.00-	4.00	.75-	1.00
☐ Venuta, Benay...................	2.00-	3.00	.75-	1.00
☐ Vera-Ellen......................	2.00-	3.00	.75-	1.00
☐ Verdon, Gwen...................	3.00-	4.00	.75-	1.00
☐ Vereen, Ben....................	2.00-	3.00	.75-	1.00
☐ Vernon, Jackie	2.00-	3.00	.75-	1.00
☐ Vigoda, Abe....................	2.00-	3.00	.75-	1.00
☐ Voight, Jon.....................	5.00-	7.00	.75-	1.00
☐ Von Furstenberg, Betsy	2.00-	3.00	.75-	1.00
☐ Von Sydow, Max.................	3.00-	4.00	.75-	1.00
☐ Waggoner, Lyle.................	2.00-	3.00	.75-	1.00
☐ Wagner, Lindsay	2.00-	3.00	.75-	1.00
☐ Wagner, Robert.................	6.00-	10.00	1.00-	1.50
☐ Walker, Clint...................	2.00-	3.00	.75-	1.00
☐ Walker, Nancy	2.00-	3.00	.75-	1.00
☐ Wallach, Eli	4.00-	6.00	.75-	1.00
☐ Walston, Ray...................	3.00-	4.00	.75-	1.00
☐ Ward, Burt	3.00-	4.00	.75-	1.00
☐ Ward, Simon	2.00-	3.00	.75-	1.00
☐ Warde, Jack....................	2.00-	3.00	.75-	1.00
☐ Warfield, William	2.00-	3.00	.75-	1.00
☐ Warner, David	3.00-	4.00	.75-	1.00
☐ Waters, Ethel...................	4.00-	6.00	.75-	1.00
☐ Wayne, David	2.00-	3.00	.75-	1.00
☐ Wayne, John	35.00-	45.00	4.00-	6.00
☐ Weaver, Dennis.................	2.00-	3.00	.75-	1.00
☐ Webb, Jack.....................	2.00-	3.00	.75-	1.00
☐ Weissmuller, Johnny	8.00-	12.00	1.50-	3.00
☐ Welch, Raquel..................	8.00-	10.00	1.00-	1.50
☐ Weld, Tuesday..................	2.00-	3.00	.75-	1.00
☐ Welk, Lawrence	2.00-	3.00	.75-	1.00
☐ Welles, Orson	8.00-	10.00	1.00-	1.50
☐ West, Adam	3.00-	4.00	.75-	1.00
☐ West, Mae.....................	30.00-	40.00	3.00-	5.00
☐ White, Betty....................	2.00-	3.00	.75-	1.00
☐ Whitman, Stuart................	2.00-	3.00	.75-	1.00

	8 × 10 Black and White Photo Signed		Plain Signature	
☐ Whitmore, James...............	3.00-	4.00	.75-	1.00
☐ Widmark, Richard	2.00-	3.00	.75-	1.00
☐ Wilde, Cornel...................	3.00-	4.00	.75-	1.00
☐ Wilder, Billy	5.00-	7.00	.75-	1.00
☐ Wilding, Michael	3.00-	4.00	.75-	1.00
☐ Williams, Cindy	3.00-	4.00	.75-	1.00
☐ Williams, Esther................	2.00-	3.00	.75-	1.00
☐ Williamson, Nicol...............	4.00-	6.00	.75-	1.00
☐ Wilson, Don....................	2.00-	3.00	.75-	1.00
☐ Wilson, Flip	2.00-	3.00	.75-	1.00
☐ Wilson, Nancy..................	2.00-	3.00	.75-	1.00
☐ Winkler, Henry	10.00-	15.00	2.00-	3.00
☐ Winters, Jonathan..............	2.00-	3.00	.75-	1.00
☐ Winters, Shelley................	3.00-	4.00	.75-	1.00
☐ Winwood, Estelle...............	2.00-	3.00	.75-	1.00
☐ Withers, Jane	2.00-	3.00	.75-	1.00
☐ Wood, Natalie	35.00-	45.00	5.00-	8.00
☐ Woodward, Joanne..............	3.00-	4.00	.75-	1.00
☐ Worley, Jo Anne................	2.00-	3.00	.75-	1.00
☐ Worth, Irene...................	4.00-	6.00	.75-	1.00
☐ Wray, Fay	6.00-	8.00	.75-	1.00
☐ Wright, Martha	2.00-	3.00	.75-	1.00
☐ Wyatt, Jane	2.00-	3.00	.75-	1.00
☐ Wyler, William	3.00-	4.00	.75-	1.00
☐ Wyman, Jane...................	6.00-	10.00	1.00-	1.75
☐ Wynn, Ed	25.00-	35.00	3.00-	5.00
☐ Wynn, Kennan	2.00-	3.00	.75-	1.00
☐ Wynter, Dana..................	2.00-	3.00	.75-	1.00
☐ York, Dick	2.00-	3.00	.75-	1.00
☐ York, Michael..................	5.00-	7.00	.75-	1.00
☐ York, Susannah	4.00-	6.00	.75-	1.00
☐ Young, Alan....................	3.00-	4.00	.75-	1.00
☐ Young, Gig	6.00-	8.00	1.00-	1.50
☐ Young, Loretta	4.00-	5.00	.75-	1.00
☐ Young, Robert..................	3.00-	4.00	.75-	1.00
☐ Youngman, Henny..............	3.00-	4.00	.75-	1.00
☐ Zanuck, Daryl	8.00-	10.00	1.00-	1.50
☐ Zimbalist, Efrem, Jr	3.00-	4.00	.75-	1.00.00

ENTERTAINMENT AUTOGRAPHS OF SPECIAL INTEREST

The following listing gives values for entertainment figure autographs of a special or unusual nature. By comparing these prices against those in the main section (above), it will be evident that the **nature of the item** counts very much toward determining value.

	PRICE RANGE	
☐ **ADAMS, JOEY.** 8 × 10 photo with Cindy Adams, signed by both...	9.00	12.00
☐ **ALLEN, WOODY.** Motion picture still, "Take the Money and Run," signed...	7.00	10.00

	PRICE RANGE	

☐ **ANDREWS, JULIE.** Colored magazine cover with her as "Eliza Doolittle," signed and inscribed.................... **6.00** **9.00**

☐ **ARNAZ, DESI.** 8 × 10 color photo with Lucille Ball, signed by both, dated on back 1954......................... **55.00** **70.00**

☐ **ARNESS, JAMES.** 8 × 10 photo as "Matt Dillon," signed "Matt Dillon," then "James Arness". **9.00** **12.00**

☐ **BACALL, LAUREN.** Magazine photo with Humphrey Bogart, signed by both. **100.00** **130.00**

☐ **BACKUS, JIM.** Color cover, "Mr. Magoo Comics," signed. **5.00** **7.00**

☐ **BAKER, CARROLL.** Motion picture still, "Jean Harlow Story," signed.. **7.00** **9.00**

☐ **BARDOT, BRIGITTE.** Photo layout from "Cavalier" magazine, signed and inscribed, 1962. .... **90.00** **115.00**

☐ **BEATTY, WARREN.** Lobby card, "Shampoo," signed. **35.00** **45.00**

☐ **BELLAMY, RALPH.** Photo as "Franklin Roosevelt," from theatrical production ("Sunrise at Campobello"), signed... **5.00** **7.00**

☐ **BERGEN, CANDICE.** Photo at age two, on knee of father, Edgar Bergen, with puppet Charley McCarthy on other knee, unsigned... **5.00** **7.00**

☐ **BERGMAN, INGRID.** 8 × 10 photo as "Joan of Arc," signed.. **50.00** **70.00**

☐ **BERLE, MILTON.** "TV Guide" cover signed, 1951......... **6.00** **8.00**

☐ **BERNARDI, HERSCHEL.** Photo with Zero Mostel and Paul Lipson, signed by all three (all played lead in "Fiddler on the Roof" at various times.).............................. **40.00** **50.00**

☐ **BIXBY, BILL.** 8 × 10 photo with Lou Ferrigno of "Incredible Hulk," signed by Bixby only. **6.00** **8.00**

☐ **BLAIR, LINDA.** Motion picture still, "The Exorcist," signed.. **12.00** **17.00**

☐ **BLOOM, CLAIRE.** Motion picture still with Charles Chaplin, "Limelight," signed by both...................... **90.00** **115.00**

☐ **BOGARDE, DIRK.** English movie annual book, signed on dust jacket.. **8.00** **10.00**

☐ **BOONE, RICHARD.** 8 × 10 photo as "Palladin," signed... **6.00** **8.00**

☐ **BORGNINE, ERNEST.** Motion picture still, "Marty," signed.. **6.00** **8.00**

☐ **BRANDO, MARLON.** Playbill, "Streetcar Named Desire," signed. Also signed by two others.................... **50.00** **65.00**

☐ **BRIDGES, BEAU.** Photo with Lloyd Bridges, signed by both.. **6.00** **8.00**

☐ **BRYNNER, YUL.** Photo from "King and I," signed........ **6.00** **9.00**

☐ **BURNETT, CAROL.** Magazine article, signed 1969....... **4.00** **5.00**

☐ **BURTON, RICHARD.** Theater poster, "Hamlet," signed; also signed by Hume Cronyn, William Redfield and three others. **350.00** **450.00**

☐ **CAAN, JAMES.** Motion picture still, "The Godfather," signed.. **15.00** **20.00**

☐ **CAESAR, SID.** 8 × 10 photo with Mel Brooks, signed by both dated 1955.. **17.00** **24.00**

☐ **CAGNEY, JAMES.** Photo as "George M. Cohan" from motion picture, signed.. **20.00** **30.00**

☐ **CANTINFLAS.** Motion picture still, "Around the World in 80 Days," signed. Also signed by David Niven and Michael Todd.. **35.00** **45.00**

PRICE RANGE

☐ **CARLISLE, KITTY.** 4 × 5 photo with Moss Hart, signed by both. **15.00** **20.00**
☐ **CARNEY, ART.** 8 × 10 photo as "Norton," signed 1956. . . **6.00** **8.00**
☐ **COBURN, JAMES.** Newspaper ad for motion picture, signed. **2.00** **3.00**
☐ **COLBERT, CLAUDETTE.** Motion picture still, "It Happened One Night," signed. **25.00** **35.00**
☐ **CONNERY, SEAN.** Photo as "James Bond," signed. **10.00** **15.00**
☐ **CONNORS, CHUCK.** Brooklyn Dodger baseball yearbook, signed. **8.00** **10.00**
☐ **COOGAN, JACKIE.** Motion picture still with Charles Chaplin, signed by Coogan. **35.00** **45.00**
☐ **CRABBE, BUSTER.** 8 × 10 photo as "Flash Gordon," signed. **15.00** **22.00**
☐ **DAVIS, OSSIE.** Photo with Ruby Dee, signed by both. . . . **7.00** **9.00**
☐ **DAY, LARAINE.** Photo with Leo Durocher, signed by both. **15.00** **20.00**
☐ **DENNIS, SANDY.** Motion picture still, "The Out-of-Towners," signed by her and Jack Lemmon. **15.00** **20.00**
☐ **DIETRICH, MARLENE.** Motion picture still, "The Blue Angel," signed and inscribed. **80.00** **100.00**
☐ **DUFF, HOWARD.** 5″ × 6½″ color photo with Ida Lupino, signed by both. **10.00** **15.00**
☐ **DUNAWAY, FAYE.** Motion picture still, "Chinatown," signed. **12.00** **17.00**
☐ **EDEN, BARBARA.** Poster photo as "Jeannie," signed. . . . **17.00** **24.00**
☐ **FALK, PETER.** Photo as "Colombo," signed. **8.00** **12.00**
☐ **FAWCETT-MAJORS, FARRAH.** Shampoo ad from magazine, signed. **9.00** **13.00**
☐ **FAYE, ALICE.** Photo with Phil Harris, signed by both, 1946. . . . . **6.00** **8.00**
☐ **FELLINI, FEDERICO.** Motion picture still, "Satyricon," signed with lengthy inscription. **30.00** **45.00**
☐ **FIELD, SALLY.** Photo as "Flying Nun," signed. **3.00** **4.00**
☐ **FISHER, CARRIE.** Motion picture still, "Star Wars," signed. **15.00** **20.00**
☐ **FONDA, HENRY.** Motion picture still, "Jesse James," signed. **50.00** **65.00**
☐ **FONDA, PETER.** Motion picture still, "Easy Rider," signed. **10.00** **15.00**
☐ **FOSSE, BOB.** Photo with Gwen Verdon, signed by both. **10.00** **15.00**
☐ **FOXX, REDD.** LP record album cover, signed, no record, 1957. . . . . **20.00** **30.00**
☐ **GABOR, EVA.** Photo with Zsa Zsa and Magda Gabor, in jewelry shop, signed by all three, c. 1950's. **12.00** **15.00**
☐ **GARDNER, AVA.** Motion picture still, "Barefoot Contessa," signed. **12.00** **15.00**
☐ **GAYNOR, MITZI.** Full-page color pin-up from magazine, signed, c. 1955. . . . . **5.00** **7.00**
☐ **GOBEL, GEORGE.** Photo with guitar at age 12, signed. **8.00** **10.00**
☐ **GORDON, RUTH.** Copy of her autobiography, signed. . . . **10.00** **15.00**
☐ **GOULET, ROBERT.** Photo with Carol Lawrence, signed by both. **6.00** **8.00**

PRICE RANGE

☐ **GREENE, LORNE.** Photo with Dan Blocker, Pernell Roberts and Michael Landon, signed by all. 30.00 40.00

☐ **GREY, JOEL.** Motion picture still, "Cabaret," signed by him and Liza Minnelli. 35.00 20.00

☐ **HAMPSHIRE, SUSAN.** Photo as Lady Churchill, signed. 8.00 10.00

☐ **HARRISON, REX.** Magazine cover with him as Henry Higgins ("My Fair Lady"), signed, 1956. .... 6.00 8.00

☐ **HAVOC, JUNE.** 8 × 10 photo with Gypsy Rose Lee, signed by both, 1942. .... 15.00 20.00

☐ **HEPBURN, AUDREY.** Motion picture still, "Breakfast at Tiffany's," signed. 7.00 10.00

☐ **HOLBROOK, HAL.** Photo as Mark Twain, signed. 6.00 8.00

☐ **HOPE, BOB.** Photo with Dwight D. Eisenhower, signed by Eisenhower. 150.00 200.00

☐ **IVES, BURL.** LP record album cover, signed, record gone. 20.00 30.00

☐ **JONES, SHIRLEY.** Photo with David Cassidy, signed by both. 10.00 15.00

☐ **KAHN, MADELINE.** Motion picture still, "Paper Moon," signed. 10.00 12.00

☐ **KAYE, DANNY.** 8 × 10 color photo with Bing Crosby, signed by both. 30.00 40.00

☐ **KEELER, RUBY.** Photo with Dick Powell, signed by both. 20.00 25.00

☐ **KELLERMAN, SALLY.** 8 × 10 photo as "Hot Lips," signed. 15.00 22.00

☐ **KELLY, GRACE.** Official Monaco wedding picture with Crown Prince Rainier, signed by both, matted and framed. 1000.00 1500.00

☐ **LANCASTER, BURT.** Motion picture still, "Elmer Gantry," signed. 10.00 12.00

☐ **LAVIN, LINDA.** Photo as "Alice," signed by her, also signed by several others in cast. 10.00 12.00

☐ **LAWFORD, PETER.** Photo with Frank Sinatra, signed.... 10.00 15.00

☐ **LEWIS, JERRY.** 8 × 10 photo with Dean Martin, signed by both, 1950. .... 30.00 40.00

☐ **LINKLETTER, ART.** Book, "Kids Say the Darndest Things," signed on front flyleaf. 6.00 8.00

☐ **LUNT, ALFRED.** Photo with Lynn Fontanne, signed by both, 1947. .... 60.00 80.00

☐ **MacLAINE, SHIRLEY.** Book, "Don't Fall Off the Mountain," signed and inscribed. 14.00 19.00

☐ **MAJORS, LEE.** Photo with Farrah Fawcett-Majors, signed by both. 18.00 25.00

☐ **MARSH, JEAN.** Photo from "Upstairs, Downstairs," signed. 5.00 7.00

☐ **MASSEY, RAYMOND.** Photo as "Abe Lincoln," signed, c. 1952. .... 10.00 12.00

☐ **MATURE, VICTOR.** Motion picture still, "One Billion B.C.," signed. 5.00 7.00

☐ **MAY, ELAINE.** Photo with Mike Nichols, signed by both, 1960. .... 15.00 20.00

☐ **MURRAY, KEN.** 8 × 10 photo with Marie Wilson, signed by both. 15.00 22.00

PRICE RANGE

☐ **NEWMAR, JULIE.** Photo from theatrical production, "Li'l Abner," signed. 6.00 8.00

☐ **NICHOLSON, JACK.** Motion picture still, "One Flew Over the Cuckoo's Nest," signed. 16.00 21.00

☐ **NIMOY, LEONARD.** 8×10 color photo as "Spock," signed. 21.00 32.00

☐ **O'BRIAN, HUGH.** Photo as "Wyatt Earp," signed. 4.00 5.00

☐ **OSMOND, DONNY.** Photo with Marie Osmond, signed by both. 6.00 8.00

☐ **PACINO, AL.** Motion picture still, "Serpico," signed. 15.00 20.00

☐ **PARKER, FESS.** 8×10 photo as "Davy Crockett," signed. 8.00 10.00

☐ **POITIER, SIDNEY.** Motion picture still, "In the Heat of the Night," signed, also signed by Tony Curtis. 12.00 15.00

☐ **POWELL, JANE.** LP record album cover (10-inch), signed, record missing, c. 1949. .... 25.00 35.00

☐ **REDFORD, ROBERT.** Motion picture still, "Barefoot in the Park," signed. 10.00 15.00

☐ **REDGRAVE, VANESSA.** Photo as "Isadora Duncan," signed. 15.00 20.00

☐ **ROONEY, MICKEY.** Photo with Judy Garland, signed by both, 1943. .... 325.00 425.00

☐ **RUSSELL, JANE.** Motion picture still, "The Outlaw," signed. 10.00 15.00

☐ **SELLERS, PETER.** Motion picture still, "Pink Panther," signed. 25.00 35.00

☐ **STEVENS, STELLA.** Nude photo from "Playboy" magazine, signed. 12.00 15.00

☐ **SWIT, LORETTA.** Photo with "Mash" cast, signed by her, Alan Alda and several others, 1977. .... 45.00 60.00

☐ **TOMLIN, LILY.** LP record album cover, signed, record gone. 15.00 20.00

☐ **VAUGHN, ROBERT.** Photo from "Man from U.N.C.L.E.," signed. 5.00 7.00

☐ **WILSON, DON.** Photo with Jack Benny, signed by both, 1945. .... 12.00 15.00

CELEBRITIES IN OTHER FIELDS

This section comprises autographs of celebrities from numerous backgrounds, excluding only Presidents and Entertainment Figures (see previous sections). A brief identification is provided for each name.

In the following listings, all items represent actual specimens sold by autograph dealers of auctioneers. Descriptions are given as they appeared in the sales offerings, though sometimes edited for space considerations.

In using this section it is important to understand that the values are for the specific items described. Similar items might, or might not, be worth similiar prices. As is always the case in the autograph hobby, any variations from item to item can influence the value. The length of a letter, for example, can be a determining factor in price. So can its date. With a signed photograph, an inscription accompanying the signature will often increase the value. The size of a photograph is important, too, and even the circumstances under which it was taken. Therefore these listings should be regarded as rough guides when used in appraising material of a similar nature. A few explanations:

HOLOGRAPH (a standard collector's term) means "in the handwriting of that person." Thus a holograph letter signed is one in which the whole letter has been handwritten by the person indicated, as well as signed by that person. A "letter signed" is signed by the person indicated, but the letter itself was either typewritten or handwritten by someone other than the signer.

NOTE. There is no clear distinction in the hobby between "letter" and a "note." Normally "note" is taken to mean a brief message without the usual embellishments of a letter such as name and address of the recipient, place of writing and so forth.

QUOTATION. This always means a quotation from a work of that individual, which the individual has handwritten at the request of a collector or fan.

TYPESCRIPT. Typewritten copy of an essay, poem, address, or some other work by the person indicated. These are of no value unless signed, as they can be reproduced at will. There is never any implication that the author actually did the typewriting, though this is often the case; it is irrelevant so far as value is concerned.

SENTIMENT. A loosely used term, which can be taken to mean a brief message, sometimes philosophical, sometimes inspirational. Not necessarily the creation of the individual writing it, but usually so. Something as standard as "Best wishes" would not be considered a sentiment.

	PRICE RANGE	
☐ **Abbey, Edwin (artist),** signature......................	18.00	24.00
☐ **Abbott, Jacob (author),** signature......................	8.00	11.00
☐ **Abel, I.W. (teamster leader),** photo signed.............	16.00	21.00
☐ **Aberdeen, First Earl of (Govenor General of Canada),** signature...	9.00	12.00
☐ **Abrams, Creighton (Allied Commander in Vietnam),** letter signed, one page, 1972...........................	16.00	21.00
☐ **Acheson, Dean (Secretary of State in Truman's cabinet),** signature on a first day cover, 1968..............	16.00	21.00
☐ **Adair, John (Commander in War of 1812 under Andrew Jackson),** signature and closing lines from a holograph letter...	24.00	31.00
☐ **Adalbert, Ferdinand B.V. (Prince of Prussia),** holograph letter signed, two pages, 1919..........................	17.00	23.00
☐ **Adams, Ansel (photographer),** bookplate, signed.......	19.00	25.00
☐ **Adams, Charles F. (Secretary of Navy, great-grandson of John Quincy Adams),** signature....................	14.00	18.00
☐ **Adams, John W. (artist),** pen and ink drawing signed, 9¾″ × 12″...	78.00	108.00
☐ **Adams, Leonie (poet),** holograph letter signed, two pages, undated...	27.00	35.00

Concluding page, with signature from a lengthy holograph letter of Hans Christian Andersen, writer of children's literature.

PRICE RANGE

☐ **Adams, Oscar F. (author)**, signature on a card dated 1892. . . . . 10.00   14.00

☐ **Addams, Jane (anti-poverty crusader)**, inscribed and signed copy of her book, "The Second Twenty Years at Hull-House". 77.00   105.00

☐ **Addison, Christopher (physician)**, signature. 10.00   14.00

☐ **Ade, George (dramatist)**, signature dated 1903. . . . . 10.00   14.00

☐ **Aicard, Jean (novelist)**, holograph letter signed, one page, 1909. . . . . 15.00   20.00

☐ **Ainsworth, Walden Lee (Admiral of World War II)**, holograph note signed. 14.00   18.00

☐ **Aks, Frank P (survivor of the Titanic)**, signature on photo of Titanic, 8 × 10. . . . . 67.00   88.00
(Aks was a ten month old baby at the time of the disaster.)

☐ **Albani, Francesco (Old Master artist)**, holograph letter signed, one page, 1659. . . . . 775.00   975.00

☐ **Albert, Carl (Speaker of the House)**, letter signed, one page, 1980. . . . . 16.00   21.00

☐ **Albert, Prince (husband of Queen Victoria of Great Britain)**, envelope addressed and signed by him. 80.00   100.00

☐ **Albrecht, Johann (Duke of Mecklenberg)**, photo signed, 1899. . . . . 23.00   31.00

☐ **Alcott, Amos (father of Louisa May Alcott)**, signature. 9.00   12.00

☐ **Alexander I (czar of Russia)**, holograph letter signed, one page, in French, 1815. . . . . 260.00   315.00
(The vast majority of Russian czarist correspondence of the eighteenth and nineteenth centuries is in French. French was regarded as the "cultured" language in Russia, while the native tongue was looked upon as vulgar.)

☐ **Alexander, Albert V. (British Lord of the Admiralty in World War II.)**, holograph quotation signed, 1955. . . . . 22.00   31.00

☐ **Alexander, John W. (artist)**, holograph letter signed, two pages, 1903. . . . . 25.00   32.00

☐ **Alexanderson, Ernst (Inventor)**, holograph quotation signed. 16.00   21.00

☐ **Alger, Russell (Governor of Michigan)**, signature on a card. 13.00   17.00

☐ **Algren, Nelson (novelist)**, inscribed and signed copy of his book, "The Man With the Golden Arm". 18.00   24.00

☐ **Ali, Muhammad (boxer)**, signature. 21.00   27.00
(A signature reading "Cassius Clay" would be worth considerably more.)

☐ **Allen, Willis (author)**, signature on a card dated 1927. . . 10.00   15.00

☐ **Atgeld, John P. (Governor of Illinois)**, document signed, 1894. . . . . 16.00   21.00

☐ **Anderson, C.E. (fighter pilot of World War II who downed sixteen axis aircraft)**, signature on a card. 14.00   18.00

☐ **Anderson, John (unsuccessful "third party" Presidential candidate in 1980)**, letter signed, one page, 1980. . . 16.00   21.00

☐ **Anderson, Kenneth (British General at Dunkirk)**, Signature on a card, 1949. . . . . 14.00   18.00

☐ **Andrew, John A. (Governor of Massachusetts)**, document signed, 1863. . . . . 16.00   21.00

Decorative signature of naturalist and artist John James Audubon.

	PRICE RANGE	
☐ **Angell, Norman (author),** holograph letter signed, two pages, undated.	18.00	24.00
☐ **Anglesley, 1st Marquis (British Field Marshall),** signature.	16.00	21.00
☐ **Anthony, Henry (Governor of Rhode Island),** signature.	14.00	18.00
☐ **Armstrong, John (Revolutionary War Officer),** holograph letter signed, one page, 1813.	95.00	115.00
☐ **Arno, Sig (cartoonist),** photo signed, 5″ × 7″.	23.00	31.00
☐ **Arnold, Sir Edwin (poet),** holograph letter signed, one page, 1883.	16.00	21.00
☐ **Atkins, Susan (member of Charles Manson cult group),** letter signed, two pages, written in prison, 1977.	115.00	145.00
☐ **Auchinleck, Sir Calude (British Field Marshall),** signature on a leaflet.	14.00	18.00
☐ **Averill, Earl (baseball player),** postcard photo, signed.	16.00	21.00
☐ **Axelrod, Julius (biochemist),** signature on a card.	14.00	18.00
☐ **Bache, Alexander (physicist),** signature.	9.00	12.00
☐ **Bacon, Robert (Secretary of State in Theodore Roosevelt's cabinet),** letter signed, one page, 1905.	18.00	24.00
☐ **Baden-Powell, Robert (founder of Boy Scouts),** signature.	50.00	65.00
☐ **Badger, George S. (Secretary of the Navy in William Henry Harrison's cabinet),** letter signed, one page, 1841.	19.00	24.00
☐ **Baer, Max (boxer),** photo signed, 1951.	37.00	48.00
☐ **Baillie, Joanna (poet),** holograph letter signed, one page, 1827.	23.00	30.00
☐ **Bainbridge, William (Commodore of War in 1812),** signed check, 1812.	47.00	60.00
☐ **Baird, Absalom (Civil War General),** holograph letter signed, one page, 1902.	18.00	24.00
☐ **Baker, "Home Run" (baseball player),** signature on a card.	55.00	70.00
☐ **Baker, Howard (Senator from Tennessee),** letter signed, 1979.	16.00	21.00
☐ **Baker, Newton (Mayor of Cleveland, associate of Woodrow Wilson),** letter signed, one page, 1924.	27.00	35.00
☐ **Balasco-Ibanez, Vincente (novelist),** signature.	14.00	18.00
☐ **Balbo, Italo (Italian aviator),** photo signed, 8 × 10.	115.00	145.00
☐ **Balfe, Michael (composer),** holograph letter signed, four pages, 1864.	85.00	105.00

Presentation inscription in a book, from J. N. Barrie to Thomas Hardy. Barrie's "Little Minister" was a fabulous best seller in the 1800s, but is all but forgotten today (he isn't by autograph collectors).

	PRICE RANGE	
☐ **Balfour, Andrew (surgeon)**, holograph letter signed, one page, 1922.	27.00	35.00
☐ **Balfour, Arthur (philosopher)**, letter signed, one page, 1890.	24.00	34.00
☐ **Ball, Thomas (sculptor)**, signature.	14.00	18.00
☐ **Bancroft, David (baseball player)**, signature with brief sentiment.	16.00	21.00
☐ **Bancroft, George (historian)**, holograph letter signed, one page, 1872.	23.00	31.00
☐ **Banfield, Gottfried (Austrian fighter pilot of World War I)**, photo signed in uniform, 4½″ × 7″.	47.00	58.00
☐ **Bankhead, William (Speaker of the House, father of Tallulah Bankhead)**, signature.	16.00	21.00
☐ **Banks, Nathaniel P. (Civil War General)**, signature on a card.	14.00	18.00
☐ **Barbour, James (Governor of Virginia)**, holograph letter signed, one page, 1828.	24.00	32.00
☐ **Baring-Gould, Sabine (composer of "Onward Christian Soldiers")**, nine lines from a holograph letter with signature.	14.00	18.00
☐ **Barlow, Francis (Civil War General)**, signature.	12.00	16.00
(One of the youngest Civil War Generals, Barlow attained the rank at 28.)		
☐ **Barnum, Phineas T. (showman)**, signature dated 1885.	24.00	32.00
(There is a considerable difference in value between Barnum's signatures and his letters. He autographed virtually anything that was thrust at him, consequently plain signatures are perhaps twenty times more common than letters.)		
☐ **Barringer, James C. (Texas Ranger)**, holograph letter signed in pencil, 1934.	32.00	43.00
☐ **Barrow, Robert (Marine General)**, signed photo, color.	32.00	43.00
☐ **Barthe, Richmond (sculptor)**, signature on a card.	14.00	18.00
☐ **Bartholdi, F.A. (French sculptor responsible for Statue of Liberty)**, holograph letter signed, 1888.	68.00	88.00
☐ **Barton, Clara (founder of American Red Cross)**, holograph quotation signed, 1899.	53.00	68.00

PRICE RANGE

☐ **Barton, William (American Revolutionary War officer who captured Prescott)**, document signed, one page, 1795. . . . . 42.00   55.00

☐ **Baruch, Bernard (financier)**, letter signed, one page, 1951. . . . . 19.00   24.00

☐ **Bass, Sam (western outlaw)**, signature. 350.00   450.00

☐ **Bates, Charlotte F. (poet, assistant of Longfellow)**, holograph letter signed, one page, 1891. . . . . 15.00   20.00

☐ **Bauer, Hans (Nazi fighter pilot of World War II)**, typescript signed, one page, undated. 45.00   60.00

☐ **Baugh, Sammy (football player)**, photo signed, 8″ × 10″. 22.00   31.00

☐ **Bayard, Thomas F. (Senator from Deleware)**, holograph letter signed, two pages, 1897. . . . . 16.00   21.00

☐ **Beahan, Kermit (crew member of A-bomb mission over Nagasaki)**, front page of newspaper signed. 27.00   35.00

☐ **Beame, Abraham (Mayor of New York City)**, photo signed. 16.00   21.00

☐ **Beard, Charles A. (Boy Scout Leader)**, signature. 10.00   14.00

☐ **Beard, William (illustrator)**, holograph letter signed, undated. 58.00   72.00

☐ **Beckwith, James (portrait artist)**, signature. 11.00   15.00

☐ **Beecher, Charles E. (paleontologist)**, holograph letter signed, one page, undated. 14.00   18.00

☐ **Beecher, Henry Ward (clergyman, anti-slavery advocate)**, signature. 9.00   12.00

☐ **Becher, Thomas K. (clergyman)**, signature on a card. . . 13.00   17.00

☐ **Beene, Geoffrey (fashion designer)**, photo signed. 16.00   21.00

☐ **Belknap, William W. (Civil War General)**, signature. 13.00   17.00

☐ **Bell, Alexander G. (inventor)**, letter signed, one page, 1921. . . . . 115.00   145.00

☐ **Bell, John (Secretary of War)**, signature. 11.00   15.00

☐ **Bellingham, Richard (colonial Governor of Massachusetts)**, holograph letter signed, 1662. . . . . 47.00   62.00

☐ **Bellomont, Earl of (colonial Governor of New York)**, signature. 78.00   102.00

☐ **Below, Ernst von (German General, World War I)**, holograph letter signed, one page, 1926. 18.00   24.00

☐ **Benavente y Martinez, Jacinto (dramatist)**, photo signed, 7″ × 9¼″. 95.00   115.00

☐ **Benes, Eduard (Czech statement)**, signature. 42.00   53.00

☐ **Bengough, Benny (baseball player)**, signature on a card. 9.00   12.00

☐ **Bergh, Henry (founder of A.S.P.C.A.)**, signature. 10.00   15.00

☐ **Berkowitz, David ("Son of Sam," notorious murderer who terrorized New York City in 1977 and 1978)**, holograph letter signed in prison, three pages, written in pencil (he was not permitted to have a pen), 1978. . . . . 300.00   375.00

☐ **Bernard, Sir Francis (colonial Governor of Massachusetts)**, portion of document signed, 1764. . . . . 31.00   42.00

☐ **Bernsdorff, Count Johann H.H. (German ambassador to U.S. during World War I)**, letter signed, one page, 1916. . . . . 15.00   20.0ⁿ

PRICE RANGE

☐ **Berstein, Theresa (artist),** ink sketch signed on 5″ × 3″ card. 31.00 42.00

☐ **Berthier, Alexandre (Marshal of France),** letter signed, one page, undated. 42.00 58.00

☐ **Bethmann-Hollweg, Theobald von (German Chancellor in World War I),** holograph sentiment signed, 1916. . . . . . 26.00 34.00

☐ **Bierstadt, Albert (artist),** signature. 42.00 54.00

☐ **Bigler, William (Governor of Pennsylvania, also Senator),** document signed, 1853. . . . . 16.00 21.00

☐ **Birdseye, Charles (frozen foods tycoon),** signature of him and his wife on an album leaf. 23.00 31.00

☐ **Bissell, William S. (Postmaster General in cabinet of Grover Cleveland),** signature. 14.00 18.00

☐ **Black, Frank S. (Governor of New York),** signature. 9.00 12.00

☐ **Black, Hugo L. (jurist),** signature. 14.00 18.00

☐ **Black, Jeremiah (Attorney General and Secretary of State),** holograph letter signed, one page, 1845. . . . . 32.00 43.00

☐ **Blackmore, Richard D. (author of "Lorna Doone"),** signature dated 1888. . . . . 17.00 23.00

☐ **Blackstone, Harry (magician),** photo signed, 1979. . . . . . 16.00 21.00

☐ **Blaine, James G. (unsuccessful Presidential candidate),** signature. 11.00 15.00

☐ **Blandy, William (Admiral of World War II),** signature on a card. 14.00 18.00

☐ **Blatchford, Samuel (jurist),** signature on a card. 26.00 34.00

☐ **Bliss, Tasker (General in Spanish-American War),** letter signed, one page, 1917. . . . . 16.00 21.00

☐ **Bloch, Flexi (physicist),** signature on a card. 16.00 21.00

☐ **Blosser, Merrill (cartoonist),** ink sketch, signed, 5″ × 8″. 19.00 24.00

☐ **Bluford, Gulon (black astronaut),** letter signed, one page, undated. 52.00 67.00

☐ **Blumberg, Baruch (scientist),** signature. 11.00 15.00

☐ **Blumenthal, Jacques (musician),** holograph manuscript signed, two bars of music, 1888. . . . . 25.00 31.00
Blumenthal was "royal pianist" to Queen Victoria.

☐ **Boardman, Russell (aviator),** letter signed, one page, 1932. . . . . 21.00 26.00

☐ **Boerne, Hermann von Dem (German General of World War I),** signature on card. 14.00 18.00

☐ **Bok, Edward W. (editor, author),** holograph note signed. 25.00 33.00

☐ **Boll, Heinrich (writer),** signature. 23.00 31.00

☐ **Bonanno, Joseph (Mafia chieftan upon whom "The Godfather" was presumably based),** signature on an album leaf. 32.00 43.00

☐ **Bonaparte, Charles (Secretary of Navy in Theodore Roosevelt's cabinet),** holograph letter signed, two pages, 1911. . . . . 17.00 23.00

☐ **Bonaparte, Lucien (brother of Napoleon),** signature. . . . 21.00 27.00

☐ **Bond, Carrie (song writer),** signed typescript. 17.00 23.00

☐ **Bone, Sir Muirhead (artist),** holograph letter signed, three pages, 1936. . . . . 16.00 21.00

PRICE RANGE

☐ **Bonheur, Rosa (artist noted for huge canvasses of animal subjects),** signature.............................. 27.00 36.00
It was not unusual for Rosa Bonejeur to paint on canvases that measured 40 to 50 feet in length; she specialized in horses and wanted them life size.

☐ **Bonney, William ("Billy the Kid," western outlaw),** no recent sales on this very rare autograph, estimated price for a signature in current market would be.............. 1550.00 2100.00

☐ **Booth, Edwin (actor, brother of John Wilkes Booth),** letter signed, 1891.. 21.00 27.00

☐ **Booth, Evangeline (Commander of Salvation Army),** signature dated 1946................................... 25.00 34.00

☐ **Borglum, Gutzon (sculptor),** photo of one of his sculptures, signed and inscribed, 7″ × 4½″................ 28.00 36.00

☐ **Borglum, James L. (photographer),** signature.......... 11.00 15.00

☐ **Borie, Adolph E. (Secretary of Navy in Grant's cabinet),** signature... 15.00 19.00

☐ **Boruwalski, Joseph (famous Polish dwarf, became international celebrity as Napoleon's court jester),** holograph quotation signed, undated. 235.00 285.00

☐ **Boutwell, George (Governor of Massachusetts),** holograph letter signed, one page, undated.................. 18.00 24.00

☐ **Boyd, John (Revolutionary War surgeon),** holograph letter signed, one page, 1766............................. 32.00 42.00

☐ **Boyd, Linn (Speaker of the House of Representatives),** signature... 14.00 18.00

☐ **Bradbury, Ray (science fiction novelist),** signature on a bookplate... 14.00 18.00

☐ **Bradfield, Roger (cartoonist),** signed sketch, 5″ × 3″... 16.00 21.00

☐ **Bradford, William (Attorney General in Washington's cabinet),** holograph document signed, one page, 1788... 120.00 145.00

☐ **Bradley, Omar (five star General),** photo signed, dated 1957... 27.00 34.00

☐ **Brady, William A. ("Diamond Jim," showman, boxing promoter),** copy of his book, "Showman," signed and inscribed... 32.00 42.00

☐ **Branch, John (Governor of North Carolina),** letter signed, one page, 1818... 31.00 41.00

☐ **Brandeis, Louis D. (jurist),** letter signed, one page, 1915... 105.00 125.00

☐ **Breese, Kidder (Naval Captain),** holograph letter signed, two pages, 1870.. 17.00 23.00

☐ **Brewer, David J. (jurist),** signature..................... 14.00 18.00

☐ **Bridgman, Frederick (artist),** signature dated 1881...... 14.00 18.00

☐ **Britten, Benjamin (composer),** photo signed............ 92.00 112.00

☐ **Brodhead, Daniel (General in Revolutionary War),** document signed, 1795....................................... 67.00 88.00

☐ **Brodie, Sir Benjamin (British surgeon),** signature dated 1859... 14.00 18.00

☐ **Brooks, John (Governor of Massachusetts),** document signed, 1823... 18.00 24.00

☐ **Brooks, Phillips (clergyman, composer),** holograph letter signed, one and a half pages, 1888.................. 29.00 37.00

PRICE RANGE

☐ **Brooks, Preston S. (Congressman from South Carolina who physically attacked and badly injured his rival, Charles Sumner, on the floor of the Senate),** signature. — 37.00 — 48.00

☐ **Brooks, Sheldon (composer),** holograph manuscript signed on card. — 93.00 — 115.00

☐ **Broskie, Sig (baseball player),** signature on a card. — 10.00 — 14.00

☐ **Brown, Edmund G. ("Pat Brown," Governor of California who defeated Richard Nixon in 1962),** signature. — 14.00 — 18.00

☐ **Brown, John (member of Ruskin circle),** holograph letter signed, one page, 1871. — 18.00 — 24.00

☐ **Brown, Walter F. (Postmaster General in Hoover's cabinet),** signature on a card. — 12.00 — 16.00

☐ **Browne, Dik (cartoonist),** ink sketch signed, 5″ × 3″. — 21.00 — 26.00

☐ **Brownell, Herbert (Attorney General in Eisenhower's cabinet),** photo signed, 8″ × 10″. — 18.00 — 24.00

☐ **Bruce, Wallace (historian),** holograph manuscript signed, four lines on a card, 1900. — 15.00 — 20.00

☐ **Bryan, William J. (unsuccessful Presidential candidate, lawyer for prosecution in Scopes "monkey trial"),** signature. — 17.00 — 23.00

☐ **Bruck, Frank (explorer, lion tamer),** holograph sentiment signed. — 18.00 — 24.00

☐ **Buck, Pearl S. (novelist),** flyleaf from a book, signed. — 14.00 — 18.00

☐ **Buckner, Simon (Civil War General),** holograph note signed, 1888. — 14.00 — 18.00

☐ **Budge, Don (tennis player),** photo signed, 8″ × 10″. — 18.00 — 24.00

☐ **Buell, Don Carlos (Civil War General),** holograph letter signed, one page, 1891. — 32.00 — 42.00

☐ **Bunche, Ralph (U.S. Ambassador to United Nations),** photo signed, 4½″ × 6½″. — 45.00 — 60.00

☐ **Bunker, Ellsworth (diplomat),** letter signed, one page, 1979. — 16.00 — 21.00

☐ **Burckhardt, H.F.K. (German fighter pilot of World War I),** holograph letter, signed, two pages, 1967. — 18.00 — 24.00

☐ **Burger, Warren (jurist),** signature on a card, also signed by other Supreme Court Justices: Douglas Brennan, Stewart, White, Marshall, Blackman, Powell, Rehnquist, undated. — 85.00 — 105.00

☐ **Burleson, Albert S. (Postmaster General in Wilson's cabinet),** signature on a card. — 14.00 — 18.00

☐ **Burnham, Clara (novelist),** holograph quotation signed, four lines, 1903. — 16.00 — 21.00

☐ **Burns, Arthur (economist),** letter signed, one page, 1980. — 21.00 — 27.00

☐ **Burns, Tommy (boxer who held heavyweight championship in early 1900s),** signature on a card. — 30.00 — 39.00

☐ **Burnside, Ambrose (Civil War General who gave name to "sideburn" whiskers),** signature on a card. — 23.00 — 30.00

☐ **Burr, Aaron (Vice President, slayer of Alexander Hamilton in infamous duel),** holograph letter signed, three pages, 1791. — 365.00 — 435.00
This letter has the address sheet present (envelopes were not used in the 1700s), with Burr's free frank.

PRICE RANGE

☐ **Burroughs, John (naturalist),** holograph letter signed, one page, undated.................................. 22.00   30.00

☐ **Burton, Harold (jurist),** letter signed, undated........... 16.00   21.00

☐ **Bush, George (Vice President under Reagan),** letter signed, one page, 1979.............................. 70.00   90.00
Bush's autograph tends to be expensive, as it may represent that of a future President.

☐ **Bussey, Cyrus (Civil War General),** holograph document signed, 1892.................................... 14.00   18.00

☐ **Butcher, Max (baseball player),** signature.............. 10.00   14.00

☐ **Butenandt, Adolph (chemist),** signature on a card...... 14.00   18.00

☐ **Butler, Benjamin (Civil War General),** letter signed, one page, 1888............................... 23.00   32.00

☐ **Butler, Matthew C. (Civil War General),** signature....... 14.00   18.00

☐ **Butler, Nicholas M. (President of Columbia University),** signed typescript, four pages, 1941................. 22.00   31.00

☐ **Buttow, Coie A. (pioneer settler in Colorado),** holograph letter signed, four pages, 1884...................... 24.00   33.00

☐ **Butz, Earl (Secretary of Agriculture in Nixon's cabinet),** letter signed, one page, 1979...................... 22.00   28.00

☐ **Byrd, Richard (explorer),** copy of his book "Little America," with signature on the titlepage....................... 60.00   75.00

☐ **Byrnes, James F. (jurist),** document signed, 1946....... 21.00   26.00

☐ **Byron, George Gordon ("Lord Byron," poet),** signature.................................... 110.00   150.00

☐ **Cabell, James B. (novelist),** signed copy of his book, "Straws and Prayer Books,"...................... 35.00   45.00

☐ **Cable, George W. (author),** signature................. 18.00   24.00

☐ **Cadman, Charles W. (composer),** holograph manuscript signed on a card.............................. 67.00   88.00

☐ **Cadwalader, George (Civil War General),** signature..... 14.00   18.00

☐ **Caldwell, Erskine (novelist),** signed photo............. 23.00   30.00

☐ **Campbell, David (lawyer),** document signed, one page, 1838................................... 42.00   53.00

☐ **Campbell, James (lawyer),** holograph letter signed one page, 1873.................................. 16.00   21.00

☐ **Campbell, Thomas (Governor of Texas),** letter signed, one page, 1907.............................. 37.00   48.00

☐ **Canby, Edward R.S. (Indian fighter),** signature........ 16.00   21.00

☐ **Cannon, Joseph G. (Speaker of House of Representatives),** letter signed, one page, 1914.............. 18.00   24.00

☐ **Canova, Antonio (sculptor),** holograph letter signed, one page, 1819................................. 285.00   340.00

☐ **Canutt, Yakima (stuntman),** photo signed, 8″ × 10″..... 21.00   27.00

☐ **Capote, Truman (novelist),** signature on a card........ 60.00   80.00

☐ **Carey, Matthew (publisher),** holograph letter signed, one page, undated.............................. 18.00   24.00

☐ **Carey, Max (baseball player),** holograph letter signed, one page, undated.............................. 34.00   45.00

☐ **Carleton, Will (poet),** signature................... 9.00   12.00

☐ **Carlisle, John (Secretary of Treasure in Cleveland's cabinet),** letter signed, one page, 1888............... 32.00   40.00

☐ **Carnegie, Andrew (Scottish-American philanthropist),** letter signed, one page, 1913..................... 23.00   31.00

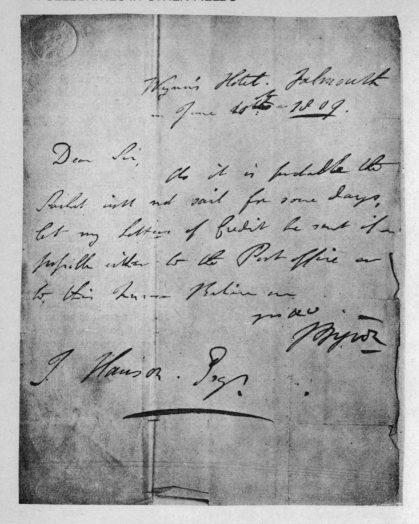

Holograph letter signed of Lord Byron, dating from 1809. The signature, "Byron," was his standard one. His real name was George Gordon Byron, and he was a Scottish nobleman.

PRICE RANGE

☐ **Carnegie, Dale (author of self-improvement books)**, signed copy of an early book of his, "Lincoln the Unknown"...	24.00	33.00
☐ **Carney, Julia (poet)**, holograph manuscript signed, sixteen lines, 1845...	105.00	130.00
☐ **Carreno, Teresa (musician)**, signature...	11.00	15.00
☐ **Cary, Alice (poet)**, holograph letter signed, one page, 1857...	18.00	24.00
☐ **Cary, Robert (Earl of Monmouth)**, in early 1600s signature...	15.00	20.00
☐ **Case, Lewis (Secretary of State)**, signature...	10.00	14.00
☐ **Casey, Silas (Civil War General)**, signature...	14.00	18.00
☐ **Cass, Lewis (General in War of 1812)**, letter signed, one page, undated...	27.00	35.00
☐ **Castle, Egerton (novelist)**, holograph letter signed, on postcard, 1901...	15.00	20.00
☐ **Catlin, George (artist, naturalist)**, signature on a card.	57.00	78.00
☐ **Catt, Carrie C. (female suffragette)**, signature...	18.00	24.00
☐ **Catton, Bruce (author)**, photo signed, 8″ × 10″...	15.00	20.00
☐ **Cayce, Edgar (writer on parapsychology)**, letter signed, one page, 1943...	150.00	190.00
☐ **Celler, Emanual (Congressman from New York)**, letter signed, one page, 1957...	13.00	17.00
☐ **Cermak, Anton J. (mayor of Chicago who was killed accidentally in 1933 by an assassin who was aiming at President Roosevelt; the two were riding together in a motorcade in Miami, Florida)**, signature...	21.00	27.00
☐ **Cernan, Eugene (astronaut)**, photo signed, color...	21.00	27.00
☐ **Chadwick, Florence (swimmer)**, signature on a plate block of postage stamps...	11.00	15.00
☐ **Chadwick, James (physicist)**, signature on card with Swedish postage stamp...	37.00	48.00
☐ **Chagall, Marc (artist)**, signed poster for Metropolitan Opera...	115.00	150.00
☐ **Chamberlain, Sir Austen (British diplomat)**, signature.	11.00	15.00
☐ **Chamberlain, Joshua (Civil War General)**, check signed, 1876...	18.00	23.00
☐ **Chamberlain, Neville (Prime Minister of Great Britain)**, signature on a card...	21.00	27.00
☐ **Chaminade, Cecile (composer)**, holograph manuscript signed, four bars of music, 1902...	70.00	90.00
☐ **Chandler, Albert (baseball commissioner)**, photo signed, 8″ × 10″...	17.00	23.00
☐ **Chandler, Zachariah (Secretary of Interior in Grant's cabinet)**, signature...	14.00	18.00
☐ **Chapman, Oscar L. (Secretary of Interior in Truman's cabinet)**, letter signed, one page, 1948...	42.00	54.00
☐ **Chapman, Ray (baseball player who died after being hit by pitched ball, only fatality in history of Major League baseball)**, signature...	42.00	54.00
☐ **Charles II (King of Spain)**, letter signed, two pages, 1698...	425.00	550.00
Signed "I, the king." In a royal letter or document this is regarded by collectors as a perfectly acceptable signature.		

PRICE RANGE

☐ **Charles, Ezzard (boxer)**, postcard photo signed......... 80.00   110.00
Scarce, as he died at an early age
☐ **Chase, Salmon P. (Secretary of the Treasury)**, signature.. 37.00   48.00
☐ **Chaves, Carlos (composer)**, photo signed.............. 21.00   27.00
☐ **Chiang Kai-shek (President of Nationalist China)**, signature..................................... 70.00   90.00
☐ **Choate, Rufus (statesman)**, holograph letter signed, 1853.. 26.00   35.00
☐ **Christina (Queen of Sweden)**, holograph letter signed, two pages, 1652.. 1550.00   2150.00
☐ **Christy, Howard C. (magazine and poster artist)**, a set of five ink sketches, three of them bearing his signature. 600.00   725.00
☐ **Clark, Thomas C. (jurist)**, first day cover signed. "American Bar Association" stamp, 1953. .... 16.00   21.00
☐ **Clarke, James (clergyman)**, holograph letter signed, two pages, 1882.. 23.00   31.00
☐ **Clay, Henry (Secretary of State, unsuccessful candidate for Presidency)**, letter signed, one page, 1827. ..... 80.00   105.00
☐ **Clay, Lucius (General in World War II)**, signature on a card.. 14.00   18.00
☐ **Clement, William T. (Marine General in World War II)**, signature on a card.................................... 11.00   15.00
☐ **Cleveland, Frances F. (wife of President Cleveland and mother of Ruth Cleveland, for whom the candy bar "Baby Ruth" was named)**, envelope addressed by her, with her free frank... 15.00   20.00
☐ **Clifford, Nathan (Attorney General)**, holograph letter signed, one page, 1872................................... 32.00   41.00
☐ **Clingman, Thomas (Civil War General)**, signature. 11.00   15.00
☐ **Clinton, George (Governor of New York, Revolutionary War hero)**, document signed, 1804...................... 135.00   175.00
☐ **Clymer, George (signer of the Declaration of Independence)**, document signed, undated.................... 115.00   140.00
☐ **Coats, Michael (astronaut on space shuttle)**, letter signed, one page, 1980. .... 65.00   85.00
☐ **Cobb, Howell (Civil War General)**, signature........... 13.00   17.00
☐ **Cobb, Ty (baseball player)**, signature on a check, 1958. 40.00   50.00
☐ **Cochran, Jacqueline (aviator)**, signature on a card. 27.00   35.00
☐ **Chochrane, John (Civil War General)**, holograph note signed, 1873.. 17.00   23.00
☐ **Cockerell, Sir Sydney (famous book collector)**, signature.. 11.00   15.00
☐ **Cockrell, Francis M. (Civil War General)**, signature..... 12.00   16.00
☐ **Cockroft, Don (football player)**, signature.............. 4.00   6.00
☐ **Coffing, Charles (author)**, holograph letter signed, one page, 1871.. 12.00   16.00
☐ **Cohan, George M. (composer)**. 23.00   32.00
☐ **Cohen, Morris (philosopher)**, holograph manuscript signed, eight pages. 32.00   43.00
☐ **Cohen, Octavus Roy (novelist)**, signature on a card. 14.00   18.00
☐ **Collins, Eddie (baseball player)**, signature on a postcard, 1947.. 27.00   35.00

PRICE RANGE

☐ **Collins, John (Governor of Rhode Island)**, signed endorsement, 1767. . . . . 28.00   36.00
☐ **Collins, Wilkie (first novelist to write who-done-it fiction)**, holograph letter signed, one page, 1888. . . . . 23.00   31.00
☐ **Colman, Norman J. (first U.S. Secretary of Agriculture)**, photo signed, undated. 17.00   23.00
☐ **Colt, Peter (Treasurer of Continental Army, father of gunmaker Samuel Colt)**, document signed, one page, 1780. . . . . 27.00   34.00
☐ **Colum, Padriac (poet)**, signed copy of his book, "Poems". 23.00   31.00
☐ **Combs, Earl (baseball player)**, signature on a postcard. 18.00   24.00
☐ **Comly, John (Quaker leader)**, holograph letter signed, one page, 1847. . . . . 21.00   26.00
☐ **Compton, Arthur H. (physicist)**, signature. 14.00   18.00
☐ **Conally, Richard (Admiral of World War II)**, signature on a card. 14.00   18.00
☐ **Condon, Richard (novelist)**, signed copy of his book, "The Manchurian Candidate". 30.00   38.00
☐ **Conlan, John ("Jocko," baseball umpire)**, signature on a postcard. 19.00   24.00
☐ **Conner, James (Civil War General)**, signature. 22.00   30.00
☐ **Connor, Selden (Civil War General)**, signature. 14.00   18.00
☐ **Constant, Benjamin (diplomat)**, holograph letter signed, one page, 1899. . . . . 28.00   36.00
☐ **Cooke, Alistair (journalist, host of "Masterpiece Theater")**, signed copy of his book, "Six Men". 26.00   35.00
☐ **Cooke, John E. (novelist)**, holograph letter signed, two pages, 1881. . . . . 18.00   24.00
☐ **Cookman, Alfred (clergyman)**, holograph quotation signed, 1866. . . . . 14.00   18.00
☐ **Coolidge, Grace (wife of President Coolidge)**, holograph note signed, in pencil. 14.00   18.00
☐ **Cooper, James F. (novelist)**, signature on a check, 1841. . . . . 52.00   67.00
☐ **Cooper, Gordon (astronaut)**, signature. 10.00   14.00
☐ **Cornell, Alonzo (Governor of New York)**, signature on a card, 1882. . . . . 14.00   18.00
☐ **Corrigan, Douglas ("Wrong Way Corrigan")**, typescript signed, one page. 25.00   33.00
☐ **Crawford, Francis M. (novelist)**, signature. 9.00   12.00
☐ **Crawford, Marion (novelist)**, holograph quotation signed. 13.00   17.00
☐ **Crawford, Sam (baseball player)**, signature on a card. 18.00   24.00
☐ **Creswell, John A. (Postmaster General in Grant's cabinet)**, signature, 1870. . . . . 14.00   18.00
☐ **Crippen, Robert (astronaut)**, photo signed, color. 21.00   27.00
☐ **Crocker, Marcelius M. (Civil War General)**, signature. . . 18.00   24.00
☐ **Croker, Richard (New York City political leader)**, signature. 14.00   18.00
☐ **Cronin, Joe (baseball player and executive)**, document signed. 27.00   36.00
☐ **Crowninshield, Benjamin (Secretary of the Navy)**, letter signed, one page, 1815. . . . . 67.00   88.00

Holograph note signed by novelist Joseph Conrad.

	PRICE RANGE	
☐ **Cullum, George W. (Civil War General)**, signature.	14.00	18.00
☐ **Cummings, Homer (Attorney General in Franklin Roosevelt's cabinet)**, signature.	14.00	18.00
☐ **Cunningham, Andrew (British Admiral of World War II)**, signature on a card.	14.00	18.00
☐ **Cunningham, Walter (astronaut)**, photo signed, color. . .	16.00	21.00
☐ **Curie, Eve (musician, daughter of Madam Curie the chemist)**, signature on a card.	14.00	18.00
☐ **Curtis, George W. (writer)**, holograph letter signed, two pages, 1883.	14.00	18.00
☐ **Curtis, N. Martin (Civil War General)**, signature.	14.00	18.00
☐ **Cushing, Caleb (statesman)**, holograph letter signed, one page, 1843.	67.00	88.00
☐ **Cushing, Richard J. (R.C. Cardinal of Boston)**, first day cover with "Religious Freedom" stamp, signed.	15.00	20.00
☐ **Custer, George Armstrong (Indian fighter)**, signature.	290.00	340.00
☐ **Custine, Comte Adam Phillippe de (Quartermaster of French Troops in American Revolutionary War)**, document signed, one page, 1793.	67.00	88.00
☐ **Cypert, Al (baseball player)**, signature.	6.00	9.00

PRICE RANGE

☐ **Dafoe, Allan R. (surgeon who delivered Dionne quintuplets)**, letter signed, one page, 1936.	42.00	53.00
☐ **Dagnan, Bouveret, Pascal (artist)**, holograph letter signed, one page, 1852.	27.00	34.00
☐ **Dahlquist, John E. (General in World War II)**, photo signed, 8″ × 10″.	18.00	24.00
☐ **d'Albert, Eugen (musician)**, holograph manuscript signed, three bars of music, 1890.	95.00	115.00
☐ **Dale, Sir Henry H. (physiologist)**, signature on a block of postage stamps.	21.00	26.00
☐ **Dali, Salvador (artist)**, photo of a Dali painting, signed by him, 4″ × 3¼″.	50.00	65.00
☐ **Dallas, George (Vice President under Polk)**, holograph letter signed, one page, 1848.	135.00	175.00
☐ **Dana, Richard H., Jr. (novelist of sea tales)**, holograph letter signed, one page, 1864.	42.00	53.00
☐ **Danforth, Dave (baseball player)**, signature.	6.00	9.00
☐ **Daniels, Josephus (Secretary of Navy in Wilson's cabinet)**, letter signed, one page, 1918.	17.00	23.00
☐ **Danilova, Alexandra (ballerina)**, signature.	10.00	14.00
☐ **Darlington, William (botanist)**, holograph letter signed, one page, 1860.	15.00	20.00
☐ **Davies, Henry (Civil War General)**, signature.	14.00	18.00
☐ **Davis, Arthur (Admiral, Commander of the Enterprise)**, photo signed.	17.00	23.00
☐ **Davis, Dwight F. (Secretary of War in Coolidge's cabinet)**, letter signed, one page, 1926.	23.00	31.00
☐ **Davis, Edmund (Civil War General)**, document signed, 1870.	47.00	60.00
Davis was from Texas but served on the Union side.		
☐ **Davis, Varina (wife of Jefferson Davis)**, signature.	11.00	15.00
☐ **Dawes, Charles (Vice President)**, signed and inscribed copy of his book, "Essays and Speeches".	52.00	67.00
This item carries extra value because the recipient was another Vice President: Charles W. Fairbanks.		
☐ **Day, Holman (novelist)**, holograph letter signed, one page, 1908.	21.00	27.00
☐ **Day, William R. (jurist)**, signature on a card.	15.00	19.00
☐ **Dearborn, Henry, A. S. (statesman)**, document signed, one page, 1812.	21.00	27.00
☐ **Debus, Adam (baseball player)**, signature on a card.	9.00	12.00
☐ **Decatur, Stephen (naval officer)**, document signed, one page, undated.	7.00	8.50
☐ **Decker, George H. (General in World War II)**, photo signed, 8″ × 10″.	22.00	30.00
☐ **DeFreese, Donald ("Clinque," leader of gang that kidnapped Patty Hearst, later slain by Los Angeles police)**, signature.	55.00	70.00
☐ **Deimling, Berthold von (German General of World War I)**, signed photo with lengthy political inscription, 1931, 9″ × 11″.	23.00	30.00
☐ **DeKoven, Reginald (composer)**, signature.	14.00	18.00
☐ **Deland, Margaret W. (novelist)**, signature on a card dated 1912.	8.00	11.00

PRICE RANGE

☐ **Dell, Floyd (novelist)**, holograph letter signed, one page, undated. ... 32.00 42.00

☐ **deMedici, Cosimo (Grand Duke of Tuscany, descendant of Lorenzo deMedici)**, letter signed, one page, 1659. ... 140.00 175.00

☐ **deMedici, Fernando (Prince of Tuscany)**, holograph letter signed, one page, 1694 ... 160.00 215.00

☐ **Dempsey, Jack (boxer)**, signature on a card. ... 14.00 18.00

☐ **Denby, Edwin (Secretary of Navy in Harding's cabinet)**, letter signed, one page, 1921. ... 17.00 23.00

☐ **Dennison, William (Postmaster General in Lincoln's cabinet)**, letter signed, one page, 1866 ... 67.00 88.00

☐ **Depew, Chauncey (lawyer)**, holograph letter signed, two pages, 1899. ... 32.00 43.00

☐ **Dern, George (Governor of Utah)**, letter signed, one page, 1926. ... 17.00 23.00

☐ **Devens, Charles (Attorney General in Hayes' cabinet)**, letter signed, one page, 1880. ... 23.00 31.00

☐ **Dewey, George (Naval Admiral)**, signature. ... 14.00 18.00

☐ **Dewey, Thomas E. (Governor of New York, twice unsuccessful Presidential candidate)**, signature on a card. ... 11.00 15.00

☐ **Dickee, Frank (Artist)**, signature. ... 9.00 12.00

☐ **Dickens, Charles (novelist)**, signature with complimentary close from a holograph letter ... 105.00 125.00

☐ **Dickerson, Mahlon (Secretary of the Navy)**, document signed, one page, 1837 ... 28.00 36.00

☐ **Dickey, James (poet)**, letter signed, one page, 1979 ... 32.00 40.00

☐ **Dickinson, Jacob M. (Secretary of War in Taft's cabinet)**, letter signed, one page, War Dept. stationery, 1909 ... 17.00 23.00

☐ **Diels, Otto (chemist)**, photo signed, 2″ × 2½″ ... 67.00 88.00

☐ **Dillon, C. Douglas (Secretary of the Treasury in Kennedy's cabinet)**, letter signed, one page, 1979. ... 21.00 27.00

☐ **Dix, John A. (Secretary of the Treasury)**, document signed, one page, 1836. ... 92.00 112.00

☐ **Doak, William (Secretary of Labor in Hoover's cabinet)**, signature. ... 14.00 18.00

☐ **Dobbin, James C. (Secretary of the Navy in Pierce's cabinet)**, letter signed, one page, 1854 ... 17.00 23.00

☐ **Dobie, J. Frank (historian of the "old west")**, holograph note signed in pencil, 1962. ... 21.00 27.00

☐ **Dodge, Henry (Governor of Wisconsin)**, signature. ... 13.00 17.00

☐ **Dodge, Mary M. (author)**. ... 18.00 24.00

☐ **Doenitz, Karl (German Nazi official)**, letter signed, one page, 1958. ... 45.00 60.00

☐ **Doisy, Edward A. (biochemist)**, signature on a card ... 14.00 18.00

☐ **Dolph, John (artist)**, holograph letter signed, one page, 1899. ... 80.00 105.00

☐ **Doolittle, James H. (aviator)**, signature ... 18.00 25.00

☐ **d'Orleans, Louis Philippe Albert (pretender to French throne)**, holograph letter signed, two pages, 1890 ... 45.00 60.00

☐ **Douglas, John Sholto (Marquis of Queensberry in late 1800's, famous for bitter vendetta against poet Oscar Wilde)**, signature. ... 21.00 27.00

To Charles Dickens from Wilkie Collins July 1865

THE MOONSTONE.

VOL. I.

A fantastic "assocation" item: Wilkie Collins' "The Moonstone," inscribed by him to Charles Dickens. In a case like this, the standard value for a Wilkie Collins autograph would not apply.

	PRICE	RANGE
☐ Dougals, Lloyd (novelist), book "White Banners," signed	25.00	35.00
☐ Douglas, Norman (author), letter signed, one page, 1926	19.00	25.00
☐ Douglas, Stephen (opponent of Lincoln in series of famous debates), signature	16.00	21.00
☐ Douglas, William O. (jurist), signature dated 1952	14.00	18.00
☐ Dow, Neal (Civil War General), holograph letter signed, one page, 1868	32.00	43.00
☐ Doyle, Sir Arthur C. (novelist, creator of "Sherlock Holmes"), holograph note on postcard, signed, 1907	135.00	175.00

PRICE RANGE

☐ **Doyle, Sir Francis (poet)**, holograph letter signed, two pages, 1872. . . . . 16.00   21.00

☐ **Draper, Charles (developer of computer gunsight)**, signature. 10.00   14.00

☐ **Dreiser, Theodore (writer)**, letter signed, one page, 1931. . . . . 45.00   60.00

☐ **Druckman, Jacob (composer)**, holograph manuscript signed, one page. 18.00   24.00

☐ **Duane, James (first Mayor of New York City)**, holograph document signed, one page, 1786. 62.00   83.00

☐ **Duane, William (journalist)**, holograph document signed, 1810. . . . . 37.00   48.00

☐ **Dumas, Alexandre (novelist)**, holograph letter signed, one page, undated. 58.00   72.00

☐ **Dundas, Deans (British naval officer)**, holograph letter signed, one page, 1834. . . . . 32.00   43.00

☐ **Dunsany, Lord (poet)**, signature. 16.00   21.00

☐ **Durant, Will (historian)**, signature. 11.00   15.00

☐ **Duvall, Gabriel (jurist)**, signature. 18.00   24.00

☐ **Dyar, Eliphalet (colonial statesman from Connecticut)**, document signed, one page, 1746/47. . . . . 32.00   43.00

This document was signed on February 11, in what we would now call 1747. At that time the new year did not officially begin until March 1. Hence the date is expressed as 1746/47.

☐ **Dyer, George C. (Admiral in World War II)**, letter signed, one page, 1948. . . . . 16.00   21.00

☐ **Eagleton, Thomas (dropped as McGovern's 1972 Vice Presidential running mate, one day after nomination)**, letter signed, one page, 1973. . . . . 13.00   17.00

☐ **Eaker, Ira (R.A.F. Commander in World War II)**, letter signed, one page, 1979. . . . . 22.00   31.00

☐ **Earhart, Amelia (aviator of 1930s)**, signature. 175.00   235.00

☐ **Earle, Alice (historian))**, holograph letter signed, three pages, 1897. . . . . 15.00   20.00

☐ **Eastman, Charles A. (physician of Sioux birth, real name Ohiyesa)**, signature. 32.00   42.00

☐ **Eastman, Dave (cartoonist)**, signed sketch, 4″ × 10″. . . 15.00   20.00

☐ **Eaton, John (early Governor of Florida)**, holograph letter signed, one page, 1836. . . . . 140.00   170.00

☐ **Eberhart, Mignon (detective fiction writer)**, holograph letter signed. 16.00   21.00

☐ **Eder, Peter (Nazi fighter pilot of World War II)**, photo signed, 4″ × 6″. 22.00   30.00

☐ **Edison, Thomas (inventor)**, document signed. 100.00   125.00

☐ **Edmunds, George (Senator from Vermont)**, holograph letter signed, one page, 1881. . . . . 43.00   55.00

☐ **Edward VIII (Duke of Windsor, King of England)**, signature on bookplate. 95.00   115.00

☐ **Einstein, Albert (mathematician, scientist)**, letter signed, one page, 1935. . . . . 325.00   425.00

☐ **Eisenhower, Mamie (wife of President Eisenhower)**, inscribed and signed greeting card, 1973. . . . . 18.00   24.00

PRICE RANGE

☐ **Eliot, Charles W. (author)**, signature....................	9.00	12.00
☐ **Eliot, T. S. (poet)**, signature.............................	21.00	27.00
☐ **Elkins, Stephen (Secretary of War in Benjamin Harrison's cabinet))**, letter signed, one page, 1892...........	18.00	24.00
☐ **Ellis, Havelock (sociologist, writer)**, holograph letter signed, three and a half pages, 1915....................	42.00	56.00
☐ **Ellsberg, Daniel (central figure of "Pentagon Paper" case in 1970s)**, signature.............................	10.00	14.00
☐ **Elman, Mischa (musician)**, signature...................	11.00	15.00
☐ **Emerson, Ralph W. (poet)**, signature..................	65.00	85.00
☐ **Ernst, August (Duke of Braunschwig)**, signature on a card..	14.00	18.00
☐ **Ervine, St. John (dramatist)**, letter signed, 1928........	14.00	18.00
☐ **Esaki, Leo (physicist)**, photo signed, 2½″ × 3½″...	15.00	19.00
☐ **Esch, Max F. (German General of World War I)**, holograph note signed, 1927......................................	11.00	16.00
☐ **Evans, Robley (officer in both Civil War and Spanish American War)**, letter signed, one page, 1898...........	67.00	88.00
Not many officers served in both wars, as they occurred more than 30 years apart.		
☐ **Evans, Ronald (astronaut)**, photo signed, color.........	26.00	34.00
☐ **Everett, Edward (orator, politician)**, seven lines in his holograph from a letter, with signature...................	15.00	19.00
☐ **Fairbanks, Charles W. (Vice President under Theodore Roosevelt)**, signature...................................	15.00	19.00
☐ **Fairless, Benjamin (industrialist)**, photo signed, 8″ × 10″..	17.00	22.00
☐ **Faisal (King of Saudi Arabia)**, photo signed, 7″ × 9½″...	40.00	50.00
☐ **Falkenhayn, Erich von (Prussian General of World War I)**, signature..	14.00	18.00
☐ **Farley, James A. (advisor to Franklin Roosevelt)**, letter signed, one page, 1935................................	21.00	26.00
☐ **Farnol, Jeffrey (novelist, cult hero)**, letter signed, one page, 1918..	14.00	18.00
☐ **Farragut, David (American Admiral)**, letter signed, one page, 1860...	260.00	315.00
☐ **Farrel, James T. (novelist)**, copy of his book, "Studs Lonigan," signed...	21.00	26.00
☐ **Ferber, Edna (novelist)**, signed copy of her book, "Cimarron"..	40.00	50.00
☐ **Ferdinand the Catholic (husband of Queen Isabella of Spain, instrumental in financing Columbus' voyages)**, document signed, one page, 1509......................	775.00	975.00
☐ **Ferdinand I (King of Bulgaria)**, letter signed, one page, 1947...	45.00	60.00
☐ **Ferguson, Miriam (female Governor of Texas)**, check signed, 1934..	37.00	48.00
☐ **Field, Cyrus (industrialist)**, letter signed, one page, 1872...	23.00	31.00
☐ **Field, Eugene (poet)**, holograph letter signed, one page, 1895...	72.00	93.00

PRICE RANGE

☐ **Fields, Jackie (boxer),** holograph letter signed, two pages, 1942. .... **17.00** **22.00**

☐ **Figl, Leopold (Austrian Chancellor),** postcard photo, signed, 1949. .... **17.00** **23.00**

☐ **Fish, Hamilton (statesman),** holograph letter signed, two pages, 1880. .... **32.00** **43.00**

☐ **Fiske, John (historian),** signature. **10.00** **14.00**

☐ **Fitzsimmons, Frank (teamster leader),** photo signed.... **21.00** **27.00**

☐ **Flavin, Martin (dramatist),** letter signed, one page, 1944. .... **15.00** **19.00**

☐ **Fleming, Sir Alexander (surgeon discoverer of penicillin),** holograph letter signed, one page, 1946............ **95.00** **115.00**
This letter was written in reply to an autograph seeker whom Fleming refers to in the letter as "pests."

☐ **Floersheim, Otto (composer),** holograph manuscript signed, four double bars of music, 1896. .... **16.00** **21.00**

☐ **Flower, Roswell (Governor of New York),** signature..... **10.00** **13.00**

☐ **Floyd, John (Governor of Virginia),** document signed, one page, 1850. .... **67.00** **88.00**
Floyd was also a General in the Confederate Army, but was relieved of his duties by Jefferson Davis.

☐ **Folger, Charles F. (Secretary of Treasury),** signature. **14.00** **18.00**

☐ **Follett, Wilson (writer),** letter signed, two pages, 1939. .... **18.00** **24.00**

☐ **Forbes, Malcolm G. (publisher),** letter signed, one page, 1979. .... **13.00** **17.00**

☐ **Ford, Betty (wife of President Ford),** signature on a first day cover, 1979. .... **32.00** **43.00**

☐ **Foreman, George (boxer),** signature.................. **23.00** **32.00**

☐ **Foreman, Grant (novelist),** holograph letter signed, one page, 1927. .... **15.00** **19.00**

☐ **Forest, Lee De (Inventor),** signature on a card along with Italian postage stamp.................... **25.00** **33.00**

☐ **Forest, Nathan B. (Civil War General),** document signed, two pages, 1869. .... **285.00** **335.00**

☐ **Forrestal, James V. (Secretary of Navy and Secretary of Defense),** signature.......................... **14.00** **18.00**

☐ **Forstmann, Walter (Nazi U-Boat pilot of World War II credited with sinking close to ½ million tons of allied ships),** signature........................... **16.00** **21.00**

☐ **Forsyth, James (Civil War General),** signature on a card. **11.00** **15.00**

☐ **Forward, Walter (Secretary of Treasury in Tyler's cabinet),** holograph letter signed, one page, 1842. .... **18.00** **24.00**

☐ **Foster, Charles (Secretary of Treasury in Benjamin Harrison's cabinet),** signature on a card.................. **14.00** **18.00**

☐ **Fowler, Gene (journalist),** holograph manuscript signed, four lines of verse.......................... **18.00** **24.00**

☐ **Fox, Henry (British Secretary of State),** document signed, 1745. .... **23.00** **30.00**

☐ **Fox, John, Jr. (novelist),** signature.................... **14.00** **18.00**

☐ **Foyt, A. J. (auto racer),** photo signed, 8″ × 10″......... **27.00** **35.00**

PRICE RANGE

- ☐ **Francis, David R. (Governor of Missouri)**, document signed, 1892. . . . . **16.00** **21.00**
- ☐ **Francis, Joseph (inventor)**, holograph letter signed, one page, 1893. . . . . **18.00** **24.00**
- ☐ **Frankau, Gilbert (writer)**, photo from a magazine, signed, 1920. . . . . **15.00** **19.00**
- ☐ **Frankfurter, Felix (jurist)**, signature, dated 1952. . . . . **32.00** **42.00**
- ☐ **Franklin, Sir John (explorer lost in Arctic)**, holograph letter signed, two pages, 1837. . . . . **65.00** **85.00**
- ☐ **Franz IV, Friedrick (Duke of Mackenburg)**, signature. . . **14.00** **18.00**
- ☐ **Frazier, Joe (boxer)**, signature on a postcard picture. **28.00** **37.00**
- ☐ **Frederick III (King of Germany)**, document signed, one page, 1880. . . . . **180.00** **230.00**
- ☐ **Frelinghuysen, Frederick (Secretary of State in Chester A. Arthur's cabinet, member of "first family of New Jersey")**, signature on a card. **14.00** **18.00**
- ☐ **Fremont, John C. (Civil War General, explorer of American West, unsuccessful Presidential candidate)**, document signed, two pages, 1872. . . . . **180.00** **235.00**
  Fremont in his later years was a featured star with the Barnum circus, in which he performed with a trained bear and troupe of "wild west" characters. He died after being dealt a fierce blow to the head by the bear, but lingered long enough to utter (very casually) this line: "Well, I guess that'll fix me."
- ☐ **French, Daniel (sculptor)**, letter signed, one page, 1904. . . . . **42.00** **53.00**
- ☐ **Frick, Ford C. (baseball commissioner)**, postcard photo signed. **18.00** **24.00**
- ☐ **Frieseler, Gerhard (German fighter pilot of World War I)**, photo signed, 8″ × 10″. **42.00** **58.00**
- ☐ **Fromme, Lynette ("Squeaky," member of Charles Manson cult group who attempted to assassinate President Ford)**, letter signed, two pages, written in prison, undated, c. 1976. . . . . **135.00** **170.00**
- ☐ **Fry, Christopher (dramatist)**, signature in the margin of a block of postage stamps. **16.00** **21.00**
- ☐ **Fullbright, John (Senator who was outspoken critic of Vietnam War)**, letter signed, one page, 1961. . . . . **9.00** **12.00**
- ☐ **Fuller, Melville (jurist)**, signature. **40.00** **50.00**
- ☐ **Furman, Richard (clergyman)**, holograph letter signed, one page, 1811. . . . . **16.00** **21.00**
- ☐ **Fyles, Franklin (author)**, holograph letter signed, one page, undated. **15.00** **19.00**
- ☐ **Gage, Thomas (colonial Governor of Massachusetts)**, signature. **42.00** **55.00**
- ☐ **Gaines, Edmund P. (General in War of 1812)**, holograph letter signed, one page, 1836. . . . . **23.00** **30.00**
- ☐ **Gale, Zona (novelist)**, holograph letter signed, two pages, 1905. . . . . **17.00** **23.00**
- ☐ **Gallagher, Ray (crew member of A-bomb mission over Hiroshima)**, holograph note signed. **27.00** **35.00**

Holograph letter signed of Francis I, King of France, dated December 22, 1545. The signature reads "Francoys." A prominent art patron, Francis I provided living quarters at his palace for Leonardo DaVinci when the latter felt he could no longer live in Italy.

PRICE RANGE

☐ **Gallatin, Albert (Secretary of the Treasury in Jefferson's cabinet),** holograph letter signed, one page, 1816....... 130.00 155.00
☐ **Galsworthy, John (novelist, author of "The Forsyth Saga"),** holograph letter signed, one page, 1914........ 33.00 42.00
☐ **Gambier, Baron (British Admiral),** signature........... 16.00 21.00
☐ **Gardner, Earl S. (detective story writer),** signature on a first day cover ("Francis Parkman" postage stamp)....... 28.00 36.00
☐ **Gardner, Isabella (famous art collector whose collection is now a public museum in Boston),** holograph letter signed, one page, 1910................................. 45.00 59.00
☐ **Gardner, Lester (aviator of World War I),** holograph letter signed, one page, undated, mentions Howard Hughes.... 23.00 30.00
☐ **Garfield, Eliza (mother of President Garfield),** signature.. 26.00 34.00
☐ **Garfield, Harry (son of President Garfield),** letter signed, one page, 1912.. 13.00 17.00
☐ **Garfield, Lucretia (wife of President Garfield),** holograph letter signed, one page, 1913.......................... 45.00 60.00
☐ **Garland, Augustus H. (Governor of Arkansas),** holograph letter signed, one page, 1878..................... 23.00 31.00
☐ **Garland, Hamlin (writer),** holograph letter signed, one page, undated.... 21.00 26.00
☐ **Garner, John N. (Vice President under Franklin Roosevelt),** signature dated 1936.......................... 16.00 21.00
☐ **Gary, Elbert (industrialist),** signature on a card, 1921... 14.00 18.00
☐ **Gatty, Harold (aviator, flying mate of Wiley Post),** letter signed, one page, 1934................................ 215.00 265.00
☐ **Gayley, Charles M. (author),** holograph letter signed, five pages, 1927... 16.00 21.00
☐ **Gaynor, William (Mayor of New York City),** letter signed, one page, 1911.. 26.00 34.00
☐ **Geary, John W. (Civil War General),** signature......... 13.00 17.00
☐ **Geddings, W. H. (Confederate surgeon in Civil War),** document signed....................................... 21.00 26.00
☐ **Gehrig, Lou (baseball player),** signature on a card...... 310.00 385.00
☐ **Genders, Sidney J. (adventurer who rowed across Atlantic in rowboat),** letter signed, one page, 1980........ 21.00 30.00
☐ **George III (King of Great Britain during American Revolution),** signature from a vellum document............. 50.00 65.00
George III's signature changed drastically in the latter period of his life, as his eyesight gradually failed.
☐ **George IV (King of Great Britain),** signature from a vellum document...................................... 45.00 60.00
☐ **George V (King of Great Britain),** signature............ 45.00 60.00
Though the reign of George V occurred a full century after that of George IV, their signatures sell for the same price. Both signed enormous quantities of documents and letters, but in the time of George IV far more royal documents reached public hands.
☐ **George, Prince of Bavaria (World War I leader),** signature on a card.. 14.00 18.00
☐ **Gerando, Baron Joseph Marie de (philosopher),** holograph letter signed, one page, undated.................. 18.00 24.00

PRICE RANGE

☐ **Gerry, Ellridge (philanthropist),** letter signed, one page, 1885. . . . . 16.00   21.00

☐ **Gershwin, Ira (composer),** signature on a card. 23.00   31.00

☐ **Geyr von Schweppenburg, Baron Le (Nazi General),** holograph letter signed, 1970. . . . . 28.00   36.00

☐ **Gibson, Charles D. (illustrator for whom "Gibson Girl" look was named),** signature. 18.00   24.00

☐ **Gide, Andre (novelist),** inscribed and signed copy of his book, "Montaigne". 56.00   77.00

☐ **Gilbert, Henry F. (composer),** holograph manuscript signed, four bars of music with lyrics, 1926. . . . . 40.00   50.00

☐ **Gilbert, Sir John (artist),** holograph letter signed, one page, undated. 18.00   24.00

☐ **Ginsberg, Allen ("beat generation" poet and cult hero),** signature on a check. 15.00   19.00

☐ **Gladden, Washington (poet),** holograph quotation signed. 9.00   12.00

☐ **Gladstone, William (eccentric British Prime Minister in Victoria's reign),** signature. 11.00   15.00

☐ **Glass, Carter (Secretary of Treasury in Wilson's cabinet),** letter signed, one page, 1918. . . . . 22.00   30.00

☐ **Glenn, John (astronaut, unsuccessful Presidential candidate),** signature. 10.00   14.00

☐ **Glubb, Sir John (British commander of Arab Legion in World War II),** holograph letter signed, two pages, war content, 1979. . . . . 42.00   54.00

☐ **Goderich, Viscount (British Prime Minister),** signature. 18.00   24.00

☐ **Godolphin, Sydney (British Prime Minister in early 1700s),** signature. 21.00   26.00

☐ **Goering, Hermann (Nazi Field Marshal),** pencil signature on a postcard photo, 1933. . . . . 88.00   110.00

☐ **Goldsborough, Louis (Admiral in Civil War),** holograph note signed, undated. 21.00   26.00

☐ **Goldschmidt, Otto (musician, husband of Jenny Lind),** holograph note signed. 16.00   21.00

☐ **Golf, Nathan (Secretary of Navy in Hayes' cabinet),** signature. 14.00   18.00

☐ **Goltz, Baron Kolmar von der (German General of World War I),** holograph sentiment signed. 17.00   23.00

☐ **Gomez, Lefty (baseball player),** signature on a postcard photo. 18.00   24.00

☐ **Gompers, Samuel (labor leader),** letter signed, one page, undated. 32.00   43.00

☐ **Good, James W. (Secretary of War in Hoover's cabinet),** letter signed, one page, 1920. . . . . 16.00   21.00

☐ **Gordon, C. G. ("Chinese Gordon," British General),** holograph letter signed, one and a half pages, 1864. . . . . 250.00   300.00

☐ **Gordon, John Brown (Civil War General),** letter signed, one page, 1886. . . . . 67.00   88.00

☐ **Gough, John (prohibition advocate),** holograph letter signed, one page, 1860. . . . . 28.00   36.00

☐ **Gould, Hannah (poet),** holograph letter signed, one page, 1841. . . . . 37.00   48.00

THE ADVENTURES
OF TOM SAWYER

Not what does or did happen
to a boy; yet nonetheless a true
portrait of a boy, because here
are the curious things Mark Twain
knew that the boy, Sam Clemens,
had longingly dreamed into a
fairyland reality.

Booth Tarkington
Sept. 1935

It was from contemplation of the outrightness
of Mark Twain that I became convinced long ago
that outrightness was the great thing in all literature
and not just in humor alone.

Robert Frost
December 1935

Usually the incriptions in books are written by their authors. Here is an example of two inscriptions by persons who had nothing to do with the book: an edition of Twain's Tom Sawyer inscribed by Booth Tarkington and Robert Frost.

PRICE RANGE

☐ **Gould, Jay (financier)**, signature. 12.00   16.00

☐ **Goyau, George S. (historian)**, holograph quotation signed, 1922. . . . . 14.00   18.00

☐ **Graham, George R. (publisher)**, holograph letter signed, one page, 1850. . . . . 15.00   19.00

☐ **Graham, William (Secretary of the Navy)**, letter signed, one page, 1852. . . . . 37.00   48.00

☐ **Grand, Sarah (novelist)**, holograph letter signed, three pages, 1911. . . . . 14.00   18.00

☐ **Granger, Gideon (Postmaster General in Jefferson's cabinet)**, address leaf from a letter with his signed free frank, 1804. . . . . 80.00   105.00

☐ **Grant, Julia D. (wife of General/President Grant)**, signature. 30.00   38.00

☐ **Grant, Lewis A. (Civil War General)**, signature. 14.00   18.00
Yes, the Union Army did have two General Grants!

☐ **Grayson, Cary (Woodrow Wilson's doctor, who lived to be 100)**, letter signed, one page, 1935. . . . . 18.00   24.00

☐ **Green, Thomas (Civil War General)**, signature. 16.00   21.00

☐ **Green, William (teamster leader)**, letter signed, one page, 1940. . . . . 18.00   24.00

☐ **Gregory, Thomas W. (Attorney General in Wilson's cabinet)**, signature. 14.00   18.00

☐ **Gresham, Walter (Civil War General)**, letter signed, five pages, 1883. . . . . 39.00   48.00
The length of this letter (five pages) has minimal influence on value because only the signature was penned by Gresham.

☐ **Grieg, Evard (composer)**, signature. 115.00   145.00

☐ **Griffith, Clark (owner of Washington Senators baseball team)**, postcard signed. 140.00   180.00

☐ **Grimes, Burleigh (baseball player and manager, last of the "spitball" pitchers)**, signature on a card. 9.00   12.00

☐ **Groener, Wilhelm (German General of World War I)**, photo signed, 5″ × 3½″. 18.00   24.00

☐ **Grofe, Ferde (composer)**, holograph manuscript signed on card. 92.00   112.00

☐ **Gruening, Ernest (Governor of Alaska Territory before statehood)**, photo of the Alaska state seal, signed. 14.00   18.00

☐ **Guardia, Ernesto de la (President of Panama)**, letter signed, one page, undated. 18.00   24.00

☐ **Guest, Edgar (poet)**, letter signed, one page, undated, responding to an autograph collector. 14.00   18.00
The quantity of celebrity letters written to autograph collectors must comprise close to half of all letters on the autograph market. Since the mid 1800s there have been collectors who have made a career of writing to every known celebrity in all fields, requesting an autograph. Since these letters go directly into collections, they reach the market more readily than celebrity letters written to relatives, friends, associates, etc. (who may pass them on to descendants).

☐ **Guinan, Texas (owner of New York nightclub in "speakeasy" days)**, photo signed, 1931. . . . . 37.00   48.00

PRICE RANGE

☐ **Guiteau, Charles (assassin of President Garfield),** holograph note signed, written while imprisoned following assassination, 1881... 350.00 425.00
Guiteau, who almost certainly would have been judged insane by today's standards, was executed.
☐ **Guiterman, Arthur (poet),** holograph verse signed....... 15.00 19.00
☐ **Guston, Philip (artist),** signed reproduction of one of his works.. 21.00 26.00
☐ **Guthrie, James (Secretary of Treasury in Pierce's cabinet),** portion of a document signed..................... 14.00 18.00
☐ **Gwinnett, Button (signer of the Declaration of Independence),** this is the most valuable autograph of any American who has ever lived. No price is given as no sales have occurred recently.
☐ **Hack, Stan (baseball player and manager),** signature... 7.00 10.00
☐ **Hafey, "Chick" (baseball player),** holograph letter signed, one page, 1971.. 32.00 43.00
☐ **Haig, Alexander M. (Secretary of State in Reagan's cabinet),** photo signed..................................... 32.00 43.00
☐ **Haines, Jesse (baseball player),** holograph letter signed, one page, 1970.. 32.00 43.00
☐ **Halas, George (football coach and owner of Chicago Bears),** photo signed, 8″ × 10″......................... 45.00 60.00
☐ **Hale, Anne (author),** holograph note signed, 1905....... 14.00 18.00
☐ **Hale, Edward E. (author),** signature................... 14.00 18.00
☐ **Hall, Willard (Governor of Missouri),** signature......... 14.00 18.00
☐ **Hailiburton, Richard (explorer),** holograph letter signed, two pages, 1931... 52.00 68.00
☐ **Hambourg, Mark (composer),** holograph manuscript signed, two bars of music, 1935......................... 18.00 24.00
☐ **Hambro, Carl J. (Norwegian statesman),** signature..... 14.00 18.00
☐ **Hamilton, Alexander (Secretary of the Treasury in Washington's cabinet, slain by Aaron Burr in duel,)** address leaf from a letter with his signed free frank, 1791... 335.00 415.00
☐ **Hamilton, A. J. (Governor of Texas),** signature......... 14.00 18.00
☐ **Hamilton, Iain (composer),** holograph manuscript signed, three bars of music.................................... 19.00 24.00
☐ **Hamilton, Paul (Secretary of Navy in Madison's cabinet),** signature....................................... 18.00 24.00
☐ **Hamlin, Hannibal (Vice President under Lincoln),** signature on a card...................................... 33.00 44.00
☐ **Hammond, William (neurologist),** holograph quotation signed, one page, undated............................. 27.00 35.00
☐ **Hammond, William A. (Civil War General),** signature... 17.00 23.00
☐ **Hamson, John (paymaster in Revolutionary War),** document signed, one page, 1778......................... 155.00 210.00
☐ **Hancock, Winfield (Civil War General, unsuccessful Presidential candidate),** signature.................... 11.00 15.00
☐ **Harder, Mel (baseball player),** holograph letter signed, one page, 1935.. 21.00 26.00

Boston 6 Decr. 1777

My dear Sir

I Recd the favr. of your letter by your Son, am much oblig'd for your attention in procuring a Load of Cyder for one, you will please to direct the Load to be brought one when it is convenient to the owner, & I will pay whatever Sum you agree for, it is uncertain whether I shall keep the Barrells, tho' rather think I must

I have not yet put off the Scarlets ornament from my foot, I am quite tir'd of it, but Mrs Gout does not incline to leave one, I wish this may meet you all in the enjoyment of every good, & be assur'd Sir in every vicissitude of life you will find me, Your Real Friend

John Hancock

Holograph letter signed of John Hancock, whose name became the byword for "signature."

Inscription from a book, by the man who wrote Jude the Obscure, The Dynasts, *and a whole roster of best sellers: Thomas Hardy.*

	PRICE RANGE	
☐ **Hardin, John Wesley (notorious "old west" desperado who is believed to have committed more murders than any other American in history),** holograph note signed.	1100.00	1375.00
A very rare signature of a man who led an unbelievable life. After serving a long prison term, Hardin renounced his former lifestyle and went to work as a lawyer. While seated in his office one day, he was shot and killed by a man who believed Hardin had uttered something libelous about him—this after having survived twenty years of shootouts, gunshot wounds, and uncountable close calls.		
☐ **Hare, Amy (composer),** holograph manuscript signed, one page, undated.	22.00	30.00
☐ **Hare, William H. (clergyman who worked among Indians),** signature on a card.	11.00	16.00
☐ **Hargreaves, Alice (the Alice for whom Lewis Carroll wrote "Alice in Wonderland"),** signature.	26.00	35.00
☐ **Harlan, James (Secretary of Interior in Andrew Johnson's cabinet),** signature.	14.00	18.00
☐ **Harmon, Judson (Attorney General in Grover Cleveland's cabinet),** letter signed, one page, 1911.	18.00	24.00
☐ **Harriman, Averell (Governor of New York),** signature on New York Executive Mansion card.	14.00	18.00
☐ **Harrington, Mark (astronomer),** signature on a card. . . .	14.00	18.00
☐ **Harris, Charles (composer),** signature.	11.00	15.00
☐ **Harrison, Caroline (wife of President Benjamin Harrison),** signature.	27.00	36.00
☐ **Harte, Bret (novelist),** holograph letter signed, one page, 1868.	45.00	60.00
Harte was the first novelist to write about the "old west."		
☐ **Hartnett, "Gabby" (baseball player),** signature on a card.	15.00	20.00

PRICE RANGE

☐ **Harts, William (advisor to Woodrow Wilson)**, holograph letter signed, two pages, 1936. . . . .   **42.00**   **54.00**

☐ **Hausen, Baron Max K. (German General of World War I)**, holograph quotation signed, two lines, 1918. . . . .   **17.00**   **23.00**

☐ **Hawkins, John (Civil War General)**, signature. **15.00**   **20.00**

☐ **Hawthorne, Julian (novelist, son of Nathaniel Hawthorne)**, holograph letter signed, one page, 1890. . . . .   **16.00**   **21.00**

☐ **Hayes, Isaac (Arctic explorer)**, holograph letter signed, two pages, 1880. . . . .   **27.00**   **35.00**

☐ **Heath, William (General in Revolutionary War)**, document signed, two pages, 1777. . . . .   **115.00**   **145.00**

☐ **Heidenstam, Verner von (Swedish poet)**, photo signed, 7″ × 9¼″. **93.00**   **112.00**

☐ **Heintzelman, Samuel (Civil War General)**, signature, dated 1867. . . . .   **14.00**   **18.00**

☐ **Hemingway, Mary W. (wife of Ernest Hemingway)**, signed and inscribed copy of her book, *How it Was*. **16.00**   **21.00**

☐ **Henderson, Arthur (statesman)**, signature. **11.00**   **15.00**

☐ **Henry, Patrick (statesman)**, signature. **180.00**   **235.00**

☐ **Henshaw, David (Secretary of the Navy)**, holograph letter signed, one page, 1843. . . . .   **31.00**   **42.00**

☐ **Herbert, Hilary A. (Secretary of Navy in Grover Cleveland's cabinet)**, letter signed, one page, 1895. . . . .   **16.00**   **21.00**

☐ **Herford, Oliver (artist)**, holograph letter signed, one page, 1899. . . . .   **54.00**   **71.00**

☐ **Herndon, William H. (law partner of Lincoln)**, holograph inscription and signature. **37.00**   **48.00**
When the building occupied by the Lincoln and Herndon office was remodeled in 1968, the original beams were cut into tiny pieces and made available to collectors.

☐ **Herrick, Myron (Governor of Ohio)**, signature on his visiting card, 1928. . . . .   **14.00**   **18.00**

☐ **Hersey, John (novelist)**, holograph letter signed, one page, 1976. . . . .   **42.00**   **54.00**

☐ **Hesse, Herman (German writer)**, signed postcard photo. **93.00**   **112.00**

☐ **Hewitt, Capt. Robert P. (pioneer commercial airline pilot)**, signature. **15.00**   **20.00**

☐ **Hill, Grace L. (novelist)**, signature on a pamphlet. **15.00**   **20.00**

☐ **Hillary, Sir Edmund (mountaineer, first conqueror of Everest)**, letter signed, one page, 1982. . . . .   **17.00**   **23.00**

☐ **Hilton, Conrad (hotel chain magnate, one-time father-in-law of Elizabeth Taylor)**, photo signed, 8″ × 10″. **25.00**   **33.00**

☐ **Hinshelwood, Sir Cyril (chemist)**, signature on a card, 1957. . . . .   **14.00**   **18.00**

☐ **Hitchcock, E. A. (Secretary of Interior in McKinley's and Roosevelt's cabinets)**, holograph letter signed, two pages, 1904. . . . .   **14.00**   **18.00**

☐ **Hitchcock, Frank H. (Postmaster General who devised "air mail")**, signature on a card. **14.00**   **18.00**

☐ **Hobart, John H. (clergyman)**, holograph letter signed, one page, 1820. . . . .   **23.00**   **31.00**

Complimentary close from a holograph letter of Ernest Hemingway.

	PRICE	RANGE
☐ Hoffa, James (teamster official who disappeared mysteriously), signature..	14.00	18.00
☐ Hogan, Ben (golfer), photo signed, 8″ × 10″............	21.00	26.00
☐ Hoinigen, Baron Ernst (German General of World War I), signature..	15.00	20.00
☐ Holmes, Larry (boxer), photo signed, 8″ × 10″.........	25.00	33.00
☐ Holmes, Oliver W. (author, essayist), signature on a card...	18.00	24.00
☐ Holyoke, Edward A. (physician), holograph document signed, one page, 1797...............................	27.00	35.00
☐ Hooker, Joseph (Civil War General), signature on a card...	18.00	24.00
☐ Hooper, Harry (baseball player), signature on a postcard...	22.00	31.00
☐ Hoover, J. Edgar (first Director of FBI), inscribed copy of his book about famous gangsters, *Masters of Deceit*..	34.00	45.00
☐ Hopper, Hedda (show business columnist), signature..	15.00	19.00
☐ Horan, Paul (novelist), typescript signed, one page.	7.00	23.00
☐ Hornung, Ernest (writer of detective fiction), signature..	14.00	18.00
☐ Horsley, John C. (artist), holograph document signed, 1893..	17.00	23.00
☐ Horthy, Mikios von N. (Hungarian Admiral in World War I), signature on a card along with a Hungarian postage stamp portraying him...................................	55.00	70.00
☐ Hough, Emerson (novelist), signature on a card........	11.00	16.00
☐ Houston, Sam (President of the Republic of Texas, prior to Texas statehood), document signed, two pages, 1844..	800.00	1050.00
☐ Howard, Benjamin (statesman), holograph letter signed, one page, 1861..	23.00	31.00

PRICE RANGE

☐ **Howard, Oliver (Civil War General)**, signature on a card. 15.00   19.00

☐ **Howe, Julia W. (composer of "Battle Hymn of the Republic")**, holograph note signed, 1884. . . . .   27.00   35.00

☐ **Howells, William D. (novelist)**. 28.00   37.00

☐ **Hoxie, Vin (sculptor)**, signature. 18.00   24.00

☐ **Hoyt, Waite (baseball player)**, letter signed, one page, 1970. . . . .   22.00   30.00

☐ **Hunt, Harold L. (industrialist, reputed to be wealthiest American citizen)**, signed copy of his book, "Alpaca," 1960. . . . .   26.00   34.00

Harold L. Hunt was the father of Nelson Bunker Hunt, who made headlines in 1980 with his investments of hundreds of millions of dollars in the silver market.

☐ **Hubbard, Cal (baseball umpire)**, signature. 18.00   24.00

☐ **Hughes, Charles E. (Governor of New York)**, signature. 14.00   18.00

☐ **Hughes, Sir Samuel (Canadian General)**, signature. 11.00   15.00

☐ **Hughes, Sarah T. (Dallas judge who swore in Lyndon Johnson as President)**, signature on a Youth Workshop program. 17.00   23.00

☐ **Hughes, Thomas (author of "Tom Brown's School Days")**, holograph note signed, 1883. . . . .   14.00   18.00

☐ **Hull, Cordell (Secretary of State in Franklin Roosevelt's cabinet)**, photo signed and inscribed, 8″ × 10″. 45.00   60.00

☐ **Humbert II (King of Italy)**, photo signed, 9″ × 12½″. 18.00   24.00

☐ **Humphrey, George (Secretary of Treasury in Eisenhower's cabinet)**, letter signed, two pages, 1955. . . . .   23.00   31.00

☐ **Humphrey, Hubert (Vice President under Lyndon Johnson)**, signature on printed announcement. 18.00   24.00

☐ **Hunt, Henry (Civil War General)**, signature. 14.00   18.00

☐ **Hunt, William H. (jurist)**, letter signed, two pages, 1881. . . . .   32.00   43.00

☐ **Hunter, R. M. T. (Jefferson Davis' Secretary of State in Confederate cabinet)**, holograph letter signed, one page, 1851. . . . .   32.00   43.00

☐ **Huntington, Jed (Revolutionary War General)**, document signed, 1782. . . . .   16.00   21.00

☐ **Hurst, Fannie (novelist)**, letter signed, one page, 1918. . . . .   16.00   21.00

☐ **Hussein (King of Jordan)**, photo signed, 7″ × 9″. 37.00   48.00

☐ **Huxley, Sir Julian (scientist)**, signature. 14.00   18.00

☐ **Hyde, Douglas (President of Ireland)**, holograph letter signed, 1927. . . . .   23.00   31.00

☐ **Ickes, Harold (Secretary of Interior in Franklin Roosevelt's cabinet)**, letter signed, one page, 1936. . . . .   22.00   30.00

☐ **Irving, Washington (first popular American novelist,)** signature. 50.00   62.00

☐ **Irwin, William (Governor of California)**, signature. 18.00   24.00

☐ **Ivanova, Anna (czaritsa of Russia)**, letter signed, three quarters of a page, 1733. . . . . 700.00   850.00

☐ **Izzet Pasa, Ahmet (Turkish General of Cavalry)**, letter signed, one page, 1918. . . . .   28.00   36.00

Sir. Long Island July 18ᵗʰ 1794 —

Last night I was honor'd by the Receipt of your Excellency's Despatch by the Express with your Appointment to a seat in the Senate of the united States vacated by the Resignation of Mr. Monroe.

It gives me great Pain to declare that existing Circumstances compel me to decline this Appointment so honorable of all Trewits, but rendered more particularly so by the Manner in which you are pleased to communicate it to me. I should be greatly wanting on this Occasion if I failed to express the highest Sense of this unmerited Honor: & I am comforted by a Reliance, that the same Goodness that dictated the Appointment, will admit my Apology for declining it, as arising from my Time of Life combined with the great Distance to Philadelphia

I want Words to express my Gratitude for the favorable Sentiments you are pleased to entertain for me; & I have only to regret

Opening page of a letter in the holograph of Patrick Henry, who was writing from Long Island, New York.

John Drinkwater

from A. E. Housman

22 Oct. 1922

Inscription in a book of poetry by A. E. Housman, author of A Shropshire Lad. *The recipient was another poet, though not of Housman's magnitude: John Drinkwater.*

	PRICE RANGE	
☐ **Jackson, Robert H. (Attorney General in Franklin Roosevelt's cabinet)**, signature	16.00	21.00
☐ **Jacobs, Helen Hull (tennis player)**, holograph note signed, six lines	15.00	19.00
☐ **James, Frank (brother of Jesse James, member of the James/Younger gang)**, holograph letter signed, two pages, in pencil, 1911.	425.00	525.00

Unlike his infamous brother, Frank James died of natural causes (in 1915). After years of hiding from the law he gave himself up, was put on trial, and acquitted of all charges, despite the presence of irrefutable proof. The reason? He had become a folk legend and a hero to the members of the jury.

☐ **James Henry (novelist)**, holograph letter signed, one page, 1893.	165.00	215.00
☐ **James, Jesse (leader of desperado gang that included his brother Frank James and Cole Younger)**, signature.	375.00	475.00
☐ **Javits, Jacob (Senator from New York)**, letter signed, one page, 1978.	16.00	21.00
☐ **Jebson, Edgar (novelist)**, holograph letter signed, one page, 1908.	18.00	24.00
☐ **Jerome, Jerome K. (novelist)**, signature	14.00	18.00
☐ **Jewett, Sarah (author)**, signature	14.00	18.00
☐ **Johannson, Ingemar (boxer)**, photo signed, 8" × 10"	31.00	42.00

An expensive autograph, for a relatively recent boxing champion (1960s) who is still living. Johannson spent little time in the U.S. and was not receptive to autograph seekers.

☐ **John VI (King of Portugal)**, document signed, three and a half pages, 1812.	93.00	112.00

PRICE RANGE

☐ **Johncock, Gordon (auto racer),** photo signed, 8″ × 10″. 26.00   35.00

☐ **Johnson, Cave (Postmaster General in Polk's cabinet),** holograph letter signed, one page, 1848. . . . .   26.00   35.00

☐ **Johnson, Jack (boxer),** signature on a card. 75.00   105.00

☐ **Johnson, Lady Bird (wife of President Lyndon Johnson),** letter signed, one page, 1964.   83.00   103.00

☐ **Johnson, Reverdy (Attorney General in Taylor's cabinet),** signature. 14.00   18.00

☐ **Johnson, Richard M. (Vice President under Van Buren),** holograph letter signed, two pages, 1834. . . . .   45.00   60.00

☐ **Johnson, Robert S. (fighter pilot of World War II),** envelope signed, 1952. . . . .   17.00   23.00

☐ **Johnson, Dr. Samuel (lexicographer, critic, poet),** signature. 750.00   950.00

☐ **Johnston, Mary (author of "gothic novels"),** holograph letter signed, 1914. . . . .   14.00   18.00

☐ **Johnstone, William H. (American General of World War I),** holograph letter signed, 1918. . . . .   16.00   21.00

☐ **Jones, Anson (last President of the Republic of Texas prior to statehood),** document signed, one page, 1845. . . . .   160.00   210.00

☐ **Jones, Frank (Texas Ranger),** document signed, 1888. . . . .   67.00   88.00

☐ **Jones, Pinckney (Texas Ranger),** holograph letter signed, one page, 1880. . . . .   32.00   43.00

☐ **Jones, William E. (Civil War General),** document signed, 1851. . . . .   35.00   45.00

A scarcer than usual signature among Civil War Generals as Jones was killed in action.

☐ **Joseph, Ferdinand (Austrian Archduke),** document signed, 1915. . . . .   31.00   42.00

☐ **Jouhaux, Leon (French labor leader),** letter signed, one page, 1938. . . . .   23.00   30.00

☐ **Jullien, Louis Antoine (composer who died in lunatic asylum),** holograph letter signed, one page, 1853. . . . .   17.00   23.00

☐ **Jung, Carl (psychiatrist, phsychologist),** holograph letter signed, one page, 1931. . . . .   475.00   600.00

☐ **Kafka, Franz (poet, novelist),** envelope addressed by him, postmarked 1912. . . . .   315.00   425.00

☐ **Kantrowitz, Adrian (physician, Nobel Prize winner),** photo signed. 21.00   27.00

☐ **Kapiolani (Queen of Hawaii),** signature. 16.00   21.00

☐ **Kaiser, Henry J. (industrialist, partner of Howard Hughes),** signature on a card. 32.00   43.00

☐ **Karpis, Alvin (gangster, "most wanted" by FBI),** letter signed, two pages, opinions on J. Edgar Hoover, 1978. . .   80.00   105.00

☐ **Karsh, Yousuf (photographer),** signature on first day cover of Churchill postage stamp, 1965. . . . .   37.00   47.00

☐ **Kathen, Hugo K. (German General in World War I),** holograph note signed, 1918. . . . .   18.00   24.00

☐ **Kauffman, James L. (Vice Admiral of World War II),** letter signed, one page, 1959. . . . .   18.00   24.00

PRICE RANGE

☐ **Kefauver, Estes (Senator from Tennessee, Adlai Stevenson's running mate)**, photo signed, 8″ × 10″........ 17.00   23.00

☐ **Keifer, J. Warren (one of the last surviving officers of
the Civil War, died in 1932 at 96)**, letter signed, one page,
1906. .... 15.00   19.00

☐ **Keller, Helen (author, lecturer)**, holograph letter in pencil,
written at the age of nine in 1889........................ 325.00   425.00

☐ **Kellert, Frank (baseball player)**, signature on a card.... 9.00   12.00

☐ **Kellogg, Frank B. (Secretary of State in Coolidge's cabinet)**, letter signed, two pages, 1925.................... 22.00   30.00

☐ **Kelly, George ("High Pockets," baseball player)**, signature. 6.00   9.00

☐ **Kelly, Walt (cartoonist, creator of Pogo)**, letter signed,
one page, 1969. .... 37.00   47.00

☐ **Kendall, Edward (scientist)**, signature on a card........ 16.00   21.00

☐ **Kennan, George (journalist)**, holograph letter signed in
pencil, one page, 1893. .... 23.00   30.00

☐ **Kershner, Glenn (pioneer newsreel cameraman)**, signa-
ture. 10.00   14.00

☐ **Kielstra, Johannes (Governor of Surinam)**, photo signed,
3½″ × 5½″. 15.00   19.00

☐ **King, Martin L., Jr. (civil rights advocate)**, signed copy
of his book, *Stride Toward Freedom*..................... 425.00   525.00

☐ **King, William R. (Vice President who died in office)**,
holograph letter signed, three pages, mentions Jenny Lind,
1851. .... 155.00   205.00

☐ **Kingstone, John J. (British Colonel of World War II who
captured Baghdad though outnumbered by 40,000 to
700)**, holograph note signed, 1945. .... 16.00   21.00

☐ **Kipling, Carrie (wife of Rudyard Kipling)**, holograph letter
signed, two pages, 1918. .... 37.00   48.00

☐ **Kipling, Rudyard (poet, novelist)**, holograph letter signed,
1896. .... 52.00   67.00

☐ **Kirkbach, Count Gunther (German General of World
War I)**, holograph quotation signed, 1918. .... 16.00   21.00

☐ **Kiss, Josef (Austrian fighter pilot of World War I)**, holograph note signed, 1917................................. 42.00   53.00

☐ **Kissinger, Henry (diplomat)**, photo signed.............. 50.00   65.00
Among living celebrities, Kissinger's autograph is one of
the most difficult to get. The vast majority of specimens are
produced by the autopen device.

☐ **Klamt, Rudolf (German fighter pilot of World War I, flew
with "Red Baron")**, holograph letter signed, two pages,
1906. .... 18.00   24.00

☐ **Klein, Calvin (fashion designer)**, letter signed, one page,
1979. .... 13.00   17.00

☐ **Klinge, Bob (baseball player)**, signature................ 6.00   9.00

☐ **Kluck, Alexander von (German General of World War I,
man for whom expression "dumb kluck" was coined)**,
signature. 16.00   21.00
Kluck's troops were about to take Paris when an error in
strategy led to their repulsion by French forces.

☐ **Kluttz, Clyde (baseball player)**, signature.............. 6.00   9.00

PRICE RANGE

☐ **Kneisel, Franz (musician)**, holograph manuscript signed, two bars of music. 13.00 17.00

☐ **Knetzer, "Baron" (baseball player)**, signature on a card. 9.00 12.00

☐ **Knox, Frank (Secretary of the Navy in Franklin Roosevelt's cabinet)**, mimeographed speech signed, 1941. . . . . 18.00 24.00

☐ **Knox, Philander (Secretary of State in Taft's cabinet)**, signature. 11.00 16.00

☐ **Konstanty, James (baseball player)**, signature. 6.00 9.00

☐ **Koufax, Sandy (baseball player)**, signature on a card. 9.00 12.00

☐ **Kreilich, Franz (Nazi fighter pilot of World War II)**, photo signed, 3¼″ × 5″. 22.00 30.00

☐ **Kroc, Ray (president of McDonald's Restaurants, owner of San Diego Padres baseball team)**, signature. 10.00 13.00

☐ **Kropotkin, Peter A. (Russian agitator for revolution during czarist age)**, holograph letter signed, one page, 1888. . . . . 93.00 112.00

☐ **Krueger, Ernie (baseball player)**, photo signed, 1920. . . 17.00 23.00

☐ **Kruell, Gustav (portrait engraver)**, engraved self-portrait signed. 23.00 31.00

☐ **Kusch, Popykarp (physicist)**, signed transcript. 17.00 23.00

☐ **Laemmle, Carl (motion picture executive in "silent" era)**, letter signed, one page, 1928. . . . . 50.00 65.00

☐ **LaFollette, Robert (unsuccessful Presidential candidate)**, Senatorial form signed. 25.00 32.00

☐ **LaGuardia, Fiorello H. (mayor of New York City)**, signature. 16.00 21.00

☐ **Lajoie, Larry "Napoleon" (baseball player)**, postcard signed. 23. 135.00 175.00

☐ **LaMotta, Jake (boxer)**, photo signed, 8″ × 10″. 32.00 43.00

☐ **Landis, Kenesaw M. (first commissioner of baseball)**, photo from a magazine, signed. 93.00 112.00

☐ **Lane, Franklin (Secretary of Interior in Wilson's cabinet)**, signature. 14.00 18.00

☐ **Langmuir, Irving (chemist)**, photo signed, 8″ × 10″. 92.00 112.00

☐ **Lansing, Robert (Secretary of State in Wilson's cabinet)**, signature on a card. 14.00 18.00

☐ **Lantz, Walter (cartoonist, creator of Woody Woodpecker, Andy Panda)**, signed ink sketch. 37.00 48.00

☐ **Laughlin, Clara (author)**, holograph letter signed. 5.00 7.00

☐ **Laumann, Arthur (German fighter pilot of World War I)**, sketch of his plane, signed, 1967. . . . . 32.00 43.00

☐ **Lavedon, Henri (dramatist)**, holograph letter signed, two pages, 1895. . . . . 15.00 19.00

☐ **Leahy, William (Fleet Admiral)**, signature. 14.00 18.00

☐ **Lee, Dudley (baseball player)**, signature on a card. 9.00 12.00

☐ **Leffers, Gustav (German fighter pilot of World War I)**, holograph letter signed, one page, 1916. . . . . 115.00 145.00
Very rare autograph, as Leffers was killed in action.

☐ **Lehand, Marguerita (secretary to Franklin Roosevelt)**, letter signed, one page, 1934. . . . . 32.00 43.00

He will need cooling off in
Vermont and he shall tell you that
the countriest country in England would
be suburbs alongside o' this ere.
Now to deal with your grosser follies — the
geographical ones
   Mississippi Bay is at the back of
Yokohama bay which is in _Japan_.
Japan is in the _East_. Thus. Q. E. D.
And so forth.
The Golden Gate is reached for choice
by rail but the sailing ship goes round
the Horn as a usual thing.
The two voyages are about the longest E. & W.
runs you can make.
As you justly remark the eagle & the snake
were both taken out under poetic license
but what can a man do. Be thankful
they weren't Typhons or Narsinghas.
I'm glad you like the new book a little
The Hansom cab rescues I couldn't
get at or else I'd have used it
somewhere for I look on that as the
crowning flower of my Pen when it
was at its best. Why can't a man do
a good thing every other week?
I am doing a lot more about the wolf man
his early life and experiences, and
some day they'll appear. Some day too
when you aren't expecting it I shall
turn up in that back den of the
Isile and pick up our rows exactly
   where we left off for there is a deal
   That you've got to learn yet

Page from a holograph letter of novelist poet and Rudyard Kipling.

PRICE RANGE

☐ **Lehman, Herbert (Governor of New York)**, signature. . . 14.00 18.00
☐ **Leman, Gerald (Belgian General of World War I)**, holograph sentiment signed, 1918. . . . . 18.00 24.00
☐ **LeMay, Curtis (Air Force commander, Vice Presidential running mate of George Wallace)**, letter signed, three pages, 1966. . . . . 65.00 80.00
☐ **Lemnitzer, Lyman (four star General)**, letter signed, one page, 1969. . . . . 21.00 26.00
☐ **Lenger, Suzanne (tennis player)**, signature. 11.00 15.00
☐ **Letcher, John (Governor of Virginia during Civil War)**, signature. 14.00 18.00
☐ **Levi, Edward (Attorney General in Ford's cabinet)**, letter signed, one page, 1980. . . . . 16.00 21.00
☐ **Lewis, Duffy (baseball player)**, signature on a card. 10.00 13.00
☐ **Lewis, John L. (teamster president)**, letter signed, one page, 1925. . . . . 17.00 23.00
☐ **Lewis, Morgan (Colonel in American Revolutionary War)**, document signed, 1833. . . . . 42.00 55.00
Lewis, who lived to 90, also served in the War of 1812.
☐ **Liddy, G. Gordon (Watergate figure)**, signature. 10.00 13.00
☐ **Lie, Trygve (Norwegian statesman, Secretary General of United Nations)**, signature. 14.00 18.00
☐ **Liliuokalini, Lydia (Queen of Hawaii)**, signature. 28.00 38.00
☐ **Lilly, Eli (industrialist, art patron)**, letter signed, one page, 1940. . . . . 40.00 52.00
☐ **Lincoln, Benjamin (General in Revolutionary War, not related to Abraham)**, document signed, one page, 1804. . . . . 23.00 32.00
☐ **Lincoln, Robert T. (son of Abraham Lincoln, holder of various public offices)**, letter signed, one and a half pages, 1908. . . . . 52.00 67.00
☐ **Lind, Jenny (operatic soprano)**, holograph letter signed, four pages, undated. 180.00 235.00
A very prolific letter-writer. Her letters would be more valuable if not so common.
☐ **Lindbergh, Charles A. (aviator)**, inscribed and signed copy of his book, *We*. 450.00 550.00
☐ **Lindsay, Vachel (poet)**, signature. 21.00 26.00
☐ **Lipton, Sir Thomas (tea tycoon and yachtsman)**, letter signed, one page, 1931. . . . . 26.00 35.00
☐ **Lloyd-George, David (British Prime Minister during World War I)**, signature on a House of Commons card. . . 11.00 15.00
☐ **Locke, Richard (author)**, signature. 13.00 17.00
☐ **Lodge, Henry C. (Senator from Massachusetts, father of Nixon's 1960 running mate)**, letter signed, one page, 1915. . . . . 17.00 23.00
☐ **Lofgren, C. E. (member of Byrd's expedition to Antarctic)**, signed postcard photo. 14.00 18.00
☐ **Long, Capt. Ira (Texas Ranger)**, holograph letter signed, two pages, 1880. . . . . 93.00 112.00

	PRICE RANGE	

☐ **Longfellow, Henry W. (poet)),** signature on a card....... **33.00** **45.00**
Not as scarce or valuable as one might guess, mainly because Longfellow was continually hounded by autograph seekers and obliged most of them.

☐ **Longworth, Buddy (photographer),** letter signed, one page, 1939. .... **21.00** **26.00**

☐ **Longworth, Nicholas (Congressman),** signed photo, dated 1928. .... **23.00** **31.00**

☐ **Louis I (King of Bavaria),** letter signed, one page, 1846. .... **140.00** **180.00**

☐ **Louis Ferdinand (Crown Prince of Prussia),** photo signed, 4″ × 5¾″.................................... **32.00** **42.00**

☐ **Louis, Joe (boxer),** signature........................... **23.00** **30.00**

☐ **Louise of Savoy (mother of Francis I),** letter signed, one page, undated, c. 1530................................ **180.00** **230.00**

☐ **Lowell, James R. (poet),** signature.................... **15.00** **20.00**

☐ **Luce, Stephen (American Naval officer),** letter signed, one page, 1887. .... **32.00** **42.00**

☐ **Luciano, "Lucky" (leader of "Murder Incorporated," New York City gang of the 1930s),** signature. **68.00** **87.00**

☐ **Luckner, Count Felix von (German naval hero of World War I),** photograph with holograph verse and signature, 1928. .... **42.00** **53.00**

☐ **Luther, Martin (lawyer for Aaron Burr in Burr's treason trial),** holograph letter signed, one page, 1809. .... **67.00** **88.00**

☐ **Luttwitz, Baron Walter von (German General of World War I),** holograph letter signed, one page, 1929.......... **17.00** **23.00**

☐ **Lyon, Nathaniel (Civil War General),** holograph letter signed, two pages, 1857............................... **135.00** **175.00**
Expensive, as he was killed in action.

☐ **Lyster, Sir Arthur (British Commander of World War II),** holograph letter signed, one page, 1955................. **16.00** **21.00**

☐ **MacArthur, Douglas (Commander of Allied Forces in the Pacific in World War II; Commander of Allied Forces in Korean War),** letter signed, one page, 1957........... **47.00** **62.00**

☐ **MacDonald, Jacques (Scotsman who became Marshal of France in Napoleonic era),** documented signed, 1818. .... **67.00** **88.00**

☐ **Machensen, August von (German General of World War II),** holograph note signed, 1928........................ **16.00** **21.00**

☐ **MacKaye, Percy (poet),** holograph quotation signed, six lines... **13.00** **17.00**

☐ **MacLeish, Archibald (poet),** last paragraph of a letter with signature.. **14.00** **18.00**

☐ **MacMahon, Comte Marie Edme (President of France),** letter signed, one page, 1861.......................... **25.00** **33.00**

☐ **MacMillan, Sir Ernest C. (composer),** signature. **14.00** **18.00**

☐ **Macomb, Alexander (General in War of 1812),** signature. **17.00** **23.00**

☐ **MacVeigh, Wayne (Attorney General in Garfield's cabinet),** letter signed, one page, 1881...................... **35.00** **44.00**

☐ **Madison, "Dolly" (wife of President Madison),** envelope with her signed free frank, undated...................... **205.00** **260.00**

PRICE RANGE

☐ **Magnan, Bernard (Marshal of France)**, part of a holograph letter with signature. 15.00 20.00

☐ **Mailer, Norman (novelist)**, letter signed, one page, 1950. .... 23.00 31.00

☐ **Malneck, Matty (composer)**, holograph letter signed, one page, 1957. .... 17.00 23.00

☐ **Mancini, Ray (boxer)**, photo signed, 8″ × 10″. 32.00 43.00

☐ **Mann, Horace (educator)**, signature. 14.00 18.00

☐ **Mann, James R. (Congressman famous for "Mann Act" against prostitution)**, photo signed, 7″ × 10″. 18.00 24.00

☐ **Manson, Charles (cult leader who ordered murder of Sharon Tate)**, envelope with his signature, written in prison, undated. 80.00 105.00

☐ **Marghiloman, Alexandru (Rumanian statesman)**, holograph sentiment signed, six lines, 1924. .... 16.00 21.00

☐ **Maris, Roger (baseball player)**, photo signed, 8″ × 10″. 25.00 33.00

☐ **Markham, Edwin (poet)**, holograph quotation signed, 1929. .... 17.00 23.00

☐ **Marquard, "Rube" (baseball player, holds record for consecutive victories by a pitcher)**, signature on a postcard. 16.00 21.00

☐ **Marshall, Peter (chemist)**, signature on a first day cover ("Chemistry" stamp), 1976. .... 16.00 21.00

☐ **Marterer, Baron Ferdinand von (Austrian Field Marshal of World War I)**, letter signed, one page, 1917. .... 23.00 31.00

☐ **Masaryk, T. G. (Czech statesman)**, signature. 83.00 102.00

☐ **Masefield, John (poet)**, holograph note on postcard, 1911. .... 27.00 35.00

☐ **Mason, A. E. W. (novelist)**, holograph letter signed, one page, 1907. .... 16.00 21.00

☐ **Mason, John Y. (Secretary of Navy in Polk's cabinet)**, letter signed, one page, 1844. .... 37.00 48.00

☐ **Mason, Walt (humorist)**, photo signed. 16.00 21.00

☐ **Massenet, Jules (composer)**, holograph letter signed, two pages, 1902. .... 42.00 55.00

☐ **Mata Hari (spy)**, holograph letter signed, three pages, undated. 1150.00 1475.00

☐ **Mathewson, Christy (baseball player)**, signature on a card. 375.00 475.00

☐ **Matthews, Francis P. (Secretary of Navy in Truman's cabinet)**, signature on a card. 14.00 18.00

☐ **Matzky, Gerhard (Nazi General of World War II)**, photo signed, 3″ × 4″. 18.00 24.00

☐ **Maurois, Andre (author)**, letter signed, one page, 1957. .... 37.00 48.00

☐ **Maxim, Hudson (inventor)**, photo signed, 9″ × 12″. 18.00 24.00

☐ **Mayer, Maria (physicist)**, concluding paragraph from a signed letter. 17.00 23.00

☐ **Maynard, Horace (Postmaster General)**, complimentary close from a holograph letter signed, 1868. .... 11.00 16.00

☐ **McCandless, Bruce (hero of World War II)**, letter signed, one page, 1947. .... 16.00 21.00

PRICE RANGE

☐ **McCarthy, Eugene (unsuccessful Presidential candidate, opponent of Vietnam War)**, signature............ 14.00 18.00

☐ **McCarthy, Joseph R. (Senator from Wisconsin)**, signature................ 28.00 36.00

☐ **McCombs, William (Chairman of Democratic National Committee)**, letter signed, one page, 1912............. 13.00 17.00

☐ **McConnell, W. J. (Governor of Iowa)**, holograph letter signed, one page, 1895................. 16.00 21.00

☐ **McCrea, John L. (Commander of the Battleship Iowa)**, letter signed, one page, 1948.......................... 16.00 21.00

☐ **McCutheon, John T. (editorial cartoonist)**, signed ink sketch............. 37.00 48.00

☐ **McDonald, Bill (Texas Ranger)**, holograph letter signed, one page, 1899......................... 45.00 59.00

☐ **McGovern, George (unsuccessful Presidential candidate)**, document signed, five pages, 1973............. 10.00 14.00

☐ **McIntosh, John B. (Civil War General)**, signature....... 14.00 18.00

☐ **McKenna, Joseph (jurist)**, signature.................. 15.00 20.00

☐ **McKinley, Ida (wife of President McKinley)**, signature on a White House card................. 80.00 105.00

☐ **McKuen, Rod (poet)**, photo signed, 8″ × 10″.......... 19.00 24.00

☐ **McLane, Louis (Secretary of State in Andrew Jackson's cabinet)**, letter signed, one page, 1833.............. 32.00 43.00

☐ **McManus, George (cartoonist, creator of "Maggie and Jiggs")**, signed ink sketchs, 1946..................... 27.00 36.00

☐ **McNeil, John (Civil War General)**, signature........... 14.00 18.00

☐ **McReynolds, James C. (jurist)**, signature on a card..... 14.00 18.00

☐ **Meany, George (teamster leader)**, photo signed........ 27.00 35.00

☐ **Meigs, Montgomery (Civil War General)**, signature..... 14.00 18.00

☐ **Meinecke, Emil (German fighter pilot of World War I)**, photo signed, 3½″ × 4½″............................ 37.00 48.00

☐ **Meitner, Lise (nuclear physicist)**, photo signed, 3″ × 4½″.............. 150.00 200.00

☐ **Mellon, Andrew W. (billionaire)**, signature............. 14.00 18.00

☐ **Mencken, H. L. (humorist)**, letter signed, one page, 1928....................... 20.00 27.00

☐ **Menninger, Karl (psychiatrist, founder of noted psychiatric clinic)**, photo signed, 1967..................... 21.00 28.00

☐ **Mensdorf, Count A. (Austrian Ambassador to England)**, document signed, 1914................. 23.00 31.00

☐ **Meredith, Edward (Secretary of Agriculture in Wilson's cabinet)**, letter signed, one page, 1920................. 18.00 24.00

☐ **Merlin, Comte Phillippe A. (jurist)**, holograph letter signed, one page, 1813.............. 67.00 88.00

☐ **Merrell, James C. (surgeon)**, signature................ 14.00 18.00

☐ **Metcalf, Victor (Secretary of Commerce in Theodore Roosevelt's cabinet)**, signature on a card, 1904........ 14.00 18.00

☐ **Michelzen, Andreas (German Commander of Submarine Forces in World War I)**, holograph letter signed, two pages, 1929............................. 16.00 21.00

☐ **Michener, James A. (novelist)**, bookplate signed........ 18.00 24.00

☐ **Mifflin, Thomas (General in Revolutionary War)**, document signed, vellum, 1792............................. 32.00 43.00

Henry Hubbard
from his old Shipmate
and Watchmate
On board the good ship
Acushnet
(Alas, wrecked at last
on the Nor' West)
Herman Melville

March 23ᵈ 1853
Pittsfield. —

A rare autograph in an even rarer book. This inscription of Herman Melville was found in a first edition of The Whale, which has become better known as Moby Dick.

If you didn't know this was written by A.A. Milne, creator of "Winnie the Pooh," you would have a hard time guessing. It's signed simply "Alan," which Milne hardly ever called himself.

	PRICE RANGE	
☐ **Mighels, Philip (author)**, holograph letter signed, one page, 1906.	16.00	21.00
☐ **Millais, John (artist)**, signature.	10.00	14.00
☐ **Millay, Edna St. Vincent (poet)**, signed copy of her book, *The King's Henchmen*.	83.00	102.00
☐ **Miller, Arthur (dramatist, husband of Marilyn Monroe)**, signature on a bookplate.	14.00	18.00
☐ **Miller, Joaquin (poet)**, holograph note signed, 1909.	19.00	24.00
☐ **Miller, Olive (ornithologist)**, signature on a card.	11.00	16.00
☐ **Mills, Ogden L. (Secretary of Treasury in Hoover's cabinet)**, signature.	11.00	16.00
☐ **Miro, Joan (artist)**, signed reproduction of one of his paintings, 7″ × 9″.	95.00	115.00
Despite the name, Joan Miro was male.		
☐ **Mitchell, Martha (wife of Watergate figure John N. Mitchell, herself a popular celebrity)**, letter signed, one page, 1972.	135.00	175.00
☐ **Mize, John (baseball player)**, photo signed, 4″ × 7″.	16.00	21.00
☐ **Moevs, Robert W. (composer)**, holograph manuscript signed, three double bars of music.	16.00	21.00
☐ **Molineux, E. L. (Civil War General)**, holograph letter signed, one page, 1885.	16.00	21.00
☐ **Montgomery, Field Marshall B. (British General who commanded tank battles against Rommel in North Africa during World War II)**, photo signed.	95.00	115.00
☐ **Moody, Dwight (evangelist)**, signature.	14.00	18.00
☐ **Moody, William H. (holder of various cabinet posts)**, letter signed, one page, 1904.	18.00	24.00
☐ **Moore, Henry (sculptor)**, photo signed, 8″ × 10″.	18.00	24.00
☐ **Moravia, Alberto (writer)**, holograph letter signed, one page, undated.	21.00	27.00
☐ **Morgan, Charles L. (novelist)**, signature dated 1943.	14.00	18.00

PRICE RANGE

☐ **Morgan, John (Civil War General)**, document signed, 1882. .... 16.00 21.00

☐ **Nansen, Fridtjof (Norwegian explorer)**, signature....... 23.00 31.00

☐ **Napoleon I Bonaparte (Emperor of France)**, letter signed, one page, 1811. .... 330.00 410.00
Napoleon was one of history's most prolific letter writers. He also had one of the worst handwritings; in the latter part of his life he seldom even bothered to sign his full name, but merely used the initial "N" as his signature.

☐ **Nash, Ogden (writer of humorous verse)**, signature.... 15.00 20.00

☐ **Nast, Thomas (influential editorial cartoonist whose cartoons focused attention on political corruption)**, signature, 1872. .... 18.00 24.00

☐ **Neiman, LeRoy (magazine illustrator)**, holograph letter signed, one page, 1979. .... 93.00 112.00

☐ **Nevers, Ernie (football player)**, photo signed, 3½ 4 × 7½". 21.00 27.00

☐ **New, Harry S. (Postmaster General in Harding's cabinet)**, signature on an official card..................... 14.00 18.00

☐ **Nightingale, Florence (nurse, author)**, holograph note signed, 1858. .... 130.00 160.00

☐ **Nin, Anais (novelist, diarist)**, holograph letter signed, one page, 1975. .... 180.00 235.00

☐ **Nixon, Pat (wife of President Nixon)**, letter signed, one page, 1972. .... 65.00 85.00

☐ **Noguchi, Yone (poet)**, holograph letter signed, two pages, 1940. .... 35.00 45.00

☐ **North, John Ringling (showman, circus promoter)**, signature dated 1950.................................... 21.00 28.00

☐ **Norton, Charles (author)**, holograph quotation signed, 1890. .... 16.00 21.00

☐ **Nosworthy, Sir Francis (British General of World War II)**, holograph letter signed, one page, 1955............. 16.00 21.00

☐ **Noyes, Alfred (poet)**, signature......................... 14.00 18.00

☐ **Nye, Bill (humorist)**, holograph quotation signed. 21.00 27.00

☐ **Oberth, Hermann (space scientist who applied to be an astronaut at age 65)**, letter signed, one page, 1974. .... 37.00 48.00

☐ **O'Casey, Sean (dramatist)**, holograph letter signed, one page, 1945. .... 90.00 110.00

☐ **Ochoa, Severo (biochemist)**, photo signed, small....... 17.00 23.00

☐ **Ochs, Adolf (publisher)**, signature. 10.00 14.00

☐ **O'Connor, Basil (associate of Franklin Roosevelt)**, photo signed, 8" × 10". 17.00 23.00

☐ **O'Dwyer, William (Mayor of New York City)**, letter signed, one page, 1947. .... 32.00 43.00

☐ **Oiumet, Francis (golfer)**, signature on a card. 11.00 15.00

☐ **Olney, Richard (Secretary of State in Cleveland's cabinet)**, holograph letter signed, one page, 1882. .... 16.00 21.00

☐ **Oppenheim, E. Phillips (novelist)**, signature on card.... 14.00 18.00

☐ **Opper, Frederick Burr (cartoonist who created "Happy Hooligan")**, signature. 14.00 18.00

☐ **Ornstein, Leo (composer)**, signature.................... 9.00 12.00

☐ **Orr, Bobby (hockey player)**, photo signed, 8" × 10". 21.00 27.00

PRICE RANGE

☐ **Osterhaus, Peter (Civil War General)**, holograph letter signed, 1904... 18.00 — 25.00

☐ **Outlaw, Edward (Naval hero of World War II)**, signature.. 11.00 — 16.00

☐ **Owens, Jesse (Olympic track star)**, photo signed....... 21.00 — 27.00

☐ **Pachmann, Vladimir (pianist)**, signature in pencil, 1892. 15.00 — 20.00

☐ **Paderewski, Ignace (musician)**, signature.............. 21.00 — 27.00

☐ **Paine, Alfred B. (author)**, holograph letter signed, two pages, 1916... 16.00 — 21.00

☐ **Palmer, Arnold (golfer)**, photo signed, color, 8″ × 10″... 18.00 — 24.00

☐ **Palmer, Innes (Civil War General)**, document signed, 1853... 22.00 — 31.00

☐ **Papagos, Alexander (Greek General in World War II)**, signature on a first day cover, 1943.................... 26.00 — 35.00

☐ **Parkhurst, Charles (radical clergyman who led anti-corruption drives in New York)**, holograph letter signed, one page, 1912.. 27.00 — 36.00

☐ **Parrish, Maxfield (magazine illustrator)**, signature...... 47.00 — 62.00
Parrish was a contemporary of Howard Chandler Christy and it seemed as though they tried to outdo each other in the elaborateness of their signatures.

☐ **Parry, Sir Charles (composer)**, holograph letter signed, one page, 1909.. 22.00 — 31.00

☐ **Pascal, Gabriel (Hungarian theatrical producer)**, letter signed, one page, 1942................................. 21.00 — 28.00

☐ **Patterson, Floyd (boxer)**, photo signed, 8″ × 10″....... 22.00 — 31.00

☐ **Patterson, Robert (Secretary of Defense in Truman's cabinet)**, signature on a card....................... 11.00 — 15.00

☐ **Pauling, Linus (chemist)**, letter signed, one page, 1976.. 16.00 — 21.00

☐ **Payne, John B. (Secretary of Interior in Wilson's cabinet)**, holograph letter signed, one page, 1892.......... 17.00 — 23.00

☐ **Peabody, Francis (Harvard professor)**, letter signed, one page, 1908.. 23.00 — 31.00

☐ **Pearson, Lester (Prime Minister of Canada)**, photo signed, 5″ × 8″.. 45.00 — 60.00

☐ **Peary, Robert (discoverer of North Pole)**, signature.... 23.00 — 31.00

☐ **Peel, Sir Robert (British Prime Minister)**, holograph letter signed, three pages, 1833........................... 18.00 — 24.00

☐ **Penn, Arthur A. (composer)**, holograph manuscript signed on a card.. 67.00 — 88.00

☐ **Penney, J. C. (department store executive)**, letter signed, one page, 1952.. 23.00 — 31.00

☐ **Perkins, Frances (social worker)**, signature on a card.. 14.00 — 18.00

☐ **Perkins, Simon (General in War of 1812)**, holograph letter signed, one page, 1839................................. 42.00 — 55.00

☐ **Peron, Evita ("Eva," wife of Argentine dictator Juan Peron)**, letter signed, one page, 1948................. 450.00 — 585.00
Evita Peron always referred to herself as "Eva" and even had the name embossed on her stationery.

☐ **Peron, Juan (Argentine dictator)**, photo signed, dated 1956.. 385.00 — 500.00

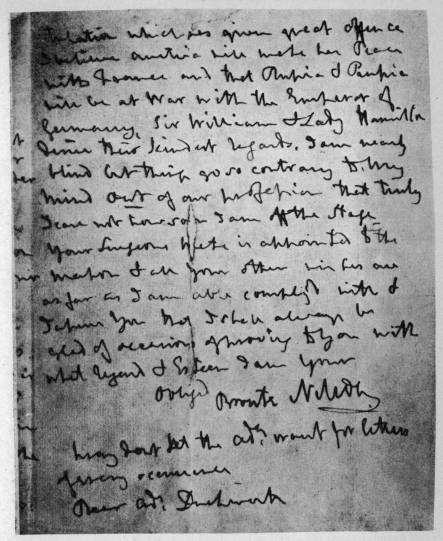

Greatest naval hero in the history of Great Britain: Admiral Lord Nelson, who won numerous sea battles and fended off Napoleon's attacks on British shipping. Never willing to take cover during an engagement, he was finally struck and killed by an enemy cannon shot.

PRICE RANGE

☐ **Perrins, C. W. Dyson (worcestershire sauce tycoon, fa-mous collector of rare books),** signature.............. 11.00 15.00
☐ **Perry Matthew (American Naval officer),** letter signed, one page, 1848.. 230.00 285.00
☐ **Pershing, John J. (Commander of Allied Forces in World War I),** letter signed, one page, 1925.................... 130.00 160.00
☐ **Phelphs, John S. (Civil War General),** signature........ 9.00 12.00
☐ **Philip II (King of Spain),** letter signed, one page, 1578.. 410.00 520.00
☐ **Philip of Edinburgh (husband of Elizabeth II of Great Britain),** signed Christmas Card, 1956.................. 115.00 145.00
☐ **Phillips, Burrill (composer),** holograph manuscript signed, two bars of music. 17.00 23.00
☐ **Phillips, Wendell (civil rights advocate),** holograph letter signed... 14.00 18.00
☐ **Phillips, William (lawyer),** document signed, one page, 1863.. 225.00 275.00
☐ **Physick, Edmund (Keeper of the Great Seal for the Commonwealth of Pennsylvania),** document signed, 1774.. 21.00 26.00
☐ **Pierrepont, Edward (Attorney General in Grant's cabi-net),** holograph quotation signed, 1864................. 18.00 24.00
☐ **Pillow, Gideon J. (Civil War General),** signature........ 28.00 36.00
☐ **Pinchot, Gifford (Governor of Pennsylvania),** signa-ture.. 13.00 17.00
☐ **Pinkerton, Allan (founder of detective agency),** photo signed... 165.00 200.00
Pinkerton once worked as bodyguard for Abraham Lincoln.
☐ **Pinkney, William (Attorney General in Madison's cabi-net),** signature..................................... 14.00 18.00
☐ **Piper, William T. (aircraft company executive),** signature dated 1945.. 27.00 35.00
☐ **Pius IX (Pope),** letter signed, one page, 1866........... 310.00 370.00
☐ **Platov, Count Matvei Invanovich (Russian General in-strumental in repelling Napoleon from Moscow),** doc-ument signed, one page, 1814........................ 450.00 585.00
☐ **Playfair, Sir Patrick (R.A.F. pilot in World War II),** sig-nature, 1961.. 14.00 18.00
☐ **Plettenberg, von (German General of World War I),** post-card photo of him, signed............................ 18.00 24.00
☐ **Poincare, Raymond (President of France),** signature on the reverse side of a calling card..................... 16.00 21.00
☐ **Poletti, Charles (Governor of New York),** letter signed, one page, 1936....................................... 14.00 18.00
☐ **Pomeroy, "Brick" (publisher),** holograph quotation signed, undated... 13.00 17.00
☐ **Pope, John (Civil War General),** holograph letter signed, one page, 1886....................................... 22.00 31.00
☐ **Porter, David (Civil War Admiral),** signature on a card.. 16.00 21.00
☐ **Porter, Linn (writer),** signature....................... 14.00 18.00
☐ **Porter, William S. ("O. Henry," short story writer),** hol-ograph letter signed, in pencil, one page, undated........ 475.00 575.00

PRICE RANGE

☐ **Post, Emily (authority on etiquette, wife of cereal tycoon Price Post)**, letter signed, one page, 1927........ 14.00   18.00

☐ **Pound, Sir Dudley (British Admiral of the Fleet)**, signature.................................... 16.00   21.00

☐ **Powell, Adam C., Jr. (Congressman from New York's Harlem district)**, signature. 11.00   15.00

☐ **Powell, Lewis F., Jr. (jurist)**, signature on a first day cover ("John Marshall" postage stamp), 1955. .... 16.00   21.00
Almost certainly signed long after the cover was postmarked in 1955; Powell would have been very young and not widely known at that time.

☐ **Power, Sir Arthur (British Admiral)**, holograph note signed.................................... 15.00   20.00

☐ **Praed, Winthrop (poet)**, signature...................... 11.00   16.00

☐ **Preston, William (Secretary of the Navy)**, letter signed, one page, 1850.. 45.00   60.00

☐ **Prudden, George (airplane designer)**, signature on a postcard photo of a Lockheed Hudson B-14. .... 13.00   17.00

☐ **Puccini, Giacomo (composer)**, holograph letter signed, one page, 1909.. 425.00   550.00

☐ **Pulitzer, Joseph (journalist who bequeathed funds for Pulitzer Price awards)**, signature on a card............. 95.00   115.00

☐ **Pyle, Howard (artist)**, letter signed, one page, 1899..... 32.00   43.00

☐ **Rabi, Isidor Isaac (physicist)**, signature................ 14.00   18.00

☐ **Radford, Arthur W. (Chairman of Joint Chiefs of Staff)**, signature on a first day cover ("P.O.W." stamp)........... 27.00   36.00

☐ **Rainger, Ralph (composer)**, holograph manuscript signed on a card.. 45.00   60.00

☐ **Ramsay, Nathaniel (Maryland statesman in Revolutionary War era)**, signature................................ 16.00   21.00

☐ **Ramsay, Sir William (chemist)**, signature dated 1885. .. 37.00   48.00

☐ **Ramsey, Alexander (Governor of Minnesota)**, signature on a War Department card................................ 14.00   18.00

☐ **Ramsey, George D. (Civil War General)**, signature...... 14.00   18.00

☐ **Randall, Alex W. (Governor of Wisconsin)**, signature. 14.00   18.00

☐ **Rasmussen, Gustav (Danish statesman)**, letter signed, one page, 1947.. 16.00   21.00

☐ **Rawlins, John (Civil War General)**, signature........... 14.00   18.00

☐ **Ray, James E. (assassin of Martin L. King)**, letter signed, one page, 1979.. 45.00   60.00

☐ **Read, George C. (Naval Commander)**, signature. 11.00   15.00

☐ **Reinchstein, Tadeusz (chemist)**, signature. 11.00   15.00

☐ **Rees, Thomas (British Commander of World War II)**, holograph letter signed, 1948. .... 17.00   23.00

☐ **Regnier, Henri (poet)**, holograph manuscript signed, one page, 1905.. 32.00   45.00

☐ **Reitsch, Hanna (female Nazi air ace in World War II)**, holograph letter signed, one page, 1970................. 27.00   36.00

☐ **Remington, Frederic (artist, sculptor of "old west" themes)**, holograph letter signed, one page, 1902........ 425.00   525.00

☐ **Reuther, Walter (teamster leader)**, signature........... 11.00   15.00

PRICE RANGE

☐ **Rexford, Eben (composer)**, holograph letter signed, one page, 1899. . . . . **27.00**   **36.00**

☐ **Reynolds, Joseph Jones (Civil War General)**, signature on a card. **14.00**   **18.00**

☐ **Rhee, Syngman (President of South Korea)**, letter signed, in English, one page, 1958. . . . . **37.00**   **47.00**

☐ **Rheman, Baron Adolf von (German General of World War I)**, signature on a printed postcard, 1918. . . . . **15.00**   **20.00**

☐ **Rice, Alexander (Governor of Massachusetts)**, holograph letter signed, one page, 1867. . . . . **28.00**   **36.00**

☐ **Rice, Cole Y. (poet)**, signature on a card. **11.00**   **16.00**

☐ **Richards, Laura (author)**, signature. **9.00**   **12.00**

☐ **Rickey, Branch (baseball executive who "broke the color line" by bringing Jackie Robinson to Major Leagues)**, document signed, one page, 1965. . . . . **52.00**   **67.00**

☐ **Ridgway, Matthew (Air Force commander in World War II and Korea)**, letter signed, one page, 1979. . . . . **47.00**   **60.00**

☐ **Riis, Jacob (anti-poverty advocate)**, holograph letter signed, one page, 1902. . . . . **37.00**   **48.00**

☐ **Ripley, Robert L. (cartoonist, creator of "Believe It or Not")**, inscribed and signed copy of his book, *The New Believe It or Not*. **35.00**   **45.00**

☐ **Ritchie, Anne (novelist)**, holograph letter signed, three pages, undated. **45.00**   **59.00**

☐ **Rivera, Diego (Mexican artist)**, photo signed, 1956. . . . . **235.00**   **290.00**

☐ **Rives, Alfred (Confederate Colonel of Engineers in Civil War)**, holograph letter signed, four pages, 1863. . . . . **67.00**   **83.00**
This war-era date of this letter, and its length (four pages), make it somewhat more valuable than the average Rives letter.

☐ **Rixley, Eppa (baseball player)**, signature. **10.00**   **14.00**

☐ **Riza Pahlevi (Shah of Iran)**, signature of him and his wife on a card, mounted on card is an Iranian postage stamp portraying both. **135.00**   **175.00**

☐ **Roberts, Dan W. (Texas Ranger)**, document signed, 1877. . . . . **67.00**   **88.00**

☐ **Roberts, Oran (Governor of Texas)**, document signed, 1877. . . . . **67.00**   **88.00**

☐ **Robinson, Brooks (baseball player)**, photo signed, color, 8″ × 11″. **16.00**   **21.00**

☐ **Robinson, Jackie (baseball player)**, signature and inscription on an album leaf. **37.00**   **48.00**

☐ **Robinson, James S. (Civil War General)**, signature. **14.00**   **18.00**

☐ **Robinson, Sugar Ray (boxer)**, photo signed, 8″ × 10″. . . **22.00**   **31.00**

☐ **Roche, James (poet)**, holograph letter signed, one page, 1903. . . . . **16.00**   **21.00**

☐ **Rochester, Earl of (court celebrity of Charles II's reign)**, signature. **18.00**   **24.00**

☐ **Rockefeller, Nelson (Vice President under Ford, Governor of New York, grandson of John D. Rockefeller)**, letter signed, one page, undated. **17.00**   **23.00**

☐ **Rockey, Keller E. (U.S. Marine Corps General of World War II)**, holograph letter signed, 1946. . . . . **18.00**   **24.00**

PRICE RANGE

☐ **Rockewell, Frank (Admiral of World War II)**, letter signed, one page, 1951.	22.00	31.00
☐ **Rockwell, Norman (artist)**, signed reproduction of his painting "The Collector," 20″ × 14″.	285.00	365.00
☐ **Roden, Henry W. (writer of detective fiction)**, letter signed, one page, 1946.	22.00	31.00
☐ **Rohde, Ruth Bryan (daughter of William Jennings Bryan)**, photo signed, 8″ × 10″.	21.00	28.00
☐ **Romains, Jules (writer)**, signature on menu, 1935.	21.00	28.00
☐ **Romney, George (Governor of Michigan, unsuccessful Presidential candidate)**, signature.	14.00	18.00
☐ **Roosevelt, Edith K. (wife of President Theodore Roosevelt)**, holograph letter signed, one page, 1931.	130.00	160.00
☐ **Roosevelt, Eleanor (wife of President Franklin Roosevelt)**, photo signed, 8″ × 10″.	55.00	70.00
☐ **Root, Elihu (statesman)**, letter signed, one page, 1904.	15.00	20.00
☐ **Rose, David (composer)**, holograph manuscript signed, three bars of music.	13.00	17.00
☐ **Ross, Sir John (explorer)**, holograph letter signed, one page, 1834.	21.00	27.00
☐ **Roth, Lillian (author and actress)**, signed copy of her book, *I'll Cry Tomorrow*.	27.00	36.00
☐ **Rubinstein, Anton (composer)**, holograph quotation signed, 1860.	625.00	825.00
☐ **Ruger, Thomas (Governor of Georgia in reconstruction days following Civil War)**, holograph letter signed, one page, 1886.	32.00	43.00
☐ **Rumsfeld, Donald (Secretary of Defense in Ford's cabinet)**, letter signed, one page, 1980.	11.00	15.00
☐ **Ruppert, Jacob (owner of Ruppert Brewery and of New York Yankees baseball club)**, document signed, 1922.	21.00	27.00
☐ **Rush, Richard (unsuccessful Presidential candidate)**, letter signed, one page, 1812.	17.00	23.00
☐ **Rusk, Dean (Secretary of State in Kennedy's cabinet)**, letter signed, one page, 1979.	21.00	27.00
☐ **Rusk, Jeremiah (Governor of Wisconsin)**, holograph letter signed, 1882.	18.00	24.00
☐ **Rusk, Thomas (Secretary of War for Texas in days of Sam Houston)**, signature.	16.00	21.00
☐ **Russell, Lord John (British Prime Minister, grandfather of Bertrand Russell)**, signature.	15.00	20.00
☐ **Russell, W. Clark (novelist)**, signature on a card dated 1900.	11.00	16.00
☐ **Rutherford, Johnny (auto racer)**, photo signed, 8″ × 10″.	27.00	36.00
☐ **Rutledge, Wiley (jurist)**, signature on a card.	16.00	21.00
☐ **Sabin, Albert (chemist)**, signature on a first day cover ("Fight Polio" stamp).	21.00	27.00
☐ **St. Gaudens, Augustus (coin designer, U.S. $20 gold piece)**, three lines from a holograph letter signed.	23.00	31.00
☐ **St. Just, Louis Antoine ("The Angel of Death," French Revolutionary leader)**, document signed, one page, "Year Two" (1794).	725.00	950.00

PRICE RANGE

The French Revolutionaries refused to use the Gregorian calendar; in their view they had ushered in a new age and it should have a new calendar. Thus they called 1793 "Year One," 1794 "Year Two," and so on.

☐ **Salisbury, Third Marquis of (British Prime Minister)**, holograph letter signed, one page, 1872.	17.00	23.00
☐ **Salk, Jonas (developer of polio vaccine)**, photo signed, 8″ × 10″.	25.00	34.00
☐ **Sandburg, Carl (poet, historian, folk singer)**, holograph letter signed, one page, undated.	95.00	115.00
☐ **Sanders, Harland (founder of fried chicken empire)**, photo signed, 1972.	24.00	32.00
☐ **Sanger, Margaret (physician, birth control authority)**, signature.	10.00	14.00
☐ **Sargent, John G. (Attorney General in Coolidge's cabinet)**, letter signed, one page, 1928.	18.00	24.00
☐ **Sarnoff, David (early radio pioneer, president of RCA)**, signature and inscription on an album leaf, 1950.	18.00	24.00
☐ **Saxe, John G. (poet)**, holograph letter signed, one page, 1852.	16.00	21.00
☐ **Saxton, Rufus, Jr. (Civil War General)**, holograph letter signed, one page, 1893.	18.00	24.00
☐ **Schencke, Robert (Civil War General)**, holograph letter signed, one page, 1874.	18.00	24.00

This letter was written to a collector who requested Schencke's autograph. In the years following the Civil War, surviving Generals from both sides were innundated with requests for their autographs. But hobbyists in that era often made the error of clipping the signature from the letter.

☐ **Schmalz, Wilhelm (Nazi General of World War II)**, color photo signed, 3½″ × 5″.	18.00	24.00
☐ **Schmeling, Max (boxer, first to defeat Joe Louis and then defeated by him in return bout)**, signature on a postcard photo.	21.00	27.00
☐ **Schoenebeck, Carl-August von (German fighter pilot of World War I)**, photo signed, 5″ × 6¼″.	42.00	55.00
☐ **Schurz, Carl (Civil War General)**, signature.	15.00	20.00
☐ **Schuyler, Philip (General in Revolutionary War)**, holograph letter signed, two pages, 1795.	265.00	315.00
☐ **Schwab, Charles (industrialist, one of America's wealthiest men in early twentieth century)**, signature.	10.00	14.00
☐ **Schwarzenegger, Arnold (bodybuilder)**, signed copy of his book, *Arnold, the Education of a Bodybuilder*.	21.00	27.00
☐ **Schwellenbach, Lewis (Secretary of Labor in Truman's cabinet)**, signature.	14.00	18.00
☐ **Scollard, Clinton (poet)**, holograph lines from a poem, signed.	15.00	20.00
☐ **Scott, Winfield (General in Mexican War)**, signature.	17.00	23.00
☐ **Seddon, James A. (Confederate Secretary of War in Civil War)**, signature.	16.00	21.00
☐ **Seddon, Margaret (female astronaut who was never assigned a flight)**, signed photo.	10.00	14.00

PRICE RANGE

☐ **Segre, Emilio (physicist)**, signature on a card. 14.00   18.00

☐ **Sellstedt, Lars (artist)**, inscribed and signed copy of his autobiography, *From Forecastle to Academy*, 1904. . . . . . .   37.00   48.00

☐ **Serno, Erich (Chief of Staff of Turkish Air Force in World War I)**, photo signed, 5″ × 7″. 28.00   36.00

☐ **Seton, Ernest T. (pioneer of Boy Scouts)**, letter signed, one page, 1923. . . . .   19.00   24.00

☐ **Seward, William H. (Secretary of State under Lincoln)**, signature. 13.00   17.00

On the night of Lincoln's assassination, an accomplice of Booth's attempted to assassinate Seward. He was admitted into Seward's home on the pretext of bringing a prescription from the drugstore and stabbed Seward a number of times. However, Seward recovered.

☐ **Seymour, Horatio (Governor of New York)**, holograph letter signed, one page, 1854. . . . .   18.00   24.00

☐ **Shafroth, John F. (Admiral of World War II)**, letter signed, one page, 1962. . . . .   45.00   60.00

☐ **Shaler, Alexander (Civil War General)**, holograph letter signed, one page, 1880. . . . .   15.00   20.00

☐ **Sharkey, Jack (boxer, only boxer to fight both Jack Dempsey and Joe Louis)**, photo signed, 8″ × 10″. 24.00   32.00

☐ **Sharp, William (poet)**, holograph letter signed, 1890. . . . .   15.00   20.00

☐ **Shaw, Anna H. (physician)**, holograph quotation signed, relating to female rights to vote. 21.00   27.00

☐ **Shaw, George B. (Irish dramatist, critic, socialist)**, holograph note signed with initials, 1917. . . . .   80.00   105.00

Shaw signed so frequently with initials that it is very difficult to get his full signature.

☐ **Sheen, Fulton (clergyman, television personality)**, letter signed, one page. 32.00   40.00

☐ **Shelley, Percy B. (poet)**, signature. 365.00   475.00

☐ **Shepard, Alan B. (astronaut, first American man in space)**, signature on first day cover, 1971. . . . .   55.00   70.00

☐ **Sheridan, Philip (Civil War General)**, signature. 18.00   24.00

☐ **Sherman, Buren (Governor of Iowa)**, document signed, 1908. . . . .   14.00   18.00

☐ **Sherman, James S. (Vice President under Taft)**, letter signed, one page, 1902. . . . .   18.00   24.00

☐ **Sherman, Roger (signer of the Declaration of Independence)**, holograph document signed, 1787. . . . . 185.00   235.00

☐ **Sherman, William T. (Civil War General)**, signature. 45.00   60.00

☐ **Shields, James (Civil War General)**, signature. 11.00   15.00

☐ **Shillaber, Benjamin (humorist who wrote under name of "Mrs. Partington")**, signature.   11.00   15.00

☐ **Shirley, William (colonial Governor of Massachusetts)**, signature. 32.00   43.00

☐ **Shonts, Theodore (transportation executive)**, letter signed, one page, 1905. . . . .   23.00   31.00

☐ **Sidmouth, Viscount (British Prime Minister)**, signature. 13.00   17.00

☐ **Siegbahn, Karl M. (physicist)**, photo signed, 3½″ × 4½″. 45.00   60.00

PRICE RANGE

☐ **Sigel, Franz (German-born Civil War General)**, signature dated 1893. .... **14.00** **18.00**

☐ **Sigourney, Lydia (author)**, holograph letter signed, 1852. .... **17.00** **23.00**

☐ **Sinclair, Sir Archibald (British Secretary of State)**, signature dated 1945. .... **14.00** **18.00**

☐ **Slayton, Donald (astronaut)**, photo signed, color. **16.00** **21.00**

☐ **Smith, Al (cartoonist)**, photo signed with ink sketches of "Mutt and Jeff," 5″ × 7″. **31.00** **42.00**
Smith was not the creator of "Mutt and Jeff." The strip was passed along to him many years after its creation by Bud Fisher.

☐ **Smith, Alfred E. (Governor of New York, defeated by Hoover in Presidential bid in 1928)**, signature. **18.00** **24.00**

☐ **Smith, Andrew (Civil War General)**, signature. **14.00** **18.00**

☐ **Smith, Charles (Postmaster General)**, letter signed, one page, 1900. .... **21.00** **27.00**

☐ **Smith, E. Kirby (Civil War General)**, holograph letter signed, two pages, 1890. .... **57.00** **74.00**

☐ **Smith, Nathan (founder of Yale Medical School)**, document signed, one page, 1821. .... **325.00** **435.00**

☐ **Smith, Robert (Secretary of the Navy in Jefferson's cabinet)**, letter signed, one page, 1808. .... **90.00** **115.00**

☐ **Snowden, Philip (politician)**, holograph letter signed, two pages, 1925. .... **17.00** **23.00**

☐ **Snyder, John W. (Secretary of Treasury in Truman's cabinet)**, photo signed, 8″ × 9″. **21.00** **27.00**

☐ **Soong Chiang, May-ling (wife of Chinese General Chiang Kai-shek)**, signature. **23.00** **31.00**

☐ **Sousa, John P. (composer, march leader)**, signature on a card. **87.00** **108.00**

☐ **Southard, Samuel (Secretary of the Navy in Monroe's cabinet)**, holograph letter signed, one page, 1837. .... **42.00** **58.00**

☐ **Soyer, Raphael (artist)**, holograph letter signed, one page, undated. **82.00** **103.00**

☐ **Speer, Albert (German Nazi official)**, signature on a bookplate. **21.00** **27.00**

☐ **Spencer, Herbert (philosopher)**, letter signed, one page, 1877. .... **22.00** **31.00**

☐ **Spillane, Mickey (detective story writer)**, photo signed, 8″ × 10″. **22.00** **31.00**

☐ **Sprague, Thomas L. (Admiral)**, letter signed, one page, 1949. .... **18.00** **24.00**

☐ **Spurgeon, Charles (clergyman)**, holograph quotation signed, 1887. .... **26.00** **35.00**

☐ **Stafford, Thomas (astronaut)**, photo signed, color. **21.00** **27.00**

☐ **Stagg, Amos A. (football coach)**, signature dated 1947. .... **14.00** **18.00**
Stagg, who won more games as a college football coach than anyone else in history, lived to be 102.

☐ **Stanbery, Henry (Attorney General in Andrew Johnson's cabinet)**, signature. **14.00** **18.00**

[handwritten manuscript text — example of Edwin M. Stanton's handwriting]

Example of the handwriting of Edwin M. Stanton, Lincoln's Secretary of War.

	PRICE RANGE	
☐ **Stanhope, Edward (British statesman)**, holograph letter signed, one page, undated.	14.00	18.00
☐ **Stanley, David (Civil War General)**, holograph letter signed, one page, 1890.	25.00	33.00
☐ **Stanley, Edward (British Prime Minister, Victorian era)**, holograph letter signed, four pages, 1852.	45.00	60.00
☐ **Stanley, Oliver (British Secretary of War in Churchill's era)**, holograph note signed, 1947.	16.00	21.00
☐ **Stanley, Wendell (scientist)**, signature on a card.	14.00	18.00
☐ **Stanton, Edwin M. (Secretary of War in Lincoln's cabinet, accused of involvement in Lincoln's assassination)**, signature on a card, 1867.	27.00	36.00
☐ **Stefansson, Vilhjalmur (explorer)**, photo signed, 4" × 6½".	22.00	30.00
☐ **Steffens, Lincoln (journalist)**, signed and inscribed copy of his autobiography, 1931.	33.00	45.00
☐ **Stein, Hermann von (German General of World War I)**, holograph letter signed, 1917.	18.00	24.00
☐ **Steinbeck, John (novelist)**, signature.	16.00	21.00
☐ **Stephen, Archduke Karl (Regent of Poland)**, holograph letter signed, four pages, 1884.	23.00	31.00
☐ **Stephen, Sir Leslie (philosopher)**, holograph letter signed, one page, 1900.	21.00	27.00
☐ **Stephens, Alice (artist)**, signature.	11.00	16.00
☐ **Stevens, John F. (chief engineer of Panama Canal)**, holograph quotation signed, one page, 1911.	17.00	23.00
☐ **Stevenson, Adlai (Vice President under Cleveland, grandfather of Adlai Stevenson who twice opposed Eisenhower for Presidency)**, signature.	12.00	16.00
☐ **Stewart, Potter (jurist)**, signature on a Supreme Court card, 1962.	16.00	21.00
☐ **Stoddert, Benjamin (Revolutionary War officer)**, holograph document signed, one page, 1783.	180.00	235.00
☐ **Stone, Harlan (jurist)**, signature on a printed Supreme Court card.	22.00	31.00
☐ **Story, Julian (portrait artist)**, signature.	11.00	15.00

For Yugoslavia:
Pour la Yougoslavie:
南斯拉夫:
За Югославию:
Por Yugoslavia:

Stanoje Simić

I Certify That the foregoing is a true copy of the Charter of the United Nations, with the Statute of the International Court of Justice annexed thereto, signed in San Francisco, California, on June 26, 1945, in the Chinese, French, Russian, English, and Spanish languages, the signed original of which is deposited in the archives of the Government of the United States of America.

In Testimony Whereof, I, Edward R. Stettinius, Jr., Secretary of State, have hereunto caused the seal of the Department of State to be affixed and my name subscribed by an Assistant Chief, Division of Central Services of the said Department, at the city of Washington, in the District of Columbia, this twenty-sixth day of June 1945.

E. R. Stettinius Jr
Secretary of State

By M L Kenestrick
Assistant Chief, Division of Central Services

The nature of an autograph specimen can drastically influence its value. This document was signed by Edward Stettinius, Jr., Secretary of State under Harry Truman. His signature is not of great value, and the second autograph, that of M.L. Kenestrick, is of even less. But this is an important United Nations charter, and is therefore of considerable collector interest and cash value.

PRICE RANGE

☐ **Stowe, Harriet B. (author of *Uncle Tom's Cabin*),** signature. 26.00   35.00

☐ **Stratten, Dorothy (centerfold model in Playboy magazine, who was murdered; her life story became the theme for a motion picture),** signature on a convention brochure, 1980. . . . . 45.00   60.00

☐ **Strauss, Richard (composer),** signature. 95.00   115.00
Strauss was well known for his unfavorable opinion of autograph seekers.

☐ **Street, Capt. George L. (Navy Commander),** holograph note signed, 1957. . . . . 16.00   21.00

☐ **Streuli, Hans (President of Switzerland),** letter signed, one page, 1957. . . . . 16.00   21.00

☐ **Strong, Caleb (Governor of Massachusetts),** document signed, 1813. . . . . 14.00   18.00

☐ **Struble, Arthur D. (World War II Admiral),** letter signed, one page, 1947. . . . . 17.00   23.00

☐ **Struther, Jan (writer),** holograph quotation signed. 16.00   21.00

☐ **Summerfield, Arthur (Postmaster General in Eisenhower's cabinet),** photo signed. 18.00   24.00

☐ **Sunday, Billy (evangelist who had been a professional baseball player),** photo signed. 110.00   135.00

☐ **Swayne, Noah (jurist),** holograph letter signed, one page, 1860. . . . . 37.00   48.00

☐ **Swayne, Wager (Civil War General),** letter signed, one page, 1894. . . . . 17.00   23.00

☐ **Swift, Jonathan (satirist, critic),** signature removed from a letter. 325.00   400.00

☐ **Swigert, John (astronaut),** photo signed, color. . . . . 21.00   ·28.00

☐ **Swinnerton, Frank (novelist),** holograph letter signed. . . 15.00   20.00

☐ **Taft, Helen (wife of President Taft),** holograph letter signed, four pages, undated. 27.00   35.00

☐ **Taft, Royal C. (Governor of Rhode Island),** signature. . . 10.00   14.00

☐ **Tallchief, Maria (ballerina),** photo signed, 8″ × 10″. 18.00   24.00

☐ **Taney, Roger B. (jurist),** document signed, one page, 1834. . . . . 40.00   51.00

☐ **Tarkington, Booth (novelist),** signature on an etching by Richard Hood, also signed by Hood, 8″ × 11″. 45.00   60.00

☐ **Taylor, Deems (music critic),** document signed, 1944. . . 16.00   21.00

☐ **Tennyson, Alfred (poet),** signature with complimentary close from a holograph letter. 67.00   88.00

☐ **Terry, Bill (baseball player),** photo signed, 8″ × 10″. 23.00   31.00

☐ **Thaxter, Celia (poet),** signature. 14.00   18.00

☐ **Theiler, Max (physician),** photo signed, 2″ × 2¾″. 45.00   60.00

☐ **Theuriet, Andre (writer),** holograph letter, three pages, 1889. . . . . 16.00   21.00

☐ **Thomas, George (Civil War General),** signature. 23.00   31.00

☐ **Thomas, Lorenzo (Civil War General),** holograph letter signed, two pages, 1865. . . . . 105.00   130.00

☐ **Thomas, Lowell (news broadcaster),** photo signed, 8″ × 10″. 22.00   30.00

☐ **Thompson, Smith (jurist),** letter signed, one page, 1820. . . . . 67.00   88.00

Here are my two books of poems. I have been a long time getting hold of them.

I do not think I told you, by the way, that my new book of poems is almost ready to send to a publisher. I hope it will appear next spring, ~~published~~ I am working very hard.

> *Yours sincerely,*
> *Dylan Thomas.*

Greatest literary figure in the history of Wales: Dylan Thomas.

	PRICE RANGE	
☐ **Thompson, Vance (author)**, holograph letter signed, one page, 1900.	15.00	20.00
☐ **Thomson, Sir Basil (English police commissioner)**, holograph letter signed, two pages, 1923.	18.00	24.00
☐ **Thomson, Virgil (composer)**, signature on a card.	18.00	24.00
☐ **Thorpe, James (athlete)**, signature on a restaurant menu, also signed by Tony Zale and several other sports figures.	115.00	145.00
☐ **Tibbets, Paul W. (pilot of the "Enola Gay" which dropped atomic bomb on Nagasaki)**, signature on a card.	16.00	21.00
☐ **Ticknor, George (author)**, holograph letter signed, one page, 1860.	14.00	18.00
☐ **Tilden, William (tennis player)**, signature.	22.00	31.00
☐ **Tinckner, Mary A. (poet)**, holograph statement signed.	14.00	18.00
☐ **Tiselius, Arne (chemist)**, signature.	14.00	18.00
☐ **Tito, Marshal (President of Yugoslavia)**, photo signed, 5" × 7".	90.00	110.00
☐ **Titus, Harold (novelist)**, letter signed, two pages, 1935.	16.00	21.00
☐ **Todd, Thomas (jurist)**, holograph document signed, two pages, 1795.	47.00	63.00
☐ **Toguri, Iva ("Tokyo Rose")**, signed greeting card.	95.00	115.00
☐ **Tojo, Admiral (Commander of Japanese Forces in World War II; though Emperor Hirohito outranked him, Tojo did most of the decision making and was virtual ruler of wartime Japan)**, signature.	105.00	135.00
☐ **Tolstoy, Leo (novelist and agitator for socialism in Russia)**, signature.	160.00	210.00
☐ **Tomlinson, Henry M. (novelist)**, holograph letter signed, one page, 1922.	16.00	21.00
☐ **Tompkins, Daniel D. (Governor of New York)**, holograph document signed, 1800.	37.00	48.00
☐ **Torrence, Ridgely (poet)**, letter signed, one page, 1925.	15.00	19.00

Do your duty to-day

& repent to-morrow.

Truly Yours

Mark Twain

Holograph quotation signed by Mark Twain.

	PRICE RANGE	
☐ **Torrey, Charles (anti-slavery advocate)**, holograph letter signed, one page, 1840	58.00	73.00
☐ **Toucey, Isaac (Secretary of the Navy)**, holograph letter signed, one page, 1857	27.00	36.00
☐ **Tower, Z. Bates (Civil War General)**, signature on a card	14.00	18.00
☐ **Trask, Katrina (poet)**, letter signed, four pages, 1915	16.00	21.00
☐ **Truman, Bess (wife of President Truman)**, letter signed, one page, 1973	28.00	37.00
☐ **Truman, Margaret (daughter of President Truman, musician, TV personality, novelist)**, letter signed, one page, 1947	28.00	37.00
☐ **Trumbull, Lyman (Senator from Illinois)**, photo signed	27.00	35.00
☐ **Tucker, Thomas (Revolutionary War surgeon)**, document signed, 1819	88.00	108.00
☐ **Tunney, Gene (boxer who dethroned Jack Dempsey as heavyweight champion)**, signature on a card along with signature of Joe E. Brown, entertainer, 1937	18.00	24.00
☐ **Twain, Mark (novelist)**, signature	52.00	68.00
☐ **Tyler, Mary E. (the Mary of "Mary Had a Little Lamb")**, signature	16.00	21.00
☐ **Tyler, Robert (son of President Tyler, holder of various public offices)**, document signed, 1841	32.00	43.00
☐ **Udall, Stewart (Secretary of Interior in Kennedy's cabinet)**, holograph letter signed, one page, undated	37.00	48.00
☐ **Untermeyer, Louis (poet, editor)**, inscribed and signed copy of his book *Burning Bush*	21.00	30.00

PRICE RANGE

☐ **Upshur, Abel (Secretary of the Navy),** letter signed, one page, 1842. . . . . 42.00   54.00

☐ **Urey, Harold (chemist),** signature on a first day cover ("Chemistry" stamp), 1976. . . . . 21.00   28.00

☐ **Utrillo, Maurice (artist),** signature on a postcard picture. 230.00   290.00

☐ **Uzelac, Emil (Austrian Major General of World War I),** letter signed, one page, 1918. . . . . 22.00   31.00

☐ **Valentine, Edward V. (sculptor),** signature. 10.00   13.00

☐ **Valentine, Lewis (Police Commissioner of New York during racketeer era),** letter signed, one page, 1934. . . . . 16.00   21.00

☐ **Vanaman, Arthur (Air Force General),** photo signed, 8″ × 10″. 23.00   33.00

☐ **VanWyck, Robert (Mayor of New York City),** letter signed, one page, 1897. . . . . 27.00   36.00

☐ **Vargas, Alberto (artist),** signed reproduction of one of his "Vargas Girls". 45.00   60.00

Recommended Reading . . .

The Official Price Guide to Old Books and Autographs is designed for the novice as well as the seasoned collector. Information on price trends, industry development, investing, and collecting techniques such as care and repair, storage, or building a collection is written in a way a beginning hobbyist will understand yet gives specific details and helpful hints the hard-core collector will find useful.

This guide also offers up-to-date prices for both rare and common collectibles that are available in the current secondary market. This guide will give any collector confidence when determining what articles to purchase at what price. With the knowledge gained from this guide, a collector will move from flea market to auction house with ease knowing which items are "hot" and which articles are definitely overpriced.

As your interest in collecting grows, you may want to start a reference library of your favorite areas. For the collector who needs more extensive coverage of the collectibles market, The House of Collectibles publishes a complete line of comprehensive companion guides which are itemized at the back of this book. They contain full coverage on buying, selling, and caring of valuable articles, plus listings with thousands of prices for rare, unusual, and common antiques and collectibles.

$10.95-5th Edition, 560 pp., Order #297-3

The House of Collectibles recommends *The Official Price Guide to Paper Collectibles,* fifth edition, as the companion to this guide.

- *Over 18,000 prices* compiled from actual dealers' lists and auction results throughout the country. Discover the current market prices for famous authors' autographs, Big Little Books, old Sears Roebuck catalogs, fruit crate art or World's Fair items.

- **MOVIE MEMORABILIA** — Paper collectible experts agree that stage and screen personalities' items are the collectibles to invest in today. Posters, press books, scripts and sheet music from your favorite movies as well as Hollywood stars' autographs are included in this comprehensive section.

- **MARKET OVERVIEW** — The paper collectibles market is flourishing. Discover what recent materials are enjoying heightened collector interest in this fascinating review.

- **A VARIETY OF MISCELLANEOUS PAPER** — Maps • magazines • greeting cards • Disneyana • aviation memorabilia • paper dolls • playing cards • sports memorabilia • stock certificates and more are included to make this the most comprehensive paper collectibles guide found on today's market.

Available from your local dealer or order direct from:
THE HOUSE OF COLLECTIBLES, see order blank

The HOUSE OF COLLECTIBLES Series

☐ Please send me the following price guides—
☐ I would like the most current edition of the books listed below.

THE OFFICIAL PRICE GUIDES TO:

☐ 753-3	American Folk Art (ID) 1st Ed.	$14.95
☐ 784-3	Silver & Silverplate (ID) 6th Ed.	$12.95
☐ 513-1	Antique Clocks 3rd Ed.	10.95
☐ 091-1	Antique & Modern Dolls (ID) 4th Ed.	12.95
☐ 287-6	Antique & Modern Firearms 6th Ed.	11.95
☐ 792-4	Antique & Modern Teddy Bears 1st Ed.	10.95
☐ 805-X	Antiques & Collectibles (ID) 11th Ed.	12.95
☐ 289-2	Antique Jewelry 5th Ed.	11.95
☐ 362-7	Art Deco (ID) 1st Ed.	14.95
☐ 447-X	Arts and Crafts: American Decorative Arts, 1894–1923 (ID) 1st Ed.	12.95
☐ 539-5	Beer Cans & Collectibles 4th Ed.	7.95
☐ 521-2	Bottles Old & New 10th Ed.	10.95
☐ 532-8	Carnival Glass 2nd Ed.	10.95
☐ 295-7	Collectible Cameras 2nd Ed.	10.95
☐ 548-4	Collectibles of the '50s & '60s 1st Ed.	9.95
☐ 803-3	Collectible Toys (ID) 5th Ed.	10.95
☐ 531-X	Collector Cars 7th Ed.	12.95
☐ 538-7	Collector Handguns 4th Ed.	14.95
☐ 748-7	Collector Knives 9th Ed.	12.95
☐ 361-9	Collector Plates 5th Ed.	11.95
☐ 296-5	Collector Prints 7th Ed.	12.95
☐ 787-8	Costume Jewelry (ID) 1st Ed.	10.95
☐ 001-6	Depression Glass 2nd Ed.	9.95
☐ 589-1	Fine Art 1st Ed.	19.95
☐ 311-2	Glassware 3rd Ed.	10.95
☐ 243-4	Hummel Figurines & Plates 6th Ed.	10.95
☐ 523-9	Kitchen Collectibles 2nd Ed.	10.95
☐ 772-X	Lunch Box Collectibles 1st Ed.	9.95
☐ 080-6	Memorabilia of Elvis Presley and The Beatles 1st Ed.	10.95
☐ 291-4	Military Collectibles 5th Ed.	11.95
☐ 788-6	Movie Memorabilia (ID) 1st Ed.	9.95
☐ 525-5	Music Collectibles 6th Ed.	11.95
☐ 313-9	Old Books & Autographs 7th Ed.	11.95
☐ 298-1	Oriental Collectibles 3rd Ed.	11.95
☐ 820-3	Overstreet Comic Book 20th Ed.	14.95
☐ 522-0	Paperbacks & Magazines 1st Ed.	10.95
☐ 297-3	Paper Collectibles 5th Ed.	10.95
☐ 809-2	*Peanuts®* Collectibles 1st Ed.	9.95
☐ 744-4	Political Memorabilia 1st Ed.	10.95
☐ 785-1	Pottery & Porcelain (ID) 7th Ed.	12.95
☐ 524-7	Radio, TV & Movie Memorabilia 3rd Ed.	11.95
☐ 819-X	Records 9th Ed.	16.95
☐ 763-0	Royal Doulton 6th Ed.	12.95
☐ 280-9	Science Fiction & Fantasy Collectibles 2nd Ed.	10.95
☐ 747-9	Sewing Collectibles 1st Ed.	8.95
☐ 358-9	Star Trek/Star Wars Collectibles 2nd Ed.	8.95
☐ 808-4	Watches 10th Ed.	16.95
☐ 248-5	Wicker 3rd Ed.	10.95

THE OFFICIAL:

☐ 760-6	Directory to U.S. Flea Markets 2nd Ed.	5.95
☐ 365-1	Encyclopedia of Antiques 1st Ed.	9.95
☐ 369-4	Guide to Buying and Selling Antiques 1st Ed.	9.95
☐ 414-3	Identification Guide to Early American Furniture 1st Ed.	9.95
☐ 413-5	Identification Guide to Glassware 1st Ed.	9.95
☐ 412-7	Identification Guide to Pottery & Porcelain 1st Ed.	$9.95
☐ 415-1	Identification Guide to Victorian Furniture 1st Ed.	9.95

THE OFFICIAL (SMALL SIZE) PRICE GUIDES TO:

☐ 309-0	Antiques & Flea Markets 4th Ed.	4.95
☐ 269-8	Antique Jewelry 3rd Ed.	4.95
☐ 807-6	Baseball Cards 10th Ed.	5.95
☐ 647-2	Bottles 3rd Ed.	4.95
☐ 544-1	Cars & Trucks 3rd Ed.	5.95
☐ 519-0	Collectible Americana 2nd Ed.	4.95
☐ 294-9	Collectible Records 3rd Ed.	4.95
☐ 306-6	Dolls 4th Ed.	4.95
☐ 800-9	Football Cards 9th Ed.	5.95
☐ 540-9	Glassware 3rd Ed.	4.95
☐ 801-7	Hockey & Basketball Cards 1st Ed.	5.95
☐ 526-3	Hummels 4th Ed.	4.95
☐ 279-5	Military Collectibles 3rd Ed.	4.95
☐ 799-1	Overstreet Comic Book Companion 3rd Ed.	4.95
☐ 278-7	Pocket Knives 3rd Ed.	4.95
☐ 527-1	Scouting Collectibles 4th Ed.	4.95
☐ 494-1	Star Trek/Star Wars Collectibles 3rd Ed.	3.95
☐ 088-1	Toys 5th Ed.	4.95

THE OFFICIAL BLACKBOOK PRICE GUIDES OF:

☐ 823-8	U.S. Coins 29th Ed.	5.95
☐ 822-X	U.S. Paper Money 23rd Ed.	5.95
☐ 821-1	U.S. Postage Stamps 13th Ed.	5.95

THE OFFICIAL INVESTORS GUIDE TO BUYING & SELLING:

☐ 534-4	Gold, Silver & Diamonds 2nd Ed.	12.95
☐ 535-2	Gold Coins 2nd Ed.	12.95
☐ 536-0	Silver Coins 2nd Ed.	12.95
☐ 537-9	Silver Dollars 2nd Ed.	12.95

THE OFFICIAL NUMISMATIC GUIDE SERIES:

☐ 254-X	The Official Guide to Detecting Counterfeit Money 2nd Ed.	7.95
☐ 257-4	The Official Guide to Mint Errors 4th Ed.	7.95

SPECIAL INTEREST SERIES:

☐ 506-9	From Hearth to Cookstove 3rd Ed.	17.95

TOTAL

SEE REVERSE SIDE FOR ORDERING INSTRUCTIONS

▭ FOR IMMEDIATE DELIVERY ▭

VISA & MASTER CARD CUSTOMERS
ORDER TOLL FREE!
1·800·733·3000

This number is for orders only; it is not tied into the customer service or business office. Customers not using charge cards must use mail for ordering since payment is required with the order—sorry, no C.O.D's.

OR SEND ORDERS TO

THE HOUSE OF COLLECTIBLES
201 East 50th Street
New York, New York 10022

POSTAGE & HANDLING RATES

First Book $2.00
Each Additional Copy or Title $0.50

Total from columns on order form. Quantity_____ $_____

☐ Check or money order enclosed $_____ (include postage and handling)

☐ Please charge $_____to my: ☐ MASTERCARD ☐ VISA

Charge Card Customers Not Using Our Toll Free Number
Please Fill Out The Information Below

Account No._____ Expiration Date_____
(All Digits)
Signature_____

NAME (please print)_____ PHONE_____

ADDRESS_____ APT. #_____

CITY_____STATE_____ ZIP_____